John William Donaldson

A Complete Latin Grammar for the use of Students

John William Donaldson

A Complete Latin Grammar for the use of Students

ISBN/EAN: 9783742804952

Manufactured in Europe, USA, Canada, Australia, Japa

Cover: Foto ©Andreas Hilbeck / pixelio.de

Manufactured and distributed by brebook publishing software (www.brebook.com)

John William Donaldson

A Complete Latin Grammar for the use of Students

TO

HENRY ANNESLEY WOODHAM, Esq., LL.D.,
LATE FELLOW OF JESUS COLLEGE, CAMBRIDGE.

My dear Woodham,

Among my friends in the two sister Universities I do not know any one whose mastery over the Latin language is greater than yours; and I have wished to inscribe this Work with your name, not only as a record of our long intimacy and as a mark of my sincere regard, but also for the purpose of directing the young student's attention to the encouraging fact, that we have still at least one Englishman, who has written Latin with as much facility and vigour, as those learned men in the 16th and 17th centuries, who used no other medium of literary communication.

Yours very truly,
J. W. DONALDSON.

PREFACE TO THE SECOND EDITION.

THE motives, which have induced me to enlarge this work very considerably, and thus to adapt it to the requirements of a higher class of students than the learners for whose use it was originally composed, are in the main identical with the considerations which led me to bestow a similar labour on the second edition of my Greek Grammar. But the present republication involved some special peculiarities both in the starting-point which it presumed, and in the object which I proposed to myself.

In its original form this Grammar was a mere sketch intended immediately, if not exclusively, to be used under my own eye in a school of which I had the entire management; and it was primarily destined, as I mentioned in the preface, to assist my pupils in the practice of Latin prose composition, which the late Bishop Blomfield, an eminent pupil of the school, had wished to encourage by the establishment of a Gold Medal. Circumstances obliged me to bring out the book with as little delay as possible, and it was printed under signal disadvantages. But in spite of its slight texture and its many defects and inequalities, the sale of a large impression has proved that it had some special recommendations in the eyes of teachers and learners; and I embrace with great satisfaction the present opportunity of giving it an extension in size, and, I hope, an exactness in detail, which will not only, as I venture to believe, satisfy the expectations of competent tutors, but also supply classical students, and especially those who wish to acquire the habit of writing Latin, with a sufficient hand-book of

PREFACE TO THE SECOND EDITION.

Latin Grammar, adapted no less for continued perusal than for reference in any case when the occasion may arise.

That such a book, as I have wished this to be, is still a desideratum in this country, is a fact which has been impressed upon me by my experience as a teacher and examiner at Cambridge and elsewhere. It is true that Latin Grammar and Latin Composition have been successfully handled in many works of first-rate merit, and at the end of this preface I have given a list of books on those subjects, which are worthy of all praise, and to which I have been directly indebted in the course of the present volume. But though a book such as I have undertaken must by the nature of the case be little more than a compilation from existing works in regard to all the ordinary details, though paradigms, lists of words, and illustrative examples belong to the *Edicta tralaticia* of Latin grammarians, which are transferred, sometimes in the mass, from one grammar to another in an unbroken succession of literary inheritance*, and though in many particulars it would not be easy to improve on the established method of presenting these facts to the reader, still there is no one of these excellent books, which contains all the information necessarily sought in such a manual as the advanced student requires; they are all defective in the statement of some details of primary importance; and the arrangement of the materials, as well as the succession of topics, introduced for the first time in the original edition of this Grammar, still seem to me to possess some material advantages in comparison with other treatises on Latin grammar. Accordingly, whether this new edition is regarded as a compilation from other sources, made by a person who has enjoyed considerable experience in regard to the practical exigencies of students; or as a result of original research in many points of detail; or as an attempt to improve the method of gram-

---

* For example, Augustus Grotefend, from whom I have taken most of the examples of subordinate sentences, says distinctly in the preface to his second volume (p. x): "damit auch Niemand versucht werde, fremden Verdienst mir beizumessen, muss ich noch bemerken, dass die meisten Beispiele unter den Regeln aus Ramshorn's grösserer Grammatik entlehnt sind." I must however remark that these examples as they appear in Grotefend, have required at my hands a good deal of sifting and revision; for in many cases the extracts were erroneously interpreted, or classified wrongly.

matical exposition; it will, I think, be found that, as a whole, it attempts at least to occupy a vacant place in this department of educational literature.

I will briefly explain some of the features of the book which I now present to the reader, referring to the table of contents for a more minute statement of the method which I have adopted.

From first to last my object has been strictly practical. Whether the information collected in these pages is the result of my own labours in the field of Latin philology, or is directly derived from the works of other grammarians, I have wished to give it in the most convenient order, with the most perspicuous exposition of the facts, and without any direct reference to speculations or reasonings, which I have exhibited in another treatise; and while I have omitted what I thought would not be immediately instructive to the student, I have enforced by repetition from different points of view those principles and facts which are most likely to be misapprehended or overlooked by an imperfect scholar.

The grammar is divided into three parts—Accidence, Syntax, and Prosody.

The *Accidence*, which has necessarily much in common with all the best Latin grammars, is distinguished by an arrangement of the declensions in accordance with the form of the genitive plural, which is the only criterion of the characteristic; a classification of the pronouns according to their real differences in meaning and usage; and an avoidance of the usual error in the order of the conjugations. The Accidence has also a peculiar feature in the attention which is paid throughout to the discrimination of synonyms, to which the student cannot pay too much attention; for without this it is impossible to attain to accuracy and perspicuity in writing Latin. In my arrangement of the declensions the greatest novelty is that of placing the nouns in -*es* or the fifth declension of the older grammars, and the nouns in -*s* preceded by a long vowel or two consonants among the -*i*- nouns. With regard to the nouns in -*es*, I refer the reader to the arguments which I have adduced elsewhere (*Varronianus*, ed. 3, p. 309). And this arrangement of nouns like *urbs, Samnis*, &c., does not depend on mere speculation, or even on the form of the genitive plural, for we have positive

PREFACE TO THE SECOND EDITION.

evidence that in their original use these words were nouns in *-is* (see the examples in Corssen, *Ausspr. Vokal. u. Beton,* II. pp. 57, 58), and the accent of the nouns in *-is* indicates a contraction no less certainly than that of *tantōn* for *tantōne*. In the arrangement of the conjugations, I have, as in the declensions, classified together those forms which end in a vowel, as distinguished from those of which the characteristic is a consonant or a semi-consonant. The ordinary system, which places the *-i-* verb in the fourth conjugation, is not only contrary to the true theory, but is practically very inconvenient. The fact, that the great majority of vowel verbs in Latin are derivative or secondary formations, corresponding to those of the Greek circumflexed verbs, which are properly placed after the barytones, does not affect the propriety of the arrangement which gives the precedence to the vowel verbs in Latin; for these verbs comprise not only the derivative formations, but also the oldest verbs, which in Greek retain the primitive conjugation in *-μι* (such as *sto, do,* and *pleo*); and it will be recollected that the Greek verbs in *-μι* are arranged according to the vowels regarded as their characteristics. I need hardly say that in this, as in the former edition, I adhere to *Priscian's* doctrine, that the Latin verb has no *futurum exactum;* and I am really surprised that good modern scholars can still maintain the paradox that *fuerit* is both indicative and subjunctive, and both future and perfect.

My *Syntax* is contained in four chapters. In the first of these I have applied to Latin grammar the general principles on which all syntax depends, and I have exhibited in a succinct form the main rules of Latin construction. This preliminary discussion is suggested by the same considerations as those which induce the teacher of Geography to place before his pupils a map of Europe before he introduces them to the examination of a particular country. Besides this, it is desirable that even the advanced student should be able to recur to a summary view of the subject which he has to pursue in such a variety of details. The three remaining chapters of the syntax are devoted to the separate and methodical investigation of the rules for construing the noun, the verb, and the sentence. In the first of these three chapters I have borrowed

PREFACE TO THE SECOND EDITION.

freely from Otto Schulz; and I am also indebted to Ramshorn for many of my examples. The chapter on the Syntax of verbs, as it stood in my first edition, seemed to me to require very little alteration. The concluding chapter of the Syntax is a supplementary collection of illustrations, arranged in an order suggested by logical considerations, and convenient for purposes of reference, as it will supply the writer of Latin with classified examples of the most usual forms of connected sentences.

The *Prosody*, which, in accordance with the usual practice in Latin grammars, discusses both quantity and metre, has nothing new to offer on the former subject, but the metres are explained, as in the first edition, with reference to certain general principles, which I investigated long ago, and which, as I conceive, are not only more true in theory than the usual expositions, but also calculated to remove the principal difficulties of versification.

The Appendices at the end of the book will speak for themselves. Although the information, which they convey, does not necessarily belong to an exposition of Latin grammar, it is convenient to a student to have these details collected in the manual to which he goes for the main facts of the language. With regard to the selection of the most usual synonyms, the grammar itself has necessarily noticed many distinctions of words and phrases, and it seemed to be desirable that the different shades of meaning with which certain common words are used, should be exhibited in a form likely to impress them on the student's memory. The *Antibarbarus*, which is mainly an abridgment of Krebs' well-known work, is added, because the writer of modern Latin must not only be cautious and discriminating in his use of good words, but should learn as soon as possible to avoid the spurious phraseology which is due to the influence of his own and other spoken languages.

Although this Grammar is designed for the use of students rather than learners, it seemed to me necessary to state all the details of the rudiments in the simplest and plainest manner, not only for the sake of method and completeness, but also because the readers, to whom I address myself, do not consist exclusively of those who have received an accurate education at school. It is my duty to examine in the course of the year some hundreds of young men, who, though not generally deficient in application or abilities, have been left by the faults of their early training in great perplexity and ignorance with regard to the most elementary principles of Latin grammar. Such persons are not likely to get what they want from the imperfect outlines compiled for the use of schools; and they would justly complain, if, in taking up a more detailed grammar, they did not find the knowledge which they want presented in a form which might enable them both to understand and recollect the general rules. It is for this reason that I have retained or introduced so many artificial helps to the memory, not shrinking from the use of the uncouth rhymes, which, when once learned, are not easily forgotten.

Such then is the plan and scope of this second edition of my Latin Grammar. And I shall willingly relinquish the claims of more ambitious authorship, if those, who are desirous of acquiring a sound and practical knowledge of the Latin language, find that I have collected in a comparatively small compass a sufficient amount of really useful and available information, so arranged as to facilitate their studies and render them permanently effectual.

J. W. D.

CAMBRIDGE, *October 16th* 1860.

ADVERTISEMENT TO THE THIRD EDITION.

In this Edition some manifest oversights and misprints have been corrected. In all other respects the book is left precisely as it came from the hand of the lamented author.

T. M.

CAMBRIDGE, *May 9th*, 1867.

WORKS

ON LATIN GRAMMAR AND COMPOSITION.

THE following is a list of all the books to which I am directly indebted for suggestions or materials in the present edition. But there is scarcely any well-known treatise on the subject of the Latin language, with which I have not made some acquaintance in the course of the last thirty years.

1. *Ausführliche Grammatik der Lateinischen Sprache von* K. L. SCHNEIDER. Berlin, 1819—21.

2. a. *Grammar of the Latin Language*, by C. G. ZUMPT; translated from the German with additions, by JOHN KENRICK, second edition, corrected and enlarged. London, 1827.

2. b. *The same*, translated from the ninth edition of the original, by Dr. LEONARD SCHMITZ. London, 1845.

3. *Ausführliche Grammatik der Lateinischen Sprache zum Schulgebrauche*, von AUGUST. GROTEFEND, 2 vols. Hannover, 1829, 1830.

4. HAND, F.: *Tursellinus seu de particulis Latinis Commentarii*, 4 vols. Lips. 1829—1845.

5. *Lateinische Synonyme und Etymologieen von* L. DÖDERLEIN, 7 vols. Leipsig, 1826—1839.

6. *Lateinische Grammatik von* LUDWIG RAMSHORN. Leipsig, 1830.

7. *Lateinische Synonymik von* L. RAMSHORN, 2 vols. Leipsig, 1831—1833.

xiv   WORKS ON LATIN GRAMMAR AND COMPOSITION.

8. Professor K. REISIG'S *Vorlesungen über Lateinische Sprach-wissenschaft, herausgegeben von* Dr. F. HAASE. Leipsig, 1839.

9. *Schulgrammatik der Lateinischen Sprache von* OTTO SCHULZ, 11th edition. Halle, 1841.

10. *Lateinische Synonymik von* D. FERDINAND SCHULZ. Arnsberg, 1841.

11. *Antibarbarus der Lateinischen Sprache von* I. P. KREBS, 2nd edition. Frankfurt am Main, 1837.

12. *Anleitung zum Lateinschreiben von* I. P. KREBS, ninth edition. Frankfurt am Main, 1842.

13. a. *Lateinische Sprachlehre für Schulen, von* Dr. I. N. MADVIG. Braunschweig, 1844.

13. b. *The same*, translated by G. WOODS. Oxford, 1849.

14. a. *Latinae Grammaticae Curriculum, or a progressive Grammar of the Latin Language for the use of all classes in Schools*, by B. H. KENNEDY, D.D. London, 1844.

14. b. *An Elementary Grammar of the Latin Language for the use of Schools*, by B. H. KENNEDY, D.D. 6th edition. London, 1851.

15. *Uber Aussprache, Vokalismus, und Betonung der Lateinischen Spruche, von* W. CORSSEN, 2 vols. Leipsig, 1858, 1859.

CONTENTS.

PART I.
ACCIDENCE, OR THE FORMS OF WORDS.

CHAPTER I.
INTRODUCTION

SECT.		PAGE
1	The Latin Language, and Latin Grammar	1
2	The Latin Alphabet and the classification of the Letters	5
3	Syllables	7
4	Parts of Speech	10

CHAPTER II.
NOUNS.

1	Declension of Substantives	12
2	First or -a Declension	14
3	Second or -o Declension	17
4	Third Declension	19
	A. First class, or Consonantal Nouns	22
	B. Second class, or Semi-consonantal Nouns	27
5	Declension of Adjectives	41
6	Degrees of Comparison	46
7	Anomalous Nouns	51
8	Numerals	59

CHAPTER III.
PRONOUNS.

1	Personal Pronouns and their Possessives	70
2	Indicative Pronouns	72
3	Distinctive Pronouns	74
4	Relative, Interrogative, Indefinite, and other connected Pronouns	75
5	Indefinite Relative Pronouns	79

xvi   CONTENTS.

CHAPTER IV.
VERBS.

SECT		PAGE
1	Regular Verbs	81
2	The Substantive Verb, or Verb of Being	89
3	Vowel Verbs. First or -a Conjugation	92
	Second or -e Conjugation	98
	Third or -i Conjugation	104
4	Consonant Verbs. Fourth or Consonant Conjugation . . .	109

TABLES OF THE REGULAR VERBS.

Table I.	Comparison of the Four Conjugations . . .	119
Table II.	Formation of the Perfect	123
Table III.	Formation of the Supines	130
Table IV.	Verbs which have i or e before the ending .	132
5	Irregular Verbs	135
	A. Additions to the Present Tense	ib.
	B. Abbreviated Forms	137
6	Defective Verbs:	
	Impersonal Verbs	140
	Deponent Verbs	142
	Specially defective Verbs	150

CHAPTER V.
UNDECLINED WORDS.

1	Adverbs	154
2	Prepositions	178
3	Conjunctions	188
4	Interjections	195

CHAPTER VI.
DERIVATION AND COMPOSITION.

1	Derivation	197
	(a) Derived Nouns	ib.
	(α) Derived Substantives	ib.
	(β) Derived Adjectives	114
	(b) Derived Verbs	119
2	Composition	222
	I. Formation of Compounds	133
	II. Classification of Compounds	225
	(A) Compound Substantives	ib.
	(B) Compound Adjectives	ib.
	(C) Compound Verbs	227

PART II.

SYNTAX, OR THE CONSTRUCTION OF WORDS.

CHAPTER I.

FIRST PRINCIPLES AND GENERAL RULES.

SECT.		PAGE
1	Subject and Predicate	219
2	Different kinds of Predicates	230
3	Accessory parts of a Sentence	231
4	Epithets and Predicates	234
5	Cases and Prepositions	235
6	Main Rules of Latin Syntax	237
7	Order of Words in a Latin Sentence, and their English Construction	247
	I. The Latin Order	248
	II. The English Construction	254

CHAPTER II.

CASES OF NOUNS.

1	The Nominative and its Adjuncts	256
	(A) Agreement of the Nominative with its Verb	257
	(B) Agreement of the Adjective with its Substantive	258
	(C) Agreement of the Relative with its Antecedent	262
	(D) Apposition of a Noun or Participle as Secondary Predicate	264
	(E) Case of the Primary Predicate, I. with the Finite Verb	266
	II. with the Infinitive	268
2	The Accusative	ib.
	(A) Accusative of the Immediate Object	269
	(B) .... of Reference	271
3	The Genitive	273
	(A) Genitive of Possession	274
	(B) .... of Quality	275
	(C) .... of the Object (1) with Substantives	277
	(D) .... of the Object (2) with Adjectives	278
	(E) .... of the Object (3) with Verbs	279
	(F) .... of Partition	281
	(G) .... of Quantity	283
	(H) .... of Number	284
	(I) .... of Price or Value	285
	(K) .... of Relation	286
4	The Dative	ib.
	(A) Dative of Limitation	287
	(B) .... of Destination	291
	(C) .... instead of a prepositional phrase	ib.

xviii CONTENTS.

SECT. | PAGE
5 The Ablative 294
  (A) Ablative of Immediate Determination . . ib.
  (B) .... of Circumstance 299
  (C) .... of the Object 300
6 The Vocative and its Substitutes 303
7 Differences of Case with the same Verb . . . 306
8 Cases in definitions of Space and Time 311
  (A) Definitions of Space . . . . . . ib.
  (B) Definitions of Time 314
9 The Cases when construed with Prepositions . . 317
  (A) Prepositions construed with the Accusative only . 319
  (B) .... Ablative only . 319
  (C) .... Accusative and Ablative . 338

CHAPTER III.

TENSES AND MOODS OF VERBS.

1 Construction of the Tenses in the Finite Verb . . 343
  (A) Indicative and Imperative 343
  (B) Subjunctive 346
2 Distinctive uses of the Indicative and Subjunctive . 350
3 Construction of the Infinitive, Participles, and other Verbals . 357
  (1) Infinitive . . . . ib.
  (2) Participles 361
  (3) Gerunds and Gerundives 364
  (4) Supines 367

CHAPTER IV.

SYNTAX OF SENTENCES.

1 Definitions 369
  (A) Co-ordinate Sentences 371
2 (a) Copulative Sentences . . . . . . ib.
3 (b) Disjunctive Sentences 373
4 (c) Adversative Sentences 374
5 (d) Distributive Sentences 376
6 (e) Distinctive Sentences 377
7 (f) Comparative Sentences 379
  (B) Subordinate Sentences 395
8 (a) Conditional Sentences . . . . . ib.
9 (b) Definitive Sentences 397
10 (c) Subjunctive Sentences 400
11 (d) Temporal Sentences 409
12 (e) Objective Sentences 414
13 (f) Illative Sentences 416
14 (g) Final Sentences 418

CONTENTS.

SECT.		PAGE
15	(b) Causal Sentences	421
16	(f) Concessive Sentences	422
17	Figures of Speech:	
	(A) Figures of Syntax	423
	(B) Figures of Style	424

PART III.

PROSODY, OR QUANTITY AND METRE.

CHAPTER I.
QUANTITY.

1	General Rules of Quantity	428
2	Quantity of Middle Syllables	432
3	Quantity of Final Syllables	434
4	Quantity of the connecting Vowel in Compounds	438
5	Quantity of Syllables as affected by Metre	439

CHAPTER II.
METRE.

1	Metrical Feet			443
2	Equal Rhythms. A. Dactylic Verse.	(a) Hexameter or Heroic Verse		444
		(b) Elegiac Verse		447
		(c) Glyconic Verse		448
		(d) Choriambic Verse		449
	B. Anapæstic Verse			ib.
3	Double Rhythms. A. Trochaic Verse			450
		(a) Ithyphallic Metre		ib.
		(b) Hipponactean Verse		ib.
		(c) Tetrameter Catalectic		451
	B. Iambic Verse			ib.
		(a) Dimeter Acatalectic		452
		(b) Trimeter Acatalectic		ib.
		(c) The Scazon		ib.
		(d) Tetrameter Catalectic		453
4	Asynartete Rhythms			ib.
	(a) Sapphic Verse			ib.
	(b) Alcaic Verse			454
	(c) Archilochian Verse			456
	(d) Elegiambus			457
	(e) Iambelegus			ib.
	(f) Galliambic Verse			ib.
5	Comic Metres			458
	(a) Iambic Trimeter Acatalectic			ib.
	(b) Iambic Tetrameter Catalectic			459

CONTENTS.

SECT.		PAGE
	(c) Iambic Tetrameter Acatalectic	159
	(d) Trochaic Tetrameter Catalectic	ib.
	(e) Trochaic Tetrameter Acatalectic	162
	(f) Bacchiac Verse	ib.
6	Accentual and Rhyming Verses	ib.
7	Poetic Style as connected with Metre	162

APPENDIX I.
CLASSIC AUTHORS ... 163

APPENDIX II.
ABBREVIATIONS ... 168

APPENDIX III.
GENERAL INFORMATION ... 472

APPENDIX IV.
DISTINCTIONS OF WORDS IN MEMORIAL VERSES.

(a) Differences of Quantity 475
(b) Differences of Form or Gender 479
(c) Synonyms, or different Words with similar meanings . . . 480

APPENDIX V.
ANTIBARBARUS 499

I. Index of Latin Words and Phrases 515
II. Index of Subjects 526

PART I.

ACCIDENCE, OR THE FORMS OF WORDS.

CHAPTER I.
INTRODUCTION.

§ 1. *The Latin Language, and Latin Grammar.*

1 A COMPLETE Latin Grammar undertakes to supply the necessary introduction to a critical study of the old Roman literature, and to furnish the rules for writing the Latin language, both in prose and verse, with elegance and correctness.

The Latin language, which was the vernacular speech of the Romans during the long continuance of their empire in Italy, derived its name from the district of Latium, lying to the southwest of the city, rather than from the city itself, because, like the right of citizenship, it received its primary development in the adjacent provinces, which first recognized the supremacy of Rome; and as this right was called the *jus Latinum*, the language obtained a corresponding designation, under which it spread itself throughout Italy and became the language of government and literature in the whole Empire. In this way it absorbed and appropriated the various old Italian dialects, some of which, as the Umbrian, the Oscan, and the Etruscan, are still preserved partially in inscriptions and fragments. Its literary form was directly affected by the Greek language, which was spoken by numerous colonists in Italy, and had many affinities with the Latin; and the Roman writers who are called *classic* were trained in the imitation of Greek models. These authors flourished in the interval between 200 B.C. and 100 A.D., and that period is divided into the golden and silver ages of the Latin language.

2   ACCIDENCE, OR THE FORMS OF WORDS.

This *best*, or, as it is sometimes termed, *golden* period of the Latin language may be regarded as extending from about the death of Sulla (B.C. 78) to the death of Augustus (A.D. 14). Before this time we have only two writers, the Comedians Plautus and Terence, whose works have come down to us in complete specimens, and these dramatists are regarded as classic, and are ranked with the authors of the golden age. The prose writers of the golden period were Varro, Cicero, Cæsar, Sallust, Cornelius Nepos, and Livy, and the poets were Lucretius, Catullus, Tibullus, Propertius, Virgil, Horace, and Ovid. The immediately succeeding period from the death of Augustus to the accession of Hadrian (A.D. 14—117) is sometimes called the *silver* age, and was one of considerable literary activity; its prose writers were Quintilian, the two Pliny's, Velleius, Seneca, Tacitus, Valerius Maximus, Curtius and Florus, and its poets Phædrus, Persius, Lucan, Martial, Silius Italicus, Statius, Juvenal, and Valerius Flaccus. The period from A.D. 117 to A.D. 476, which is called the *iron* age, produced the prose writers Justin, Ammianus Marcellinus, Gellius, Macrobius, Appuleius, and a number of ecclesiastical authors, and the poets Ausonius and Claudian; but their style, when it was most correct, was merely an imitation of that of the classical period[1].

It is generally stated that Latin is a dead language, because it is no longer the vernacular speech of any nation. But as a written language it was used by learned men long after it ceased to be spoken, and there is no reason why it should lose its functions in this respect. Accordingly, it is still an important object with the Latin grammarian to provide for the practical use of the language as a vehicle of literary communication, and the present Grammar in particular is composed with a special reference to this result.

§ 2. *The Latin Alphabet, and the classification of the Letters.*

2   The Latin Alphabet differs from the English only by the omission of the letter W.

(1) It consists therefore of the following twenty-three letters (*litteræ*):

A B C D E F G H I (J) K L M N O P Q R S T U (V) X Y Z.
a b c d e f g h i (j) k l m n o p q r s t u (v) x y z.

[1] A list of the best Latin Authors with their names in full is given in Appendix I.

ACCIDENCE, OR THE FORMS OF WORDS.

All these letters occur in the following line:

Gasifrequens Libycos duxit Karthago triumphos.

Obs. 1 Cicero (*de natur. Deor.* II. 37, § 93) speaks of only 21 letters, but in his time the Greek letters Y and Z were imported under the forms of Y and Z. The emperor Claudius introduced three additional characters: ⅃ to give the sound of *v* in *servus* and *vulgus;* the antisigma Ↄ or ↃC to represent the Greek ψ or *ps;* and Ⱶ to express the middle sound between *u* and *i*. But these characters did not remain long in use.

Obs. 2 The Romans wrote C for both C and G until about B.C. 230, when the latter was distinguished by the addition of a tail. And the names *Gāius, Gnaeus* were to the last indicated by the initials *C.* and *Cn.*, though those words were always pronounced with a G.

Obs. 3 The letters I and U are written J and V to indicate the change of pronunciation specified below; but the Romans did not consider that I or J and U or V were distinct pairs of letters, and they are not placed separately in the best dictionaries.

Obs. 4 As in English, the letter Q is always followed by U.

Obs. 5 We pronounce the Latin alphabet as we do our own, taking care, however, in reading words to articulate every syllable according to the rules given below. It cannot be doubted, however, that our pronunciation is very unlike that of the ancient Romans.

Obs. 6 While the true pronunciation of the Latin letters is for the most part left to conjecture, their correct use in writing, which is termed *orthography* or exact spelling, is also in many cases very vague and uncertain. We have very few manuscripts, which are earlier than A.D. 400, and even the inscriptions seem to have been left to ignorant workmen, who are not always consistent in the spelling of the same words in the same document. The most usual vacillations are found in the vowels and diphthongs *e, ae, oe; i, u, y; e, i; u, o;* in the consonants *h* at the beginning or in the middle of a word; *b* and *p* before *s; c* and *ch; p* and *ph; t* and *th; ct* and *t; mp* and *m; ci* and *ti; c* and *qu; d* and *t* at the end of a word; *s* after *x;* and in the double consonants *ll, mm, nn, cc, tt, pp, ss.*

The following table contains a list of the words, which are most frequently given with an erroneous or inconvenient orthography. The spelling here recommended either rests on the best manuscripts and inscriptions, or it is suggested by the derivation of the words and the analogy of the Latin language.

Write	rather than	Write	rather than
Ægæus (Αἰγαῖος)	Ægeus.	cælare	celare.
amœnus } Inscr.	amenus	cælum	cælum.
Camœna }	Camœna.	crementum } (cædo)	cœmentum.
cæcus	crecus.	cræpes }	cœspes.
Cæcilia	Cœcilia.	crepa (Cæpio)	cæpa.

ACCIDENCE, OR THE FORMS OF WORDS.

Write	rather than	Write	rather than
cerimonia	ceremonia.	satira	satyra.
cæruleus } Inscr.	cœruleus.	lanx satura	lanx satira.
cæsius	cædus.	silva	sylva.
ceteri	cæturi.	Silvius	Sylvius.
cœna	cœna and cena.	stilus	stylus.
cœpi	copi.	tiro	tyro.
heres	hæres.	moriendum	moriundum.
levis	lævis.	dicendum	dicundum.
Lævinus (lœvus)	Levinus.		
mæreo } (maroso)	mœreo.	benevolus	benivolus.
mæstus	mæstus.	malevolus	malivolus.
musæum (μουσεῖον)	musæum.	deminutio	diminutio.
fœcundus	fœcundus.	deverto	diverto.
fenus	fœnus.	valetudo	valitudo.
felix	felix.	Vergilius	Virgilius.
femen } feo	fœmen.	Vergilius	Virgilius.
femina	fœmina.	Herculeus	Herculius.
femur	fœmur.	Cæsareus	Cæsarius.
fetialis	fetialis.	vindico (vindex)	vendico.
fœdus } Inscr.	fœdus.	intelligo	intellego.
fœnum	fœnum.	comissari	comessari.
pene	pene.	protinus	protenus.
penitus } Inscr.	pœnitus.	genitrix	genetrix.
pænitet	pænitet.	querimonia	queremonia.
pæna	pæna.	Mauritania	Mauretania.
pomœrium (murus)	pomerium.	omnes (Acc.)	omnis.
prœlium (prœlium)	prælium.	urbes (Acc.)	urbis.
prelum (premo)	prælum.	ultim	ultem.
obscænus (from obscus = cæcus) }	obscænus.		
		epistola	epistula.
scæna	scæna.	adolescens (oleo)	adulescens.
sepes	sæpes.	suboles (sub)	soboles.
septus	sæptus.	jucundus (juvo)	jocundus.
Æmilius	Æmilius.	alec (alex)	halec.
Brundisium (Βρεντέσιον) }	Brundusium.	irpex (sirpex)	hirpex.
clipeus	clypeus.	Etruria	Hetruria.
cupressus	cypressus.	Ilerda	Hilerda.
hiemps	hyems.	Iber	Hiber.
inclutus (cluo)	inclytus.	Ister	Hister.
lacrima	lacryma.	Istria	Histria.
lubet	libet.	Hadria	Adria.
manubiæ } Inscr.	manibiæ.	Hadrianus	Adrianus.
monumentum	monimentum.	hariolus	ariolus.
		haruspex	aruspex.
		hedera	edera.
ocius	ocyus.	heluo	eluo.
optimus	optumus.	hercisco	ercisco.
Jupiter optumus maxumus	Jup. optimus maximus.	herctum	erctum.
		hibiscus	ibiscus.

ACCIDENCE, OR THE FORMS OF WORDS.

Write	rather than	Write	rather than
hordeum	ord.	Bosporus	Bosphorus.
Hadrumetum	Adr.	sulfur	sulphur.
Hamilcar	Am.	tropæum	trophæum.
Hammon	Amm.	Rhipæus	Riphæus.
Hannibal	Ann.	triumphus	triumpus.
Hanno	Anno.		
Hasdrubal	Asdr.	letum	lethum.
Hebræus	Ebr.	postumus	posthumus.
Hiarba	Jarb.	Postumius	Posthumius.
Hiempsal	Jemps.	Sulla	Sylla.
Himilco	Im.	tensa	thensa.
Hecate	Ecate.	Trasimenus	Thrasim.
Henna	Enna.	torus	thorus.
halcedo	alcedo.	tus	thus.
halcyon	alcyon.	Tuscia	Thuscia.
have	ave.	Tusculum	Thusculum.
Istæc (-oc, -ic)	Isthæc (-hoc, -hic).	Cethegus	Cetegus
		Matho	Mato.
excdra	exhedra.	Otho	Oto.
Panormus	Panhormus.	Spinther	Spinter.
synodus	synhodus.	Thorius	Torius.
aheneus	ahæneus.	Viriathus	Viriatus.
ahenus	ahænus.	Karthago	Cartago.
Ahenobarbus	Ahænob.	Gothi	Goti.
Polyhymnia	Polymnia.	Jugurtha	Jugurta.
polyhistor	polyistor.		
		Ræti	Rhæti.
apsis	absis.	Ramnes	Rhamnes.
apsinthium	absinth.	Remi	Rhemi.
Apsyrtus	Absyrt.	Regium Lepidi (rex)	Rheg. L.
opsonium (ὄψον)	obsonium.	Rhegium in Bruttiis (ῥήγνυμι)	Reg. in Br.
carus	charus.		
caritas	charitas.	Rhenus	Renus.
corona	chorona.	Rhodanus	Rodanus.
ancora	anchora.	rhetor	retor.
lacrima	lachrima.		
sepulcrum	sepulchrum.	auctor	autor.
fulcrum	fulchrum.	autumnus	auctumnus.
cocles	cochles.	conjux	conjunx.
pulcherrimus	pulcerrimus¹.	Quintus	Quinctus.
pulcher	pulcer.	Quintius	Quinctius.
bracæ (bracco)	bracchæ.		
Chilo	Cilo.	Murtia ⎫	Murcia.
Stilicho	Stilico.	nuntio ⎪	nuncio.
charta	carta.	fetialis ⎬ Insee.	fecialis.
Chatti	Catti.	negotium ⎪	negocium.
Chauci	Cauci.	solatium ⎪	solacium.
Cherusci	Cerusci.	planities ⎭	planicies.

¹ But the h is dropt if the r immediately follows the c, as in pulcra, pulcrum, &c.

ACCIDENCE, OR THE FORMS OF WORDS.

Write	rather than	Write	rather than
Domitius	Domicius.	exanguis	exanguis.
Horatius	Horacius.	exsurgo	exurgo.
Lucretius	Lucrecius.		
Vegetius	Vegecius.	Allia	Alia.
Apicius	Apitius.	allium	alium.
Cædicius (Inser.)	Cæditius.	Appulejus	Apulejus.
Mæcius	Mætius.	Appulus	Apulus.
Mauricius	Mauritius.	Attis	Atis.
Minucius	Minutius.	bacca	baca.
Mucius	Mutius.	bellua	belua.
Sulpicius	Sulpitius.	buccina	bucina.
Porcius	Portius.	Elissa	Elisa.
ditio (do)	dicio.	Gracchus	Grachus.
conditio (condo)	condicio.	idcirco	iccirco.
convitium (-icit-)	convicium.	immo	imo.
suspitio (-icit-)	suspicio.	ligurrio	ligurio.
Martius (Mars)	Marcius.	Messalla	Messala.
Martialis	Marcialis.	paullum	paulum.
Marcius (Marcus)	Martius.	Paullus	Paulus.
Marcianus	Martianus.	querella	querela.
infitiae (fateor)	inficiae.	relligio	religio.
segnities	segnicies.	rettuli	retuli.
justitia	justicia.	Sallustius	Salustius.
servitium	servicium.	sollennis	solemnis.
And the like.		sollers	solers.
		sollicitus	solicitus.
novitius (-itio-)	novicius.	Sollitaurilia	Solitaur.
patricius	patritius.	villicus	vilicus.
tribunicius	tribunitius.	Atilius	Atilius.
adventicius	adventitius.	bissextus	bisextus.
And the like.		braccæ	braccæ.
		caussa	caussa.
quum or quom[1] (cf. qui)	cum.	Cybèle	Cybelle.
cum (cf. con)	quum.	disyllabus	disyll.
secutus	sequutus.	Duilius	Duillius.
locutus	loquutus.	flammeus	flameus.
reliquus[2]	reliquus.	Juppiter	Jupiter.
coquus	cocus.	littera	litera.
quotidie	cotidie.	litus	littus.
sōtius (sectius)	sequius.	pedisequus	pedissequus.
sed	set.	quattuor	quatuor.
apud	aput.	squaleo	squalleo.
haud	haut.	squama	squamma.
assisto	existo.	supellex	suppellex.
		vicesimus	vigesimus.

[1] See Quintil. l. 7, § 5. Priscian, I. p. 45, Krehl.

[2] In the comedians *relicŭus* is a word of four syllables; it never occurs in Virgil, Horace, &c.; and first appears under the form *reliquus* in Martial (IV. 43) and Juvenal (V. 153): see Bentley ad Phaedr. pp. 20, 21.

(2) The twenty-three letters of the Latin alphabet are divided into vowels and consonants.

(a) There are six letters called 'vowels,' *vocales*, or 'producing a sound:' A, E, I, O, U, Y. Of these, A, E, O, are pure vowels; but as I, U, in all original forms, represent the consonants J, V, it is most convenient to designate them in these forms as semi-consonants. Y is found only in words immediately derived from the Greek.

(b) There are nineteen letters called 'consonants,' *consonantes*, or 'sounding with' (*i.e.* not without) a vowel. Of these, Z is found only in words immediately derived from the Greek; J and V are only the strongest forms of the semi-consonants, I and U; K is used only before *a*, in abbreviations of such words as *Kalendae*, *Kaeso;* the remaining fifteen are arranged as follows:

		Labial	Guttural	Dental
I. Nine mutes, which are—	*tenues*	P	C, Q	T
	mediae	B	G	D
	aspiratae	F	H	

II. Six semi-vowels, which are—(a) *sibilants* S, X (or KS).
(b) *liquids* L, M, N, R.

Obs. The distinctions of the mutes, as Labial, Guttural, and Dental, may be extended to the other letters; thus M and V are labials, K is a guttural, and is included in X; L, N, R, are dental; the last seems to have had a pronunciation like our *th*, and it was constantly substituted for D and S; S at the end of a word is dental, as approximating to R = *th*, but at the beginning it is guttural, as another form of H. We may consider J as belonging to the gutturals, and we pronounce it as we do G before E or I; but it is properly termed a palatal sound.

§ 3. *Syllables.*

3 Syllables are parts of words, and words are parts of speech.

(1) A Syllable is a vowel, or a consonant and vowel, or two vowels, pronounced in a breath.

(2) As one vowel makes a sound, two vowels joined in one syllable are called a *diphthong*, or double sound, and there are five diphthongs in Latin—AE, or Æ; OE, or Œ[1]; AU, EI, and EU. Of these, Æ stands for AI, which is rarely used; Œ for OI, which scarcely ever occurs; and EI, EU, are not often found. In longer words Æ and Œ are turned into I, AU into Ú, Ó, or É.

[1] To avoid confusion the diphthongs *ae*, *oe* are written with the letters separate whenever they are printed in Italics in the present grammar; but the united letters are retained when the Roman type is used.

ACCIDENCE, OR THE FORMS OF WORDS.

(3) Besides these diphthongs we have only a single syllable when I stands before another vowel in the same syllable; and when U precedes a vowel at the beginning of a word, or follows NG, L, R, and in some words an initial S; but in these cases the semi-consonants are pronounced as consonants, like our J and V or W.

Obs. 1 It will be observed that in the two cases in which a concurrence of vowels makes a single syllable, one of the vowels is always I or U, and these are also used as consonants.

Obs. 2 The diphthong AE resumes its original form of AI only when there is a *diaeresis* or division of the component vowels, as in the poetic genitives *auldī*, *pictī* for *aulae*, *pictae*. In longer forms we have *ex-īquus* from *aequus*, *ex-latimo* from *aestimo*, &c.

Obs. 3 The diphthong OE is invariably substituted for OI when both vowels are represented, except in the particles *proin*, *proinde*. In the proper name *Oileus* there is no diphthong. We find OE for OI even in a compound with a preposition, as in *coetus* for *coïtus*. And this is generally the case in transcriptions from the Greek, even when the ō is long, as in *tragoedia* for τραγῳδία. Sometimes, however, the I is omitted, and the O alone retained, as in *pōēma* for ποίημα; *prosodia* for προσῳδία. In many Latin words a long U represents an original OI or OE, as *unus* for *oinus*; *uti* for *oetier*; and we have both forms together in *poena* and *pūnio*. But we have UI for OI in *Chuilius* by the side of *Cloelius*. In a few cases OI becomes I, as in *cimeterium* for κοιμητήριον.

Obs. 4 The diphthong AU is changed into long U in *ex-clūdo* from *daudo*; into O in *codex* by the side of *caudex*, and *Clodius* by the side of *Claudius*; and into long E in *obēdio* for *ob-audio*. We have AV for AU in some Greek transcriptions, as *Agāve* from Ἀγαυή.

Obs. 5 The diphthong EI is found only in the interjection *hei* and a few obsolete forms, as *nareis* for *nares*, *heic* for *hic*, &c. In Greek words it is represented by I, as in *Euclides*, *Epirus* for Εὐκλείδης, Ἤπειρος; or by E, as in *Darēus* or *Darius* for Δαρεῖος.

Obs. 6 The diphthong EU is found only in Greek words like *Euclides*, *Orpheus*, and in *heu*, *eheu*, *heus*, *ceu*, *seu*, *neu*, *neuter*, *neutiquam*. In some Greek names EV is written for EU, before A, as in *Evander*, *Evadne*, *Evangelium*, from Εὔανδρος, Εὐάδνη, Εὐαγγέλιον.

Obs. 7 When I begins a Latin word, and is followed by another vowel, it becomes consonantal and is written J. And the same is the case when it stands between two vowels in the middle of a word. Thus we have *jejunus*, *major*, &c. The only exception at the beginning of a word is the participle *iens*, and of course we have *ieram*, &c. for *ierunt*, &c. This rule does not apply to Greek words like *iambus*, *Iolaus*, &c. The I is not consonantal when it follows U, as in *tenuia*, *tenuior*; and though we have *Troja*, we have *Troïus* for *Trojius*. So also we have *Gāīūs* for *Gaiēīs*. On the other hand I sometimes begins a syllable or becomes J after a consonant, as in *abjets, consiljum*, &c. which appear as trisyllables in poetry.

Obs. 8 The consonantal use of U mentioned in the rule is shown in the following examples: at the beginning of a word we have it in *vado, venio, video, volo, vilis, vultus;* in the middle of a word, as in *anguis, solvo, arvum;* also *suavis, suadeo, sursco, Suetonius.* But in forms like *coldi, voldi, conserdi,* the U is a vowel, because these words, as we shall see, involve *fui.* And there are some instances of a *diaeresis* or separation of vowels after S and L, as in *silemus, silda, dissolsto.*

Obs. 9 The Greek Y when followed by I makes one syllable, as in *Ilithyia, Harpyia, Thyios.*

(4) In every syllable the vowel is considered short (˘) or long (¯); it is said to be short or long by nature when it is followed by a single consonant; but it may become long by position when followed by two consonants. Diphthongs, contracted syllables, and vowels before X and Z, are always long. The rules for the quantity of syllables are given in Part III.

(5) In dividing a word at the end of a line it is most convenient to adopt the following rules:

(a) A single consonant between two vowels belongs to the second of them, as in *pa-ter.*

(b) Two or more consonants may be placed after the division if they can begin a Latin word; this applies to any mute followed by *l* or *r*, to *g* followed by *n*, to *s* followed by a tenuis, and to a followed by a tenuis and *l* or *r*; but if any other consonant precedes these combinations it must be placed before the division; thus we divide *im-plico, pa-tris, i-gna-rus, ne-scio, a-spi-ro, a-sto, re-splen-det, con-scri-bo, a-spra-tum, de-stric-tus;* but *emp-tus, ef-fluo, ax-is, ip-se, scrip-si.*

(c) The final consonant of a preposition does not pass on to the first syllable of the word with which it is compounded; thus we divide *ab-eo, ad-eo, prod-eo, prod-est, abs-tineo, trans-eo, praeter-eo.*

(6) Although the tone or accent is not written in Latin, some one syllable of every word, except a preposition before its case, has either an acute (´) or circumflex (^), according to the following rules:

(a) Monosyllables have the circumflex if the vowel is long by nature; otherwise the acute.

(b) Dissyllables have a circumflex on the first syllable if the vowel be long by nature, and the last syllable short; otherwise the acute; thus we have *Rômā, Rômŭl, hômo, ŭctus*.

(c) Words of more than two syllables have the circumflex on the last syllable but one (*penultima*), if this is long by nature, and the last syllable is short; they have the acute on the *penultima* if it is long by position and the last syllable is short; they have the acute on the last syllable but two (*antepenultima*) if the penultima is short, whether the last syllable is short or long; thus we have *Romānŭs, Metellus, môribus, carmĭnibus, hôminēs*.

(d) If *que, ne, ve* are used as enclitics, the accent falls on the last syllable of the main word; but if *que* is a constituent part of the word, the general rule is adopted; thus we have *ĭtăque*, 'therefore,' but *ĭtăque*, 'and so;' similarly we have *Musăque, Musăque*, but *ŭterque*.

(e) If an enclitic loses its vowel or suffers *apocope*, as it is called, the accent remains as before; thus we have *audĭn, tantĭn* for *audĭsne, tantĭsne*. The same is the case with nouns in *-ds* for *-ătis*.

(f) Compounds of *facio* with other words than prepositions retain the accent on the verb, as though it were uncompounded; thus we have *calefácit, palamfécit*.

§ 4. *Parts of Speech*.

4. There are eight parts of speech, or different kinds of words; four declined, or admitting of an inflexion or change of form; and four undeclined, or uninflected. The inflexions or changes of form express the differences of case, number, and gender in the noun, and the distinctions of person, number, tense, mood, and voice in the verb. When the inflexions are removed, we say that the declinable word is in its *crude or uninflected form;* thus *dominŏ* is the crude or uninflected form of *dominu-s = dominŏ-s, dominō = domino-i*, and *dominŭ-m = dominŏ-m;* and *mone-* is the crude or uninflected form of *monē-s = mone-is, mone-at*, and *mon-ui = monefui*. The uninflected form may or may not admit of further reduction to a monosyllabic form called a *root;* thus *ped-* is both the

root and the uninflected form of *pes = ped-s*, 'a foot;' but while the same *ped-* is the root, *tri-pud-io-* is the uninflected form of *tri-pudiu-m = tri-pudiŏ-m*. An uninflected form is contained in every inflected word, and the variable terminations are appended to it; but it may appear also without an inflexion, and even without a characteristic vowel. Thus, *tenerŏ-* is the uninflected form of *tener*, which has lost its termination *-us* in the nom. sing. masc.

(1) The declined parts of speech are,

(a) The *noun*, which is called *substantive* when it is the name of a person or thing, as *puer*, 'a boy,' *equus*, 'a horse,' *mensa*, 'a table;' and *adjective* when it is the name of a quality, as *bonus*, 'good,' *celer*, 'swift.'

(b) The *pronoun*, which indicates a position, and generally refers to some noun expressed or understood; as *ille*, 'that one there' (e. g. either *puer* or *equus*).

(c) The *verb*, which denotes an act; as *discit*, 'he learns,' *currit*, 'it runs.'

(d) The *participle*, which combines the meaning of a verb with the form of a noun; as *discens*, 'learning,' *currens*, 'running.'

(2) The undeclined parts of speech are,

(a) The *adverb*, which qualifies the verb; as *discit bene*, 'he learns *well*,' *currit celeriter*, 'it runs *swiftly*.'

(b) The *preposition*, which defines the relation of a noun; as *cum puero*, '*with* a boy,' *ex equo*, '*from* a horse.'

(c) The *conjunction*, which joins words and sentences; as *puer et equus*, 'the boy *and* horse.'

(d) The *interjection*, which expresses an exclamation; as *O bone puer!* 'O good boy!'

(3) The rules for the change of form in declinable words are arranged according to the division of letters into vowels and consonants, and according to the division of consonants into *labials*, *gutturals*, *dentals*, *liquids*, and *semi-consonants*, namely, according to the nature of the letter which terminates the crude or uninflected form of the declinable word.

CHAPTER II.

NOUNS.

§ 1. *Declension of Substantives.*

5 RULES of declension are rules for the formation of cases in particular nouns.

(1) There are six regular cases in the Latin noun, which are called the *nominative*, or case of 'naming,' the *genitive*, or case of 'sonship,' the *dative*, or case of 'giving,' the *accusative*, or case of 'accusing,' the *vocative*, or case of 'calling,' and the *ablative*, or case of 'removing.'

Obs. These names seem to be derived from the proceedings in a law-court; thus, the *nominative*, or case of 'naming,' 'names' the party, as *Gāius accusat*, 'Gaius accuses;' the *genitive*, or case of 'sonship,' says '*of* whom' or 'what,' as *accusatio furti*, 'an accusation of theft,' *filius Marci*, 'son of Marcus;' the *dative*, or case of 'giving,' states '*to* or *for* whom,' as *mihi*, '*to* me;' the *accusative*, or case of 'accusing,' indicates the person accused, or the object of the action, as *Gaius accusat Lucium*, 'Gaius accuses Lucius;' the *vocative*, or case of 'calling,' addresses a person, as *judex*, 'O judge;' and the *ablative*, or case of 'removal,' states the place from which or the person from whom an action or thing proceeds or is taken, as *ablatum a me*, 'taken *from* me;' *factum a me*, 'done *by* me.' But although the names of the cases admit of this explanation, their distinctive value is best given with reference to the English prepositions, which express their meaning. Thus omitting the nominative, which is never indicated by a preposition, the other cases are defined as follows: the *genitive* is expressed by 'of,' and denotes possession, as *magistri liber*, 'the book of the master,' or 'the master's book,' i.e. possessed by him; the *dative* is expressed by 'to' or 'for,' and denotes limitation, as *datum magistro*, 'given to or for the master,' i.e. limited to him; the *accusative* is expressed by 'unto' or 'towards,' or by this meaning contained in the verb on which it depends, and denotes motion towards an object, as *venit Romam*, 'he comes unto Rome;' *accusat Lucium*, 'he brings an accusation unto, in the direction of, against Lucius;' *verberat servum*, 'he beats, bestows a beating on, directs his blows unto or towards the slave;' the *ablative* is expressed by 'from' or 'by,' and denotes motion from an object or agent, as *venit Romā*, 'he came from Rome;' *verberatur a me*, 'he is beaten by me,' i.e. 'receives a beating from me.' Besides these cases, some nouns, especially names of places, have a *locative*, or case of position, which in form corresponds to the G. in the sing. of vowel nouns, and to the Ab. in the sing. of consonant nouns, and in the plural of all nouns; thus we have *Romae*, '*at* Rome;' *domi*, '*at* home;' *Carthagine*, '*at* Carthage;' *Athenis*, '*at* Athens;' but, generally, this is superfluous, as the same meaning is expressed by the ablative with *in*, as in *domo*, '*in* the house.' The nominative is called the *direct* case, and all the others are termed *oblique* cases.

(2) There are three *genders*,—*masculine*, *feminine*, and *neuter*; and two *numbers*, *singular* and *plural*, in most nouns.

Obs. The gender of a noun is known either by its meaning or by its form. The latter distinction depends upon the declension, and will be treated in its proper place. According to the meaning (a) the following nouns are generally masculine: names of *Gods*, *men*, *male animals*, and the *inhabitants of different countries*, as *Jupiter*, *consul*, *taurus*, *Iberus;* of *mountains*, *rivers*, *winds* and *months*, as *Olympus*, *Tiberis*, *Boreas*, *September*. (b) The following are generally feminine: names of *Goddesses*, *women*, *female animals*, *countries*, *islands*, *cities*, and *plants*, as *Juno*, *virgo*, *vacca*, *Italia*, *Naxos*, *Pharsalia*, *salix*. (c) The following are neuter: all indeclinable substantives, as *fas*, 'right;' *nefas*, 'wrong;' and all verbs, &c. used as substantives, as *scire tuum nihil est*, 'your knowing or knowledge is nothing;' because we supply in our thoughts '*the thing* called *right*, *wrong*, *knowing*.' (d) The following are either masculine or feminine, and are called common: nouns which may denote indifferently either a male or female person or animal, as *civis*, 'a male or female citizen;' *adolescens*, 'a young man or woman;' *testis*, 'a witness;' *parens*, 'a parent;' *bos*, 'an ox or cow;' *sus*, 'a hog or sow,' &c.

(3) There are two great classes of Latin nouns,—vowel nouns in *-a* or *-o*, and consonant nouns. The semi-consonant nouns in *-i* and *-u* are properly appended to the latter class:

(4) The following rules apply to all declensions :

(a) The N. A. V. pl. end in *-a* in all neuter nouns.

(b) The A. sing. ends in *-m* in all m. and f. nouns, and the A. pl. ends in *-s* in all but neuter nouns.

(c) The G. pl. ends in *-um* in all nouns.

(5) The following rules distinguish vowel nouns from consonant nouns of all kinds:

14 NOUNS.

I. (a) Vowel nouns always form the G. pl. in -ā-rum or -ō-rum, which is rarely contracted into -um.

(b) They form their D. Ab. pl. in -is, which is rarely uncontracted in -bus.

(c) Their A. sing. is always -am or -um, and their A. pl. f. and m. -ās or -os.

(d) Their Ab. sing. is always -ā or -ō.

II. (a) Consonant nouns generally omit r before -um in the G. pl.

(b) Conversely, they retain -bus in the D. Ab. pl.

(c) The A. sing. m. and f. is always -em or -im, the Ab. sing. is always -e or -i, and the A. pl. always -ēs in m. and f. nouns, except where the characteristic is u.

6 The characteristic letter of the declension may be always seen in the G. pl.; but when a-i is contracted into -ē, the G. pl. is ē-rum, thus forming a new characteristic. Accordingly, the following formula overrules all exceptions, and furnishes the criterion of the Latin declensions:

Declension-characters are those which come
In genitives before the -rum or -um.

§ 2. *First or -a Declension.*

7 The first declension includes Latin nouns in -ă masculine and feminine, and Greek words in -ās or -ēs = -eas masculine and -ē feminine; as *agricŏla*, 'a husbandman;' *musa*, 'a muse;' *Æneas* and *Anchises*, the names of men; and *crambē*, 'a cabbage.' With regard to the gender of this declension, it is to be observed that all Latin -a nouns are feminine except (a) designations of men, as *agricŏla*, 'a husbandman;' *scriba*, 'a secretary;' *nauta*, 'a sailor;' *convīva*, 'a guest;' *aurīga*, 'a chariot-driver;' *incŏla*, 'an inhabitant;' *collēga*, 'a colleague;' *advĕna*, 'a stranger;' &c.: (b) some names of rivers, as *Sequăna, Garumna, Cremĕra;* but *Allia, Matrŏna,* and *Albŭla* are feminine : (c) *Hadria,* the name of the

NOUNS.   15

Adriatic sea: (d) *dama*, 'a deer;' *talpa*, 'a mole,' which are of both genders, the latter being most frequently masculine.

8
Singular.
N. agricola	musa
G. agricolæ	musæ
D. agricolæ	musæ
A. agricolam	musam
V. agricola	musa
Ab. agricolâ	musâ

Plural.
N. agricolæ	musæ
G. agricolArum	musArum
D. agricolis	musis
A. agricolās	musās
V. agricolæ	musæ
Ab. agricolis	musis.

Obs. In committing to memory the declension of a Latin noun, it may be advantageous to the learner that he should be taught to repeat the English of every case. One of the two following methods may be adopted, according as it is thought desirable or not to express the gender as well as the number and case of the inflexion:

(*a*) To express the number and case only.

Sing.	Plur.
N. mensa, a table	mensæ, tables
G. mensæ, of a table	mensarum, of tables
D. mensæ, to or for a table	mensis, to or for tables
A. mensam, unto a table	mensas, unto tables
V. mensa, O table	mensæ, O tables
Ab. mensa, by or from a table	mensis, by or from tables

(*b*) To express gender, number and case.

Masc. Sing.	Masc. Plur.
N. puer, he—the boy	pueri, they—the boys
G. pueri, of him—the boy	puerorum, of them—the boys
D. puero, to or for him—the boy	pueris, to or for them—the boys
A. puerum, him—the boy	pueros, them—the boys
V. puer, O thou—the boy	pueri, O you—the boys
Ab. puero, by or from him—the boy	pueris, by or from them—the boys

NOUNS.

Fem. Sing.
- N. *filia*, she—the daughter
- G. *filiae*, of her—the daughter
- D. *filiae*, to or for her—the daughter
- A. *filiam*, her—the daughter
- V. *filia*, O thou—the daughter
- Ab. *filia*, by or from her—the daughter

Fem. Plur.
- *filiae*, they—the daughters
- *filiarum*, of them—the daughters
- *filiabus*, to or for them—the daughters
- *filias*, them—the daughters
- *filiae*, O you—the daughters
- *filiabus*, by or from them—the daughters

Neut. Sing.
- N. *regnum*, it—the kingdom
- G. *regni*, of it—the kingdom
- D. *regno*, to or for it—the kingdom
- A. *regnum*, it—the kingdom
- V. *regnum*, O thou—the kingdom
- Ab. *regno*, by or from it—the kingdom

Neut. Plur.
- *regna*, they—the kingdoms
- *regnorum*, of them—the kingdoms
- *regnis*, to or for them—the kingdoms
- *regna*, them—the kingdoms
- *regna*, O you—the kingdoms
- *regnis*, by or from them—the kingdoms

9 Greek nouns of the first declension differ from the Latin only in the singular number, as in the following examples :

N.	Æneäs	Anchisēs	crambē
G.	Æneæ	Anchisæ	crambēs
D.	Æneæ	Anchisæ	crambæ
A.	Æneam or -än	Anchisem or -ēn	cramben
V.	Ænea	Anchisā	crambē
Ab.	Æneā	Anchisē	crambē

Obs. Some Greek nouns in *-as* or *-es* are occasionally written in *-a;* thus we have *Mida, cometa, Scytha, Æeta, pycta,* by the side of *Midas, cometes, Scythes, Ætes, pyctes,* the latter, however, being the more usual forms.

For variations between the first and third declension in the forms of some of the cases of these Greek nouns, see below, 30 (b).

10 Some feminine nouns retain the original D. and Ab. pl. in *-abus;* as *deabus, filiabus, animabus;* and in the poets, the older form of the G. sing. in *āī* is still found, as in *aulāī, pictāi:* the original *s* of the G. sing. is retained only in *familias* following *pater, mater, filius,* as in *paterfamilias,* 'the father of a family.' The genitive plural is sometimes shortened into *-um,* as in *caelicolum, amphorum.*

NOUNS. 17

§ 3. *Second or o- Declension.*

11 The characteristic δ is changed into *ŭ* in the N. A. sing., but retained in the D. Ab. sing. and G. pl. The termination *-ros* or *-eros* is shortened into *-er*, as we see in *ager*, compared with ἀγρός, *Alexander* compared with 'Αλέξανδρος. Thus we have masculine nouns in *-us* or *-er* (*-ir, -ur*), and neuter nouns in *-um*; as *dominus*, 'a lord;' *populus*, 'a people;' *magister*, 'a master;' *puer*, 'a boy;' *liber*, 'a book;' *ager*, 'a field;' *vir*, 'a man;' *regnum*, 'a kingdom;' *bellum*, 'a war.'

Singular.

N. dominus	magister	puer	regnum
G. domini	magistri	pueri	regni
D. domino	magistro	puero	regno
A. dominum	magistrum	puerum	regnum
V. domine	magister	puer	regnum
Ab. domino	magistro	puero	regno

Plural.

N. domini	magistri	pueri	regna
G. dominOrum	magistrOrum	puerOrum	regnOrum
D. dominis	magistris	pueris	regnis
A. dominos	magistros	pueros	regna
V. domini	magistri	pueri	regna
Ab. dominis	magistris	pueris	regnis

Obs. 1 *Liber*, 'a book,' is declined like *magister*; but *Liber*, 'Bacchus,' and *liberi*, 'children,' like *puer*.

The only word which ends in *-ir* is *vir*, 'a man;' and this, as well as its compounds *triumvir*, &c. and the national name *Trevir*, will follow the declension of *puer*, thus: *vir, viri, viro, virum, viri, virorum, viris, viros*. The only word which ends in *-ur* is the adjective *satur*, which also follows the declension of *puer*, as is the case with most adjectives in *-er*, as *asper, tener, miser;* with those in *-fer* and *-ger*, as *signifer, armiger;* and with the substantives *socer, gener, adulter, vesper*. We have both *dexteri* and *dextri* from *dexter;* both *Mulciberi* and *Mulcibri* from *Mulciber*.

Obs. 2 Although most Greek names in *-pos* preceded by a consonant follow the declension of *Alexander* and *magister*, the Greek form is occasionally retained, especially by the poets. Thus we have *Meleagros* in Ovid, *Evandrus*, and *Codrus*. And while we write *hexameter*, we also write *diametrus*.

D. L. G.

16   NOUNS.

12 *Deus*, "God," makes *O Deus* in the vocative singular. The plural is thus declined:

    N. V. Di (seldom Dei)
    G.   Deûm or Deorum
    D.   Dis (seldom Deis)
    A.   Deos
    Ab.   Dis (seldom Deis)

13 The genitive plural in *-um* for *-orum*, as in *Deum* for *Deorum*, is particularly common in nouns denoting trades, as *fabrum*, 'of carpenters,' from *faber*; coins, as *sestertium numum*, 'of sesterces;' and in poetry in adjectives and national names, as *magnanimum Rutulum*, 'of the courageous Rutuli.'

14 In Classical Latinity, substantives in *-ius* and *-ium* made the G. sing. in *-i*, as *Vergilius*, G. *Vergili*; *ingenium*, 'disposition,' or 'natural abilities,' G. *ingeni*. But this rule does not apply to adjectives, for we have in the same line of Horace:

egregii altiquo silenti.

15 Roman proper names in *-ius*, together with *filius*, 'a son,' and *genius*, 'a tutelary spirit,' make the vocative in *i*; as *Vergilius* V. *Vergili*; *Mercurius* V. *Mercūri*; *filius* V. *fili*. So also we have *mi* for *mee* from *meus*. This rule does not apply to Greek names or adjectives, as *Cynthius* V. *Cynthīe*, or to nouns in *-ius* Gr. *-ειος*, as *Sperchius* V. *Sperchie*. The vocative *Gāi* exposes the common error of pronouncing *Gā-ius* as a word of two syllables. The poets use *Pompei* as a dissyllable.

16 Greek nouns in *-ŏs*, *-ŏn* retain the *ŏ* in the N. and A. as:

    N.   Delos   colŏn
    G.   Deli   coli
    D.   Delo   colo
    A.   Delŏn or Delum colŏn
    V.   Dele   colŏn
    Ab. Delo   colo

17 Those, which, in the original, end in *-ως*, sometimes retain the *ŏ* throughout; as:

    N. V. Androgeōs
    G.   Androgeo or -i
    D.   Androgeo
    A.   Androgeon or -o or -ōna
    Ab.   Androgeo

18 Greek nouns in *-eus* (*-εύς*) sometimes follow the second declension in Latin; as:

    N. Orpheus (dissyllable)
    G. Orphĕŏs, -ĕi, -ei
    D. Orphĕī, -ĕi, -eo
    A. Orpheă, -eum
    V. Orpheu
    Ab. Orpheo

We have also *Achillei* and *Ulixi* in the G., though in other cases *Achilles* and *Ulixes* follow the third declension.

19 Contracted Greek nouns are contracted also in Latin; as:

    N. Panthūs
    G. Panthi
    D. Ab. Pantho
    A. Panthum
    V. Panthū

20 Neuter nouns corresponding to Greek words in *-ος* follow this declension; as *pelagus*, 'the surface of the sea;' *virus*, 'poison.' *Vulgus*, 'the multitude,' is generally neuter; but sometimes also masculine.

21 The following nouns in *-us*, *-ŭs* are feminine:

(1) Names of countries; as *Ægyptus, Cyprus, Samos*, &c.

(2) *Alvus*, 'belly;' *colus*, 'distaff,' or 'spinning-rock;' *humus*, 'ground;' *vannus*, 'winnowing fan.'

(3) Certain Greek words, as *periodus*, 'period;' *dialectus*, 'dialect;' *abyssus*, 'a bottomless pit,' &c.

(4) All names of trees, and some of shrubs; as *pŏpulus*, 'the poplar' (distinguished by quantity also from *pŏpulus*, 'the people;') *fagus*, 'the beech;' *pirus*, 'the pear-tree;' *mālus* and *pōmus*, 'the apple-tree' (but *pirum*, 'the pear;' *mālum* and *pōmum*, 'the apple;') *buxus* 'the box-tree' (but *buxum*, 'box-wood;') &c.

§ 4. *Third Declension, or consonantal and semi-consonantal nouns.*

22 Nouns of the third declension are arranged according to the nature of the characteristic consonant which precedes the case-

NOUNS.

ending; and they fall into two great classes, according as they retain the consonant or vocalize it into *i* or *u*. The characteristic of the crude form is often lost in the nominative singular, but is always seen in the genitive plural, as the following table will show:

Nom.	Gen. Plural.	Example.		Crude-form.	No. of Rule.
a	aTum	*poema*	poemaTum	poemaT	25
e	Ium	*mare*	marIum	marI	28
o -o (1)	ōNum	*leo*	leoNum	leoN	27
-o (2)	nIum	*caro*	carnIum	carnI	28
-o (3)	iNum	*virgo*	virgiNum	virgiN	27
-o (4)	ŏNum	*Macedo*	MacedoNum	MacedoN	27
c	ctIum	*lac*	lactIum	lactI	28
l	Lum	*pugil*	pugiLum	pugiL	27
n -an (1)	āNum	*Titan*	TitaNum	TitaN	27
-en (2)	ēnIum	*ren*	renIum	renI	28
-en (3)	iNum	*carmen*	carmiNum	carmeNT	25
-on (4)	ŏNum	*sindon*	sindoNum	sindoN	27
r -ar (1)	arIum	*calcar*	calcarIum	calcarI	28
-er (2)	ēRum	*carcer*	carceRum	carceR	27
-ter (3)	tRum	*pater*	patRum	patrR	27
-or (4)	ōRum	*honor*	honoRum	honoR	27
-or (5)	ŏRum	*arbor*	arboRum	arboR	27
-ur (6)	ŭRum	*fulgur*	fulguRum	fulguR	27
s -as (1)	ātIum	*Arpinas*	ArpinatIum	ArpinatI	28
-as (2)	sIum	*as*	assIum	assI	28
-as (3)	Dum	*lampas*	lampaDum	lampaD	25
-as (4)	NTum	*gigas*	gigaNTum	gigaNT	25
-as (5)	Tum	*aetas*	aetaTum¹	aetaT	25
-es (6)	Ium	*nubes*	nubIum	nubI	28
-es (7)	ĕDum	*pes*	peDum	peD	25
-es (8)	ēDum	*haeres*	haereDum	haereD	25
-es (9)	iDum	*obses*	obsiDum	obsiD	25
-es (10)	ĕTum	*seges*	segeTum	segeT	25
-es (11)	iTum	*comes*	comiTum	comiT	25
-is (12)	ĕRum	*cinis*	cineRum	cineR	27
-is (13)	iNum	*sanguis*	sanguiNum	sanguiN	27
-is (14)	Ium	*puppis*	puppIum	puppI	28
-is (15)	Dum	*lapis*	lapiDum	lapiD	25

¹ The form *aetatium* is found in some MSS., but it is not the usual spelling.

NOUNS.

Nom.	Gen. Plural.	Example.		Crude-form.	No. of Rule.
-is (16)	Ium	vis	virIum	virI	28
-is (17)	itIum	Quiris	QuiritIum	QuiriT	28
-os (18)	ŏtIum	dos	dotIum	dotI	28
-os (19)	ŏRum	mos	moRum	moR	27
-os (20)	ŏDum	custos	custoDum	custoD	25
-os (21)	sIum	os	ossIum	ostI	28
-us (22)	[V]um	bos	bo[V]um	boV	29
-us (23)	ūTum	virtus	virtuTum	virtuT	25
-us (24)	ŭDum	palus	paluDum	paluD	25
-us (25)	ŭDum	pecus	pecuDum	pecuD	25
-us (26)	ûrIum	mus	murIum	murI	28
-us (27)	u[cR]um	sus	su[cR]um	sueR	27
-us (28)	ĕRum	opus	opeRum	opuT	25
-us (29)	ŏRum	tempus	tempoRum	tempoT	25
-æs (30)	a·Rum	aes	æRum	æR	26
-ais = ēs (31)	Erum	dies	diErum	diaI	28
-aus (32)	Dum	laus	lauDum	lauD	25
-bs (33)	Ium	urbs	urbIum	urbI	28
-bs (34)	Bum	caelebs	cæliBum	cæliB	23
-ps (35)	Pum	forceps	forciPum	forccP	23
-mps (36)	Mum	hiemps	hicMum	hicM	26
-ns (37)	Ium	serpens	serpentIum	serpentI	28
t	Tum	caput	capiTum	capuT	25
x -ax (1)	Cum	fax	fãCum	faC	24
-ex (2)	Cum	vervex	vervĕCum	verveC	24
-ex (3)	Cum	judex	judiCum	judiC	24
-ex (4)	Gum	rex	rĕGum	reG	24
-ex (5)	Gum	grex	grĕGum	greG	24
-ex (6)	Gum	remex	remiGum	remiG	24
-ix (7)	Cum	cornix	corniCum	corniC	24
-ix (8)	Gum	strix	striGum	striG	24
-ox (9)	Cum	vox	vŏCum	voC	24
-ux (10)	Cum	dux	dŭCum	duC	24
-ux (11)	Gum	conjux	conjŭGum	conjuG	24
-yx (12)	Cum	bombyx	bombyCum	bombyC	24
-yx (13)	Gum	Phryx	PhryGum	PhryG	24
-nx (14)	Cum	lynx	lynCum	lynC	24
-rx (15)	Ium	arx	arcIum	arcI	28

NOUNS.

A. *First class, or consonantal nouns.*

23 (a) Labial nouns are m. or f.; *caelebs*, c. 'an unmarried person;' *auceps*, c. 'a fowler;' *forceps*, c. 'a pair of tongs,' which change *e* into *i* in the oblique cases. If the characteristic is proceded by *r*, the noun really belongs to the *i* declension; thus we have *urbs*, G. pl. *urb-I-um*; also in some other instances, as *trabs*, G. pl. *trab-I-um*, &c.: see below, 26. Although *hiemps* is written with an inserted *p*, it is properly a liquid noun; below, 26.

Singular.

N. V.	caelebs	forceps
G.	caelibis	forcipis
D.	caelibi	forcipi
A.	caelibem	forcipem
Ab.	caelibe	forcipe

Plural.

N. A. V.	caelibes	forcipes
G.	caeliBum	forciPum
D. Ab.	caelibibus	forcipibus

24 (b) Guttural nouns are m. or f.; as *dux*, *dŭcis*, c. 'a leader;' *judex, judĭcis*, c. 'a judge;' *conjux, conjŭgis*, c. 'a consort.' The following are irregular: *senex, sĕnis*, c. 'an old man or woman;' *sŭpellex, supellectĭlis*, f. 'household furniture.' *Nix, nĭvis*, f. 'snow,' and *merx, mercis*, f. 'merchandise,' and some others in *x*, are really nouns in *i*, like *urbs* and *pars;* see below, 28.

Singular.

N. V.	dux	judex	conjux
G.	ducis	judicis	conjugis
D.	duci	judici	conjugi
A.	ducem	judicem	conjugem
Ab.	duce	judice	conjuge

Plural.

N. A. V.	duces	judices	conjuges
G.	duCum	judiCum	conjuGum
D. Ab.	ducibus	judicibus	conjugibus

25 (c) Dental nouns are of all genders: (a) as *lapis, lapĭdis*, m. 'a stone;' *cuspis, cuspĭdis*, f. 'a point;' *cōmes, comĭtis*, c. 'a companion.' *Vāt-ēs*, 'a prophet,' inserts a long *e* in the N. sing.

only. Apparently dental nouns, in which the characteristic *t* is preceded by *n*, *r*, or a long vowel, are really nouns in *i*. This is the case with *fons, pars, lis* (*lit-i-*), &c.; see below, 28. But feminines in *-tât-*, *-tût-*, as *boni-tas, vir-tus*, are dentals.

Singular.

N. V.	lapis	comes
G.	lapidis	comitis
D.	lapidi	comiti
A.	lapidem	comitem
Ab.	lapide	comite

Plural.

N. A. V.	lapides	comites
G.	lapiDum	comiTum
D. Ab.	lapidibus	comitibus

(β) Dental nouns of the neuter gender properly end in *t*, but *caput, capitis*, 'a head,' and its compounds, are the only words which still retain the genuine characteristic in the nominative. It is sometimes preserved in the oblique cases, as in *poēma, poemătis*, 'a poem;' *lac, lactis*, 'milk;' or under the medial form *d*, as *cor, cordis*, 'the heart.' But in most instances it is either omitted altogether, as in *carmen, carmĭnis*, 'a poem' (cf. *carmentis*, 'a poetess'); *agmen, agmĭnis*, 'a troop' (cf. *armentum*, 'a herd'); or softened into *s* or *r* (2, (2) b. *Obs.*), as in *corpus, corpŏris*, 'a body;' *tempus, tempŏris*, 'time;' *opus, opĕris*, 'a work;' some,—as *jecur* (for *jecinor*), *jecinŏris*, 'the liver;' *iter* (for *itiner*), *itinĕris*, 'the journey;' *jubar, jubăris*, 'a ray of light;' *nectar, nectăris*, 'nectar;' *far, farris*, 'corn;'—probably had both *l* and *t*, and *r* and *t* in the original form.

Singular.

N. A. V.	caput	carmen	corpus	opus
G.	capitis	carminis	corporis	operis
D.	capiti	carmini	corpori	operi
Ab.	capite	carmine	corpore	opere

Plural.

N. A. V.	capita	carmina	corpora	opera
G.	capiTum	carmin[T]um	corpoRum	opeRum
D. Ab.	capitibus	carminibus	corporibus	operibus

24   NOUNS.

26 (d) Liquid nouns are generally of dental origin, and very much resemble some of the neuters, which have just been mentioned. Thus we have nouns in *-ān*, as *Titan, Titānis*, m. 'a Titan;' in *-ōn*, as *sermo, sermōnis*, m. 'a discourse;' *ratio, ratiōnis*, f. 'an account,' 'a reason;' in *-īn*, as *ordo, ordĭnis*, m. 'an order;' *homo, homĭnis*, m. 'a man' (whence *nemo = ne-homo*); *virgo, virgĭnis*, f. 'a virgin;' in *l*, as *sol, sōlis*, m. 'the sun;' *consul, consŭlis*, m. 'the consul;' *mel, mellis*, n. 'honey;' in *r*, as *pater, patris*, m. 'a father;' *ver, vēris*, n. 'spring;' to which class belong *Cĕres, Cerĕris*, f. 'the goddess of corn;' *os, ōris*, n. 'a face;' *rus, rūris*, n. 'the country;' *flos, flōris*, m. 'a flower;' *mos, mōris*, m. 'a custom;' *aes, aeris*, n. 'copper;' and the exceptional nouns, *cinis, cinĕris*, m. 'ashes;' *pulvis, pulvĕris*, m. 'dust.' *Canis*, 'a dog;' and *juvenis*, 'a young man,' insert an articulation *i* in the N. sing. only.

Singular.

N. V.	sermo	virgo	pater	mos	os
G.	sermonis	virginis	patris	moris	oris
D.	sermoni	virgini	patri	mori	ori
A.	sermonem	virginem	patrem	morem	os
Ab.	sermone	virgine	patre	more	ore

Plural.

N. A. V.	sermones	virgines	patres	mores	ora
G.	sermoNum	virgiNum	patRum	moRum	oRum
D. Ab.	sermonibus	virginibus	patribus	moribus	oribus

27 The genders of consonantal nouns, when not positively determined by the meaning (above 5 (2) b, *Obs.*), may be known by the terminations as follows:

(1) Labial nouns are either feminine or common.

(2) Of guttural nouns (a) those in *-ax* are feminine, as *pax, pācis*, 'peace;' *fax, făcis*, 'a torch:' (b) those in *-ex, -ĭcis* are masc., as *codex, codĭcis*, 'a trunk of a tree,' also 'a book;' *apex, apĭcis*, 'the extreme point;' but *curex*, 'sedge;' *forfex*, 'a pair of shears;' *ilex*, 'holm-oak;' *pellex*, 'a concubine;' and *vitex*, 'a withy,' are feminine; and *imbrex*, 'a tile,' *obex*, 'a bolt' (not used in the nom. sing.); *rumex*, 'sorrel;' and, in poetry, *cortex*, 'bark,' and *siler*, 'flint,' are common: (c) those in

-nex, -necis; *-ex, -ecis;* *-ex, -egis* are fem., as *faex, faecis*, 'lees;' *nex, necis*, 'death;' *lex, legis*, 'law;' but the following are masculine: *grex, gregis*, 'a herd;' *rex, regis*, 'a king;' *aquilex, aquilegis* and *-icis*, 'a person skilled in discovering springs;' *remex, remigis*, 'a rower;' *cervex, vervecis*, 'a wether sheep;' *faenisex, faenisecis*, 'a haycutter:' (d) those in *-ix, -icis*, are feminine, as *fulix*, 'a coot;' but *calix*, 'a cup,' and *fornix*, 'a vault,' are masc., and *varix*, 'a varicose vein' is common: (e) those in *-ix, -icis* are feminine, as *cervix*, 'a neck;' and to this class belongs *vibex, vibicis*, 'the mark of a blow or stripe,' i.e. 'a weal;' but *spadix*, 'a palm-branch,' and *Phoenix*, 'a fabulous bird,' are masculine; (f) *bombyx, bombycis*, 'a kind of wasp,' also 'a silkworm,' is masculine; (g) *strix, strigis*, 'a screech-owl,' is feminine; (h) *vox, vocis*, 'voice,' and *celox, celocis*, 'a pinnace,' are feminine: (i) those in *-ux, -ucis* and *-ucis, -ugis* and *-ugis*, are feminine, as *nux, nucis*, 'a nut;' *lux, lucis*, 'light;' *conjux, conjugis*, 'a wife' (but com. when it denotes 'a consort'); *frux, frugis*, 'fruit' (not used in nom. sing.); *faux, faucis*, 'throat' (not used in nom. sing.). But *dux, ducis*, 'a leader;' *tradux, traducis*, 'the layer of a vine,' are masc.

(3) Of dental nouns (a) those in *-as, -ădis* are fem., as *lampas*, 'a lamp;' but *vas, vădis*, 'a surety in criminal cases,' and its derivatives *praes, praedis*, 'a surety in money matters;' *custos, custodis*, 'a guardian,' are common: (b) *heres, heredis*, 'an heir,' is c., and *merces, mercedis*, 'wages' (derived from *merx*, 'merchandise'), is fem.: (c) *obses, obsidis*, 'a hostage;' *praeses, praesidis*, 'a protector;' *pes, pedis*, 'a foot,' are masc.: (d) those in *-is, -idis* are fem., as *cuspis*, 'a point;' but *lapis*, 'a stone,' is masc.: (e) those in *-es, -itis* are masc., as *miles*, 'a soldier;' but *comes*, 'a companion,' and *ales*, 'a bird,' are common; and *merges*, 'a sheaf of corn,' is feminine: (f) *paries, parietis*, 'a party-wall,' is masc.; but *seges, segetis*, 'a corn-field,' is fem.: (g) those in *-us, -ătis, -es, -etis, -us, -ŭtis* are fem.; as *aetas*, 'an age;' *quies*, 'quiet;' *virtus*, 'virtue,' or 'manliness;' so also *anas, anătis*, 'a duck;' but *sacerdos*, gen. *sacerdotis*, 'a priest or priestess,' is common: (h) *laus, laudis*, 'praise;' *palus, palūdis*, 'a marsh;' *pecus, pecūdis*, 'a beast' (distinguished from *pecus, pecŏris*, n. 'cattle'), and the Greek *chlamys, chlamydis*, 'a cloak,' are feminine; (i) those in *-as, -antis* are masculine, as *adamas*, 'steel;' *elephas*, 'an elephant;' *gigas*, 'a giant.' The neuter dentals are those mentioned in rule 25 (β), and

all others of the same class. *Pecten, pectĭnis,* 'a comb,' and *flamen, flamĭnis,* 'a priest,' are masculine.

(4) Of liquid nouns, (a) the Greek nouns in *-an, -ănis, -en, -ĕnis, -in, -ĭnis,* are masc., as *Titan,* 'a Titan;' *splen,* 'the spleen;' *attagen,* 'a heathcock;' *delphin,* 'a dolphin:' (b) those in *-o, -ōnis* are masc., as *sermo,* 'a discourse:' (c) those in *-io, -iōnis* are fem., as *ratio,* 'reason;' except *papilio,* 'a butterfly;' *pugio,* 'a dagger;' *scipio,* 'a staff;' *septentrio,* 'the north;' *vespertilio,* 'a bat;' *unio,* 'a pearl;' *senio,* 'the number six;' *ternio,* 'the number three:' (d) those in *-do, -dĭnis, -go, -gĭnis,* are fem., as *hirundo,* 'a swallow;' *origo,* 'an origin;' but *cardo,* 'a hinge;' *ordo,* 'an order;' and generally *margo,* 'a margin,' are masculine: (e) those in *-or, -ōris* are masculine, as *honor,* or *honos,* 'honour;' but *uxor,* 'a wife;' *soror,* 'a sister,' are necessarily feminine, and so is *arbor,* or *arbos, arbŏris,* 'a tree;' but *aequor, -ŏris,* 'a surface;' *ador, -ŏris,* and *-ōris,* 'spelt;' *marmor, -ŏris,* 'marble;' *os, ōris,* 'a face,' are neuter: (f) those in *-er, -ĕris* or *-ris* are masc., as *pater, patris,* 'a father;' *carcer,* 'a prison;' to this class belong *cinis* and *pulvis,* and the two Greek words *aër* and *aether;* but the following are neuter: *cadaver,* 'a corpse;' *tuber,* 'a swelling or a truffle;' *uber,* 'an udder;' the plur. *verbera,* 'blows,' and botanical names, as *papaver,* 'poppy:' but *tuber,* 'an apple,' is masculine; and *mulier,* 'a woman;' *mater, matris,* 'a mother,' and *Ceres,* are necessarily feminine: (g) those in *-ur, -ŭris, -ur, -ŏris* are neuter, as *fulgur,* 'lightning;' *robur,* 'strength:' (h) *fur, fūris,* 'a thief,' is masc., but *jus, jūris,* 'right,' and *rus, rūris,* 'the country,' are neuter; and *tellus, tellūris,* 'the earth,' is feminine; *furfur,* 'bran;' *turtur,* 'a turtle-dove;' *vultur,* 'a vulture;' and *augur,* 'a soothsayer,' which form the gen. in *-ŭris,* are masculine: (i) *aes, aeris,* 'copper,' and *ver, veris,* 'spring,' are neuter: (k) *sol, sōlis,* 'the sun,' is masculine; *sal, sălis,* 'salt,' is masc. in the plur., and masc., or rarely neuter, in the singular (when masc. it is for *sal-is,* when neuter for *sal-t*); *fel,* 'gall;' *mel,* 'honey,' are neuter: (l) those in *-il, -ĭlis,* as *pugil,* 'a boxer;' and in *ul, ŭlis,* as *consul,* 'a consul,' are masculine: (m) *sanguis, sanguĭnis* is masculine: (n) *sus, suis* (for *sueris,* Fest. p. 330), 'a sow;' *grus, gruis* (for *gŭr-is?*), 'a crane,' are more frequently fem. than masc.: (o) *hiem-p-s, hiem-is,* which is fem., is the only noun of which the crude form ends in *-m*: (p) the following Greek nouns in *-on, -ŏnis* are feminine: *Gorgon,* 'a Gorgon;' *halcyon,* 'a king-fisher;' *sindon,* 'muslin.'

NOUNS.

B. *Second class, or semi-consonantal nouns.*

28 (α) Nouns ending in -*i* ought properly to retain this vocalized consonant throughout all the cases; but in ordinary Latin the characteristic is often omitted or changed into *e* in all cases except the G. pl., and this too exhibits *e* in the contracted nouns in *ê = ai*. This declension must therefore be subdivided as follows:

(a) Characteristic retained in the N. and A. sing.; as *sitis*, f. 'thirst;' *Tiberis*, m. 'the Tiber;' *febris*, f. 'a fever;' *puppis*, f. 'the stern of a ship;' *sinapis*, f. and *sinapi*, n. 'mustard.'

(b) Characteristic omitted or changed into *e* in the N. sing., as *mare*, n. 'the sea;' *animal*, n. 'an animal;' *calcar*, n. 'a spur;' *lac*, also written *lacte*, n. 'milk;' *os, ossis*, n. 'a bone,' which has *ossa* in the N. A. V. pl.

(c) Characteristic omitted or changed into *e* in the N. A. Ab. sing., as *urb-s*, f. 'a city;' *nubes*, f. 'a cloud;' *merx (merc-i-)*, f. 'merchandise;' *pars (part-i-)*, f. 'a part;' *Quiris, (Quirit-i-)*, m. 'a Roman citizen.'

Obs. 1 The nouns, in which the characteristic is thus disguised, are:

(a) The apparently liquid nouns, *imber*, 'a shower;' *linter*, 'a bark;' *uter*, 'a leathern bottle;' *Insuber*, an inhabitant of Gallia Transpadana; and *caro*, gen. *carnis*, 'flesh;' for which a nom. *carnis* also occurs (Liv. XXXVII. 3).

(b) Monosyllables in *s* or *x* preceded by a consonant, as *merx*, 'merchandise;' *mons*, 'a mountain;' *arx*, 'a citadel;' *stirps*, 'a stock;' *trabs*, 'a beam;' and the nouns, *as*, 'a pound,' *asslum; glis*, 'a dormouse,' *glirlum; lis* (for *stlis*), 'a law-suit,' *litlum; dos*, 'a free gift,' *dotlum; cos*, 'a whet-stone,' *cotlum; mas*, 'a male,' *marlum; os* (for *osti*), 'a bone,' *osslum; mus*, 'a mouse,' *murlum; vis*, 'force,' *virlum; faux* (not used in sing. nom.), 'a throat,' *fauclum; nix* (for *niqvis*, cf. *ninguo*), 'snow,' *nivlum; nox*, 'night,' *noctlum; fraus*, 'harm,' *fraudlum; frons*, 'a leaf,' *frondlum; frons*, 'a brow,' *frontlum; glans*, 'an acorn,' *glandlum; urb-s, urblum; nubes*, also *nub-s, nublum*.

(c) Words of more than one syllable in *-ns* and *-rs*, as *cliens*, 'a client,' *clientlum; serpens*, 'a serpent,' *serpentlum; cohors*, 'a battalion,' *cohortlum*.

(d) Nouns in *-as, atis, -es, -etis, -is, -itis*, as *Arpinas*, 'a man of Arpinum,' *Arpinatlum; locuples*, 'a man of substance,' *locupletlum; Samnis*, 'a man of Samnium,' *Samnitlum*. In many of these cases the original nouns in *-tis* are still extant.

Obs. 2 The nouns in -*i* which retain this characteristic in the accusative singular are thus given in memorial lines:

> The following will always give
> I-M in the accusative:
> *Vis, ravis, pelvis, sitis, tussis,*
> *Sinapis, cannabis, amussis,*
> *Praesepis, tigris,* and *securis.*
> Together with *charybdis, buris;*
> And rivers' names, which end in *is,—*
> For instance, *Albis, Tiberis.*
> In certain nouns the ending is
> Both *im* and *em;* as *strigilis,*
> *Sementis, turris, puppis, navis,*
> *Aqualis, febris, restis, clavis.*

amussis, a rule	*puppis,* the stem of a ship
aqualis, a water-pot	*ravis,* hoarseness
buris, a plough-tail	*restis,* a rope
cannabis, hemp	*securis,* an axe
charybdis, a whirlpool	*sementis,* sowing
clavis, a key	*sinapis,* mustard
febris, a fever	*sitis,* thirst
navis, a ship	*strigilis,* a scraper
pelvis, a pan	*turris,* a tower
praesepis, a stall	*tussis,* a cough
	vis, force, violence.

Obs. 3 The abl. sing. ends in *i* in all nouns of an adjectival nature, as *Atheniensis, sodalis, natalis, September;* but *juvenis, Ædilis,* and adjectives used as proper names, as *Martialis, Pertinax,* make the abl. in *e.* Those which have the accusative in *im* have the abl. in *i;* those which have the accus. in *im* or *em* have the abl. in *i* or *e.* The abl. in *i* is found in certain usages of *ignis,* as *aqua et igni interdicere alicui; rure,* 'from the country,' is distinguished from *ruri,* 'in the country;' and the abl. in -*i* is rare in *amnis, civis, finis, fustis, imber, orbis, supellex.*

Obs. 4 The gen. plur. always retains its characteristic *i,* though there are some cases in which the MSS. vary, and others in which the exigences of metre require a contraction in *um.* The following rhymes give most of the nouns in which the termination is regularly -*um,* and which must therefore be excluded from this declension:

(a) Monosyllables.

> *Crux, dux* and *nux, Thrax, fax* and *grex,*
> *Gryps, Phryx, vox, lynx,* and *rex* and *lex,*
> *Fur, splen,* and *laus,* and *strix,* and *mus,*
> *Crus, grus* and *sus, praes, pes* and *flos.*

NOUNS.   20

(b) Polysyllables.
Vates, senex, puter, panis,
With *accipiter* and *canis,*
Frater, mater, juvenis,
And often *apis, volucris.*

Certain plural nouns in *-alia,* as names of feasts, *Floralia,* &c. and the word *rectigalia,* sometimes have a gen. plur. in *-aliorum,* as from an adjective in *-alius.*

Obs. 5 The accusative plural of nouns in *-i* is written *-eis* or *-is* in some editions of the best authors.

(d) Characteristic absorbed by contraction of *a-i* into *ē,* as *res,* f. 'a thing;' *dies,* c. 'a day;' *materies,* f. 'mother-stuff,' or 'materials.'

Singular.

	(a)	(b)		(c)	
N.V.	puppis	mare	animal	urbs	nubes
G.	puppis	maris	animālis	urbis	nubis
D.	puppi	mari	animāli	urbi	nubi
A.	puppim & -em	mare	animal	urbem	nubem
Ab.	puppi	mari	animāli	urbe	nube

Plural

N.A.V.	puppes (īs)	maria	animalia	urbes (īs)	nubes (īs)
G.	puppIum	marIum	animalIum	urbIum	nubIum
D.Ab.	puppibus	maribus	animalibus	urbibus	nubibus

(d)
Singular.

N.V.	dics	res	materies	(materia)
G.	diēi	rēi	materiēi	(materiāī)
D.	diēi	rēi	materiēi	(materiae)
A.	diem	rem	materiem	(materiam)
Ab.	diē	rē	materiē	(materiā)

Plural

N.A.V.	diēs	rēs	*materies	(materiae)
G.	diErum	rErum	*materiErum	(materiArum)
D.Ab.	diēbus	rēbus	*materiēbus	(materiābus)

Obs. The gen. of nouns in *es* exhibits occasional varieties. It was originally in *e-is,* like that of other *i* nouns, and this was contracted into es in *Dies-piter* for *Diei-pater*. Similarly *ei* was contracted into *ē*, as in *dis* for *diei* (Virgil, *Georg.* I. 208; Hor. 3 *Carm.* VII. 4; Ovid, *Met.* III. 311); in *fide* for *fidei* (Ovid, *Met.* VII. 728); in *acie* for *aciei* (Cæs. *Bell. Gall.* II. 23); and we have a similar contraction of the dative, as in *fide* (Hor. 1, *Serm.* III. 95); and *pernicie* (Liv. v. 13). Both gen. and dat. are sometimes contracted into *i*, as in the gen. *plebi* for *plebei* (Liv. II. 42), and in the dative *pernicii* (Nep. *Thrasyb.* 2). Both in the gen. and dat. the *e* is long before *i*, if it is preceded by another vowel, as in *diei*, *maciei*; but short after a consonant, as *fidei*, *rei*. Only *dies*, *res*, and *species* have their plural complete, and Cicero does not allow even the forms *specierum* and *speciebus* (*Topic.* 7). The words *facies*, *effigies*, *series* and *spes*, are not found in any good authors except in the nom. and accus. pl.; and others from their signification have no plural.

(1) All nouns in *es* are fem., like the nouns of the *a* declension, with which most of them are connected. But *dies* is always m. in the plural; and though almost always f. in the singular, when it denotes a *period*, it is m. when it signifies a *day* in particular. This distinction is carried so far, that while we have *certa*, *constituta*, *præstituta*, *dicta*, *finita dies* of definite periods of time, we have always *stato condicto die* of a particular day legally fixed (*Fest.* p. 314). The compounds *meridie*, *postridie*, &c. are necessarily masc., as they stand for *medii die*, &c., just as we have *die septimi* (Plaut. *Men.* 1156); *die crastini* (Id. *Mostell.* 884), &c.

(2) The gender of the other nouns in -*i*, so far as it can be reduced to rule, may be defined as follows:

(a) Nouns in -*e*, -*i*, -*al*, and -*ar* are neuter, and to this class belongs *os* for *oste* or *osti*, 'a bone.'

(b) Nouns in -*er*, -*ris*, as *imber*, 'a shower;' in -*ns*, -*ntis*, as *dens*, 'a tooth;' *mons*, 'a mountain;' *pons*, 'a bridge;' *fons*, 'a fountain;' in -*as*, -*ātis*, -*is*, -*itis*, as *Arpinas*, 'a man of Arpinum;' *Quiris*, 'a Roman citizen,' are masculine. But although *bidens*, 'a hoe;' *tridens*, 'a three-pointed spear;' are masculine, *bidens* for *ambidens*, 'a sheep fit for sacrifice,' is feminine; and *frons*, 'a brow,' is hardly ever masculine.

(c) Nouns which omit the *i* between *s* and any consonant but *n*, or change it into *e*, are feminine; to this class belong the apparently labial nouns, *trabs*, 'a beam or rafter;' *stirps*, 'the root of a tree;' *urbs*, 'a city;' *scobs* or *scobis*, 'saw-dust;' *scrobs* or *scrobis*, 'a ditch' (sometimes also fem.); *stips*, anciently *stipes*, 'a small piece of money;' *plebs* or *plebes*, 'the common people.' The apparently guttural nouns, *merx* for *mercis*, 'merchandise;' *nix* for *niguis*, 'snow;' the apparently dental nouns, *pars*, *partis*, 'a part;' *sors* (also *sortis*), 'a lot;' *cos, cotis*, 'a whetstone;' *fraus, fraudis*, 'a loss or damage,' are feminine; and we have also with the inserted *e, nubes, nubis*, 'a cloud' (anciently written *nubs*); *caedes*, 'a cutting;' and the like. *Acinaces*, 'a Persian dagger,' is masc., perhaps with reference to *pugio* or *gladius*.

(d) Nouns which retain the termination -*is* in the nominative are generally feminine, as *febris*, 'a fever;' *avis*, 'a bird;' *puppis*, 'the stern of a ship;' some are common, as *corbis*, 'a basket;' *clunis*, 'the hinder part;' some more frequently masculine than feminine, as *anguis*, 'a snake;' *canis*, 'a dog;' some essentially masculine from the signification, as *hostis*, 'an enemy;' *Lucretilis*, the name of a mountain; *Tiberis*, the name of a river; *manes*, *manium*, 'the spirits of the dead;' as for *assis*, properly an adjective agreeing with *numus*, and signifying 'a pound of coined copper,' with its derivatives, *semissis*, 'half a pound,' *decussis*, 'ten pounds,' &c. All nouns ending in -*nis* are masculine, as *amnis, crinis, canis, finis, funis, ignis, panis*, together with a number of words, as *fustis, canalis, callis, torquis, torris*, which cannot be reduced to any common rule, but are given in the memorial lines at the end of this section.

Even some of these, as *canalis*, are found in the feminine: this is rarely the case with *callis* and *torquis*, also written *torques*; and *finis* is used as a feminine only in the singular and with the meaning, 'an end, purpose, or termination;' in the sense 'a boundary,' it is always masculine.

Obs. *Ren* for *renis*, also written *rien*, was generally used only in the plural *renes*, for which the ancient Romans wrote *nefrendines*, from the Greek *νεφροί*. The Greek *σπλήν* was used as well as its Latin equivalent *lienis*.

29 (*B*) Nouns in *u* originally terminated in the consonant *v*, and were declined like other consonant-nouns. Of this class only two remain: *bos, bŏvis*, c. 'an ox, bull, or cow;' and *Jup-piter (Juvs-pater), Jŏvis*, m. 'the king of the gods.' The others retain *u* throughout the cases, as *fructus*, m. 'fruit;' but the dative and ablative plural change this into *i*, except in the nouns: *artus*, m.

'a joint;' *partus*, m. 'a birth;' *tribus*, f. 'a tribe;' *cornu*, n. 'a spit;' and in those which have *c* before *u*, as *arcus*, m. 'a bow.'

Obs. The nouns which form the D. and Ab. pl. in *ubus* may be recollected by the following rhymes:

*Arcus, artus,
Portus, partus,
Quercus, cornu, lacus,
Specus, tribus, acus.*

Or by the hexameters:

*Arcus, acus, portus, quercus, ficus, lacus, artus,
Et tribus, et partus, specus, adde veruque pecuque.*

But of these *quercus* does not occur in the Dat. and Abl. pl. in the best writers; *ficis* is more common than *ficubus*; and we have both *portubus* and *portibus*.

Singular.

N. V.	bos	fructus	cornu	tribus
G.	bovis	fructūs	cornūs	tribūs
D.	bovi	fructui	cornu (for cornui)	tribui
A.	bovem	fructum	cornu	tribum
Ab.	bove	fructu	cornu	tribu

Plural.

N. A. V.	boves	fructūs	cornua	tribūs
G.	bo[v]um	fructuum	cornuum	tribuum
D. Ab.	bubus	fructibus	cornibus	tribubus

Nouns in *u* are neuter, and those in *us* masculine, with the exception of the following ten substantives, which are feminine:

Domus, 'a house;' *acus*, 'a needle;' *porticus*, 'a porch;' *tribus*, 'a tribe;' *Idus, Iduum*, 'the middle of the month;' *Quinquatrus, Quinquatruum*, 'a feast of Minerva;' *manus*, 'a hand;' *socrus*, 'a mother-in-law;' *anus*, 'an old woman;' *nurus*, 'a daughter-in-law.'

Obs. 1 It used to be believed that nouns in -*u* were indeclinable in the singular, but this opinion is now relinquished (see Freund's Append. in the Pref. of his *Lat. Dict.*). The dat. in -*ui* is recognised by Martian. Capella, III.; but Liv. XLII. 58, gives us only the contracted form *cornu*.

Obs. 2 Certain nouns in -*us* are sometimes declined throughout like the second declension, and sometimes take certain cases of the *u* declension, as *laurus*, f. 'the laurel,' Ab. a. *lauru*, A. pl. *laurus*. *Domus*, f. 'a house,' exhibits peculiar irregularity:

	Singular.	Plural.
N. V.	domus	domus
G.	domûs	domUum, domOrum
D.	domui (rarely domo)	domibus
A.	domum	domos (rarely domūs)
Ab.	domo (rarely domu)	domibus

We have also the locative *domi*, 'at home.' These irregularities are generally remembered by the line:

'Tolle *me, mu, mi, mis* si declinare *domus* vis.'

30. Greek nouns of the consonant declension sometimes retain the Greek forms, as *lampas*, A. sing. *lampăda*, A. pl. *lampadăs*; *heros*, A. sing. *heröa*, N. pl. *herŏës*. This, however, is more common in poetry than in prose, with the exception of proper names, and the words *aer, aether,* which generally retain the Greek accusative in -a, as *Agamemnŏna, Babylŏna, aëra, aethera.*

The following are peculiarities of the declension of Greek nouns of the third declension, when adopted by the Latin writers:

(a) The gen. sing. frequently ends in -*i*, as *Achilli, Ulixi* (above, 19), from nouns in -*eus,* and *Aristoteli, Pericli,* from nouns in -*es;* but this is not usually the case with nouns increasing in the gen., as *Laches, Lachītis.*

(b) Conversely, the genitive of nouns in -*es* of the first declension is frequently in -*is,* as *Æschines, Æschinis; Alcibiades, Alcibiadis; Xerxes, Xerxis;* but this does not take place in real patronymics, as *Atrides, Atridae;* and in the accus. these nouns have -*en* as well as -*em,* which is also admitted in nouns in -*es* of the third declension, as *Xenocraten,* where the Greek has both Ξενοκράτη and Ξενοκράτην. Some nouns in -*tes,* as *Orestes,* follow both the third and first declensions, preferring however the third; *acinaces,* 'a Persian dagger,' follows the third declension; *satrapes,* 'a Persian governor,' follows the first declension, but has *satrapis* in the gen. sing.; *sorites,* 'a kind of fallacious argument,' follows the third declension in the sing., and the first in the plural.

(c) The gen. sing. in -*os* is sometimes retained by the poets in such words as *Pallas, Palladŏs; Tethys, Tethyŏs; Peleus, Peleŏs;* and feminines in -*o* have gen. sing. in -*ûs* for the Greek -*ους,* as *Sappho, Sapphus;* the acc. dat. and abl. of these nouns generally end in -*o,* the forms *Sapphonem, Sapphoni, Sapphone* being less common.

34 NOUNS.

(d) Nouns in *-is* have in the accus. sing. either *-im* or *-in*, as *Charybdim*, *Charybdin*; those which have *-ιν* and *-ιδα* in Greek have *-im* or *-in*, and rarely *-idem* or *-ida*, as *Paris*, *Parim*, *Parin*, rarely *Paridem*; but those in *-tis* have both forms, as *Phthiotis*, *Phthiotim* or *Phthiotin*, *Phthiotidem* or *Phthiotida*; and those which have only *-ιδα* in Greek have only *-idem* or *-ida* in Latin, as *tyrannis*, *tyrannidem*, *tyrannida*.

(e) Nouns in *-is*, *-ys*, *-eus*, *-as*, *-es*, may drop the *s* in the vocative sing.; as: *Phyllis*, *Phylli*; *Cotys*, *Coty*; *Orpheus*, *Orpheu*; *Calchas* (*-antis*), *Calcha*; *Carneades* (*-ae*), *Carneade*; *Chremes* (*-etis*), *Chreme*.

(f) We have sometimes *-es*, *-is*, for *-es*, in the nom. and accus. pl. of Greek words, and of certain barbarous names which resemble the Greek, as *Allobrōgis*, *Lingŏnas*, from *Allobrox*, *Lingon*. But *Sardis* is written for Σάρδεις.

(g) The gen. pl. in *-ōn* is written only in the titles of books, as *Metamorphoseōn libri*.

(h) The dat. pl. in *-si* (*-sin*) is occasionally used by the poets, as in *Troasin*, *Charisin*.

(i) The nom. and acc. pl. in *-ē* is used in a few Greek words, as *melē*, *Tempē*.

(k) The final *-n* of proper names in *-ων*, *-ωνος*, or *-ονος*, is generally dropped, as in *Plato*; but some others retain it, as *Conon*; and in the proper names of towns this is almost always done, as in *Babylon*, *Lacedaemon*: so also in nouns in *-ων*, *-οντος*, or *-ωντος*, as *Xenophon*, *Laocoon*; though we sometimes find *Antipho*, *Antiphōnis*, and instead of *Antiphon*, *Antiphōntis*, &c.

The following tables exhibit the most usual forms of the Greek nouns of the third declension:

	Singular.	Plural.
N.	poëma	poëmata
G.	poëmatis	poëmatum *also* poëmatorum
D.	poëmati	poëmatis (*-ibus*)
A.	poëma	poëmata
Ab.	poëmate	poëmatis (*-ibus*)

NOUNS.

	Singular.	Plural.
N.	poësis	poëses
G.	poësis (-ĕos)	poëseŏn
D.	poësi	poësibus, not found
A.	poësim (-in)	poëses
Ab.	poësi	poësibus, not found

	Singular.	Plural.
N.	Erinnys	Erinnyes (-ges)
G.	Erinnyis (-ys, -yos)	Erinnyum
D.	Erinnyi (-ÿ)	—
A.	Erinnyn (-ym)	Erinnyas (-ys)
Ab.	Erinnye (-y)	—

	Singular.	Plural.
N.	Nerĕis	Nerëides
V.	Nerëi	
G.	Nereidis (-os)	Nereidum
D.	Nereidi	Nereidibus
A.	Nereidem (-a)	Nereides (-as)
Ab.	Nereide	Nereidibus

	Singular.	Plural.
N.	chlamys	chlamydes
G.	chlamydis (-os)	chlamydum
D.	chlamydi	chlamydibus
A.	chlamydem (-a)	chlamydes (-as)
Ab.	chlamyde	chlamydibus

	Singular.	Plural.
N.	tigris	tigres and tigrides
V.	tigris and tigri	
G.	tigridis (-os)	tigridum (?)
D.	tigridi	tigribus (?)
A.	tigridem (-a) tigrim (-in)	tigres and tigrides
Ab.	tigride	tigribus (?)

	Singular.	Singular.
N.	Echo	Dido
G.	Echus	Didus and Didonis
D.	Echo	Dido and Didoni
A.	Echo	Dido and Didonem
Ab.	Echo	Dido and Didone

30 NOUNS.

	Singular.	Singular.
N.	(Achilleus) Achilles	(Ulixeus) Ulysses, Ulixes
G.	Achillis, Achilli (Achilleos, Achillǽi)	Ulyssis, Ulixěi, Ulixi
D.	Achilli (Achilěi)	Ulyssi, Ulixi, Ulixěi
A.	Achillem (Achillen, Achillea)	Ulyssem, Ulixen (Ulixea)
Ab.	Achille, Achillí	Ulysse (-i), Ulixe (-i)
V.	Achille	Ulysse, Ulixe

	Singular.	Singular.
N.	Pericles	Chremes
G.	Periclis, -i	Chremis, -i, Chremētis
D.	Pericli	Chremi, -ēti
A.	Periclem, -ea	Chremem, -en, -ētem, -ēta
Ab.	Pericle	Chreme
V.	Pericles, -e	Chremes and Chreme

Obs. It may be advisable to express the rules for the genders of nouns of the third declension in memorial lines accompanied by alphabetical lists of the special exceptions.

I. First general rule:

> Nouns in *-o, -or, -os, -er, -es,*
> Increasing in the genitive
> The number of their syllables,
> Will *masculinum genus* give.

Exceptions: (1) Most of those in *-go* and *-do*
Are feminine; save *harpāgo,*
And *margo, ligo, udo,*
With *ordo, cardo, cudo.*

Hence the following are masculine:

cardo, -ĭnis, hinge, main-post
cudo, -ōnis, helmet
harpago, -ōnis, hook
ligo, -ōnis, mattock

margo, -ĭnis, rim
ordo, -ĭnis, order
udo, -ōnis, a sock made of goat-skin

(2) In *-io* masculines are such,
As eyes can see, or hands can touch.

Thus the following are masculine:

curculio, weevil
papilio, butterfly
pugio, dagger

scipio, staff
septentrio, one of the seven stars, the north

NOUNS.

stellio, lizard
struthio, ostrich
titio, fire-brand

unio, pearl
vespertilio, bat

Other nouns in *-io*, being chiefly verbal nouns, and denoting abstractions of the mind, are feminine, as *ratio*, 'reason,' &c.

(3) Four neuter nouns, which end in *-or*,
Are: *aequor, ador, marmor, cor;*
And only *arbor, arbŏris*,
Is *feminini generis*.

ador, -ōris, spelt
aequor, -ŏris, surface, the sea
arbor, -ŏris, tree

cor, cordis, the heart
marmor, -ŏris, marble

(4) There are three feminines in *os*,
Cos, dos, in *t;* the r- noun *glos:*
But *os*, 'a mouth,' and *os*, 'a bone,'
Are *generis neutrius* alone.

cos, cōtis, a whet-stone
dos, dōtis, a dowry
glos, glōris, a brother's wife

os, oris, a mouth
os, ossis, a bone

(5) Many neuters end in *-er;*
For instance: *laser, laver, tuber,*
Siler, siser, spinther, uber;
Acer, cicer, et *cadaver,*
Iter, piper, et *papaver;*
Suber, et amoenum *ver,*
Verber, atque *zingiber.*

acer, acĕris, the maple-tree
cadaver, -ĕris, corpse
cicer, vetch
iter, itinĕris, journey
laser, -ĕris, the silphium and its juice
laver, water-cress
papaver, poppy
piper, pepper

siler, a withy, or osier
siser, skirret, or parsnip
spinther, armlet
suber, cork-tree
tuber, swelling, truffle
uber, udder
ver, the spring
verber, blow
zingiber, ginger

(6) There are eight feminines in *-es,*
With lengthened genitives: *requiēs,*
And *quiēs, merges, mercēs, teges,*
With *compes, inquies,* and *seges.*

compes, -ĕdis, fetter
inquies, -ētis, unrest
merces, -ēdis, wages
merges, -ĭtis, sheaf

quies, -ētis, rest
requies, -ētis, repose
seges, -ĕtis, sown-corn
teges, -ĕtis, a covering

But *aes, aeris*, bronze, copper, is neuter.

NOUNS.

II. Second general rule:

Nouns, in which a final *-s*
A consonant preceding has,
For instance, *stirps*, or *ars*, or *frons*,
With those in *-x*, or *-ans*, or *-as*,
Increasing in the genitive,
Will *femininum genus* give.

Exceptions: (1) Sex masculina sunt in *-as*,
Vas, (*vadis*), *gigas*, *elephas*,
As, (*assis*), *mas* et *adamas*.
Sed neutra sunt *artocreas*,
Fas, *nefas*, *erysipelas*,
Vas, *vasis* atque *buceras*.

adamas, *-antis*, diamond, steel
as, *assis*, the Roman pound of copper
elephas, *-antis*, the elephant
gigas, *-antis*, a giant
mas, *maris*, a male
vas, *vadis*, a surety

artocreas, *-atis*, a pasty
buceras, a cabbage
erysipelas, *-atis*, a red eruption
fas, right
nefas, wrong
vas, *vasis*, a vessel

(2) Most of the nouns which end in *-ex*,
Are masculines, as *grex* and *rex*;
But feminine are *carex*, *nex*,
Supellex, *forfex*, *forpex*, *lex*,
With *halex*, *ilex*, *vitex*, *fucx*.

carex, *-icis*, sedge
faex, *faecis*, lees
forfex, *-icis*, scissors
forpex, *-icis*, curling tongs
halex, *-ecis*, herring
ilex, *-icis*, holm-oak

lex, *legis*, law
nex, *necis*, death
supellex, *-ectilis*, household furniture
vitex, *-icis*, a shrub

(3) In *-ix*, *-yx* masculine are *sorix*,
And *culix*, *fornix*, *phoenix*, *oryx*,
With *bombyx*, *coccyx*, *calyx*, *varix*,
And sometimes *onyx*, *natrix*, *larix*.

bombyx, *-ycis*, silk-worm
culix, *-icis*, cup
calyx, *-ycis*, cup of a flower
fornix, arch
larix, larch

natrix, water-snake
onyx, a precious stone
oryx, a gazelle
phoenix, a fabulous bird
varix, a distended vein

(4) Among the masculines are *mons*,
With *chalybs*, *hydrops*, *dens*, and *fons*,
So also *rudens*, *gryps*, and *pons*.

chalybs, -ybis, steel
dens, -tis, a tooth
fons, -tis, fountain
gryps, grȳphis, a griffin

hydrops, -ōpis, dropsy
mons, -tis, mountain
pons, -tis, bridge
rudens, -tis, cable

Adeps, fat, and *scrobs,* a ditch, are common.

III. Third general rule:

> Nouns in *-is* or *-es,* as *avis,*
> *Nubes, ratis, puppis, naris,*
> With equal length of genitive
> Will *femininus* genus give.

Exceptions: Two and thirty nouns in *-is*
Are masculini generis:
Callis, cassis, caulis, cullis,
Fascis, fustis, funis, follis;
Anguis, unguis, cenchris, crinis,
Sentis, vectis, atque *finis;*
Piscis, postis, panis, ensis,
Torris, torquis, orbis, mensis;
Ignis, amnis, et *canalis,*
Axis, cossis, et *sodalis;*
Adde *lienis,* et si vis,
Penis atque *mugilis.*

amnis, a river
anguis, a snake
axis, an axle
callis, a path
canalis, a canal
cassis, a hunter's net
caulis, a stalk
cenchris, a kind of snake
collis, a hill
cossis, a wood-worm
crinis, hair
ensis, a sword
fascis, a bundle
finis, an end
follis, a leather-bag or bellows
funis, a rope

fustis, a club
ignis, fire
lienis, the spleen
mensis, a month
mugilis, a mullet
orbis, a circle
panis, bread
penis, a tail
piscis, a fish
postis, a door-post
sentis, a bramble
sodalis, a companion
torris, a fire-brand
unguis, a finger-nail
vectis, a lever
vermis, a worm

IV. Fourth general rule:

> Nouns in *-u* are neuters all;
> And nouns in *-us* with genitive
> In *-ūs* for *-uis* or for *-ris,*
> Will *genus masculinum* give.

Exceptions: Feminina sunt in *-us,*
Domus, acus, porticus,

40   NOUNS.

　　　　　Idus et Quinquatrus, manus,
　　　　　Tribus, nurus, socrus, anus.

acus, a needle　　　　　　　*nurus,* a daughter-in-law
anus, an old woman　　　　　*porticus,* a porch
domus, a house　　　　　　　*Quinquatrus,* a feast of Minerva
idus, the middle of the month (i.e. *socrus,* a mother-in-law
　the 13th or 15th day)　　　　*tribus,* a tribe or division of the
manus, a hand　　　　　　　　Roman people

　　V. Fifth general rule:

　　　　　Nouns in *-ar, -ur, -us, -a, -e,*
　　　　　In *-c* and *-l,* in *-n* and *-t,*
　　　　　Will generally neuter be.

Exceptions: (1) Masculine in *-l* are *mugil,*
　　　　　Sol, consul, praesul, sal and *pugil;*
　　　　　With five in *-ur,* as *furfur, fur,*
　　　　　With *astur, vultur,* and *turtur;*
　　　　　And two of those which end in *-us,*
　　　　　As *lepus, lepōris,* and *mus.*

consul, -ŭlis, a Roman consul　　*astur,* a buzzard
mugil, -ĭlis, a mullet (also *mugilis*) *fur,* a thief
pugil, -ĭlis, a boxer　　　　　*furfur,* bran
Praesul, -ŭlis, chief of the Salii, or *turtur,* a turtle-dove
　priests of Mars　　　　　　　*vultur,* a vulture
sal, sălis, salt, *sales,* wit　　*mus, mŭris,* a mouse
sol, sōlis, the sun　　　　　　*lepus, lepōris,* a hare

　　(2) These are masculines in *-n:*
　　　　　Pecten, Hymen, attagen,
　　　　　Lien, lichen, ren et *splen;*
　　　　　Daemon, horizon et *canon,*
　　　　　Python, gnomon, atque *agon,*
　　　　　To which we add *chamaeleon.*
　　　　　But feminine are *aëdon,*
　　　　　Sindon, icon, halcyon.

aëdon, -ŏnis, a nightingale　　*Hymen, -ĕnis,* the God of marriage
agon, -ōnis, a contest　　　　*icon, -ŏnis,* an image
attagen, -ĕnis, a woodcock　　*lichen, -ĕnis,* ringworm
canon, -ŏnis, a rule　　　　　*lien, -ēnis,* spleen (also *lienis*)
chamaeleon, -ŏnis and *-ontis,* a kind *pecten, -ĭnis,* a comb
　of lizard　　　　　　　　　*python, -ōnis,* a mythical serpent
daemon, -ŏnis, a spirit　　　　*ren, rēnis,* a kidney (generally used
gnomon, -ŏnis, index of a sun-dial　only in the plural, *renes*)
halcyon, -ŏnis, kingfisher　　　*sindon, -ŏnis,* linen
horizon, -ontis, the limit of the *splen, -ēnis,* the spleen
　view.

NOUNS.

(3) Nine substantives which end in -us:
Juventus, virtus, servitus,
With incus, subscus, tellus, palus.
And also these: senectus, salus;
(To which add pecus, pecudis)
Are *feminini generis.*

incus, -ūdis, an anvil
juventus, -ūtis, youth
palus, -ūdis, marsh
pecus, -ŭdis, a sheep
salus, -ūtis, health, safety
senectus, -ūtis, old age

servitus, -ūtis, servitude
subscus, -ūdis, a dovetail in carpentry
tellus, -ūris, the earth
virtus, -ūtis, virtue

§ 5. *Declension of Adjectives.*

31 Adjectives have either distinct terminations for the three genders, or only two sets of terminations, by which the neuter is distinguished in the N. A. V. from the masculine and feminine.

(a) *Adjectives of three terminations.*

32 We have (a) masculines in -us or -er, like *dominus* and *puer* or *magister;* feminines in -a, like *musa;* and neuters in -um, like *regnum:* or (β) masculines in -er, like *pater;* feminines in -is, like *puppis;* and neuters in -e, like *mare.* Thus, we have (a) *bŏnus,* 'good;' *tĕner,* 'tender.'

Singular.

	M.	F.	N.
N.	bonus	bona	bonum
G.	boni	bonæ	boni
D.	bono	bonæ	bono
A.	bonum	bonam	bonum
V.	bone	bona	bonum
Ab.	bono	bonā	bono

Plural.

N.	boni	bonæ	bona
G.	bonOrum	bonArum	bonOrum
D.	bonis	bonis	bonis
A.	bonos	bonas	bona
V.	boni	bonæ	bona
Ab.	bonis	bonis	bonis

NOUNS.

Singular.

	m.	f.	n.
N.V.	tener	tenera	tenerum
G.	teneri	tenerae	teneri
D.	tenero	tenerae	tenero
A.	tenerum	teneram	tenerum
Ab.	tenero	tenera	tenero

Plural.

	m.	f.	n.
N.V.	teneri	tenerae	tenera
G.	tenerOrum	tenerArum	tenerOrum
D.	teneris	teneris	teneris
A.	teneros	teneras	tenera
Ab.	teneris	teneris	teneris

If the fem. has no *e* before *r*, the *e* is omitted in the oblique cases, as in *niger, nigra, nigrum,* 'black;' *pulcher, pulcra, pulcrum,* 'beautiful.' The only adjective of this class, in which *r* is preceded by *ŭ* for *ĕ* is *satur, satŭra, satŭrum,* 'full,' 'sated,' 'stuffed.'

33 (β) There are thirteen adjectives of this class, namely: *ācer,* 'keen;' *alăcer,* 'active;' *campester,* 'belonging to the field;' *celĕber,* 'much frequented;' *celer,* 'swift;' *equester,* 'belonging to horsemen;' *paluster,* 'marshy;' *pedester,* 'going on foot;' *puter,* 'rotten;' *salŭber,* 'wholesome;' *silvester,* 'wooded;' *terrester,* 'belonging to the land;' *volŭcer,* 'winged.' All of these, except *celer,* drop the *e* of the termination in every case except the nom. sing. masc. For example, *acer,* 'keen,' is thus declined by the side of *celer,* 'swift.'

Singular.

	m.		f.		n.	
N.V.	acer	celer	acris	celeris	acre	celere
G.	acris	celeris	acris	celeris	acris	celeris
D.	acri	celeri	acri	celeri	acri	celeri
A.	acrem	celerem	acrem	celerem	acre	celere
Ab.	acri	celeri	acri	celeri	acri	celeri

Plural.

	m.		f.		n.	
N.V.	acres	celeres	acres	celeres	acria	celeria
G.	acrIum	celerIum	acrIum	celerIum	acrIum	celerIum
D.Ab.	acribus	celeribus	acribus	celeribus	acribus	celeribus
A.	acres	celeres	acres	celeres	acria	celeria

NOUNS.   43

But we have *celerum* in the gen. pl., where *celeres* signifies 'the old Roman knights.'

Obs. 1 Some of these adjectives have *-ris* for *-er* in the nom. sing. masc., as in *annus salubris, collis silvestris;* but this is of rare occurrence, and mostly poetical.

Obs. 2 The names of months, as *September*, are masc. substantives in the nom. sing., but are used as adjectives agreeing with fem. nouns in such phrases as *Kalendae Septembres, libertate Decembri*, &c.

(b) *Adjectives of two terminations.*

34 Some, as *tristis*, 'sad' (declined like *puppis* and *mare*), *melior*, 'better' (declined like *flos* and *os, oris*), distinguish the masculine from the neuter in the N. A. V. of both numbers; but if the N. sing. ends in *-x, -rs, -us,* or *-ns,* it serves for all three genders, as in *felix*, 'happy;' *sollers*, 'sagacious;' *Larinas*, 'of Larinum;' *ingens*, 'big' (declined like *urbs* and *animal*). In the comparative the neuter plural always ends in *-ra*, but although *plus* makes *plura, complures* makes both *compluria* and *complura*. The only adjective of this class, which has *-a* for *-ia* in the neuter plural of the positive, is *vetus*, for *veter*, 'old,' which is declined like *opus*, and has *vetera* in the plural. Of those adjectives, which have a neuter plural, only *vetus, bĭpes, quadrupes, versicolor, anceps,* and *praeceps* have the gen. pl. in *-um* for *-ium*. But this form is regularly adopted for adjectives which have no neuter plural, and thus we have *cuelebs, caelĭb-um; dires, dirit-um; inops, inŏp-um; pauper, paupĕr-um; memor (immemor), memŏr-um; sospes, sospĭt-um; uber, ubĕr-um; compos, compŏt-um; supplex, supplĭc-um; anceps, ancipit-um; vigil, vigil-um; degener, degenĕr-um;* &c. Some nouns in *-ns* and even *-is* occasionally shorten the gen. pl. from *-ium* to *-um*, in the poets, as *parentum* for *parentium, sapientum* for *sapientium,* and *caelestum* for *caelestium*. The following are the rules for the ablative singular of this class of adjectives:

(1) The regular form of the ablative in adjectives of classes *a, β,* and *b* is the same as that of the dative; but the comparatives and adjectives of one ending in the nom. sing. have both *-e* and *-i* in the ablative; thus we have *celer,* abl. *celeri; tristis,* abl. *tristi;* but *melior,* abl. *meliore* and *meliori; felix,* abl. *felice* and *felici;* though in the comparative the abl. in *-e* is more usual.

(2) The adjectives *par, memor, immemor* have only *-i* in the abl.; the compounds *compar, impar, dispar* have both *-e* and *-i*.

(3) The following adjectives have *-e* only: *compos, impos*, abl. *compŏte, impŏte; hospes, sospes*, abl. *hospĭte, sospĭte; pauper, puber*, abl. *paupĕre, pubĕre; senex, superstes*, abl. *sĕne, superstĭte*. So also the compounds of *corpus* and *pes*, e. g. *bicorpor, tricorpor, bipes, tripes*; but *quadrūpes* has both *quadrupĕde* and *quadrupĕdi*.

(4) The present participle in *-ns*, when it is not used as a mere adjective or epithet, but refers at once to the meaning of its verb, has generally an abl. in *-e* only; thus, although we may write either *sapiente* or *sapienti* from *sapiens* the participle of *sapio*, used as a mere adjective signifying 'wise,' we must write *imperante Augusto*, 'when Augustus was ruling.'

(5) Adjectives of one ending in the nom. sing., which are sometimes used as substantives, generally have an abl. in *-e* in that usage, but an abl. in *-i* when they are construed with other substantives; such words are *artifex, nutrix, rictrix, vigil*.

The adjectives, which have a gen. plur. in *-ium*, form their accus. pl. m. and f. in *-is* or *-eis* in some MSS. of the best Latin authors, e. g. we have *tris, omnis, fortis* instead of *tres, omnes, fortes*.

Singular.

	M. F.	N.	M. F.	N.
N. V.	tristis	triste	melior	melius
G.	tristis		melioris	
D.	tristi		meliori	
A.	tristem	triste	meliorem	melius
Ab.	tristi		meliore	
			(more rarely *meliori*)	

Plural.

N. A. V.	tristes	tristia	meliores	meliora
G.	tristium		meliorRum	
D. Ab.	tristibus		melioribus	

Singular.

N. V.	felix		ingens
G.	felicis		ingentis
D.	felici		ingenti
A.	felicem felix		ingentem ingens
Ab.	felici		ingente, or ingenti

Plural.

	M. F.	N.	M. F.	N.
N. A. V.	felices	felicia	ingentes	ingentia
G.		feliclum		ingentIum
D. Ab.		felicibus		ingentibus

Obs. 1 Some adjectives in *-is* have by-forms in *-us*; as *acclivis, acclivus,* 'rising,' 'sloping upwards;' *hilaris, hilarus,* 'merry;' *bijugis, bijugus,* 'with two horses' (similarly, *quadrijugus* or *-is*); *exanimis, exanimus,* 'lifeless;' *imbecillis* (rare), *imbecillus,* 'weak;' *inermis, inermus,* 'unarmed;' *unanimis, unanimus,* 'of one mind,' &c.

Obs. 2 A few adjectives in *-ns* have by-forms in *-ntus*, as *opulens, opulentus,* 'rich;' *violens, violentus,* 'violent.'

Obs. 3 *Dives,* 'rich,' makes *ditia* in the neuter plural.

Obs. 4 Some adjectives, which have no neuter plural of the nom. and accus., are construed with neuter-substantives in the dat. and abl. pl.; thus we have *discoloribus signis, supplicibus verbis, puberibus foliis.*

Obs. 5 Substantives are occasionally used as adjectives with various degrees of irregularity; thus *artifex,* which means 'one who makes by art,' is used as an adjective in the sense 'artificial,' i. e. 'made by art;' as *artifices motus,* 'artificial motions;' *artifices boves,* 'oxen made by art.' By a curious apparition, we have *incola turba,* 'a crowd of inhabitants;' and even *agricola aratrum,* 'the plough which cultivates the fields.'

Obs. 6 Substantives in *-tor* have feminines in *-trix,* and both are used as adjectives with corresponding masculine and feminine nouns; as *victor exercitus, Mars ultor, victrix causa, ultrices deae.* But the poets treat the feminine as a regular adjective after the model of *felix,* and we have neuter plurals, as *victricia arma,* 'the victorious arms;' *ultricia tela,* 'the avenging weapons.' So also *hospes,* 'the guest,' gives a neuter plural, as in *hospita aequora,* 'the hospitable seas.'

35 Certain distinctive adjectives, which might be termed pronouns, follow the declension of the pronouns in the G. and D. singular, which they form in *-ius* and *-i;* such as *unus,* 'one;' *alius,* 'another;' *uter,* 'which of two;' *alter,* 'one of two;' *ullus,* 'any at all;' *nullus,* 'none at all;' *solus,* 'alone;' *totus,* 'whole;' *neuter,* 'neither;' *uterque,* 'both;' *utervis, uterlibet,* 'whichever you please,' &c. *Alius* (like *ille,* 'that other,' of which it is a by-form; see below, G2) makes the N. A. sing. neut. in *-ud.*

N.	unus	una	unum
G.		unius	
D.		uni	
A.	unum	unam	unum
Ab.	uno	una	uno
N.	alius	alia	aliud
G.		alius	
D.		alii	
A.	alium	aliam	aliud
Ab.	alio	alia	alio
N.	uter	utra	utrum
G.		utrius	
D.		utri	
A.	utrum	utram	utrum
Ab.	utro	utra	utro
N.	alter	altera	alterum
G.		alterius	
D.		alteri	
A.	alterum	alteram	alterum
Ab.	altero	altera	altero

Obs. Unus has of course no plural, except when it is combined with a word which has no singular, as *unae litterae*, 'an epistle,' or when it signifies 'alone,' or 'the same,' as *uni Ubii*, 'the Ubians alone' (Caes. B. G. iv. 16), *unis moribus*, 'with the same manners' (Cic. Flacc. 26).

§ 6. *Degrees of Comparison.*

36 In its simple form an adjective is said to be in the positive degree; when we wish to express that the quality denoted by the adjective is possessed in a higher degree, we modify the form and call it the comparative degree; when we wish to express that the quality is possessed in the highest degree, we introduce another modification of the form, and call it the superlative degree. Regularly the comparative and superlative are formed by substituting *-ior* and *-issimus* for the *-i* or *-is* of the genitive singular of the positive; thus from *dur-us*, 'hard,' gen. sing. *dur-i*, we have *dur-ior*, 'harder,' or 'more hard,' *dur-issimus*, 'hardest,' or 'most hard;' from *moll-is*, 'soft,' gen. sing. *moll-is*, we have *moll-ior*, 'softer,' or 'more soft,' *moll-issimus*, 'softest,' or 'most soft;' from *felix*, 'happy,' gen. sing. *felic-is*, we have *felic-ior*, 'happier,' or 'more happy,' *felic-issimus*, 'happiest,' or 'most happy.'

37 Adjectives in *-er* form the comparative regularly, but add *-rimus* to the nom. sing. of the positive as a substitute for the usual form of the superlative; thus we have *pulch-er*, 'beautiful,' gen. sing. *pulcr-i*, *pulcr-ior*, 'more beautiful,' *pulcher-rimus*, 'most beautiful;' *celer*, 'swift,' gen. sing. *celer-is*, *celer-ior*, 'swifter,' or 'more swift,' *celer-rimus*, 'swiftest,' or 'most swift.' So also *retus*, 'old,' gen. sing. *reter-is*, superlative *veter-rimus*, 'oldest,' or 'most old.'

Obs. This rule sometimes applies to nouns in *-rus*; thus we have *prosper-rimus* from *prosper-us*, and both *matur-rimus* (especially in the adverb *maturrime*) and *matur-issimus* from *matur-us*.

38 Certain adjectives in *-ilis* form the comparative regularly, but change *-ilis* into *-illimus* for the superlative. Thus we have *facilis*, 'easy,' *facilior*, 'easier,' *facillimus*, 'easiest.' The remaining adjectives which follow this rule are *difficilis*, 'difficult;' *gracilis*, 'slender;' *humilis*, 'low;' *similis*, 'like;' *dissimilis*, 'unlike.' Other adjectives in *-ilis*, if they have a superlative, form it in *-issimus*; as *utilis*, 'useful,' *utilissimus*, 'most useful.'

Obs. As *imbecillis* has a by-form *imbecillus* (34, *Obs.* 1), we have both *imbecillimus* from the former, and *imbecillissimus* from the latter.

39 Verbal adjectives which end in *-dicus*, *-ficus*, *-vilus*, form their comparatives and superlatives from the participles of their verbs; thus *maledicus*, 'slanderous,' *maledicent-ior*, 'more slanderous,' *maledicent-issimus*, 'most slanderous.' Similarly the verbal adjectives *egenus*, 'needy,' and *providus*, 'exercising forethought,' form their comparative and superlative from the participles *egens*, and *providens*, or *prudens*; as *egentior*, 'more needy,' *egentissimus*, 'most needy.'

40 Some comparative adjectives have a diminutive form in *-culus*, as *grandiusculus*, 'a little older.'

41 Philology shows (*Varron.* p. 394) that the superlative termination *-issimus*, *-errimus*, *-illimus* is an assimilation of *ed-timus*, *er-timus*, *il-timus*, resulting from *-timus* affixed to the corresponding

adverb in *-ed* or the neuter of the adjective (below, 108). But the comparative and superlative adjective have adverbial forms, generally in *-ius* and *-e*, which are referred to positive adverbs; thus we have:

digne, 'worthily;' *dignius, dignissime.*
breviter, 'briefly;' *brevius, brevissime.*
certo, 'certainly;' *certius, certissime.*
saepe, 'often;' *saepius, saepissime.*
diu, 'long;' *diutius, diutissime.*

The following have no positive:

magis, 'more;' *maxime*, 'most.'
ocius, 'more swiftly;' *ocissime.*
potius, 'rather;' *potissimum.*
prius, 'sooner;' *primum.*

The following have no comparative:

belle, 'prettily;' *bellissime.*
merito, 'deservedly;' *meritissime.*
ob, 'upon;' *optime*, 'uppermost,' i.e. 'best.'
nuper, 'lately;' *nuperrime.*

The following have no superlative:

satis, 'sufficiently;' *satius*, 'better.'
secus, 'otherwise;' *sequius*, 'more otherwise,' for which *setius*, originally *sectius*, is more frequently used.

42 Many adjectives have either no forms for the comparative and superlative, or express one only of these degrees of comparison.

(1) The following have no degrees of comparison:

(a) Those which have a vowel before *-us* in the positive, as *dubius*, 'doubtful;' *idoneus*, 'fitting or suitable.'

Obs. This rule does not always apply to the semi-consonants *u* and *i* before a vowel, for we have *antiquus*, 'ancient;' *antiquior, antiquissimus; egregius*, 'remarkable;' *egregior*, and more rarely *egregiissimus*; also *tenuis*, 'thin;' *tenuior, tenuissimus*, and the superlatives *assiduissimus, piissimus, strenuissimus*.

(b) Verbal compounds, except those which use the participle for the formation of their comparison (above, 39), have no forms for the comparative and superlative; thus we do not compare such compounds as *furci-fer, armi-ger, igni-romus, arti-fex*.

(c) Compounds, of which the last part is a noun, generally have no forms of comparison; thus we do not compare *in-ops*, 'poor;' *versi-color*, 'of different colours;' *de-gener*, 'degenerate;' *magn-animus*, 'highminded.' But, those which involve *-ars*, *-cor*, *-mens*, as *in-ers*, 'helpless;' *con-cors*, 'harmonious;' *de-mens*, 'frantic,' admit of comparison.

(d) Derivatives from other nouns in *-ālis*, *-īlis*, *-āris*, *-īcus*, *-īnus*, *-īvus*, *-ōrus*, *-ūlus*, *-īmus*, with those which have the form of a passive participle in *-ātus* or *-ĭtus*, are not usually found in the comparative or superlative; such words are *naturālis* (but *hospitālis* and *liberālis* have both degrees, and *aequālis*, *capitālis*, *regālis* have the comparative), *hostīlis* (but *civīlis* has the comparative), *familiāris* (but *populāris* and *salutāris* have the comparative), *civĭcus* (but *rustĭcus* has the comparative), *peregrīnus* (but *divīnus* has both degrees of comparison), *furtīvus* (but *tempestīvus* has the comparative), *canōrus*, *querŭlus*, *finitīmus*, *barbātus*, *crinītus*.

(e) Certain adjectives, which imply a definite quality, do not admit of comparison; such are words denoting a material, as *aureus*, 'of gold;' a nation, as *Graecus*, 'belonging to Greece;' a time, as *aestivus*, 'belonging to the summer;' a special employment, as *equester*, 'belonging to the cavalry;' an absolute state, as *vivus*, 'alive;' *incolumis*, *sospes*, 'safe;' *merus*, 'absolute;' *memor*, 'mindful;' *ferus*, 'savage' (though *ferox* is compared); *gnarus*, 'knowing;' *mirus*, 'wonderful;' *gnarus*, 'active' (though we have *ignavissimus*); *rudis*, 'unskilled;' *trux*, 'harsh' (though *atrox* is compared regularly). On the other hand *verus*, 'true,' and *dirus*, 'dreadful,' are regularly compared; and not only is this the case with *clarus*, 'illustrious,' but (although adjectives qualified by *per* and *prae* do not generally admit of comparison) we have both the comparative and superlative of *praeclarus*, 'exceedingly illustrious.'

(2) The following have a superlative, but not a comparative: *falsus*, 'false;' *inclitus*, 'renowned;' *novus*, 'new' (*novissimus* means 'the last'); *sacer*, 'sacred;' *serus*, 'late' (*serissimus* is of rare occurrence); *vetus*, 'old' (*veterrimus*, above, 37). But *vetustus* is compared regularly.

(3) The following have a comparative, but not a superlative: *agilis*, 'active;' *docilis*, 'teachable;' *credibilis*, 'credible;' *proba-*

bilis, 'satisfactory;' *ater,* 'relatively black' (as distinguished from *niger,* 'absolutely black'); *caecus,* 'blind;' *jejunus,* 'fasting;' *longinquus,* 'distant,' and *propinquus,* 'near' (but we have *propior, proximus,* from *prope;* below, 43); *proclivis,* 'sloping downwards,' 'inclined;' *surdus,* 'deaf;' *teres,* 'rounded and tapering' (*teretior*), &c.

Obs. When it is necessary in any of the excepted cases to express the degree of comparison, we prefix the adverbs *magis* for the comparative, *maxime* or *summe* for the superlative, as *idoneus,* 'suitable,' *magis idoneus,* 'more suitable,' *maxime* or *summe idoneus,* 'most suitable.'

43 The following adjectives, adverbs, and adverbs used as adjectives, are compared irregularly:

bonus, 'good;' *melior,* 'better;' *optimus,* 'best' (from the preposition *ob;* above 41).
malus, 'bad;' *pejor,* 'worse;' *pessimus,* 'worst.'
magnus, 'great;' *major,* 'greater;' *maximus,* 'greatest.'
multus, 'much;' sing. *plus,* G. *pluris,* 'more;' *plurimus,* 'most.'
        plur. *plures, plura,*
                plurium, pluribus, 'several.'
parcus, 'little;' *minor,* 'less;' *minimus,* 'least.'
nequam, 'worthless;' *nequior,* 'more worthless;' *nequissimus,* 'most worthless.'
frugi, 'honest;' *frugalior,* 'more honest;' *frugalissimus,* 'most honest.'

44 *Senex,* 'old,' *juvenis,* 'young,' have the comparatives *senior, junior,* which are used to express the relative age of two classes, as *juniores patrum,* 'the younger' or 'more recently elevated patricians.' Gradations of age are properly expressed by the phrases *major natu, minor natu, maximus natu, minimus natu,* or with *natu* omitted, as *Fabius Maximus.*

45 Some adjectives expressing relations of space, time, or degree, have either no regular positive, or have it only in some prepositional form, or with some limitation of inflexion or meaning; thus we have the comparative and superlative *citerior, citimus,* 'more' or 'most on this side,' but only the preposition *citra* for the positive. Though we might imagine a form *de-ter, detra* (cf. *dexter, dextra, dexterior*) from the preposition *de,* we have only the com-

parative and superlative *deterior,* 'worse,' i.e. 'more downward,' *deterrimus,* 'worst' (cf. *optimus* from *ob*). The poetic *ocior,* 'swifter,' *ocissimus,* have no positive except the unusual adverb *ociter* (41); and *potior,* 'preferable,' *potissimus,* are used in a somewhat different sense from their positive *potis,* 'able.' *Exterior,* 'outer,' *extremus,* 'last' or 'utmost,' have in the plural of the positive *exteri,* 'foreigners,' and *exterae nationes, extera regna,* and also the prep. *extra,* 'out.' Similarly, *superior,* 'higher,' *supremus,* 'extreme,' 'last in time,' or *summus,* 'highest;' and *inferior,* 'lower,' *infimus* or *imus,* 'lowest,' have for the positive the prepositions *supra* and *infra,* or the adjectives found in the phrases *superum mare,* 'the Adriatic or upper sea,' and *inferum mare,* 'the Etruscan or lower sea;' *superi,* 'the gods above,' *supera,* 'the upper parts of the world;' *inferi,* 'the dead as inhabitants of the lower world,' *infera flumina,* 'the rivers of the infernal regions,' *inferae partes,* 'the subterraneous regions.' In the same way, *posterior,* 'later' or 'hinder,' *postremus,* 'last,' are referred immediately to the preposition *post,* 'after:' but we have *posterum diem, posterā nocte, postera aetas,* where the 'following' or 'subsequent' in order of time is referred to: *posteri* are 'descendants,' and *postumus,* 'last-born,' means 'a child born after its father's death.' The following also have only adverbial or prepositional positives:

ante, 'before,' *prior,* 'former,' *primus,* 'first.'
intra, 'within,' *interior,* 'inner,' *intimus,* 'most inward.'
prope, 'near,' *propior,* 'nearer,' *proximus,* 'nearest' (*propinquus*).
ultra, 'beyond,' *ulterior,* 'further,' *ultimus,* 'last.'

§ 7. *Anomalous Nouns.*

46 Anomalous nouns may be divided into four classes: (I.) those which are used in the plural or singular only; (II.) those which vary, or have more than one form, in the plural or singular, or both; (III.) those which employ the plural in a special or separate sense; (IV.) those which appear in one case or in some only of their cases.

Obs. In the older grammars anomalous nouns are divided into two main classes: the (A) *defectiva,* and the (B) *abundantia.* (A) The *defectiva* are (a) undeclined, when they do not admit of case-endings, although they occur in all cases; such are the names of Greek letters, *alpha, beta, &c.*; foreign proper names, as *Adam, Elizabeth;* some few words, as *cepe,* 'an onion,' *gausape,* 'a napkin,' and the cardinal numbers from *quattuor* to *centum*; (b) they are *defectiva numero* in the following classes I. and III.; and they are *defectiva casibus* in class IV., when the old grammarians call them *monoptota*, *diptota*, *triptota*, *tetraptota*, *pentaptota*, according as they occur in one only, or in two, three, four, or five cases. (II) The *abundantia* have either two forms in the same declension, as *baculus* and *baculum*, 'a stick;' or two forms in different declensions, as *elephantus*, *elephanti*, and *elephas*, *elephantis*, 'an elephant.' If the difference of form appears in the plural only, the nouns which exhibit this variety are called *heteroclita*; as *vas*, *vasis*, 'a vessel;' plur. *vasa*, *vasorum*: if the gender varies in the plural, they are termed *heterogenea*, as *carbasus*, *carbasi*, fem. 'flax,' *carbasa*, *carbasorum*, 'a sail.' In some cases the *heteroclita* are also *heterogenea*, as *epulum*, 'a public entertainment,' *epulae*, 'a feast.'

I. (1) The following have no singular:

47 (a) *First Declension.*

angustiae, straits.
argutiae, refinements.
balneae, the public bath-house[1].
bigae,   } a carriage, with two
quadrigae,} or four horses respectively.
calendae or *kalendae*, the first of the month.
clitellae, panniers.
cunae, a cradle.
delicias, an object of delight[2].
dirae, a curse.
divitiae, riches.
epulae, a feast.
excubiae, the watch.
exequiae, funeral solemnities.
exuviae, spoils (lit. strippings).
facetiae, pleasantries.
feriae, a holiday.
habēnae, reins.
induciae, an armistice.
ineptiae, silliness.

inferiae, funereal offerings.
inimicitiae, enmity.
insidiae, an ambuscade.
lapicidinae, a quarry.
manubiae, booty.
minae, threats.
minutiae, details.
nonae, the fifth or seventh of the month (50, (b), *Obs.* 5).
nugae, trifles.
nundīnae, the market-day.
nuptiae, nuptials.
phalērae, trappings (of a horse).
prestigiae, tricks.
primitiae, first-fruits.
quisquiliae, rubbish.
relliquiae, relics.
scalae, the stairs.
scopae, a broom.
sulebrae, unpolished diction.
salinae, a salt-work.
tenebrae, darkness.

[1] *balneum*. pl. *balnea*, is 'a private bath.'
[2] *delicium* occurs very rarely in the same sense, e. g. Phædr. IV. 1. 8. Mart. VII. 50.

NOUNS. 53

thermae, a warm-bath.
tricas[1], trifles, minor annoyances.
valvae, folding-doors.
vindiciae, a defence.

48   (b) Second Declension.

bellaria, dainties.
cancelli, a lattice.
cani, white hairs.
castra[2], a camp.
clathri, a trellis or grate.
crepundia, toys.
codicilli[3], writing tablets.
cunabula, } a cradle.
incunabula, }
exta, entrails.
fasti, annals.
fori, benches or seats (in a ship or in the circus).

inferi (45).
justa, funereal offerings.
lamenta, lamentations.
liberi, children.
loculi, a closet, a coffer.
lustra, a thicket.
munia, duties.
posteri (45).
praecordia, the diaphragm.
sata, corn-fields.
superi (45).
tesqua, wild-places.

49   (c) Third Declension.

ambāges, a circuit (Ab. s.).
antes, rows or ranks (of vines, soldiers, &c.).
artus, limbs, joints.
brevia, shoals.
caelĭtes, the gods above.
cervices, the hinder part of the neck[4].
compĕdes, fetters (Ab. s.).
fauces, the throat (Ab. s.).
fides, a lute.
fores, a door.
lactes, the chitterlings.
idus, the thirteenth or fifteenth of a month (50, (b), Obs. 5).
lemŭres, goblins.
majores, ancestors.
moenia, the collective buildings of a city.
minores, posterity.
obĭces, a bolt (Ab. s.).
preces, supplications (Ab. s.).
procĕres, nobles.
sentes, a thorn-bush.
sordes, dirt.
vepres, a bramble.
verbera, stripes.
viscera, the intestines.

---

[1] *Apisa* and *Trica* were two small towns in Apulia: hence *apinae* (once) and *tricae* are used to signify the contemptible but annoying vulgarity of a country place.
[2] *castrum* is used in the names of places, as *Castrum Novum*.
[3] *codicillus*, which occurs only once (in Cato), denotes the trunk of a little tree.
[4] *cervix* occurs in poetry in this sense; in prose, it means the neck of a vessel, &c.

54   NOUNS.

The following proper names also have no singular: cities, as *Arbĕla, Athēnae, Gades, Hierosŏlyma, Leuctra, Syracūsae, Thebae, Argi, Gabii, Veii, Philippi, Treveri;* feasts, as *Bacchanalia, Floralia, Olympia, Palilia, Quinquatrus, Saturnalia, Suovetaurilia,* &c.

50 I. (2) The following have no plural:

(a) Words denoting substances; as *aurum*, 'gold;' *lignum*, 'wood;' *aes*, 'bronze;' *oleum*, 'oil;' *sanguis*, 'blood:' plurals are sometimes used to denote pieces of the material, as *aera*, 'bronze statues;' *cerae*, 'wax tablets;' *ligna*, 'billets of wood.'

(b) Abstract nouns; as *senectus*, 'old age;' *pietas*, 'affection' or 'duty;' *quies*, 'rest;' *fames*, 'hunger;' *indoles*, 'disposition.'

(c) Words denoting objects, which are necessarily collective or undistributable; as *vulgus*, 'a crowd;' *tellus*, 'the earth;' *supellex*, 'furniture;' *aerum*, 'time;' *ver*, 'the spring;' *vesper*, 'the evening,' &c.

(d) Names of towns and countries; as *Roma, Italia.*

51 II. (1) The following vary or have more than one form in the plural:

jocus, a jest, pl. *joci, joca.*
locus, a place, pl. *loca,* places, but *loci,* passages in books, objects, and topics of argument.
frenum, a bit or bridle, pl. *freni* and *frena.*
caelum, heaven, pl. *caeli.*
ostrea, an oyster, pl. *ostrea, ostreae.*
porrum, a leek or chive, pl. *porri.*
rastrum, a mattock, pl. *rastri* and *rastra.*
siser, n. skirret, phir. *siseres,* m.
sestertius, 2½ ases or pounds, pl. *sestertii* and *sestertia.*
sibilus, a hissing, pl. *sibili,* poet. *sibila.*
vas, vasis, a vessel, also *vasum, vasi,* pl. *vasa, vasorum, vasis,* and rarely *vasibus.*

Several proper names have a sing. in *-us,* and a plur. in *-a,* as *Dindỹmus, Ismărus, Gurgŭrus, Maenălus, Pangaeus, Pergamus, Taenarus, Tartarus, Taygĕtus.*

(2) The following vary or have more than one form in both numbers:

alimonia, alimonium, nourishment.
buccĭna, buccīnum, a trumpet.
cingula, cingulum (-us), a girdle.
essĕda, essĕdum, a war-chariot.
menda, mendum, a fault.
mulctra, mulctrum, a milk-pail.
terricula, terriculum, a scarecrow.

hebdomas, -ădis, hebdomada, -ae, a week.
juventus, -tūtis, poet. jurenta, youth.
senectus, -tūtis, poet. senecta, old age.

capus, -i, and capo, -ōnis, a capon.
lanius, -i, and lanio, -onis, a butcher.
ludius, -i, and ludio, -onis, a stage-player.
parus, -i, and paro, -onis, a peacock.
palumbus, -i, and palumbes, -is, a wood-pigeon.
scorpius, -i, and scorpio, -ōnis, a scorpion.

architectus, -i, and architecton, -ŏnis, an architect.
baptismus, -i, and baptisma, -ătis, baptism.
delphīnus, -i, and delphin, -īnis, a dolphin.
elephantus, -i, and elephas, -antis, an elephant.
spasmus, -i, and spasma, -ătis, cramp.

consortium, -i, and consortio, -onis, fellowship.
contagium, -i, and contagio, -onis, infection.
occipitium, -i, and occiput, occipitis, back of the head.
praesepium, -i, and praesepe, -is, a stall.
tapētum, -i, and tapes, -ĕtis, a carpet.

angiportum, -i, and angiportus, -us, a lane.
incestum, -i, and incestus, -us, incest.
praetextum, -i, and praetextus, -us, a pretence.
sinum, -i, and sinus, -us, a pail.
suggestum, -i, and suggestus, -us, a platform.

gibbus, -i, and gibbus, -ĕris, a hump.
glomus, -i, and glomus, -ĕris, a clue.
pecus, -ŏris, and pecu, n. cattle.
penus, -ŏris, n. and penus, peni, m. provision.
specus, -ŏris, n. and specus, g. specus, m. a den.

The noun *jugerum*, an acre, is declined fully according to the second declension, but has also some forms from the third, as gen. *jugeris*, abl. *jugere*; dat. and abl. plur. *jugeribus*. The gen. plur. *jugerum* may be regarded as belonging to either declension.

52 III. The following employ the plural in a separate or special sense:

Singular.	Plural.
aedes, a temple.	*aedes*, a. temples. b. a house.
aqua, water.	*aquae*, a. waters. b. mineral spring.
auxilium, help.	*auxilia*, auxiliary troops.
bonum, a good or blessing.	*bona*, goods, property.
carcer, a prison.	*carceres*, starting-post.
cera, wax.	*cerae*, a waxen tablet.
comitium, a place in the forum at Rome.	*comitia*, the election-meeting.
copia, abundance.	*copiae*, a. stores. b. troops.
facultas, a power or faculty.	*facultates*, means or resources.
finis, an end.	*fines*, boundaries.
fortuna, fortune (in the abstract).	*fortunae*, the gifts of fortune.
gratia, favour or gratitude.	*gratiae*, thanks.
hortus, a garden.	*horti*, a. gardens. b. a pleasure-garden, or country-house.
impedimentum, a hindrance.	*impedimenta*, a. hindrances. b. baggage.
littera, a letter of the alphabet.	*litterae*, an epistle, or literature.
ludus, play, or a fencing-school.	*ludi*, a public spectacle, or games.
lustrum, a term of five years.	*lustra*, haunts of wild beasts, a brothel.
mors, death.	*mortes*, fatal attacks or kinds of death.
naris, the nostril.	*nares*, the nose.
natalis, a birth-day.	*natales*, pedigree.
opera, exertion.	*operae*, workmen.
ops (not used in the nominative), help.	*opes*, power, riches.

Singular.	Plural.
pars, a part.	*partes*, a. parts. b. the part of an actor in a play, side, party.
rostrum, a beak, the beak of a ship.	*rostra*, the pulpit for speaking in the Roman forum, adorned with the beaks of captured ships.
sal, salt.	*sales*, wit (cf. *facetiae*).
tubula, a board.	*tubulae*, a. boards. b. an account-book, a document.

53 IV. Certain nouns appear only in one case or in some only of their cases.

(1) Those found only in one case are the following:

(a) Some are indeclinable; as *fas*, 'right;' *nefas*, 'wrong;' *nihil*, 'nothing;' *instar*, 'equality' or 'likeness;' *necesse*, 'necessity;' *opus*, 'need;' *caepe*, 'an onion;' *mane*, 'the morning' (also in the abl.); *gummi*, 'gum.'

(b) Greek neuters in *-os* have only the N. A. sing. and plur.; as *melos*, *mele*, 'songs.' The same is the case with the plur. of the following words, which however are fully declined in the singular: *farra*, 'corn;' *mella*, 'honey;' *mĭtus*, 'fears;' *murmura*, 'murmurs;' *rura*, 'countries;' *situs*, 'abodes;' *spes*, 'hopes;' *tura*, 'frankincense,' &c.

(c) Some are used only in the ablative, as *pondo*, which is employed either to denote a single pound in weight, as *coronam auream, librum pondo*, 'a crown of gold, a pound in weight,' or to signify a number of pounds, as *quinquagena pondo data consulibus*, '50 lbs. of copper were given to each of the consuls.' From the same root we have *sponte*, signifying an impulse or inclination, which is used with possessives; as *med sponte*, 'by my own free inclination,' 'of my own accord.'

(d) Similarly, we have many verbal substantives or supines with a genitive or possessive pronoun, as *jussu populi*, 'by order of the people;' *meo rogatu*, 'at my request.' To the same class belong *natu*, 'in respect of birth;' as *grandis natu*, 'advanced in years;' *maximus natu*, 'oldest.'

NOUNS.

(e) Some of these verbals are used in the dat. only, and in particular combinations, as *derisui esse*, 'to be a laughing-stock;' *ostentui esse*, 'to be shown.'

(f) *In promptu*, 'ready to be drawn upon,' *in procinctu*, 'prepared for fighting,' are used only in these prepositional phrases.

(g) The dative *frugi*, and the locative *nequam*, are used as regular adjectives, equivalent to *frugālis* and *vilis*, thus *homo frugi*, 'an honest man;' *homo nequam*, 'a worthless fellow' (see 43).

(h) Others are used only in the accus., as *suppetias ferre*, 'to bring assistance;' *infitias ire*, 'to deny;' *ad incitas redigere*, 'to reduce to extremity;' *venum ire*, *dāre*, 'to be sold,' 'to sell;' others only in the G., as *non nauci facere*, ' to estimate at less than a nutshell,' i.e. 'to hold cheap;' *dicis causā*, 'for form's sake.'

(i) *Secus* is either a synonym of *sexus*, and used only in the nom. and accus. with *virīle* or *muliēbre*, or it is an adverb signifying 'otherwise.'

(k) The following words are used in the ablatives only of the singular, though, as has been mentioned above, they are inflected throughout in the plural: *ambāge*, *compede*, *fauce*, *vice*, *prece*, *verbere*, and with the exception of the last two the abl. sing. is limited to the poets.

(2) The following are found in some only of their cases:

(a) *fors*, 'chance,' only in the nom. abl. sing. (*forte*, as an adverb, 'by chance').

(b) *fides*, 'a lyre,' only in the gen. acc. abl. sing. *fidis, fidem, fide*, and then only by the poets; otherwise in the pl. *fides, fidium, fidibus*.

(c) *impes*, 'violence,' only in the gen. and abl. sing., *impĕtis, impĕte*; no plural.

(d) *lues*, 'a disease,' only in the nom. accus. and abl.; no plural.

(e) *ops*, 'help,' only in the gen. accus. abl. *opis, opem, ope*, but *opes*, 'riches,' regularly inflected in the plural.

(f) *sordes*, 'dirt,' only in the acc. and abl. *sordem, sorde*, both rare; the plural regularly inflected.

(g) *repres*, 'a bramble,' only in the acc. and abl. *reprem, repre*, both rare; plural regularly inflected.

(h) *vix* or *vicis*, 'change,' only in the gen. acc. abl. *vicis, vicem, vice*; in the plur. only nom. acc. *vices*, dat. abl. *vicibus*.

(i) *vis*, 'force,' only nom., and the accus. and abl. *vim, vi*; but complete in the plural *vires, virium, viribus*.

(3) The following want only the nom. singular: (*daps*) *dapis*, 'food;' (*ditio*) *ditionis*, 'dominion;' (*frus*) *frugis*, 'fruit;' (*internecio*) *internecionis*, 'utter destruction;' (*pollis* or *pollen*) *pollinis*, 'fine flour.'

Obs. The old grammarians (*e. g.* Priscian, vi. 15, p. 273, Krehl) give the neuter nom. accus. *tonitru*, 'thunder;' but there is no authority for any cases except the abl. sing. *tonitru*, the nom. acc. pl. *tonitrua*, gen. *tonitruum*, dat. abl. *tonitribus*. The form *tonitrua* might also be referred to *tonitruum*, which occurs in Plin. *N. H.* xxxvi. 13; and *tonitribus* might come from a form *tonitrus*, of which we seem to have the acc. pl. in Statius, *Theb.* i. 258.

§ 8. *Numerals.*

54 Numerals are partly adjectives and partly adverbs, and are divided into six classes: (a) *Cardinals*, which answer to the question, how many? (b) *Ordinals*, which combine the idea of number with that of order or arrangement; (c) *Distributives*, which indicate the number of things to be taken together; (d) *Multiplicatives*, which state out of how many parts a whole is composed; (e) *Proportionals*, which state the rate of increase; and (f) *Numeral Adverbs*, which indicate how often a thing is repeated in time.

55 (a) *Cardinals.*

1.	I.	*unus.*
2.	II.	*duo.*
3.	III.	*tres.*
4.	IV.	*quattuor.*
5.	V.	*quinque.*
6.	VI.	*sex.*
7.	VII.	*septem.*
8.	VIII.	*octo.*
9.	IX or VIIII.	*novem.*

NOUNS.

10.	X.	decem.
11.	XI.	undecim.
12.	XII.	duodecim.
13.	XIII.	tredecim.
14.	XIV.	quatuordecim.
15.	XV.	quindecim.
16.	XVI.	sedecim.
17.	XVII.	septendecim.
18.	XVIII.	duodeviginti.
19.	XIX.	undeviginti.
20.	XX.	viginti.
30.	XXX.	triginta.
40.	XL.	quadraginta.
50.	L.	quinquaginta.
60.	LX.	sexaginta.
70.	LXX.	septuaginta.
80.	LXXX.	octoginta.
90.	XC.	nonaginta.
99.	XCIX or IC.	{nonaginta novem, novem et nonaginta, undecentum.
100.	C.	centum.
200.	CC.	ducenti, -ae, -a.
300.	CCC.	trecenti.
400.	CCCC.	quadringenti.
500.	D or IƆ.	quingenti.
600.	DC or IƆC.	sexcenti¹.
700.	DCC or IƆCC.	septingenti.
800.	DCCC or IƆCCC.	octingenti.
900.	DCCCC.	nongenti.
1000.	M or CIƆ.	mille or mile.
2000.	MM or CIƆCIƆ.	duo millia.
5000.	IƆƆ.	quinque millia.
7000.	IƆƆCIƆCIƆ or IƆƆMM.	septem millia.
10000.	CCIƆƆ.	decem millia.
100000.	CCCIƆƆƆ.	centum millia.

Obs. I The declension of *vnus* has been already given (35). *Duo* and its correlative *ambo*, 'both,' are thus declined:

¹ *sexcenti* is used to denote an indefinite but large number, as when we say 'hundreds,' 'thousands.'

N. V.	duo	duæ	duo
G.	duorum	duarum	duorum
D. Ab.	duobus	duabus	duobus
Acc.	duos or duo	duas	duo
N. V.	ambo	ambæ	ambo
G.	amborum	ambarum	amborum
D. Ab.	ambobus	ambabus	ambobus
Acc.	ambos or ambo	ambas	ambo

Tres is declined like the plural of *tristis* (34), thus:

	M. F.	N.
N. A. V.	tres	tria
G.	trium	
D. Abl.	tribus	

The other cardinals up to *ducenti* are undeclined. *Mille* is undeclined in the singular, but the plural *millia* is declined as a substantive, like *maria*.

Obs. 2 For 13, 16, 17, 18, 19 we may also write *decem et tres, d. et sex, d. et septem, d. et octo, d. et novem*.

Obs. 3 The number added to 20, 30, &c., is either prefixed with, or affixed without, *et;* thus 21 is either *unus (-a, -um) et viginti*, or *viginti unus (-a, -um)*, and 25 is either *quinque et viginti*, or *viginti quinque*. For the last two numbers in the decad, we may subtract, as in the case of *duodeviginti* and *undeviginti;* thus 28 and 29 are generally *duodetriginta* and *undetriginta*. But although 99 may be *undecentum*, 98 is either *nonaginta octo*, or *octo et nonaginta*.

Obs. 4 In combinations with numbers above 100 the smaller number follows with or without *et;* thus 304 is *trecenti et quatuor*, or *trecentiquatuor*.

Obs. 5 In order to express numbers exceeding 1000, we either prefix the digits to the declinable plural *millia*, as *duo millia*, or couple it with the distributives, as *bina millia*. In this case *millia* is regarded as a neuter substantive. The poets sometimes prefix the numeral adverb, as *bis mille, quinquies mille*. When smaller numerals follow *millia* in a detailed enumeration, the objects specified are put in the same case, if the numerals precede; as *cum sunt tria millia trecenti milites; Cæsar cepit duo millia trecentos sex Gallos*. But if the objects specified precede the numerals, they are generally put in the genitive, as *Cæsar Gallorum duo millia quingentos sex cepit*. The same case, however, is sometimes used even when the object of the enumeration precedes, as *omnes equites, quindecim millia numero, convenire jussit;* or *Gallos cepit duo millia quingentos sex*.

Obs. 6 The numeral adverbs are always used to denote millions, which are expressed as so many times a hundred thousand; thus *decies centena millia*, or *decies centum millia*, is 'a million;' *vicies centena millia* is 'two millions;' *bis millies centena millia* is 'two hundred mil-

62   NOUNS.

lions,' and so forth. To these the single thousands and smaller numbers are added in order, as *decies centena millia triginta sex millia centum nonaginta sex*, 'one million, thirty-six thousand, one hundred and ninety-six,' i.e. 1,036,196. In reckoning with *sestercos* (below, 56, *Obs.* 4), the rule is to omit *centena millia*, and to prefix the numeral adverb alone to the genitive *sestertiûm*, i.e. *nummûm* (13). Thus *decies sestertiûm* is 'one million of sesterces;' *vicies sestertiûm* is 'two millions of sesterces;' *centies sestertiûm* is 'ten millions of sesterces,' &c. These phrases are regarded as equivalent to singular nouns of the neuter gender, which are even declined in the different cases; thus we have in the nom., *sestertium quadragies relinquitur*, 'six millions of sesterces are left;' in the gen., *argentum ad summam sestertii decies in aerarium rettulit*, 'he transferred to the treasury a sum of silver to the amount of a million of sesterces;' in the accus., *sestertium ducenties accepi*, ' I received twenty millions of sesterces;' in the abl., *senatorum censum duodecies sestertio taxavit*, 'he fixed the senatorial census at 1,200,000 sesterces.' The adverb alone is sometimes put without *sestertium*. And in combining greater and smaller numbers, the word *nummos* may be used without *sestertium*, as in Cic. Verr. 1. 14 : *accepi vicies ducenta triginta quinque millia quadringentos decem et septem nummos*, ' I received two millions, two hundred and thirty-five thousand, four hundred and seventeen sesterces.'

Obs. 7 Cardinal numbers are sometimes expressed by compound nouns; thus 'two,' 'three,' 'four days,' are expressed by *biduum, triduum, quadriduum;* 'two,' 'three,' 'four,' 'six,' 'seven years,' are expressed by *biennium, triennium, quadriennium, sexennium, septennium* (which is more correct than *septuennium*); commissions or bodies consisting of 'two,' 'three,' 'four,' 'five,' 'six,' 'seven,' 'ten,' 'fifteen men,' are expressed by *duoviri, tresviri, quattuorviri, quinqueviri, sexviri or sexviri, septemviri, decemviri, quindecimviri*. A single member of a commission of two or three functionaries was called *duumvir*, 'a man of two;' *triumvir*, 'a man of three.' The plural forms *duumviri, triumviri*, are in themselves ungrammatical; and though *duomviri* occurs once in an inscription, there is no authority for *triumviri*, and both forms should be avoided in writing Latin.

56 (b) Ordinals.

1st,	*primus.*
2nd,	*secundus*, or *alter* of two only.
3rd,	*tertius.*
4th,	*quartus.*
5th,	*quintus.*
6th,	*sextus.*
7th,	*septimus.*
8th,	*octavus.*
9th,	*nonus.*
10th,	*decimus.*

11th,	undecimus.
12th,	duodecimus.
13th, 14th, &c.	tertius, quartus decimus, &c.
20th,	vicesimus or vigesimus.
30th,	tricesimus or trigesimus.
40th,	quadragesimus.
50th,	quinquagesimus.
60th,	sexagesimus.
70th,	septuagesimus.
80th,	octogesimus.
90th,	nonagesimus.
100th,	centesimus.
200th,	ducentesimus.
300th, 400th, &c.	trecentesimus, quadringentesimus, &c.
1000th,	millesimus or milesimus.

Obs. 1. The numbers between 13 and 20 may also be expressed by prefixing *decimus* with or without *et*, as *decimus et tertius*, or *decimus tertius*, 'the thirteenth;' and for '18th,' and '19th,' we may say not only *octavus decimus*, *nonus decimus*, but also, with the usual subtraction, *duodevicesimus*, *undevicesimus*.

Obs. 2. In adding digits to the tens after 20, we either prefix the smaller number with *et* or affix it without *et*. Thus 'the 21st' is either *primus et vicesimus*, or *vicesimus primus*. When *alter* is used for *secundus* it is generally connected by *et*, whether it precedes or follows; thus for 'the 22nd' we may write either *alter et vicesimus*, or *vicesimus et alter*. The cardinals are often used in combination with the tens of the ordinal numbers; thus 'the 21st' may be expressed by *unus et vicesimus*. The usual subtraction may take place in the last numbers of the decad; thus 'the 28th,' 'the 39th,' may be written *duodetricesimus*, *undequadragesimus*.

Obs. 3. The numeral adverbs must be used for numbers above 1000, as *bis millesimus*, 'the two-thousandth;' *decies millesimus*, 'the ten-thousandth.'

Obs. 4. Fractional parts are expressed by an addition of *pars* to the ordinal; as *tertia pars*, 'the third part.' But *pars* is often omitted, and *tertia, quarta*, &c. are used alone, as in English, to signify 'a third,' 'a fourth,' &c. With *dimidia*, however, *pars* is always added to signify 'a half;' otherwise we have *dimidium* with a genitive, as *dimidium facti*, 'half the thing done;' or *dimidius* agrees with the noun denoting the integer, as *dimidius modius*, 'half a bushel;' *dimidia hora*, 'a half-hour.' We may express 'a sixth,' either by *sexta* or by *dimidia tertia;* 'an eighth,' either by *octava* or *dimidia quarta*. The numerator of a fraction is expressed, as in English; thus we have *duae septimae*, i. e.

64 NOUNS.

partes, 'two sevenths.' But $\frac{1}{2}, \frac{2}{3}$, may be expressed by *duae partes, tres partes,* i. e. 'of a whole consisting of four parts.' The addition of two fractions is stated at length; thus 'Capito is heir to five-sixths of the estate' (to $\frac{1}{2} + \frac{1}{3}$) is given *heres ex parte dimidia et tertia est Capito* (Cic. *ad Div.* xiii. 29); and '14 hours and $\frac{14}{60} = 14 \frac{1}{6} + \frac{1}{30}$' is given *horae quattuordecim atque dimidia cum trigesima parte unius horae.* When a fraction is added to one or more integers, the ordinal of the divided number or measure is merely appended to *as* or *asque,* where *as* is a contracted form of *semis,* Gr. ἥμισυ, 'a half;' thus *sesquialter* is 'one and a half,' i. e. 'one and the second a half;' *sesquipes* is 'a foot and a half,' i. e. 'a foot and half a foot;' *sestertius* scil. *nummus* is 'two *asses* or *librae* and the third halved,' which is accordingly written IIS or IIS, i. e. *duae librae et semis.* The *as* or *libra (pondo),* which weighed originally nearly a pound (Troy) of copper, was reduced in B.C. 217 to one-twelfth, and ultimately, by the *Lex Papiria,* to one twenty-fourth of its original weight, i. e. to half an ounce, which continued to be the standard ever after. It has the following special designations for the 12 *unciae,* or ounces, into which it was subdivided, and the same nomenclature is used with reference to every thing, which admits of the same number of fractional parts (e. g. *heres ex dodrante,* 'heir to three-fourths of the property'):

1. Uncia.
2. Sextans = $\frac{1}{6}$.
3. Quadrans = $\frac{1}{4}$.
4. Triens = $\frac{1}{3}$.
5. Quincunx.
6. Semis, -issis.
7. Septunx.
8. Bes or bessis (from *bis*) = $\frac{2}{3}$.
9. Dodrans = de-quadrans = $\frac{3}{4}$.
10. Dextans = de-sextans; also decunx (Priscian, *de pond.* II. p. 391 Krehl).
11. Deunx.
12. As.

Since the word *as* signified essentially a copper coin, the word *aes* was used as its equivalent; thus we find such phrases as (Liv. xxiv. 11): *qui millibus aeris quinquaginta census fuisset,* 'who had been rated at 50,000 *asses.*' But in order to distinguish between *as* meaning a pound of copper, and *as* denoting a coin ultimately weighing only half an ounce, the phrase *aes grave* was introduced to denote the full pound of copper as (Liv. xxii. 33): *indici data libertas et aeris gravis viginti millia,* 'his liberty and 20,000 actual pounds of copper were given to the informer.' Silver money was first coined at Rome, B.C. 269, five years before the first Punic war, in three different pieces, *numi,* called from the number of *asses* which they contained, namely:

The *Denarius* i. e. *numus* = 10 asses.
The *Quinarius* = 5 asses.
The *Sestertius* = 2½ asses.

When the *as* was reduced in B.C. 217 to one ounce, the *denarius,* though retaining its name, was made equivalent to 16 asses, the *quinarius* being 8, and the *sestertius* of course 4 asses; and this continued to be the relation between these silver coins and the *as.* The computation of money was regularly by *sestertii,* and *nummus* always meant 'a sesterce,' unless some epithet was prefixed, as when we read (Liv. xxii. 52): *nummis quadrigatis,* where the adjective shows that *denarii* are meant, from the figure of a chariot with four horses *(quadrigae)* which sometimes took the place of the *Dioscuri* on the *denarius*. The value of the *sestertius* may be reckoned at twopence sterling, and in estimating the value in English money in large sums, it may be convenient to the student to recollect that 600 *sestertii* = £5, consequently that any large sum may be reduced to English money by striking off one cypher and dividing by 12, e.g. 100,000 HS = £833. 6s. 8d. In counting by thousands of sesterces it was equally correct to say *mille sestertii* and *mille sestertium* (gen. plur.). It was perhaps from some mistaken analogy suggested by this genitive that *sestertia* in the neuter plural was used to denote sums of one thousand sesterces. It cannot be shown that the neuter *sestertium* was ever used in the singular, but we have *septem sestertia* in Horace (1 *Epist*. VII. 80), and Juvenal says (IV. 15): *mullum sex millibus emit, nequantem sane puribus sestertia libris*, 'he bought a mullet for 6000 sesterces, matching, you observe, the thousands of sesterces with pounds.' The method of counting very high numbers by using the numeral adverb has been already mentioned (above, 55, *Obs*. 6). As interest was paid monthly the part of the *as* or number of *unciae* paid for every hundred *asses* gave the rate per cent. per annum; thus *sextantes usurae* would be six per cent., *quadrantes usurae*, four per cent., *asses usurae*, twelve per cent.; the last rate was also called *centesimae usurae*, or one hundredth per month, whence we have *binae centesimae* = 24 per cent., *quinae centesimae* = 60 per cent. The *unciarium fenus*, or one-twelfth of the capital, being ⅚ per cent. of the old year of 10 months, was 10 per cent. for the year of 12 months.

Obs. 5 The ordinals are used in a peculiar manner in stating the day of the month, which was reckoned backwards according to the following subdivisions. The first of every month was designated *Kalendae*, 'the Calends,' from the old verb *calare*, 'to call;' the 5th or 7th was named *Nonae*, 'the Nones,' i.e. the 9th before the *Ides*; and the 13th or 15th was known as *Idus*, 'the Ides,' i.e. the division or middle of the month (Hor. 1 *Carm*. IV. 11—14). All other days were calculated backwards from the Nones or Ides of the month in question, or from the Calends of the following month, the day *from* which, and the day *to* which they reckoned, being both included in the sum.

The days on which the Nones and Ides fall in particular months may be remembered by the following rhymes:

> 'The 5th or 13th day divides
> A Roman month at the Nones or Ides;
> But in March, October, July, May,
> Count back from the 7th or 15th day.'

Thus, 'on the 2d Jan.' is 'on the 4th day before the Nones,' that is, in strict grammatical propriety, *die quarto ante Nonas Januarias*, or, omitting *die* and *ante*, *quarto Nonas*, or, in figures, *IV. Nonas*. In Cicero, however, and Livy, a curious attraction takes place, and this date is written *a. d. IV. Non. Jan.*, i.e. *ante (diem quartum) Nonas Januarias*, where *die quarto* is inserted between the preposition *ante* and its case, and changed by attraction into *diem quartum*, so that the whole is regarded as one phrase, which may be governed by another preposition;

thus, *ex ante diem III. Non. Jun. usque ad pridie Kalendas Septembres*, 'from the 3rd day before the Nones of June up to the day before the Calends of September.' This adverbial usage was carried so far that we have even *ante Idus* for *Idibus*, where the Ides themselves are intended, as in Liv. III. 40: *ante Idus Maias decemviros abiere magistratu*. From the previous example it will be observed that the day before the Nones, Ides, and Calends was designated by the adverb *pridie*, and not by an ordinal number. And the use of this locative in the phrase in question shows that the other days must have been originally expressed in the same case.

The number of days in the Roman months according to the Julian year was the same as ours, but although February had, as with us, one day more in leap-year, it was not added at the end of the month, but was inserted after the 23rd of February, so that the 24th of February, or the sixth day before the Calends of March, was reckoned twice, and was accordingly called *bis sextus;* whence the leap-year itself got the name of *bis sextus* or '*bis-sextile*.'

The following table, drawn up by Bröder, will save the trouble of calculating the Roman date in any particular case.

Days of English Month.	Martius, Maius, Julius (Quintilis), October, 31 Days.		Januarius, Augustus (Sextilis), December, 31 Days.		Aprilis, Junius, September, November, 30 Days.		Februarius, 28 Days—In every fourth Year 29.	
1	Kalendis		Kalendis		Kalendis		Kalendis	
2	a.d. VI.		a.d. IV.		a.d. IV.		a.d. IV.	
3	a.d. V.	Nonis	a.d. III.	Nonis	a.d. III.	Nonis	a.d. III.	Nonis
4	a.d. IV.		Pridie		Pridie		Pridie	
5	a.d. III.		Nonis		Nonis		Nonis	
6	Pridie		a.d. VIII.		a.d. VIII.		a.d. VIII.	
7	Nonis		a.d. VII.		a.d. VII.		a.d. VII.	
8	a.d. VIII.		a.d. VI.		a.d. VI.		a.d. VI.	
9	a.d. VII.		a.d. V.		a.d. V.		a.d. V.	
10	a.d. VI.	Idus	a.d. IV.	Idus	a.d. IV.	Idus	a.d. IV.	Idus
11	a.d. V.		a.d. III.		a.d. III.		a.d. III.	
12	a.d. IV.		Pridie		Pridie		Pridie	
13	a.d. III.		Idibus		Idibus		Idibus	
14	Pridie		a.d. XIX.		a.d. XVIII		a.d. XVI.	
15	Idibus		a.d. XVIII.		a.d. XVII.		a.d. XV.	
16	a.d. XVII.		a.d. XVII.		a.d. XVI.		a.d. XIV.	
17	a.d. XVI.		a.d. XVI.		a.d. XV.		a.d. XIII.	
18	a.d. XV.		a.d. XV.		a.d. XIV.		a.d. XII.	
19	a.d. XIV.		a.d. XIV.		a.d. XIII.		a.d. XI.	
20	a.d. XIII.		a.d. XIII.		a.d. XII.		a.d. X.	
21	a.d. XII.	Kalendas	a.d. XII.	Kalendas	a.d. XI.	Kalendas	a.d. IX.	Kalendas
22	a.d. XI.		a.d. XI.		a.d. X.		a.d. VIII.	
23	a.d. X.		a.d. X.		a.d. IX.		a.d. VII.	
24	a.d. IX.		a.d. IX.		a.d. VIII.		a.d. VI.	
25	a.d. VIII.		a.d. VIII.		a.d. VII.		a.d. V.	
26	a.d. VII.		a.d. VII.		a.d. VI.		a.d. IV.	
27	a.d. VI.		a.d. VI.		a.d. V.		a.d. III.	
28	a.d. V.		a.d. V.		a.d. IV.		Pridie	
29	a.d. IV.		a.d. IV.		a.d. III.			
30	a.d. III.		a.d. III.		Pridie			
31	Pridie		Pridie					

NOUNS. 67

Obs. 6 All the ordinals are adjectives of three genders.

Obs. 7 From the feminines of certain ordinals we have adjectives in *-anus* to denote the soldiers of the Roman legions, which were known, like our regiments, by their numbers; thus *primanus* is a soldier of the first legion (*prima sc. legio*); similarly we have *secundanus, quintanus, decumanus, tertiadecimanus, quartudecimanus, unaetvicesimanus, duoetricesimanus,* &c., for 'belonging to the 2nd, 5th, 10th, 13th, 14th, 21st, 22nd legion,' &c. Besides this meaning, *quintana* and *decumana* (sc. *via*) mean the passages after the fifth and tenth lines of tents in a Roman camp; and as the rear-wall of the camp bounded this tenth road, the gate in that wall was called the *decumana porta.* There are other applications of the adjective *decumanus*; for *decumanus ager* was land that paid tithes (*decimae* or *decima pars*); the *decumanus fluctus* was the tenth wave; and as this was supposed to be the largest, *decumanus* came to signify 'very large,' as *decumana scuta,* 'very large shields' (Fest. p. 4), and *decumanus acipenser,* 'a very large sturgeon' (Lucilius, *ap. Cic. Fin.* II. 8, § 24).

57 (c). *Distributives.*

1. *singuli.*
2. *bini.*
3. *terni.*
4. *quaterni.*
5. *quini.*
6. *seni.*
7. *septeni.*
8. *octoni.*
9. *noveni.*
10. *deni.*
11. *undeni.*
12. *duodeni.*
13, 14, &c. *terni deni, quaterni deni,* &c.
20. *viceni.*
30. *triceni.*
40. *quadrageni.*
50. *quinquageni.*
60. *sexageni.*
70. *septuageni.*
80. *octogeni.*
90. *nonageni.*
100. *centeni.*
200. *duceni.*
300. *treceni.*
400. *quadringeni.*
500. *quingeni.*
600. *sexceni.*
700. *septingeni.*
800. *octogeni.*
900. *nongeni.*
1000. *singula millia.*

Obs. 1 These distributives seem to be formed from the numeral adverbs (below, 59) from which they borrow their signification; thus *bini* refers itself to *bis, terni* to *ter, quaterni* to *quater,* and as *bis, ter, quater* mean 'twice' (i.e. two times), 'three times,' 'four times,' we can see that the corresponding distributives mean 'two at a time,' 'three at a time,' 'four at a time,' &c.

Obs. 2 In combinations of the units with numbers above 20, the usual plan is to put the smaller number second, without *et;* as *viceni*

eni, '26 at a time, by twenty-sixes;' but the smaller number may also be prefixed with or without *et*; as *quini et viceni*, or *quini viceni*, 'by twenty-fives.' The usual subtraction takes place in the case of 8 and 9: thus, 18, 19 may be written *duodeviceni, undeviceni; 28, 29, duodetriceni, undetriceni;* and 99 is *undecenti*. It will be observed that there is no distributive for 1000: but we say *singula millia*, 'by thousands at a time;' just as we say *singulis annis*, 'every year;' or *singulis diebus*, 'day by day.'

Obs. 3 Distributives are used instead of cardinals with words which have no singular; with the exception of *singuli*, for which *uni* is used (35, *Obs.*). Thus we say, *una moenia,* 'a wall;' *binae litterae*, 'two epistles.' With such words *trini* is used for *terni;* as *trina castra*, 'three camps.'

Obs. 4 The adjectives *bimus, trimus, quadrimus*, 'two, three, four years old,' are derived from *bis-hiems, ter-hiems, quater-hiems* ('quasi a *bis, ter, quater* ab ista a hieme dicta.' Eutyches, *ap. Cassiod.* p. 231), and so count the years by the winters (*hiemes*). It is not known with certainty what is the derivation of the correlative adjective *hornus*, 'of this year;' but it is probable that it is merely formed from *hujus*, anciently *hoius*: cf. *hodier-nus* from *hodius, tacitur-nus* from *tacitus*. According to Nonius, p. 83, it means *ipsius anni*.

58 (d) *Multiplicatives* and (e) *Proportionals*.

(d) *Multiplicatives*.

Of these words, which are formed by the addition of *-plex, -plicis*, to the root denoting the number, only the following are in use: *simplex*, 'simple;' *duplex*, 'double;' *triplex*, 'triple;' *quadruplex*, 'four-fold;' *quincuplex*, 'five-fold;' *septemplex*, 'sevenfold;' *decemplex*, 'ten-fold;' *centumplex*, 'one hundred-fold.'

Obs. Poets and later writers, like Pliny, use the distributives as multiplicatives; thus we have Lucan, VIII. 455: *septeno gurgite* for *septemplice*, and Plin. *N. H.* XVII. 3: *campus fertilis centena quinquagena fruge* for *centumplice quincuplice*.

(e) *Proportionals*.

These words add *-plus* to the root denoting the number, and are generally used in the neuter gender. The following only are in use: *simplus, duplus, triplus, quadruplus, quinquiplus, septuplus, octuplus.* There is but a slight difference in meaning between the proportional and the multiplicative; *duplex* means that which is double in itself, as *duplex ficus*, 'a double fig,' i.e. 'two growing together;' but *duplum* is the double of something else; as *poena dupli*, 'a penalty of double the amount.'

59 (f) *Numeral Adverbs.*

1. *semel.*		19. *novies decies* or *undevicies.*
2. *bis.*		20. *vicies.*
3. *ter.*		30. *tricies.*
4. *quater.*		40. *quadragies.*
5. *quinquies.*		50. *quinquagies.*
6. *sexies.*		60. *sexagies.*
7. *septies.*		70. *septuagies.*
8. *octies.*		80. *octogies.*
9. *novies.*		90. *nonagies.*
10. *decies.*		100. *centies.*
11. *undecies.*		200. *ducenties.*
12. *duodecies.*		300. *trecenties.*
13. *ter decies* or *tredecies.*		400. *quadringenties.*
14. *quater decies* or *quartum decies.*		500. *quingenties.*
		600. *sexcenties.*
15. *quinquies decies* or *quindecies.*		700. *septingenties.*
		800. *octingenties.*
16. *sexies decies* or *sedecies.*		900. *noningenties* or *nongenties.*
17. *septies decies.*		
18. *octies decies* or *duodevicies.*		1000. *millies.*

Obs. 1 These adverbs answer to the question *quoties?* 'how many times?' of which *toties,* 'so many times,' is the demonstrative, and *aliquoties,* 'a certain number of times,' the indefinite expression. Hence *semel* is 'once,' i. e. a single time; *bis,* 'twice,' i. e. two times; *ter,* 'thrice,' i. e. three times; *quater,* 'four times,' and so on.

Obs. 2 For intermediate numbers in the tens, the smaller number is either prefixed with *et;* as *semel et vicies,* or affixed with or without *et;* as *vicies et semel,* or *vicies semel.*

Obs. 3 From the ordinals we have adverbs answering to the question 'of what number?' or 'in what number?' Two forms were adopted, one in *-um,* the other in *-o,* and the old grammarians themselves could not decide which was preferable (Aul. Gell. *N. A.* x. 1). In the best writers the form in *-um* is the more common, except that while both *primum* and *primo* are used to signify 'for the first time,' *primum* alone signifies 'firstly,' and *primo* means also 'at first;' and while *secundum* is generally used as a preposition, *iterum* is used to signify 'a second time;' and *secundo,* 'in the second place,' or 'secondly,' is not so common as *deinde.*

CHAPTER III.

PRONOUNS.

§ 1. *Personal Pronouns and their Possessives.*

60 THE personal pronouns, which are used instead of nouns, as the nominative cases or subjects of verbs, are *ego,* 'I,' for the first person, and *tu,* 'thou,' for the second. The third person is not expressed in the nominative by a pronoun, but is either omitted, or expressed by a noun substantive. When, however, it is necessary to use a pronoun referring to the nominative case of the verb, we employ the pronoun *sui,* 'of himself, herself, itself, themselves,' which is called 'a reflexive pronoun,' because it refers, or is reflected back for its explanation, to the principal word in the sentence. Thus, if we wish to express in Latin, 'Alexander said that he, namely, Alexander, was the son of Jove,' we must write, *Alexander dicebat* SE *Jovis filium esse.* These personal pronouns, and their supplement the reflexive, have corresponding adjectives in *-us,* which are called *possessives.* The personal pronouns have possessives corresponding to their different numbers; but the reflexive makes no difference between the singular and plural.

61 First person.   Second person.   Reflexive.

	Singular.			Singular.			Sing. and Plur.	
N.	ego	Posses-	tu		Posses-	—		Posses-
G.	mei (mis obsol.)	sive.	tui (tis obsol.)		sive.	sui (sis obsol.)		sive.
D.	mihi	meus.	tibi		tuus.	sibi.		suus.
A. Ab.	me		te			se		

	Plural.		*Plural.*	
N.		Possess-		Possess-
A.	nos	ive.	vos	ive.
V.				
G.	nostri or	noster.	vestri or	vester.
	nostrûm		vestrûm.	
D.	nobis		vobis	
Ab.				

Obs. 1 The possessives *meus, tuus, suus* are regularly declined like *bonus,* except that *meus* makes *mi* in the voc. sing. masculine.

Obs. 2 The genitives *mei,* and *nostri* or *nostrûm, tui,* and *vestri* or *vestrûm,* are really the genitives singular and plural (13) of the possessives *meus, noster,* and *tuus, vester,* which are used instead of them, and in direct agreement with the noun, in all instances except when a particular emphasis of personality is required; as *non meus hic sermo est,* 'this discourse is not mine;' but *si tibi cura mei, sit tibi cura tui,* 'if thou hast a care for *me,* care for *thyself;*' and the two forms may stand side by side; as *memoria nostri tua,* 'your remembrance of us;' or they may be opposed; as *paramus tui lateat corpore clausa meo,* 'a part of you may lie hid, shut up in my body.' In the plural, *nostri, vestri,* are used when we speak of the persons as a whole; as *memoria nostri tua,* 'your recollection of us,' as a single object of thought: *habetis ducem memorem vestri, oblitum sui,* 'you have a general mindful of you, forgetful of himself.' But we use *nostrûm, vestrûm,* when we speak of the persons as a collection of separate elements; thus these genitives are used with *omnium;* as *patria est communis omnium nostrûm parens,* 'our native land is the common parent of all of us,' many and separable as we are. That this is an attraction appears from such passages as *hi ad vestrûm omnium caedem Romae restiterunt,* 'these men remained at Rome for the massacre of you all.'

Obs. 3 The personal pronouns are sometimes strengthened by the addition of the syllable *-met;* as *ego-met,* 'I myself;' *vos-met,* 'you yourselves.' This affix is not directly attached to *tu,* though we have *tuté* and *tutémet;* and it is never appended to the genitives *nostrum* and *vestrum.*

Obs. 4 The abl. sing. of the possessives (especially *suus*) may be strengthened by the affix *-pte,* as in *meopte ingenio,* 'by my own particular talents;' *suopte pondere,* 'by its very own weight.' The affix *-met* is also found with the ablative of *suus* and more rarely of *meus,* especially when the pronoun *ipse* follows; as *suamet ipse fraude.*

Obs. 5 From *noster, vester* we have the adjective in *-as* (for *-ati-s,* above, 28 (c), *Obs.* (d)), *nostras, vestras,* 'of our country,' 'of your country.'

§ 2. *Indicative Pronouns.*

62 The pronouns *hic, iste, ille,* indicate, as objects, the three persons, 'I,' 'thou,' 'he.' *Hic,* 'this,' indicates the speaker and all close to him; *iste,* 'that of yours,' indicates the person addressed and those in his proximity; *ille,* 'that other,' indicates all distant persons and objects. They correspond respectively to the Greek ὅδε, οὗτος, and ἐκεῖνος, and are thus declined:

(a) *Hic,* 'this' (here, by me).

Singular.

	M.	F.	N.
N.	hic	haec	hoc
G.		hujus	
D.		huic	
A.	hunc	hanc	hoc
Ab.	hoc	hâc	hoc

Plural.

	M.	F.	N.
N.	hi	hae	haec
G.	horum	harum	horum
D.		his	
A.	hos	has	haec
Ab.		his	

(b) *Iste,* 'that' (there, by you).

Singular.

N.	iste	ista	istud
G.		istius	
D.		isti	
A.	istum	istam	istud
Ab.	isto	ista	isto

Plural.

N.	isti	istae	ista
G.	istorum	istarum	istorum
D.		istis	
A.	istos	istas	ista
Ab.		istis	

(c) *Ille*, 'that other.'

Singular.

	M.	F.	N.
N.	*ille*	*illa*	*illud*
G.		*illius*	
D.		*illi*	
A.	*illum*	*illam*	*illud*
Ab.	*illo*	*illâ*	*illo*

Plural.

	M.	F.	N.
N.	*illi*	*illae*	*illa*
G.	*illorum*	*illarum*	*illorum*
D.		*illis*	
A.	*illos*	*illas*	*illa*
Ab.		*illis*	

Obs. 1 The *c*, which is found at the end of certain cases in the ordinary declension of *hic*, is a remnant of a pronominal particle *ce* also found in *ec-ce*, *cis*, *ci-tra*, *ce-teri*, &c. The original form must have been *hi-ce*, *ha-ce*, *ho-ce*, and the diphthong in the nom. sing. fem. and the nom. accus. pl. neut. has arisen from a transposition of the final vowel. This diphthong is represented only by a long *a* in *posthac*, 'after these things.' The full form of the affix *-ce* is found occasionally after the cases ending in *-s*, as in *hujusce*, *hosce*, and in old Latin we have *han-ce legem*, *ha-ce lege*. In the nom. plur. we have *hic* for *hi* or *hi-ce*, in Varr. *L. L.* VI. 73, and *haec*, for *hae* or *hae-ce* in the comedians (Plaut. *Aul.* III. 5, 59; Ter. *Eun.* III. 5, 34, &c.). When the interrogative particle *ne* is added, we have the forms *hicine*, *haecine*, *hocine*, &c.

Obs. 2 In old Latin the affix *-ce* is found with *iste* and *ille* in the forms *istic*, *istuec*, *istoc*; *illic*, *illaec*, *illoc*. The cases in which this addition is found are the same as those which end in *-c* in the common declension of *hic*, except the dative. Cicero has only *istuc* and *istaec*. We rarely find even in old Latin the full forms *istisce*, *istisce*, *illuce*, *illisce*, *illosce*, *illasce*. The interrogative *ne* may be added as in the case of *hic*, so that we get the forms *istucine*, *istocine*, *illicine*, *illuncine*, *istoscine*.

Obs. 3 *Istius* and *illius* sometimes appear in the forms *isti* and *illi*; the dat. sing. fem. is written *istae*, *illae*; and the nom. pl. fem. is found with an appended *c*; as *istace*, *illace* (Bentl. *ad Ter. Hec.* IV. 2, 17).

Obs. 4 *Ille* was anciently written *olle*, or *ollus*, *-a*, *-um*, from which we have the dat. sing. and nom. plur. *olli* in Virgil, the plur. *ollos* and *ollos* in Cicero (*Legg.* II. 9, where he is reproducing the obsolete legal forms), and the locative adverb *olim*, i. e. 'at that time,' whether past (which is the more common meaning) or future. *Alius*, 'another,' is in constant use, as a by-form of *ille*, which it resembles in declension (35). The only difference between them is that *alius* means 'another' indefinitely; *ille*, 'the,' or 'that other' definitely; as *alio die*, 'another day;' *illo die*, 'the other day,' i. e. 'on that day.'

§ 3. *Distinctive Pronouns.*

63 The pronoun *is* and its derivatives *i-dem* and *i-pse* (sometimes *ipsus*) define or distinguish particular objects. The meaning of all three is conveyed by different usages of the Greek αὐτός. *Is* is either the correlative and antecedent to *qui*, so that *is qui* means 'the particular person who,' or it is used as a mere pronoun of reference, like the oblique cases of αὐτός; as *uxor ejus*, 'his wife,' ἡ γυνὴ αὐτοῦ, 'the wife of a person already mentioned and referred to.' *I-dem*, means more emphatically, 'the very he,' 'the same man,' like ὁ αὐτός; and *i-pse* signifies 'the man himself,' or 'the man as distinguished from others,' like αὐτός in apposition without the article (see *Gr. Gr.* Art. 444, (*d*), *aa*). *Is* and *i-dem* are declined as follows:

Singular.

	M.	F.	N.
N.	is	ea	id
G.		ejus	
D.		ei	
A.	eum	eam	id
Ab.	eo	ea	eo

Plural.

	M.	F.	N.
N.	ii (ei)	eae	ea
G.	eorum	earum	eorum
D. } Ab.}		iis (eis)	
A.	eos	eas	ea

Singular.

	M.	F.	N.
N.	idem	eadem	idem
G.		ejusdem	
D.		eidem	
A.	eundem	eandem	idem
Ab.	eodem	eadem	eodem

Plural.

	M.	F.	N.
N.	iĭdem	eaedem	eădem
G.	eorundem	earundem	eorundem
D. Ab. }		iisdem	
A.	eosdem	easdem	eădem

Ipse (in old Latin *ipsus*) is declined like *ille* and *iste*, except that in the singular the N. and A. neut. end in -*um* instead of -*ud*, as though it were *ipsus, ipsa, ipsum*.

Obs. 1 The declension of *is* seems to bear the same relation to that of *hic*, that *quis* does to *qui* (below, 64, *Obs.*); namely, *is* belongs to the -*i*, and *hic* to the -*o* declension. There can be little doubt that they are different forms of the same pronoun. There are no distinct traces of an appendage *ce* in the case of *is*; but this must have been the case originally, for there is no other explanation of the long *a* in *interred, postea, praeterea, &c.* than that which applies to *posthăc*, namely, that it represents a diphthong arising from the transposition of the final vowel of *ce*, so that *eā* is for *eāce = eāce*. Although the final *ce* is obsolete with *is*, yet we have in colloquial Latin such combinations as *eccum, eccam, eccos, eccos*, for *ecce eum, ecce eam, ecce eos, ecce eas*, just as we have *eccillum* or *ellum*, for *ecce illum*, or *en illum*, and *eccistam* for *ecce istam*, from which comes the modern French and Italian *cet* for *cest*, and *questo, cel* and *quello*.

Obs. 2 The dat. sing. fem. of *is* was written occasionally *eae* in old Latin; the obsolete dat. sing. *ibi* is in common use as a particle signifying 'there;' and the dat abl. plur. appeared in the forms *ibus, eibus*. In the nom. plur. masc. *ei* is rare. As *eidem* never appears for *iidem*, and as *iidem* and *iisdem* are generally written with one *i* in the MSS., and are always treated as one syllable in poetry, it is probable that *ii, iis* were the genuine spelling, and that the double *ii* in these forms as in *dii, diis* merely represented a long *i*.

§ 4. *Relative and Interrogative Pronouns and their Correlatives or Antecedents.*

64 The relative *qui*, 'who,' connects with the indicative or distinctive pronouns, and especially with *is*, its regular correlative and antecedent, some fuller description or explanation of the person or thing indicated or intended; as *vidi eum, qui haec scripsit*, 'I saw him, i.e. the man, who wrote these things,' i.e. 'the writer' (τὸν γράψαντα). *Qui* is thus declined:

PRONOUNS.

Singular.

	M.	F.	N.
N.	qui	quae	quod
G.		cujus (quojus, obsol.)	
D.		cui (quoi, obsol.)	
A.	quem	quam	quod
Ab.	quo	quâ	quo

Plural.

	M.	F.	N.
N.	qui	quae	quae
G.	quorum	quarum	quorum
D.		quibus (queis)	
A.	quos	quas	quae
Ab.		quibus (queis)	

Obs. It seems that there were originally two forms of this pronoun, one of which followed the *-o*, while the other belonged to the *-i* declension, the former being of adjectival and the latter of substantival signification. Traces of both forms exist, with a distinct reference to this difference of usage. In old Latin we have a plural *ques* corresponding to the *-i* form, and the particle *quia,* 'because,' seems to be a corresponding neuter plural. There was also an ablative *qui* for all genders. By itself it is used only as an interrogative, in such phrases as *qui fit?* 'how does it happen?' *qui convenit?* 'how does it agree?' *qui ista intellecta sint, debeo discere,* 'I ought to learn in what manner these things are understood;' *habeo, qui utar,* 'I have what I can use;' *vix reliquit, qui efferretur,* 'he scarcely left wherewith to bury him.' Otherwise, we have *quicum* for *quocum* or *quacum,* with an indefinite antecedent, as Cic. *Lael.* 6: *quid dulcius quam habere, quicum omnia audeas sic loqui ut tecum?* 'what is more agreeable than to have some one, with whom you may venture to say all things just as if you were speaking with yourself?' Virgil, *Æn.* XI. 821 : *fida ante alias quae sola Camillae, quicum partiri curas,* 'singularly distinguished by her fidelity, being such a one that Camilla could impart to her all her thoughts.' There are traces of a locative in the particle *quum* or *quom* (also found in *quon-iam = quom-jam*), which signifies 'when,' i. e. 'at what time,' and is sometimes written *cum,* a mode of spelling, which, however sanctioned by authority, is to be avoided as leading to a needless confusion with the preposition.

65. The proper interrogative is *quis?* 'who?' which may be lengthened by prefix into *ecquis, numquis,* and by affix into *quisnam, numquisnam.* But all the relatives may be used as interrogatives. The declension of *quis* is the same as that of *qui,* except that it has *quid* as well as *quae,* and even more commonly, in the nom. sing. fem., and the nom. and accus. neut. plural; otherwise, it merely

substitutes *quis* for *qui*, and *quid* for *quod* in the singular; thus, N. *quis, quae* or *quā, quid;* A. *quem, quam, quid.* *Uter,* 'which of the two?' (35) is also used as an interrogative.

Obs. A possessive pronoun *cujus, cuja, cujum* is formed from the relative, as is, *cuja res est*, 'he whose property it is.' This form is also used as an interrogative, as *cujum pecus?* 'whose flock is it?' The only cases of this possessive which are used are the nom. and acc. sing., the abl. fem. sing., and the nom. and acc. pl. fem. Like the possessives *noster, vester*, this possessive has a collateral form in *-as (-ātis)* to express its interrogative use when applied to a man's country, as *cujas*, 'of which nation?'

66 The other correlatives are *talis*, 'of such a kind,' *qualis*, 'of which kind' (declined like *tristis*); *tantus*, 'so great,' *quantus*, 'how great' (declined like *bonus*); *tot*, 'so many,' *quot*, 'how many' (undeclined).

67 The affix *-cunque* may be subjoined to any relative and to the interrogative *uter* in the sense of our '-ever,' or '-soever;' as *qui-cunque*, 'whoever,' *qualis-cunque*, 'of what kind soever,' *utercunque*, 'whichever of the two,' &c.

68 The indefinite pronouns are *quis, quispiam*[1], 'any one;' *aliquis, aliquispiam*, 'some one' in particular; *quisquam, ullus*, 'any one at all;' *quidam*, 'a certain person;' *alteruter*, 'one or the other' (of two); *quisque*, 'every one;' *unusquisque*, 'each individual;' *uterque*, 'each of two,' also 'both' (*uterque frater*, 'both brothers;' *uterque eorum*, 'each of them;' *utrique*, 'both of them'); *quivis, quilibet*, 'any one you please' (out of a larger number); *utervis, uterlibet*, 'any one you please' (of two); with which may be classed the negatives, *nemo, neminis*, 'no one' (27); *nihil*, 'nothing;' *nullus*, 'no, none;' *neuter*, 'neither' (of two).

Obs. 1 In all indefinite pronouns the form *quod* is used as an adjective, and the form *quid* as a substantive; thus we say *aliquod monstrum*, 'some monster,' but *aliquid monstri*, 'something of the monster.' This rule applies to *quoddam, quiddam; quodpiam, quidpiam; unumquodque, unumquidque*, &c. But *quisquam* is always substantive, and forms the neuter in *quidquam* or *quicquam*. It has neither fem. nor plural, and uses *ullus* as its adjective.

[1] Some old grammarians (as Festus, p. 254), and many modern scholars, regard *quispiam* as a synonym of *aliquis*, but this is not its usage, and the occurrence of *aliquispiam* or *aliquipiam* (Cic. Tusc. Disp. III. 9, § 19; pro Sext. 39), shows that *quispiam* rather corresponds to the indefinite *quis*.

Obs. 2 The indefinite *quis* may be written *qui*, chiefly in an adjective sense, and only after *si, nisi, ne, num;* and *quis* itself is seldom used except in suppositions, as *dicat quis = dicat quispiam*, 'suppose any one says,' or after the particles just mentioned, and others of a similar meaning, such as *quum, quanto, quo*. The fem. sing. or neuter plur. is either *quae* or *qua*, but more commonly the latter.

Obs. 3 *Ali-quis* for *alius-quis = ille-quis* (35, 62) always indicates 'some one in particular,' though the object is not named: and the English 'some' must be introduced into the translation of all pronominal words to which the syllables *ali-* are similarly prefixed; thus *aliquot* is 'some few,' *ali-quantus*, 'of some considerable size,' *ali-quando*, 'at some time.' Consequently, *aliquis* is only a degree less definite than *quidam*, which may be explained as *certus aliquis*. The word 'any' cannot therefore be used in translating *aliquis* or the other words compounded with *ali-*. If by 'any' we merely grant or suppose the existence of the person or thing, we use *quis* or *quispiam* (above, *Obs.* 2), and we denote without naming the person or thing, when we prefix *ali-* to either of these words. If by 'any' we mean to include within the range of our choice all the objects referred to, we must use *quivis, quilibet*. If by 'any' we mean to exclude all the objects specified, in which case we say 'any at all,' we must use *quisquam* or *ullus*. Such sentences are in effect negative. And as we find *ullus* used in the negative form *nullus*, so *quisquam* and *ullus* are found chiefly in combination with such particles as *non, haud, ne, num, an, sine*, and *absque;* and we may even have *nihil quicquam*, or *nec quisquam unus*, and in colloquial Latin, *quicquam* may even stand alone for *nihil quicquam*, as in the phrase *aeque quicquam* for *aeque ac nihil quicquam* (Ter. *Andr.* II. 6, 3). We have thus two pairs of words, (1) *quis* and *quispiam* opposed to *aliquis* and *aliquispiam*, as 'any one' is distinguished from 'some one;' (2) *quivis* and *quilibet* opposed to *quisquam* and *ullus*, as 'any you please' is opposed to 'any at all.' These distinctions, which are very important, will be remembered by the following rhymes:

(1) *Quis, quispiam*, 'any,' esse dant
Vel ponunt; non determinant;
Aliquis, 'some one,' denotat
Quampiam, sed non nominat.

(2) *Quivis, quilibet*, 'any you please,'
Continebunt cunctas res;
Quisquam, 'any at all,' et *ullus*,
Excludunt omnes, sicut *nullus*.

Obs. 4 In *utervis, uterque*, &c., *uter* is declined as above (35), and *ullus, nullus*, follow the same form of declension. *Nemo* is a substantive of the masculine gender, and is declined like *homo* which it includes (26); it may however be used as a general adjective, except that the gen. and abl. are rarely found in the best writers, who substitute *nullius* and *nullo*. *Nihil* occurs only as nom. and accus. But *nihili* and *nihilo* from *nihilum* are sometimes found.

PRONOUNS.   79

Obs. 5   *Utervus* means 'both the one and the other' (Gr. ἑκάτερος);
ambo means 'both together' (Gr. ἄμφω, ἀμφότεροι); *quisque* means
'each' or 'every one' of a larger number (Gr. ἕκαστος); *unusquisque*
means 'each' or 'every one' taken singly (Gr. εἷς ἕκαστος or ὡς ἕκαστος
opposed to σύμπας, Herod. vi. 128; Thucyd. i. 3); *omnis* means 'all, as
many as there are,' 'all, as a collection of individuals' (Gr. πᾶς); *cuncti*,
for *conjuncti*, means 'all in a body,' i.e. 'all conjoined and united for
a particular purpose and at a particular time' (Gr. ἅπαντες); *universus*
means 'all acting by common consent,' i.e. all going in the same direction (*una versus*) and generally combined (Gr. σύμπας, συνάπας), so that
it is opposed both to *unusquisque* (Cic. *de Off.* III. 6), and to *singuli* (Cic.
de Nat. Deor. II. 17); and *totus* means 'the whole,' i.e. that all the parts
are so combined that they are regarded as forming a new unit (Gr. ὅλος).

§ 5. *Indefinite Relative Pronouns and their Correlatives.*

69 Indefinite relatives are those formed by the addition of
-cunque to any relative (67), and to the interrogative *uter.* The
reduplicated *quisquis* is used both relatively and as an adjective
signifying 'every.' It is commonly found only in the nom. masc.
and in the nom. and accus. neuter *quidquid* or *quicquid.* The
phrase *cujuscuĭmŏdi*, 'of whatever kind,' has sprung from an abridge-
ment of the gen. of this pronoun coupled with the gen. of *modus.*
Several of these indefinite relatives have correlative forms, as
follows:

Demonstr.	Rel. and Interrog.	Indef. Rel.	Indef.
talis, 'of such a kind.'	*qualis,* 'of which (what ?)' kind.	*qualiscunque,* 'of what-soever kind.'	*qualislibet,* 'of any kind you please.'
tantus, 'so great.'	*quantus,* '(so great) as,' 'how great ?'	*quantuscunque,* 'how great soever.'	*aliquantus,* 'of some consi-derable size.'
tot, 'so many.'	*quot,* '(so many) as,' 'how ma-ny ?'	*quotcunque, quotquot,* 'how many soever.'	*aliquot,* 'a cer-tain number, some.'
tŏtus, 'such in number.'	*quŏtus,* 'of what number,' 'which in the series ?'	*quŏtuscunque,* 'never so little.'	
totĭdem, 'just so many.'			

Obs. 1 *Aliquantus* is generally used in the neuter (*aliquantum, aliquanto*) as a substantive. From *tantus* and its correlatives we have the diminutives, *tantillus*, 'so little,' *quantulus*, 'how little,' &c. &c.; from *tantum* we have *tantundem* (nom. acc. neut.), 'just so much,' gen. *tantidem*.

Obs. 2 The use of *quisquis* for *quisque*, in the sense 'every,' is of comparatively rare occurrence, though it is found in the best writers; e. g. in Cicero, *ad Famil.* VI. 1, § 1, we have *quocunque in loco quisquis est*, and in the same, book IV. § 3, *ubi quisque sit* in the same sense. In the neuter modern scholars write *quicquid* when it means 'every,' but *quidquid* when it means 'whatsoever;' thus in Lucret. v. 304: *et primum quicquid fulgoris perdere semper*, 'that they always lose every first grab of light;' but Virgil, *Æn.* II. 49: *quidquid id est*, 'whatever that is.' Similarly they distinguish between *quidque* in the sense of *et quid*, and *quicque* the neuter of *quisque*.

Obs. 3 The adjective *quotus* signifies 'what in number?' 'of what number, order,' &c.; as *hora quota est?* 'what o'clock is it?' And *quotus quisque* means 'what one amongst many;' as *quotus quisque philosophorum invenitur*, 'how few philosophers there are.' The meaning of *titus* is shown by the line of Lucretius, VI. 652: *nec tota pars homo terrai quota totius unus*. And that of *quotuscunque* by the line of Tibullus, II. *El.* ult. *ad fin.*: *moreris e votis pars quotacunque deos*.

CHAPTER IV.

VERBS.

§ 1. *Regular Verbs.*

70 A REGULAR verb is that which may be inflected through all its *voices, moods, tenses, numbers, persons, participles, gerunds,* and *supines.*

(a) *Voices.*

There are two voices, the *active*, in -*o* (with the exception of *sum*, 'I am;' *inquam*, 'I say'), which means that the *subject* or nominative *does* something; the *passive*, in -*or*, which expresses that the subject or nominative *suffers* something, or has something *done to him, her,* or *it*, and so becomes an *object;* thus, *amo*, 'I am loving' some object—i.e. I am the *subject* of love; *amor*, 'I am loved,' or some one loves me—i.e. I am the *object* of love. If the action of a verb is confined to itself, it is called *intransitive;* if it passes on to something else, it is called a *transitive* verb. Thus *curro*, 'I am running,' *caleo*, 'I am warm,' *sto*, 'I stand,' are intransitive verbs; but *amo*, 'I love,' *scribo*, 'I write,' are transitive verbs, because they generally imply and require some object expressed in the accusative to which the action immediately passes, as *amo Deum*, 'I love God,' *scribo epistolam*, 'I write a letter.' If a verb is active in form, but intransitive in sense and usage, it is called *neuter*, that is, neither active nor passive; if it is transitive in sense and usage, but passive in form, it is called *deponent* ('laying aside,' from *depono*, because it lays aside its active form); and while the neuter verb is never used in a passive form, except when it is impersonal, the deponent verb has no active form, except in a few cases where both forms are used with the same signification. Thus *curro*, 'I run,' is a neuter verb; for though its form is active, and though it denotes an action, it is intransitive in sense and usage, and it cannot have a passive form except in the impersonal construction, as *curritur a me,* 'it is run by me' (below, 100). On the other hand, *hortor,* 'I exhort,' is deponent, for it is essentially transitive, and has not, by the nature of the case, any form to express a passive signification.

Obs. A transitive verb may be used intransitively; thus we may say absolutely *amo,* 'I am in love,' as well as *amo te,* 'I love thee;' and conversely an intransitive verb may have a transitive usage; thus we may say *excedo modum,* 'I exceed bounds,' as well as absolutely *excedo,* 'I go forth.'

(b) *Moods.*

There are four *moods* or ways (*modi*) in which an action or circumstance may be stated:

A. The *indicative,* which declares a fact, as *puer scribit,* 'the boy is writing.'

B. The *imperative,* which gives a command, as *scribe,* 'write!'

C. The *subjunctive,* which states a wish or possibility, as *scribat puer,* 'may the boy write?' or, 'the boy may write.'

D. The *infinitive,* by which the mere action or circumstance is described in a general and indefinite manner, as *scribere,* 'to write,' or 'writing.'

(c) *Tenses.*

There are five *tenses* or times (*tempora*) in the indicative and subjunctive:

I. The *present,* which indicates that the action is going on at the time of speaking, as *amo,* 'I am loving.'

II. The *imperfect,* which indicates that the action was going on at a time specified, as *amabam,* 'I was loving' at some particular time.

III. The *perfect,* which declares that the action is past and gone now, as *scripsi,* 'I have written,' or 'I wrote.'

Obs. There are three forms of the perfect active, which do not, however, differ in signification : (a) reduplicated, as *do, de-di;* (b) aorist in *-si,* as *scribo, scrip-si;* (c) composite, in *-vi* or *-ui* from *fui,* as *ama-vi* for *ama-fui.*

IV. The *pluperfect*, which speaks of an action done and ended at some specified time now past, as *scripseram*, 'I had written' at some specified time.

V. The *future*, which indicates some action as coming or about to be, as *amabo*, 'I shall love.'

(d) *Numbers and Persons.*

In every one of these tenses there are two *numbers*, singular and plural; and in each number three *persons*, corresponding to the personal and indicative pronouns: (1) *ego, nos*; (2) *tu, vos*; (3) *hic, hi, iste, isti, ille, illi*. The regular forms of the person-endings in the active singular are: (1) -*m*, (2) -*s*, (3) -*t*; plural: (1) -*mus*, (2) -*tis*, (3) -*nt*. Thus we have, sing. (1) *diceba-m*, (2) *diceba-s*, (3) *diceba-t*; plur. (1) *diceba-mus*, (2) *diceba-tis*, (3) *diceba-nt*. There is no doubt that these affixes represent the elements of the personal pronouns. But while they are liable to some disfigurement in the active, they are almost undistinguishable in the passive verb. The -*m* of the first person singular is always lost in the perfect indicative active, and in the future indicative of the first two conjugations. It is occasionally lost in the transition from -*im* to -*o* in the perfect subjunctive, and, with the exception of two verbs—*sum*, 'I am,' and *inquam*, 'I say'—the first person of the present indicative active always ends in -*o*. The second person singular always ends in -*s*, except in the imperative, when it is either omitted or written -*to*; and in the perfect indicative, when it is written -*is-ti*, as in *amav-is-ti, scrips-is-ti*; just as we have *amav-is-tis, scrips-is-tis*, in the second person plural. The syllable -*is*- is constantly omitted both in these inflexions of the perfect indicative of the fourth conjugation and in the corresponding form of the perfect infinitive in -*is-se*. Thus we have *direxti* for *direx-is-ti* (Virgil, *Æn*. VI. 57), *accestis* for *access-is-tis* (Virgil, *Æn*. I. 201), *surrexe* for *surrex-is-se* (Hor. 1 *Serm*. IX. 73), *traxe* for *trax-is-se* (Virg. *Æn*. V. 786). The second person plural is changed from -*tis* to -*te*, or -*tote*, in the imperative; and the third person plural of the perfect indicative sometimes substitutes -*re* for -*runt*. In the passive voice the affix of the first person singular is invariably wanting. Thus we have not only *amo-r* as the passive of *amo*, but *amaba-r* as the passive of *amaba-m*, and *ame-r* as the passive of *ame-m*. The second person singular substitutes -*ris*, or more rarely -*re*, for the

84   VERBS.

-*s* of the active, as *ama-ris* or *ama-re* for *ama-s*. The third person singular and plural change -*t* and -*nt* into -*tur* and -*ntur*, as *amatur* for *ama-t*, or *ama-ntur* for *ama-nt*. The first person plural substitutes -*mu-r* for -*mu-s*, as *ama-mur* for *ama-mus*; and the second person plural presents the peculiar form in -*mini*, or -*minor* in the imperative, which has no relation to the active of the same person; thus we have *ama-mini*, *ama-minor*, by the side of *ama-tis* and *ama-ts*, *ama-tote*. In the perfect and pluperfect of the indicative and subjunctive passive there is no regular inflexion of the verb itself, but only a combination of the participle with the persons of the substantive verb *sum*.

(*v*) *Participles and Gerunds*.

Participles, which are so called from partaking of the nature of the noun and verb, are nominal forms, expressing the undefined and general action of the verb, like the infinitive mood, for which they are sometimes used. The participles are either active and present (E. I.), as *amans*, *amandus*, *amabundus*, 'loving;' or active and future (E. V.), as *amatūrus*, 'about to love;' or passive and past (E. III.), as *amātus*, 'loved.' The neuter of the present participle, under the form -*ndus*, is used to make oblique cases of the infinitive, and is then called a *gerund* (F.); as *amandum*, 'to love;' *amandi*, 'of loving;' *amando*, 'in or by loving.'

Obs. 1 The active verb has no past participle; but the deponent verb has a present participle in -*ns*, and a past participle in -*tus*, both of them with an active signification; thus *hortans* means 'exhorting,' and *hortatus* means 'having exhorted.' If we wish to express the past participle of an active verb, for instance *amo*, we must say either *quum amasset*, 'since he had loved,' i. e. 'having loved,' *qui amabat* or *amavit*, 'he who loved,' or in the ablative absolute, *filio amato*, 'his son having been loved,' i. e. 'having loved his son.' On the other hand, the passive verb has no present participle, and 'being loved,' for instance, must be expressed by *quum amaretur*, 'since he was being loved.'

Obs. 2 The participle in -*ndus* is not used as equivalent to the participle in -*ns*, except in some few forms, as *secundus* = *sequens*, 'following' (of a fair wind), 'second' (in order); *oriundus*, 'rising,' 'originating;' and in those in -*bundus*, as *lacryma-bundus*, 'weeping.' This participial or verbal form is generally employed as a present infinitive, with four modifications of construction.

(*a*) Its neuter constitutes a *substantival* infinitive, and is then called a *gerund*, as above.

(b) This may be made to agree with the case governed by the verb, as *consilium urbis capiendae*, 'the design of taking the city;' and it is then an *attracted* infinitive, and is called a *gerundive*.

(c) It may be used as a direct assertion with the verb *sum*; as *nunc est nobis pulsanda tellus*, 'now it is for us to beat the earth;' and it is then a *predicated* infinitive.

(d) It may be used as an epithet or attribute, as *reges timendi*, 'kings to fear,' or 'objects of fear,' and it is then an *adjectival* infinitive.

In the last two cases the English idiom admits the passive infinitive also. But we must be careful not to suppose that the Latin participle in *-ndus* is ever passive, for these constructions occur in the case of deponent verbs, which have no passive (98), as *proelia conjugibus loquenda*, 'battles for wives to talk about.'

(f) *Supines.*

There are also verbals in *-tus*, which correspond in meaning to the infinitive; and these, when used in the accusative and ablative in *-tum* and *-tu*, are called *supines* (G.), and correspond in meaning to the gerunds in *-dum* and *-do*, as *amātum*, 'to love;' *amātu*, 'in or by loving.' The supine in *-tum* is used with *iri*, the infinitive of the impersonal *itur*, 'things are going,' to express the future passive of that mood, thus *audio eum monitum iri*, 'I hear that things are going to admonish him'—i.e., that he will be admonished.

71. The conjugations are arrangements of verbs according to the form of the syllable to which the terminations are appended, and, like the declensions, depend upon the distinctions pointed out before (14). There are three vowel conjugations in *-a*, *-e*, *-i*, respectively, and one consonant conjugation, to which the semi-consonant conjugations in *-i* and *-u* are properly appended. A vowel conjugation is known by its infinitive *-āre*, *-ārī*; *-ēre*, *-ērī*; *-īre*, *-īrī*; as *amo, amāre, amārī; audio, audīre, audīrī*. Consonant and semi-consonant conjugations are distinguished by their infinitive in *-ĕre*, *-i*, as *scribo, scribĕre, scribi; rapio, rapĕre, rapi*.

The following scheme shows the formation of the *moods, tenses, numbers,* and *persons* in both *voices*, and in all four *conjugations* of the regular Latin verb:

VERBS.

Active.

		Indicative I.	II.	III.	IV.	Subjunctive I.	II.	III.	IV.
Present. Sing.	1.	-o	-eo	-io	-o	-em	-eam	-iam	-am
	2.	-as	-es	-is	-is	-es	-eas	-ias	-as
	3.	-at	-et	-it	-it	-et	-eat	-iat	-at
Plur.	1.	-āmus	-ēmus	-ĭmus	-īmus	-ēmus	-eāmus	-iāmus	-āmus
	2.	-ātis	-ētis	-ĭtis	-ītis	-ētis	-eātis	-iātis	-ātis
	3.	-ant	-ent	-iunt	-unt	-ent	-eant	-iant	-ant
Imperfect. Sing.	1.	-abam	-ebam	-iebam	-ebam	-ārem	-ērem	-īrem	-ĕrem
	2.	-abas	-ebas	-iebas	-ebas	-āres	-ēres	-īres	-ĕres
	3.	-abat	-ebat	-iebat	-ebat	-āret	-ēret	-īret	-ĕret
Plur.	1.	-abamus	-ebamus	-iebamus	-ebamus	-ārēmus	-ērēmus	-īrēmus	-ĕrēmus
	2.	-abatis	-ebatis	-iebatis	-ebatis	-ārētis	-ērētis	-īrētis	-ĕrētis
	3.	-abant	-ebant	-iebant	-ebant	-ārent	-ērent	-īrent	-ĕrent
Perfect. Sing.	1.	-i				-ero, -erim			
	2.	-isti				-eris			
	3.	-it				-erit			
Plur.	1.	-imus				-erimus			
	2.	-istis				-eritis			
	3.	-ērunt, -ēre				-erint, -erunt			

Passive.

		Indicative I.	II.	III.	IV.	Subjunctive I.	II.	III.	IV.
Present. Sing.	1.	-or	-eor	-ior	-or	-er	-ear	-iar	-ar
	2.	-āris	-ēris	-ĕris	-īris	-ēris	-eāris	-iāris	-āris
	3.	-ātur	-ētur	-ĭtur	-ītur	-ētur	-eātur	-iātur	-ātur
Plur.	1.	-āmur	-ēmur	-ĭmur	-īmur	-ēmur	-eāmur	-iāmur	-āmur
	2.	-āmini	-ēmini	-ĭmini	-īmini	-ēmini	-eāmini	-iāmini	-āmini
	3.	-antur	-entur	-iuntur	-untur	-entur	-eantur	-iantur	-antur
Imperfect. Sing.	1.	a-	e-	ie-	e-bar	ā-	ē-	ī-	ĕ-rer
	2.				-baris				-reris
	3.				-batur				-retur
Plur.	1.				-bamur				-remur
	2.				-bamini				-remini
	3.				-bantur				-rentur
Perfect. Sing.	1.	-tus, &c. sum				-tus, &c. sim			
	2.	es				sis			
	3.	est				sit			
Plur.	1.	sumus				simus			
	2.	estis				sitis			
	3.	sunt				sint			

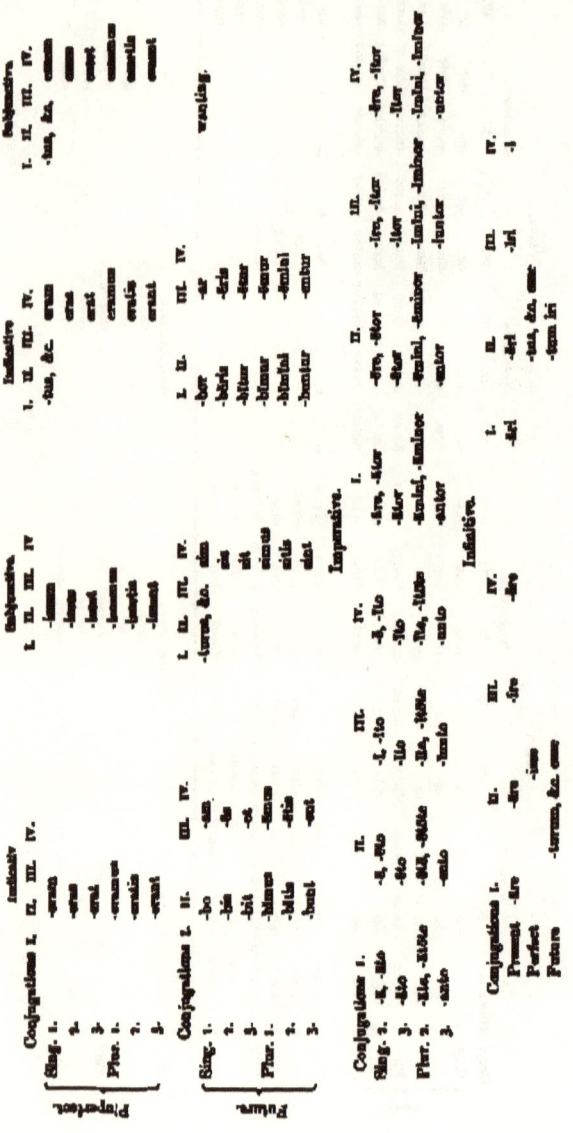

VERBS.

	Active.				Passive.			
		Participles.						
Conjugations	I.	II.	III.	IV.	I.	II.	III.	IV.
Present	-ans,	-ens,	-ens,	-ens	wanting.			
Perfect	wanting.				-tus, &c.			
Future	-turus, &c.				wanting.			

It will be remarked in the scheme, which is here given, that (1) in the tenses the imperfect and future may be formed from the present, the pluperfect from the perfect; (2) that the subjunctive mood may be formed from the corresponding tenses of the indicative; and the indicative and imperative from the infinitive; and (3) that the passive voice may be formed from the active. Thus, (1) from the present *amo=ama-o* we get imp. *ama-bam*, fut. *ama-bo*; from *mone-o* we get *mone-bam* and *mone-bo*; from *audi-o* we get *audi-ebam* and *audi-am*; from *reg-o* we get *reg-ebam* and *reg-am*; from the perf. *amav-i* we have the plup. *amav-eram*; from *monu-i*, *monu-eram*; from *audiv-i*, *audiv-erum*; from *scrips-i*, *scrips-eram*: (2) from the present indic. *am-o*, *mone-o*, *audi-o*, *scrib-o* are formed the pres. subj. *am-em*, *mone-am*, *audi-am*, *scrib-am*; from the imp. indic. *ama-bam*, *mone-bam*, *audi-ebam*, *scrib-ebam* are formed the imp. subj. *ama-rem*, *mone-rem*, *audi-rem*, *scrib-erem*; from the perf. ind. *amav-i*, *monu-i*, *audiv-i*, *scrips-i*, the perf. subj. *amav-erim*, *monu-erim*, *audiv-erim*, *scrips-erim*; from the plup. ind. *amav-eram*, *monu-eram*, *audiv-eram*, *scrips-eram*, the plup. subj. *amav-issem*, *monu-issem*, *audiv-issem*, *scrips-issem*; from the infin. *amare*, *mone-re*, *audi-re*, *scrib-ere*, we have the indic. and imper. *amao=amo*, *ama*; *mone-o*, *mone*; *audi-o*, *audi*; *scrib-o*, *scrib-e*: (3) from the active *amo*, *amaba-m*, *ama-bo*, the pass. *amo-r*, *amaba-r*, *amabo-r*; and similarly in the other conjugations.

Obs. In this mode of forming the tenses &c. of the verb attention is paid only to the convenience of the learner. Theoretically the formation of the Latin verb is a question of considerable difficulty. It is probable that the forms in *-bam*, *-bo*, like those in *-ri* or *-ui*, are compounded with the verb of existence *fu-*. The changes within this verb itself, and in the tenses of other verbs which do not involve it, are effected by an insertion of the letters *s* and *i*, either separately or combined, the former being turned into *r* between two vowels, but resuming its form when reduplicated or thrown back on another consonant. Thus from *fui* we have *fue-ram* for *fue-sam*; from *amo=ama-o* we have *amem=ama-iam*; from *mone-o* we have *mone-am=mone-iam*; from *audi-o* we have *audi-am=audi-iam*; from *scrib-o* we have *scrib-am=scrib-iam*. Then again from *amem=ama-iam* we have *ama-r-em=ama-s-iam*; from *scrib-am=scrib-iam* we have *scrib-e-r-em=scrib-e-s-iam*; from *fui* we

VERBS. 89

have *fue-rim = fue-sim*; and from this again *fuissem = fue-se-siom*. As
we have an omission of the syllable *is* in *direxti* for *direx-is-ti*, and
surrexe for *surrex-is-se*, so we may have an omission of the syllable
er = es in the perfect subjunctive. Thus for *jusserim = jus-se-sim*, we
have *jusrim* (Plaut. *Rud.* 1248); for *aus-erim = aus-se-sim* always *ausim*
or *aussim* (Plaut. *Bacch.* 1086); for *faxerim = fac-se-sim* (which is obsolete) we have *faxim*; for *dixeris = dix-se-sis* we have *dixis* (Plaut. *Aul.*
IV. 10. 14); and so in the pluperfect for *intellexissem* we have *intellexem*
(Plaut. *Cist.* II. 3. 81); for *extinxissem* we have *extinxem* (Virg. *Æn.* IV.
606); for *crepuissemus* we have *crepemus* (Hor. 1 *Sat.* V. 79). The forms
in *-asso, -assim* from verbs of the first conjugation, as *servasso* (Plaut.
Most. 228), *negassim* (*Asin.* 503), seem, from the infinitives in *-assere*, as
expugnassere (Plaut. *Amph.* I. 1. 55) to be agglutinate forms compounded
with *sino* (see below, 97, a). Perhaps *prohibessis* (Plaut. *Aul.* IV. 2. 4)
belongs to this class.

§ 2. *The Substantive*[1] *Verb, or Verb of being.*

sum, 'I am.'

72 All the conjugations make some use of the verb *sum*,
which is thus inflected:

A. (*Indicative Mood.*)

I. (*Present Tense.*)

Singular.	Plural.
1. *sum*, I am	*sŭmus*, we are
2. *ĕs*, {thou art / you are}	*estis*, ye are
3. *est*, he is	*sunt*, they are.

II. (*Imperfect.*)

1. *ĕram*, I was	*ĕrāmus*, we were
2. *ĕras*, {thou wert / you were}	*ĕrātis*, ye were
3. *ĕrăt*, he was	*ĕrant*, they were.

III. (*Perfect.*)

1. *fŭi*, I have been	*fŭĭmus*, we have been
2. *fuisti*, {thou hast been / you have been}	*fuistis*, ye have been
3. *fŭit*, he has been	*fŭērunt*, or *fŭēre*, } they have been.

---

[1] This name is derived from *substantia*, by which the school-doctors translated οὐσία, 'essence,' 'being.'

VERBS.

IV. (*Pluperfect.*)

Singular.
1. *fuĕram*, I had been
2. *fuĕras*, {thou hadst been / you had been}
3. *fuĕrat*, he had been

Plural.
fuerāmus, we had been
fuerātis, ye had been
fuĕrant, they had been.

V. (*Future.*)

1. *ĕro*, I shall be
2. *ĕris*, {thou wilt be / you will be}
3. *ĕrit*, he will be

ĕrĭmus, we shall be
ĕrĭtis, ye will be
ĕrunt, they will be.

B. (*Imperative Mood.*)

2. *ĕs, esto*, be thou
3. *esto*, be he, or let him be

este, estōte, be ye
sunto, be they, or let them be.

C. (*Subjunctive Mood.*)

I. (*Present Tense.*)

1. *sim* (*siem, fuam*, obsol.), I may be
2. *sis*, {thou mayest be / you may be}
3. *sit*, he may be

sīmus, we may be
sītis, ye may be
sint, they may be.

II. (*Imperfect.*)

Singular.
1. *essem, fŏrem*, I might be
2. *esses, fŏres*, {thou mightest be / you might be}
3. *esset, fŏret*, he might be

Plural.
1. *essēmus, fŏrēmus*, we might be
2. *essētis, fŏrētis*, ye might be
3. *essent, fŏrent*, they might be.

III. (Perfect.)

Singular.

1. *fuero, fuerim*, I shall or may have been
2. *fueris*, {thou wilt or mayst have been / you will or may have been}
3. *fuerit*, he will or may have been

Plural

1. *fuerĭmus*[1], we shall or may have been
2. *fuerĭtis*[1], ye will or may have been
3. *fuerint*, they will or may have been.

IV. (Pluperfect.)

Singular.

1. *fuissem*, I should or might have been
2. *fuisses*, {thou wouldest or mightest have been / you would or might have been}
3. *fuisset*, he would or might have been

Plural

1. *fuissēmus*, we should or might have been
2. *fuissētis*, ye would or might have been
3. *fuissent*, they would or might have been.

V. (Future.)

Singular.

1. *futūrus sim*, I may be about to be
2. *futūrus sis*, {thou mayest be about to be / you may be about to be}
3. *futūrus sit*, he may be about to be

Plural

1. *futūri simus*, we may be about to be
2. *futūri sitis*, ye may be about to be
3. *futūri sint*, they may be about to be.

As *futurus* is a participle, it will, according to the syntax, alter with the gender of the nominative to the verb.

[1] The quantity of *-rimus* and *-ritis* in this tense has been a cause of dispute to the old grammarians. Usage and philological reasoning are in favour of the long i. See *Varronianus*, p. 133. Ed. 3.

D. (*Infinitive Mood.*)

I. (*Present.*)   III. (*Perfect.*)
esse, to be   fuisse, to have been.

V. (*Future.*)
fŏre vel fŭtūrum esse, to be about to be.

The present participle *sens*, occurs only in some compounds: as *ab-sens*, 'being away or at a distance,' from *ab-sum*.
The future participle is *futūrus*, 'about to be.'

§ 3. *Vowel Conjugations.*

73 The vowel conjugations contain contracted verbs only, and are known by the long *ā, ē*, and *ī* respectively of the infinitive: thus we have *āmāre* for *ama-ĕre*, *monēre* for *mone-ĕre*, and *audīre* for *audi-ĕre*. Hence we see that the irregular *do, das, dedi, dăre, dătum* does not belong entirely to the vowel verbs, but partly also to the same class as its compounds: *condo, condis, condidi, condĕre; trado, tradis, tradidi, tradĕre;* &c. And similarly we distinguish from this class the semi-consonant verbs in -io, as *fug-io, fugis, fūgi, fugĕre; rapio, rapis, rapui, rapĕre;* &c.

First or -a Conjugation.

74 Active voice : *amo*, 'I love' or 'am loving.'

A.

I. I (thou or you, he, &c.) 'love,' 'do love' or 'am loving.'

Singular.   Plural.
1. ămo   ămāmus
2. ămās   ămātis
3. ămăt   ămant.

II. I (&c.) 'did love' or 'was loving.'

1. ămābam   ămābāmŭs
2. ămābās   ămābātis
3. ămābat   ămābant.

III. I (&c.) 'loved' or 'have loved.'

1. ămāvi   ămāvĭmus
2. ămāvisti   ămāvistis
3. ămāvĭt   ămāvērunt v. ămāvērĕ.

VERBS.

IV. I (&c.) 'had loved.'

Singular.	Plural.
1. ămāvĕram	ămāvĕrāmus
2. ămāvĕrās	ămāvĕrātis
3. ămāvĕrat	ămāvĕrant.

V. I (&c.) 'shall' or 'will love.'

1. ămābo	ămābĭmus
2. ămābis	ămābĭtis
3. ămābit	ămābunt.

B. 'Love thou,' (&c.)

2. ămā, ămāto	ămāte, ămātōte
3. ămāto	ămanto.

C.

I. I (&c.) 'may love.'

1. ămem	ămēmus
2. ămēs	ămētis
3. ămĕt	ăment.

II. I (&c.) 'might love.'

1. ămārem	ămārēmus
2. ămārēs	ămārētis
3. ămārĕt	ămārent.

III. I (&c.) 'shall' or 'may have loved.'

1. ămāvĕro, ămāvĕrim	ămāvĕrĭmus
2. ămāvĕris	ămāvĕrĭtis
3. ămāvĕrit	ămāvĕrint.

IV. I (&c.) 'should' or 'might have loved.'

1. ămāvissem	ămāvissēmus
2. ămāvisses	ămāvissētis
3. ămāvisset	ămāvissent.

V. I (&c.) 'may be about to love.'

1. ămātūrus, -a, -um, sim	ămātūri, -æ, -a, simus
2. sis	sitis
3. sit	sint.

VERBS.

āmāro

D.
I. 'to love.'

III. 'to have loved.'
āmāvisse

V. 'to be about to love.'
amaturum, -am, -um, esse v. fore.

E.
I. amans, 'loving.'   V. āmātūrus, 'about to love.'

F.
amandum, 'to love.'
amandi, 'of loving.'
amando, 'in' or 'by loving.'

G.
amatum, 'to love.'
amatu, 'in' or 'by loving.'

75 Passive voice: *amor*, 'I am being loved.'

A.
I. I (&c.) 'am loved' or 'being loved.'

Singular.	Plural.
1. amor	āmāmur
2. āmāris v. āmāre	āmāmini
3. āmātur	āmāntur.

II. I (&c.) 'was being loved.'

1. āmābar	āmābāmur
2. āmābāris v. āmābāre	āmābāmini
3. āmābātur	āmābantur.

III. I (&c.) 'was, have been loved.'

Singular.
1. āmātus, -a, -um, sum v. fui [1]
2.   es v. fuisti
3.   est v. fuit

[1] The auxiliary *fui* is rarely, if ever, used by good authors to form the perfect passive, and the same remark applies to *fuerum*.

VERBS.

Plural.
1. ămāti, -æ, -a, sŭmus v. fuĭmus
2.   estis v. fuistis
3.   sunt, fŭĕrunt v. -ēre

IV. I (&c.) 'had been loved.'

Singular.
1. ămātus, -a, -um, eram v. fŭĕram
2.   eras v. fŭĕras
3.   erat v. fŭĕrat

Plural.
1. ămāti, -æ, -a, ĕrāmus v. fŭĕrāmus
2.   ĕrātis v. fŭĕrātis
3.   ĕrant v. fŭĕrant.

V. I (&c.) 'shall, will be loved.'

Singular.	*Plural.*
1. ămābor	ămābĭmur
2. ămābĕris v. ămābĕre	ămābĭmĭni
3. ămābĭtur	ămābuntur.

B. 'be thou (&c.) loved.'

| 2. ămāre, ămātor | ămāmĭni, ămāmĭnor |
| 3. ămātor | ămantor. |

C.

I. I (&c.) 'may be loved.'

1. ămer	ămēmur
2. ămēris v. ămēre	ămēmĭni
3. ămētur	ămentur.

II. I (&c.) 'might be loved.'

1. ămārer	ămārēmur
2. ămārēris v. -ēre	ămārēmĭni
3. ămārētur	ămārentur.

96   VERBS.

III. I (&c.) 'shall' or 'may have been loved.'
Singular.
1. amātus, -a, -um, sim, fuero, fuerim
2. sis, fueris
3. sit, fuerit

Plural.
1. amāti, -æ, -a, simus, fuerīmus
2. sitis, fuerītis
3. sint, fuerint.

IV. I (&c.) 'should' or 'might have been loved.'
Singular.
1. amātus, -a, -um, essem, fuissem
2. esses, fuisses
3. esset, fuisset

Plural.
1. amāti, -æ, -a, essēmus, fuissēmus
2. essētis, fuissētis
3. essent, fuissent.

D.
I. 'to be loved.'
amāri (obsol. amarier).
III. 'to have been loved.'   V. 'to be about to be loved.'
amātum esse v. fuisse   amātum iri

E.
III. amātus, 'loved.'

76 *Remarks on the -a Conjugation.*

(1) *Perfect.* (a) It has been already mentioned (above, 70, (c) III. *Obs.*) that there are three forms of the perfect active in Latin: (a) the proper or reduplicated perfect; (β) the aorist-perfect in -*si*; (γ) the composite perfect, which adds -*vi* or -*ui*, for *fui*. In this composite tense the *v* may be dropt when *avi* is followed by *s* or *avs* by *r*; thus we have *amavisti, amāsti; amavissem, amāssem; amavisse, amāsse; amaveram, amāram; amavero, amāro; amavērunt, amārunt;* but not *amāre* for *amavere*, lest there should be a confusion with the infinitive. The only verbs of the -a conjugation, which take the proper perfect, are *do* and *sto*, which have for their

perfects *dĕdi* and *stĕti*. *Do*, which is otherwise irregular, and of which an older form *dĭno* is still in existence (e. g. Plautus, *Most.* III. I. 34. *Pseud.* III. 1. 1), exhibits the following forms: A. I. *do, das, dut, dămus, dătis, dant,* II. *dăbam,* v. *dăbo,* B. *da, dăto,* C. I. *dem, des, det, dēmus, dētis, dent,* II. *dărem,* D. *dăre,* supine *dătum*. We occasionally find in the comic poets and in antiquated phrases the forms *duim,* &c. for *dem,* &c., and *duitor* for *dator* (see p. 434). In the compounds we have *creduam* and *creduis* for *credam, credas,* &c., and *perduint* for *perdant* is used even by Cicero (*pro Deiot.* VII. 21) in an imprecation.

(b) All other -*a* verbs take the composite perfect from *fui*, which is written -*vi* if the *a* of the root is retained, and -*ui* if the *a* is elided; and the *v* is absorbed or represented only by a lengthening of the first vowel of the verb, if in the latter case it comes in contact with another *v* (below, (d)). In the pluperfect, -*ave-* or -*avi-* may be contracted into *ā*; as *amārat, amāsset,* for *amaverat, amavisset.*

(c) The following are the only verbs which elide the characteristic -*a*: *crĕpo, crepui,* 'rattle;' *cŭbo, cubui,* 'lie;' *dŏmo, domui,* 'tame;' *frĭco, fricui,* 'rub;' *mĭco, micui,* 'move rapidly;' *nĕco, necui,* 'kill;' *plĭco, plicui,* 'fold;' *sĕco, secui,* 'cut;' *sŏno, sonui,* 'sound;' *tŏno, tonui,* 'thunder;' *vĕto, vetui,* 'forbid;' and their compounds. In some of these verbs the *a* is occasionally retained in the perfect. Thus *applico, complico, implico* have also the perfects *applicavi,* &c. The simple verb *neco* has generally the perfect *necavi,* though its compounds, as *eneco, enecui,* most frequently omit the characteristic. The only compound of *mico,* which retains the form in -*avi,* is *dimico,* 'I fight.'

(d) In the verbs *jŭvo,* 'I assist;' *lăvo,* 'I wash,' the affix of the perfect is represented only by a lengthening of the root syllable; thus we have *jūvi* for *jŭv-ui* and *lāvi* for *lăv-ui.* In old Latin (e. g. in Ennius, ap. *Cic. Cat. Maj.* init.), we have a double omission of the *v* of the *juvo,* for in *adjuro* for *adjuvero* we have lost both the *v* of the perfect and the *v* of the root.

(e) Verbs derived from adjectives in -*plex,* as *duplīco* from *duplex,* and *supplīco* from *supplex,* must be carefully distinguished from the compounds of *plĭco*. These verbs always retain their characteristic in the perfect, which is *duplicavi, supplicavi,* &c.

(2) *Supine and passive participle.* Verbs, which omit the characteristic *a* in the perfect, generally omit it in the supines, or

rather substitute for it a short *i*. Thus *cubo* makes *cubĭtum*, *domo*, *domĭtum*, *plico*, *plicĭtum*, &c. But the compounds of *plico* sometimes retain *a* in the supine as they do in the perfect; thus we have *applicatum*, *complicatum*, *explicatum* as well as *applicitum*, &c. *Frico*, *neco*, and *seco* omit even the *i*, and their supines are *frictum*, *nectum*, *sectum*, though *fricatum*, *necatum* also occur. The same is the case with *jŭvo*, *jŭvi*, *jŭtum*; *lăvo*, *lăvi*, *lautum* or *lōtum*. *Pōto*, although it has a regular perfect, has both *potatum* and *potum* in the supine, and its participle is *potus*, which means both 'being drunk' and 'having drunk.' *Mico* has no supine, and its compounds always retain the characteristic in the supine; as *emicātum*, *dimicātum*.

Second or -e Conjugation.

77 Active voice: *mŏneo*, 'I put in mind.'

A.

I. 'I (&c.) am putting in mind.'

Singular. Plural.
1. moneo monēmus
2. monēs monētis
3. monet monent.

II. 'I (&c.) was putting in mind.'
1. monēbam monēbāmus
2. monēbas monēbātis
3. monēbat monēbant.

III. 'I (&c.) have put in mind.'
1. monui monuĭmus
2. monuisti monuistis
3. monuit monuērunt v. monuēre.

IV. 'I (&c.) had put in mind.'
1. monuĕram monuerāmus
2. monuĕras monuerātis
3. monuĕrat monuĕrant.

V. 'I (&c.) shall' or 'will put in mind.'
1. monēbo monēbĭmus
2. monēbis monēbĭtis
3. monēbit monēbunt.

VERBS.

B. 'Put thou (&c.) in mind.'

Singular.	Plural.
2. monē, monēto	monēte, monētōte
3. monēto	monento.

C.

I. 'I (&c.) may put in mind.'

1. moneam	moneāmus
2. moneas	moneātis
3. moneat	moneant.

II. 'I (&c.) might put in mind.'

1. monērem	monērēmus
2. monēres	monērētis
3. monēret	monērent.

III. 'I (&c.) shall' or 'may have put in mind.'

1. monuĕro, monuĕrim	monuĕrĭmus
2. monueris	monuĕrĭtis
3. monuerit	monuĕrint

IV. 'I (&c.) should' or 'might have put in mind.'

1. monuissem	monuissēmus
2. monuisses	monuissētis
3. monuisset	monuissent.

V. 'I (&c.) may be about to put in mind.'

1. moniturus, -a, -um, sim	monitūri, -æ, -a, simus
2. sis	sitis
3. sit	sint.

D.

I. monēre, 'to put in mind.'
III. monuisse, 'to have put in mind.'
V. moniturum esse v. fore, 'to be about to put in mind.'

E.

I. monens, 'putting in mind.'
V. moniturus, 'about to put in mind.'

100 VERBS.

F.
monendum, 'to put in mind.'
monendi, 'of putting in mind.'
monendo, 'in or by putting in mind'

G.
monĭtum, 'to put in mind.'
monītu, 'in or by putting in mind.'

78 Passive voice: monĕor, 'I am being put in mind.'

A.

I. 'I (&c.) am being put in mind.'

Singular. *Plural.*
1. moneor   monēmur
2. monēris v. monēre   monēmĭni
3. monētur   monentur.

II. 'I (&c.) was being put in mind.'
1. monēbar   monēbāmur
2. monēbāris v. monēbāre monēbāmĭni
3. monēbātur   monēbantur.

III. 'I (&c.) have been put in mind.'
1. monĭtus, -a, -um, sum   monĭti, -æ, -a, sumus
2.   es   estis
3.   est   sunt.

IV. 'I (&c.) had been put in mind.'
1. monĭtus, -a, -um, eram   monĭti, -æ, -a, eramus
2.   eras   eratis
3.   erat   erant.

V. 'I (&c.) shall' or 'will be put in mind.'
1. monēbor   monēbĭmur
2. monēbĕris (-e) monēbĭmĭni
3. monēbĭtur   monēbuntur.

B. 'Be thou &c. put in mind.'

2. monēre, monētor   monēmĭni, monēmĭnor
3. monētor   monentor.

C.

I. 'I (&c.) may be put in mind.'

Singular.
1. monear
2. moneāris (-e)
3. moneātur

Plural.
monæāmur
monēamini
moneantur.

II. 'I (&c.) might be put in mind.'

1. monērer
2. monērēris (-e)
3. monērētur

monērēmur
monērēmini
monērentur.

III. 'I (&c.) shall' or 'may have been put in mind.'

Singular.
1. monĭtus, -a, -um, sim, fuĕro, fuĕrim
2. sis, fuĕris
3. sit, fuĕrit

Plural.
1. monĭti, -æ, -a, simus, fuĕrĭmus
2. sitis, fuĕrĭtis
3. sint, fuĕrint.

IV. 'I (&c.) should' or 'might have been put in mind.'

Singular.
1. monĭtus, -a, -um, essem, fuissem
2. esses, fuisses
3. esset, fuisset

Plural.
1. monĭti, -æ, -a, essēmus, fuissēmus
2. essētis, fuissētis
3. essent, fuissent.

D.

I. monēri (obs. *monerier*), 'to be put in mind.' III. monĭtum, -am, -um, esse, 'to have been put in mind.' V. monĭtum iri, 'to be about to be put in mind.' E. III. monĭtus, 'put in mind.'

79 *Remarks on the -e Conjugation.*

(1) *Perfect.* (a) The only verbs of this conjugation, which take the proper or reduplicated perfect, are *mordeo,* 'I bite,' *mŏmordi; pendeo,* 'I am hanging,' *pependi; tondeo,* 'I shear,' *totondi; spondeo,* 'I promise,' *spŏpondi.*

(b) Most of the -*e* verbs elide this characteristic in the perfect, and take the composite form (γ) in -*ui,* as *mon-eo, mon-ui, hab-eo, hab-ui.*

(c) The only verbs, which form the perfect in -*ē-vi,* are *deleo,* 'I destroy,' *delēvi; fleo,* 'I weep,' *flēvi; neo,* 'I spin,' *nēvi;* the compounds of *oleo,* 'I grow,' as *ab-oleo, ab-olēvi, ad-oleo, ad-olēvi;* the compounds of *pleo,* 'I fill,' as *compleo, complēvi, impleo, implēvi;* and *vieo,* 'I bind with twigs,' *vēvi.* This form of the perfect may lose its *v,* like the perfect in -*avi* of the first conjugation; thus we have *nevisti, nēsti, neverunt, nērunt; complevissem, complêssem;* &c.

(d) Some of the verbs which omit the characteristic -*e* take the aorist-perfect in -*si,* (β), which, as we shall see, is the usual form with consonant-verbs. The only labial verb which exhibits this perfect alone is *jubeo,* which has *jussi* for *jub-si;* but *sorbeo* may have *sorpsi,* as well as its more common perfect *sorbui.* The following guttural verbs have the perfect in -*si,* which, in combination with the preceding letter, becomes -*xi: augeo,* 'I increase,' *auxi; frigeo,* 'I freeze,' *frixi; luceo,* 'I shine,' *luxi; lugeo,* 'I bewail,' *luxi;* to which must be added *conniveo* for *conniqueo,* 'I wink,' *connixi,* also *connivi,* as in *caveo* mentioned below.

(e) If the liquid *l* or *r* precedes the guttural, this characteristic is omitted before -*si:* as in *algeo,* 'I am cold,' *alsi; fulgeo,* 'I shine,' *fulsi; indulgeo,* 'I indulge,' *indulsi; mulceo,* 'I soothe,' *mulsi; mulgeo,* 'I milk,' *mulsi; tergeo,* 'I wipe,' *tersi; torqueo,* 'I twist,' *torsi; turgeo,* 'I swell,' *tursi; urgeo,* 'I press,' *ursi.*

(f) When a dental precedes the -*e,* it is omitted before -*si,* as in *ardeo,* 'I burn,' *arsi; rideo,* 'I laugh,' *risi; suadeo,* 'I advise,' *suasi.*

(g) The same rule applies to the *r* of *haereo,* 'I stick,' perf. *haesi;* but *maneo,* 'I remain,' makes *mansi.*

(h) *Sĕdeo,* 'I sit,' *video,* 'I see,' merely add *i* and lengthen the first syllable, the perfects being *sēdi, vīdi;* and the same alsorption has really taken place in *prandeo*, 'I dine,' perf. *prandi*; *strideo*, 'I hiss,' perf. *stridi*; where the root-vowel is already long by position or by nature.

(i) The same is generally the case when the root ends with *v*; thus we have *careo*, 'I take care,' *cāvi*; *faveo*, 'I am favourable,' *fāvi*; *foveo*, 'I make warm, cherish,' *fōvi*; *moveo*, 'I move,' *mōvi*; *paveo*, 'I dread,' *pāvi*; *voveo*, 'I vow,' *vōvi*. The compounds of *movi* sometimes syncopate *vi*-, as in *commōssem* for *commovissem*. But *ferveo*, 'I glow,' makes *fervui* as well as *fervi*, and *conniveo*, as we have seen, makes *connixi* as well as *connīvi*.

(2) *Supine and passive participle*. The characteristic -*s* is retained only in those verbs which exhibit it in the perfect; as *deleo*, *delēvi*, *delētum*: even in one of these it is elided; for we have *adoleo*, *adolēvi*, *adultum*, and another compound of *oleo*, namely, *aboleo*, has *abolĭtum*, substituting a short *ĭ* for the *ē*, which is generally the case in verbs which form the perfect in -*ui*; thus we have *moneo*, *monui*, *monĭtum*; *habeo*, *habui*, *habĭtum*, &c. The deponent *tueor*, 'I protect,' sometimes forms its participle *tutus* as well as *tuĭtus*, and the shorter form is always adopted, when the participle is used as an adjective, and *tutus*, 'protected,' means 'safe.' Guttural verbs often form the supine and participle passive in *ct*; thus, from *augeo*, *doceo*, *lugeo*, we have *auctus*, *doctus*, *luctus*. If *l* or *r* precedes the guttural, the latter is omitted and the *t* changed into *s*; thus, from *mulceo*, 'I soothe,' *mulgeo*, 'I milk,' *tergeo*, 'I wipe,' we have *mulsus* and *tersus*. But the *t* is retained in *indulgeo* and *torqueo*, which make *indultus* and *tortus*. All other verbs of this kind want the supine and passive participle. *Misceo*, 'I mix,' makes both *mistus* and *mixtus*. *Ardeo*, *fateor*, *mordeo*, *pendeo*, *sedeo*, *suadeo*, *video*, have for their supines, *arsum*, *fassum*, *morsum*, *pensum*, *sessum*, *suasum*, *visum*. *Teneo* gives *tentum*, *misereor* both *misertus* and *miserĭtus*, *torreo*, *tostum*; *caveo*, *moveo*, *voveo*, give *cautum*, *mōtum*, *vōtum*; *censeo* has *censum*, but *recenseo* makes *recensĭtum* as well as *recensum*. *Haereo* has only *haesum*, *maneo*, *mansum*, and *jubeo*, *jussum*. *Cieo*, 'to stir up,' makes *cĭtum*, to be distinguished from the synonymous *citum*, which belongs to *cio*. The deponent *reor*, 'I think,' has the irregular form *rătus*, whence *ratio*; but the compound *ir-rĭtus = non ratus*, 'not ratified,' 'of no effect,' follows the model of *monĭtus*.

104 VERBS.

Third or -i Conjugation.

80 Active voice: *audio*, 'I hear.'

A.

I. 'I (&c.) am hearing.'

Singular.	Plural.
1. audio	audīmus
2. audīs	audītis
3. audit	audiunt.

II. 'I (&c.) was hearing.'

1. audiēbam	audiēbāmus
2. audiēbas	audiēbātis
3. audiēbat	audiēbant.

III. 'I (&c.) have heard.'

1. audīvi	audīvimus
2. audīvisti	audīvistis
3. audīvit	audīvērunt v. audīvēre.

IV. 'I (&c.) had heard.'

1. audīveram	audīverāmus
2. audīveras	audīverātis
3. audīverat	audīverant.

V. 'I (&c.) shall hear.'

1. audiam	audiēmus
2. audies	audiētis
3. audiet	audient.

B. 'Hear thou,' (&c.)

2. audī, audīto	audīte, audītōte
3. audīto	audiunto.

C.

I. 'I (&c.) may hear.'

1. audiam	audiāmus
2. audias	audiātis
3. audiat	audiant.

VERBS. 105

II. 'I (&c.) might hear.'

Singular.	Plural.
1. audīrem	audīrēmus
2. audīres	audīrētis
3. audīret	audīrent.

III. 'I (&c.) shall' or 'may have heard.'

1. audīvĕro, audīverim	audīvĕrīmus
2. audīvĕris	audīverītis
3. audīverit	audīvĕrint.

IV. 'I (&c.) should' or 'might have heard.'

1. audīvissem	audīvissēmus
2. audīvisses	audīvissētis
3. audīvisset	audīvissent.

V. 'I (&c.) may be about to hear.'

1. audītūrus, -a, -um, sim	audītūri, -æ, -a, simus
2. sis	sitis
3. sit	sint.

D.

I. audīre, 'to hear.' III. audīvisse, 'to have heard.'
V. audītūrum esse v. fore, 'to be about to hear.'

E.

I. audiens, 'hearing.' V. audītūrus, 'about to hear.'

F.   G.

audiendum, 'to hear'   audītum, 'to hear'
audiendi, 'of hearing'
audiendo, 'in or by hearing'   audītu, 'in or by hearing.'

§1 Passive voice: *audior*, 'I am being heard.'

A.

1. 'I (&c.) am being heard.'

1. audior	audīmur
2. audīris (-e)	audīmini
3. audītur	audiuntur.

VERBS.

II. 'I (&c.) was being heard.'

Singular.	Plural.
1. audiēbar	audiebāmur
2. audiēbāris (-e)	audiebāmini
3. audiēbātur	audiebantur.

III. 'I (&c.) have been heard.'

1. audītus, -a, -um, sum	audīti, -æ, -a, sumus
2. es	estis
3. est	sunt.

IV. 'I (&c.) had been heard.'

1. audītus, -a, -um, eram	audīti, -æ, -a, erāmus
2. eras	erātis
3. erat	erant.

V. 'I (&c.) shall be heard.'

1. audiar	audiēmur
2. audiēris (-e)	audiēmini
3. audiētur	audientur.

B. 'Be (&c.) thou heard.'

2. audire, auditor	audimini, audiminor
3. auditor	audiuntor.

C.

I. 'I (&c.) may be heard.'

1. audiar	audiāmur
2. audiāris (-e)	audiāmini
3. audiātur	audiantur.

II. 'I (&c.) might be heard.'

1. audīrer	audirēmur
2. audirēris (-e)	audirēmini
3. audirētur	audirentur.

III. 'I (&c.) shall' or 'may have been heard.'

Singular.

1. audītus, -a, -um, sim, fuero, fuerim
2. sis, fueris
3. sit, fuerit.

VERBS.

Plural.
1. audīti, -æ, -a, sīmus, fuerĭmus
2.   sītis, fuĕrĭtis
3.   sint, fuĕrint.

IV. 'I (&c.) should' or 'might have been heard.'

Singular.
1. audītus, -a, -um, essem, fuissem
2.   esses, fuisses
3.   esset, fuisset.

Plural.
1. audīti, -æ, -a, essēmus, fuissēmus
2.   essētis, fuissētis
3.   essent, fuissent.

D.

I. audīri (obs. audirier, 'to be heard'). III. audītum, -am, -um, esse, 'to have been heard.' V. audītum iri, 'to be about to be heard.' E. III. audītus, 'heard.'

82. *Remarks on the -i Conjugation.*

(1) *Imperfect.* The imperfect almost always adds -ēbam, &c. to the characteristic *i*, but the poets contract *ie* into *i*: thus Virgil has *leniībat* from *lenio*, *polībant* from *polio*, &c.; and *eo*, *queo*, as we shall see, have always *ībam*, *quībam*.

(2) *Perfect.* (a) The perfect is generally in -īvi, which may be shortened into -ii, and even contracted in the pluperfect subjunctive into -i: thus we may have not only *audīvi*, *audīverat*, *audīvissent*, but also *audīi*, *audierat*, *audīssent*. It is, however, to be observed that, although *v* is often omitted even in the best prose writers between *i* and *e*, as in *audierunt*, *definieram*, &c., the concurrence of two *i*'s, as in *audīit*, *mugīit*, *munīit*, except in the compounds of *eo*, is generally confined to the poets, and especially occurs in cases like *impĕdii*, *oppĕtii*, where the hexameter verse would not admit the full form. The contraction of the two *i*'s, as in *audīsti*, *audīsse*, *audīssem*, is common even in prose, and in the silver age the contracted form was the most usual.

(b) The aorist perfect in -si is not uncommon, especially with guttural verbs; thus, *amicio*, 'I clothe;' *sancio*, 'I ordain;' *vincio*,

'I bind;' make *amixi, sanxi,* and *vinxi;* but *amicio* has also *amicui* and *sancio* has sometimes *sancivi.*

(c) If *l* or *r* precedes the guttural, it produces the same effect as in the -*s* conjugation, for the guttural is omitted before -*si*; thus *farcio,* 'I stuff;' *fulcio,* 'I support;' *sarcio,* 'I mend;' make *farsi, fulsi, sarci.*

(d) The labial verbs *sepio,* 'I hedge in,' *cambio,* 'I exchange,' have the perfects *sepsi, campsi.*

(e) The dental *sentio,* 'I feel,' makes *sensi.*

(f) Of the liquid verbs *haurio* makes *hausi* (like *haerco*); *aperio,* 'I open,' and *operio,* 'I cover,' make *aperui, operui;* *salio,* 'I leap,' makes *salui* and sometimes *salii;* *sarrio,* 'I weed corn with a hook,' *sarrivi* and *sarrui;* and *vĕnio,* 'I come,' perf. *vēni,* is the only verb of this class, which represents the absorbed affix of the perfect by a lengthening of the root syllable.

(3) *Future.* In the -*i* conjugation, as in the consonant-verbs, the only future in common use is a stronger form of the present subjunctive, to which it corresponds in the first person singular. The true form in -*bo* is obsolete except in *eo* and *queo.*

(4) *Supine and passive participle.* The regular supine and passive participle retain the characteristic *i,* as in *audītus,* and, of course, when this is the root-vowel, as in *accītus* from *accio,* to be distinguished from *concĭtus, incĭtus, percĭtus,* which belong to *concieo, incieo, percieo.* The *i* is omitted in those cases in which it is omitted in the perfect; thus we have *amicio, amixi, amictus; sancio, sanxi, sanctus* (but *sancivi, sancitus*); *vincio, vinxi, vinctus.* Similarly *farcio, farsi, fartus* (also *farsus*); *fulcio, fulsi, fultus; sarcio, sarsi, sartus.* Verbs with *r* before the characteristic *i* omit the latter before the *t:* thus we have *apertus, compertus, expertus, opertus, ortus, repertus,* from *aperio, comperio, experior, operio, orior, reperio.* But *haurio* makes *haustus, hausum,* and *hausurus.* *Salio* and *venio* make *saltus* and *ventus; sentio* has *sensus,* and *sepelio* forms its participle *sepultus.*

83. The verb *eo,* 'I go,' belongs to the -*i* conjugation, but changes *i* into *e* before *a, o, u.* It is inflected thus:

A. I. *eo, is, it, īmus, ītis, eunt.*
II. *ibam, -as, -at, -amus, -atis, -ant.*
III. *ivi* (in compounds *ii), ivisti, &c.*

VERBS. 109

IV. *iveram, iveras,* &c. (in compounds *ieram*).
V. *ibo, ibis,* &c.

B. *i, ito; ito; ite, itōte, eunto.*

C. I. *eam, eas, eat,* &c.
II. *irem, ires, iret,* &c.
III. *ivero* or *iverim, iveris,* &c. (in compounds *iero,* &c.)
IV. *ivissem* (in compounds *iissem* or *issem*).

D. *ire.* Part. *iens,* gen. *euntis.* Fut. *iturus.* Gerund *eundum,* &c. Supine *itum.*

In the same way is inflected *vēneo* for *venum eo,* which is used as the passive of *vendo,* 'I sell.'

Obs. 1 Except in the poets the shortened form in *ii* is not used in the simple verb; on the other hand, there are very few instances in which compounds of *eo* retain the *v* in the perfect and its derivatives. Sometimes the *ii* is still farther contracted into *i,* as in *ablāti, abistis, abisse.*

Obs. 2 *Eo* has no passive except when used as an impersonal; as *itur a me,* 'I go,' and in the infinitive *iri,* when in conjunction with the supine of a verb, it forms the future passive, as *amatum iri,* 'to be about to be loved' (70). Some of its compounds, however, are regularly formed in the passive; as *praetereor,* 'I am passed by,' *adeor,* 'I am approached,' &c. That *eo* had also the form *ino* may be inferred from *prodinunt* for *prodeunt* (Ennius, *op. Fest.* p. 220).

Obs. 3 *Queo,* 'I can,' and *nequeo,* 'I am unable,' are inflected like *eo,* but the original forms were *queno* and *nequino,* which contain the root of our 'can.' In common Latin the perfect *quivi* is obsolete. The imperf., plup., and future are also of very rare occurrence, and while *queo* is generally employed in negative propositions only, *quis* and *quit* are used only with *non.* When a passive or deponent infinitive follows we find in the older Latin an occasional attraction of *queo* into the passive form; thus we have in Terence, *Hec.* IV. 1. 57 : *forma in tenebris nosci non quita est.* Sallust, *Jug.* 31 : *quidquid sine sanguine civium ulcisci nequitur.* Lucret. I. 1045 : *dum veniant aliae ac suppleri summa queatur.*

§ 4. *Fourth or Consonant Conjugation.*

84 Regular consonant verbs are divided into different classes according to the nature of the consonant which is their characteristic. Thus there are mute verbs and liquid verbs; and the mute verbs are either labial, guttural or dental; and to these must be added the semi-consonantal verbs in *-i* and *-u.* Accordingly we have the following arrangement:

VERBS.

A. *Mute Verbs*:
(a) *Labial* verbs; as *scribo*, 'I write,' *scripsi, scriptum*.
(b) *Guttural* verbs; as *dico*, 'I speak,' *dixi, dictum*.
(c) *Dental* verbs; as *ludo*, 'I play,' *lusi, lusum*.

B. *Liquid Verbs*:
L verbs; as *colo*, 'I till,' *colui, cultum*.
M verbs; as *gemo*, 'I groan,' *gemui, gemitum*.
N verbs; as *cano*, 'I sing,' *cecini, cantum*.
R verbs; as *gero*, 'I carry,' *gessi, gestum*.
S verbs; as *texo*, 'I weave,' *texui, textum*.

C. *Semi-consonantal Verbs*:
I verbs; as *facio*, 'I make,' *feci, factum*.
U verbs; as *ruo*, 'I throw down,' *rui, ruitum* or *rūtum*.

We will take the first of these, as a specimen of the regular conjugation of verbs which form their infinitive in *-ěre*.

85 Active voice: *scribo*, 'I am writing.'

A.

I. 'I (&c.) am writing.'

Singular.	Plural.
1. scrībo	scrībĭmus
2. scrībis	scrībĭtis
3. scrībit	scrībunt.

II. 'I (&c.) was writing.'

1. scrībēbam	scrībēbāmus
2. scrībēbas	scrībēbātis
3. scrībēbat	scrībēbant.

III. 'I (&c.) have written.'

1. scripsi	scripsĭmus
2. scripsisti	scripsistis
3. scripsit	scripsērunt v. scripsēre.

IV. 'I (&c.) had written.'

1. scripsěram	scripsěrāmus
2. scripsěras	scripsěrātis
3. scripsěrat	scripsěrant.

VERBS. 111

v. 'I (&c.) shall write.'

Singular.	Plural.
1. scrībam	scrībēmus
2. scrībes	scrībētis
3. scrībet	scrībent.

B. 'Write thou' (&c.)

| 2. scrībe, scrībĭto | scrībĭto, scrībitote |
| 3. scrībĭto | scrībunto. |

C.

I. 'I (&c.) may write.'

1. scrībam	scrībāmus
2. scrības	scrībātis
3. scrībat	scrībant.

II. 'I (&c.) might write.'

1. scrībĕrem	scrībĕrēmus
2. scrībĕres	scrībĕrētis
3. scrībĕret	scrībĕrent.

III. 'I (&c.) shall' or 'may have written.'

1. scripsĕro, scripsĕrim	scripsĕrīmus
2. scripsĕris	scripsĕrītis
3. scripsĕrit	scripsĕrint.

IV. 'I (&c.) should' or 'might have written.'

1. scripsissem	scripsissēmus
2. scripsisses	scripsissētis
3. scripsisset	scripsissent.

v. 'I (&c.) may be about to write.'

1. scripturus, -a, -um, sim	scripturi, -æ, -a, simus
2. sis	sitis
3. sit	sint.

D.

I. scrībĕre, 'to write.' III. scripsisse, 'to have written.' V. scriptūrum esse, 'to be about to write.'

E.

i. scribens, 'writing.'   v. scripturus, 'about to write.'

F.

scribendum, 'to write.'
scribendi, 'of writing.'
scribendo, 'in or by writing.'

G.

scriptum, 'to write.'

scriptu, 'in or by writing.'

Passive voice: *scribor*, 'I am being written.'

A.

i. 'I (&c.) am being written.'

Singular.	Plural.
1. scribor	scribimur
2. scriberis (-e)	scribimini
3. scribitur	scribuntur.

ii. 'I (&c.) was being written.'

1. scribebar	scribebamur
2. scribebaris (-e)	scribebamini
3. scribebatur	scribebantur.

iii. 'I (&c.) have been written.'

1. scriptus, -a, -um, sum	scripti, -æ, -a, sumus
2. es	estis
3. est	sunt.

iv. 'I (&c.) had been written.'

1. scriptus, -a, -um, eram	scripti, -æ, -a, eramus
2. eras	eratis
3. erat	erant.

v. 'I (&c.) shall be written.'

1. scribar	scribemur
2. scriberis (-e)	scribemini
3. scribetur	scribentur.

B. 'Be thou (&c.) written.'

2. scribere, scribitor	scribimini, scribiminor
3. scribitor	scribuntor.

C.

I. 'I (&c.) may be written.'

Singular.
1. scribar
2. scribāris (-e)
3. scrībātur

Plural.
scrībāmur
scrībāmĭni
scrībantur.

II. 'I (&c.) might be written.'

1. scrīberer
2. scrīberēris (-e)
3. scrīberētur

scrīberēmur
scrīberēmĭni
scrīberentur.

III. 'I (&c.) shall' or 'may have been written.'

Singular.
1. scriptus, -a, -um, sim, fuero, fuerim
2.   sis, fueris
3.   sit, fuerit

Plural.
1. scripti, -æ, -a, simus, fuerĭmus
2.   sitis, fuerĭtis
3.   sint, fuerint.

IV. 'I (&c.) should' or 'might have been written.'

Singular.
1. scriptus, -a, -um, essem, fuissem
2.   esses, fuisses
3.   esset, fuisset

Plural.
1. scripti, -æ, -a, essēmus, fuissēmus
2.   essētis, fuissētis
3.   essent, fuissent.

D.

I. scribi (ols. scrībier), 'to be written.' III. scriptum, -am, -um, esse, 'to have been written.' V. scriptum iri, 'to be about to be written.' E. III. scriptus, 'written.'

Remarks on the Consonant Conjugation.

A. Mute Verbs.

86 (a) Labial Verbs.

(1) *Perfect.* (a) The form is generally the aorist (*S*) in -*si*, before which *b* is changed into *p*; thus we have *carpo*, 'I pluck,' *carpsi*; *nubo*, 'I put on the veil,' *nupsi*.

(b) Some verbs take the composite form in -*ui*; as *cumbo*, 'I lie down,' *cubui* (cf. *cubo*); *strepo*, 'I make a noise,' *strepui*.

(c) Some verbs merely add *i* to the root, which, if possible, is lengthened; as *lambo*, 'I lick,' *lambi*; *rumpo*, 'I break,' *rūpi*; *scabo*, 'I scratch,' *scābi*.

(d) *Bibo*, 'I drink,' perf. *bĭbi*, has lost its reduplication.

(2) *Supine and passive participle.* Generally the *t* is immediately attached to the *p* of the perfect; thus we have *nubo*, *nuptum*, *rumpo*, *ruptum.* But *bibo*, *cumbo*, *lambo*, *strepo* insert a short *i* in *bibĭtum*, *cubĭtum*, &c. And the deponent *lābor*, 'I glide down,' makes the participle *lapsus*.

87 (b) Guttural Verbs.

(1) *Perfect.* (a) The general form of the perfect is that in -*si*, and the -*s* combined with the preceding guttural becomes -*x*. Thus we have *dico*, 'I say,' *dixi*; *cingo*, 'I gird,' *cinxi*; *coquo*, 'I cook,' *coxi*; *distinguo*, 'I distinguish,' *distinxi*.

(b) The same rule applies when the guttural is reduced to a mere aspirate, and when *qu* is represented by *v* or *u* only; thus we have *veho*, 'I carry,' *vexi*; *traho*, 'I draw,' *traxi*; *vivo* for *viguo*, 'I live,' *vixi*; *fluo* for *fluguo*, 'I flow,' *fluxi*; *struo* for *struguo*, 'I build,' *struxi*; and the deponent *fruor*, 'I enjoy,' *fructus sum*.

(c) If *r* precedes the characteristic, the latter is omitted before -*si*: thus *mergo*, 'I dip,' makes *mersi*; *parco*, 'I save up,' *parsi*; *spargo*, 'I scatter,' *sparsi*. In the sense of 'I spare,' *parco* makes *peperci*.

(d) The perfect affix is sometimes represented by a mere lengthening of the root-vowel, which may be changed from *a* to *e*, and in this case an euphonic *n* may be omitted. Thus we have *ago*, 'I drive,' *ēgi*; *frango*, 'I break,' *frēgi*; *linquo*, 'I leave,' *liqui*; *vinco*,

'I conquer,' *vici; lego*, 'I read,' *lēgi*. But three compounds of *lego* take the form in *-si*; thus we have *diligo*, 'I love,' *dilexi*; *intelligo*, 'I understand,' *intellexi*; *negligo*, 'I neglect,' *neglexi*.

(c) *Pungo*, 'I pierce,' has *pupŭgi*, but its compounds, as *interpungo*, 'I distinguish with points,' take the form in *-si*, as *interpunxi*. *Tungo*, 'I touch,' makes *tetĭgi*, but its compounds omit the reduplication; thus we have *contingo*, *contĭgi*. *Pango*, 'I fix,' makes *panxi*, and in the compounds *-pĭgi:* but in the sense 'I bargain' (for which *paciscor* is generally used in the present) we have the perfect *pepĭgi*.

(2) *Supine and passive participle.* As a general rule *-t* is subjoined to the guttural, which is changed into *c;* thus we have *coctum* from *coquo*, *lectum* from *lego*, &c. But *mergo*, *parco*, *spargo* omit the guttural, as in the perfect, and make *mersum*, *parsum*, *sparsum:* and the euphonic *n* is omitted in *fractus*, *lictus*, *pactus*, *rictus*, from *frango*, &c. The deponents *loquor* and *sequor* vocalize the *u* in the participles *locutus*, *secutus*, and also in *secundus*, 'following,' for *sequendus*.

88   (c) Dental Verbs.

(1) *Perfect.* (a) The usual form is that in *-si*, before which the dental is always omitted. Thus, *claudo*, 'I shut,' makes *clausi*; *divido*, 'I divide,' *divisi*; and even *mitto*, 'I send,' *misi*. *Cedo*, 'I yield,' and *quatio*, 'I shake,' retain the dental under the form of *s* in their perfects *cessi*, *quassi* (in compounds *-cutio*, *-cussi*).

(b) If the characteristic is *ct*, the perfect follows the rule of the guttural verbs; thus *flecto*, 'I bend,' *necto*, 'I knit,' *pecto*, 'I comb,' make *flexi*, *nexi*, *pexi*.

(c) *Cado*, 'I fall,' *caedo*, 'I cut down,' 'fell,' take the reduplicated perfect, *cecĭdi* and *cecīdi*, the reduplication being as usual omitted in the compounds, as *incĭdo*, 'I fall upon,' *incĭdi*; *concīdo*, 'I cut to pieces,' *concīdi*.

(d) The same rule applies to some verbs which take an euphonic *n* before *d* in the present; as *pendo*, 'I weigh,' *pependi*; *tendo*, 'I stretch out,' *tetendi*; *tundo*, 'I beat,' *tŭtŭdi*. But *findo*, 'I split,' makes *fĭdi*; *scindo*, 'I cut,' *scĭdi*, without any reduplication even in the uncompounded verbs; and the same is the case with *accendo*,

'I inflame,' *mando*, 'I chew,' *offendo*, 'I stumble against,' *prehendo*, 'I seize,' *verto*, 'I turn,' which have for their perfects the simple forms *accendi, mandi, offendi, prehendi, verti*.

(e) *Ĕdo*, 'I eat,' *fŏdio*, 'I dig,' and *fundo*, 'I pour out,' have *ēdi, fōdi, fūdi*: and *cūdo*, 'I forge,' *sīdo*, 'I sit down,' *strīdo*, 'I hiss,' have *cūdi, sīdi, strīdi*.

(f) *Fido*, 'I trust,' has no active perfect, but uses the passive *fisus sum*.

(g) The only dental verbs which take the composite perfect form *-fui* are *frendo*, 'I gnash with the teeth,' *sterto*, 'I snore,' which make *frendui* and *stertui;* and *meto*, 'I reap,' *peto*, 'I seek,' *rudo*, 'I bray,' which have the elongated forms *messui, petivi, rudivi*.

Obs. The later writers have the forms *rugio* and *rugitus*, as well as *ruditus*, which seem to be suggested by the pronunciation of an original *rudio* pronounced *rudjo*. An approximation to this change is first seen in Persius, III. 9, who makes the first syllable of *rudere* long, as though he had written *rudjere*, whereas Virgil (*Georg*. III. 374 ; *Æn*. VII. 16) and Ovid (*A. A.* III. 290) make the first syllable short.

(2) *Supine and passive participle*. The *t* of the affix is generally changed into *s;* thus from *ludo* we have *lusum;* and if *c* precedes the characteristic, it becomes *x;* thus from *flecto* we have *flexum*. The following have a double *s* in the supine : *cedo, cessum; findo, fissum; fodio, fossum; meto, messum; mitto, missum; quatio, quassum; scindo, scissum; sido, sessum;* to which may be added the deponents *gradior*, 'I go,' *gressum*, and *patior*, 'I suffer,' *passum*. But *tendo* has *tentus* as well as *tensus*, *comedo* has *comestus* as well as *comēsus*, and *peto* and *rudo* have the elongated forms *petītus, ruditus*.

B. *Liquid Verbs*.

89 *L Verbs*.

(1) *Perfect*. (a) The usual form is *-ui*, as *alo*, 'I rear,' *alui*. Some merely add *-i*, as *vello*, 'I pull,' *velli;* but the compounds of this verb retain the *-si*, as *convello, convulsi*.

(b) Some few take the proper or reduplicated perfect, as *fallo*, 'I deceive,' *fefelli; pello*, 'I drive,' *pepŭli;* and *tollo*, 'I take up,' omits the reduplication in its perfect *tŭli* for *tetŭli*.

(2) *Supines.* The usual form is *-t* appended to the *l*; as *alo, altum; colo, cultum.* The former verb has also *alĭtum*, and this is the case with *molo*, 'I grind,' *molĭtum.* Verbs with a double *l* generally change *t* into *s*, as *fullo, falsum; pello, pulsum; percello, perculsus;* but *excello, excelsus. Tollo* has the peculiar form *latus* for *tlatus* or *toltus.*

90 *M* Verbs.

(1) *Perfect.* (a) Generally the perfect is formed in *-ui;* as *tremo,* 'I tremble,' *tremui.*

(b) But *ĕmo,* 'I take up,' thence 'I buy,' with its compounds *adĭmo,* 'I take away,' *coemo,* 'I buy up,' *interimo,* 'I take out of the way, i. e. destroy,' form the perfect by a lengthening of the root-vowel; thus *ēmi, adēmi, coēmi, interēmi:* and when the preposition in the compound coalesces with the first syllable of *emo,* the perfect is formed in *-si,* the liquid *m* being followed by the corresponding muto *p;* thus we have *como = coēmo,* 'I take and put together' (the hair), *compsi; dēmo = de-emo,* 'I take away from,' *dempsi; prōmo = pro-emo,* 'I take out' (from a store), *prompsi; sumo = sub-emo,* 'I take up' (for use), *sumpsi.*

(c) *Premo,* 'I press,' makes *pressi,* the liquid *m* being assimilated.

(2) *Supines and passive participles.* Perfects in *-ui* have a supine in *-ĭtum;* as *gemo, gemui, gemĭtum.* All others have the supine in *-ptum;* as *emo, emptum;* except *premo, pressi,* which makes *pressum.*

91 *N* Verbs.

There are only two *n* verbs: the reduplicated *gigno,* 'I beget,' 'bring into being,' 'cause to be,' which makes *genui, genĭtum;* and *cano,* 'I sing,' which makes *cĕcĭni, cantum.*

Obs. Three of the compounds of *cano,* namely, *concino, occino* (or *occano*) and *praecino,* take the composite perfect in *-ui,* as *occinui;* others, as *accino,* have no perfect.

92 *R* Verbs.

Curro, 'I run,' makes *cŭcurri, cursum; gero,* 'I carry,' and *uro,* 'I burn,' make *gessi, gestum* and *ussi, ustum. Sero,* 'I place in rows,' makes *serui, sertum;* and *verro,* 'I sweep,' makes *verri, versum.* The deponent *quĕror,* 'I complain,' makes *questus.*

93 S Verbs.

Depso, 'I knead,' makes *depsui, depstum; texo,* 'I weave,' *texui, textum,* and so all the others except *viso,* 'I visit,' which makes *visi.*

C. *Semi-consonantal Verbs.*

94 I Verbs.

Many of these have been already mentioned under the characteristic which precedes the *i.* They are such as *allicio,* 'I entice' (and other compounds of *lacio*), *allexi, allectum; capio,* 'I take,' *cēpi, captum; cupio,* 'I desire,' *cupīvi, cupītum; facio,* 'I make,' *fēci, factum; fŏdio,* 'I dig,' *fŏdi, fossum; fŭgio,* 'I flee,' *fūgi, fugĭtum; gradior,* 'I go,' *gressus; jacio,* 'I throw,' *jēci, jactum; morior,* 'I am dying,' *mortuus; pario,* 'I bring forth,' *pĕpĕri, partum; patior,* 'I suffer,' *passus; quatio,* 'I shake,' *quassus; rapio,* 'I snatch,' *rapui, raptum; sapio,* 'I have a taste,' hence 'I have sense, I am wise,' *sapui* (no supine); *specio,* 'I see' (obsol.), *spexi, spectum* (hence *aspicio, conspicio,* &c.).

95 U Verbs.

Many of these verbs belong to the guttural class, and have been discussed in their proper place. Others, as *juro, caveo,* have *a* or *e* after their characteristic *v,* and therefore belong to the vowel-verbs. *Ruo,* 'I overthrow,' makes *rui, ruitum* or *rūtum; minuo,* 'I break into small pieces,' makes *minui, minūtum.* Compounds of *nuo,* 'I nod,' as *abnuo,* 'I refuse,' i. e. 'express dissent by nodding,' make *abnui, abnuĭtum,* &c. *Arguo,* 'I put to the test,' makes *argui, argūtum.*

Obs. For the imperatives of *dico, duco, facio, fero* and *scio,* see below, p. 435.

Tables of the Regular Verbs.

Table I. Comparison of the Four Conjugations.

I. Finite Moods.

A. Primary Formations.

(1) Present and its Derivatives.

Indicative Active.

1. Present.

	Conj. 1. (love)	Conj. 2. (teach)	Conj. 3. (hear)	Conj. 4. (read)
Sing.	amo	doceo	audio	lego
	amas	doces	audis	legis
	amat	docet	audit	legit
Pl.	amamus	docemus	audimus	legimus
	amatis	docetis	auditis	legitis
	amant	docent	audiunt	legunt

2. Imperfect.

Sing.	amabam	docebam	audiebam	legebam
	amabas	docebas	audiebas	legebas
	amabat	docebat	audiebat	legebat
Pl.	amabamus	docebamus	audiebamus	legebamus
	amabatis	docebatis	audiebatis	legebatis
	amabant	docebant	audiebant	legebant

3. Future.

Sing.	amabo	docebo	audiam	legam
	amabis	docebis	audies	leges
	amabit	docebit	audiet	leget
Pl.	amabimus	docebimus	audiemus	legemus
	amabitis	docebitis	audietis	legetis
	amabunt	docebunt	audient	legent

Indicative Passive.

1. Present.

Sing.	amor	doceor	audior	legor
	amaris (-e)	doceris (-e)	audiris (-e)	legeris (-e)
	amatur	docetur	auditur	legitur
Pl.	amamur	docemur	audimur	legimur
	amamini	docemini	audimini	legimini
	amantur	docentur	audiuntur	leguntur

VERBS.

2. Imperfect.

	Conj. 1. (love)	Conj. 2. (teach)	Conj. 3. (hear)	Conj. 4. (read)
Sing.	amabar	docebar	audiebar	legebar
	amabaris (-e)	docebaris (-e)	audiebaris (-e)	legebaris (-e)
	amabatur	docebatur	audiebatur	legebatur
Pl.	amabamur	docebamur	audiebamur	legebamur
	amabamini	docebamini	audiebamini	legebamini
	amabantur	docebantur	audiebantur	legebantur

3. Future.

Sing.	amabor	docebor	audiar	legar
	amaberis (-e)	doceberis (-e)	audieris (-e)	legeris (-e)
	amabitur	docebitur	audietur	legetur
Pl.	amabimur	docebimur	audiemur	legemur
	amabimini	docebimini	audiemini	legemini
	amabuntur	docebuntur	audientur	legentur

(2) Perfect and its derivative.

Indicative Active.

1. Perfect.

Sing.	amavi	docui	audivi	legi
	amavisti	docuisti	audivisti	legisti
	amavit	docuit	audivit	legit
Pl.	amavimus	docuimus	audivimus	legimus
	amavistis	docuistis	audivistis	legistis
	amaverunt	docuerunt	audiverunt	legerunt
	(amarere)	(docuere)	(audivere)	

2. Pluperfect.

Sing.	amaveram	docueram	audiveram	legeram
	amaveras	docueras	audiveras	legeras
	amaverat	docuerat	audiverat	legerat
Pl.	amaveramus	docueramus	audiveramus	legeramus
	amaveratis	docueratis	audiveratis	legeratis
	amaverant	docuerant	audiverant	legerant

VERBS. 121

B. Secondary Formations.

(1) Present and its derivatives.

Subjunctive and Imperative Active.

1. *Subjunctive Present* (from the pres. indic.).

	Conj. 1. (love)	Conj. 2. (teach)	Conj. 3. (hear)	Conj. 4. (read)
Sing.	amem	doceam	audiam	legam
	ames	doceas	audias	legas
	amet	doceat	audiat	legat
Pl.	amemus	doceamus	audiamus	legamus
	ametis	doceatis	audiatis	legatis
	ament	doceant	audiant	legant

2. *Subjunct. Imperfect* (from the imp. indic.).

Sing.	amarem	docerem	audirem	legerem
	amares	doceres	audires	legeres
	amaret	doceret	audiret	legeret
Pl.	amaremus	doceremus	audiremus	legeremus
	amaretis	doceretis	audiretis	legeretis
	amarent	docerent	audirent	legerent

3. *Imperative* (from the pres. infin.).

Sing.	{ama	doce	audi	lege
	{amato	doceto	audito	legito
	amato	doceto	audito	legito
Pl.	{amate	docete	audite	legite
	{amatote	docetote	auditote	legitote
	amanto	docento	audiunto	legunto

Subjunctive and Imperative Passive.

1. *Subj. Present* (from the pres. indic.).

Sing.	amer	docear	audiar	legar
	ameris (-e)	docearis (-e)	audiaris (-e)	legaris (-o)
	ametur	doceatur	audiatur	legatur
Pl.	amemur	doceamur	audiamur	legamur
	amemini	doceamini	audiamini	legamini
	amentur	doceantur	audiantur	legantur

VERBS.

2. *Subj. Imperfect* (from the imp. indic.).

	Conj. 1. (love)	Conj. 2. (teach)	Conj. 3. (hear)	Conj. 4. (read)
Sing.	amarer	docerer	audirer	legerer
	amareris (-e)	docereris (-e)	audireris (-e)	legereris (-e)
	amaretur	doceretur	audiretur	legeretur
Pl.	amaremur	doceremur	audiremur	legeremur
	amaremini	doceremini	audiremini	legeremini
	amarentur	docerentur	audirentur	legerentur

3. *Imperative* (from the pres. infin.).

Sing.	amare	docere	audire	legere
	amator	docetor	auditor	legitor
	amator	docetor	auditor	legitor
Pl.	amamini	docemini	audimini	legimini
	amaminor	doceminor	audiminor	legiminor
	amantor	docentor	audiuntor	leguntor

(2) Perfect and its derivative.

Subjunctive Active.

1. *Perfect* (from the perf. indic.).

Sing.	amaverim	docuerim	audiverim	legerim
	amaveris	docueris	audiveris	legeris
	amaverit	docuerit	audiverit	legerit
Pl.	amaverimus	docuerimus	audiverimus	legerimus
	amaveritis	docueritis	audiveritis	legeritis
	amaverint	docuerint	audiverint	legerint

2. *Pluperfect* (from the plup. indic.).

Sing.	amavissem	docuissem	audivissem	legissem
	amavisses	docuisses	audivisses	legisses
	amavisset	docuisset	audivisset	legisset
Pl.	amavissemus	docuissemus	audivissemus	legissemus
	amavissetis	docuissetis	audivissetis	legissetis
	amavissent	docuissent	audivissent	legissent

II. Infinitive Mood and its adjuncts.

1. *Supine.*

amatum	doctum	auditum	lectum
amatu	doctu	auditu	lectu

2. Infinitive.

	Conj. 1. (love)	Conj. 2. (teach)	Conj. 3. (hear)	Conj. 4. (read)
Pres. Act.	amare	docere	audire	legere
Pres. Pass.	amari	doceri	audiri	legi
Perf. Act.	amavisse	docuisse	audivisse	legisse

3. Gerund.

Nom. Acc.	amandum	docendum	audiendum	legendum
Gen.	amandi	docendi	audiendi	legendi
Abl.	amando	docendo	audiendo	legendo

4. Participles.

Part. Pr. Act.	amans	docens	audiens	legens
Part. Perf. Pass.	amatus, -a, -um	doctus	auditus	lectus
Part. Fut. Act.	amaturus, -a, -um	docturus	auditurus	lecturus
Part. Fut. Pass.	amandus, -a, -um.	docendus	audiendus	legendus

TABLE II.
Formation of the Perfect.
First Conjugation.

1. *Perfect in -ui.*

crepo, crepui, rattle
cubo, cubui, lie down
domo, domui, tame
frico, fricui, rub
juvo, jūvi (for juv-ui), help
(so also lavo, lavi, wash)

mico, micui, move quickly
seco, secui, cut
sono, sonui, sound
tono, tonui, thunder
veto, vetui, forbid

2. *Perfect in -ui and -avi.*

neco, necui and necavi, kill
discrepo, discrepui and discrepavi, differ
increpo, increpui and increpavi, chide
plico, plicui and plicavi, fold

124 VERBS.

but *supplico* has only *supplicavi*, supplicate
multiplico only *multiplicavi*, multiply
duplico only *duplicavi*, double
dimico only *dimicavi*, fight.

3. *Reduplicated Perfect.*

do, dĕdi, give
circumdo, surround
renundo, roll
pessundo, overthrow
satisdo, satisfy

sto, stĕti, stand
circumsto, surround
antesto, stand before
intersto, stand between
supersto, stand above

Second Conjugation.

1. *Perfect in* -evi.

deleo, delevi, destroy
neo, nevi, spin

fleo, flevi, cry
vieo, vievi, bind with twigs

and the verbs from *oleo*, cause to grow; *pleo*, fill, and *sueo*, am
accustomed.

2. *Perfect in* -i.

caveo, cavi, take care
faveo, favi, favour
ferveo, fervi and ferbui, glow
foveo, fovi, cherish

moveo, movi, move
niveo, nivi, wink with eyes
paveo, pavi, quake with fear
voveo, vovi, vow

but *conniveo* has *connixi*

prandeo, prandi, dine
sedeo, sedi, sit
strideo, stridi, hiss, creak

video, vidi, see
langueo, langui, languish
liqueo, liqui and licui, am clear

3. *Perfect in* -si.

jubeo, jussi, order
sorbeo, sorpsi, sup up, suck in

mulceo, mulsi, soothe
algeo, alsi, am cold
indulgeo, indulsi, indulge
fulgeo, fulsi, shine
mulgeo, mulsi, milk
turgeo, tursi, am swollen
urgeo, ursi, press
torqueo, torsi, twist

luceo, luxi, shine
augeo, auxi, increase
frigeo, frixi, am cold
lugeo, luxi, bemoan

ardeo, arsi, am burning
suadeo, suasi, advise

maneo, mansi, remain
haereo, haesi, adhere

4. Reduplicated Perfect.

mordeo, momordi, bite
pendeo, pependi, am hanging
spondeo, spopondi, promise
tondeo, totondi, cut with shears

5. Neuter Passive.

audeo, ausus sum, dare
gaudeo, gavisus sum, rejoice, am glad
soleo, solitus sum, am accustomed, am wont

Verbs of the Second Conjugation without any Perfect.

areo, desire
calveo, am bald
flaveo, am yellow
foeteo, stink
hebeo, am dull
humeo, am moist
liveo, am livid

immineo, hang over
maereo, am sorrowful
polleo, am strong
renideo, shine
scateo, bubble forth like water
squaleo, am rough with hair, &c.
vegeo, excite

Third Conjugation.

1. Perfect in -i.

venio, veni, come
reperio, repperi, find.
comperio, comperi, discover

2. Perfect in -ui.

salio, salui (salii) spring up, jump
aperio, aperui, open
operio, operui, cover

3. Perfect in -si.

amicio, amixi, clothe
farcio, farsi, stuff
fulcio, fulsi, support
haurio, hausi, draw out
raucio, rausi, am hoarse

sancio, sanxi, ordain
sarcio, sarsi, mend, patch
sentio, sensi, feel
sepio, sepsi, hedge in
vincio, vinxi, bind

4. Perfect wanting.

ferio, strike
ferocio, am fierce

Fourth Conjugation.

Perfect in -i.

(a) Without alteration of the root.

A. *acuo, acui*, sharpen
    arguo, argui, test
    congruo, congrui, agree
    imbuo, imbui, imbue
    induo, indui, put on
    luo, lui, pay
    metuo, metui, fear
    minuo, minui, lessen
    pluo, plui, rain

    ruo, rui, overthrow
    spuo, spui, spit out
    statuo, statui, establish
    sternuo, sternui, sneeze
    suo, sui, sew or stitch
    tribuo, tribui, assign
    solvo, solvi, loosen, pay
    volvo, volvi, roll

and the verbs formed from *nuo*, I nod, *abnuo, annuo, innuo, renuo*.

B. *mando, mandi*, chew
    pando, pandi, open

    prehendo, prehendi, seize
    scando, scandi, climb

and the verbs formed from *cando* and *fendo, accendo, succendo, incendo; defendo* and *offendo*.

C. *bĭbo, bĭbi*, drink
    cūdo, cūdi, hammer
    dĕgo, dēgi, live
    lambo, lambi, lick
    psallo, psalli, play on a stringed instrument

    scābo, scābi, scratch
    sĭdo, sĭdi, settle myself
    vello, velli (vulsi), pluck
    verro, verri, sweep
    verto, verti, turn myself
    viso, visi, visit

(b) With an alteration of the root.

A. *ĕdo, ēdi*, eat
    ĕmo, ēmi, buy (90, (1), (b))
    lĕgo, lēgi, read
    fŏdio, fōdi, dig
    fŭgio, fūgi, flee

    cǎpio, cēpi, take
    făcio, fēci, do, make
    jăcio, jēci, throw
    ăgo, ēgi, do, act

B. *findo, fĭdi*, cleave
    frango, frēgi, break
    fundo, fūdi, pour out
    linquo, liqui, leave
    percello, perculi, beat down

    rumpo, rūpi, burst
    scindo, scĭdi, split
    vinco, vīci, conquer
    sisto, stĭti, stop

VERBS. 127

C.   With reduplication.

cado, cecidi, fall   *parco, peperci,* spare
caedo, cecidi, fell   *pario, peperi,* bring forth
cano, cecini, sing   *pello, pepŭli,* drive away
credo, credidi, believe   *pendo, pependi,* weigh
curro, cucurri, run   *pungo, pupugi,* prick
disco, didici, learn   *posco, poposci,* demand
fallo, fefelli, deceive   *tango, tetigi,* touch
pango, pepigi, make a con-   *tendo, tetendi,* stretch
    tract   *tundo, tutudi,* thump

and the derivatives of *-do,* as *condo, abdo, indo,* &c., *condidi, abdidi, indidi,* &c.

2. Perfect in *-si.*

(a) Without any essential alteration of the root.

A. *glubo, glupsi,* strip   *carpo, carpsi,* pluck
nubo, nupsi, put on a veil (as   *repo, repsi,* creep
    a bride)   *scalpo, scalpsi,* scrape
scribo, scripsi, write   *sculpo, sculpsi,* carve in stone
ango, anxi, vex
cingo, cinxi, gird   *frigo, frixi,* roast
figo, fixi, fix   *jungo, junxi,* join
fingo, finxi, form   *lingo, linxi,* lick

and the derivatives of *fligo, flixi, affligo, confligo,* &c.

mingo, minxi, make water   *plango, planxi,* beat the breast
mungo, munxi, wipe the nose   *rego, rexi,* direct
ningo, ninxi, snow   *stringo, strinxi,* strip
pingo, pinxi, paint

and the derivatives of *stinguo,* i. e. *exstinguo, restinguo.*

sugo, suxi, suck   *dico, dixi,* say
tego, texi, cover   *duco, duxi,* lead
tingo, tinxi, dye   *coquo, coxi,* cook
ungo, unxi, anoint
                           flecto, flexi, turn
traho, traxi, draw   *necto, nexi,* and *nexui,* link to-
veho, vexi, carry   gether
                           pecto, pexi, comb

VERBS.

como, compsi, adorn
demo, dempsi, take away
promo, prompsi, put forth
sumo, sumpsi, take up
contemno, formed from temno, tempsi.

B. claudo, clausi, shut
divido, divisi, divide
laedo, laesi, hurt
ludo, lusi, play
plaudo, plausi, clap the hands
mitto, misi, send
rado, rasi, scrape
rodo, rosi, gnaw
trudo, trusi, thrust

and evado, evasi, invado, pervado, formed from rado, go.

(b) With an alteration of the root.

cedo, cessi, go, yield
gero, gessi, carry
uro, ussi, burn

and concutio, percutio, incutio, &c., concussi, percussi, &c.,
formed from quatio, shake;

premo, pressi, press.

mergo, mersi, sink
spargo, sparsi, scatter
tergo, tersi, wipe;

those formed from the obsolete specio, behold:

conspicio, conspexi, look at
adspicio, adspexi, regard

those formed from lacio:

al'icio, allexi, entice
pellicio, pellexi, seduce;

besides

diligo, dilexi, love
intelligo, intellexi, understand.

3. Perfect in -ui.

(a) Without alteration of the root.

alo, alui, nourish
colo, colui, pay attention to
concino (-ui), sing in concert
consulo, consului, consult, deliberate
molo, molui, grind
occino (-ui), sing
occulo, occului, conceal
volo, volui, wish
nolo, nolui, am unwilling
malo, malui, prefer
praecino (-ui), sing before

VERBS. 120

those from *cello*, raise up:

excello, excellui, ⎫
antecello, ⎬ excel
praecello, ⎭

rapio, rapui, snatch
sapio, sapui, have a savour, am wise

fremo, fremui, roar
gemo, gemui, groan
tremo, tremui, tremble
vomo, vomui, vomit

gigno, genui, beget

elicio, elicui, draw out
compesco, compescui, restrain
dispesco, dispescui, separate

depso, depsui, knead
pinso, pinsui, pound
sterto, stertui (sterti), snore

and those formed from *sero*, put in rows:

consero, conserui, join together *dissero, disserui,* discourse.

(b) With an alteration of the root (-*si* and -*vi*).

meto, messui, mow
pono, posui, put, lay down
(see 97, (a), p. 134)
cerno, crevi, distinguish
lino, levi, smear
sino, sivi, leave, suffer
sperno, sprevi, despise
sterno, stravi, strew
sero, sevi, sow

tero, trivi, rub

cresco, crevi, grow
nosco, novi, know
pasco, pavi, feed
quiesco, quievi, rest
suesco, suevi, am accustomed

and the other inchoatives (97, (c)).

4. Perfect in -*xi*.

fluo, fluxi, flow
vivo, vixi, live.

struo, struxi, build up

5. Perfect in -*ivi* (see 97, (a), p. 134).

peto, petivi, make for
quaero, quaesivi, seek, inquire
cupio, cupivi, desire

capesso, capessivi, undertake
facesso, facessivi, cause
lacesso, lacessivi, provoke
incesso, incessivi, attack

arcesso, arcessivi, send for

6. One Neuter-passive.

fido, fisus sum, trust.

D. L. G.   9

130 VERBS.

7. Verbs without any perfect (see 97, (c), (2), (a), p. 136).

furo, rage
quatio, shake
stinguo, extinguish
aegresco, grow sick or infirm
ditesco, grow rich
dulcesco, grow sweet
grandesco, grow large
gravesco, } grow heavy
ingravesco,

incuresco, become crooked
integrasco, become renovated
juvenesco, grow young
mitesco, grow mild
mollesco, grow soft
plumesco, get feathers
puerasco, become a child (again)
sterilesco, become barren
teneresco, become tender

fero, bear, perfect *tuli*
tollo, raise up, perfect *sustuli*.

TABLE III.
Formation of the Supines.
First Conjugation.

frico — *fricatum* and *frictum*
seco — *sectum*
juvo — *jutum* and *juvatum* (both rare)
adjuvo — *adjutum* and *adjuvatum* (the latter rare)
lavo — *lavatum*, *lautum* and *lotum*
applico — *applicātum* and *applicĭtum*

explico — *explicātum* and *explicĭtum*
implico — *implicātum* and *implicĭtum*
poto — *potum* and *potatum*
do — *dătum*
sto — *stătum*
praesto — *praestĭtum* and *praestātum* (rare)

Several compounds with *sto* have no Supine.

Second Conjugation.

doceo — *doctum*
teneo — *tentum*
misceo — *mixtum* and *mistum*
torreo — *tostum*
censeo — *censum*
recenseo — *recensum* and *recensĭtum*

jubeo — *jussum*
sedeo — *sessum*
indulgeo — *indultum*
torqueo — *tortum*
augeo — *auctum*
cieo — *citum*

The last is the same word as *cio*, sup. *citum*, which occurs only in compounds and when the idea of 'calling' is included;

e.g. *excitus* is 'called forth,' but *excĭtus*, 'aroused:' we have only *accitus*, 'summoned forth,' from *accio*.

Verbs without any Supine, besides those which have no Perfect.

algeo, am chilled   *arceo*, keep off

but *coerceo* and *exerceo* have Supine in -*Itum*.

calleo, am inured	*pateo*, stand open
egeo, need	*paveo*, quake for fear
emineo, project forward	*rigeo*, am stiff
ferveo, am hot	*rubeo*, blush
floreo, flourish	*sileo*, am silent
frigeo, am cold	*sorbeo*, sup up
frondeo, grow green	*sordeo*, am dirty
fulgeo, shine	*splendeo*, glitter
horreo, shudder	*studeo*, am eager
luteo, lie hid	*stupeo*, am amazed
langueo, languish	*timeo*, fear
luceo, am bright	*torpeo*, am torpid
lugeo, lament	*tumeo*, swell
madeo, am wet	*turgeo*, grow big
niteo, shine	*vigeo*, am strong
conniveo, wink at	*vireo*, am green
oleo, smell of something	*urgeo*, press on
palleo, am pale	

Obs. All these verbs except *sorbeo* are neuter.

Third Conjugation.

eo — Itum	*sancio — sanctum* and *sancitum*
queo — quitum	*sarcio — sartum*
sepelio — sepultum	*sentio — sensum*
farcio — fartum	*sepio — septum*
fulcio — fultum	*venio — ventum*
haurio — haustum	*vincio — vinctum*
raucio — rausum	*amicio — amictum*
salio — saltum	*aperio — apertum*

Verbs without any Supine.

ferio and *ferocio*.

Fourth Conjugation.

frendo — fressum
pando — passum (rarely pansum)
vello — vulsum
bibo — bibitum

fugio — fugitum
parco — parsum
credo — creditum
abdo — abditum

also condo, edo, indo, &c.

sisto — stitum
fingo — fictum
mingo — mictum
pingo — pictum
stringo — strictum
figo — fixum
flecto — flexum
necto — nexum
pecto — pexum
gero — gestum
uro — ustum
colo — cultum
consulo — consultum

rupio — raptum
sero — sertum
alo — altum and alitum
depso — depstum and depsitum
pinso — pinsitum and pistum
pono — positum
lino — litum
sino — situm
sero — satum
pasco — pastum
cognosco — cognitum
fero — latum
tollo — sublatum

Verbs without any Supine.

congruo	mando	psallo	pluo
sido	dego	sternuo	lambo
viso	metuo	scabo	posco
disco	ango	compesco	tremo
dispesco	sapio	volo	antecello
nolo	praecello	malo	excello
incesso	fio		

Table IV.

(a) Verbs of the Third Conjugation, which have *i* before the ending.

facio, make
jacio, throw
fodio, dig
fugio, flee
capio, take

cupio, desire
sapio, am wise
pario, bring forth
quatio, shake,

whence *percutio, discutio, concutio,* &c.

Those formed from *licio,* pull about:

elicio, draw out   allicio, draw on   pellicio, allure

VERBS. 133

Those formed from *spacio*, see:
adspicio, look at   *conspicio*, gaze on

Three deponents:
morior, die   *patior*, suffer   *gradior*, approach,
whence *congredior, aggredior,* &c.

(b) Verbs of the First Conjugation which have *e* or *i* before the ending:

beo, bless   *ablaqueo*, lay bare the roots
calceo, put on shoes   *illaqueo*, ensnare
creo, create   *malleo*, hammer
cuneo, wedge in   *meo*, go to and fro
collineo, aim in a straight line   *nauseo*, feel sick
delineo, draw a line or outline   *enucleo*, take out the kernel
lanceo, fling a lance   *screo*, hawk in spitting

amplio, increase   *hio*, gape
ascio, hew   *medio*, divide in the middle
brevio, shorten   *nuntio*, announce
centurio, divide into centuries   *pio*, atone
decurio, divide into tens   *satio*, satiate
crucio, torture   *saucio*, wound
ebrio, intoxicate   *socio*, confederate
sobrio, make sober   *spolio*, spoil
ferior, enjoy a holiday   *strio*, groove or make chan-
furio, rage   nels
glacio, freeze   *tertio*, repeat thrice

§ 5. *Irregular Verbs.*

96 Irregularities, in the inflexion of verbs through their moods and tenses, arise either from the use of some strengthening affix in the present tense, which is neglected in the perfect, or from the practice of making up the tenses by forms derived from different, but synonymous roots, or from some syncope or abbreviation in the inflexions themselves.

A. *Additions to the Present Tense.*

97 (a) *N added.* Those in which an euphonic *n* (or *m* before a labial) is inserted before the characteristic of the verb,

often retain this letter in the perfect; as in *jungo*, root *jug-*, *junxi*; *fungor*, root *fug-*, *functus sum*. Others omit it, as *rumpo*, *rupi*. These verbs have been discussed under their proper characteristics. When the inserted *n* is added to the root, it is always omitted in the perfect and supine; thus we have *cerno*, 'I separate,' *crēvi*, *certum*; *sperno*, 'I despise,' *sprēvi*, *sprētum*; *sterno*, 'I strew,' *strāvi*, *strātum*; in which verbs there is a change in the place of the vowel. Similarly, we have *contem-no*, 'I despise,' *contemp-si*, *contemp-tum*; *li-no*, 'I besmear,' *li-vi*, *li-tum*; *sino*, 'I let, suffer, or cause to be,' *sivi*, *situm*. The last verb is used, without the inserted *n*, as the affix to a class of compound verbs signifying 'to cause or allow an action.' These are known from other verbs in *-so* by their meaning and by the perfect *-sivi*. They are *arcesso* or *accerso* for *accedere sino*, 'I send for,' i.e. 'cause to approach,' *arcessivi*, *arcessitum*; *cupesso* for *cupere sino*, 'I let myself take,' i.e. 'I undertake,' *capessivi*, *capessitum*; *lacesso* for *lacere sino*, 'I let myself pull about,' 'I provoke or irritate,' *lacessivi*, *lacessitum*; *pōno* for *po-sino*, 'I let down,' 'I place,' *posui* for *po-sivi* (Plaut. Trin. 1. 2. 108), *positum* and *postum*; *quaero* (from *quaeso*, which occurs in the sense of 'prithee') for *quere* (see *in-quam*) *sino*, 'I cause to speak,' i.e. 'I ask,' *quaesivi*, *quaesitum*.

(b) *R added*. The only verb of this class is *se-ro*, 'I sow,' *sēvi*, *sātum*.

(c) *Sc added*. This affix is inchoative, i.e. it expresses the beginning of an action, and therefore is necessarily omitted in the perfect, which declares the completion or perfection of an action. If the termination follows *a, e, i*, the perfect is formed according to the rule of the vowel-verbs: thus *pasco*, 'I feed,' makes *pā-vi* (though its compounds *compesco*, 'I feed together,' 'keep in the same field,' 'restrain,' *dispesco*, 'I separate,' make *compescui*, *dispescui*); *cre-sco*, 'I grow,' makes *crē-vi*; *sue-sco*, 'I am accustomed,' *suē-vi*; *contice-sco*, 'I become silent,' *contic-ui*; *exurde-sco*, 'I grow hot,' *exar-si*; *sci-sco*, 'I inquire,' *sci-vi*, like corresponding verbs in *a, e, i*. But *di-sco* for *dic-sco*, 'I learn,' makes *didici*. The only verb which has *o* before *sc* is *no-sco*, 'I get knowledge,' and its derivatives *agno-sco*, 'I acknowledge,' *cognosco*, 'I become acquainted,' *dignosco*, 'I distinguish,' *ignosco*, 'I pardon,' i.e. 'take no knowledge of;' and these make *nōvi*, 'I am acquainted with' (always used as a present), *agnōvi, cognōvi*, &c., in which *ov* may be syncopated, as in *nōrunt, nōrim, nōsse*, &c.; compare *commōssem* for *commovissem*, &c. (79, (i)). In the supine we have *nōtum, dignōtum, ignōtum*, but *agnĭtum, cognĭtum*. If the original verb has a consonant for its characteristic, *i* is inserted before *sc*; thus from *vivo* we have *revivisco*, 'I revive,' *revixi*; and from *facio* we have *profici-scor*, 'I cause myself to set forth,' 'I set out,' *profectus sum*. The peculiar verb *ob-liv-i-scor* (from *liv-o*, 'to blacken,' whence *livor, liveo, livesco*), 'I make for myself a black mark,' 'I obliterate,' 'I forget,' has the perfect *oblītus sum*.

The following lists contain most of the inchoative verbs in common use:

(1) Verbal inchoatives which adopt the perfect of the original verb.

Acesco (aceo) acui, grow sour; *coacesco, peracesco*.
Albesco and *exalbesco (albeo) albui*, become white.
Aresco (areo) arui, grow dry.
Calesco (caleo) calui, become warm.
Canesco (caneo) canui, become grey.
Conticesco (taceo) conticui, become silent, hold one's peace.
Contremisco (tremo) contremui, tremble.
Defervesco (ferveo) deferbui, grow cool gradually.
Delitesco (lateo) delitui, lurk.
Effervesco (ferveo) efferbui, grow hot.
Excandesco (candeo) excandui, grow of a white heat; figuratively, am enraged.
Extimesco, pertimesco (timeo) extimui, am terrified.
Fatisco (fateor) perf. pass. part. *fessus*, give in, begin to confess, yield, and, physically, open or gape.
Floresco, de-, ef- (floreo) florui, burst into flower.
Haeresco, ad-, in- (haereo), ad-, in-, haesi, stick to.
Horresco, exhorresco, perhorresco (horreo) horrui, am struck with horror.
Ingemisco (gemo) ingemui, groan.
Intumesco (tumeo) intumui, swell up.
Irraucesco (raucio) irrausi, become hoarse.
Lactesco (lacteo, no perfect), turn to milk, begin to give suck.
Languesco, elanguesco, relanguesco (langueo) elangui, become feeble.
Liquesco (liqueo) licui, melt away.

Madesco (madeo) madui, become wet.
Marcesco (marceo) comp. *commarcesco; emarcesco*, perfect, *emarcui*, fade.
Occallesco (calleo) occallui, become hard on the surface.
Pallesco, expallesco (palleo) pallui, turn pale.
Putresco (putreo) putrui, moulder.
Resipisco (sapio) resipui and *resipiri*, grow wise again.
Rubesco, erubesco (rubeo), grow red, blush.
Senesco, consenesco (seneo) consenui, grow old.
   (The part. *senectus*, grown old, is rare).
Stupesco (obstupesco, stupeo) obstupui, am struck dumb.
Tabesco (tabeo) tabui, pine, waste away.
Tepesco (tepeo) tepui, grow lukewarm.
Viresco, comp. *conviresco, eviresco, reviresco (vireo), virui*, grow green.

(2) Inchoatives apparently derived from Nouns.

(a) Having no perfect.

Aegresco (aeger), grow sick or infirm.
Ditesco (dives), grow rich.
Dulcesco (dulcis), grow sweet.
Grandesco (grandis), grow large.
Gravesco and *ingravesco (gravis)*, grow heavy.
Incurvesco (curvus), become crooked.
Integrasco (integer), become renovated.
Juvenesco (juvenis), grow young.
Mitesco (mitis), grow mild.
Mollesco (mollis), grow soft.
Pinguesco (pinguis), grow fat.
Plumesco (pluma), get feathers.
Puerasco, repuerasco (puer), become a child (again).
Sterilesco (sterilis), become barren.
Teneresco, tenerasco (tener), become tender.

(β) Having a perfect.

Crebresco, in-, per- *(creber) crebrui*, grow frequent.
Duresco, ob-, in- *(durus) durui*, grow hard.
Evanesco (vanus) evanui, disappear.
Innotesco (notus) innotui, become known.
Macresco (macer) macrui (rare), grow lean.

Maturesco (maturus) maturui, grow ripe.
Nigresco (niger) nigrui, grow black.
Obmutesco (mutus) obmutui, become dumb.
Obsurdesco (surdus) obsurdui, become deaf.
Recrudesco (crudus) recrudui, to open again (of a wound that had been closed).
Vilesco, evilesco (vilis) evilui, become cheap or worthless.

Obs. Mansuesco, mansuevi, 'grow tame,' 'get used to the hand,' is a compound of *manus* and *suesco* (p. 129).

(3) Verbal Inchoatives which have the supine as well as perfect of the root.

{ *Abolesco, abolevi, abolitum*, censo, am annihilated.
{ *Exolesco, exolevi, exolĕtum*, grow useless by age.
{ *Adolesco, adolevi, adultum*, grow up.
Coalesco (alere) coalui, coalitum, grow together.
Concupisco (cupere) concupivi, concupitum, desire.
Convalesco (valere) convalui, convalitum, recover health.
Exardesco (ardere) exarsi, exarsum, am inflamed.
Indolesco (dolere) indolui, -itum, feel pain.
Inveterasco (inveterare) inveterari, -atum, grow old.
Obdormisco (dormire) -iri, -itum, fall asleep, *edormisco*, sleep out.
Revivisco (vivere) revixi, revictum, recover life.
Scisco (scire) scivi, scitum, resolve, decree.
(Hence *plebiscitum, populiscitum*.)

Obs. The first three are from *oleo*, the neuter of *alo*, root *al-* or *ol-*, which must be distinguished from *oleo*, 'smell,' root *ol-=od-*, cf. *od-or*.

B. *Abbreviated Forms.*

98. The following verbs are liable to syncope or abbreviation in many of the inflexions: *possum* for *potis sum*, 'I am able,' which prefixes an abridged form of the adjective to a complete inflexion of the verb *sum*, except that in the perfect and pluperfect the *f* of *fui* is omitted, as in the verbs which take this form of the perfect; *volo*, 'I wish,' and its compounds—*nolo* for *non volo*, 'I do not wish;' *malo* for *magis volo*, 'I prefer;'—*ědo*, 'I eat;' *fěro*, 'I bear or suffer.' The latter is also irregular in having no perfect of its own, for *tollo* gives it the perfect and supine, *tŭli* for *tetŭli* and *lātum* for *t'latum* or *toltum*, and takes to itself the compound forms *sus-tŭli* and *sub-lātum*.

VERBS.

A.
I.

Singular.

possum	pŏtĕs	pŏtest
vŏlo	vis	vult
nōlo	nonvis	nonvult
mālo	māvis	māvult
ĕdo	ĕdis v. es	ĕdit v. est
fero	fers	fert

Plural.

possŭmus	potestis	possunt
vŏlŭmus	vultis	vŏlunt
nōlŭmus	nonvultis	nōlunt
mālŭmus	mavultis	mālunt
ĕdĭmus	ĕdĭtis v. estis	ĕdunt
ferĭmus	fertis	fĕrunt

II.

	Singular.			Plural.	
poteram	poteras	poterat	poterāmus	poterātis	poterant
vŏlē-bam					
nōlē-bam					
mālē-bam	-bas	-bat	-bāmus	-bātis	-bant
ĕdē-bam					
fĕrē-bam					

III.

potu-i					
vŏlu-i					
nōlu-i	-isti	-it	-imus	-istis,	-ērunt v. -ēre
mālu-i					
ĕd-i					
tŭl-i					

IV.

potu-eram					
volu-eram					
nolu-eram	-eras	-erat	-erāmus	-erātis	-erant
malu-eram					
ed-eram					
tul-eram					

VERBS.

V.

	Singular.			*Plural.*	
potero	poteris	poterit	potĕrĭmus	potĕrĭtis	potĕrunt
vol-am					
nol-am					
mal-am	-es	-et	-ēmus	-ētis	-ent.
ed-am					
fer-am					

B.

2. nōlī, nōlīto   2. nōlīte, nōlītōte
2. ede, edito *v.* es, esto   2. ĕdĭte, ĕdĭtōte *v.* esta, estote
3. edito *v.* esto   3. ĕdunto
2. fer, ferto, 3. ferto   2. ferte, fertōto, 3. ferunto.

Obs. Possum, volo, and malo have no imperative.

C.

I.

poss-im					
vel-im					
nol-im	-is	-it	-īmus	-ītis	-int.
mal-im					
ed-am	-as	-at	-āmus	-ātis	-ant.
fer-am					

II.

poss-em					
vell-em					
noll-em					
mall-em	-es	-et	-ēmus	-ētis	-ent.
eder-em *v.*					
ess-em					
ferr-em					

III.

potuer-o, -im					
voluer-o, -im					
noluer-o, -im	-is	-it	-īmus	-ītis	-int.
maluer-o, -im					
eder-o, -im					
tuler-o, -im					

IV.

Singular.			Plural.	
potu-issem				
volu-issem				
nolu-issem } -isses	-isset	-issēmus	-issētis	-issent.
malu-issem				
ed-issem				
tul-issem				

D.
I.
posse, velle, nolle, malle, edere v. esse, ferre.

III.
potuisse, voluisse, noluisse, maluisse, edisse, tulisse.

V.
ēsūrum esse, lātūrum esse.

The supines of *edo* and *fero* are *ēsum* and *lātum*.

The abbreviated forms of *fero* are found in the passive also; thus we have, A. I. *feror, ferris, fertur*, and B. *ferre, fertor;* C. II. *ferrer, ferrēris*. In the passive of *edo*, we have *estur* for *editur*. In *fero* the shortened forms alone are used, but in *edo* both forms are common. In *volo* we have the still further abbreviations, *sīs* for *si vis, sultis* for *si vultis*.

§ 9. *Defective Verbs.*

99. All impersonal verbs are defective in the first and second persons, though they are regularly inflected through the moods and tenses; thus we have

oportet me, it behoves me, or I ought.
miserebat te, it pitied you, or you pitied.
licuit mihi, it was allowed to me, or I could.
pigeret eum, it would vex him, or he would be vexed.

The following lists contain the most common impersonal verbs:

1. Impersonals never used personally.

oportet, it is proper.   *licet*, it is lawful.
libet, it is pleasing.   *piget*, it is wearisome.

paenitet, it repents.
pudet, it shames.
miseret, it pities.
taedet, it disgusts.

rēfert (i.e. *rei fert*), it is for the interest.
diluculat, it dawns.

2. Impersonals also used personally in the 3rd sing. or pl.

tonat, it thunders.
pluit, it rains.
ningit, it snows.
fulgurat, it lightens.
grandinat, it hails.

fulminat, it thunders.
rorat, it bedews.
lapidat, it rains stones.
vesperascit, it grows late.
lucescit, or *luciscit*, it is light.

Obs. In a secondary or figurative sense *tono* and *lapido* are used as personal verbs in the 1st and 2nd persons. Otherwise when used personally the subject of these words is some word implying the heavenly phenomena, as *Jupiter* (the sky) *pluit; astra rorant; dies luciscit, vesperascit.*

3. Personal verbs used impersonally in a particular signification.

(a) in the active.

stat, it is determined.
constat, it is known.
praestat, it is better.
restat, it remains.
delectat, it pleases.
juvat, it is agreeable.
vacat, there is leisure.
placet, it is agreed.
attinet, pertinet, it concerns.
appāret, it is plain.
decet, it is becoming.
dedecet, it is unbecoming.
liquet, it is clear.
patet, it is manifest.
latet, it is hidden.

solet, it is wont.
accidit, it happens.
accedit, it is added.
excidit, it falls out.
conducit, confert, it is advantageous.
contingit, it succeeds.
sufficit, it suffices.
interest, it concerns.
crebrescit, it is spread abroad.
evenit, it happens.
expedit, it is useful.
fit, it comes to pass.
convenit, it suits.

(b) in the passive.

ridetur, it seems.
dicitur, it is said.
itur, one goes.
venitur, one comes.
scitur, one knows.
statur, one stands.

favetur, people are well disposed.
estur, people eat.
bibitur, people drink.
creditur, the world believes.
&c.

142   VERBS.

100 All neuter and deponent verbs are defective in voice, except in the usage just mentioned, i.e. when the former are defective in person: thus *curro*, 'I run,' is not inflected in the passive, except as an impersonal, when we also have the gerund; as

curritur a me, it is run by me, i.e. I run.
currendum est vobis, ye must run.

101 These verbs, *fio*, 'I become,' *vapulo*, 'I cry out for pain,' 'I am beaten,' *veneo*, 'I go for sale,' 'I am sold,' are strictly passive in their signification and construction, and may be called neuter-passives. *Fio*, which is used as the passive of *facio*, 'I make,' is thus inflected:

A. I.
fīo, fīs, fit
fīmus, fītis, fīunt.

II.
fīēbam, &c.

III.
factus sum, &c.

IV.
factus eram, &c.

V.
fīam, fīes, fiet, &c.

C. I.
fīam, fīas, &c.

II.
fīĕrĕm, &c.

III.
factus sim, fuero, fuerim, &c.

IV.
factus essem, &c.

B.
2. fi, fīto, 3. fīto.   2. fīte, fītōte, 3. fiunto.

D.
I. fĭĕri.   III. factum (-am, -um) esse.   V. factum iri.

Veneo, which is a compound of the supino *venum* and the verb *eo*, is used as the passive of *ven-do* or *venum do*. We have seen that the passive infinitive of *eo* may be used with the supine of any verb to form the future infinitive passive; as *amatum iri*, 'to be about to be loved,' from *itur* [*a me*, &c.] *amatum*, 'there is a going [by me, &c.] to love' = 'I am going to love' (70).

102 A deponent verb is inflected like a passive, but has an active supine and participle; and its participle of the passive form is merely past in signification; thus *loquor*, 'I am speaking,' *locū-*

tus sum, 'I have spoken,' *loquens,* 'speaking,' *locūtūrus,* 'about to speak,' *locūtus,* 'having spoken,' *loqui* and *locūtum,* 'to speak,' *locūtum esse,* 'to have spoken,' *locūtūrum esse,* 'to be about to speak.' A deponent verb may be either *transitive,* as *veneror deum,* 'I worship God;' or *intransitive,* as *morior,* 'I am dying.'

(1) The following paradigm will suffice to show the contrast between the form and signification of a deponent verb.

Loquor, 'I speak.'

Indicative.	Subjunctive.
A.	C.

I. Present.

loquor, I am speaking	*loquar,* I may speak
loquĕris (-e), thou art speaking	*loquaris (-e),* thou mayest speak
loquĭtur, he is speaking	*loquatur,* he may speak
loquĭmur, we are speaking	*loquamur,* we may speak
loquĭmini, ye are speaking	*loquamini,* ye may speak
loquuntur, they are speaking	*loquantur,* they may speak.

II. Imperfect.

loquēbar, I was speaking	*loquĕrer,* I might speak
loquēbāris (-e), thou wast speaking	*loquĕrēris (-e),* thou mightest speak
loquēbātur, he was speaking	*loquĕrētur,* he might speak
loquēbāmur, we were speaking	*loquĕrēmur,* we might speak
loquēbāmini, ye were speaking	*loquĕrēmini,* ye might speak
loquēbantur, they were speaking	*loquĕrentur,* they might speak.

III. Perfect.

locutus (-a, -um) sum, I have spoken	*locutus (-a, -um) sim,* I may have spoken
locutus (-a, -um) es, thou hast spoken	*locutus (-a, -um) sis,* thou mayst have spoken
locutus (-a, -um), he (she, it) has spoken	*locutus (-a, -um) sit,* he (she, it) may have spoken
locuti (-ae, -a) sumus, we have spoken	*locuti (-ae, -a) simus,* we may have spoken
locuti (-ae, -a) estis, ye have spoken	*locuti (-ae, -a) sitis,* ye may have spoken
locuti (-ae, -a) sunt, they have spoken	*locuti (-ae, -a) sint,* they may have spoken.

Indicative. *Subjunctive.*

IV. Pluperfect.

Indicative	Subjunctive
locutus (-a, -um) eram, I had spoken	locutus (-a, -um) essem, I might have spoken
locutus (-a, -um) eras, thou hadst spoken	locutus (-a, -um) esses, thou mightest have spoken
locutus (-a, -um) erat, he (she, it) had spoken	locutus (-a, -um) esset, he (she, it) might have spoken
locuti (-ae, -a) eramus, we had spoken	locuti (-ae, -a) essemus, we might have spoken
locuti (-ae, -a) eratis, ye had spoken	locuti (-ae, -a) essetis, ye might have spoken
locuti (-ae, -a) erant, they had spoken	locuti (-ae, -a) essent, they might have spoken.

V. Future.

loquar, I shall speak	locuturus (-a, -um) sim, I may be about to speak
loquēris (-e), thou wilt speak	locuturus (-a, -um) sis, thou mayest be about to speak
loquētur, he (she, it) will speak	locuturus (-a, -um) sit, he (she, it) may be about to speak
loquēmur, we shall speak	locuturi (-ae, -a) simus, we may be about to speak
loquēmĭni, ye will speak	locuturi (-ae, -a) sitis, ye may be about to speak
loquentur, they will speak	locuturi (-ae, -a) sint, they may be about to speak.

Imperative.

B.

loquĕre, loquĭtor, speak thou
loquimini, loquiminor, speak ye.

Infinitive.

D.

I. loqui, to speak
III. locutum (-am, -um) esse, to have spoken
V. locuturum (-am, -um) esse, to be about to speak.

VERBS. 145

Participles.
E.
I. *loquens*, speaking. III. *locutus*, having spoken. V. *locūturus*, about to speak.

Gerunds.
F.
loquendum, to speak, *loquendi*, of speaking, *loquendo*, in or by speaking.

Supines.
G.
locutum, to speak, *locutu*, in or by speaking.

The following lists give the principal verbs of this class:

1 *Deponent Verbs of the First Conjugation.*

Abominor, express abhorrence
Adminiculor, aid
Adversor, oppose myself
*Adūlor, flatter
Æmulor, rival
Allucinor, also *aluc-* and *haluc-*, dote, talk idly
*Altercor, quarrel
Amplexor, embrace
Ancillor, am a handmaid
Apricor, sun myself
Aquor, fetch water; *frumentor*, collect corn; *lignor*, collect wood; *materior*, fell timber; *pabulor*, forage
Arbitror, think
Architector, build (am *architectus*)
Argumentor, test by proofs
Argutor, chatter (am *argutus*)
Aspernor, despise
Assentor, agree, flatter

Astipulor, agree
Auctiōnor, sell at auction
Aucūpor, catch birds (am *auceps*)
Aversor, dislike, avoid with horror
Auguror (*augur*)   ⎫
*Auspicor (*auspex*) ⎬ practise soothsaying
Hariolor (*hariolus*) ⎬
Vaticinor (*vates*) ⎭
Auxilior, aid
Bacchor, revel as a Bacchanal
*Cachinnor, laugh aloud
Calumnior, cavil
Cavillor, ridicule
Caupōnor, deal in retail
Causor, allege
Circulor, form a circle round me
Comissor, feast
*Comitor, accompany (active only in the poets)

D. L. G.

Commentor, reflect upon, dispute
Concionor, harangue
*Conflictor, contend
Conor, attempt
Consilior, advise
Conspicor, behold
Contemplor, contemplate
Convicior, revile
Convivor, feast (am *conviva*)
Cornicor, chatter as a crow
Criminor, accuse
Cunctor, delay
Depeculor, plunder
Despicor, despise; but *despricatus* is passive, despised
Deversor, lodge
Digladior, fight
Dignor, think worthy (Cicero sometimes uses it as a passive)
Dedignor, disdain
Dominor, rule (am *dominus*)
Elucubror, produce by dint of labour
Epulor, feast
Exsecror, execrate
*Fabricor, fashion
Fabulor, *confabulor*, talk
Famulor, serve (am *famulus*)
Foeneror, lend at interest (in later writers active in the same sense as deponent, but *foenero* in Terence means 'to restore with interest')
Ferior, keep holiday
Frustror, disappoint
Furor, *suffuror*, steal
Glorior, boast
Graecor, live like a Greek, i.e. luxuriously
Grassor, advance quickly, attack

Gratificor, comply with
Grator and *gratulor*, give thanks, present congratulations
Gravor, think heavy (passive of *gravo*)
Helluor, gluttonize
Hortor, exhort; *adhortor*, *exhortor*, *dehortor*
Hospitor, am a guest, lodge
Jaculor, throw, dart
Imaginor, imagine
Imitor, imitate
Indignor, am indignant, spurn
Infitior, deny
Insidior, plot
Interpretor, explain (am an *interpres*)
Jocor, jest
Jurgor, quarrel
Lacrimor, shed tears
Laetor, rejoice
Lamentor, lament
Latrocinor, rob
Lenocinor (*alicui*), flatter
Libidinor, am voluptuous
Licitor, bid at an auction
Lucror, gain
Luctor (*ob-*, *re-*), strive, wrestle
*Ludificor, ridicule
Luxurior, am luxurious
Machinor, devise
*Medicor, heal
*Meditor, meditate
Mercor, buy
*Meridior, repose at noon
Metor, measure out
Minor and *minitor*, threaten
Miror (*de-*, *ad-*), wonder
Miseror, *commiseror*, pity
Moderor, restrain, temper

VERBS.

Modulor, modulate
Morigeror, comply
Moror (com-), delay; trans. and intrans.
**Muneror, remuneror* (*aliquem aliqua re*), reward
Mutuor, borrow
Negotior, carry on business
Nidulor, build a nest
Nugor, trifle
Nundinor, deal in buying and selling
Nutricor, nourish
Odoror, smell out
Ominor, prophesy
Operor, bestow labour on
Opinor, think
Opitulor, lend help
*Oscitor, yawn
Osculor, kiss
Otior, have leisure
Palor, wander
*Palpor, stroke, flatter
Parasitor, act the parasite (am *parasitus*)
Patrocinor, patronize
Percontor, inquire
Peregrinor, dwell as a stranger
Periclitor, try, am in danger
Philosophor, philosophize
*Pigneror, take a pledge, bind by a pledge
Pigror, am idle
Piscor, fish
*Populor, lay waste
Praedor, plunder
Praestolor, wait for
Praevaricor, walks crookedly (figur. act dishonestly as an advocate)

Precor, pray; *comprecor, deprecor, imprecor*
Proelior, fight a battle
Ratiocinor, reason
Recordor, remember
Refragor, oppose
Rimor, examine minutely
Rixor, wrangle
*Ruminor, chew the cud
*Runcor, eructate
Rusticor, live in the country
Scitor and *sciscitor*, inquire
Scortor, live unchastely
Scrutor, perscrutor, search
Scurror, play the buffoon
Sector, follow (frequentative of *sequor*); *assector, consector, insector*
Sermocinor, hold discourse
Solor, consolor, comfort
Spatior, exspatior, walk
Speculor, keep a look out
Stipulor, make a bargain
Stomachor, am indignant
Suavior, kiss
Suffragor, assent to
Suspicor, suspect
Tergiversor, shuffle
Testor (de-, ob-) and *testificor*, bear witness
Tricor, make unreasonable difficulties (*tricas*)
Tristor, am sad
Trutinor, weigh (*trutina*)
Tumultuor, make uproar
Tutor, defend
Vador, summon to trial
Vagor, wander
*Velificor, steer towards (fig. promote an object; with dat.)

10—2

Velitor, skirmish with light troops
Veneror, venerate
Venor, hunt
Verecundor, feel shame at doing
Versor (properly passive of *verso*), dwell, am occupied in; *aversor, conversor, obversor*
Vociferor, vociferate
Urinor, dive under water (to void urine is *urinam facere* or *reddere*)

2 Deponents of the Second Conjugation.

Fateor, fassus sum, fateri, acknowledge.

Confiteor, confessus sum, confess; *profiteor*, profess; *diffiteor* (no participle), deny.

Obs. This word properly means 'I give in, own that I have had enough,' like the Greek ἀπαυδῶ: and in this sense the inchoative *fatisco*, E. III. *fessus sum*, is regularly used.

Liceor, licitus sum, bid at an auction.

Polliceor, promise.

Medeor, no participle, for which *medicatus* is commonly used.

**Mereor, meritus sum*, more commonly *meritus*, deserve. The active used in the sense of earning or securing, as *merere stipendia; quid mereas?* But the forms are often interchanged.

Commereor, demereor, promereor, have the same meaning.

Misereor, miseritus or *misertus sum*, pity.

Reor, ratus sum, reri, think; has no imperfect subjunctive (Cic. *de Or.* III. 38; Quint. VIII. 3. 26).

Tueor, tuitus sum, look upon, fig. defend.

Contueor, intueor, look upon. There was an old form *tuor*.

Vereor, veritus sum, fear.

Revereor, reverence; *subvereor*, slightly fear.

3 Deponents of the Third Conjugation.

Adsentior, adsensus sum, adsentiri, assent. (The active form, *adsentio, adsensi, adsensum, adsentire*, is not so common).

Blandior, blanditus sum, blandiri, flatter.

Experior, expertus sum, experiri, experience, try.

*Comperior is used in the present tense, as well as *comperio;* the other tenses are formed only from the active verb; *comperi*, not *compertus sum*.

Largior, largitus sum, largiri, give money; *dilargior*, distribute money.

Mentior, mentitus sum, mentiri, lie; *ementior*, the same.

Metior, mensus sum, metiri, measure.

   Dimetior, measure out; *emetior*, measure completely; *permetior*.

Molior, molitus sum, moliri, move a mass; plan.

   Amolior, remove from the way; *demolior*, demolish, and others.

Opperior, oppertus sum, opperiri, wait for.

Ordior, orsus sum, ordiri, begin.

   Exordior, the same; *redordior*, begin over again.

Orior, ortus sum, oriri. See this verb in the list of the Fourth Conjugation.

Partior, partitus sum, partiri, divide (rarely active).

   **Dispertior, dispertitus sum* (more frequently active), distribute; *impertior (also *impertio, impartio, impartior*), communicate.

Potior, potitus sum, potiri, possess myself of.

   It is not uncommon, especially in the poets, for the present indicative and the imperfect subjunctive to be formed after the fourth conjugation; *potitur, potimur, poteretur, poteremur*.

*Punior. This verb is also found as an active verb; but is used as a deponent by Cicero, *Off.* L 25, *punitur*; *Tusc. Disp.* L 44, *puniantur*; *Phil.* VIII. 3, *puniretur*; *Mil.* 13, *punitus es*; *Invent.* II. 27, *punitus sis*.

Sortior, sortitus sum, sortiri, cast lots.

4. *Deponents of the Fourth Conjugation.*

Adipiscor, adeptus sum, and *indipiscor*, obtain (from the obsolete *apiscor, aptus sum, apisci*).

Divertor, turn aside, and *revertor*, return, are used as deponents, though *vertor* is passive only. They take the perfect from the active form, except the participle *reversus*; *reversus sum* occurs, but much more rarely than *reverti*.

Expergiscor, experrectus sum, expergisci, awake.

Fruor, fructus, and *fruitus sum, frui*, enjoy.

   Perfruor, perfructus sum, strengthens the meaning.

Fungor, functus sum, fungi, perform, discharge.

   Defungor, completely discharge, finish.

150   VERBS.

Gradior, gressus sum, gradi, proceed, is obsolete, except in the compounds.

Aggredior, aggressus sum, aggrĕdi, assail; *congredior*, meet; *digredior*, depart; *egredior*, go out of; *ingredior*, enter on; *progredior*, advance; *regredior*, return.

Invĕhor, invectus sum, invĕhi, inveigh against, properly passive of *veho*.

Irascor, irasci, properly an inchoative, grow angry; *iratus sum*, I am angry. I have been or was angry, is *succensui*.

Lābor, lapsus sum, lābi, fall.

Collābor, sink together; *dilābor*, fall in pieces; *elābor*, slip away; *illābor*, fall on; *relābor*, fall back.

Liquor, liquefactus sum, liqui, melt away.

Loquor, locutus sum, loqui, speak.

Allŏquor, address; *colloquor*, speak with; *eloquor, interloquor; obloquor*, speak against, revile.

Comminiscor, commentus sum, comminisci, devise, imagine (from the obsolete *miniscor*); *reminiscor* has no perfect; *recordatus sum* is used for the perfect.

Morior, morĕris, imperative *morere; moriebar, mortuus sum, moriar, morerer* (participle future, *moriturus*), *mori*, die (*moriri* poetical).

Emorior, commorior, demorior.

Nanciscor, nactus sum, nancisci, obtain. The participle is written *nanctus* in many passages of Livy and other writers.

Nascor, natus sum, nasci, nasciturus, am born (passive in sense, but without an active).

Innascor, renascor.

Nitor, nisus or *nixus sum, niti*, lean upon, strive.

Adnitor, strive for; *connitor*, and *enitor*, exert myself; in the sense of 'having brought forth,' *enixa* is the preferable form of the participle; *obnitor*, strive against, commonly *obnixus; renitor, reinit.*

Obliviscor, oblītus sum, oblivisci, forget.

Orior, ortus sum (participle future, *orīturus*), has in the infinitive *orīri*, and in the imperfect subjunctive both *orerer* and *orīrer* (Liv. XXIII. 16; Tac. *Annal*. II. 47, XI. 23). The present indic. follows the fourth conjugation, *orēris, orĭtur, orĭmur*.

Coorior, and *exorior* are formed in the same way (*exoreretur*, Lucret. II. 516); of *adorior, adorīris* and *adorĭtur* are certain, whereas *adorēris, adorĭtur* are only probable.

VERBS. 151

Paciscor, pactus sum (or *pepigi;* see 87, (1)), make a bargain.
Depaciscor or *depeciscor, depactus sum,* same meaning.
Pascor, pastus sum, feed; intransitive. (Properly passive of *pasco.*)
Patior, passus sum, pati, suffer.
Perpetior, perpessus sum, perpeti, endure.
Amplector and *complector, complexus sum,* embrace (from *plecto,* twine).
Proficiscor, profectus sum, proficisci, set out (from *facio,* 97, (c)).
Quĕror, questus sum, quĕri, complain.
Conqueror, lament.
Ringor (no perfect or participle), *ringi,* grin, show the teeth.
Sĕquor, secutus sum, sĕqui, follow.

    Assĕquor and *consequor,* overtake, attain; *exsequor,* execute; *insequor,* follow; *obsequor,* comply with; *persequor,* pursue; *prosequor,* attend; *subsequor,* follow close after.

Vescor (no perfect or supine), *vesci,* eat. *Edi* is used as the perfect.
Ulciscor, ultus sum, ulcisci, revenge, punish.
Utor, usus sum, uti, use.
Abutor, abuse.

5 Many deponents occur also in the active form, and these are denoted by an asterisk (*) in the above lists. This explains the fact, that many deponents are occasionally found also in a passive signification, e. g. *adulor, criminor, dignor, partior, testor* in Cicero. On the other hand, some active verbs are occasionally used as deponents, namely, *bello* (Virg.); *communico* (Livy); *peragro* (Vell. Put.); *multo* (Suet.); *elucubro, punio,* and *suppedito* (Cicero). The perfect participle (E. 111.) of the deponent verb is very often used in a passive sense, as the following list will show:

arbitratus, thought	*machinatus,* devised
comitatus, accompanied	*meditatus,* considered
conatus, attempted	*mercatus,* bought
dominatus, ruled	*metatus,* measured
frustratus, frustrated	*moderatus,* moderated
imitatus, imitated	*modulatus,* modulated
lamentatus, lamented	*moratus,* delayed

152   VERBS.

opinatus, thought
populatus, laid waste
stipulatus, agreed on

blanditus, flattered
largitus, bestowed
mentitus, lied
partitus, divided
meritus, deserved

tentatus, proved
veneratus, honoured

pactus, agreed on
mensus, measured
ortus, begun
ausus, dared

Also the compounds:

abominatus, detested
commentatus, devised
consolatus, consoled
deprecatus, deprecated
despicatus, despised
exhortatus, encouraged
execratus, cursed
insectatus, pursued
interminatus, threatened
interpretatus, explained
testificatus, proved

velificatus, sailed over
adeptus, obtained
aggressus, attacked
confessus, admitted
professus, made known
commentus, imagined
complexus, embraced
expertus, experienced
exsecutus, carried out
oblitus, forgotten

On the other hand, some active participles are used in a reflexive or middle sense, as *vertens*, 'turning oneself,' *volvens*, 'rolling oneself' or 'being rolled,' *vehens*, 'carrying oneself, carried,' *rotans*, 'wheeling oneself' (of a wheel).

103 Four verbs, *audeo*, 'I dare,' *ausus sum*; *fido*, 'I trust,' *fisus sum*; *gaudeo*, 'I am glad,' *gavisus sum*; *soleo*, 'I am accustomed,' *solitus sum*, have a passive form but active signification in the perfect, and might therefore be called *neuter deponents*. To the same class belong the participles *exosus* and *perosus*, 'having hated;' *pertaesus*, 'weary of;' *pōtus*, 'having drunk;' *juratus*, 'having sworn;' *coenatus*, 'having dined;' and the quasi-adjectives *consideratus* (Cic. *Caecin.* 1, § 1), *circumspectus*, *cautus*, *falsus*, *tacitus*, *nupta*, &c., which belong to active verbs.

104 The following verbs are specially defective:

(a) *Aio*, 'I say.'

A. 1.   aio,   ais, ait   aiunt.

II. aiē-bam, -bas, -bat, -bamus, -batis, -bant.
III. ait.
Part. aiens.

(b) *Inquam*, 'say I,' 'quoth I,' only used between words quoted as spoken by another.

A. I.
inquam inquis inquit inquĭmus inquĭtis inquiunt.

II.
inquiē-bam -bas -bat -bamus -batis -bant.

III.
inquisti inquit   inquistis

V.
inquies inquiet.

B.
inque   inquĭto   inquĭte.

(c) *Fari*, 'to speak,' has only *fatur*, 'he says,' *fare*, 'say thou,' *fatus*, 'having said,' *fando*, 'by saying.'

(d) *Quaeso*, 'I pray,' 'prithee,' has only this form and *quaesŭmus*; but the verb *quaero*, which is merely another orthography, is complete (above, 97, (a)).

(e) *Coepi*, 'I begin,' *memĭni*, 'I remember,' *odi*, 'I hate,' have only the perfect and pluperfect of the indicative, subjunctive, and infinitive; but *coepi* has also a perfect passive *coeptus sum*, *coepi* and *odi* have the future participles *coepturus* and *osurus*, and *memĭni* has the imperative *memento*, *mementōte*.

(f) *Forem* and *fore* are used as synonyms of *essem* and *futurum esse* (above, 72).

(g) *Aus-im*, *-is*, *-it*, *-int* are used for corresponding persons of *audeam*, 'I may dare,' and *faxim*, *faxis*, *faxit*, *faxĭmus*, *faxĭtis*, *faxint* are synonymous with *faciam*, *facias*, &c. 'I may make.'

(h) The following verbs are used only as imperatives: *apage*, *apagĕte*, 'begone,' *ave*, *avēte*, 'hail,' *salve*, *salvēte*, 'good morrow,' fut. *salvēbis*, infin. *salvēre*; *vale*, *valēte*, 'farewell,' infin. *valēre*; to which may be added *cĕdo*, 'give me,' 'tell me,' with its obsolete plural *cette* for *cedite*.

CHAPTER V.

UNDECLINED WORDS.

§ 1. *Adverbs.*

105 AN adverb is a word used in a fixed case for the purpose of qualifying by some secondary statement that which is already expressed by a verb, an adjective, or even another adverb; thus in the phrases *feliciter vivit*, 'he lives happily;' *eximie doctus*, 'exceedingly learned;' *satis bene scripsit*, 'he wrote sufficiently well;' the adverb *feliciter* qualifies the verb *vivit* by a secondary or accessory statement, of the manner of the life; the adverb *eximie* qualifies the adjective *doctus* by a secondary statement of the degree of the learning; the adverb *satis* qualifies the other adverb *bene* by the secondary, or, in this case, the tertiary statement, that the writing was not only well done, in regard to quality, but that it exhibited a sufficient amount of that quality. The prepositions, conjunctions, and interjections, which are given as separate varieties of undeclined words, are, in regard to their origin and primitive use, neither more nor less than adverbs; but they are classed as separate parts of speech, because they have peculiar functions in the syntax of an inflected language. With regard to their etymology, adverbs are either (1) primitive, or (2) derivative. Primitive adverbs are those which cannot be referred to any declinable words as their immediate origin. Derivative adverbs are those which may be formed regularly from adjectives or participles. The latter are much the most numerous, and their meaning is generally given by that of the corresponding declinable words. The former, though a less extensive class, constitute some of the most important machinery in the Latin language, and involve a considerable amount of philological difficulty. It will be sufficient in a practical grammar to classify the adverbs in common use according to the nature of the secondary qualifications which they express, and to add observations on those which are most deserving of the student's attention. But it will be desirable in the first place to make some remarks on the formation of those adverbs, which belong to the class of derivatives.

106 The great majority of adverbs are cases of substantives, adjectives, and participles.

(a) From adjectives and participles in *-us, -a, -um*, and adjectives in *-er, -a, -um*, we have adverbs in *-ē*, which is the commonest form, as *longē* from *longus*, or *pulcrē* from *pulcer*; or *-ō*, as *raro* from *rarus*, *subito* from *subitus*. But we have *benĕ* and *malĕ* from *bonus* and *malus*. Some adjectives have two forms of the adverb with a difference of meaning; thus *certe* means 'at any rate,' *certo*, 'certainly;' *vere* means 'truly;' *vero* is either the conjunction 'but,' or it is added to another word in the sense of 'indeed;' as *ego vero, minime vero*. *Sanē* from *sanus* is nearly equivalent in meaning to *certo*, and has many idiomatic uses as a concessive particle, in which case it may even be opposed to *certe*; as *sint falsa sane, invidiosa certe non sunt*, 'let them be false, *if you please; at any rate* they are not malicious' (Cic. *Acad. Prior.* II. 32, § 103).

(b) Other adjectives and participles form their adverbs, if they have any, in *-ter* which is the common form, or else use their neuter as an adverb; thus we have *celeriter* from *ce'er*, *amanter* from *amans*, &c., or *dulcĕ* from *dulcis*, and *recens* instead of *recenter*. Some adjectives in *-us* have adverbs in *-ter* as well as in *-ē*; thus we find both *firme* and *firmiter* from *firmus*. From *violentus* we have *violenter* only, although *violens* is never used in prose. *Vehementer* is used, like *oppido*, as a merely intensive adjunct in the sense of 'very' or 'very much;' as *haec res vehementer ad me pertinet*, 'this matter very much concerns me.'

(c) Adverbs in *-tim* or *-sim* have a sort of participial meaning, but are apparently derived from nouns as well as verbs; thus we have *cursim*, 'cuttingly,' i. e. 'with a cut,' *catervā-tim*, 'troopingly,' i. e. 'in troops,' *ricis-sim*, 'in turns,' *fur-tim*, ' by stealth,' &c. *Partim* is merely the locative of *pars*; it means not only 'partly,' but, substantively, 'a part of;' as *partim e nobis timidi sunt, partim averri*, 'some of us are cowardly, others unfriendly.'

Saltim, 'jumpingly,' is generally used as a concessive particle = 'at least,' 'at all events;' and *statim*, 'standingly,' means not only 'firmly,' 'stably,' but also and more commonly 'on the spot,' 'immediately,' as a particle of time.

(d) Adverbs in *-tus* denote origin; as *coeli-tus*, 'from heaven,' *fundi-tus*, 'from the bottom,' *peni-tus*, 'from within,' hence 'entirely,' 'thoroughly,' like *plane* and *prorsus* = *pro-versus*, which have the same meaning.

(e) Many adverbs are merely cases of nouns; as *diu*, *noctu*, *palam*, *forte*, *frustra*, *vulgo*; and some include more than one word, as *denuo* = *de novo*, *profecto* = *pro facto*, *nimirum* = *mirum ni*, *postridie* = *posteri die*, *meridie* = *medii die* (where *posteri*, *medii* are locatives, like *domi*), *hodie* = *hoc die*, *magnopere* = *magno opere*. Others are formed from verbs, as *scilicet*, *videlicet*, for *scire licet*, *videre licet* = 'it is clear,' *dumtaxat* = 'provided one estimates it exactly,' 'only,' 'at least,' 'as far as that goes.'

(f) New adverbs are formed by prefixing prepositions, as *exinde*, *deinde*, *subinde*, *adhuc*, &c. But *antea*, *postea*, *posthac*, &c. are merely obsolete forms of the pronoun added to the preposition; thus *antea* is for *ante ea*, *posthac* for *post haec*, &c.

107 According to their signification adverbs fall into five principal classes: (A) Adverbs of negation, affirmation, and interrogation; (B) adverbs of place; (C) adverbs of time, which answer to the question, 'when?' (D) adverbs of time, which answer to the question, 'how long?' or 'how often?' (E) adverbs of manner or degree.

(A) Adverbs of negation, affirmation, and interrogation.

(a) Negative particles.

Non, no, not
Haud, quite the reverse
Ne-quidem, not even
Neutiquam, by no means

Immo, nay rather
Ne, the prohibitive or final negation

(b) Affirmative or concessive particles.

Nae, verily
Etiam, yes
Quidem, at least, at all events

Equidem, surely
Utique, at any rate
Vel, if you please

UNDECLINED WORDS. 157

Sic plane, quite so
Nempe, to be sure
Nimirum,
Scilicet, } doubtless
Videlicet,

Certe, certainly, at least
Profecto, of a truth, doubtless
Quippe, of course
Sane, assuredly
Recte, quite right.

(c) Interrogative particles.

-ne, is it so?
Nonne, is it not so?
Num, it is not so, is it?
Utrum (num) -ne (an), is this the case, or that?

Quare,
Cur,   } why?
Quid,

Qui,
Quomodo, } how?

(B) Adverbs of place.

*Ubi, where
Ibi, there
Ibidem, at the same place
Alibi, elsewhere
Nusquam, nowhere at all
Hic, here (by the speaker)
Istic, there (by the person addressed)
Illic, at that other place
Utrobique, at both places
Ubivis,
Ubilibet, } everywhere
Ubique,
Alicubi, somewhere
Uspiam, anywhere
Usquam, anywhere at all
Ubiubi,
Ubicunque, } wherever
*Unde, whence
Inde, thence
Indidem, from the same place
Aliunde, from another place
Hinc, from hence (from the speaker)
Istinc, from thence (from the person addressed)

Illinc, from that other place
Utrinque, from both sides
Undique, from all sides
Undevis,   } from any place you
Undelicet, } please
Alicunde, from some other place
Undeunde,   } from whencesoever
Undecunque, }
*Quo, whither
Eo, thither
Eodem, in the same direction
Alio, in another direction
Citra, on this side
Ultra, on that side, beyond
Citro, in this direction
Ultro, in that direction
Prae, before
Pone, } behind
Retro,
Longe, far (a considerable distance in length)
Late, widely (a considerable distance in breadth)
Longe lateque, far and wide
Procul, afar (relative distance and separation)

* Words marked with an asterisk are used also as interrogatives.

Huc, hither (to the speaker)
Istuc, thither (to the person addressed)
Illuc, in that other direction
Quovis, } whither you please
Quolibet,
Aliquo, some whither
Quopiam, any whither
Quoquam, any whither at all
Quoquo, } whithersoever
Quocunque,
*Qua, in what way
Eâ, in that way
Eadem, in the same way
Alia, in a different way
Hac, in this way
Istac, in that way
Illac, in that other way

Quavis, } in any way
Qualibet,
Aliqua, in some way
Quaqua, } in any way soever
Quacunque,
*Quorsum, in what direction (for *quoversum*)
Aliorsum, in another direction
Illorsum, in that direction
Dextrorsum, to the right
Sinistrorsum, to the left
Introrsum, inwards
Retrorsum, backwards
Sursum, upwards
Deorsum, downwards
Quoquoversus, in any direction whatsoever

(C) Adverbs of time, which answer to the question 'when?'

Quum, } when
*Quando,
Hŏdie, to-day
Heri (*here*), yesterday
Nudiustertius, the day before yesterday
Cras, to-morrow
Perendie, the day after to-morrow
Pridie, the day before
Postridie, the day after
Propediem, within a few days, shortly
Interdiu, by day
Noctu, by night
Mane, in the morning
Vesperi, in the evening
Abhinc, from this time (counting backwards)
Alias, at another time

Aliquando, sometimes (opposed to *nunquam*)
Ante, antea, before (*multo ante*, long before)
Actutum, with all despatch, without waiting
Cito, soon
Confestim, in all haste
Continuo, immediately, opposed to *ex intervallo* (also, 'from the first')
Extemplo, now, on the spur of the moment (opposed to *mox* and *postremo*)
E vestigio, without delay
Illico, } at once, without hesitation or slowness
Ilicet,
Dein, deinde, then
Deinceps, in succession

Diu, long ago
Dudum, sometime before (but with *haud*, *quam*, and *jam*, *dudum* implies a long time)
Jam, now, already (*jam amplius*, any longer)
Interim, *interea*, in the meantime
Modo, just now
Commode, *commodum*, just at that moment, but that moment
Mox, soon, presently (between *extemplo* and *postremo*)
Nondum, not yet (οὔπω)
Non jam, no longer (οὐκέτι)
Nunc, now
Nunc demum, not until now
Nunc denique, now at last
Etiam nunc, still, even now (without any idea of duration), distinguished from
Adhuc, still, until now (with an idea of duration)
Olim, formerly (also 'sometimes' and 'hereafter')

Paullo post, shortly after
Posthac, hereafter
Postremo, at last
Postremum, for the last time
Pridem, long ago
Protinus, straightway, forthwith
Quam primum, as soon as possible
Quandoque, sometimes
Quondam, once upon a time
Repente, suddenly (i.e. unexpectedly)
Subito, suddenly (i.e. unforeseen)
Statim, now, at once (opposed to *deinde* and *postea*)
Tandem, at length
Tum, then, thereupon (opposed to *quum*, when)
Tunc, then, at that time (opposed to *nunc*, now, at this time)
Tunc demum, not until then
Tunc denique, then at last
Unquam, ever at all
Vix, scarcely
Vixdum, but now (followed by *quum*)

(D) Adverbs of time, which answer to the question 'how long?' or 'how often?'

*Quamdiu, how long, as long as
Aliquamdiu, } rather a long
Aliquantisper,} time
Adhuc, still, until now (to be distinguished from *etiam nunc*)
Diu, a long time
Paulisper,} a little while
Parumper,}
*Quousque, how long
Tantisper, so long, such a short while

Quoties, how often, as often as
Aliquoties, several times
Crebro, frequently (opposed to *raro*)
Frequenter, on numerous occasions, or by many persons
Iterum, again, a second time (in the same direction back again)
Rursus, again, over again
Denuo, anew

UNDECLINED WORDS.

De integro, quite afresh, from the beginning
Identidem, repeatedly
Subinde, in quick succession, one after the other
Interdum, sometimes, now and then (opposed to *saepe*)
Nonnunquam, not unfrequently (opposed to *raro*)
Plerunque, generally, in most cases (opposed to *semper*)
Quotannis, every year
Quotidie, every day
Raro, seldom
Saepe, often (opposed to *semel*, *nonnunquam*, and *semper*)
Toties, so often
Semper, always (of duration)
Usque, always (of continuance up to a certain point)

To these may be added the numeral adverbs (above, 59).

(E) Adverbs of manner or degree.

Abunde, even more than enough (*satis superque*)
Adeo, to such an extent
Admodum, considerably
Affatim, sufficiently (in regard to the person satisfied)
Aliter, otherwise (*non aliter quam si*, just as if)
Alioqui(n), in other respects (also 'besides')
Apprime, by far, especially
Imprimis, very much, exceedingly
Æque ac, just as much as
Ceterum, ceteroqui, for the rest, in other respects
Ceu, as it were
Dumtaxat, precisely, solely, at least
Fere, ferme, almost
Forte, fortasse, forsitan, perhaps
Frustra, incassum, nequidquam, in vain
Gratis, freely, for nought
Ita, so
Item, itidem, likewise, in the very same manner
Magnopere (*magne* does not occur), *majore opere, maximopere*, much, more, most
Magis, more
Maxime, chiefly
Minus, less
Minime, least
Modo, only
Omnino, altogether
Paene, almost
Pariter ac, just as well as
Nimis, nimium, too much (also 'very much')
Parum, too little
Penitus, to the very bottom
Perinde ac, } just as if
Proinde ac,
Perquam, very much, exceedingly
Plane, quite
Potius, rather
Potissimum, chiefly
Praecipue, } especially
Praesertim,

Prope, nearly	*Secus*, otherwise
Praeut, prout, just as	*secus ac,* } otherwise than
Prorsus, entirely	*secus quam,*
Quam, as, how much	*Sic*, so
Quantopere, how greatly	*Sicuti*, just as
Tantopere, so much	*Solum*, only
Quasi, as if	*Tanquam*, as though
Quatenus, as far as	*Tantum,* } only
Eatenus, so far as	*Tantummodo,*
Hactenus, thus far	*Tantum non*, all but
Aliquatenus, to a certain extent	*Ut*, as, for example
Saltim, at least	*Utique*, in any case, at any rate
Sanequam, very much	*Valde*, very much
Satis, sat, enough (in regard to the thing in question)	*Velut, veluti*, just as
	Vix, scarcely.

108. Many of these adverbs create special difficulties, either because the synonyms require to be carefully discriminated, or because there is a tendency on the part of the English student to introduce into the Latin language the vagueness which he finds in his own vernacular idiom. In these cases it is desirable to add some observations to the lists given above.

(A)

(a) A negative either *denies*, i.e. affirms that the thing is not so, or *prohibits*, i.e. forbids that it should be so: thus, *non* and *haud* deny, but *ne* prohibits: *non dico*, 'I do not say,' *haud dico*, 'I am the very reverse of saying,' but *ne dic*, 'say not,' *ne dicam*, 'let me not say,' 'that I may not say,' 'lest I say.' The difference between *non* and *haud* is, that, while the former merely denies, the latter contradicts; thus, *auctor haud quaquam spernendus*, means 'an author the very reverse of despicable;' and *haud scio* does away with the ambiguity of the question which follows, so that *haud scio an*, means 'I am rather inclined to think.' Although *ne* by itself is always used in prohibitive, optative, or final sentences, *ne* or *nec* (*neg-*) in composition amounts to a simple negative; as *ne-scio*, 'I know not,' *neg-otium*, 'no leisure,' *neg-ligo*, 'I neglect,' *nec-opinato*, 'unexpectedly,' &c.: and when followed by some other word and *quidem* it amounts to the intensive negative, 'not even;' as *ne musca quidem*, 'not even a fly.'

Obs. The following rhymes will exemplify the usage, and remind the young student, that *quidem* must not immediately follow the negative:

'*Ne unus quidem locus est*
In all the authors, reckoned best,
Where *ne—quidem* 'not even' mean,
Without some words these words between.'

The reason is, however, because *quidem* qualifies only the word which it immediately succeeds.

We have sometimes *nec* in the same sense as *ne-quidem*, especially in Quintilian, e.g. *alioqui nec scriberem*, 'otherwise I should not even write.' If *ne-quidem*, or *nec—nec* follow another negative, the force of the negation is not lost; thus we may say *nihil nec utilius nec jucundius fieri potest*, 'nothing can be done either more usefully or more pleasantly.'

In conditional and final sentences *minus* sometimes stands for *non* or *ne*; as *si minus*, 'if not;' *quo-minus*, 'lest,' 'so as not;' and in the conjunction *qui-n* the negative is represented by a single letter.

The particle *immo* (or *imo*) primarily means 'in the lowest degree' (from *imus*). In answers it is used as a corrective negation; thus *Cic. de Off.* III. 23: *si patriam prodere conabitur pater, silebitne filius? immo vero obsecrabit patrem, ne id faciat*, 'if a father shall attempt to betray his native land, will the son remain silent? Nay rather' (in the lowest degree in accordance with that supposition, on the contrary), 'he will earnestly beseech his father not to do so.' Ter. *Andr.* III. 5. 11: *Expedies! Certe Pamphile. Nempe ut modo. Immo melius spero.* 'You will deliver me? Yes, certainly. No doubt as you did just now. On the contrary, better I hope.' In some cases, where *immo* has been thought to mean 'yes,' it really contradicts the previous remark by the intimation that it does not go far enough; thus in Hor. 1 *Serm.* III. 20: *quid tu? nullane habes vitia? Immo alia et fortasse minora*, 'What of yourself? have you *no* faults? On the contrary, I *have* faults, but they are of a different kind, and perhaps less than those of Tigellius.' In general *immo* approaches very nearly to the corrective use of μὲν οὖν (*Greek Grammar*, 567). In simply answering 'no!' to a question, we must use *non, non vero, non ita, minime,* or *minime vero*.

(b) The affirmative adverbs do not create much difficulty. The simple answer 'yes,' is not very commonly expressed in Latin.

UNDECLINED WORDS.

It may be given by *sane, utique, vero, ita,* or *ita est.* But perhaps the only single particle, which exactly bears this meaning, is *etiam.* Thus Cic. *Acad. Pr.* II. 32: *ut probabilitatem sequens, ubicunque haec occurrat aut deficiat, aut 'etiam,' aut 'non' respondere possit,* 'to answer either yes or no.' Plin. *Ep.* VI. 2: *at quaedam superracua dicuntur. Etiam. Sed satius est et haec dici.* 'Yes, but it is better that even these things should be mentioned.' When *quippe* stands alone in an answer, it implies that the question or observation is assented to as obvious; thus Cic. *pro Caecin.* 19: *recte igitur diceres te restituisset quippe,* 'Yes, of course.' To express an ironical assent, the particles *nempe, nimirum, scilicet, videlicet* are commonly used; thus Ter. *Andr.* I. Sc. ii. 5; *meum nutum rumor est amare. Id populus curat scilicet,* 'Oh! of course the world cares much for that.'

(c) The simple interrogative particles are *num, utrum, an, -ne* (which is enclitic and may be added to the three preceding) and *nonne,* to which we may add the prefix *ec-* found in *ecquid,* and *numquid.* Of these *-ne* appended to a verb merely inquires; *num* expects the answer 'no,' and *nonne* the answer 'yes;' *numquid* follows the meaning of *num,* and *ecquid* is quite general; *utrum* always implies an alternative, and *an* can only stand before the second of two questions. Thus we have the following usages:

aegrotasne? 'are you ill?'
num aegrotas? 'you are not ill, are you?'
nonne aegrotas? 'you are ill, are you not?'
utrum ea vestra an nostra culpa est? 'is that your fault or ours?'

The same rules apply to indirect questions. Of double questions there are only four modes:

1. *utrum (num) an:* 'non refert *utrum* sit aureum poculum, *an* vitreum, *an* manus concava,' 'it matters not whether it be a gold cup, or a silver one, or the hollow of the hand.'
2.   *an:* 'recte *an* secus fecerim nescio,' 'whether I have done rightly or otherwise, I know not.'
3. *ne,* enclitic, *an:* 'taceamne *an* prodicem nescio,' 'I know not whether to hold my tongue *or* to speak out.'
4.   *ne:* 'experiri voluit verum falsum*ne* esset relatum,' 'he wanted to find out whether the story was true or false.'

164   UNDECLINED WORDS.

Sometimes both interrogative particles are omitted in the indirect double question, as *velit, nolit, scire difficile est,* 'it is difficult to know whether he wishes it or not.'

Obs. Young students must remember that only *an* and *ne* can render 'or' in questions:

'In double questions *an* and *ne*
Not *aut* or *vel* the word must be.'

If the second member of the double question, whether direct or indirect, is merely the opposite of the first, we have in Latin either *annon* or *necne*; thus, *num tabulas habet, annon?* 'has he got the document or not?' *Antigonus nondum statuerat, conservaret Eumenem necne,* 'Antigonus had not yet determined whether to preserve Eumenes or not.' *Quaeritur, Corinthiis bellum indicamus annon,* 'it is asked whether we ought to declare war against the Corinthians or not.' *Di utrum sint, necne sint, quaeritur,* 'the question is whether the Gods exist or not.'

(B)

Adverbs of place do not generally require any special explanation, but *ultro,* which properly answers to *quo,* as *ultra* does to *qua,* has some usages which deserve particular attention. Its primary meaning is 'to a place beyond;' as *ultro istum a me,* 'take him far from me;' and *ultro citroque* is 'thither and hither;' hence it signifies 'still farther,' 'over and above,' 'besides;' as *his lacrimis vitam damus et miserescimus ultro,* 'to these tears we grant his life, and pity him besides.' But the commonest use of the word is as an apparent synonym for *sponte,* which must be distinguished from it. For *sponte,* which is the ablative of *s-pons* or *expons,* a derivative of another form of *pondus,* means 'by its own weight or inclination,' 'of its own accord,' 'unbidden:' hence we have (Hor. I Epist. XII. 17): *sponte sua jussuene:* but *ultro* means 'going still farther,' 'going beyond expectation,' 'without waiting,' 'to our surprise;' hence (in the same *Epist.* v. 22) we have: *si quid petet, ultro defer,* 'if he wants any thing, give it at once,' 'surprise him with it.' This distinction may be remembered by the following line:

'*Sponte*—quod injussus; necopinus quod facis,—*ultro.*'

In many passages *ultro* may be best rendered by our particle 'even.' Thus in Hor. 4 *Carm.* IV. 51: *sectamur ultro quos opimus fallere et effugere est triumphus,* 'we even pursue those whom it is the greatest triumph to deceive and avoid.' Liv. I. 5: *captum regi Amulio tradidisse latrones ferunt, ultro accusantes,* 'they say that the robbers, having captured Remus, delivered him to king Amulius, and even accused him (i. e. although they were brigands themselves)'. It may sometimes even be rendered 'on the contrary.' Thus in Virgil, Æn. IX. 120: *at non audaci cessit fiducia Turno: ultro animos tollit dictis, atque increpat ultro,* 'bold Turnus did not abate his confidence; on the contrary (far beyond that) he rouses their courage with his words, and he even chides them.' Similarly, Æn. V. 55: *Hunc (diem) ego Gaetulis agerem si Syrtibus exsul, &c. annua vota tamen exsequerer, &c. Nunc ultro ad cineres ipsius et ossa parentis adsumus,* 'if I were an exile, I should keep the anniversary; now, on the contrary (when the case is so different), we are come even to the ashes and bones of my father.' The true force of *ultro* is also given in the opposition between *ultro tributum* and *vectigal;* for while the latter denotes a tax, for the privilege of collecting which the farmer-general had to pay a fixed sum to the treasury, the *ultro tributum* was some public work for which the state had *even* to advance money to the contractor (see e.g. Liv. XXXIX. 44). Hence we may explain Seneca's illustration when he says (*De Beneficiis,* IV. 1) that virtue *in se impendere jubet et saepius in ultro tributis est,* 'bids us spend money upon itself, and generally belongs to those contracts which presume an initiatory outlay.'

(C) and (D)

Many of the adverbs of time, which are apparently synonyms, require to be carefully distinguished, for even some of those which answer to the question 'when?' are not unfrequently confused by the student with the adverbs which answer to the question 'how long?' or 'how often?' It will be desirable therefore to consider these two classes together.

(a) *Jam* and *nunc* both signifying 'now,' and *tum* and *tunc* both signifying 'then,' are frequently confused in writing Latin. *Nunc* signifies the actually present time of the speaker as opposed to the past or the future, but *jam* only indicates the immediate occurrence of an incident, whether it belongs to the present, the past, or the future. Hence it is prefixed not only to *nunc,* but to *tunc, dudum, pridem* of past time; and while *jam amplius* means

'any longer,' *non jam* means 'no longer,' and *non jam ut ante* is
'no longer as before.' The general distinction between *tum* and
tunc, which is sometimes lost from the careless writing of the
manuscripts, is suggested by the difference between *jam*, which,
as well as *quum*, is the correlative of the former, and *nunc*, which
is the regular antithesis of the latter. The following examples[1]
will illustrate these distinctions: Erat *tunc* excusatio oppressis,
misera illa quidem, sed tamen justa: *nunc* nulla est. Cic. *Phil.*
VII. 5. Quae quidem multo plura evenirent, si ad quietem integri
iremus: *nunc* onusti cibo et vino perturbata et confusa cernimus.
Cic. *Divin.* I. 29. Jam Horatius, caeso hoste victor, secundam
pugnam petebat. *Tum* clamore Romani adjuvant militem suum.
Liv. 1. 24. Cedo, quid postea? Eum ego meum esse aio.
Quid *tum*? Cic. *Mur.* XII. Haec non noram *tum*, quum cum
Democrito tuo locutus sum. Cic. *Att.* VI. 1. Id tu, Brute, *jam*
intelliges, quum in Galliam veneris. Cic. *Brut.* 46. Quo autem
pacto deceat incise membratimve dici, *jam* videbimus; *nunc* quot
modis mutentur comprehensiones dicendum est. Cic. *Or.* 63. Sunt
duo menses *jam*. Cic. *Rosc. Com.* 3. *Jam* a prima adolescentia. Cic.
Divers. 1. 9. Consilium istud *tunc* esset prudens, si nostris rationes
ad Hispaniensem casum accommodaturi essemus. Cic. *Att.* X. 8.

(b) *Mŏdŏ* (for *mi dato*, 'grant me this,' *Trans. Phil. Soc.* 1854,
p. 97) implies the concession of the very shortest time preceding
the present; *commode* or *commodum* expresses exact coincidence in
time; and *nuper* indicates that the time referred to is absolutely
distinct from the present, and may be relatively long gone by.
The following passages make good these distinctions: In qua urbe
modo gratia, auctoritate, gloria floruimus, in ea *nunc* his omnibus
caremus. Cic. *Div.* IV. 13. *Commodum* discesseras heri, *quum*
Trebatius venit, 'you had but just gone yesterday, when Trebatius
came.' Cic. *Att.* XIII. 9. Haec *nuper*, id est, *paucis ante saeculis*,
medicorum ingeniis reperta sunt. Cic. *N. D.* II. 50. *Nuper* homines
ejusmodi, et quid dico *nuper*? immo vero *modo* ac plane paulo ante
videmus. Cic. *Verr.* IV. 3.

(c) *Olim*, 'at another time'[2] (properly the locative of *ille =
ollus*), refers to a distant time, whether past or future, and is opposed

---

[1] Most of the examples illustrating the distinctive use of the particles are taken from F. Nebula's *Lateinische Synonymik*.
[2] In Hor. 1 *Serm.* l. 25; Virgil, *Aen.* VIII. 391, *olim* means 'sometimes,' and after *si* it is equivalent to *quando* in Virgil, *Ecl.* I. 33.

to *nuper; quondam* (properly the locative of *quidam*) refers in good Latin prose only to the past, and is opposed to *nunc; aliquando* denotes at some definite time, and is opposed to *nunquam*, whether past, present, or future. It loses its first two syllables after *ne* and *si*. Thus we have: Quid ostenta Lacedæmonios *olim*, nuper nostros adjuverunt? Cic. *Divin.* II. 25. Utinam coram tecum *olim* potius, quam per epistolas (sc. colloquar)! Cic. *Att.* XI. 4. Omnia fere, quæ sunt conclusa nunc artibus, dispersa et dissipata *quondam* fuerunt. Cic. *Or.* I. 42. Populus Romanus, qui *quondam* lenissimus existimabatur, hoc tempore domestica crudelitate laborat. Cic. *Rosc. Am.* 53. Tandem *aliquando* Catilinam ex urbe ejecimus. Cic. *Cat.* II. 1. Si placet, sermonem alio transferamus, et nostro more *aliquando*, non rhetorico, loquamur. Cic. *Or.* I. 29. Illucescet *aliquando* ille dies. Cic. *Mil.* 26. Inquiritur, sitne *aliquando* mentiri boni viri? Cic. *Or.* III. 29. Si, num, ne ... *quando*. Cic. *Rosc. Am.* 13, 50; *Am.* 16, 19. Si *quando* de amicitia disputabunt. *Am.* 15.

(d) *Semper* denotes 'always,' as a continued duration of time, during which the events referred to happened either continually or in every possible case; *usque* denotes 'always,' as an uninterrupted continuance up to a given time; *perpetuo* denotes 'always,' as an uninterrupted continuance without any limitation. Thus: Ea quum tempore commutantur, commutatur officium, et non *semper* est idem. Cic. *Off.* I. 10. Quod *semper* movetur, æternum est. Cic. *Tusc.* I. 30. Mihi *usque* curæ erit, quid agas, *dum* quid egeris sciero. Cic. *Div.* XII. 1. *Usque* animadverti, judices, Erucium jocari atque alias res agere, antequam Chrysogonum nominavi. Cic. *Rosc. Am.* 22. Ut eam opinionem *perpetuo* retineatis. Cic. *Agr.* III. 1.

Obs. It is observed by teachers that young scholars frequently confuse between *semper* and *unquam*, because they are both occasionally rendered by the English 'ever.' The following rhyme may assist in correcting this gross mistake :

Dum pro *semper* scribis *unquam*
Probo stylo scribes nunquam.

But it may perhaps be sufficient to state to an intelligent student that *semper* means 'ever' in the sense 'for ever,' but that *unquam*, which is liable to the rule about *quisquam* and *ullus* (68, *Obs.* 3), is only used in negative sentences, in questions implying a negation, and in conditions excluding the affirmative result, so that it may always be rendered 'ever

168 UNDECLINED WORDS.

at all.' It sometimes follows *quando* in the phrase *si quando unquam*, 'if at any particular time at all' (Liv. VIII. 4). In Ovid, *Amor.* VI. 23, it seems that we ought to read *si cunquam* for *sic unquam* (like *sicubi*, &c.); for otherwise it would be impossible to reconcile the use of *unquam* with the established signification of the word; the passage will therefore run:

Excute, *sicunquam* ('if ever at all') longa relevere catena,
Nec tibi perpetuo serva bibatur aqua.

(e) The distinctions between *statim, illico, e vestigio, extemplo, continuo, protinus, actutum, confestim*, as given in the list, are illustrated by the following examples: Verres simulac tetigit provinciam, *statim* literas Messanam dedit. Cic. *Verr.* I. 10. Ad vadimonium non venerat; *illicone* ad prætorem ire convenit? Cic. *Quint.* 15. Repente *e vestigio* ex homine, tamquam aliquo Circæo poculo, factus est Verres. Cic. *Caecil.* 17. Quod fingat *extemplo*, non habet. Cic. *Rosc. Com.* 3. Alia subito *ex tempore* conjectura explicantur. Cic. *Divin.* I. 33. Ignis in aquam conjectus *continuo* extinguitur. Cic. *Rosc. Com.* 6. Te hortor et rogo, ut Romam *protinus* pergas et properes. Cic. *Qu. Fr.* I. 3. Heus! heus! aperite aliquis *actutum* ostium. Ter. *Ad.* IV. 4. 26. Cæsar cohortes, quæ in stationibus erant, secum proficisci; reliquas armari et *confestim* se subsequi jussit. Cæs. *B. G.* IV. 32. Scribis, si secundum mare ad me ire cœpisset, te *confestim* ad me venturum. Cic. *Att.* VIII. 12.

(f) The distinction between *repente* and *subito*, as given above, is shown by the following passages: Cæsar, accusata *acerbitate* Marcelli, *repente praeter spem* dixit, se senatui roganti de Marcello non negaturum. Cic. *ad div.* IV. 4. Divinus hic adolescens, *subito praeter spem* omnium exortus, prius exercitum confecit, quam quispiam hoc cum cogitare suspicaretur. Cic. *Phil.* V. 16. Etsi utile est, *subito* sæpe dicere, tamen illud utilius, sumto spatio ad cogitandum, parntius atque accuratius dicere. Cic. *Or.* I. 33. Hostium repens (often *repentinus*) adventus magis aliquanto conturbat, quam exspectatus; et maris *subita* (in Liv. often *subitarius*) tempestas, quam ante provisa, terret navigantes vehementius. Cic. *Tusc.* III. 22.

(g) *Adhuc* and *etiamnunc*, being both rendered by the same English word 'still,' are occasionally confused by modern writers of Latin. As has been shown above, they belong to different classes; for while the former answers to the question, 'how long?' by expressing the duration of time down to the present moment, *etiamnunc* answers to the question, 'when?' and does not express the duration of time at all. There is a similar distinction between *usque eo*, 'up to that time,' and *etiamtunc* or *etiamtum*, 'even then;' which is used regularly with the imperfect, and describes a state which existed at a former time, but has since ceased. It is to be observed that *etiamnunc* may be used with verbs in a past and future tense; as, Qua valetudine quum *etiamnunc* premeretur, C. Flaminium Cos. occidit. Corn. Nep. *Hannib.* 4. Aut ad to conferam me aut *etiamnunc* circum hæc loca commorabor. Cic. *Att.* III. 17. In this usage we may render it by our particle 'yet.' Similarly *adhuc* may be used of the relative duration of time past; thus, Scipio, quamquam gravis *adhuc* vulnere erat, tamen quarta vigilia noctis insequentis profectus ad Trebiam fluvium castra movet. Liv. XXI. 48. For 'yet' or 'still,' after a negative, the best writers use *dum*, and not *adhuc*. *Etiam dum* is rejected by many critics. *Adhuc* seems to mean *eatenus* in one or two passages, e.g., Ipse Cæsar erat *adhuc* impudens, qui exercitum et provinciam invito senatu teneret. Cic. *ad div.* XVI. 11. But generally while *adhuc* refers to time, *hactenus* and *hucusque* are used to express place or degree, 'up to this place,' 'up to this point.' The following examples illustrate the distinctions between *adhuc*, *hactenus*, *etiam nunc* and *dum*: Non commovi me *adhuc* Thessalonica; sed jam extrudimur. Cic. *Att.* III. 14. Cæsari, sicut *adhuc* feci, libentissime pro te supplicabo. Cic. *ad div.* VI. 14. Ergo hæc *hactenus:* redeo ad urbana. Cic. *Att.* V. 13. *Hactenus* fuit, quod caute a me scribi posset. Cic. *Att.* XL 4. Quum iste *etiam* cubaret, in cubiculum introductus est. Cic. *Verr.* III. 23. Quamdiu *etiam* furor iste tuus nos eludet? Cic. *Cat.* I. 1. Quæ spes si manet, *etiam* nunc salvi esse possumus. Cic. *Rosc. Com.* 52. Ille autem quid agat si scis, *neque dum* Roma es profectus, scribas ad me velim. Cic. *Att.* XIV. 10. Gabinium statim, *nihildum* suspicantem, ad me vocavi. Cic. *Cat.* III. 3.

(h) The distinction between *rursus* and *iterum* is often neglected. *Rursus* is opposed to *prorsus*, 'in the same line,' just as *transvorsus* or *trames* is opposed to *prorsus* as cutting it at right angles. Thus we have: Trepidari sentio et cursari *rursus prorsus*, 'backwards and forwards.' Ter. *Hec.* III. 1. 35. While then *rur-*

sus implies returning along the same line, *iterum* means going for a second time in the same direction (*prorsus*). Accordingly, *iterum* (αἶθις) means repetition, or doing the same again; but *rursus* (πάλιν) is reversing the operation. Hence *iterum* is generally used instead of *secunda vice*, which is barbarous, or *secundum*, *secundo*, in the sense of 'the second time;' and *iterum consul*, 'consul for the second time,' is a very common phrase by the side of *tertium* (&c.) *consul*. It is never used as a substitute for *denuo*, though this confusion is often made by modern Latinists. Nor is *denuo* ever written in its full and original form *de novo*, which is also a common moderuism. The difference between *denuo* and *de integro* is as follows: *denuo* implies that the first attempt was not complete or successful, and must be regarded as though it was not available; while *de integro* means that the act must be repeated with the same vigour as when it was first performed. Although *iterum* properly denotes only the second occurrence, we may have *iterum iterumque* of successive repetitions for any number of times (Virgil, *Æn.* II. 770). And although *rursus* properly signifies 'backwards,' it may be used to indicate the recurrence of a similar act after an interval. The following examples illustrate these usages: *Facis, ut rursus plebs in Aventinum sevocanda esse videatur.* Cic. *Mur.* 7. *Quid est autem se ipsum colligere, nisi dissipatas animi partes rursum in suum locum cogere?* Cic. *Tusc.* IV. 36. *Æstimatio, quæ ἀξία dicitur, neque in bonis numerata est, neque rursus in malis.* Cic. *Fin.* III. 10. *Nemo est, quin sæpe jactans Venerium jactum jaciat aliquando, nonnunquam etiam iterum atque tertium.* Cic. *Divin.* II. 59. *Quinto quoque anno Sicilia censetur. Censa erat prætore Peducæo. Quintus annus quum te prætore incidisset, censa denuo est.* Cic. *Verr.* II. 56. *Quæ deinde interceptio poculi? cur non de integro datum?* Cic. *Cluent.* 60.

(E)

Of the adverbs which introduce the qualification of manner or degree, the following require particular attention on the part of the student:

(a) The adverbs expressing the highest degree may be thus distinguished: *plane* is 'quite,' 'entirely,' opposed to 'almost' (*pæne, propemodum*), or 'scarcely' (*vix*); *omnino*, 'altogether,' 'in all,' is opposed to 'in part' (*ex parte*); *prorsus* (*proversus*), 'all through,' 'throughout,' 'in short,' 'absolutely,' is a general summing up opposed to general statements; *utique*, 'howsoever,' 'in any case,' which is also a concessive or affirmative particle, implies that something holds good or must be done, whatever else may possibly occur, and in Cicero at least is generally used with the subjunctive or imperative; *penitus*, 'thoroughly,' 'deeply,' 'to the very bottom,' is opposed to 'superficially,' 'on the surface.' Thus we have: Effice id, quod jam propemodum, vel *plane* potius effeceram. Cic. *Brut.* 97. Has res sustinere *vix* possum, vel *plane* nullo modo possum. Cic. *Att.* XI. 9. Defensionum laboribus senatoriisque muneribus aut omnino, aut magna ex parte liberatus sum. Cic. *Tusc.* I. 1. Sane frequentes fuimus, omnino ad ducentos. Cic. *Qu. Fr.* II. 1. Si id dicis, nihil esse mundo sapientius, nullo modo prorsus assentior. Cic. *N. D.* III. 8. In philosophos vestros si quando incidi, verbum prorsus nullum intelligo. Cic. *Or.* II. 14. Quo die venies, *utique* cum tuis apud me sis. Cic. *Att.* IV. 4. Si quid acciderit, quid censens mihi faciendum, *utique* scribito. Cic. *Att.* X. 1. *Penitus* ex intima philosophia hauriendam juris disciplinam putas. Cic. *Leg.* I. 5. Euhemerus videtur relligionem *penitus* totam sustulisse. Cic. *N. D.* I. 42.

(b) *Valde* is 'very much,' and is used both with adjectives and verbs; *perquam* means 'in an extraordinary degree,' 'exceedingly;' *admodum* is 'to a considerable extent,' and may be used with numerals and *nihil*; as, mille *admodum* occidit, Liv. XXVII. 30, 'quite a thousand;' *magnopere*, 'greatly,' is generally used with verbs. The other adverbs expressing different degrees of exaggeration, as *mire*, *mirifice*, *mirum quantum*, *eximie*, *vehementer*, do not admit of accurate discrimination. The same may be said of *oppido*, which is a rare synonym of *plane*. The following examples illustrate *valde*, *perquam*, *admodum*, and *magnopere*: De Hispania novi nihil; sed exspectatio *valde* magna. Cic. *ad div.* XV. 17. Gaudeo, vos significare literis, quam *valde* probetis ea, quæ apud Corfinium sunt gesta. Cic. *Att.* IX. 6. Ille, quam ille, dignior: *perquam* grave est dictu. Cic. *Planc.* 6. *Perquam* flebiliter lamentatur. Cic. *Tusc.* II. 21. Equidem etiam *admodum* adolescentis Rutilii familiaritate delector. Cic. *Am.* 27. Alter non multum, alter nihil *admodum* scripti reliquit. Cic. *Or.* II. 2. Hi me *admodum* diligunt. Cic. *ad div.* IV. 13. *Magnopere* volo. Cic. *ad div.* II. 6. Ut nunc est, nulla *magnopere* exspectatio est. Cic. *ad div.* VIII. 1. *Magnopere* is frequently divided into its two parts; thus, Quum puerorum formas *magno* hic *opere* miraretur. Cic. *Invent.* II. 1. We have also *majore opere* and *maximopere* or *maximo opere*.

(c) The distinctions of *satis*, *affatim* and *abunde*, as given in the list, are illustrated by the following examples: Sum avidior, quam *satis* est, gloriæ. Cic. *ad div.* IX. 14. Hæc hominibus *satis* multa esse debent. Cic. *Rab. Posth.* 16. *Satis* temporis habere. Cic. *Verr.* II. 1. Seminibus et homines *affatim* vescuntur, et terræ ejusdem generis stirpium renovatione complentur. Cic. *N. D.* II. 51. *Satis* est et *affatim* prorsus. Cic. *Att.* XVI. 1. Puto, me Dicæarcho *affatim satis* fecisse. Cic. *Att.* II. 10. Toti huic quæstioni *abunde* satisfactum erit. Cic. *ad div.* II. 1.

(d) *Apprime* (which belongs rather to the older Latinity) and *imprimis* apply to a distinction in some quality possessed in common with other persons, and indeed with the foremost of the class; *praecipue* is opposed to *communiter*, and does not admit that there is the same classification; it therefore means more than *apprime* and *imprimis*; *praesertim* is used to mark a special ground or condition; hence we have *praesertim quum*, *praesertim si*, though the conjunction may be omitted, and the ground or condition may be expressed by an adjective or participle; *potissimum*, which differs from all the adverbs just mentioned, has the same signification in reference to many that *potius* has in reference to two, namely, the separation and exaltation of some one person or act to the exclusion of all others; *maxime* does not involve any comparison, but merely strengthens the predicate. Thus we have: Albutius homo *apprime* doctus. Varro, *R. R.* III. 2. Id arbitror in vita *apprime* esse utile, ut ne quid nimis. Ter. *Andr.* L 1. 34. Lentulum quum ceteris artibus, tum *imprimis* imitatione tui fac erudias: quem nos *imprimis* amamus earumque habemus. Cic. *ad div.* I. 7. Auditor Platonis Ponticus Heraclides, vir doctus *imprimis*. Cic. *Tusc.* V. 3. Labor in hoc defendendo *praecipue* meus est, studium vero conservandi hominis *commune* mihi vobiscum esse debebit. Cic. *Rab. Posth.* 1. Dicendi ars in omni libero populo, maximeque in pacatis tranquillisque civitatibus, *praecipue* semper floruit semperque dominata est. Cic. *Or.* I. 8. Sera gratulatio reprehendi non solet, *praesertim* si nulla negligentia praetermissa est. Cic. *ad div.* II. 7. Non tam ista me sapientiæ fama delectat, falsa *praesertim* (i. e. præsertim si falsa est). Cic. *Am.* 4. E quibus (philosophandi generibus) nos id *potissimum* consecuti sumus, quo Socratem usum arbitramur. Cic. *Tusc.* v. 4. Missi sunt, qui consulerent Apollinem, quo *potissimum* duce uterentur. Nep. *Milt.* I. Hoc ad rem mea sententia *maxime* pertinet. Cic. *Rosc. Am.* 31.

(e) *Æque* and *pariter* (with *atque, ac*) denote an actual equality, the former of validity, and the latter of efficacy; *perinde ac*, on the other hand, indicates only an assumed or supposed equality. *Tanquam*, 'as though,' 'as much as,' *quasi*, 'as if' (for *quam si*¹), and *tanquam si*, 'as much as if,' denote not an equality, but a comparison; but while *tanquam* generally requires the expression of something corresponding to the antecedent *tam*, we may have *quasi* alone; thus we might say, *est quasi parens*, where *tanquam* could not stand, but would require some adjunct, as in *est benignus tanquam parens*, i. e. *tam benignus quam parens*. Thus, Præsens me adjuvare potuisses et consolando et prope *aeque* dolendo. Cic. *ad div.* IV. 6. Me colit et observat *aeque* atque illum ipsum suum patronum. Cic. *ad div.* XIII. 69. De industria elaboratur, ut verba verbis quasi dimensa respondeant...et ut *pariter* extrema terminentur eundemque referant in cadendo sonum. Cic. *Or.* 12. Domi tuæ *pariter* accusatorum atque judicum greges videt. Cic. *Par.* VI. 2. Brutus illud non *perinde* atque ego putaram, arripere visus est. Cic. *Att.* XVI. 5. Is, qui pecuniam debuerit, *perinde* habeatur, *quasi* eam pecuniam acceperit. Cic. *Leg.* II. 19. E vita discedo, *tamquam* (just as) ex hospitio. Cic. *Sen.* 23. Dolabella quod scripsi, videas suadeo, *tamquam* si tua res agatur. Cic. *ad div.* II. 16. Artium omnium *quasi* (to a certain extent) parens philosophia judicatur. Cic. *Or.* 1. 3.

Obs. It is to be observed that, while *atque* or *ac* is used after words expressing equality or difference, when the degree is indicated, we have *quam* instead of *atque* or *ac*, when a negative precedes *alius* or *aeque*. Thus we have *ac* after *aeque, juxta* and *par, pariter, perinde* and *proinde, pro eo, similis* and *dissimilis, similiter, alius, aliter, talis, idem, totidem, contra, secus, contrarius*, in such phrases as Dissimulatio est quum *alia* dicuntur *ac* sentias. Virtus *eadem* in homine *ac* Deo est. *Simile* fecit *atque* alii. Honos *talis* paucis delatus est *ac* mihi. But we have *quam* in such phrases as Virtus nihil *aliud* est *quam* in se perfecta natura. Nihil *aeque* eos terruit, *quam* robur et calor im-

¹ We have *quamsi* for *quasi* in the *Lex Thoria*, see *Varron.* p. 281, L 34, 3rd Ed.

peratoria. Nihil *aliud* agit *quam* ut *non* decipiat. Neque id *aliter* fieri potest, *quam* si omnes nervos contenderis. We have *quam* after *perinde* without a negative in Tacit. *Ann.* VI. 30; *perinde ac quam* Tiberium falli potuisse.

(f) *Aliter* is the common particle for expressing difference of manner; it may be strengthened by *multo* or *longe*; it may be used comparatively, as already explained, with *atque* (*ac*) or *quam*; *non aliter quam si* occurs, though not in any prose-writer earlier than Livy, in the sense 'just as if,' and the jurists use *non aliter ac si* in the same manner. It is certain that in the best writers *alias* is as much an adverb of time as *alibi* is an adverb of place; but in later authors, as Pliny, it means 'in other respects,' and modern Latinists often follow this mistaken usage. This meaning is given by *alioqui*(*n*), in Livy and later writers; thus, Triumphatum de Tiburtibus; *alioquin* mitis victoria fuit, Liv. VII, 19, 'in other respects the victory was gently used.' But Cicero uses *alioqui*(*n*) much in the same way as *aliter*, 'otherwise,' 'else;' thus, Credo minimum olim istius rei fuisse cupiditatem: *alioquin* multa exstarent exempla majorum, 'otherwise there would be many examples.' To signify 'in other respects,' Cicero generally uses *ceterum* or *ceteroqui*. To imply that the circumstance is not only otherwise, but wrongly so, we use *secus*. A provisional exception is expressed by *aliter nisi*, 'except on the condition.' The following examples will illustrate these distinctions: *Alias* pluribus; nunc ad institutam disputationem revertamur. Cic. *Divin.* II. 2. Ego in Cumano et in Pompeiano praeterquam quod sine te, *ceterum* satis commode me oblectabam. Cic. *Qu. Fr.* II. 15. Falernum mihi semper visum est idoneum deversorio; si modo tecti satis est ad comitatum nostrum recipiendum. *Ceteroquin* mihi locus non displicet. Cic. *ad div.* VI. 19. Tu si *aliter* existimes, nihil ernbis. Cic. *ad div.* III. 7. Jus semper est aequabile; neque enim *aliter* jus esset. Cic. *Off.* II. 12. Tecum agam non *secus* ac si meus frater esses. Cic. *Mur.* 4. Recte an *secus* faciant, nihil ad nos. Cic. *Fin.* 28. Nobis *aliter* videtur; recte *secus*ne postea. Cic. *Fin.* III. 13. Quod *aliter* non potest fieri, *nisi* spatium habuero. Cic. *ad div.* XII. 14.

(g) *Fere* is used to deprecate an expectation of accuracy, as when it is used with a definite number, in the sense 'about,' when *circiter* is also used; or with *ad*, if we wish to intimate that the amount was approached rather than equalled. So also *fere fit* would mean that the circumstance generally, not always, happens; *nemo fere* means 'hardly any one.' *Ferme* has much the same signification as *fere*; but although it is often used by Livy and later writers, Cicero hardly ever employs it except in a negative sentence. *Paene*, 'almost,' and *prope* or *propemodum*, 'nearly,' qualify a strong expression, or intimate that something is still wanting, or that there is only an approximation to the truth. Thus, Probabile est, quod *fere* fieri solet. Cic. *Inv.* t. 29. Ex victoria bellica non *fere* quemquam est invidia civium consecuta. Cic. *Sest.* 51. Brutum abjectum, quantum potui, excitavi: quem non minus amo, quam tu, *paene* dixi, quam te. Cic. *Att.* v. 20, post med. Dicendi Latine maturitas jam ad summum *paene* perducta est, ut eo nihil *ferme* quisquam addere possit, nisi qui a philosophia, a jure civili, ab historia fuerit instructior. Cic. *Brut.* 43. *Prope* desperatis his rebus te in Græciam contulisti. Cic. *ad div.* VII. 28. *Propemodum* justioribus utimur illis, qui omnino avocant a philosophia. Cic. *Fin.* I. 1.

(h) *Forte* by itself denotes merely 'by chance,' like *casu*, which is opposed to *consulto*, 'designedly,' 'intentionally;' it sometimes approaches in meaning to *temere*, 'at random,' and to *fortuito*, which is opposed to *causa*; and *forte fortuna* means 'by good luck.' If, however, *forte* is combined with *ne, num, si, nisi, quo*, &c., it may be rendered 'perhaps,' 'perchance.' Otherwise, we must use *fortasse* and *forsitan* to express mere possibility of occurrence; and with this distinction, that while *fortasse*, which is generally used with the indicative, intimates that there are probable grounds for our belief, *forsitan*, even in the few cases in which it is found with an indicative, generally implies that there is only a possibility; or it is used in anticipating some objection which is answered in a sentence beginning with *sed* or *rerum tamen*. A sentence often begins with *et* (*ac, aut*) *fortasse*. It has been mentioned above (108, (A), (a)) that *haud scio an* indicates a belief that the thing is so. Thus, *fortasse rerum est* is 'perhaps it is true— it is probably true;' *forsitan verum sit* is 'it may be true perhaps —it is possibly true;' *haud scio an verum sit* is 'I think it is true, though I will not positively assert it.' The following examples illustrate the distinctions between *forte, fortasse,* and *forsitan:* Est, est profecto illa vis divina; nisi *forte* idcirco esse non putant, quia non apparet, nec cernitur. Cic. *Mil.* 31. Heri veni in Cumanum;

cras ad te *fortasse*. Cic. *ad div.* IX. 23. Raras tuas quidem (*fortasse* non perferuntur), sed suaves accipio literas. Cic. *ad div.* II. 5. *Forsitan* quærratis, qui iste furor sit et quæ tanta formido. Cic. *Rosc. Am.* 11. *Forsitan* meliores illi accusatores habendi sunt; sed ego defensorem in mea persona, non accusatorem, maxime laudari volo. Cic. *Verr.* I. 38.

(i) *Frustra, nequidquam*, and *incassum* are all translated 'in vain,' but with the following distinction: *frustra* implies the disappointment of the *agent; nequidquam* refers to the *thing* which has been unsuccessfully attempted; and *incassum* ('into emptiness,' also *casse*, 'emptily,' Liv. XXIV. 26) intimates that the undertaking was idle from the first,—that it was only a beating of the air. Thus we have: Neque enim ipse auxilium suum sæpe a viris bonis *frustra* implorari patietur, neque id æquo animo feret civitas. Cic. *Or.* II. 35. Dic, inquam, diem. Pudet dicere. Intelligo; verum et sero et *nequidquam* pudet. Cic. *Quint.* 25. Senatus *nequidquam* Pompeii auxilium imploraturus est. Cæs. *B. C.* I. 1. *Incassum* missæ preces. Liv. II. 49. Galli vana *incassum* tela jactare. Liv. X. 29. If we compare the first and third of these examples, we shall see that the *frustra auxilium implorari* refers to the fruitlessness of the request, and the *nequidquam auxilium implorare* to the ill-success of the application. *Incassum*, which is a figurative expression, does not seem to occur in Cicero. It is to be observed that *frustra* occasionally indicates that want of proper forethought which leads to the frustration of a design, so that it is equivalent to *sine consilio, temere;* thus, Nec *frustra* ac sine causa quid facere dignum Deo est. Cic. *Divin.* II. 60. And in the comic poets *frustra habere* (=*fraudem facere*) is ' to deceive,' and *frustra esse* is ' to be deceived.'

(k) *Modo*, the same as the temporal particle, signifying 'just now' (108, (c), (D), (b)), is used also as a particle of restriction in the sense 'only.' As it originally means 'grant me' (*mi dato*), it is properly used before *ut, ne*, &c., and with imperatives and subjunctives. *Tantum*, which properly denotes ' so much,' is used in the sense ' so much only,' to oppose the part to the whole. *Solum*, ' alone,' opposes the thing itself to all others as one of a number of different objects. Both *tantum* and *solum* may have *modo* added, but *solummodo* is not used by writers of the best ages. *Nonnisi* gives the sense of 'only' in a conditional sentence. *Dumtaxat* ('provided one estimates it,' i.e. *dum aliquis taxat*) denotes 'only,' as expressing a limitation in the judgment of the speaker; it means, therefore, 'not less than,' i.e. 'at least;' or 'not more than,' i.e. 'at most.' Thus we have: Veniat *modo*, explicet suum illud volumen. Cic. *Rosc. Am.* 35. Vide *modo*. Cic. *Caecil.* 14. Videtur posse opprimi, *modo* ut salva urbe. Cic. *ad div.* XVI. 12. In hac arte, si *modo* est ars, nullum est præceptum, quomodo verum inveniatur. Cic. *Or.* II. 33. Nomen *tantum* virtutis usurpas; quid ipsa valeat ignoras. Cic. *Par.* 2. Dixit *tantum;* nihil ostendit. Cic. *Flacc.* 15. Quasi vero atra bile *solum*, ac non sæpe vel iracundia graviore, vel timore, vel dolore moveatur. Cic. *Tusc.* III. 5. Amicitia *nisi* inter bonos esse *non* potest. Cic. *Am.* 5. Antonius *nil nisi* de rei publicæ pernicie cogitabat. Cic. *Phil.* IV. 2. Hac tamen in oppressione sermo in circulis *dumtaxat* et conviviis est liberior, quam fuit. Cic. *Att.* II. 18. Valde me Athenæ delectarunt, urbs *dumtaxat* et urbis ornamentum. Cic. *Att.* V. 10. *Non modo —sed* or *non solum—sed* may be used like our 'not only—but.' If, however, the propositions are negative, and both clauses have a common verb, *non modo—sed ne-quidem* is used for *non modo non —sed ne-quidem*. Otherwise *non modo non* is expressed in the first clause; and *non modo nullus, nihil, nemo, nunquam, nusquam*, are the general forms, even when both clauses are negative. Thus we have: In privatis rebus si quis rem mandatam *non modo* malitiosius gessisset, sui quæstus aut commodi causa, *verum etiam* negligentius; eum majores summum admisisse dedecus existimabant. Cic. *Rosc. Am.* 38. O rem indignam, in qua *non modo* docti, *verum etiam* agrestes erubescant! Cic. *Leg.* I. 14. Tullus Hostilius *non solum* proximo regi dissimilis, *sed* ferocior *etiam* Romulo fuit. Liv. I. 22. Qua in re Cæsar *non solum* publicas, *sed etiam* privatas injurias ultus est. Cæs. *B. G.* I. 12. Tu non *solum* ad negligendas leges et quæstiones, *verum etiam* ad evertendas perfringendasque voluisti. Cic. *Cat.* I. 7. Talis vir *non modo* facere, *sed ne* cogitare *quidem* quidquam audebit, quod non honestum sit. Cic. *Off.* III. 19. Regnum video, *non modo* Romano homini, *sed ne* Persæ *quidem* cuiquam tolerabile. Cic. *Att.* X. 8. If the negative in the first clause belongs to a single verb, it must necessarily stand by itself after *non modo*. Thus we have: Cæsaris ac Pompeii *non modo* res gestas *non* antepono meis, *sed ne* fortunam *quidem* ipsam. Cic. *Att.* X. 4.

§ 2. *Prepositions.*

109 Prepositions are merely adverbs used in connexion with cases of the noun, from which they derive their principal application. The doctrine of the cases belongs to syntax; but the meaning of the prepositions may be explained here.

(a) *A (ab, absque), ad, adversus, apud, versus.*

A or *ab* (more rarely *absque*, which signifies 'without') denotes separation or removal from the side or surface of an object; it may generally be rendered by 'from' or 'by,' and takes the ablative. As the act of separating implies nearness at the time of separation, we find that *a* (*ab*) is used to express relative positions, as *a fronte*, 'in front,' *a tergo*, 'behind;' and our word 'amanuensis' comes from the Latin phrase for a secretary: *libertus a manu*, 'a freed-man at the hand,' i. e. 'who had to do with writing.'

Ad signifies the act of addition, or motion with a view to conjunction or juxtaposition; it may generally be rendered by 'to' or 'at,' and takes the accusative. It is often combined with *versus* or *versum* in the sense of 'towards' or 'against,' as *adversus leges*, 'against the laws.' And *versus* alone may be used with names of places; as *Brundisium versus*, 'towards Brundisium.'

Apud, which is compounded of *ab* and *ad*, combines the meanings of these two prepositions, for it signifies 'being by the side of but not part of an object,' and this implies both juxtaposition and separation; it may generally be rendered by 'at' or 'with,' and always takes the accusative.

(b) *Ante, in, inter, intra.*

In denotes position 'upon' or 'within' an object. It takes an accusative when it denotes 'into,' 'unto,' 'to,' and an ablative when it signifies 'in' or 'upon.' In the former case it may be followed by *versus*, as in *Galliam versus*, 'towards Gaul.'

Inter signifies 'between' or 'among,' and governs the accusative. It is also used to express mutual agency, as *inter se diligunt*, 'they love one another.'

Intra, which is only another form of *inter*, means 'within,' and governs the accusative.

Ante means 'before,' in place, time, or degree, and takes the accusative.

(c) *De, e (ex), extra.*

E or *ex* denotes motion from the interior of an object; it may generally be rendered 'out of,' and takes the ablative.

Extra, 'beyond' or 'without,' is the opposite of *intra*, and like it takes the accusative.

De implies descent and derivation, and takes the ablative. Its proper meaning is 'down from,' as *de rostris descendit*, 'he came down from the pulpit;' but it is very commonly used to denote the subject from which an action or writing is derived, i. e. the source of agency; thus, *scripsit de republica*, 'he wrote about or concerning the commonwealth,' that was the source or subject from which he derived his book.

(d) *Cis (citra), circa (circum, circiter), trans, ultra.*

Cis or *citra*, 'on this side,' and its opposites *ultra*, 'on that side,' 'beyond,' and *trans*, 'across,' take the accusative.

Circa, circum, 'around' or 'about,' express approximate nearness in space or time. The derivative *circiter* denotes indefinite time or number. These take the accusative.

(e) *Contra, erga.*

Contra, 'against,' and its opposite *erga*, 'towards' (of affection), take the accusative.

(f) *Juxta, ob, pĕnes, prŏpe, propter.*

Juxta, 'close to,' and *pĕnes*, 'in the power of,' approach in meaning to *apud*, and take the accusative.

Ob properly means circumposition at some height from the ground, i. e. 'upon' (whence *op-timus*, 'uppermost'), but is practically used, like *propter*, with the accusative, to signify 'on account of.' *Ob* also means 'before,' and *propter*, like *prope*, from which it is derived, and which also takes the accusative, signifies 'near.'

(g) *Per, prae, praeter, pro.*

Per denotes 'through,' either in space or time, or as the instrument. It takes the accusative.

Pro, which signifies 'for,' 'before,' or 'proportionally to,' and *prae*, which denotes 'before,' 'in comparison with,' and 'owing to,' take the ablative. The derivative *praeter*, 'before,' 'beside,' 'beyond,' or 'except,' takes the accusative.

12—2

UNDECLINED WORDS.

(h) *Cum, pone, post, secundum, sine.*

Post, 'after,' 'behind,' or 'since,' and *pone,* 'behind,' take the accusative.

Cum, 'with,' and *sine,* 'without,' take the ablative.

Secundum, 'along,' 'according to,' 'following the course of,' sometimes agrees in meaning with *cum,* and sometimes with *post.* It takes the accusative.

(i) *Clam, coram.*

Clam, 'without the knowledge of,' 'concealed from,' stands in a sort of opposition to *coram,* 'in the presence of,' 'before the eyes of,' and both take the ablative.

(k) *Infra, sub, subter, super, supra.*

Sub, 'under,' and *super,* 'above;' take the accusative when they denote motion, and the ablative when they imply rest. *Supra,* 'above,' is always used with the accusative, and *subter,* 'under,' generally with the accusative, but occasionally with the ablative. *Infra,* 'beneath,' is always construed with the accusative.

110. It may be desirable to illustrate by a few examples the distinctions in meaning of these prepositions, which are most nearly synonymous, in regard to the English prepositions by which they are generally expressed.

(a) The preposition 'from' may be used to render by *a (ab), abs, de, e (ex),* but with marked differences of meaning or reference. For *a* refers to the exterior, or to the thing regarded as a whole; *de* to an elevation; and *e (ex),* generally and properly, to the interior. These distinctions are given in the following passage: Quum *de* vi interdicitur, duo genera causarum esse intelligebant, ad quæ interdictum pertineret; unum si qui *ex* eo loco, in quo esset; alterum si *ab* eo loco, quo veniret, vi dejectus esset...Si qui meam familiam *de* meo fundo dejecerit, *ex* eo loco me dejecerit. Si qui mihi præsto fuerit cum armatis hominibus extra meum fundum, et me introire prohibuerit; non *ex* eo loco, sed *ab* eo loco me dejecerit... Unde utrumque declarat, et *ex* quo loco, et *a* quo loco. Unde dejectus Cinna? *Ex* urbe. Unde dejecti Galli? *A* Capitolio. Unde qui cum Graccho fuerunt? *Ex* Capitolio, &c. Cic. *Cæcin.* 30.

(b) *Ad, apud, penes, juxta, propter* may all be rendered by the synonymous expressions 'at,' 'with,' 'by,' or 'close by;' but with these distinctions: *ad* denotes the approximation or proximity chiefly with reference to place or time; *apud* denotes approximation or proximity chiefly with reference to a person; *penes*, which is limited to a person, implies not only proximity, but dependence on his will or power; *juxta*, for which Cicero uses *propter*, is used only with inanimate objects. Thus, Deinde iter faciam *ad* exercitum, ut circiter Idus Sextiles putem me *ad* Iconium fore. Cic. *ad div.* fIL 5. Ab hora octava *ad* vesperum secreto collocuti sumus. Cic. *Att.* VII. 8. Fuisti *apud* Lcccam illa nocte. Cic. *Cat.* I. 4. Hoc *apud* Platonem est in philosophos dictum. Cic. *Off.* I. 9. *Apud* eosdem judices reus est factus. Cic. *Cluent.* 22. Hi servi centum dies *penes* accusatorem (in his house, in his power) quum fuissent, ab eo ipso accusatore producti sunt. Cic. *Mil.* 22. Eloquentia non modo eos ornat, *penes* quos est, sed etiam universam rem publicam. Cic. *Or.* 41. Atticus sepultus est *juxta* viam Appiam *ad* quintum lapidem. Nep. *Att.* 22. *Propter* Platonis statuam consedimus. Cic. *Brut.* 6.

(c) *Adversus, in, contra* may all be rendered by 'against,' and *adversus, in, erga* may all be rendered 'towards,' a rendering, which, in a certain sense, may also be applied to *contra;* but while *adversus* (and *versus*) or *in* may retain their original meaning of actual motion towards a place, *contra* and *erga*, especially the latter, are used in a secondary sense, namely, *contra* implies 'against' or 'towards,' in a hostile signification, *erga* has this meaning with a friendly reference. *Adversus* and *in* may be used generally in the expression of kindly feelings or the reverse. Thus, Quonam modo me gererem *adversus* Cæsarem, usus tuo consilio sum. Cic. *ad div.* XI. 27. Manlius perindulgens fuit *in* patrem; idem acerbe severus *in* filium. Cic. *Off.* III. 31. Te ex Asia Romam *versus* profectum esse constabat. Cic. *ad div.* II. 6. Detrahere aliquid alteri est *contra* naturam. Cic. *Off.* III. 5. Ea nos utimur *pro* salute bonorum *contra* amentiam perditorum. Cic. *Mil.* 5. Præcipiunt, ut eodem modo *erga* amicos affecti simus, quo *erga* nosmet ipsos. Cic. *Am.* 10.

(d) *Ante, prae, coram* may all be rendered 'before;' but while *ante* signifies 'before' in space or time, *prae* is 'before' with an implication of direct contrast and comparison; and *coram* is used specially of some person, before him, in his presence or sight, in conversation with him. When we speak of appearing 'before the people,' 'before the court,' &c., we must use *apud*. The phrase *prae se ferre* is very common in the sense 'to carry before us, to exhibit,' and *prae* has often a causal signification. As denoting a contrast or comparison we may have *praeter ceteros* for *prae ceteris*, and this is a various reading in the passage from Cic. *Am.* 1, quoted below. But Cicero and Caesar avoid *ante ceteros* in this sense, though the phrase is found in Livy. The following are examples: *Ante* tribunal tuum, M. Fanni, *ante* pedes vestros, judices, caedes futurae sunt. Cic. *Rosc. Am.* 5. Jam *ante* Socratem omnes paene veteres ad ignorationis confessionem adducti sunt. Cic. *Ac.* I. 12. Comitia in *ante* diem VI. Kal. Sextil. dilata sunt. Cic. *Att.* I. 16. Beata vita praedicanda et *prae* se ferenda est. Cic. *Tusc.* V. 17. Stillantem *prae* se pugionem tulit. Cic. *Phil.* II. 12. Romani *prae* sua Capua irridebunt. Cic. *Agr.* II. 35. Cato in ipsa senectute *prae* ceteris floruit. Cic. *Am.* I. Solem *prae* jaculorum multitudine et sagittarum non videbitis. Cic. *Tusc.* I. 42. *Prae* gaudio ubi sim nescio. Ter. *Heaut.* II. 3. 67. Reliqua *prae* lacrimis scribere non possum. Cic. *Att.* IX. 12. Mihi ipsi *coram* genero meo quae dicere ausus es? Cic. *Pis.* 6. *Coram* tecum eadem haec agere conantem me deterruit pudor. Cic. *ad div.* V. 12.

(e) *Pone, post,* and *secundum* may all be rendered 'after;' but *pone,* which is of comparatively rare occurrence, is used only of place; *post,* as the opposite of *ante,* is used both of place and time; and *secundum* means 'next,' or 'immediately after,' 'closely following,' 'in the steps of,' 'according to,' and is not used of time. Thus, Totum animal movebatur et ante et *pone.* Cic. *Tim.* 13. Nam sic fac existimes, *post* has miserias nihil esse actum aliud cum dignitate. Cic. *ad div.* IV. 4. Repente *post* tergum equitatus cernitur. Caes. *B. G.* VII. 88. Proxime et *secundum* deos homines hominibus maxime utiles esse possunt. Cic. *Off.* II. 3. Vultus *secundum* vocem plurimum potest. Cic. *Or.* 18. Finis bonorum est *secundum* naturam vivere. Cic. *Fin.* V. 9.

(f) *Circum, circa, circiter* may all be rendered 'about;' but while *circum* implies actual motion in a circle about an object, *circa* merely denotes the vicinity within a certain circle; and *circiter,* in Cicero, corresponds to our 'about' or 'nearly' in an estimate of time. Livy uses *circa* also in this sense. Thus we

have: Terra *circum* axem se summa celeritate convertit. Cic. *Ac.*
II. 39. Nævius pueros *circum* amicos dimittit. Cic. *Quint.* 6.
Verres multa sibi opus esse aiebat, multa canibus suis, quos *circa* se
haberet. Cic. *Verr.* I. 48. Nos *circiter* Kalendas aut in Formiano
erimus aut in Pompeiano. Cic. *Att.* II. 4.

(g) *Cis* and *citra, in* and *intra, sub* and *infra*, all signify
'within,' in reference to an outer limit designated in the first
case by *trans* and *ultra*, in the second by *ex* and *extra*, in the
third by *super* and *supra*. But there are several distinctions to
be noticed. In the first class of opposites *cis, citra*, mean 'within,'
and *trans, ultra*, 'without,' 'on this or that side of a boundary
line,' in reference to horizontal extension; in the second class *in,
intra*, mean 'within,' and *ex, extra*, 'without,' in reference to a
surrounding circle; in the third class *sub* and *infra* mean 'within,'
and *super, supra*, mean 'without,' in reference to a boundary line
above us. And in the same class we distinguish *cis, trans, in,
ex, sub, super*, as indicating that which is nearer with reference
to a defined locality, from *citra, ultra, intra, extra, infra, supra*,
which do not imply a definition of the place; for example, *cis
Alpes, trans Alpes*, indicate local proximity to the Alps on this
or that side of the mountains, but *citra Alpes*, means anywhere
between us and the Alps, and *ultra* may denote any extent beyond. When we say *in urbe* or *ex urbe*, we consider the city
as a point, and therefore the locality indicated is sufficiently defined; but if we write *intra* or *extra urbem*, we regard only the
outer bounds indicated, and do not refer to any definite place
within those limits. When we use *sub* and *super*, we presume
a proximity to the objects above and below respectively; but
when we write *infra* and *supra*, any distance from the limits
given may be implied. Thus, Me omnium illarum diœcesium,
quæ *cis* Taurum sunt, omniumque earum civitatum magistratus
legationesque conveniebant. Cic. *ad div.* III. 8. Gallia *Ci*salpina,
*Cis*padana; *Trans*alpina, *Trans*padana. Decretum est, ut exercitum *citra* flumen Rubiconem educeret, dum ne propius urbem
Romam CC millia admoveret. Cic. *Phil.* VI. 3. Belgæ proximi sunt
Germanis, qui *trans* Rhenum incolunt. Cæs. *B. G.* I. 1. Cæsar
paulo *ultra* eum locum castra transtulit. Cæs. *B. C.* III. 66. Memi-
nistine me hoc dicere *in* senatu? Cic. *Cat.* I. 3. *Intra* parietes
meos de mea pernicie consilia inibantur. Cic. *Att.* III. 10. Ampius.

conatus erat tollere pecuniam Epheso *ex* fano Dianæ, ejusque rei causa senatores omnes *ex* provincia evocaverat. Cæs. *B. C.* III. 105. Apud Germanos latrocinia nullam habent infamiam, quæ *extra* fines cujusque civitatis fiunt. Cæs. *B. G.* VI. 23. *Sub* radicibus montis vi summa prœlium commiserunt. Nep. *Mil.* 5. Res quædam ita sunt parvæ, ut *sub* sensum cadere non possint. Cic. *Ac.* I. 8. *Infra* lunam nihil est, nisi mortale et caducum; *supra* lunam sunt æterna omnia. Cic. *Rep.* VI. 17. Demetrius *super* terræ tumulum noluit quid statui, nisi columellam, tribus cubitis ne altiorem. Cic. *Leg.* II. 20. To indicate the place at table the proper words are *supra* and *infra*. *Supra* me Atticus accubuerat, *infra* Verrius. Cic. *ad div.* IX. 20.

(h) The following pairs of words may be rendered respectively by the same English prepositions: *in, inter,* 'among;' *sub, subter,* 'under;' *præ, præter,* 'before;' *prope, propter,* 'near;' but the first in each pair indicate *a point*, and the second *an extension*; compare the compound verbs *interjicere, subterfugere, prætermittere,* with *injicere, suffugere, præmittere,* and the following examples of the separate prepositions: Codrus so *in* medios inimisit hostes. Cic. *Tusc.* I. 48. Classis communis Græciæ *inter* Eubœam continentemque terram cum classiariis regiis conflixit. Nep. *Them.* 3. Virtus omnia, quæ calere in hominem possunt, *subter* se habet. Cic. *Tusc.* V. 1. *Subter* tertium orbem mediam fere regionem sol obtinet. Cic. *Rep.* VI. 17. Servi hæc omnia *præter* oculos Lollii ferebant. Cic. *Verr.* III. 35.

(i) Both *usque ad* and *tenus* may be rendered 'up to,' 'as far as;' but *usque ad* (sometimes *ad* or *usque* alone) denotes both the extension and the direction; it stands always with reference to the starting-point, generally indicated by the preposition *a (ab)*; and it may refer to time as well as space; on the other hand, *tenus* denotes only the further limit, the nearer being assumed as known, and refers only to space. In the phrase *verbo tenus*, we understand 'only as far as words go' in opposition to the truth. The following are examples: Ab hora octava *ad* vesperum secreto colloquuti sumus. Cic. *Att.* VII. 8. Nihil difficilius est, quam amicitiam *usque ad* extremum vitæ spiritum permanere. Cic. *Am.* 10. *Usque* Ennam profecti sunt. Cic. *Verr.* IV. 49. Antiochus Magnus Tauro *tenus* regnare jussus est. Cic. *Deiot.* 13. Nam veteres *verbo tenus,* acute illi quidem, sed non ad hunc usum popularem atque civilem de re publica disscrebant. Cic. *Leg.* III. 0.

(k) *Ob, propter, causa,* and even *de* and *per* may be rendered 'on account of;' but *ob* denotes the cause or reason as it appears to our mind; *propter* the real or actual ground; *causa* the motive alleged or supposed: and when *de* is rendered 'on account of,' we mean the immediate occasion, and when *per me* is rendered 'on my account,' we mean that there is a permission or hindrance to be accounted for. The preposition *ob* is frequently used with the words *res* and *causa,* as *quam ob rem, hanc ob causam,* &c. The following are examples: *Ob* aliquod emolumentum suum cupidius dicere videntur. Cic. *Font.* 8. Multa mihi veniebant in mentem, quam *ob* rem istum laborem tibi honori fore putarent. Cic. *ad div.* III. 10. Tironem *propter* humanitatem malo salvum, quam *propter* usum meum. Cic. *Att.* VII. 5. Me autem, *propter* quem ceteri liberi sunt, tibi liberum non visum demiror. Cic. *ad div.* VII. 27. Qui sui defendendi *causa* telo est usus, non hominis occidendi *causa* telum habuisse putatur. Cic. *Mil.* 4. Sophistæ appellabantur ii, qui ostentationis aut quæstus *causa* philosophabantur. Cic. *Ac.* II. 33. Flebat uterque non *de* suo supplicio, sed pater *de* filii morte, *de* patris filius. Cic. *Verr.* I. 30. His *per* to frui libertate non licet. Cic. *Flacc.* 29. Consequatur summas voluptates, non modo parvo, sed *per* me nihilo, si potest. Cic. *Fin.* II. 48.

111 Most of the prepositions are used in composition, and generally add their own meaning to that of the verb; they are occasionally affected by the contact. The following list will show their employment and modifications.

Ab, 'from,' appears as *a* (before *m* and *v*), *abs* (before *c* and *t*), and *ab* in other cases; as *amitto, averto; abscondo, abstineo; abeo, abduco, abrado.* We have *au* for *ab* in *aufero, aufugio,* and *as* for *abs* in *aspello, asporto.*

Ad, 'to,' remains unaltered before vowels and *j, m, v,* as in *adeo, adjaceo, admiror, advolvo;* it is changed into *ac* before *qu,* as in *acquiro;* it is shortened into *d* in *aperio, amoenus, adeps, atrox;* in most other cases it is assimilated to the first consonant of the following word, as in *af-fero, ag-grego, al-loquor, an-numero, ap-pono, as-sequor, at-tingo;* but the *d* is retained in some editions of the best authors; and this is generally the case before *sc*, and *sp*, as in *ad-scisco, ad-spicio*. In old Latin it was written *ar-*, and this form is retained in *ar-biter* (from *ad-bio*, 'to approach'), in *ar-cesso* (for *ac-cedso*, also written *accerso*), and in *ar-guo* for *ad-gruo*. In *approbo* and *affirmo*, the preposition *ad* merely strengthens the sense.

Ante, 'before;' as *antepono*.

Circum, 'around;' as *circumeo*.

Cum, 'with,' written *con*, is changed into *co* before vowels and *h*, as in *coalesco, cohibeo*, and with an absorption of the following vowel in *cogo* for *co-igo* from *ago*; it is changed into *com* before *b, m*, and *p*, as in *combibo, commoveo, compono*; it is assimilated to the liquids *l, n, r*, as in *colloquor, conniveo, corrumpo*; in other cases it is always written *con*, as in *conjungo, convivo*.

De, 'down from,' sometimes *des-* before *t*, as in *destino*; before a vowel either shortened, as in *dĕorsum*, or with an absorption of the vowel, as *dēmo* for *de-imo*; in other cases unaltered, as in *detraho, descendo*. It is sometimes used with a negative force, as in *demens*.

E, *ex*, 'out of,' retains the full form *ex* before vowels and *c, p, q, s, t*; it becomes *ef-* before *f*, and *e* in all other cases; as *exigo, excipio, expono, exquiro, exspecto, extraho, effero, emitto*. We have also *e* for *ex* in *epoto, escendo*. This preposition sometimes denotes completion; as in *efficio, enarro, exōro*.

In, 'into,' 'upon,' 'against,' is written *im-* before *b* and *p*, and assimilated before *l, m* and *r*; otherwise it remains unchanged; as *imbibo, impono; illido, immisceo, irrideo; incurro, induco*. In old writers or their imitators we have *endo*, or *indu* for *in*. With adjectives *in* is a negative prefix; as *incautus, imparātus*.

Inter, 'between;' as *interpono*: it is assimilated in *intelligo*.

Ob, 'upon,' 'against,' 'around,' is assimilated before *c, f*, and *p*, as in *occurro, offero, oppono*; it is shortened to *ŏ* in *ŏmitto, ŏperio*; and is written *obs* or *os*, in *obs-olesco, obs-tinutus, os-tendo*; in other cases it remains unaltered, as in *objicio, obtineo*. With some verbs it denotes perseverance, as in *obtineo, occupo*, and our word 'obstinate.'

Per, 'through;' as in *perlego, perago*; but we have *pergo* for *perrigo*; the *l* is assimilated in *pellicio, pellectio, pellucidus*, and shortened in *pĕjero* for *perjuro*, and *pĕjor* for *pĕrior*.

Post, 'after;' as in *postpono;* but we have *pomoerium, pomeridianus,* and *pōno, posui* for *post-sino.*

Obs. Post seems to denote 'beyond' in *post-moerium,* or *po-moerium,* 'the space beyond the wall;' *postliminium,* 'the space beyond the threshold,' within which a resumption of rights is possible.

Prae, 'before;' as *praefero, praebeo* for *praehibeo.*

Praeter, 'by;' as *praetereo.*

Pro, 'before;' as *profero, projicio, promoveo;* but we have *probeo* for *prohibeo* (Lucret.); *pro* is shortened before vowels, or separated by an inserted *d,* as in *prodeo, prodigo,* and in some forms of *prosum,* as *prodest;* and it suffers metathesis and assimilation in *pol-liceo, por-rigo.*

Sub, 'under,' assimilates *b* to *c, f, g, m, p, r;* as in *succedo, sufficio, suggero, summoveo, suppono, surripio;* but we have always *sub-rideo* and *subrado. Sub* passes into *sus,* probably from *subs,* in *sus-cipio, sus-cito, sus-pendo,* and while *suscipio* was anciently written *succipio* (Servius, *ad Verg. Æn.* l. 148), some MSS. on the other hand give us *suscenseo* for *succenseo* (Drakenb. *ad Liv.* xxv. 6, p. 951), and this form is adopted by Bentley in his Terence. In composition with some verbs *sub* implies secrecy, as in *subornare testem;* in others, as *sufficio, succedo, substituo,* it implies putting one thing in the place of another.

Super, 'upon,' 'in addition;' as *supersto, supersum.*

Trans, 'beyond,' sometimes *trā;* as *transeo, transjicio* or *trajicio;* but generally *trādo, trāno.*

The following prepositions are used only in composition:

Amb- (another form of *ob*), also *am-* or *an-,* 'around;' as *ambio, amplector, anceps.*

Dis-, 'asunder,' retains its full form before *c, j, p, q, t,* and *s* followed by a vowel; as in *discedo, disjicio, displiceo, disquiro, distraho, disseco;* the *s* is assimilated to *f,* as in *differo, diffundo;* it becomes *r* in *dīrimo;* and we use *di* in *dijudico,* and before all consonants except those mentioned above, as in *digero, dimitto,* &c.

Re-, 'back,' also *red-* or *ret-;* as *revertor, redeo, rettuli.* With verbs of covering, closing, &c., it has the meaning of our prefix *un-* or *dis-,* as *re-tego,* 'to un-cover,' 'dis-cover,' *re-velo,* 'to un-veil,' *re-cludo,* 'to un-close,' 'dis-close,' *re-sero,* 'to un-lock,' &c. Sometimes *re-* denotes *repetition* or 'doing a thing over again,' as in *re-peto,* 'to repeat,' *re-lego,* 'to reperuse,' &c.

Sē- (another form of *sine*), 'apart,' 'without;' as *sēcerno*, *sēcurus*. It is shortened into *sĕ* in *sŏrsim* and also with a change of vowel in *sŏcors*, *sŏcordia*¹. We have *sēditio* from *se* and *eo*, and this is the only instance of *se* used in composition before a vowel, and retaining its full form and a long vowel: but *sudus*, 'warm,' 'dry,' is said by Festus (p. 294) to be for *se-udus*, and some derive *solus* from *se-alius* or *se-olus*.

Vē- or *vehe-*, 'away,' 'out of;' as *ve-cors* or *vehe-mens*, 'out of mind,' i.e. 'stupid or impatient,' *ve-stibulum*, 'that which stands out from the house.'

§ 3. *Conjunctions.*

112 Conjunctions are adverbs especially used for the purpose of joining together words and sentences, from which circumstance they derive their name (i.e. from *conjungo*, 'I yoke together'). In regard to their form conjunctions are either simple or compound. Thus *et*, *at*, *sed*, *nam* are simple conjunctions, but *atque*, *itaque*, *attamen*, *siquidem*, *enimvero*, &c. are compound conjunctions. According to their position in the sentence, conjunctions are, (1) *postpositive*, if they cannot stand first in the sentence, as *enim*, *autem*, *vero*, *quidem*, *quoque*; (2) *prepositive*, if they must stand first, at least in prose, as *sed*, *at*, *verum*, *etenim*, *nec*, *sin*, *sive*, *quare*, &c.; (3) *common*, if they may stand either first or second, as *tamen*, *igitur*, *itaque*; (4) *enclitic*, when they are necessarily appended to some other word, as *-que* and *-ve*. According to their signification and usage, they are divided into the following classes: (A) Copulative Conjunctions, which join words and sentences on an equal footing; and these again are (1) Positive; (2) Negative; (3) Disjunctive; (4) Alternative; (B) Adversative Conjunctions, which oppose words and sentences; (C) Inferential Conjunctions, which introduce a conclusion or inference; (D) Causal Conjunctions, which introduce a statement of the ground or reason; (E) Conditional Conjunctions, which introduce an hypothesis or assumption; (F) Concessive Conjunctions, which introduce an admission; (G) Final Conjunctions, which introduce an expression of the purpose, object, or result; (H) Temporal Conjunctions, which introduce a definition of time.

¹ [Marked in the lexicons *sĭcors*, *sĭcordia*. Neither word is often, if ever, found in classical poets. Prudentius has *sŏcordia*.]

(A) Copulative Conjunctions.

(1) Positive, *et*
  atque (ac) } and
  -que
  quoque } also
  etiam
  quinetiam, moreover
  neque non } and besides
  necnon
  itidem, item } likewise.
  simul

(2) Negative, *neque, nec,* and not.

(3) Disjunctive, *aut* }
  vel } or.
  -ve

(4) Alternative, *sive, seu,* or whether.

Copulative conjunctions of every kind are very frequently doubled, as follows:

et—et, 'both—and,' 'as well—as,' 'partly—partly' (this is a common usage).

et—que, 'both—and' (common in later writers, but of rare occurrence in Cicero).

que—et (connect single words, but this combination is not found in Cicero).

que—que (only in poetry).

et—neque, 'on the one hand,' i.e. 'partly so' —'not on the other,' i.e. 'partly not so' } (this a very common usage).

neque—et, 'in part not so—partly so'

nec—que (of rarer occurrence).

modo—modo } 'at one time—at another time.'
modo—nunc

non modo—sed etiam } 'not only—but also.'
non solum—sed etiam

quum—tum
tum—tum
qua—qua } 'both—and.'
simul—simul

neque (nec)—neque (nec) (very common). }
neque—nec (not unfrequent).
nec—neque (of rare occurrence).
aut—aut }
vel—vel } 'either—or.'
sive (seu)—sive (seu), 'whether—or.'

(B) Adversative Conjunctions.

autem, however
at (ast), but yet
atqui, but for all that
attamen, but still
at vero, but in fact
enim vero, but really now
sed, but on the contrary

nihilominus }
tamen } nevertheless
vero, in fact, however
verum }
verumtamen } still in fact
verum enim vero, but in solemn truth.

(C) Inferential Conjunctions.

ergo, therefore
idcirco, on that account
ideo, for that reason
igitur, therefore
itaque, accordingly
cur, why?

quare, on what account?
quamobrem }
quapropter } on which account
proinde, wherefore
propterea, on that account
quocirca, wherefore.

(D) Causal Conjunctions.

quum, seeing that
enim, for
etenim, for indeed
nam }
namque } for
quando, whilst
quandoquidem, since

quia }
quod } because
quoniam }
si quidem } since, inasmuch as
quippe, forasmuch as
ut pote (with relative), seeing that, considering that.

(E) Conditional Conjunctions.

si, if
si forte, if perchance
si modo, if only
si tamen, if otherwise
sin, but if

sin autem, if, however, on the contrary
sin minus, if not
sin vero, but if really
nisi, ni, or even nisi si, unless

nisi forte, unless perchance
dummodo ⎫
modo ⎬ provided only
dum ⎭

dum ne ⎫
modo ne ⎬ if only not, provided only not
dummodo ne ⎭
quod si, but if
quod nisi, but unless.

(F) Concessive Conjunctions.

et si ⎫
etiam si ⎬ even if
tametsi ⎫
tamenetsi ⎬ if ever so much
licet, though it be supposed that
quamquam, although

quamvis ⎫
quantumvis ⎬ however much
quamlibet
quantumlibet ⎭
ut, to whatever extent
quum, all the while that.

(G) Final Conjunctions.

ne, lest, to the end or extent that not
ne forte, lest perchance
neve, neu, and lest
quin, so that—not

quo, in order that
quominus, in order that—not
ut, uti, to the end that
ut ne, to the end that—not
ut non, to the extent that—not.

(H) Temporal Conjunctions.

antequam, before
donec, until
priusquam, before
quamdiu, as long as

quoad ⎫
dum ⎬ until
postquam, after
quoties, as often as
simul, simulatque (ac), as soon as.

The use of the conjunctions, considered according to these different classes, is best learned from their employment in the corresponding forms of co-ordinate or subordinate sentences. It will be sufficient here to subjoin a few remarks on those conjunctions which require and admit of a special discrimination as synonymous words.

(A)

(a) The copulative conjunctions *et*, *-que*, and *at-que* may be distinguished as follows:

Et, which is another form of *ad*, merely denotes the addition of one thing to another; *-que*, which contains the same root as the relative, places two objects on a parallel footing, and combines them in one idea; *at-que*, which is compounded of the other two, implies that there is not only an addition, but also an intimate connexion between the things coupled together, and therefore indicates cause and effect, antecedent and consequent, &c. *Ac* is another form of *atque*, as *nec* is of *neque*, and never stands before vowels or *h*, although *nec* and *neque* are used indifferently before vowels or consonants. The following examples, taken from the first chapter of Cæsar, *de Bello Civili*, will show the use of *et*, *-que*, *atque* (*ac*). The chapter might be headed *de causa et origine belli civilis*, because they are separate subjects; and in the context we find *senatu reique publicae*, because the senate and the state form one connected, complex notion; but we have *audacter ac fortiter,—sin Caesarem respiciant atque ejus gratiam sequantur,—gratiam atque amicitiam*, because the word or phrase which follows *atque* (*ac*) is an extension or supplement of that which precedes. In some copulative phrases the *et* is always omitted; for example, in *Patres Conscripti*, for *Patres et Conscripti*, 'Patricians and new Senators;' *sarta tecta*, 'sound in wall and roof;' *Populus Romanus Quirites*, 'the people of Roman and Sabine origin;' *lis vindiciae*, 'plaint and claim,' &c. In these phrases we might of course insert *atque* as correctly as *et*; for it is sometimes a matter of indifference whether we use *et* or *atque* in coupling similar objects; thus in Cic. *Parad.* 3 fin., we have: Perturbationo peccetur *rationis atque ordinis*; perturbata autem *ratione et ordine*, &c. In introducing the sentence 'and that too,' we may write either *atque id, et id*, or *idque*, but with *hic, idem, adeo, potius, utinam*, &c. it is more common to use *atque*. The use of *atque* as a comparative particle has been noticed above (p. 173). The explanation of the idiom seems to be this,—that *atque* in itself may express a meaning similar to *atque id*. Thus we find in answers such usages as the following: *Cognostine hos versus?* 'do you know these lines?' *ac memoriter*, 'yes, I do, and that too by heart.' *Num hic duae Bacchides habitant*, 'surely two women of the name of Bacchis do not live here.' *Atque ambae sorores*, 'yes they do, and what is more they are both sisters.' So in the comparative sentence, *atque* may be rendered 'and indeed;' thus, *is tibi notus est aeque ac mihi*, 'he is known to you equally, and that too (i.e. and besides) to me;' *aliud mihi ac tibi videtur*, 'it appears a different thing to you, and that too (i.e. and besides) to me,' in other words, 'both you and I perceive the thing as different.'

(b) The difference between *etiam* and *quoque* consists in this, that while *etiam* introduces a new circumstance, *quoque* merely denotes the addition of something similar; so that *etiam* may be rendered 'and farther;' *quoque*, 'and also.' Hence *etiam* may qualify a particular word, in which case it precedes, or may give emphasis to a sentence, in which case its position is optional; but *quoque* always qualifies some single word, which it necessarily follows. Thus, Cæsar splendidam quamdam dicendi rationem tenet, voce, motu, forma *etiam* magnifica et generosa quodammodo. Cic. *Brut.* 75. Me scilicet maxime, sed proxime illum *quoque* fefellissem. Cic. *Rab. Post.* 12. These particles are so different in meaning that they may occur together; thus, Ego pol *quoque etiam* timida sum, Ter. *Hecyr.* v. 1. 7, where *quoque* belongs to *ego*, and *etiam* to *timida;* and this may of course happen when *etiam* is a particle of time, as, Egomet *quoque* ejus causa in funus prodeo nihil suspicans *etiam* mali. Ter. *Andr.* L 1. 89.

(c) *Item* expresses only similarity, and is often a particle of comparison followed by *ut; itidem* presumes a repetition; and *identidem* a repetition after a short interval. Thus, Fecisti *item*, uti prædones solent. Cic. *Verr.* IV. 9. Placuit Scævolæ *itemque* ceteris. Cic. *Leg.* II. 21. Spectaculum uni Crasso jucundum fuit, ceteris *non item.* Cic. *Att.* II. 21. Nunc *itidem* (ut in Aratio carmine) ab eodem Jove et a ceteris diis immortalibus sunt nobis agendi capienda primordia. Cic. *Leg.* II. 3; cf. Cic. *Top.* 22. Recitabatur *identidem* Pompeii testimonium. Cic. *Rab. Post.* 12.

(d) *Nec (neque) non* is not used in good prose as a mere substitute for *et* to connect nouns together, but only to couple propositions, and the two negatives are often separated; thus, Nemo Attico minus fuit ædificator, *neque* tamen *non* imprimis bene habitavit. Nep. *Att.* 13. Cicero has *nec vero non*, &c.; and in the later writers, from Quintilian downwards, *necnon* is written as one word, and used as precisely equivalent to *et*.

(e) We have *nec* rather than *et non*, if the negation belongs to the whole sentence; as, Expurgandus est sermo et adhibenda tamquam obrussa ratio, quæ mutari non potest, *nec* utendum pravissima consuetudinis regula (Cic. *Brut.* 74), 'we must make our style pure, and employ as our touchstone reason, which is not liable to change; and we must not act upon custom, the most faulty of all standards,' because all that follows *nec* is included in the negation. But if the negation belongs to a single word or constitutes an antithesis, we must have *et non* or even *ac non*; thus, Athenis apud Demetrium Syrum, veterem *et non* ignobilem dicendi magistrum, exerceri solebam (Cic. *Brut.* 91), because *non* belongs only to *ignobilem*. Patior *et non* moleste fero (Cic. *Verr.* I. 1), because *non* belongs to *moleste*. Si quam Rubrius injuriam suo nomine, *ac non* impulsu tuo fecisset, because *ac non*, 'and not rather,' belongs to *impulsu tuo*, directly opposed to *suo nomine*. If *et* precedes, it is more usually followed by *et non* than by *nec*; thus, Manlius *et* semper me coluit, *et* a studiis nostris *non* abhorret. Cic. *ad div.* XIII. 23. And we may have *et non* even when *neque* precedes; as, Africanus *neque* cessabat unquam, *et* interdum colloquio alterius *non* egebat. Cic. *Off.* III. 1.

(*f*) Of the disjunctives, *aut*, which is another form of *haud* or *haut*, expresses total separation, *vel* suggests a choice, and *-ve* conveys an unimportant distinction; thus, Quidquid dicam *aut* erit *aut* non, 'whatever I shall say will either be, or, *which is quite a different thing*, it will not.' Hor. 2 *Serm.* V. 59. Hanc mihi *vel* vi *vel* clam *vel* precario fac tradas (Ter. *Eun.* II. 3. 28), 'take care to procure her for me either by stealth or, *if you please*, by entreaty,' meaning that the mode was entirely indifferent and optional; for he adds, *mea nihil refert dum patiar modo*. Cf. Hor. 2 *Epist.* II. 173: *nunc prece, nunc pretio, nunc vi*. And compare *si plus minusve dixero*, 'if I shall have said more or less,' the difference being small (Cic. *pro Flacco*, 5), with *aut plus aut minus*, quam opus erat, multo, where the difference is expressly stated to be great (Plautus, *Menaechmei*, IV. 2. 27). From the exclusive force of *aut*, it is often used after negatives; as, *Non* mehercule unquam apud judices *aut* dolorem *aut* misericordiam *aut* invidiam *aut* odium excitare dicendo volui. Cic. *de Oratore*, II. 43, 189.

(g) The only pronoun used for the expression of an alternative is *sive* (shortened into *seu*), which is really a combination of the conditional *si* with the disjunctive *ve*. This word is sometimes used as a substitute for *vel si*, as in Ter. *Andr.* I. 2. 19: Postulo, *sive* aequum est, te oro. *Ib.* I. 5. 58: Si te in germani fratris dilexi loco, *sive* haec te solum semper fecit maximi, *seu* tibi morigera fuit, where we must translate *sive* or *seu* by 'or if.' The alternative is therefore to be understood as the option between two conditions. This is readily seen when the alternative sentence contains a verb; as, Cretum leges, quas *sive* Juppiter *sive* Minos sanxit, laboribus erudiunt juventutem (Cic. *Tusc.* II. 14), 'either if it was Juppiter or if it was Minos who made these laws, take which alternative you please; they produce the same effect.' But if there is no verb the conditional sentence is lost, and we must translate *sive—sive* by 'whether—or.' Thus we have this conjunction repeated with an oblique case: *Sive* certaminis periculo, *sive* subito adventu, *sive* exspectatione nostri consilii. Cæs. *B. G.* VIII 9. Or alone, in the sense of 'or:' Adjungit agros in Macedonia, qui regis Philippi *sive* Persæ fuerunt. Cic. *Agr.* II. 19. Or in a sentence containing *si*: His in rebus *si* apud te plus auctoritas mea quam tua *sive* natura paulo acrior *sive* quædam dulcedo iracundiæ, *sive* dicendi sal facetiæque valuissent, nihil sane esset quod nos pœniteret. Cic. *Quint. Fr.* I. 2. By a singular change of application *sive* is regarded as equivalent to an indirect interrogative particle, and is followed by *an*; thus, Sed Plautum ea nou movere; *sive* nullam opem providebat inermis atque exsul, *seu* tædio ambiguæ spei; *an* amore conjugis et liberorum. Tac. *Ann.* XIV. 59. If the second alternative is merely the negative of the first, it may be expressed simply by *sive non;* thus, Sive referent ad me *sive non,* mea tamen benevolentia fidesque præstabitur. Cic. *ad div.* XII. 2.

Obs. How far we are at liberty to substitute the form of the double question (above, 108, (A), (c)) for the expression of the alternative by means of *sive* may be regarded as an open question. Hand thinks (*Turssellinus,* I. p. 300) that the use of *an* for *dubium an* was a colloquialism, and he adds: 'interpositum *an* non mutat verborum constructionem, quæ, ut incepit, pergit per indicativum.' When he maintains that in the former member of the disjunctive sentence the particle is necessarily omitted, it is to be remarked that although this is the most usual form, it is not and cannot be invariable. Thus in Cic. *Resp.* II. 15, we have a variety of reading: 'verene hoc memoriæ proditum sit [*sit*] regem istum Numam Pythagoræ [ne] ipsius discipulum *an* certe Pythagoreum fuisse!' On this Hand remarks: 'est vero bimembris dubitatio verbis expressa, nec debebat illud *an* pro *aut* accipi, ut fecit Moserus.' He adds the following quotations with the accompanying comments: 'Plin. *Ep.* v. 4, 2, dixerunt se deceptos, lapsine verbo, *an* quia ita sentiebant. Vidit Gesnerus hæc verba addi a Plinio tanquam interpositam interrogationem: sed eodem modo Dictys Cret. I. 19: neque multo post irans cælesti, *an* ob imitationem aeris corporibus portentatis, lues invadit; ubi Meserus multa exempla affert per *ne—an* formata.' That these

sentences are not dependent, but that the indicative construction is
proper, appears from such passages as the following:

> O felix, tantis quam primum industria rebus
> Prodidit auctorem, deus ille, an proxima divis
> Mens fuit, in cæcas aciem quæ magna tenebras
> Egit, et ignarum perfudit lumine vulgus.
> Gratius Faliscus, *Cyneget*. 95—98.

In Varro, *L. L.* 8, 61: quod ait *an* non, nihil commovet analogiam, the last words are equivalent to *nihil refert*, so that the double interrogative is dependent, and the subjunctive is in its proper place. Schwartz renders this passage 'allein es mag dies seyn oder nicht, so thut es doch der Analogie nichts;' and adds, 'versio quidem nostra loci Varroniani docet, quod lingua nostra vernacula aut ferat aut postulet.' And as Hand tells us, 'Facciolatus in *Epist. Meieri*, p. 12, notaverat in Varronis loco an eleganter quidem, non pro *sive* positum esse. "Si quid," inquit, "pro *an non* reponi posset, non *sive* reponeretur sed *necne*."' But Hand himself (p. 302) supposes the *sit annon* of Varro to be equivalent to *sive sit sive non sit*, and quotes besides Ovid, *Remed. Amoris*, 797: Daunius an Libycis bulbus tibi missus ab oris, an veniat Megaris, noxius omnis erit. He remarks that in Statius, *Silva.* L 3, 40, 'per *an* exprimitur sententia, quæ antea, v. 34, per *ve* dicta erat;' and he quotes many passages in which *sive, seu*, and *an* are placed in juxtaposition, e. g. Tac. *Ann.* XI. 26; Ovid, *Fasti*, III. 773: *sive—sive quia —sive—an quia*, cf. I. 327; III. 231. In Tac. *Annal.* XIV. 7, we have: Igitur longum utriusque silentium, ne irriti dissuaderent *an* eo descensum crederent, ut, &c., where *an* appears to be equivalent to *an quia*. On the whole it seems that the transition from the mere alternative expressed by the conditional *sive* to the interrogation expressed by *an* must be reserved for those cases in which the alternative suggests some question, as in Milton's phrase: 'or hear'st thou rather pure ethereal stream, whose fountain who shall tell?' There can be no doubt at any rate that the use of *sive* is much more common, and the young student may safely confine himself to this mode of expressing the alternative sentence.

(B)

Sed, which is another form of *sine* and the prefix *se-*, conveys a direct opposition or contradiction; *autem*, which is a lengthened form of *aut*, states that the new matter is different, but not necessarily inconsistent; *at*, which is another form of *ad* and *et*, merely denotes continuance, or the addition of something farther, so that the contrast is produced not by any thing in the meaning of *at*, but in the assertion of contemporaneous but opposite phenomena, which it introduces. Thus *sed* means 'but on the contrary;' *autem*, 'but, which is a different matter;' and *at* 'joined even to that,' 'still,' 'yet,' 'notwithstanding;' as in the following examples: Non mihi, *sed* tibi, 'not to me, but, *on the contrary*, to you;' Gyges a nullo videbatur, ipse *autem* omnia videbat, 'Gyges was seen by no one, but he himself, *which was quite a different matter*, saw all things;' Cæsar fuit vir fortis, prudens, clemens: *at* ambitiosus, *at* patriæ proditor, 'Cæsar possessed fortitude, prudence, and clemency, *still, yet, continuing all this state of things, and in addition to them* he was, *at the same time*, ambitious, and a traitor to his country.' Sometimes *at* means 'therefore' or 'well then,' as in Livy, I. 38: *at* ego recipio, '*well then, therefore*, as a continuance, necessary and expected, I receive the surrender,' which is the natural consequence of the capitulation; and so in imprecations, as in Virg. Æn. II. 538: *At* tibi pro scelere, &c., '*therefore* may the gods punish thy wickedness.' *Verum* and *vero* are merely corrective, but *verum etiam* and *sed etiam* are synonymous. *Tamen* comes as nearly as possible to our 'nevertheless;' and the compounds *attamen, sed tamen, veruntamen* combine the notion of an objection, a correction, or a corroboration, with that of a concession, which is more or less contained in *tamen*. The following examples will illustrate these usages: Atque hunc ille summus vir scelere solutum periculo liberavit; insidiatori *vero* et latroni quæ potest inferri injusta nex...Est enim hæc, judices, non scripta, *sed* nata lex; quam non didicimus, suscepimus, legimus, *verum* ex natura ipsa arripuimus, hausimus, expressimus; ad quam non docti, *sed* facti; non instituti, *sed* imbuti sumus: ut, si vita nostra in aliquas insidias...incidisset, omnis honesta ratio esset expediendæ salutis. Cic. *Mil.* 4. Nunc quod agitur agamus; agitur *autem*, liberine vivamus, an mortem obeamus. Cic. *Phil.* XI. 10. Quid *porro* quærendum est? factumne sit? *At* constat. A quo? *At* patet. Cic. *Mil.* 0. Canes aluntur in Capitolio, ut significent, si fures venerint. *At* fures internoscere non possunt. Cic. *Rosc. Am.* 20. Ego (Crassus), quamquam memet mei pænitet, cum hoc (Antonio) maxime *tamen* in comparatione conjungar. Cic. *Or.* III. 9. *Verum enimvero* legibus id prohiberi, id demum contumeliosum est plebi. Liv. IV. 4.

(C)

Ergo is the most appropriate word to express our 'therefore' in its logical sense; *igitur*, which originally meant 'thereupon,' 'thereafter,' merely continues the thought by some inference obvious at first sight; *itaque*, 'and so,' 'accordingly,' introduces an explanation naturally flowing from the previous statement; *proinde* generally confines the inference to the wish of the speaker, and is used in good prose only with the imperative or subjunctive; and all these four particles strictly refer to what has gone before. On the other hand, *ideo*, *idcirco*, and *propterea*, which do not indicate a fact, but an aim and object, connect themselves with what follows, and are generally supplemented by *quod*, *ut*, *ne*, &c. Although *idcirco* is properly the antecedent of *quocirca*, the two words are not used in combination; but *quocirca* takes the place of *proinde* when we express 'wherefore' with an indicative. The same may be said of *quare*, *quamobrem*, *quapropter*, which do not follow the corresponding antecedent expression, *propterea*, but introduce a sentence in much the same way as *quocirca*. Quare is also an interrogative particle, demanding the cause or reason why; and this is properly the use of *cur*. Thus we have: A. Malum mihi videtur esse mors. M. Iisne, qui mortui sunt, an iis, quibus moriendum est? A. Utrisque. M. Est miserum *igitur*, quoniam malum. A. Certe. M. *Ergo* et ii, quibus evenit jam, ut morerentur, et ii, quibus eventurum est, miseri. A. Mihi ita videtur. M. Nemo *ergo* non miser. A. Prorsus nemo. Cic. *Tusc.* I. 5. Est *igitur* ambulantibus ad hunc modum sermo ille institutus. Cic. *Tusc.* II. 4. Bestiolæ quædam unum diem vivunt: ex his *igitur* hora octava quæ mortua est, provecta ætate mortua est. Cic. *Tusc.* I. 39. Est enim metus, ut ægritudo præsentis, sic ille futuri mali. *Itaque* nonnulli ægritudinis partem quandam metum esse dicebant. Cic. *Tusc.* IV. 30. Si quis rem mandatam gessisset negligentius, eum majores nostri summum admisisse dedecus existimabant. *Itaque* mandati constitutum est judicium, non minus turpe, quam furti. Cic. *Rosc. Am.* 38. Quæ resecanda sunt, non patiar ad perniciem civitatis manere: *proinde* aut exeant aut quiescant. Cic. *Cat.* II. 5. *Proinde* fac tantum animum habeas, quanto opus est. Cic. *ad div.* XII. 6. Quis unquam crederet, Verrem mulierum adversarium futurum? an *ideo* aliquid contra mulieres fecit, ne totum edictum ad Chelidonis arbitrium scriptum videretur? Cic. *Verr.* L 41. Ergo *idcirco* turpis hæc culpa est, quod duas res sanctissimas violat, amicitiam et fidem. Cic. *Rosc. Am.* 39. Hæc *propterea* de me dixi, ut mihi Tubero conquiesceret. Cic. *Lig.* 3. Affers hæc omnia argumenta, *cur* dii sint. Cic. *N. D.* III. 4. Afferunt rationem, *cur* negent. Cic. *ad div.* VI. 8. Quid est, *cur* sedeas? Cic. *Cluent.* 53. *Cur* Marcellum

Hannibal interemit? *cur* Paulum Cannæ sustulerunt? *cur* Africanum domestici parietes non texerunt? Cic. *N. D.* III. 32. *Quare* nihil potuit confici? Cic. *Att.* XL 13. Utendum est excusatione, *quare* id necesse fuerit. Cic. *Off.* II. 19. Agusius fuit omnium periculorum meorum socius... *Quare* sic eum tibi commendo, ut unum de meis domesticis et maxime necessariis. Cic. *ad div.* XIII. 71. Permulta sunt, quæ dici possunt, *quare* illud intelligatur. Cic. *Rosc. Am.* 33. Honos virtutis est præmium. *Quamobrem*, mi Planci, incumbe toto pectore ad laudem. Cic. *ad div.* X. 10. Meminero, me recepisse, quem defenderem: *quapropter* nihil est, quod metuas. Cic. *Verr.* II. 73. Meas cogitationes omnes explicavi tibi superioribus literis; *quocirca* hæ sunt breves. Cic. *Att.* X. 0.

Obs. *Ergo* is sometimes an expression of sorrow; as, *Ergo Quintilium perpetuus sopor urget!* 'So then eternal sleep oppresses Quintilius!'

(D)

(a) *Nam* is our 'for,' when it introduces a proof or reason; *enim* is 'for,' when it merely explains; accordingly *nam* is used to strengthen a preceding negative sentence, whereas *enim* explains a positive clause; and conversely, while *nam non* is of rare occurrence, nothing is more frequent than *non enim* or *neque enim*; *nam* has frequently an adversative sense, nearly equivalent to *sed*; but *enim* in an adversative clause must be preceded by *at* or *sed*, and we have even *at enim vero*, or *verum enim vero*. With the addition of the copulative conjunctions, *que* and *et*, *namque* and *etenim* not only refer to the preceding sentence, but introduce as something fresh the first clause of a new argument. We often find *nam* before *etsi*, *quod* (=*quod ad id attinet*), but *etenim* before *si*. Thus we have: Exiguum hoc tempus tamen mihi nimium longum videtur. Habeo enim nihil, tentatis omnibus robus, in quo acquiescam. *Nam* dum illud tractabam, de quo antea scripsi ad te, quasi fovebam dolores meos......Solitudinem meam non obturbavit Philippus. *Nam*, ut heri me salutavit, statim Romam profectus est......Sed omnia, ut voles. Ego *enim*, quidquid feceris, id quum recte, tum etiam mea causa factum putabo. Cic. *Att.* XII. 18. *Nam* (elliptically for *sed supervacanea dico*; *nam*) quid argumentamur, quo pecunia ista pervenerit. Fecit ipse judicium. Cic. *Verr.* L 57. Tum ille:

Namque quod tu non poteris aut nescies, quis nostrum tam impudens est, qui se scire aut posse postulet? Cic. *Or.* L 22. Intelligetis, nullis hominibus quemquam tanto odio, quanto istum Syracusanis et esse et fuisse. *At enim* (elliptically for *at hoc nihil efficit; nam*) istum soli Siculi persequuntur, cives Romani salvum esse cupiunt. Cic. *Verr.* II. 6. Similarly, *Sed enim*. Cic. *Arch.* 3.

(b) *Quia* gives the grounds, as resting on absolute fact, which is supposed to be known; otherwise we must use *nam; quod* gives the grounds, as merely our own or some other person's thought, and the verb is subjunctive, if it is left uncertain whether we really accept the implied reason, but indicative, if the conviction of the speaker is expressed. *Quippe*, like our 'as,' merely expresses the correspondence of the alleged ground with the facts of the case; it is both used alone in this sense, and is also frequently joined with *quum, quod, quia* and the relative *qui*, in the sense of 'inasmuch as.' The same remark applies to *utpote*. *Quum* is properly an adverb of time, and is not used as a causal conjunction, except so far as the effect follows in course of time. *Quoniam=quum jam* expresses the motive as springing from the existing state of the case. *Quando* is almost always a mere particle of time, and this is the predominant meaning where it seems to be a causal conjunction. *Quandoquidem*, owing to the concessive *quidem*, makes the present state of affairs a reason for an admission of the grounds. And *siquidem* similarly passes from the condition to the concession. Thus, Tertia est urbs, quæ, *quod* in ea parte Fortunæ fanum antiquum fuit, Tycha nominata est. Quarta est urbs, quæ, *quia* postrema ædificata est, Neapolis nominatur. Cic. *Verr.* IV. 53. Dolorem ob id ipsum, *quia* dolor sit, fugiendum putat. Cic. *Tusc.* V. 33. Aristides expulsus est patria, *quod* prætor modum justus esset. Cic. *Tusc.* v. 36. Num propterea nulla est rei publicæ gerendæ ratio atque prudentia, *quia* multa Pompeium, quædam Catonem, nonnulla etiam te ipsum fefellerunt? Cic. *Divin.* I. 14. Minari denique divisoribus ratio non erat, propterea *quod* eos intelligere videbam (nearly=quod illi intelligebant), me hoc judicio districtum atque obligatum futurum. Cic. *Verr.* I. 9. Prædia mea tu possides; ego aliena misericordia vivo. Concedo, et *quod* animus æquus est, et *quia* necesse est. Cic. *Rosc. Am.* 50. Sol Democrito magnus videtur, *quippe* homini erudito in geometriaque perfecto. Cic. *Fin.* I. 6. Convivia cum patre non inibat, *quippe qui* ne in oppidum quidem, nisi perraro, veniret. Cic. *Rosc. Am.* 18. Non intelligo, quare Rullus quemquam intercessurum putet; *quum* intercessio stultitiam intercessoris significatura sit. Cic. *Agr.* II. 12. *Quoniam* semel suscepi, succurram atque subibo. Cic. *Rosc. Am.* 11. Itaque *quando* vestræ cautiones infirmæ sunt, Græculam tibi misi cautionem. Cic. *ad div.* VII. 18. *Quandoquidem* tu istos oratores tanto opere laudas, vellem aliquid Antonio, plura Crasso libuisset scribere. Cic. *Brut.* 44. Confiteor, jure mihi contigisse, *quandoquidem* tam iners sum. Ter. *And.* III. 5. 2. Quare non οἴχεται tua industria, sed præclare ponitur; *siquidem* id egisti, ut ego delectarer. Cic. *Att.* VI. 1.

(E)

The distinction between *nisi* (*ni*) and *si non* deserves the best attention of the student. A negative assumption or concession can only be expressed by *si non*, and this is generally followed by *tamen*, *at*, or some other particle of limitation. On the other hand, *nisi*, which seems to contain the prohibitive *ne*, rather than the direct negative, implies rather an exception, than a negation of the condition; and the frequent addition of another *si* shows that it is used rather as an adverb than as a conjunction. It is often found after *non*, but not immediately, or as a compound particle. We have also very frequently the combination *nisi forte*, *nisi vero*. The shortened form *ni* is for the most part poetical, but it occurs in Cicero. If it is necessary to negative a preceding condition, we use *si non* when the verb is repeated; but *sin minus*, when we do not repeat the verb. Thus, Memoria minuitur, *nisi* exerceas ('except when'). Cic. *Sen.* VI. Non tam perspicue istorum maleficia videremus, *nisi* ipsos cæcos redderet cupiditas. Cic. *Rosc. Am.* 35. Dolorem justissimum, *si non* potero frangere, occultabo. Cic. *Phil.* XII. 8. Perfectionis laudem *si non* assequimur, at quid deceat videmus. Cic. *Or.* 30. Si feceris, magnam habebo gratiam; *si non* feceris, ignoscam. Cic. *ad div.* V. 19. Moriar, *ni*, quæ tua gloria est, puto te malle a Cæsare consuli, quam inaurari. Cic. *ad div.* VII. 13. Is sponsionem fecit, *ni* vir bonus esset. Cic. *Off.* III. 19. Quod si assecutus sum, gaudeo; *sin minus*, tamen me consolor. Cic. *ad div.* VII. 1, extr. Dolores si tolerabiles sint, feramus; *sin minus*, æquo animo e vita excamus. Cic. *Fin.* I. 15.

(F)

Etsi and *etiamsi*, 'even if,' express the concession in the form of a restricted condition, and take their colour from the sentence which follows. *Tametsi* or *tamenetsi*, 'if ever so much,' throw a greater emphasis on this restriction. *Quamquam*, 'although,' presumes that the statement conceded is true. *Licet* merely allows the supposition. *Quamvis, quantumvis*, with the less usual *quamlibet, quantumlibet*, concede an unlimited amount of assumption. *Quum*, when used as a concessive particle, falls back on its meaning as an adverb of time, and implies a contemporary existence of the circumstance conceded. *Ut*, like our phrase 'all the while,' indicates the extent to which the concession reaches, and may be rendered by 'granting that—going to the extent of allowing.' All these particles of concession may be followed by the adversative *tamen* or even *tamen nihilominus*, which are found especially after the correlative *tametsi*. Thus we have: Optimi homines faciunt, quod honestum est, *etsi* nullum emolumentum consecuturum vident. Cic. *Fin.* II. 14. Habet res deliberationem; *etsi* ex parte magna tibi assentior. Cic. *Att.* VII. 3. *Etiamsi* quod scribas non habebis, scribito tamen. Cic. *ad div.* XVI. 26. Neque ea quisquam, nisi diu multumque scriptitarit, *etiamsi* vehementissime se in his subitis dictionibus exercuerit, consequetur. Cic. *Or.* I. 33. *Tametsi* statim vicisse debeo, tamen de meo jure decedam. Cic. *Rosc. Am.* 27. Rem publicam more nostro tuebimur, *quamquam* admodum sumus defatigati. Cic. *ad div.* XII. 25. *Quamquam* quid loquor? *Quamquam* quis ignorat? Cic. *Cat.* I. 8; *Flacc.* 27. *Quamvis* prudens ad cogitandum sis, sicut es; tamen, nisi magnae curae tibi esset,... nunquam ea res tibi tam belle in mentem venire potuisset. Cic. *Att.* XII. 37. *Quam volet*, jocetur. Cic. *N. D.* II. 17. Non enim possis, *quantumvis licet* excellas, omnes tuos ad honores amplissimos perducere. Cic. *Am.* 20. *Licet* omnes in me terrores impendeant, tamen succurram atque subibo. Cic. *Rosc. Am.* 11. Has tabulas Marcellus, *quum* omnia profana fecit, non attigit. Cic. *Verr.* IV. 55. *Ut* illud non cogitares, tamen ad ejusdem ordinis homines te judices esse venturum. Cic. *Verr.* III. 45.

(G)

Either *ut* or *quo* may be used to express affirmatively the end of an action. Thus we may say either *ut sit studiosior*, or *quo sit stu-*

diosior, to signify 'in order that, to the end that, he may be more studious.' To express the end negatively, the most common particle is *ne*, for which we may have the fuller form *ut ne*, when the sentence is really final, but *ut non*, *ut nunquam*, &c., when we denote rather the consequence or extent of the action. If we wish to couple two final sentences dependent on one main sentence, we introduce the second by *neve* (*neu*), which means 'or in order that not' or 'and in order that not.' For *ne*, *ut ne*, *ut non*, we substitute *quin* or *quominus*, when the main sentence implies a negation, prohibition, omission, or prevention. The distinction between these particles demands the best attention of the student. *Quin* is properly the old ablative *qui* (above, 64, *Obs.*) with the negative *ne* for *non*, and it may be used interrogatively in the sense 'why not?' as *quin imus!* 'why do we not go?' But it is also used relatively in the sense 'in what manner not,' 'in such manner that not.' *Quominus* is the common ablative *quo* with *minus* used negatively, as in *sin minus*, &c., and therefore means 'in what manner the less,' 'in such manner that so much the less.' Generally therefore these conjunctions may seem to agree in meaning; but practically *quin* is rather used to denote a consequence, and *quominus* to denote a purpose. Accordingly, *quin* is used rather than *quominus*, when the main sentence is negative, or when the negative force of the impersonal verb *abest* or of a verb or phrase signifying to doubt or omit, is destroyed by a negative or interrogative particle; thus we have *quin* after *nemo, nullus, nihil, non, nunquam, nusquam, vix, aegre*, &c.; after interrogatives; after *nihil, paulum, non procul, haud multum abest; non dubito, non est dubium, non ambigo; non possum; non, vix, aegre abstineo, me contineo; nihil praetermitto*, and the like; and we have also *quin* after negative expressions of time. But we have *quominus* (or *ne*) rather than *quin* after verbs signifying to hinder or refuse, such as *impedio, prohibeo, intercedo, interdico, detineo, per me fit* or *stat, moror* or *in mora sum, recuso, repugno*, and the like. The following examples will suffice to illustrate the distinction: *Nihil est quod aeneum habeat quin id intereat.* Cic. *N. D.* III. 13. *Haud multum abfuit, quin Ismenias interficeretur.* Liv. XLII. 44. Num *dubitas quin specimen naturae capi deceat ex optima quaque natura?* Cic. *Tusc.* I. 14. *Vix me contineo quin involem in eum.* Ter. *Eun.* V. 2. 20. *Nihil praetermisi, quin enucleate ad te perscriberem.* Cic. *Quint. Fr.* III. 3. *Neque ullum fere totius hiemis tempus intercessit sine sollicitudine*

Cæsaris, *quin* aliquem de conciliis et motu Gallorum nuntium acciperet. Cæs. *B. G.* v. 51. Hiemem credo adhuc *prohibuisse, quominus* de te certum haberemus. Cic. *ad div.* XII. 5. *Deterrere* eum voluit, *quominus* medicamentum biberet. Curt. VI. 40. Cæsar cognovit *per* Africanum *stare, quominus* dimicaretur. Cæs. *B. C.* I. 41. *Non recusabo quominus* omnes meas scripta legant. Cic. *Fin.* I. 3.

(H)

The temporal adverb *quum* and the local adverb *ubi* are also used as temporal conjunctions. It is to be observed that *quoad, donec, dum,* and *usque dum* signify both 'as long as' and 'until.' In *quoad* the end is regarded rather than the duration; this particle always implies limitation, and may be rendered 'and then no longer or farther.' *Donec,* which is not used by Cicero, expresses the whole of the intervening period, and may be rendered 'continually or uninterruptedly until.' *Dum* always expresses a contemporaneous occurrence, and must be rendered 'whilst.' These three words may denote any lapse of time, whether long or short; to express exclusively a long time we must use *quamdiu,* which is also distinguished from the other particles by its use as an interrogative 'how long?' *Quoad* or *quousque* (the former only in the poets) is used to signify not 'how long?' but 'up to what time?' Thus we have: *Quoad exspectatis?* Ter. *Phorm.* I. 2. 08. *Quousque?* inquies; *quoad* erit integrum. Cic. *Att.* XV. 23. Tam diu velle debebis, *quoad* te, quantum proficias, non pænitebit. Cic. *Off.* I. 1. Ea vero continebis, *quoad* ipse te videam. Cic. *Att.* XIII. 21. Scire autem nos oportet, coguitis, *quoad* possunt ab homine cognosci, bonorum et malorum finibus, nihil a philosophia posse aut majus aut utilius optari, quam hæc, quæ a nobis hoc quatriduo disputata sunt. Cic. *Tusc.* IV. 38. *Quoad* facere potui, or *quoad* ejus facere potueris. Cic. *Or.* II. 72; *Div.* III. 2. *Donec* armati confertique abibant, peditum labor in persequendo fuit. Liv. VI. 13. Nunquam destitit orare, *donec* perpulit. Ter. *Andr.* IV. 1. 37. Catilina erat unus timendus, *dum* mœnibus urbis continebatur. Cic. *Cat.* III. 7. Exspecta, *dum* Atticum conveniam. Cic. *Att.* VII. 1. Subtrahendi sunt iratis ii, in quos impetum conantur facere, *dum* se ipsi colligant. Cic. *Tusc.* IV. 30. *Quamdiu* etiam furor iste tuus nos eludet? Cic. *Cat.* I. 1. Se oppido tam diu tenuit, *quamdiu* in provincia Parthi fuerunt. Cic. *ad div.* XII. 19.

§ 4. *Interjections.*

113 Interjections or exclamatory words, which are used parenthetically for the expression of strong emotions, may be divided into three classes: (1) indeclinable words, which are never used except in these forms and for this purpose; (2) other parts of speech occasionally used in this way; (3) invocations of the gods.

(1) Interjections exclusively so used are the following:

  (a) Of joy: *io, iu, ha, he, hoi, hahahe, euoe, euax.*
  (b) Of pain or grief: *heu, eheu, vae, vah, au, hei, proh, ohe.*
  (c) Of astonishment: *o, en, ecce, hui, hem, ehem, aha, atat, papae, vah, tatae.*
  (d) Of disgust: *phui, apage.*
  (e) Of calling: *heus, eho, ehodum, o.*
  (f) Of attestation: *proh.*
  (g) Of encouragement: *eia.*
  (h) Of praise: *euge, eugepae, heia.*
  (i) Of calling attention: *en, ecce.*
  (k) Of enjoining silence: *st!*

(2) Other parts of speech, which may be used as interjectional words, are nouns, as *malum, indignum, turpe, miserabile, nefas;* and in the vocative, as *macte, macti;* verbs, as *quaeso, obsecro, amabo, oro, precor,* used in entreaties. So also the hortative *age, agite, cedo, sodes = si audes, sis = si vis, sultis = si vultis, agesis = age si vis, agedum, agitedum, &c.* And the adverbs *nae, profecto, cito, bene, belle.* Of the last, *nae* stands only before pronouns in the best writers, as, *Nae ego, si iterum eodem modo vicero, sine ullo milite in Epirum revertar.*

(3) Invocations of the gods have sometimes passed into mere interjections or even adverbs. Of this class the following are the most usual: *mehercule, mehercle, hercule, hercle, mehercules, hercules, medius fidius, mecastor, ecastor, pol, edepol, per deum, per deum immortalem, per deos, per Jovem, proh Juppiter, proh sancte, supreme Juppiter, proh dii immortales, proh deum fidem, proh deum*

atque hominum fidem, proh deum (scil. *fidem*), &c. Of these, *mehercule*, 'may you help me, O Hercules,' is the form approved by Cicero (*Orat.* 47); and this, or *Hercule*, is the emphatic interjection most frequently found in his writings. *Me deus fidius*, 'may Jove's son (*fidius* for *filius*) help me,' is also an appeal to *Hercules*. The weakest adjuration is *pol*, i.e. 'by Pollux,' and this is the woman's interjection in comedy. *Edepol* or *Epol*, &c., stand for *per aedem Pollucis*, &c.

CHAPTER VI.

DERIVATION AND COMPOSITION.

§ 1. *Derivation.*

(a) *Derived Nouns.*

114 (a) DERIVED SUBSTANTIVES.

(1) Substantives derived from Verbs.

(aa) In some cases the formative syllable is represented merely by the vowel *a*, the sibilant *s*, or the termination *-us*, appended to the root of the verb; thus we have *scrib-a* from *scrib-o*, *in-col-a* from *in-col-o*, *ad-vēn-a* from *ad-ven-i-o*, *per-fug-a* from *per-fug-i-o*, &c.; also, *dux* from *duc-o*, *rex* from *reg-o*, *pel-lex* from *pel-lic-io*, *ob-ses* from *ob-sid-o*, &c.; and *coqu-us* from *coqu-o*, *merg-us* from *merg-o*; with a number of words like *dol-us*, *riv-us*, *mod-us*, which seem to involve the roots of verbs no longer extant in a simple form.

(bb) Nouns in *-or*, so far as they can be referred to simple verbs, denote the action of the verb, as *fur-or*, 'a raging,' from *fur-o*, *am-or*, 'habitual choice, selection or preference,' from *emo*, 'to select or take up;' the majority of these words, though with a verbal meaning, cannot be referred to any known simple verb, but have on the contrary contracted verbs derived from them; thus from *am-or* we have *amo* = *ama-o*, 'to love,' from *fav-or*, which we refer conjecturally to a root *fav-o* (cf. *fav-onius*), we have *fav-eo*, 'to be favourable,' and from *lăb-or*, which we refer to an original *lăb-o* (cf. *lăb-or*), we have the derivative verbs *lăb-o* = *lub-ao* and *lăbor-o* = *labor-ao*.

(cc) Nouns in *-us* (gen. *-ūs*) formed like those, which appear as supines, express the action of the verb. Thus from *latro* we have *latra-tus*, 'a barking;' from *moveo* we have *mo-tus*, 'a moving;' from *audio* we have *audi-tus*, 'a hearing;' from *video* we have *vi-sus*, 'a seeing;' from *haurio* we have *haus-tus*, 'a drawing;' from *traho* we have *trac-tus*, 'a dragging;' from *orior* we have *or-tus*, 'a rising;' from *utor* we have *u-sus*, 'a using.'

(dd) From the same source we have masculines in *-or* (*-ōris*), denoting the agent; thus from *amo* we have *ama-tor*, 'a lover;' from *moneo* we have *moni-tor*, 'an adviser;' from *audio* we have *audi-tor*, 'a hearer;' from *scribo* we have *scrip-tor*, 'a writer;' from *curro* we have *cur-sor*, 'a runner;' from *peto* we have *peti-tor*, 'a seeker;' from *fodio* we have *fos-sor*, 'a digger.' Many of these have corresponding feminines in *-trix* from nouns in *-tor*, as *venator, vena-trix, vic-tor, vic-trix*, or, more rarely in *-strix* from nouns in *-sor*, as *ton-sor, ton-strix*; but *expul-sor* makes *expul-trix*.

Obs. 1. Some of these nouns in *-tor* appear to be derived from other nouns, as *gladiator* from *gladius, viator* from *via, funditor* from *funda*. But the affix seems to indicate that there may have been verbs from which they were formed like the others.

Obs. 2. Nouns in *-o, ōnis* coexist with verbs of the first conjugation, and seem to be derivatives; thus from *cachinnare* we have *cachinno*, 'a laugher;' from *errare, erro*, 'a wanderer;' from *palpare, palpo*, 'a flatterer.'

(ee) By a further extension, nouns in *-tor* (*-sor*) have derivatives in *-tura, -sura*, indicating the particular employment of the agent designated by the form in *-or*; thus we have *prae-tor, prae-tura, merca-tor, mercu-tura, pic-tor, pic-tura*. It will be observed that, as the noun of action in *-us* corresponds to the supine, those in *-ura* correspond to the fut. participle in *-rus*.

(ff) We have also nouns of action in *-io* formed on the basis of the supine, as *tracta-tio* from *tracto, cau-tio* from *caveo, largi-tio* from *largior, divi-sio* from *divido*.

(gg) From the root of the verb are formed nouns in *-ium* expressing the action, as *imper-ium* from *impero, gaud-ium* from *gaudeo, colloqu-ium* from *colloquor*.

(hh) In the same way are formed nouns in *-ies*, as *conger-ies* from *con-ger-o, ef-fig-ies* from *ef-fi-n-go*, &c.; but these rather express the result of the action, than the action itself.

(ii) We have also some few in *-ela* or *-ella*, either formed directly from the verb, as *med-ella, quer-ela*, from *medeor, queror;* or from the basis of the supine, as *corrupt-ela*.

(kk) A few verbal derivatives are found in *-igo* (*-iginis*), as *origo* from *orior*, or in *-ido* (*-idinis*), as *cupido* from *cupio*.

(ll) A sort of instrumental agency is expressed by a limited number of verbal derivatives in *-mus* and *-ma*, as *re-mus* (root *ret* or *rot*), 'a turning round' (in the water), i.e. 'a rowing thing,' 'an oar;' *ani-mus*, 'a blowing thing;' *al-mus*, 'that which nourishes' (from *alo*); *ar-mus*, 'that which joins,'—'the shoulder;' *fa-ma*, 'that which speaks' (*fāri*); *flam-ma*, 'that which burns' (*flag-rare*); *tra-ma*, 'a drawing, or that which draws' (*trah-o*), i.e. 'a web,' &c.

(mm) By an extension of these last forms we have a certain number of derivatives in *-mnus*, which seem to pass from the instrumental agency to its result, or to stand to the others in the relation of passive to active; thus by the side of *al-mus*, 'that which nourishes,' we have *alu-mnus*, 'he who is nurtured,' 'a foster-child,' 'a pupil;' similarly, *vertu-mnus*, 'that which is turned' (*verto*), i.e. 'the year in spring,' cf. *auctu-mnus;* *colu-mna*, 'that which is raised up' (*cello*) by the side of *cul-mus*, 'that which raises,' i.e. 'the stalk;' *da-mnum*, 'that which is given' (*do*), i.e. 'a penalty, a loss,' &c.

(nn) The derivatives in *-mnus, -a, -um*, appear also in the neuter form *-men*, originally *-men-t* (above, 25, (β)), as *car-men* = *quod creatur* (Gr. ποίη-μα); *cri-men* = *quod cernitur;* *legu-men* = *quod legitur;* *se-men* = *quod seritur;* *su-men* = *quod sugitur;* *volu-men* = *quod volvitur*.

(oo) Of these last we have a fuller form in *-mentum*, to denote the thing which carries out the action of the verb; thus we find *ali-mentum*, 'that which nourishes' (*alo*); *argu-mentum*, 'that which tests' (*arguo*); *ar-mentum*, 'that which ploughs' (*aro*); *atra-mentum*, 'that which makes a black mark' (*atrol*), i.e. 'ink;' *condi-mentum*, 'that which seasons' (*condio*); *docu-mentum*, 'that which shows' (*doceo*); *fo-mentum*, 'that which warms' (*foveo*); *leni-mentum*, 'that which alleviates' (*lenio*); *monu-mentum*, 'that which reminds' (*moneo*); *nutri-mentum*, 'that which nurtures' (*nutrio*); *orna-mentum*, 'that which adorns' (*orno*); *pig-mentum*, 'that which paints' (*pi-n-go*); *testa-mentum*, 'that which testifies' (*testor*); *vesti-mentum*, 'that which clothes' (*vestio*), &c.

(pp) Nouns in *-bulum*, and in *-culum* or *-clum*, denote either the implement or the place necessary for the completion of the verb's action; as *in-fundi-bulum*, 'an implement for pouring in liquid' (*in-fundo*), 'a funnel;' *sta-bulum*, 'a place for standing' (*sto*), 'a stall;' *oper-culum*, 'a thing for covering' (*operio*), 'a lid;' (*coena-culum*, 'a place for dining' (*coeno*). If the verb has an *l* within a syllable or two of the affix, we have *-brum* for *-bulum*, and *-crum* for *-culum* or *-clum*; thus we have *fla-brum* from *flo*; *sepul-crum* from *sepelio*. Sometimes these derivatives end in *-bula*, *-bra*, as *fā-bula* from *fari*, *dola-bra* from *dolare*. If the verb ends in *c* or *g*, the termination is *-ulum* only, as in *jac-ulum* from *jacio*, *vinc-ulum* from *vincio*, *cing-ulum* from *cingo*. In some few instances we have a termination *-lum* only, as in *cae-lum*, 'the hollowed vault of heaven' (from an obsolete verb *ca-io*), *tem-p-lum*, 'the divided heaven' (from *tem-no*, in its old sense, 'to cut').

(qq) There are a few verbal nouns in *-tis* and *-tus* which cannot be referred to the form of the supine, but have the same meaning as those mentioned above (cc), as *pes-tis*, 'a destroying,' *ves-tis*, 'a clothing,' *spiri-tus*, 'a breathing.'

(rr) A very few with the same meaning end in *-sa*, as *noxa*, 'hurt,' from *noc-eo*, *cau-sa*, 'an excuse,' from *cav-eo*. Most verbal nouns in *-sa* are really feminines of the passive participle; such are *fossa*, *sponsa*, *tonsa*.

(2) Substantives derived from other Substantives.

(aa) Nouns in *-ium*, denoting a condition or employment, are formed from substantives of various kinds denoting personal agency; thus from *collega*, 'a colleague,' we have *colleg-ium*, 'an association of colleagues;' from *conviva*, 'a guest,' *convio-ium*, 'a meeting of guests;' from *sacerdos* (*-tis*), 'a priest,' *sacerdot-ium*, 'a priesthood.' We have *mater-ia* or *mater-ies* from *mater*.

(bb) Nouns in *-tor*, *-ter* have occasionally derivative forms in *-trum*, *-tērium*, *-tōrium*, denoting the instrument, the office, or place appropriate to the agency; thus we have *ara-tor*, 'a ploughman,' *ara-trum*, 'a plough;' *minister*, 'a subordinate agent,' *minis-terium*, 'a subordinate office;' *audi-tor*, 'a hearer,' *audi-torium*, 'a place for hearing.' Hardly any of the nouns in *-trum* can be immediately referred to nouns in *-tor*; some have corresponding verbs; but others are of uncertain origin. Of those in *s-trum* several owe the *s* to *d* or *r* in the verb to which they belong, as *claus-trum* (*claud-o*), *haus-trum* (*haur-io*), *plaus-trum* (*plaud-o*), *ras-trum* (*rad-o*), *rostrum* (*rod-o*); but we have not this means of accounting for *fenestra*, 'a window,' *mons-trum*, 'a prodigy.' In *cas-trum* we have probably the same element as in *cas-a*, 'a house,' *cas-tus*, 'religiously protected,' and in the Greek κάσ-τωρ, 'a mailed warrior.' *Antrum* is the Greek ἄντρον.

(cc) The termination *-monium* is found only in the words *merci-monium* from *merx*, *testi-monium* from *testis*, *vadi-monium* from *vas* (*vădis*), in which it bears the same meaning as the termination in *-ium* (*an*); and in *matri-monium*, 'marriage,' *patrimonium*, 'inheritance,' in which the meaning is exceptional.

(dd) The termination *-atus* indicates the office or functions of the person indicated by the noun, which is thus extended; as *consul-atus* from *consul*, *tribun-atus* from *tribunus*, *triumvir-atus* from *triumvir*.

(ee) Nouns in *-arius* denote an employment, as *statu-arius* from *statua*, *tabern-arius* from *taberna*, *vexill-arius* from *vexillum*, &c.; those in *-arium* signify a place or receptacle, as *aer-arium*, 'a place for money,' *avi-arium*, 'a place for birds;' or a thing, as *calend-arium*, 'an almanack,' *sud-arium*, 'a napkin.'

(ff) Nouns in *-ina* or *-inum* denote the place or employment of the person indicated by the primary noun; thus from *tonsor* we have *tonstr-ina*, 'a barber's shop,' from *medicus* we have *medic-ina*, 'the art of healing,' from *pistor* we have *pistr-ina* or *pistr-inum*, 'the grinding-house.' These words seem to be only the feminines of adjectives in *-inus* (below, 115, (2), (ζ)), and in *reg-ina*, 'a queen,' we have merely an indication of a female person; compare the names of goddesses, *Luc-ina*, *Libit-ina*, &c. In other cases the noun in *-ina* seems to refer immediately to a verb, though we have perhaps lost the intervening substantives: thus we have *rap-ina*, *ru-ina*, by the side of *rapio* and *ruo*.

(gg) Nouns in *-al*, *-ar* (properly the neuters of adjectives in *-alis*, *-aris*, below, 115, (2), (δ)) denote a derivative object, as *anim-al,* 'a living thing,' from *animus, calc-ar,* 'a spur,' from *calx,* 'the heel.'

(hh) Nouns in *-tum* or *-ētum* are generally formed from the names of plants, and denote the places where they grow; as *salic-tum* from *salix, arbus-tum* from *arbos, oliv-ētum* from *oliva, frutic-ētum* from *frutex.*

(ii) The affix *-īle* added to the names of animals denotes their stall, as *orīle* from *ovis.* This is only the neuter of the adjective in *-ilis.* In *cub-īle,* 'a place to recline,' and *sed-īle,* 'a place to sit,' it seems to be referred directly to the verb. The primitive of *mon-īle,* 'a necklace,' is the Greek μάνος or μάννος.

(kk) Diminutives in *-lus* and *-cūlus* are formed as follows:

(α) Nouns of the first and second declensions have diminutives in *-lus* (*-la*), as *arcula* from *arca, serv-ŭ-lus* from *servus.* If the primitive nouns terminate in two vowels, the diminutive is formed in *-olus* (*-ola, -olum*), as *fili-olus* from *filius, lineola* from *linea, ingeniolum* from *ingenium.* If the primitive form ends in *-n,* in *-r* preceded by a consonant or *e,* or in *-ul,* we generally have diminutives in *-ellus* (*-a, -um*); as *agnellus* from *agnus, asellus* from *asinus, corolla* from *corona, labellum* from *labrum, puella* from *puera* (obsol.), *ocellus* from *oculus, tabella* from *tabula.* These last sometimes appear under the form *-illus* (*-a, -um*); as *sigillum* from *signum, bacillum* from *baculum.* Sometimes we have a double or triple diminutive in *-ulus, -ellus, -ellulus* (*-a, -um*), as *cista, cist-ula, cist-el-la, cist-el-lu-la.* From *equus* we have the irregular diminutive *eculeus.*

(β) Nouns of the third declension have diminutives in *-culus.*

(αα) This affix is appended without a connecting vowel and without any change in the word itself to nouns in *l, r,* and *s* for *r;* as *animal-culum, tuber-culum, flos-culus, frater-culus, opus-culum;* so also *vas-culum,* and *os-culum* from *os, oris;* but *ossi-culum* from *os, ossis,* which is an *-i* noun.

(ββ) The affix is appended with a change of vowel to the crude form of nouns in *-o*(*-ōnis*), *-o*(*-ĭnis*), as *sermun-culus* from *sermo* (*-ōnis*), *homun-culus* (also *homuncio*) from *homo* (*-ĭnis*), *carun-cula* from *caro* (*-nis*), *pectun-culus* from *pecten* (*-ĭnis*), and we have a similar formation in *rumus-culus* from *rumor, arbus-cula* from *arbor, gran-dius-culus* from *grandior.*

DERIVATION AND COMPOSITION. 213

Obs. The diminutives *ovun-culus, ranun-culus, furun-culus* presume secondary forms of *arus, rana, fur*, such an *avo* (*-ōnis*), (cf. *patronus* from *pater, matrona* from *mater*), *rano* (*-onis*), (cf. *bufo*), *furo* (*-onis*) (cf. *latro*).

(γγ) The affix *-culus* is appended to the crude-form of nouns in *-es, -is, -s* (preceded by a consonant), gen. *-is,* retaining the characteristic vowel of the nominative when *s* is preceded by a vowel, and otherwise adopting the *-i* of the genitive, as *nube-cula, die-cula, pisci-culus, ponti-culus, parti-cula*, and so also *ventri-culus* from *venter* (*ventris*). But the shorter form *-ulus* (*-a, -um*) is adopted if the letter before *s* is *c* or *g*, and so we have *fac-ula, voc-ula, radi-cula, reg-ulus* from *fax, vox, radix, rex.*

(δδ) The affix *-culus* is appended to *-u* nouns, which, however, change their characteristic to *-i*, as *versi-culus* from *versus, corni-culus* from *cornu;* but *lacus* makes *lacus-culus*, and the fem. *acus* gives us the masc. *acu-leus.*

(εε) Greek patronymics in *-ĭdes* (fem. *-is*), *-ĭdes* (fem. *-ēis*), *-oĭdes, -iĭdes* (fem. *-iĭs*), are rather borrowed ready made than formed from the primitives; thus we have *Priamīdes*, 'a son of Priam,' *Tantalīs,* 'a daughter of Tantalus,' *Atrīdes,* 'a son of Atreus,' *Nerēis,* 'a daughter of Nereus,' *Æneĭdes,* 'a son of Æneas,' *Atluntiĭdes,* 'a son of Atlas,' *Thestĭs,* 'a daughter of Thestius.'

(3) Substantives derived from Adjectives.

(aa) Nouns in *-tas* (*-tatis*), or more rarely in *-tus* (*-tutis*), denote the quality indicated by the adjective, like our nouns in *-ness,* &c. Generally we have the form *-itas*, as *bon-i-tas,* 'goodness,' from *bonus; asper-i-tas,* 'harshness,' from *asper; crudel-i-tas,* 'cruelty,' from *crudelis.* Adjectives in *-ius* give us the form *-ĕtas,* as *pi-ětas* from *pius, vari-ětas* from *varius.* Some few adjectives, especially those in *r* or *l,* omit the connecting vowel, as *pauper-tas* from *pauper, difficul-tas* from *difficilis.* Some substantives, which have occasionally an adjectival meaning, take this ending, as *auctor-ĭtas* from *auctor, civi-tas* from *civis, juven-tus* from *juvenis, vir-tus* from *vir* (cf. *virili-tas*). Adjectives already formed in *-stus* give us a substantive in *-stas,* as *honestas, venustas.* It would seem that *potestas* must be formed from a lost adjective of this class.

(bb) Nouns in *-ia,* of much the same signification as the last, are formed from adjectives of one termination or participles in *-us* and -*dus*; thus we have *audac-ia* from *audax* (but *felici-tas* from *felix*), *elegant-ia* from *elegans*, *magnificent-ia* from *magnum faciens* (cf. *magnificentior*, the comparative of *magnificus*), *iracund-ia* from *iracundus* (but *jucund-ĭtas* from *jucundus*).

(cc) Nouns in -*itia*, also of the same signification, are generally formed from adjectives of three terminations, as *just-itia* from *justus*, *pigr-itia* from *piger*. But we have *moll-itia* and *moll-ities* from *mollis*, and *pauper-ies* as well as *pauper-tas* from *pauper*.

(dd) Nouns in -*ĭ-tūdo*, with the same meaning, are formed from adjectives in -*us* (-*er*) or -*is*, as *magn-i-tudo* from *magnus*, *aegr-i-tudo* from *aeger*, *pingu-i-tudo* from *pinguis*. By the side of these we have synonymous forms in -*ēdo*, as *dulc-ēdo* instead of *dulc-ĭ-tudo* from *dulcis*, *pingu-ēdo* instead of *pingu-ĭ-tudo*, &c.

(ee) A few nouns of this kind are formed in -*monia*, as *casti-monia* from *castus*, *sancti-monia* from *sanctus*, *acri-monia* from *acer*. We have also *parsi-monia* for *parci-monia* from *parcus*, and *queri-monia* from a lost adjective, which may be presumed in *querulus*. It will be observed that these words differ in meaning from the neuters in -*monium* (above, (2), (cc)).

115 (β) Derived Adjectives.

(1) Adjectives derived from Verbs.

(aa) Participles of all kinds are used as regular adjectives.

(a) The regular and ordinary participles in -*ns* (-*ntis*) for the active and -*tus* (-*a*, -*um*) for the passive not only appear as adjectives, but are even employed as substantives. Thus *sapiens*, *obediens*, *conveniens*, *constans*, &c. are constantly found as epithets; *adolescens*, *serpens*, *parens*, &c., *natus*, *dictum*, *scriptum*, *praeceptum*, *consultum*, *placitum*, *furtum*, &c. are to all intents and purposes nouns substantive; and many participles have their degrees of comparison, as *sapientior*, *potentior*, *appetentior*, *appetentissimus*. Some passive participles are almost confined to an adjectival use, as *acutus*, *argutus*, *altus*, &c., and *secundus*, whether it means following as next in order ('second'), or following as a wind blowing from the stern ('fair,' 'prosperous'), is always distinguished from *sequens* by one of these applied and adjectival senses.

(β) Participles in -*bundus*, as *lacrima-bundus*, *pudi-bundus*, *mori-bundus*, *freme-bundus* are used as adjectives or epithets.

(γ) A smaller class of adjectives in *-cundus* seem to be really extended participles from inchoatives in *-sco* or *-scor*. It is true that the *s* is always wanting, and though its absorption is sometimes represented by a long vowel, as in *irā-cundus*, *fā-cundus*, *verē-cundus*, *fē-cundus*, it has not even this substitute in *rubi-cundus*. Still the existence of *ira-scor*, the probability of such forms as *fa-scor* (φάσκω), *fui-sco* (xυἱ-σκω), &c., and the meaning of these adjectives, which always denote a general tendency, inclination or habit, justify their reference to inchoative verbs, and there are no verb-forms ending in a simple *c*. In *jū-cundus* and perhaps in *fe-cundus* (for *fuvi-scundus*) we have an absorption of *v*.

(bb) Verbal adjectives in *-ĭ-dus* correspond in meaning to participles, and are generally formed from intransitive verbs in *-eo;* thus we have *cal-ĭ-dus=calens* from *caleo*, *tim-ĭ-dus=timens* from *timeo*, &c. They are also formed from other verbs, as *turb-ĭ-dus=turbans* from *turbo*, *cup-ĭ-dus=cupiens* from *cupio;* and some, as *lepĭdus, trepĭdus, gravĭdus*, cannot be referred directly to any existing verbs.

(cc) Verbal adjectives in *-bĭlis* express capability, either actively, as *terri-bĭlis*, 'capable of frightening,' passively, as *placa-bĭlis*, 'capable of being appeased,' or both, as *penetra-bĭlis*, 'capable of penetrating or of being penetrated.' In the shorter form in *-ĭlis*, which is attached only to consonant verbs, we have only the passive sense of capability, as *facĭlis*, 'capable of being done,' i.e. 'easy,' *fragĭlis*, 'capable of being broken,' i.e. 'fragile.' Both of these forms are generally attached to the root of the verb with the connecting vowel *ĭ*, but we have *volūbĭlis* for *volvĭ-bĭlis*, *mōbĭlis* for *movi-bĭlis*, *nobĭlis* for *nosci-bĭlis*. They are sometimes formed from the supine, as *comprehens-ĭbilis, flex-ĭbilis, plaus-ĭbilis, fiss-ilis, versat-ilis*. Of those in *-ilis*, some have much the same signification as the mere passive participle, for instance, *alt-ĭlis, coct-ĭlis, fict-ĭlis*. To this class belong *subtilis* for *subtex-ĭlis*, and *exĭlis* for *exigĭ-lis*.

(dd) Verbal adjectives in *-ax* (*-ācis*) express inclination or disposition, as *loqu-ax*, 'inclined to talk,' *pugn-ax*, 'inclined to fight.' Some of them have much the same signification as the active participle, for instance *fall-ax*, 'deceiving,' *min-ax*, 'threatening.'

(ee) Verbal adjectives in -*ŭlus* have much the same meaning as those in -*ax*; compare *garr-ŭlus*, 'inclined to talk,' with *loqu-ax*; so also we have *pat-ŭlus*, 'opening or tending to open,' *quer-ŭlus*, 'inclined to complain,' *cred-ŭlus*, 'inclined to believe,' &c.

(ff) Verbal adjectives in -*uus* have sometimes the sense of the active participle, as *congr-uus* = *congruens*, *innoc-uus* = *innocens*; sometimes that of the passive participle, as *conspic-uus*, 'seen,' in-*dividuus* (cf. *viduus*), 'undivided.'

(2) Adjectives derived from Substantives.

(aa) The following adjectives denote possession, and may be rendered by 'of' or 'belonging to.'

(α) in -*ius* (generally from nouns in -*or*), as *ora-tor-ius*; also *patr-ius*, *reg-ius*, &c.

(β) in -*icus*, as *bell-icus*, *civ-icus*, *host-icus*.

(γ) in -*ilis*, as *civ-ilis*, which is more common than *civ-icus* in prose, except in *corona civica*; and *host-ilis*, which is preferred to *hosticus*, except in *ager hosticus*. We have *curulis* from *currus*, *tribūlis* from *tribus*, *fidēlis* from *fides*, and *humĭlis*, *partĭlis*, from *humus*, *pars*.

(δ) in -*ālis*, which is more common even than -*ilis*, and is appended not only to substantives, as *reg-ālis* from *rex*, *nav-ālis* from *navis*, *ann-ālis* from *annus*, *judici-ālis* from *judicium*, but even to an adjective, as *liber-ālis* from *liber*, 'free.' If the primary noun involves an *l* within the influence of the termination, we have -*āris* instead of -*ālis*, as in *popul-āris*, *milit-āris*; but *pluvius* and *fluvius* make *pluviālis*, *fluviālis*.

(ε) in -*ārius* (see above, (2), (ee)), which are perhaps an extension of those in -*aris*, as *agrārius*, *gregārius*, *auxiliārius*, *tumultuārius*.

(ζ) in -*anus*, -*inus*, -*enus*, and -*unus*, as *oppid-anus*, 'belonging to a town,' *urb-anus*, 'belonging to the city,' *mont-anus*, 'belonging to the mountain,' *hum-anus* (for *hominanus*), 'belonging to man,' *germ-anus* (for *germinanus*), 'belonging to the same stem,' *mar-inus*, 'belonging to the sea,' *terr-ēnus*, 'belonging to the land,' *tribūnus*, 'belonging to the tribe,' &c. From numerals we have the adjectives in -*anus* derived from ordinals (56, Obs. 7), and the distributives in -*enus* from the numeral adverbs (57, Obs. 1).

DERIVATION AND COMPOSITION. 217.

(η) in -*ensis*, which seem to be an extension of the last (see below, (4), (cc), (δ)), as *castr-ensis*, 'belonging to the camp.'

(θ) in -*trus*, as *furt-īvus*, 'belonging to theft,' from *furtum*, *aest-īvus*, 'belonging to summer or heat,' from *aestas* or *aestus*.

(ι) in -*ātilis*, as *aquā-tilis*, 'belonging to water,' *umbr-ātilis*, 'belonging to the shade.'

(bb) The following denotes the material, and may be rendered by ' made of,' ' consisting in.'

(a) in -*eus*, as *lign-eus*, 'made of wood,' *ign-eus*, 'consisting in fire.'

(β) in -*Inus*, -*nus*, or -*neus*, as *fag-īnus*, ' of beech wood,' *ebur-nus* or *ebur-neus*, ' of ivory,' *quer-nus* (for *querc-nus*) or *quer-neus*, ' of oak.'

(γ) in -*āceus*, -*icius* and -*ūceus*, as *chart-aceus*, ' of paper;' *later-icius*, 'of brick,' *pannuceus*, ' of rags, ragged.'

Obs. 1 If the primary noun does not denote a material, these adjectives may be rendered by 'like' or 'belonging to,' as *virgin-eus*, ' like a virgin;' *pater-nus*, ' belonging to a father;' *tribun-icius*, 'belonging to a tribune.'

Obs. 2 Some adjectives in -*icius* are formed from verbals in -*tus*, as *comment-icius* 'feigned,' from *commentum*, &c. In the same way *novicius* is for *nov-it-icius*, as *nuntius* is for *novi-vent-ius*.

(cc) The following denote abundance, and may be rendered by ' full of.'

(a) Those in -*idus*, as *herb-idus*, ' abounding in grass.'

(β) those in -*ōsus*, as *pericul-osus*, ' full of danger.'

(γ) those in *lentus* preceded by ŭ, or by ŏ after n and i, as *op-ŭ-lentus*, ' loaded with wealth,' *sanguin-ŏ-lentus*, ' full of blood,' *vi-ŏ-lentus*, ' full of violence.' These are properly compounds with the adjective *lentus*.

(dd) Adjectives in -*tĭmus* denote direction of motion, as *fini-timus*, ' towards the borders,' *mari-timus*, ' towards the sea.' Many, superlatives take this form, as *in-timus*, ' most inward,' *op-timus*, ' most upward.'

(ee) Adjectives in -*rnus* denote a state at a particular time, as *noctu-rnus*, ' a condition relating to night,' *hodie-rnus*, ' a condition of to-day,' *tacitu-rnus*, ' a condition of silence after speaking.'

(ff) Adjectives in *-ātus, -ītus, -ūtus*, have the form of passive participles, and may have been derived from verbs no longer existing; but they refer to the possession of that which is indicated by the primary noun, as *barb-ātus*, 'having a beard,' 'bearded,' *crin--ītus*, 'having long hair,' 'long-haired,' *corn-ūtus*, 'horned.' The secondary verb is still seen in *sta-tūtus, cinc-tūtus, ver-sūtus*, and the particle *act-ūtum*.

(gg) Adjectives in *-tus* like the corresponding substantives in *-tas* (above, (3), (aa)), denote a quality, as *hones-tus*, 'honourable, virtuous,' *onus-tus*, 'heavy,' *modes-tus*, 'moderate, modest.'

(hh) Adjectives in *-s-ter, -s-tris*, signify locality, as *campes-ter*, 'in the fields,' *palus-tris*, 'in the marshes.' The isolated word *seques-ter* from *secus* (cf. *sequior*) means 'one who is not interested, a mediator or umpire between two parties.'

(3) Adjectives derived from other Adjectives.

(aa) Some adjectives are diminutives formed according to the rules given above; thus we have *parv-ulus* from *parvus, levi-culus* from *levis, misel-lus* from *miser*. Also the irregular forms *bellus* from *bonus, novellus* from *novus, paullus* from *parvus*.

(bb) Adjectives in *-ox (-ōcis), -ūcus* and *-icus*, seem to be extensions of simpler adjectives, which are often lost; thus *fer-ox* is clearly an extension of *fer-us, cad-ūcus* must be referred to some form like *cud-uus* (above, (1), (ff); cf. *oc-cid-uus*); *ant-īcus, post-īcus*, seem to fall back on some derivative of *anteo, posteo; am-īcus, pud-īcus*, point to intermediate forms like *ex-im-ius*. As the substantive from *ferox* is *ferōcia*, whereas *amicus, pudicus* make *amicitia, pudicitia*, the solitary form *fidūcia* seems to imply an extension of *fidus* in the form of *fidux*, rather than an adjective *fidūcus*. As we have *Apr-īlis* by the side of *apr-īcus*, we may refer them both to some one derivative from *aperio*.

(cc) Comparatives and superlatives (above, 36) are derived not only from positive adjectives but from adverbial forms.

(4) Adjectives derived from Proper Names.

(aa) The gentile name in *-ius* (below, Appendix III. (a)) is used as an adjective to denote a man's public doings; thus we have *via Appia*, 'the road constructed by Appius,' *Liciniae rogationes*, 'the bills brought in by Licinius,' *circus Flaminius*, 'the circus made by Flaminius.'

(bb) Derivatives in *-anus* from the gentile name express transference by adoption from the family so named, as *Scipio Æmilianus*, the younger Scipio Africanus, who had belonged to the *gens Æmilia*, but was transferred by adoption to the *gens Cornelia*. The same affix also expresses the possessive relation in any case except those mentioned under (aa); for example, 'Pompey's law' is *lex Pompeia*, but 'Pompey's fleet' is *classis Pompeiana*. Sometimes in the latter case we have derivatives from the cognomen in *-ianus, -anus*, or *-inus*, *Ciceron-ianus, Gracch-anus, Verr-inus*.

(cc) From names of towns we have the following derivative adjectives:

(a) in *-anus* from words in *-a, -ae, -um*, as *Romanus, Formianus, Tusculanus*, from *Roma, Formiae, Tusculum*.

(β) in *-inus* from words in *-ia, -ium, -e*, as *Amerinus, Lanuvinus, Praenestinus*, from *Ameria, Lanuvium, Praeneste*.

(γ) in *-us* (*-atis*) from Roman names only in *-a, -ae, -um*, as *Cupēnas, Fidēnas, Arpīnas*, from *Cupēna, Fidēnae, Arpīnum*.

(δ) in *-ensis* from Roman and foreign words in *-o* (*-onis*), and from some in *-a, -ae, -um*, as *Sulmonensis, Bononiensis, Cannensis, Atheniensis*, from *Sulmo, Bononia, Cannae, Athenae*.

Obs. 1 Adjectives in *-ensis* sometimes represent a temporary as distinguished from a fixed residence in a country. Thus *Siculus, Corinthius* are natives of *Sicilia* and *Corinthus*, but *Siciliensis, Corinthiensis*, are foreigners settled or living in Sicily and Corinth.

Obs. 2 Greek names in *-ius*, as *Corinthius*, in *-enus*, as *Cyzicenus*, in *-aeus*, as *Erythaeus* (*Cumanus* in prose, but *Cumaeus* in poetry), in *-tes*, as *Abderites, Spartiates* (but the adjective is *Spartanus*), *Tegeates, Heracleates*, are retained in Latin.

Obs. 3 Greek feminine forms in *-is* (*-idis*), *-as* (*-adis*), and in *-ssa*, as *Pelias, Hesperides, Cilissa, Cressa*, retain their place as Latin adjectives.

(b) *Derived Verbs.*

116 Derivative verbs are either extensions of other verbs, or are formed immediately from nouns. In either case the variety in form is conjugational, and, as such, has been already discussed. The proper classification of these derivative verbs is attended with certain philological difficulties, for the loss of intermediate forms of the verb has led grammarians to refer immediately to nouns more than one class of verbs, which are really derived from other verbs, and, on the other hand, to derive immediately from primary verbs those derivative forms which rest on verbal substantives. Thus, in the former case they have divided verbs in *-sco* into *inchoativa verbalia* and *inchoativa nominalia*; for instance, *in-cale-sco* is an extension of *caleo*, but *mature-sco* is supposed to be a derivative from the adjective *maturus*. As, however, the formation in *-sco* is limited to the present in both cases, and as the primitive *caleo* is reproduced in the perfect *in-calui*, so the perfect *maturui* leads us to a lost primitive in *-eo*, which is the neuter correlative of the transitive *maturare* (below, 117, (2), (cc)). A similar inference may be drawn from the perfects *obmutui, percrebui, irrausi, vesperavi, iratus sum*, &c., although these have no present in use except the inchoatives *obmutesco, percrebresco, irraucesco, vesperasco, irascor*, &c. In the second case, when the grammarians say that the frequentative verbs in *-ito* are derived from their primitives by the mere addition of this syllable, they forget that *mil-it-are*, for example, has no primitive verb, but that it is formed directly from *miles* (*-Itis*), which is formed from *miles* and *eo*, and that the same is the case with *interpretari* from *interpres;* and they forget also that there are frequentatives in *-to*, *-so*, which are directly formed from the supine or verbal noun derived from the primitive verb, as *curso* from *cursus* the verbal of *curro*. The following arrangement places first the verbs really derived from nouns, whether those nouns are or are not themselves verbal forms, and secondly, the verbs which are really extensions of other verbs, without an intervening noun.

117 (1) Verbs derived from Nouns.

These are always contracted verbs in *-a*, *-e*, *-i*; and it is to be observed, that while most verbs thus derived in *-a* and *-i* are transitive, *-e* verbs formed from nouns are always intransitive. Thus, from *emo*, 'to take up,' comes *amor*, 'habitual selection or preference,' and from this again, *amo* (*-ao*), 'to love;' but from *favor* comes *faveo*, 'to be favourable.'

(aa) Transitive verbs in *-are* are derived from substantives of all kinds, as *curare, numerare, fraudare, onerare, vulgare*, from *cura, numerus, fraus, onus, vulgus*. Some few of these are intransitive, as *militare, cursare, laborare, germinare,* from *miles, cursus, labor, germen.*

(bb) Transitive verbs in *-are* are also formed from adjectives, as *cavare, maturare, lēvare* (for *leviare*), *ditare* (for *divitare*), *probare, celebrare, memorare,* from *cavus, maturus, lēvis, dīves (-ĭtis), probus, celeber, memor.* Some few of these are intransitive, as *nigrare,* 'to be black,' from *niger; concordare,* 'to be agreed,' from *concors;* and *durare,* from *durus,* means both 'to make hard' and 'to last or endure.'

(cc) Deponents in *-ari* are formed from substantives and adjectives to denote an occupation or situation; generally in an intransitive sense, as *piscari,* 'to be occupied in fishing,' *philosophari,* 'to play the philosopher,' *laetari,* ' to be glad;' rarely with a transitive signification, as *interpretari,* 'to interpret,' *furari,* 'to steal,' *osculari,* 'to kiss.'

(dd) A few transitive verbs in *-ire* are formed from substantives of all kinds, as *punire, audire, finire, vestire, custodire,* from *poena, auris, finis, vestis, custos;* but *servire* is intransitive. A few also from adjectives in *-is,* as *lenire, mollire, stabilire,* from *lenis, mollis, stabilis;* but *superbire, ferocire, blandiri,* from *superbus, ferox, blandus,* are intransitive.

(ee) Intransitive verbs in *-eo* are formed from substantives, as *ardēre, florēre, frondēre, lucēre,* from *ardor, flos, frons, lux,* and a few from adjectives, as *albēre, canēre,* from *albus, canus.*

(ff) Desiderative verbs in *-ūrio* are formed from the future participle in *-ūrus,* with a shortening of the penultima, as in *minister* compared with *ministerium.* Thus, from *edo, esūrus,* we have *esūrio,* 'to desire to eat;' from *pario, partūrus,* we have *partūrio,* 'to desire to bring forth.' With the exception of these two, the desideratives are not in very common use. The verbs *ligūrio* or *ligurrio,* and *scatūrio* or *scaturrio,* are not desideratives, but derived from some lost verbals.

(gg) A few verbs in *-ūtio,* as *caec-utio, balb-utio,* are derived not immediately from the adjectives (as *caecus, balbus*) which they include, but from participial adjectives, *caecūtus, ba'būtus,* of the class mentioned above (115, (2), (ff)).

(hh) Some verbs in *-tlo* are derived from diminutives in *-ŭlus,* as *modūlo* from *modulus;* others, as *postulo,* are, as we shall see ((2), (bb)), verbal extensions.

(2) Verbs formed from other verbs.

(aa) Verbs in *-sco* are generally formed from *-e* verbs, which exist or may be presumed; and they very often appear with prepositions prefixed, as *taceo, conticesco; valeo, convalesco; frigeo, refrigesco,* &c.; but they are also formed from other verbs, the *a* and *i* being retained in the conjugations characterized by those vowels, and the vowel *i* being inserted before the affix in derivatives from consonant verbs; thus, from *labare* we have *labasco;* from *gelo, congelasco;* from *dormio, obdormisco;* from *gemo, ingemisco;* from *vivo, revivisco,* &c.

(bb) Some few verbs are formed in *-illo (-āre)* and *-ŭlo (-āre)*; in the former case, as it seems, from the infinitive, as in *cavillor* for *cavere-lor*, 'I let myself take care;' *conscribillo* for *conscribere-lo*, 'I let write, I write at random;' sometimes from the supine, as *postu-lo* for *poscitum-lo*, 'I let ask,' *cantillo* for *cantum-lo*, 'I let sing,' &c.

(cc) A change in the form of the verb produces sometimes a change in the meaning from transitive to intransitive, and it is not easy in every case to determine the process of derivation by which the change is effected. Sometimes it is merely conjugational, as when we have the neuter verbs, *fugio*, 'I flee;' *jaceo*, 'I lie;' *liqueo*, 'I am clear;' *pendeo*, 'I hang;' *sedeo*, 'I sit;' by the side of the transitive verbs, *fugo (-are)*, 'I put to flight;' *jacio*, 'I throw;' *liquo (-are)*, 'I make clear;' *pendo*, 'I weigh' (by hanging up in a scale); *sedo (-are)*, 'I pacify.' Sometimes the form of the root-syllable is changed, as in *caedo*, 'I fell' or 'cause to fall,' by the side of *cado*, 'I fall;' and we have both differences in *pando*, 'I open;' *scando*, 'I climb;' by the side of *pateo*, 'I am laid open;' *scateo*, 'I rise up' (of water, &c.). In *ven-do*, 'I give for sale, I sell,' by the side of *ven-eo*, 'I go for sale, I am sold,' we have probably a combination with the verbs *do* and *eo;* cf. *per-do* and *per-eo*.

§ 2. *Composition.*

118 A compound is an union of two or more words of which the last only is inflected, the preceding word or words being in a dependent or construct state, and having consequently lost all inflexion. If both parts retain their inflexion, or, if the first part, though an oblique case, is separable, the composition is only appa-

rent; thus, *respublica*, 'the commonwealth,' *jusjurandum*, 'an oath,' in which both parts are declined throughout, and *senatusconsultum*, 'a resolution of the senate,' *verisimilis*, 'like the truth,' are not compounds, but juxtapositions of separable elements, and we may say *resque publica, senatusve consulta*.

Obs. Even in regular compounds this *tmesis* or separation may take place in poetry; thus we have in Virgil *inque ligatus* for *illigatusque*, *inque salutatus* for *insalutatusque;* and the emphatic prefix *per* may suffer *tmesis* even in prose, as *per mihi mirum videtur; pergratum perque jucundum est*, &c. The adverbial combinations *hactenus, eatenus, quadamtenus*, are also divisible into their component parts; as *est quadam prodire tenus, si non detur ultra;* and the affix *cunque* may be detached from its relative, as *qua re cunque possum; quo ea me cunque ducet; quam rem cunque ferox miles gesserit*.

I. *The formation of compounds.*

119 The first part of a true compound is either an indeclinable word, or a noun, whether substantive, adjective, or numeral, and the latter part of the word always determines to what part of speech the whole belongs.

(a) When the first part is a particle, the vowels and diphthongs *a, e, ae, au* in the root of the word which follows are liable to be changed into *i, e, i, u* or *u* respectively (above, p. 8); thus, from *amīcus, capio*, we have *in-imicus, ac-cipio;* from *teneo* we have *con-tineo;* from *aequus, aestimo*, we have *in-iquus, ex-istimo;* from *claudo, causa, ex-cludo, ac-cuso;* from *audio, obedio*, &c.; but before two consonants, and sometimes before a consonant and the semi-consonant *i, a* is represented by *e;* compare *barba, im-berbis; scando, as-cendo; spargo, con-spergo;* &c., with *facio, pro-fic-iscor, pro-fectus; jacio, ab-jicio, ab-jectus; cano, concino, con-centus; pario, peperi;* and before *l* and a consonant *a* may become *u:* compare *calco, con-culco*, with *colo, cultura*. In some cases an *e* is retained, as in *peto, ap-peto; tego, con-tego; fremo, per-fremo;* and *lego* exhibits in its compounds both *e* and *i*, as *per-lego, intel-ligo;* the compounds of *traho, caveo* and *haereo* retain the vowel or diphthong unaltered, and the same applies to all the compounds of *maneo*, and to the adjective *concarus*.

Obs. 1 The particles, which may form the first part of a compound, are either adverbs, prepositions, or the inseparable words mentioned above (111). Of these latter, it seems that *amb-* sometimes appeared in the fuller form *ambi-*, more directly referring to *ambo*, and in one particular case, that of *ambidens*, scil. *ovis*, 'a sheep having both the upper and lower teeth,' and therefore of fit age for sacrifice (Festus, p. 4), this form has suffered apocope, and under the usual form *bidens* this name of a sheep is liable to confusion with *bidens*, 'a mattock' (from *bis-dens*, cf. *tridens*). The word *ambiegnus*, 'having a lamb on both sides' (Varro, L. L. VII. 31), was also written *ambrynus* (Fest. p. 4). *Nemis*, 'a half,' appears in compounds as *semi-*, e.g. in *semi-supinus; sesqua*, 'and a half,' appears as *sesqui-*, e.g. in *sesquipes*; and we have also *ses-*, as in *sestertius*.

Obs. 2 The negative prefixes in Latin are *in-* and *ne-* or *nec-*. The prefix *in-* is found only with adjectives, adverbs, and a few participles used as adjectives, as *incultus, indoctus;* or with derivatives from substantives, as the adjective *informis* from *forma*, and the substantive *injuria* from *jus*. It is liable to the same modifications as the preposition *in*, from which it must sometimes be distinguished, as *infectus*, 'undone,' by the side of *infectus* (from *inficio*), 'dyed, stained;' *indictus*, 'unsaid,' by the side of *indictus* (from *indico*), 'enjoined.' The prefix *ne-* or *nec-* is of rather rare occurrence. We have *ně-* in *něqueo, něfas, něfarius, něfandus, něfastus; ně-* in *nequam, nequitia, nequaquam, nequicquam, nědum; nec-* in *necopinatus, necopinus, negligo, nego (nec-aio), negotium*.

(b) When the first word is a noun and the second begins with a vowel, an elision takes place, as in *magn'animus;* but if the second begins with a consonant, the connecting vowel is generally *i*, as *caus-dicus, corni-ger, aedi-fico*. Sometimes, however, the *i* is omitted, as in *naufrāgus* (from *navis* and *frango*), *puer-pera* (from *puer* and *pario*), *mus-cipula* (from *mus* and *capio*), and sometimes a characteristic letter and its preceding vowel are left out before *i*, as in *lap-ĭ-cida* for *lapĭdĭ-cĭda, hom-ĭ-cĭda* for *homĭnĭcĭda, op-ĭ-fex* for *opĕrĭfex,* &c. When the first is a numeral, it is either unchanged as in *decemvir*, or is specially changed, as in *biceps, triumvir*, 'on man of three.' In some few cases the connecting vowel is *ŏ=ŭ; e. Aheno-barbus, Troju-gena, rio-lentus, opu-lentus, turbŭ-lentus, quadrŭpes;* and in *tibī-cen* for *tibī-i-cen*, we have a contracted *i*, though *tub-ĭ-cen* follows the general rule. In some compounds with *man* the second vowel is represented by *u* or *i*, as *manu-pretium* o *mani-pretium, mani-festus, mani-plus,* &c.; and we have a contraction in *manubrium* for *manu-hibrium*. In other compounds with this word the *n* alone is retained, and, in some cases, assimilated to a succeeding consonant; thus we have *man-do, man-ceps, mansuetus, man-tele, mal-lurium*. The adverbs *bene, male*, retain the final *e* in *bene-ficus, male-ficus,* but change it into *i* in *beni-gnus, mali-gnus*.

II. *The classification of compounds.*

Considered as a declinable whole, a compound word is either a substantive, an adjective, or a verb.

(A) Compound Substantives.

(1) Most compound substantives are derivatives of compound verbs, as *ad-ven-a* (*advenio*), *trans-fug-a* (*transfugio*), *de-lec-tus* (*deligo*), *pro-gres-sus* (*progredior*), &c.

(2) Some are compounded of a substantive and a verb, as *arti-fex* (*arte facio*), *auriga* (*aureum ago*), *lani-ficium* (*lana facio*), *au-spicium* (*aves specio*), *agri-cola* (*agrum colo*), *agri-peta* (*agrum peto*), *caeli-cola* (*caelum colo*), *homi-cida* (*hominem caedo*), *caussi-dicus* (*caussam dico*), &c.

(3) Some are compounded of a preposition and a noun, as *ab-avus*, *ag-nomen* (*ad-nomen*), *com-mercium* (*cum-merx*), *pro-consul*, &c.

(4) Some are compounded of a numeral and a noun, as *decem-vir*, *tri-duum*, *quadri-ennium*.

(5) Some are compounded of two substantives, as *rupi-capra* from *rupes* and *capra*.

(6) Some of an adjective and a substantive, as *rect-angulum*, *stulti-loquium*; but these generally belong to Latinity of a later age.

(B) Compound Adjectives.

(a) The last part is a substantive.

(α) If the last part is a substantive, and is a consonantal noun masc. or fem., it often remains unchanged, as in *bi-pes*, *bi-color*, *de-mens*; and then it retains the inflexions of the original substantive, except that *ex-sanguis* has for its gen. *exsanguis*, not *exsanguinis*; acc. *exsanguem*, not *exsanguinem*. If the substantive involved is neuter, or of the 1st or 2nd declension, or of the semi-consonantal declension, the compound adjective ends in *-is*, *-e*, or *-us*, *-a*, *-um*, as *de-vius* (*via*), *e-nervis* (*nervus*), *bi-maris* (*mare*), *centi-manus* (*-a*, *-um*), *cog-nominis* (*nomen*).

Obs. Except the compounds with *caput*, as *bi-ceps, bi-cipitis*; with *corpus*, as *bi-corpor, bi-corporis*; and with *cor*, as *con-cors, con-cordis*; which retain the inflexions of their primitives.

(β) The first part of a compound adjective, whose last part is derived from a substantive, is either

(aa) Another substantive, as in *aeri-pes, angui-manus.*

(bb) An adjective or numeral, as in *bi-linguis, long-aevus, lati-fundium.*

(cc) A preposition or other particle, as in *a-mens, per-vius, in-ers.*

(b) The last part is a verb.

(α) If the last is a verb, the compound adjective generally ends in *-us, -a, -um* appended to the verb-root, as *luci-fugus, fati-loquus, monti-vagus.* But compounds with *gero* and *fero* generally end in *-ger* and *-fer*, those from *capio* end in *-ceps*, and those from *frango* and *dico* shorten the ending into *-frăgus, -dĭcus*; thus we have *igni-fer, flammi-ger, parti-ceps, nau-frăgus, veri-dĭcus.*

(β) The first part of a compound adjective, whose last part is derived from a verb, is either

(aa) A substantive, which is generally an accusative, more rarely an ablative dependent on the verb, as *caduci-fer (caduceum ferens), igni-vomus (ignem vomens), monti-vagus (in monte vagans), nocti-vagus (nocte vagans),* &c.

(bb) An adjective, either substantively, as the object of the verb, or adverbially, as a secondary predicate; thus we have *falsi-dicus (falsa dicens), multi-loquus (multa or multum loquens), alti-sonus (alte sonans), soli-vagus (solus vagans), bene-ficus (bene faciens),* &c.

(c) The last part is an adjective.

If the last part of the compound adjective is itself an adjective, the first part is either a preposition or an inseparable particle; thus we have *per-difficilis, prae-dives, sub-agrestis, sub-pallidus, im-memor, im-prudens, in-imicus,* &c.

(C) Compound Verbs.

A compound verb is either (α) a primary compound or (β) a derivative compound.

(α) A primary compound retains, with occasional abbreviations, the conjugation of the original verb which stands at the end; it is

(aa) The original verb with a prepositional prefix, as *damno, con-demno; moneo, ad-moneo; salio, de-silio; scribo, de-scribo,* &c.

(bb) The original verb with an adverb prefixed, as *volo, magis-volo = malo, non-volo = nolo; lego, nec-ligo; satis-do, sat-ago,* &c.

(cc) The original verb, with another verb prefixed; as *assue-facio, pate-facio, condoce-facio, perterre-facio, arces-so* (for *arcessino), venum-do,* &c.

(β) A derived compound verb is of the first or fourth conjugation; it is formed from a compound noun, and changes the conjugation of the verb which stands at the end, if the compound noun ended in a verb-root, unless the original verb was also of the first conjugation; thus we have *per-nocto* (-āre) from *pernox, tergi-versor* (-āri) from *tergum vertens, im-pedio* (-īre) from *in pede, ir-retio* (-īre) from *in reti, il-laqueo* (-āre) from *in laqueum, e-rudio* (-īre) from *e rudibus,* 'out of foils;' *aedi-fico* (-āre) from *aedem faciens, multi-plico* (-āre) from *multi-plex, ampli-fico* (-āre) from *amplum facio, mori-geror* (-āri) from *morem gerere,* &c.

Obs. Verbs, which have reduplicated perfects, generally lose the reduplication when they are compounded with a preposition. Thus from *tundo, totondi* we have *detundo, detondi.* But compounds with *do, sto, disco, posco,* and most of those with *curro,* retain their reduplication; thus we have *circumdedi, astiti, edidici, repoposci, accucurri.* But in *circumcurro, recurro, succurro, transcurro* we have no reduplication of the perfect.

120 Compounds are called (a) *determinative* when the first part of the word defines the second; as *interrex, cognomen, benefīcus, latifundium, laticlāvus,* &c.; (b) *syntactical,* when the first word is governed by the second; as *agricŏla, opulentus, signifer,* *æquiparo, breviloquens*, &c.; (c) *auxiliary*, when two verbs come together, and the second helps the former; as *ama-ri* for *ama-fui*, *ven-do* for *venum do*, *arcesso* for *ac-cedere sino*; (d) *possessive*, when the first part denotes the manner of the thing possessed; as *crassipes*, 'thick-footed,' *alipes*, 'wing-footed,' and the negatives *aspers*, 'without a share in,' *inermus*, 'without arms,' &c. Those compounds which consist of more than two constituent parts are called *decomposita*; as *su-ove-taur-ilia*, *in-de-feunus*, &c.; and those which are made up of words from different languages are termed *hibridae*; as *epiredium* or *epirrhedium*, from ἐπί and *rheda*, *dextrocherium* from *dexter* and χείρ, *monoculus* from μόνος and *oculus*.

PART II.

SYNTAX, OR THE CONSTRUCTION OF WORDS.

CHAPTER I.

FIRST PRINCIPLES AND GENERAL RULES.

§ 1. *Subject and Predicate.*

121 (1) *Syntax* or *construction* (i.e. 'arrangement' or 'putting together in order') gives the rules of speech or speaking.

(2) Speech or speaking consists of sentences or thoughts expressed in words.

(3) A sentence or expression of thought (*propositum effatum*) is called a Proposition or Enunciation, and consists of, or may be resolved into, three parts—the *Subject*, the *Copula*, and the *Predicate*.

(4) The *Subject* is some noun substantive, pronoun, or other designation of a person or thing, about which we say, predicate, or tell something; the *Copula* is some finite mood and tense of the verb 'to be,' or some other verb not involving a distinct predicate; and the *Predicate* is some adjective or other general term, which is predicated or asserted of the subject: thus, in the sentence, *Deus est bonus*, 'God is good,' *Deus* is the subject, *est* the copula, and *bonus* the predicate.

(5) The Predicate and Copula are very often included in some form of a finite verb, thus *equus currit*, 'the horse runs,' is equivalent to *equus est currens*, 'the horse is running.'

(6) The whole sentence may be contained in a finite verbal form. This is especially the case when the nominative is one of the personal pronouns; indeed, these are never expressed unless some emphasis is intended; as in the lines of Terence (*Adelph.* III. iv. 10 sqq.):

'In *te* spes omnis, Hegio, nobis sita est:
Te solum habemus; *tu* es patronus, *tu* pater;
Si deseris *tu*, perimus.'

But Cæsar, writing to the senate, after his victory over Pharnaces, says, *Veni, vidi, vici*, where three complete sentences, 'I came, I saw, I conquered,' are included in three words: because every one knew who was the agent.

(7) The nominative is also very frequently omitted when the verb shows what it must be: thus we say *pluit*, 'it rains,' i.e. *caelum; advesperascit*, 'it grows towards evening,' sc. *dies:* sometimes with a pronoun; as *luciscit hoc jam*, 'this is growing light,' sc. *caelum* (Plautus, *Amphitr.* I. iii. 45).

(8) Impersonal verbs supply their nominative from the particular word, phrase, or sentence which depends upon them; as *pudet me errare*, 'to err shames me,' 'the fact of erring causes shame unto me,' i.e. 'I am ashamed to err;' *pudet me facti*, 'that which belongs to the action causes me shame,' i.e. 'I am ashamed of the action;' *curritur a me*, 'it is run by me,' 'there is running caused by me,' i.e. 'I run.'

§ 2. *Different kinds of Predicates.*

122 There are three different kinds of Predicates:

(A) *Primary*, when there is nothing between the subject and predicate except the copula, either expressed or implied; as in the instances given above.

(B) *Secondary*, when the predicate is connected with the subject through a verb, which already contains a primary predicate; as *pii orant taciti*, 'the pious pray in silence;' which is equivalent to *pii sunt orantes et sunt taciti*, 'the pious are (1) praying and they are (2) silent,' or 'the pious are silent when they pray.'

(C) *Tertiary,* when the secondary predicate is used in an oblique case; thus in *tu solus es,* 'you are alone,' *solus* is a *primary* predicate; in *tu solus adjuvisti nos,* 'you alone have assisted us,' i. e. 'you have assisted us, and you are alone in that,' *solus* is a *secondary* predicate; but in *te solum habemus,* 'we have you alone,' i. e. 'we have you, and you are the only one whom we have,' *solum* is a *tertiary* predicate.

According to these definitions, (A) *primary* predicates are *direct;* (B) *secondary* predicates are *oblique* or *adverbial;* and (C) *tertiary* predicates are both *oblique* and *adverbial:* in other words, (A) *primary* predicates are either finite verbs including a copula, or the nominatives of nouns and participles predicated through a copula; (B) *secondary* predicates are either adverbs, nouns used adverbially, or the oblique cases of nouns with or without a preposition; (C) *tertiary* predicates are words in agreement with oblique cases of nouns.

§ 3. *Accessory parts of a sentence.*

123 In order to understand fully the application of the doctrine that there are three kinds of predicates, it is desirable to enumerate here all the accessory parts which can enter into a simple sentence in Latin, and also the most obvious of the subordinate sentences which serve as secondary predications.

A simple sentence may consist of the following parts in addition to the subject and primary predicate:

(1) The object or person addressed in the vocative case, which is merely interjectional.

(2) A verb in the infinitive mood, when the verb which contains the primary predicate does not convey a complete conception; as *qui non vult intelligi non debet legi,* 'he who is not willing to be understood, is not entitled to be read.'

(3) A noun or pronoun in the accusative case expressing the immediate object of a transitive verb; as *manus manum lavat,* '(one) hand washes (another) hand;' *ego amo te,* 'I love thee;' *panem et aquam natura desiderat,* 'nature requires bread and water.'

(4) A noun or pronoun in the dative case limiting the action to or for a particular object; as *pater filio librum emit,* 'the father

bought a book *for* his son;' dedi *tibi* pecuniam, 'I gave money *to* you;' non *scholae*, sed *vitae* discimus, 'we learn not *for* the school, but *for* life.'

(5) A noun in the ablative case, indicating the time, the means, or the instrument of the action; as *hieme* bella conquiescunt, 'wars rest in the winter;' *concordia* parvæ res crescunt, 'little things grow *by means of* concord;' Alexander Clitum *gladio* interfecit, 'Alexander slew Clitus *with* (by the instrumentality of) a sword.'

(6) When the verb is changed from active to passive, the accusative of the immediate object may become the subject, and the subject of the active verb may be expressed by the ablative with *ab*; thus: *Alexander vicit Darium*, 'Alexander conquered Darius,' may be turned into *Darius victus est ab Alexandro*, 'Darius was conquered by Alexander.'

(7) Any noun, whether subject or object, may be defined by an adjective or adjectival word agreeing with it in case, gender, and number; as Alexander *magnus fidelem* Clitum gladio suo interfecit, 'the *great* Alexander slew the *faithful* Clitus with *his own* sword.'

(8) The functions of the defining adjective may be represented

(a) By another substantive in the genitive case; as amor *patriae* nobis insitus est, 'the love *of our country* is implanted in us,' where *patriae*, 'of our country,' defines the word *amor* just as an adjective would have done; maximum *tui* desiderium me tenet, 'the great love of *you* possesses me,' where *tui* might be written in the adjectival form *tuum*, 'thine.'

(b) By a relative sentence; as Alexander, *qui tot populos vicerat*, iræ succubuit, 'Alexander *who had conquered so many nations*, gave way to passion,' where the relative sentence merely describes Alexander, as *magnus* had done, with a particular reference.

(c) By an apposition of another noun in the same case; as Alexander, *Macedonum rex*, 'Alexander, *the king of the Macedonians*,' for which we might substitute a relative sentence, as *qui fuit rex Macedonum*, 'who was king of the Macedonians.'

(9) Any predicate or even epithet may be qualified by an adverb; as *longe pessimum consilium,* '*by far* the worst counsel;' *mens ejus est valde prava,* 'his mind is *very* depraved;' *equus cito currit,* 'the horse runs *swiftly.*' Some adverbs, as those of affirming or denying, are construed rather with the whole sentence than with single predicates; such are *sane, certo, fortasse, non, minime, nequaquam, neutiquam,* &c.

(10) An adjective may take the place of an adverb and appear as a secondary or even tertiary predicate; as lupus gregibus *nocturnus* obambulat, 'the wolf prowls about the flocks *at night;*' where *nocturnus* is equivalent to *noctu,* and is therefore a secondary predicate; to *solum* habemus, ' we have thee alone,' where *solum* is equivalent to *solummodo, dumtaxat,* or some adverb of similar signification. But sometimes the sense is changed when the predicative adjective stands for the adverb; thus, Cicero *primus* hoc fecit, means 'Cicero was the first who did this,' i. e. 'he did it before all other men;' but, Cicero *primo* hoc fecit, means 'Cicero first did this,' and he did other things after it; and, Cicero *primum* hoc fecit, means 'Cicero did this for the first time,' but he may have done it several times afterwards. Similarly we have, Thrasybulus non *solum* princeps, sed et *solus* initio bellum tyrannis indixit, 'Thrasybulus not *only* was the first, but also at the beginning was the *only* person who declared war against the tyrants.'

(11) A participle is regularly used as a secondary predicate, both in the same case with one of the ordinary members of the sentence, and in the ablative absolute; as omne malum *nascens* facile opprimitur, *inveteratum* plerumque fit robustius, 'every evil, *when still growing,* is easily kept down; but *when it has grown old* it generally becomes stronger;' Horatius, *occisis tribus Curiatiis, et duobus amissis fratribus,* domum se victor recepit, 'Horatius, the three Curiatii *having been killed,* and having himself lost his two brothers, returned home victorious.'

(12) As the Latin language has no past participle of the active voice, unless the verb is deponent in form, a secondary predication of time in this tense, is either expressed in the ablative absolute, as in the example just given, or it is expressed by *quum* and the pluperfect subjunctive; as *quum haec dixisset,* hostes adortus est, 'having said these things he attacked the enemy.' Similarly

contemporary time may be expressed by *quum* with the imperfect subjunctive; as *Cæsar, quum iterum esset consul, multas res gessit,* 'Cæsar being consul for the second time, performed many exploits.'

(13) A mere apposition of the same case is sometimes equivalent to a secondary predication of contemporary time, and in that case we may use the adverb of time by the side of the noun in apposition; as *Cæsar iterum* consul, 'Cæsar being consul *for the second time;'* Appius *tum* decemvir, 'Appius being *at that time* decemvir.'

(14) A word or phrase dependent on a preposition may serve to qualify an epithet or secondary predicate, or may constitute an additional predication; as *amor in me tuus,* 'your love *towards me;'* Augustus *erga* omnes benignus *in* multorum reprehensionem incurrit, 'Augustus, being kind to all, fell under the censure of many;' *pro patria quodvis periculum adeas oportet,* 'you ought to encounter any danger on behalf of your native country.' In the first of these passages *in me* qualifies the epithet *tuus;* in the second, *erga omnes* qualifies the secondary predicate *benignus,* and *in multorum reprehensionem incurrit* constitutes the main statement or primary predication, 'he was blamed by many;' and in the third example, *pro patria* is equivalent to a secondary predication of the condition, namely, 'if our country is at stake.'

(15) The substitution of a sentence dependent on a relative or conjunction, for an epithet (8, (b)) or secondary predicate (12), may be carried to any extent, and the rules for the application of this machinery are called the doctrine of co-ordinate and subordinate sentences.

§ 4. *Epithets and Predicates.*

124. It is of the utmost consequence that a predicate should be distinguished from an epithet, and for this we give the following rule: An adjective, or oblique case, or relative sentence, if dependent merely on a noun, is an epithet or description; if dependent also on a verb, it is a secondary or tertiary predicate, according as its case is direct or oblique. Thus, *Gălĭas* is merely described, or we have merely epithets, attributes, or appositions, when we add to this name such phrases as *bonus puer,* 'a good

boy;' *Marci filius,* 'the son of Marcus;' *qui est bonus,* 'who is good;' *qui est Marci filius,* ' who is the son of Marcus.'

125 That all adjectives, oblique cases, and relative sentences dependent on verbs are subsidiary or accessory predicates, i. e. adverbs, may be shown by a few examples. We have seen this in the example *pii orant taciti,* 'the pious pray in silence,' i.e. 'silently.' The meaning of this would not be altered if we wrote in *silentio,* or *silenter,* or *tacito ore,* which are adverbial phrases, or *itu orant, ut taciti sint,* which is a relative sentence dependent on *orant,* and of the nature called illative. In fact, the only difference between an undeclinable adverb, and the other forms of secondary and tertiary predication, consists in the fact, that the adverb is *general,* while the others denote *special* affections. Thus if we say, *habitabat ibi,* 'he dwelt there,' we do not specify the place; but if we say, *habitabat Romae,* 'he dwelt at Rome,' we state where he lived. Again, if we say, 'he beat him violently,' we merely express the manner; but if we say, 'he beat him with a stick,' or 'so as to kill him,' we add the instrument and the extent or consequences. Again, if we say, 'he will go to London *conditionally,*' it is a general predication of condition, but not more adverbial than the specific condition in 'he will go to London, if you will accompany him,' i.e. 'on the particular condition that you accompany him.'

§ 5. *Cases and Prepositions.*

126 The general meanings of the cases have been given above, 5 (1); and we may now add that the nominative or direct case is *subjective,* but the oblique cases are *objective.* Regarded as adverbial words or secondary predicates, the oblique cases ought to denote 'motion *from,*' 'rest *at,*' and 'motion *to,*' an object. This distinction is accurately observed only in the nouns mentioned below (128, VII. (b)). All others express motion *from* by some preposition signifying 'from' or 'out of' prefixed to the ablative; motion *to,* by some preposition signifying 'to' or 'towards,' with the accusative; and rest *at,* by some preposition signifying 'in,' 'upon,' 'before,' or 'in presence of,' with the ablative; or by some preposition signifying 'at,' 'before,' 'behind,' 'besides,' &c., with the accusative.

127 The general meanings of the prepositions have been given above (109). In the following lists, arranged according to the case with which the prepositions are construed, *f* denotes 'motion *from*,' *t* denotes 'motion *to*,' and *r* signifies 'rest *at*.' But all prepositions construed with the accusative, whether they denote motion or rest, imply extension, or that the thing is stretched out or extended; and all prepositions construed with the ablative, though they denote that there has been derivation or motion *from* the object, imply that the motion is terminated.

(a) Prepositions construed with the accusative are the following:

Adversum (*adversus*),' *cis* (*citra*),' *apud*,' *ante*,' *penes*'-*que*.
Intra,' *infra*,' *contra*,' *supra*,' *post*,' *circiter*,' *inter*.'
Circa' (*circum*), *ultra*,' *juxta*,' *erga*,' *praeter*,' et *extra*.'
Ob,' *prope*,' *per*,' *propter*,' *versus*,' *trans*,' *pone*,' *secundum*,' *ad*.'

These may also be remembered by the following arrangement in lines of four words each:

Ante, apud, ad, adversus,
Circum, circa, citra, cis,
Erga, contra, inter, extra,
Infra, intra, juxta, ob,
Penes, pone, post, and praeter,
Prope, propter, per, secundum,
Supra, versus, ultra, trans.

(b) Prepositions construed with the ablative are the following:

'*De*,' *a*' (quod et *ab*'), *cum*,' *absque*,' *e*' (quod et *ex*'), *prae*,' *pro*,' *sine*,' *coram*."

Or those given in the rhymes:

A, ab, absque, abs and *de,*
Coram, clam, cum, ex and *e,*
Sine, tenus, pro, and *prae.*

Of these, however, *coram, clam,* and *tenus,* with *procul, simul,* and some adverbs construed with the genitive, can be regarded only as quasi-prepositions (see below, 169).

(c) Prepositions construed with an accusative, if motion or extension is implied, with an ablative, if rest is signified, are the following:

'*In, super, et subter*, pro quâ *sub* crebrius exstat;' that is: *In*, 'into,' 'towards,' 'to,' 'upon,' 'against,' governs the accusative; but *in*, 'in,' 'among,' governs the ablative.

Sub, or *subter*, 'under,' 'beneath,' 'about,' requires the accusative; but *sub*, or *subter*, 'just under,' 'just at,' requires the ablative.

Super, 'above,' 'over,' takes the accusative; but *super*, 'upon,' 'concerning,' takes the ablative.

§ 6. *Main Rules of Latin Syntax.*

128 The main rules of Latin Syntax are the following:

A. *Tres Concordantiae.*

I. *Verbum personale cum nominativo concordat numero et personâ.*—A personal verb agrees with its nominative case in number and person; as *equus currit*, 'a horse runs;' *nos pueri discimus*, 'we boys learn.'

II. *Adjectivum cujuscunque modi cum substantivo concordat genere, numero, et casu.*—An adjective, whether nominal, pronominal, or participial, and whether predicate or epithet, agrees with its substantive in gender, number, and case; as *Deus est bonus*, 'God is good,' *celeres equi*, 'swift horses:' where *bonus* is the predicate of *Deus*, and *celeres* is a descriptive epithet of *equi*.

III. *Relativum cum antecedente concordat genere, numero, et personâ.*—The relative agrees with its antecedent, i.e. with the substantive which it helps to define, in gender, number and person, but derives its case from the verb with which it is construed; as *adsum, qui feci*, 'I, who did it, am here;' *urbs, quam condiderunt*, 'the city which they founded;' *phaselus ille, quem videtis*, 'that skiff which ye see.'

These are called the three concords.

B. *Casus Nominum.*

IV. *Nomina ejusdem relationis aliis nominibus in eodem casu apponuntur.*—When two substantives refer to the same person or thing, they are put in the same case by apposition; as *Æneas filius,* 'Æneas the son.'

V. *Nomina diversae relationis aliis nominibus in genitivo subjunguntur.*—When one substantive depends upon another, it is put in the genitive case; as *Æneas filius Anchisae,* 'Æneas the son of Anchises.'

VI. *Praedicata primaria subjecti casum obtinent.*—When two nouns are connected by a verb signifying 'to be, become, be called, thought, or appointed,' and serving only as copula, they stand in the same case; as *perpusilli vocantur nani,* 'very little men are called dwarfs.'

VII. (a) *Accusativo casu stat*
Objectum, ad quod transeat
Transitivorum actio;
Ut: 'filios meos amo.'

(b) *Latina praepositio*
Designat 'ubi,' 'unde,' 'quo.'
Exceptis his
Vocabulis:
'Militia,' 'humus,' 'domus,' 'rus;'
Et urbium nominibus.

(c) *Accusativus exprimit*
Id tempus, quod extentum fit;
In ablativo casu sit
Hora ipsa, qua quid evenit.

(d) *Agentia rei gestae, quorum*
Nominativi rite stant
Pro subjectis activorum,
'A, ab' cum ablativo dant.

(e) *Sed postulat Latinitas*
Ut ablativis exprimas
Causas, modos, formas agendi,
Et instrumenta faciendi;
Et cave unquam scribas 'cum'
Doctoris ad fastidium.

MAIN RULES OF LATIN SYNTAX. 239

(f) *Id quod eodem pertinet—*
Sententiis quibuslibet
Ablativus assidet,
Ut absolute praedicet.

These rules are classed together, because they tell the young scholar when to use and when to omit a Latin preposition in rendering an oblique case, which is always his greatest difficulty.

(a) The immediate object of a transitive verb is put in the accusative case, without a preposition; as *pater amat filium*, 'a father loves his son,' i.e. his son is the object of his love. As the case of extension the accusative denotes distance in space, as *sub monte consederunt millia passuum ab ipsius castris octo*, 'they posted themselves under the mountain 8000 paces distant from his camp.' But the gen. and abl. may also be used with adjectives, to express a measure, as *fons latus pedibus tribus*, 'a fountain three feet wide;' *area lata pedum denum*, 'a floor ten feet broad.' As the case of the object it may denote the part affected, as *tremit artus*, he 'is trembling *in* or *as to* his limbs.'

(b) We must add a Latin preposition signifying 'in' or 'at,' 'from' or 'out of,' 'to' or 'into,' if we wish to express the place *where, whence*, or *whither*; as *restat in hoc loco*, 'he remains in this place;' *profectus est ab illo loco*, 'he set out *from* that place;' *venit ad hunc locum*, 'he came *to* this place:' except the nouns *militia* (or *bellum*), *humus, domus*, and *rus*, and the names of cities, which express these relations without the assistance of prepositions; as *una semper militiae et domi fuimus*, 'we were always together *on* service and *at* home;' *Roma profectus est*, 'he set out *from* Rome;' *ego rus ibo*, 'I will go into the country.' (For the form of the locative in different declensions, see p. 13.)

(c) As a general rule, the accusative expresses duration of time, in answer to the question, 'how long?' but the ablative expresses the exact time of an occurrence in answer to the question 'when?;' as *proxima nocte castra movit*, 'he marched on the following night;' *septem horas dormiebat*, 'he slept (to the extent of) seven hours.'

(d) We may put the object of the active verb in the nominative case of the passive, and substitute for the subject an ablative, which must be accompanied by *a, ab;* as *filius a patre amatur,* 'a son is loved by his father.'

(e) While the *person* by whom the action is performed is thus expressed in the ablative with *a, ab,* the *thing* (whether cause, manner, form, or instrument) *by* or *with* which the action is effected must be expressed in the ablative *without any preposition,* and the young scholar must be careful to resist the temptation to use *cum,* 'with,' which denotes only an accompaniment; thus *securi percussus est a Pisone,* 'he was smitten by Piso with an axe,' as an instrument; but *magnâ cum curâ scripsit,* 'he wrote with (i. e. under the accompaniment of) great care.' In accordance with this rule, the ablative expresses the price or materials. And, as we have seen (above, (c)), the ablative alone is also used to express the time in answer to the question 'when?'

(f) To the same idiom we may refer the use of the ablative absolute to express a subordinate predication of time, cause, or circumstance; as *magnâ comitante catervâ, ibat ad tumulum,* 'he went to the tomb with a great crowd accompanying him;' *nihil de hâc re agi potest, salvis legibus,* 'nothing can be done in this matter without violating the laws,' i. e. 'with the laws in their integrity.'

VIII.   *Si quis quid, diserte datum*
      Ut propositum effatum,
      Infinitivo scripserit,
      Subjecta res objecta fit.
      Nam 'quod vales' idem fere
      Valet, atque 'te valere.'

The infinitive presents merely the objective notion of the verb, without any personal relation. If, therefore, its subject is expressed, it must be in an objective case, or *in regimine verbi finiti.* This case will generally be the accusative, which is the most usual expression of objectivity or regimen. Thus we say, *gaudeo te valere,* 'I am glad as to you being well,' i. e. 'that' or 'with reference to the fact that you are well,' which is much the same as *quod tu vales, gaudeo,* 'as to the circumstance that you are well, I am glad.' But if the main verb requires a dative, the subject of the infinitive may be in this case; as *licet tibi esse beato* or *beatum,* 'it is permitted to you to be happy,' or 'that you should be happy.'

This objective construction is not affected by the fact that the main verb may be impersonal, in which case the whole clause explains the subject of the verb; thus, *pudet me errare,* 'with reference to the fact that I am in error, there is a feeling of shame,' i. e. 'to err causes me shame.' The same rules apply to the case when the infinitive is used without any finite verb in a narrative.

IX. *Dativus limitationem qualemcunque denotat.*—The limitation or destination of an action, whether expressed or not by 'to' or 'for' in English, may always be conveyed by the dative in Latin; as *dedit mihi librum,* 'he gave me the book,' i.e. 'he gave the book *to* me,' or 'the book was the object given, but I was the limitation or destination of the gift.' We may even have two datives; as *exitio est mare nautis,* 'the sea is *destined* or designed *for* destruction *to* sailors.' This rule finds a particular application in the use of the *adjectival* infinitive in *-ndus* (79, *Obs.*), which has the force of an active infinitive, and expresses the limitation to a particular subject by the dative case; as *proelia conjugibus loquenda,* 'battles *for* wives to talk about.'

C. *Verborum Modi.*

X. (a) *Relativa praedicant,*
    Si cum subjunctivo stant.

 . (b) *Si cum primo modo sunt,*
    '*Qui, quae, quod*' *definiunt.*

(a) A relative sentence with the subjunctive mood is a secondary predication of *end, cause, consequence,* or *concession* (below, 205, (*β*)).

(b) A relative sentence with the indicative mood is equivalent to a definition or epithet (below, 204).

Thus we have *missi sunt, qui urbem oppugnarent,* 'they were sent, and I will *predicate,* or tell the *end* for which they were sent—to besiege the city;' but, *qui urbem oppugnabant Romani erant,* 'those who besieged the city (i. e. the particular persons so *defined*) were Romans.' Again: *stultus es qui hoc feceris,* 'you are foolish, and I will *predicate* or tell you the *cause*—because you did this;' but, *qui hoc fecit stultus est,* 'he who did this (i. e. the particular person so *defined*) is foolish.' *Quod rules*, mentioned above, expresses the object or reference of the action, not a fresh predication of cause; and the same may be said of all causal sentences with the indicative.

> XI. *Relativa, quae conceptus
> Alienos exprimunt
> In sententiis obliquis,
> Subjunctivum exigunt.*

The subjunctive is invariably used when the relative sentence is oblique, or expresses the thoughts or words of a third person; as *Socrates dicebat omnes in eo, quod scirent, satis esse eloquentes,* because *in eo quod scirent* depends on the oblique expression of the opinion of Socrates. Again: *Socrates accusatus est quod corrumperet juventutem,* 'Socrates was accused of corrupting the young;' not that it was a fact, but the accuser said so (below, 205, (γ), (δ)).

> XII. *Interrogatio obliqua subjunctivum requirit.*—The indicative is always used in direct questions; as *quis est,* 'who is it?' But the subjunctive is invariably found in indirect or oblique questions; as *nescio quis sit,* 'I know not who it is' (below, 205, (a)).

> XIII. *Ut finalis et illativa subjunctivum postulat.*—The subjunctive is necessarily used after *ut*, (a) in final sentences denoting the end, or (b) in illative sentences signifying the extent or consequence; as (a) *missi sunt, ut specularentur,* 'they were sent to the end that they might act as spies;' (b) *Titus ita facilis fuit, ut nemini quidquam negaret,* 'Titus was so good-natured that, as a consequence, he could not deny anything at all to anybody.' The final *ut* is sometimes omitted before the subjunctive, especially after *fac, velim, licet, necesse est,* and *oportet;* as *tu velim animo sapienti sis* (for *velim ut sis*), 'I wish that you may be wise.'

> XIV. *Ne prohibitiva vel imperativum vel subjunctivum admittit; ne pro ut ne finalis, pro ut non illativa, subjunctivum deposcit.*—Properly speaking, the prohibitive is a remnant of the final sentence with *ut ne;* but in this case the *ut* is regularly omitted, as in the idioms mentioned at the end of the last rule; and if *cave* precedes, even *ne* may be dropt in the final prohibition; as *cave scribas,* for *cave ne scribas,* 'take care, to the end that you may not write.' In the full final sentence, when the end is prohibited, it is a matter of indifference whether we write *ne* or *ut ne;*

and in the illative sentence, we may have either *ne* alone (as in *vos adepti estis ne quem civem metueretis*, 'you have gained an advantage to such an extent or consequence that you are not obliged to fear any one of your fellow-citizens') or *ut non*, *ut nunquam*, and the like.

Obs. It is to be observed that *ut* and *ne* are regularly opposed in expressing wishes and fears. Thus *ut* or *utinam* introduces a wish, while *ne* forbids it. For *ut* or *utinam veniat* means 'O that he may come!' But *ne veniat* signifies 'I wish that he may not come.' As this is tantamount to a prohibition, it may be said that *ne veniat*, as the opposite of *ut veniat*, must be equivalent to *ut ne veniat*. But this explanation will not apply to the opposition of *ut* and *ne* after verbs of fearing; for *vereor ut veniat* means 'I fear, how he can come,' i.e. 'I fear he will *not* come;' whereas *vereor ne veniat* means 'I fear lest he come,' i.e. 'I fear he will come.' If we said *efficio ut veniat*, we should mean 'I manage to the end that he may come,' and *efficio ne veniat* or *ut ne veniat* would mean 'I manage to the end that he may not come.' And as the dependent sentence in each case is the same, the opposite meaning given by the use of *ut* and *ne* after verbs of fearing must be caused by the peculiar force of the main verb, namely, by the fact that a verb of fearing qualifies the whole sentence with a negative or prohibitive meaning, which annuls the dependent wish or prohibition; so that *vereor ut veniat* means 'O that he may come! but I fear that he will not;' and *vereor ne veniat* means 'may he not come! but I fear that he will.' This construction belongs to the indirect interrogation (below, 205, (a), (bb)).

XV. *Consecutio temporum valet in subjunctivo.*—If one sentence is dependent on another, the verbs must be in congruous tenses. Thus (1) a present or future is followed by a present, a perfect, or a periphrastic future, to express that something predicated in the subjunctive is still continuing, is completed, or is about to happen. The imperative is regarded as a present or future. Hence we may write:

Nemo est, { quem oratio tua non *delectet*.
quem oratio tua non *delectaverit*.
cui carmina tua non *placitura sint*.

Scribam tibi { quid frater tuus *agat*.
quid frater tuus *egerit*.
quid frater tuus *facturus sit*.

Veniam, ubi *cognovero* { quid *agas*.
quid *egeris*.
quid *facturus sis*.

244   MAIN RULES OF LATIN SYNTAX.

Scribe mihi { quid rerum *agas.*
{ quid consilii *ceperis.*
{ quando *profecturus sis.*

(2) The historical tenses, as they are called, namely, perfect, imperfect, and pluperfect, which narrate a past occurrence, are followed by the imperfect, if the event predicated in the subjunctive was contemporary with the main action; by the pluperfect, if it was anterior to the main action; by the imperfect of the periphrastic future, if it was subsequent or was so regarded. Hence we may write:

Quaesivit ex me { quid rerum *agerem.*
{ quid rerum *egissem.*
{ quid *facturus essem.*

Dubitabam { num *faceret,* quod jusseram.
{ num *fecisset,* quod jusserum.
{ num *facturus esset,* quod jusseram.

Scripserat mihi { quamobrem non *venirel.*
{ quamobrem non *venisset.*
{ quamobrem non *venturus esset.*

The following special cases must be noticed:

(a) The perfect subjunctive may be used for the imperfect, after a perfect indicative, when we wish to limit the dependent circumstances to a single act; as Aristides, quum tantis rebus praefuisset, in tanta paupertate *decessit,* ut qui efferretur, vix *reliquerit,* because we should certainly have used *reliquit,* and not *relinquebat,* to express the fact that he left very little at the moment of his death.

(b) If the present indicative is used historically to describe a past event, it may be followed by a present subjunctive; as Tum ille *scribit* ad quosdam Melitenses, ut ea vasa *perquirant.* But the imperfect may be used by the side of the other construction; thus in the passage from which the last example is taken (Cic. *Verr.* IV. 18) we read: Diodorus ad propinquum suum *scribit,* ut iis, qui a Verre *venissent, responderet,* illud argentum se paucis illis diebus misisse Lilybaeum.

(3) As the perfect may be used, not only as an historical tense, but also as indicating the completed result of past actions, it may

be followed by the present subjunctive; thus we may say both *cognovi ex tuis litteris, quam tibi carus essem,* 'I *learned* from your letter, how dear I *was* to you,' and also, *cognovi ex tuis litteris, quam tibi carus sim,* 'I *have learned* (i.e. I know) from your letter, how dear I am to you.'

(4) In the *oratio obliqua* (above, XI),

(a) if the verb declaring the thought or opinion is in a finite mood, its tense will generally regulate that of the dependent verbs; as Sapientissimum *dicunt* eum, cui quid opus *sit*, ipsi *veniat* in mentem. But a present tense may be followed by an imperfect or pluperfect, if a definite time is specified, which requires these tenses; and a perfect is followed by a present or perfect, when a proverb or some saying perpetually applicable is cited; thus we find: Verres ita *dictitat*, iis esse metuendum, qui quod ipsis solis satis *esset surripuissent; se* tantum *surripuisse* (i.e. habere), ut id multis satis *sit*. Turnum *dixisse* ferunt, nullam breviorem esse cognitionem, quam inter patrem et filium; ni *pareat* patri, habiturum infortunium esse.

(b) If the verb of declaration appears as an infinitive or participle, the tense of the subjunctive verb is regulated by that of the verb on which the infinitive depends or by that of the temporal sentence into which the participle might be resolved; thus we have *Negabat* Cato quidquam utile *esse*, quod idem non *esset* honestum, because *negabat* defines the tense of *esse*, and we have *Cogitanti* mihi, quid optimum factu *esset*, litterae tuae allatae sunt, because *cogitanti* is equivalent to *dum cogitabam*.

XVI. *Quatuor sunt conditionalium formulae.*—The same rule of congruity is of course applicable to the different forms of conditional sentences, which imply respectively,

(1) Possibility, without the expression of uncertainty; as *Si quid habet, dat*, 'if he has anything, he gives it.'

(2) Uncertainty, with some small amount of probability; as

(a) *Si quid habeat, dabit*, 'if he shall have anything (which is not improbable), he will give it.'

(b) *Si quid habuerit, dederit*, 'if he shall have (on a particular occasion) had anything, he will have given it (once for all).'

(3) Mere assumption, without any subordinate idea; as *Si quid habeat, det*, 'if he were to have anything (i.e. as often as he had anything), he would give it.' The present tense is used because the results are supposed to be still within the reach of the speaker.

(4) Impossibility, or when we wish to indicate that the thing is not so; as

(a) *Si quid haberet, daret*, 'if (which is not the case) he had anything, he would give it.'

(b) *Si quid habuisset, dedisset*, 'if (which was not the case) he had had anything, he would have given it.'

The four modes of expressing a condition and its results may be regarded as supplying the general rules for such expressions. It will be found, however, that they admit of certain modifications, which do not violate the principle that, in all conditional propositions, the present or the perfect, properly so called, is used to intimate that the circumstance assumed is possible or at least conceivable, and the imperfect or pluperfect is employed to express that, in the opinion at least of the speaker, it is impossible. Precisely the same distinction is observable in the use of the subjunctive as an optative, i.e. as the expression of a wish. For in this case, we have merely a condition without a statement of the result. And if we say *si* or *ut* or *utinam veniat*, 'if' or, 'O that he would come,' we merely suspend the expression of our consequent satisfaction. The rule for the tense of the subjunctive in this optative use is therefore the same as that in the conditional clause. Accordingly, if we say *cupiam scire*, 'I may wish to know,' we imply that our desire might be realized; but if we say *cuperem scire*, 'I might wish to know,' we imply that the condition of possibility is not forthcoming. Similarly, *quam velim hoc fiat*, or *utinam hoc fecerit*, imply a possibility that the wish may be fulfilled; but *quam vellem hoc fieret*, or *quam vellem hoc factum esset*, exclude the possibility. In carrying out this distinction in the uses of the present or perfect, and of the imperfect or pluperfect tenses of the subjunctive mood, the student experiences two difficulties. On the one hand, he finds that the past tense is used in English to translate both the present and the imperfect in these sentences; and on the other hand, the present is used in Latin, where there seems to

ORDER OF WORDS IN A SENTENCE.   247

be no actual possibility in the condition. Both of these difficulties are illustrated by cases like the following. We may say, *tu si hic sis, aliter sentias*, 'if you were in my place, you would think otherwise;' *si exsistat hodie ab inferis Lycurgus*, 'if Lycurgus were to stand forth to-day from the shades below.' Here the corresponding English phraseology would imply that the hypothesis in either case was not within the reach of possibility; but the mere use of the present in Latin shows that the circumstance, however improbable in itself, is at least supposable for the sake of argument, and we have the same use of the Greek optative, which is regularly appropriated to this form of the conditional sentence (see *Greek Grammar*, 502, (γ), p. 539).

These are the main or general rules of Latin Syntax. For convenience sake, the details of their application will be exhibited afterwards in the order suggested by the accidence. But we may from the first presume a knowledge of the constructions here explained.

§ 7. *Order of Words in a Latin Sentence, and their English Construction.*

129 Among the peculiarities of the Latin language, the arrangement or order of the words demands the earliest attention of the student, because it is the necessary converse of the process of construing Latin into English, which is one of the first duties of a learner. There are no two languages which differ more in this respect than the English and the Latin. For while the merely syntactical condition, to which modern English has been reduced, by the loss of nearly all its inflexions, obliges us to maintain the logical and grammatical construction of every sentence, the Latin language, which has not even a definite article, and depends entirely upon its inflected forms, not only admits, but requires a considerable variety in the relative position of the words, in order to make the inflexions as serviceable as may be in giving perspicuity, emphasis, and harmony to the style. We must here consider separately (I.) the order to be adopted, when we translate English into Latin; (II.) the process of construing Latin into English.

I. The Latin Order.

The two general rules by which the Latin order is governed are the following:

(a) That the most emphatic words take precedence in the sentence.

(b) That, if emphasis does not interfere, the explanatory or additional word follows the subject but precedes the predicative word or phrase to which it belongs.

From this it will follow that the subject will generally stand first and the predicative verb last, while the intervening particles, dependent cases, &c., will stand between them in an order regulated by their weight in the sentence. That the verb is most properly and naturally placed last, is expressly stated by Quintilian (*I. O.* IX. 4, § 26): *Verbo sensum cludere, multo, si compositio patiatur, optimum est. In verbis enim sermonis vis.* How regularly this is the case in Latin prose may be seen in such a passage as the following (Cic. *Leges*, I. 9): Hominem natura non solum celeritate mentis *ornavit*, sed etiam sensus tanquam satellites *attribuit* ac nuntios; figuramque corporis habilem et aptam ingenio humano *dedit*. Nam quum ceteras animantes *abjecisset* ad pastum, solum hominem *erexit*, ad caelique quasi cognationis domiciliique pristini conspectum *excitavit*; tum speciem ita *formarit* oris, ut in ea penitus reconditos mores *effingeret*. The words intervening between the subject and predicate in this natural order may change their relative places and form new permutations according to the emphasis intended. Thus we may say, *Romani Jovi templum in Capitolio condiderunt*, 'the Romans to Jove a temple in the Capitol erected,' if we mean to direct attention to the fact that the god to be honoured was the distinctive circumstance; but we might say also: *Romani* templum in Capitolio *Jovi Junoni Minervae condiderunt*, if we wished to lay a stress on the foundation of the temple without such a special reference to the worship to be carried on in it. The same law of emphasis will even qualify the position of the subject and predicative verb themselves, and we not unfrequently find that the subject concludes the sentence, if we wish to make it bear a particular stress; as *sensit in se iri Brutus* (Liv. II. 5); *cujus in oratione plerumque efficit numerum ipsa concinnitas* (Cic. Orat. 50); *in Academia recentiore exstitit divina quadam celeritate ingenii dicen-*

dique copia Carneades (Cic. *de Orat.* III. 18); *semper oratorum moderatrix fuit oratorum prudentia* (Cic. *Orat.* 8).

Obs. In Latin poetry the natural order of the words is disturbed not only by a greater variety of intended emphasis, but also by the occasional exigencies of the metre. Ausonius apologizes for a deviation from the usual order of the epistolary address by saying (*Ep.* 20, 1):

Paulino Ausonius. Metrum sic suasit ut esses
Tu prior, et nomen prægrederere meum.

130. As the Latin language has no article, the definite epithet cannot very well precede its noun, unless it has some distinctive emphasis of its own. The same rule applies to the genitive case in regimen, and to the apposition of a title or definition. Hence, in all ordinary cases, the adjective follows the noun, the genitive its governing substantive, and the apposition the word which it qualifies; as

(a) *res familiaris*, 'property;' *res publica*, 'the state;' *bellum sociale*, 'the social war;' *jus civile*, 'the civil law;' *civis Romanus*, 'a Roman citizen;' *senatus populusque Romanus*, 'the senate and people of Rome;' *aes alienum*, 'debt;' *via Appia*, 'the Appian road,' &c.

(b) *filius Anchisae*, 'the son of Anchises;' *magister equitum*, 'master of the knights;' *tribunus militum*, 'tribune of the soldiers;' *jus gentium*, 'the right of nations;' *lex naturae*, 'the law of nature;' &c.

(c) *Q. Mucius augur, M. Tullius Cicero consul, Cyprus insula, Tiberis flurius.*

But although this arrangement is the most natural, it is abandoned, whenever the emphasis or perspicuity requires a different order. Thus, although we should say, *ager Tuscus, ager Romanus*, if those phrases stood alone, we must put the epithet first when we wish to give prominence to the distinction which it involves, for example, in such a sentence as *Tuscus* ager *Romano* adjacet. Similarly, *mors fratris tui*, and *fratris tui mors*, are equally allowable, but the former lays the stress on the death as contrasted with the previous life, and the latter makes an emphatic reference to the particular person, whose death is mentioned. Again, in some cases the adjective or qualifying word is so essential to the idea, which we wish to convey, that it necessarily precedes. Thus Pliny's great work is styled *Libri Naturalis Historiae*, because it is the adjective which gives its distinctive subject, so that the noun and its epithet might be regarded as one compound word; so also we have *Theodosianus codex, Julium sidus, Mariani consulatus*, because the emphasis necessarily falls on the adjective. For the same reason the genitive precedes its noun in such combinations as *animi motus, terrae motus, corporis partes*, &c., because the specific meaning is given by the genitive. And this is particularly the case with certain adjectives which get their special meaning from the genitive of a noun, as *juris prudens, juris consultus*, &c.; hence we have even in the same sentence: *reipublicae peritus et juris consultus* (Nep. xxiv. 3). On the other hand, when the genitive denotes the object, it properly follows; thus we write *expugnatio urbis, indagatio veri, scientia linguae, amor patriae, cura rerum alienarum, fiducia virium suarum*, &c. If the same noun has both a genitive of the subject and a genitive of the object dependent on it, the former generally precedes and the latter may either precede or follow; thus we have *cognoscite hominis principium rerum gerendarum; hominis amplissimi causam tanti periculi repudiare; Atheniensium populi potestatem omnium rerum*, &c. In appositions too the general rule that the defining word follows, is neglected in certain cases. Thus *rex* as an hereditary title, and *Imperator*, when it became a regular designation of the chief of the Roman empire, are prefixed to the name, and we have *rex Deiotarus, Imperator Titus*. So also we have *urbs Roma*, not *Roma urbs*.

131 If a substantive is explained by a genitive case or other adjunct, as well as by an adjective, the combined epithet is sufficiently definite to precede the noun, and the adjective generally stands first; thus, *summum eloquentiae studium, nocturnus in urbem adventus*, &c. Between the preposition and its case we may have not only an epithet or genitive case, but a relative sentence or any other merely explanatory insertion; as *propter Hispanorum, apud quos consul fuerat, injurias; in summa bonorum ac fortium, qui tunc aderant, virorum copia; ex illo caelesti Epicuri de regula et judicio volumine*.

132 (a) A demonstrative pronoun will of course regularly precede the noun to which it calls attention; as *haec mulier, ille vir, hujus fratris mei*. But if there is also an adjective, the pro-

noun and adjective may follow as in Greek; thus, ἀνὴρ ὁ μέγας
= *vir ille magnus*, or *magnus ille vir*; and if the emphasis falls
upon the noun, the pronoun is placed after it; as *disputationem
hanc de oratore malo tibi et Bruto placere; caedem hanc ipsam
contra rempublicam senatus factam esse decrevit; virginem ego hanc
sum ducturus; ab intimo sinu excurrit tumulus is ipse in quo
condita urbs est.*

(b) The relative pronoun regularly stands first in the sentence,
and so completely appropriates this position, that it takes the place
of a demonstrative with *et*; hence we have *qui* for *et is*, *qualis* for
et talis, *quo* for *et eo*, &c. It is even substituted for the demonstrative when there is not only an *et*, but some particle such as
quum, si, quamvis, utinam, or another inflected relative: thus we
find *quod quum audivissem, quod si audivissem, quod quamvis non
ignorassem, quam palmam utinam dii immortales vobis reservent,
quod qui facit*, &c. for *et quum hoc, et si hoc, et quamvis hoc, et
utinam hanc, et qui hoc facit*, &c. From this usage arose the practice of using *quod* before certain particles, especially *si* and *nisi*,
without any force as a pronoun, and merely as equivalent to our
'but' or 'and.' Thus we find *quod si illinc profugisses*, 'but if
you had fled from thence;' *quod nisi Metellus hoc tam graviter
egisset*, 'unless however Metellus had done this with such energy;'
quod etsi quidam dicendi copiam sine ratione consequuntur, 'and
although some attain to fluency without theoretical study.' We
have also *quod quum, quod ubi, quod quia, quod quoniam, quod ne,
quod utinam*. But even a relative may lose its place at the beginning of a sentence, if emphasis requires it, and if its antecedent
follows; as *Romam quas asportata sunt ad aedem Honoris et Virtutis
videmus.*

(c) If *quisque* follows a reflexive pronoun, the distribution is
expressly signified; but the distribution is already given by some
other word, if *quisque* precedes; thus we say on the one hand,
minime sibi quisque notus est, et difficillime de se quisque sentit;
and on the other hand, *Gallos Hannibal in civitates quemque suas
dimisit.*

133 (a) Adverbs (according to 129, rule (b)) regularly precede the predicative word to which they are attached. This is
always the case with the categorical negative *non*, and almost
always with the adverbs expressing a degree, though the latter

are sometimes separated from their adjective, in order to increase the emphasis; as *hoc si Sulpicius noster faceret, multo ejus oratio esset pressior*, where the adverb *multo* is placed at the beginning of the clause merely to strengthen the assertion.

(b) Prepositions, especially monosyllables, are frequently placed between an adjective or pronoun and its substantive; as *multis de causis, paucos post menses, magna ex parte, summa cum cura, ea de re;* especially in the case of the relative, as in *qua de re, quam ob rem, quem ad modum,* &c. And the tendency of the relative to take the first place allows it to appear before a preposition even of two syllables when there is no following substantive in agreement with it; thus we have *quorum de virtutibus, quos inter erat, quem contra venerat, quo de agitur.* This usage is found, but less commonly, with other pronouns, as *hunc post, hunc propter, hunc juxta, hunc adversus.* The Latin language generally requires a repetition of the preposition in sentences connected with *et—et, nec—nec, aut—aut, vel—vel,* and also after *nisi* and *quam,* but not with words connected by enclitics; and it is not the usage to refer a substantive to two connected prepositions; thus we say *et in bello et in pace;* and *ante aciem postve eam,* not *ante postve aciem.*

(c) Conjunctions generally precede the sentence, which they introduce; but *ut* and *ne* have sometimes several words before them; as *Catilina postulabat, patres conscripti ne quid de se temere crederent;* and the illative *ut* is not unfrequently preceded by a negative or qualifying adverb such as *vix, nemo, nihil, nullus, prope, puene;* thus we have *erant optimi cives judices, vix ut mihi tenuis quaedam venia daretur excusationis.*

134 Repeated words are placed in juxtaposition, the subject preceding the oblique case (129 (b)); thus, *nulla virtus virtuti contraria est; vir virum legit; ex domo in domum migrare; diem ex die exspectare; nihil est unum uni tam simile; laudando omnes omnium imagines; Titus Berenicen ab urbe dimisit invitus invitam; sequere quo tua te virtus ducet.* The same rule applies to contraries; thus, *quaedam falsa veri speciem habent; mortali immortalitatem non arbitror contemnendam; in custodia socer generi periit morbo.*

Antithesis sometimes exhibits an inverted order, which is called *chiasmus* (from χιάζειν, 'to put cross-wise,' like the letter χῖ); thus, *ratio nostra consentit, repugnat oratio; fateor vulgi judicium a judicio meo dissensisse; quae me moverunt movissent eadem te profecto; fragile corpus animus sempiternus movet; leges supplicio improbos afficiunt, defendunt ac tuentur bonos; errant, quod solum, quod Attice, non falluntur.*

135 Certain words have a fixed place in the clauses to which they belong.

(a) *Nam* always stands first: generally also *namque*.

(b) *Enim* always after at least one word, seldom after two. In the compound *enimvero* it may commence a sentence.

(c) *Ergo* either at the beginning or after another emphatic word. *Igitur* always follows, and may be last word. *Itaque* generally begins the sentence.

(d) *Quoque* and *autem* immediately after the word which they add or oppose.

(e) *Etiam* before the word to which it belongs, unless this word is very emphatic.

(f) *Quidem* after the word which it qualifies, and to which it is closely attached. If *ne* precedes, the meaning is 'not even' (above, 105, (a)).

(g) *Tamen* stands at the beginning, unless a single word is to be made emphatic.

(h) *Autem* always follows the first word in the sentence.

(i) No enclitic can stand first in a sentence[1].

(k) The verb *inquit,* 'says he,' or 'said he,' is always inserted parenthetically in the course of the words quoted; as *Tum Cocles, ' Tiberine pater,' inquit, ' te sancte precor haec arma et hunc virum propitio flumine accipias.'* If the nominative of *inquit* does not thus precede the citation of the words spoken, it is placed immediately after the verb; as *'mihi quidem,' inquit Cotta, 'videtur.'* We may place *ait* either before the words cited, or in the citation, like *inquit*. The poets alone use *dicit* and *dixit* in this way.

---

[1] Here learners may find it convenient to recollect the memorial lines:

Quoque, autem, quidem, que,
Second words must always be.

136. These are the general rules, and it seems unnecessary to multiply illustrations, or to collect instances of the exceptions necessitated by the variations of emphasis; for after all it is only a continued perusal of the best writers, and adequate practice in prose composition, which can give that perception of rhetorical symmetry on which so much depends, or enable the student to frame perspicuous and harmonious periods. And even those who have gone through a long course of reading and writing Latin too often fail in producing a pleasing effect by the structure of their sentences, when they have not received from nature the susceptible and fastidious delicacy of ear (*aures teretes et relligiosae*) which Cicero (*Orator.* 9) regards as a distinguishing peculiarity of the Attic orator.

II. *The English Construction.*

137. As the Latin order in most cases differs entirely from the English, it is necessary that a student should acquire betimes the art of reducing the elements of the Latin sentence to their proper places in English syntax. This, although it is a process of decomposition, as far as the Latin is concerned, is called *construing* or *construction*, a term absolutely equivalent to the Greek word represented by the word *syntax*. The method to be adopted is presumed, in what has been already said on the parts of the sentence (above, § 3). The order, therefore, of Latin construing will be as follows:

(1) The interjection with its vocative.

(2) The conjunction.

(3) The subject of the sentence, with all that belongs to it, whether it be a relative sentence, an epithet, an apposition, or a dependent genitive.

(4) The copula with the predicate, that is either

    (a) *sum* with a noun, and all that belongs to it;

    or (b) a finite verb;

    or (c) a finite verb and its dependent infinitive.

(5) The adverb or other secondary predicate.

(6) The accusative, as expressing the immediate object, and all that belongs to it.

(7) The dative, as expressing the limitation, and all that belongs to it.

(8) The ablative, as expressing the means or instrument, and all that belongs to it.

It will be observed that, if the main verb is impersonal, it will precede any expression of the subject, which is generally given in the accusative case; that an adverb will often be taken immediately before the verb, especially a negative particle; that prepositions, with their cases, will follow the word which they define; and that the accusative, dative, and ablative may be taken in an order different from that given above, if the verb requires that either the dative or ablative should immediately follow it, rather than the accusative.

The beginning of Cæsar's speech (Sallust, *Cat.* 51) will serve as an example of these rules. The Latin order is: *Omnes homines, Patres Conscripti, qui de rebus dubiis consultant, ab odio, amicitia, ira atque misericordia vacuos esse decet. Haud facile animus rerum providet, ubi illa officiunt; neque quisquam omnium lubidini simul et usui paruit.* The English construing will be as follows: *Patres Conscripti* (vocative), *decet* (impersonal verb) *omnes homines* (accusative of the immediate object with its epithet), *qui* (relative with its sentence, conveying an additional epithet or definition of the accusative *homines*, which is here the real subject of the infinitive which follows) *consultant* (verb, containing the primary predicate of the relative clause) *de dubiis rebus* (ablative with its epithet, dependent on *de*, and expressing the object of *consultant*), *esse* (copula of the sentence dependent on *decet*) *vacuos* (predicate of *homines*) *ab odio*, &c. (ablatives dependent on *ab* and explanatory of *vacuos*). *Animus* (subject) *haud facile* (adverbs) *providet* (verb containing predicate) *rerum* (accusative of the immediate object), *ubi* (adverb of place, equivalent to case of relative) *illa* (subject) *officiunt* (verb containing predicate); *neque* disjunctive conjunction) *quisquam* (subject) *paruit* (verb containing predicate) *simul* (adverb of time) *lubidini et usui* (datives of limitation) *omnium* (dependent genitive).

CHAPTER II.

CASES OF NOUNS.

§ 1. *The Nominative and its Adjuncts.*

138 THE nominative is used to express not only the subject of the sentence, but also the predicate, whenever the copula appears in the form of a verb denoting existence and the like. In either case it carries along with it the accompanying adjective, whether it be an epithet or a secondary predicate, and the explanatory adjunct, whether it be another noun in apposition or a relative sentence. It is true that most of these adjuncts may be found with oblique cases as well as with the nominative; indeed, any nominative, which appears as the subject of a finite verb, may be turned into the accusative when it appears as the subject of a verb in the infinitive mood; but it will be most convenient that all these qualifying expressions should be discussed once for all in connexion with the nominative, not only because they belong primarily to the subject, but also because they are sometimes referred to a department of Latin syntax which is formally distinguished from that which treats of the oblique cases. In some grammars it is the practice to consider separately the *Syntaxis Convenientiae*, which treats of the concord or agreement of the separate parts of a proposition, and the *Syntaxis Rectionis*, which treats of the dependence of one part of the sentence upon another, so that one member is said 'to govern' (*regere*) another member in the same clause. It will be in accordance with this arrangement, if, in speaking of the nominative, we consider in order (A) the agreement of the nominative with its verb; (B) the agreement of the adjective with its substantive; (C) the agreement of the relative with its antecedent; (D) the apposition of a noun or participle in the same case; (E) the agreement of the subject and predicate.

SYNTAX OF THE NOMINATIVE.

(A) *Agreement of the Nominative with its Verb.*

139 (a) The number and person of the verb are regulated by the number and person of the nominative or subject; as

Ego reges ejeci, vos tyrannos introducitis; ego libertatem peperi, vos partam servare non vultis, 'I have expelled kings, you are introducing tyrants; I have procured liberty, you, after it has been procured, are unwilling to keep it.'

(b) If there are two or more nominatives, the verb which follows is in the plural, provided the nominatives indicate persons; but if the verb precedes, or if the nominatives do not indicate persons, the verb may be either singular or plural; as

Pompeius, Scipio, et Africanus foede perierunt, 'Pompey, Scipio, and Africanus perished disgracefully.'
Beneficium et gratia sunt vincula concordiae, 'kindness and good feeling are the bonds of harmony.'
Virtus et honestas et pudor cum consulibus esse cogebat, 'virtue, honour, and shame compelled me to be with the consuls.'
Tempus necessitasque postulat, 'time and necessity demand it.'
Dixit hoc Zosippus et Ismenias, 'Zosippus and Ismenias said this.'

(c) Collective nouns like *pars, turba, vis, multitudo,* when they denote a number of persons, are construed with a plural verb. The same is the case with distributive words and phrases like *quisque, pro se quisque, neuter, uterque, alius-alium, vir-virum,* which must be regarded as a sort of parenthetical apposition to the plural subject of the verb. The same principle explains the use of a plural verb when another subject is added with the preposition *cum.* Thus we have

Magna pars vulnerati aut occisi sunt, 'they,' i.e. 'a great part of them, were wounded or slain.'
Magna vis hominum segetem fuderunt in Tiberim, 'a great mass of men cast the corn into the Tiber.'
Pro se quisque miles gaudio alacres fremunt, 'excited by joy they shout, each soldier of them.'
Uterque exercitum ex castris educunt, 'both the one and the other lead their armies from the camp.'

Ilia cum Lauso de Numitore sati sunt, 'they, that is, Ilia together with Lausus, were sprung from Numitor.'

But *unus et alter* may have a verb in the singular; as, *dicit unus et alter breviter,* 'one and the other,' i.e. 'one after the other, speaks briefly.'

(d) When the substantive verb stands between two nouns of different numbers, it takes its number from that with which it is most closely connected in meaning or position; as

Praecipuum robur Rhenum juxta octo legiones erant, 'the main force near the Rhine consisted in eight legions.'

Magnae divitiae sunt lege naturae composita paupertas, 'poverty regulated by the law of nature constitutes great riches.'

(e) With regard to the person of the verb, if the pronouns *ego, nos, tu, vos,* appear together, or by the side of some subject in the third person, the verb is plural, but takes its person from the pronoun which stands first in the usual order of reference, that is, the first in preference to the second person, and the second in preference to the third; as

Pater, ego, fratresque mei terra marique pro vobis arma tulimus, 'my father, myself, and my brothers (we) have borne arms for you by land and sea.'

Si tu et Tullia valetis, bene est; ego et Cicero valemus, 'if you and Tullia are (both of you) in good health, it is well; I and Cicero (both of us) are in good health.'

(B) *Agreement of the Adjective with its Substantive.*

140 (a) The adjective, whether it be epithet or predicate, agrees with its substantive in gender, number, and case; as

Amicus certus in re incerta cernitur, 'a sure friend is distinguished in an uncertain matter.'

Sera nunquam est ad bonos mores via, 'the way to good conduct is never too late.'

Sapientia est rerum divinarum et humanarum scientia, 'wisdom is the knowledge of things human and divine.'

SYNTAX OF THE NOMINATIVE. 259

The apparent exceptions to this rule are the following:

(a) An adjective taken substantively in the neuter singular may appear as the predicate to a masculine or feminine noun, either singular or plural; as

Triste lupus stabulis, maturis frugibus imbres, 'the wolf is a baneful thing to the folds, and showers [are a baneful thing] to ripened corn.'

Mors omnium rerum extremum est, 'death is the last thing of all events.'

Varium et mutabile semper femina, 'a woman is always a fickle and changeable creature.'

(β) If a substantive denotes a person of a different gender, the adjective will generally agree with it in gender, when used as a mere epithet; but will take the gender of the person signified, when used as a primary predicate; as

Dicaearchus, meae deliciae, 'Dicaearchus, my favourite author;' but, *mea Glycerium*, 'my dear Glycerium.'

And, *Millia triginta servilium capitum dicuntur capti*, 'thirty thousand slaves are said to have been taken.'

(γ) A predicative adjective is always in the neuter singular when the subject is an infinitive verb or a sentence; as

Errare humanum est, 'to err is human.'

Dulce et decorum est pro patria mori, 'it is sweet and noble to die for one's country.'

(b) An adjective in agreement with the noun very often expresses the secondary predicate, or is used in cases when we should employ an adverb of time, place, manner, or degree; as *Roma parentem, Roma patrem patriae Ciceronem libera dixit*, 'Rome, while still free, called Cicero parent, and father of his country.' *Prudens, sciens, imprudens, invitus, frequens*, and words of order or position are most commonly used in this way. In some cases it is quite optional whether we use an adjective or an adverb; thus we may say either *tardus* or *tarde ad me venisti*, 'you were slow in coming to me,' i.e. 'you came to me slowly;' either *laetus* or *laete vivit*, 'he lives cheerfully;' either *libens* or *libenter hoc feci*, 'I did this gladly.' But sometimes it makes a great difference whether we use the adjective or the adverb (123, (10)), especially in the case of *primus* and *solus*, which are used in Latin where we should employ a relative sentence; as

Pericles primus adhibuit doctrinam, 'Pericles was the first who brought in learning.'

And this predicative use occurs in a relative sentence; as

Æsculapius, qui primus vulnus obligavisse dicitur, 'Æsculapius, who is said to have been the first who bound up a wound.'

In the same way we may employ *ultimus, summus, imus, medius, solus,* and other adjectives denoting position. Sometimes the secondary predicate bears all the stress of the passage; as

Verebar, ne molestus vobis intervenirem, 'I feared lest I should be troublesome to you by intruding.'

Sometimes it implies that the quality denoted by the adjective is conveyed to the subject by the verb; as

Stomachus flagitat immorsus refici, 'the stomach craves to be restored by being stimulated.'

Paullatimque anima caluerunt mollia saxa, 'by little and little the stones softened and grew warm with life.'

This use is also found in an oblique case, where we have a tertiary predicate; as

Liquido cum plasmate guttur mobile collueris, 'when you have rinsed your throat with a liquid gargle, so as to make it flexible.'

Praetor effusum agmen ad Mutinam ducit, 'the praetor leads his army to Mutina, without keeping it together.'

The predicative adjective is particularly common with participles used as substitutes for a temporal sentence; as

Mortuo Socrati magnus honos habitus est, 'great honour was paid to Socrates after his death.'

Quamdiu affuit, ne qua sibi statua poneretur restitit, absens prohibere non potuit, 'as long as he was present he opposed the erection of a statue to himself, when absent he could not prevent it.'

It will generally be found that the predicative adjective is more common in poetry than in prose; thus Horace says: *Per meos fines lenis incedas abeasque parvis aequus alumnis,* 'may you gently pass over my boundaries and depart without hurt to my rising flock.' *Domesticus otior,* 'I pass my time idly at home.' *Mane forum, vespertinus pete tectum,* 'repair to the forum in the morning, and retire to your home in the evening.' Virgil has: *Volat avia longe,* 'she flies far from the road.' Lucretius: *Avius longe vagaris,* 'you wander far from the road.'

(c) An adjective agreeing with two or more substantives of different genders is in the plural number, and if one or more of the subjects denotes a person, the adjective takes its gender from the substantive which stands first in the usual order of priority, namely, masculine, feminine, neuter; as

Pater mihi et mater mortui sunt, 'my father and my mother are dead.'

Domus, uxor, liberi inventi sunt invito patre, 'a house, a wife, and children have been found against his father's will.'

Rex regiaque classis una profecti, 'the king and the royal fleet started together.'

(d) If, in the case just mentioned, all the substantives denote things, and not persons, the adjective is in the neuter plural; as

Labor et voluptas societate quadam naturali inter se juncta sunt, 'labour and pleasure are (things) connected together by a sort of natural society.'

Catilinae bella intestina, rapinae, discordia civilis grata fuere, 'intestine wars, plunder, civil discord, were (things) agreeable to Catiline.'

(e) A neuter plural adjective may agree with two or more nouns of the same gender, and not neuter, and even when persons are in part denoted, if we can regard the subjects as implying things rather than agents; thus we may say,

Stultitiam et temeritatem, injustitiam et intemperantiam dicimus esse fugienda, 'we say that folly and rashness, injustice and intemperance, are things to shun.'

Patres et plebem, invalida et inermia, cunctatione ficta ludificatur, 'by a feigned reluctance he sports with the senate and the commonalty, as things of no power.'

(f) An adjective really referring to two or more substantives may be made to agree with the word to which it stands nearest; as

Verres perspicua sua consilia conatusque omnibus fecit, 'Verres made his plans and efforts plain to all.'

Thrasybulus contemptus est a tyrannis atque ejus solitudo, 'Thrasybulus was despised by the tyrants, and so was his isolation.'

Invidi virtutem et bonum alienum oderunt, 'the envious hate the virtue and goodness which do not belong to themselves.'

(g) If a participle stands between two substantives, it agrees generally with the word to which it stands nearest; but if the subject is a person, the natural gender is retained; thus we have

Non omnis error stultitia est dicenda, 'not every error is to be called folly.'

Paupertas mihi onus visum est et miserum et grave, 'poverty has appeared to me as a miserable and heavy burthen;' but

Semiramis sexum mentita, puer esse credita est, 'Semiramis, having belied her sex, was believed to be a boy.'

Tulliae moriendum fuit, quoniam homo nata fuerat, 'Tullia had to die, because she had been born a human being.'

Obs. Although the Latin language has no article, the adjective may be used as a substantive, or with some substantive tacitly referred to, especially in the masculine or neuter gender; as *Est miserorum, ut malevolentes sint, atque bonis invideant,* 'it is the part of the miserable (i.e. of miserable men) to be malevolent and to envy the good (i.e. rich or worthy men).' *Tria genera sunt bonorum, maxima animi, secunda corporis, externa tertia,* 'there are three kinds of blessings (i.e. good things), the greatest those of the mind, the second those of the body, and external advantages the third.' *Multi nihil prodesse philosophiam, plerique etiam obesse arbitrantur,* 'many (men) think that philosophy is of no use, most (men) think that it is even hurtful.' *Omne tulit punctum qui miscuit utile dulci,* 'he has gained every vote, who has mixed the useful with the pleasant.' *Honestum praetulit utili, rejecit alto dona nocentium vultu,* 'he has preferred the honourable (thing) to the useful, has rejected the bribes of the guilty (men) with uplifted countenance.'

(C) *Agreement of the Relative with its Antecedent.*

141 (a) The relative pronouns, *qui, qualis, quantus,* take their gender and number from the word which they define, and which is called the antecedent, but are placed, like nouns, in the case, whether direct or oblique, which the sentence requires; thus we have

Accepi ab Aristocrito tres epistolas, quas ego lacrimis prope delevi, 'I have received from Aristocritus three letters, which (letters) I have almost blotted out with my tears.'

Nullus dolor est, quem non longinquitas temporis minuat ac molliat, 'there is no sorrow such that length of time does not lessen and assuage it (the sorrow).'

Obs. 1 If the antecedent, though expressed figuratively as a thing, really means a person, the relative agrees in gender with the person signified; as *Habebam inimicum non Marium, sed duo importuna prodigia, quos egestas tribuno plebis constrictos addixerat,* 'I had for my enemy not Marius, but two strange monsters, whom their poverty had made the bond-slaves of the tribune of the commons.'

Obs. 2 If the relative does not refer to a particular antecedent, but to the general purport of the main sentence, it is put in the neuter singular, or its antecedent may be expressed parenthetically by *id;* as *Rufus sponte decessit,* [*id*] *quod meum dolorem exulcerat,* 'Rufus has departed voluntarily, a circumstance which aggravates my grief.'

Obs. 3 A relative may be attracted into the case of its antecedent, if it is easy to supply the necessary construction from the main sentence; as *Quum scribis et agis aliquid eorum quorum consuesti* (*aliquid scribere et agere*), 'when you write and do some one of those things (some one) of which you are accustomed (to write and do).' *Consulibus senatus permisit, ut de his rebus legem, quam* (*dicere*) *ipsis videretur, dicerent,* 'the senate permitted the consuls to propose a law about these things such as it might seem good to them (to propose).'

Obs. 4 Conversely, the antecedent is attracted into the case of the relative, when the latter stands first; as *Ad Cæsarem quam misi epistolam, ejus exemplum fugit me tibi mittere,* 'I forgot to send you a copy of the letter, which I sent to Cæsar.'

In the poets we have this attraction even when the noun stands first; as *Urbem quam statuo vestra est,* i.e. In prose, *quam statuo urbem, vestra est,* 'the city, which I am establishing, is yours.'

Obs. 5 A relative may have for its antecedent a personal pronoun included in a possessive; as *Omnes laudare fortunas meas, qui natum haberem tali ingenio praeditum,* 'all men cried up my good luck (the good luck of me), who had a son blest with such a disposition.'

(b) When the relative refers to two or more nouns of different genders, its concord follows the rule given for adjectives in the similar case (140, (c)); and the neuter plural is similarly used (140, (d)); as the following examples will show:

Duilius, rediens a coena, delectabatur crebro funali et tibicine, quae sibi nullo exemplo privatus sumpserat, 'Duilius, on returning from supper, was regaled frequently with torches and flute-players, which things no man out of office had taken to himself in any previous example.'

Fortunam nemo ab inconstantia et temeritate sejunget, quae digna certe non sunt deo, 'no one will separate fortune from fickleness and rashness, which things certainly are not worthy of a divinity.'

(c) If a relative stands between two substantives, it generally takes its gender and number from that which is in the relative sentence, especially if the relative sentence is parenthetical; as

Animal plenum rationis, quem vocamus hominem, 'an animal fraught with reason, which we call man.'

Thebae quod Boeotiae caput est, 'Thebes, which is the capital of Boeotia.'

But we also find the relative in agreement with its grammatical antecedent; as

Apud vicum, qui Cannae appellatur, ambo Consules ab Hannibale vincuntur, 'both the Consuls are conquered by Hannibal, at the village which is called Cannae.'

(d) If the relative sentence also contains an apposition to the main sentence, the gender of the relative is regulated by the apposition; as

Ipse ex flumine, quam proximam oppido aquam diximus, jumenta onerat, 'he himself loads the beasts of burthen from the river, which we have mentioned as the stream nearest to the town.'

To this class belong the idiomatic phrases, *qui tuus est erga me amor,* 'such is your love towards me;' *quae tua est humanitas,* 'such is your courtesy;' for which we might write, *pro tuo in me amore; pro tua humanitate.*

(D) *Apposition of a Noun or Participle as secondary Predicate.*

142 The relative sentence corresponds to the use of the adjective as a defining epithet. Accordingly, the apposition of a noun or participle in the same case corresponds to the use of the adjective adverbially or as a secondary predicate; and it is always possible to pass from one construction to the other by substituting the predicate of the relative sentence, in the form of a noun or participle, for the whole sentence with the relative, and putting it in the same case, and, so far as possible, in the same gender and number with the antecedent. Conversely, the apposition may be

expressed by restoring the form of the relative sentence or substituting a conjunction for the relativa. As the difference between the relative sentence and the apposition is just that between the epithet and the secondary predicate, and as the Latin language has no definite article to mark this distinction in the case of single words, the student should observe that the relative sentence, of which the predicate alone may constitute an apposition, has necessarily a definite antecedent, and that the relative sentence into which the apposition may be resolved has necessarily an indefinite antecedent, which constitutes it a subordinate or dependent sentence. The following examples will show the processes of forming an apposition from the predicate of a relative sentence, and of resolving an apposition into a subordinate or dependent sentence apparently relative.

(a) If the predicate of the relative sentence is a noun, it admits of direct apposition to the antecedent; thus from the sentence, *Aristides, qui fuit Lysimachi filius*, which means, 'the Aristides, who was the son of Lysimachus,' and gives us a definition of a particular person, we may make the apposition, *Aristides, Lysimachi filius*, which means, 'Aristides, being the son of Lysimachus,' or tells us, as a piece of information, *who* was his father; and this might be expressed in a subordinate sentence by *Aristides, quum esset Lysimachi filius*, if we wished to make any thing follow from the secondary predication. Similarly, we might say, *Cicero, qui tunc praetor fuit, legem Maniliam suasit*, 'Cicero, who, as is well known, was then praetor, recommended the Manilian law,' where we define Cicero by a notorious circumstance; from this we might make the apposition, *Cicero praetor legem Maniliam suasit*, which means, 'Cicero, being praetor (or when he was praetor), recommended the Manilian law,' and tells us, as a piece of information, when it was that Cicero did this; or we might resolve the apposition into a subordinate sentence, and say, *Cicero quum praetor esset, legem Maniliam suasit*, if we mean that by being praetor at the time he had some special advantage in regard to what he then did.

(b) If the predicate of the relative sentence is contained in a finite verb, a direct apposition will be effected by substituting the participle for the verb in question; thus from the relative sentence in *Quam miser est virtutis famulatus, quae servit voluptati*, 'how wretched is the thraldom of that virtue which serves pleasure,' we might make the apposition, *Quam miser est virtutis fumulatus servientis voluptati*, 'how wretched is the thraldom of virtue, when (or if) it serves pleasure;' which might be resolved into a subordinate sentence, thus, *Quam miser est virtutis famulatus, si voluptati serviat*, with a more distinct expression of the condition. By changing the voice we may get a participial apposition from a subordinate sentence which has a subject of its own; thus for *Hannibal Gracchum sustulit posteaquam eum in insidias duxit*, 'Hannibal cut off Gracchus, after he had drawn him into ambush,' we might write with much the same meaning, *Hannibal Gracchum in insidias ductum sustulit* (see above, 140, (b)).

Obs. It has been remarked that the noun in apposition will agree with the main noun, so far as possible, in gender and number; thus we should say, *philosophia, inventrix legum*, not *inventor*, and the like. The following are necessary exceptions to the general rule:

(1) When the noun in apposition does not admit of a change of gender; as *Vitas philosophia dux*.

(2) When the main noun is a collective word, or has no singular; as *Athenae urbs celeberrima; Aborigines, genus hominum agreste; opes, irritamenta malorum*.

(3) When a locative, preserved in the name of a town, is followed by the ablative of the common word used locatively; as *Archias natus est Antiochiae, celebri quondam urbe et copiosa*.

(4) The words *urbs, oppidum, flumen, mons, arbor* may be followed by a genitive of the name with which they would otherwise be in apposition; as *oppidum Antiochiae, flumen Rheni, arbor fici*.

(E) *Case of the Primary Predicate.*

143 As a general rule the case of the subject is repeated in that of the primary predicate (above, 128, vi.), and this case in most propositions is the nominative. It will be desirable, however, to consider the primary predication both with the finite verb and with the infinitive.

I. Case of the Predicate with the Finite Verb.

(a) A nominative of the predicate, as well as of the subject, is used with finite verbs, denoting existence or coming into being; such as *sum, existo, maneo, appareo, videor, fio, nascor, evado*.

SYNTAX OF THE NOMINATIVE. 267

The subject indicates *who* any person or thing is; the predicate tells *what* he is or becomes. For example:

Ætas praeterita irrevocabilis est, 'past time is irrevocable.'
Nemo nascitur dives, 'no one is born rich.'
M. Brutus per se magnus homo evaserat, 'Marcus Brutus had turned out a great man by himself.'

(b) A nominative of the predicate, as well as of the subject, is used with finite verbs denoting 'to be named, chosen, considered,' &c. The subject indicates *who* is named, &c., and the predicate tells us *how* he is named, *to what* he is chosen, *in what light* he is considered, &c. For example:

Qui erant cum Aristotele Peripatetici dicti sunt, 'those who associated with Aristotle were called Peripatetics.'

Themistocles quum in epulis recusasset lyram habitus est indoctior, 'Themistocles having declined the lyre at an entertainment was considered deficient in education.'

Servius Tullius magno consensu rex est declaratus, 'Servius Tullius with much unanimity was declared king.'

Obs. 1 The ablative with *pro*, or the genitive with *loco, in numero,* may sometimes be used instead of the predicative nominative with some of these verbs; thus we may have *videri pro, haberi pro, haberi loco, haberi in numero;* thus, *Cur stulti non muciunt, ut, quae mala perniciosaque sunt, habentur pro bonis et salutaribus?*

Obs. 2 If we substitute the active for the passive of a verb signifying 'to be named,' &c., the two nominatives will be represented by two accusatives. Similarly, if the finite verb is expressed in the infinitive mood and the subject is therefore (128, VIII.) placed in the accusative, the predicate will be in the accusative also. And in the same way we shall have two ablatives in the ablative absolute; thus, *Romani Ciceronem creaverunt consulem; nuntiatum est Ciceronem consulem creatum esse; Cicerone consule creato.*

Obs. 3 The subject of the infinitive after the impersonal expressions, 'it seems,' &c., ought to be in the accusative. But *videor* is always construed as a personal verb; for we do not say, *videtur me, fratri tuo carum esse,* 'it seems that I am dear to your brother;' but, *videor fratri tuo carus esse, videris fratri carus esse, videtur fratri carus esse, videmur fratri cari esse, videmini fratri cari esse,* &c. Similarly we may construe the verbs *credor, dicor, putor,* &c.; for example, *crederis hoc fecisse; diceris mihi iratus esse; luna solis lumine collustrari videtur.* But we may also say, *dicunt, ferunt, tradunt,* &c. with the accusative and the infinitive.

SYNTAX OF THE ACCUSATIVE.

II. Case of the Predicate with the Infinitive.

(a) When verbs, which take the double nominative, as *esse, fieri, appellari, creari, haberi, videri,* &c. are used in the infinitive, the predicate stands in the nominative, if the infinitive depends on a personal verb, as, for instance, the passive verbs *videor, credor, putor, habeor, dicor,* &c.; as

Socrates parens philosophiae jure dici potest, 'Socrates may rightly be called the parent of philosophy.'

Cato bonus esse quam videri malebat, 'Cato preferred to be, rather than to seem, good.'

Xanthippe, Socratis uxor, morosa admodum fuisse fertur et jurgiosa, 'Xanthippe, the wife of Socrates, is reported to have been very ill-tempered and quarrelsome.'

(b) With the infinitive of the verbs just mentioned, the predicate stands in the accusative, if the infinitive depends on an impersonal verb, or is regarded as an independent expression; thus

Aliud est, iracundum esse, aliud iratum, 'it is one thing to be (that a man should be) passionate, another thing to be (that a man should be) angry.'

Nulla est laus, ibi esse integrum, ubi nemo est, qui aut possit aut conetur corrumpere, 'there is no merit that a man should be upright, when there is no one who would be willing or would attempt to corrupt him.'

(c) If a dative of the person is expressed after the impersonal verbs *licet, contingit, conceditur, expedit, necesse est, satius fuit,* the predicate is generally in the dative, though it may occasionally appear in the accusative; thus,

Illis timidis et ignavis licet esse, vobis necesse est fortibus viris esse, 'it is allowed to them to be timid and cowardly, it is necessary for you to be brave men.'

Civi Romano non licet esse Gaditanum, 'it is not allowed to a Roman citizen to be (that he should be) a citizen of Gades.'

§ 2. *The Accusative.*

144 The transition from the nominative to the accusative is immediate; for any sentence may become *objective,* that is, dependent in the infinitive mood on another verb; and in this case the nominative, or *subject,* becomes the accusative or *object;* thus the sentence, *Æneas filius fuit Anchisae*, might become the object of the verb *dixit*, 'he said,' and we should then write, *dixit*, 'he said,'—what? *Æneam Anchisae filium esse*, 'that Æneas was the son of Anchises'—*that is what he said*, or the object of his speaking (see above, 128, VIII.). But although the accusative represents the subject of the verb in the infinitive mood, it cannot be said that its use is *subjective*, for the whole sentence in which it appears is objective, and is governed by the main verb, so that the accusative, in this as in other usages, is a secondary predicate according to the principle explained above (125). The idiomatic usages of the Latin accusative fall into two main classes, which may be distinguished by a reference to this relation between the accusative and the nominative; for the Latin accusative denotes either (A) the immediate object of the action, or, as we might say, the *patient* as opposed to the *agent;* or (B) the object to which the action refers, or which defines the immediate object or patient. The distinction between *the accusative of the immediate object* and *the accusative of reference* depends upon the following simple consideration. In the former instance, the accusative becomes the nominative when the governing verb is changed from active to passive; but in the latter instance, the accusative is retained even with the passive. Thus we have an accusative of the immediate object in *dux urbem militibus diripiendum tradidit*, because this may be expressed in the passive by *urbs militibus a duce diripienda tradita est;* and so also when there is the apposition of a secondary predicate; as *invidiam di fortunae comitem dederunt*, which is expressed in the passive by *invidia fortunae a dis comes data est*. But we have an accusative of reference in *rogo te sententiam*, because the passive expression would be *rogaris sententiam*.

(A) *Accusative of the Immediate Object.*

145 (a) All transitive verbs, whether their form be active or deponent, and whether their use be personal or impersonal, require an accusative of the immediate object; thus,

Haec studia adolescentiam agunt, senectutem oblectant, secundas res ornant, adversis perfugium et solatium praebent, 'these studies occupy youth, charm old age, embellish prosperity, supply a refuge and consolation to adversity.'

Conqueri adversum fortunam, non lamenturi decet, 'it is proper to regret adversity, not to lament it.'

Pudet regem facti, 'it shames the king (the king is ashamed) of the action.'

Oratorem irasci minime decet, 'it by no means becomes an orator to be angry.'

Obs. 1 Many intransitive verbs, when compounded with prepositions, become completely transitive, and not only govern the accusative, but may be used in the passive voice; thus we have both *inire consilia*, or *societatem*, and *consilia ineuntur, societas initur;* both *circumvenit hostem,* and *ab hoste circumventus est.* Some of these verbs change their meaning, when instead of the accusative they repeat their preposition with the appropriate case; thus, *aggredi ad aliquam rem* means, 'to attempt some business,' but *aggredi aliquem* is 'to attack some one;' *egredi e castris* is 'to go forth from a camp,' but *egredi modum* is 'to overstep the limit.'

Obs. 2 Some writers, chiefly poets, use intransitive verbs in a secondary signification, which is to all intents transitive; thus we have *ardere aliquem,* 'to burn for somebody,' i.e. 'to be in love with him;' *olere antiquitatem,* 'to have a smack of antiquity;' *sapere crocum,* 'to savour of crocus;' *saltare Ledam,* 'to dance Leda,' i.e. to 'represent her in a dance;' *ambulare mare,* 'to traverse the sea;' *desinere artem,* 'to give up an art;' *perseverare inediam,* 'to continue a fast;' *vigilare noctem,* 'to pass the night awake,' &c.

(b) Intransitive verbs may often be followed by an accusative of cognate signification, if it is accompanied by an epithet which bears the stress of the secondary predicate; thus we may say, *vivere vitam jucundissimam,* 'to live a most pleasant life,' where we might have written *vivere jucundissime,* 'to live most pleasantly;' *mirum somniare somnium,* 'to dream a strange dream;' *risum ridere sardonium,* 'to laugh a sardonic laugh,' i.e. 'to laugh sardonically;' *pugnam pugnare nobilissimam,* 'to fight a most noble fight,' i.e. 'to fight most nobly.' It has been mentioned already (125) that all oblique cases are secondary predicates; and in this usage, which is called the *figura etymologica,* the secondary predication is virtually contained in the adjective.

(c) A double accusative of the object is used after verbs of demanding, naming, choosing, regarding, &c., the passives of which take the double nominative (140, (b)); as

Artaxerxes Iphicratem ab Atheniensibus petivit ducem, 'Artaxerxes demanded Iphicrates from the Athenians as (to be) general.'

Invidiam fortunae di comitem dederunt, 'the gods have given envy as a companion to fortune.'

Obs. This construction, in which the second accusative is really a tertiary predicate, is especially common in such phrases as *habere aliquem amicum; praestare se virum; facere aliquem certiorem; planum facere aliquid; reddere aliquem caecum, felicem, infelicem; dare alicui pecuniam mutuam.*

(d) A double accusative of the object is used after such verbs as *curo, do, loco, conduco, suscipio, trado,* which denote the assignment or undertaking of a work; and here one of the accusatives denotes the object and the other is a gerundive denoting the act assigned or undertaken; as

Antigonus Eumenem mortuum propinquis sepeliendum tradidit, 'Antigonus gave over Eumenes when dead to his friends for burial.'
Diomedon Epaminondam pecunia corrumpendum suscepit, 'Diomedon undertook Epaminondas, to corrupt him with money.'
Conon dirutos a Lysandro muros reficiendos curat, 'Conon provides for the repair of the walls destroyed by Lysander.'

(B) *Accusative of Reference.*

146 The accusative of reference is very frequently supported by one of the prepositions, which will be examined in their proper place. It is found by itself in the following usages.

(a) Verbs of asking, begging, demanding, teaching, and concealing, take two accusatives, of which one refers to the person, as the immediate object, and the other is the accusative of reference; thus we have

Meo jure te hoc beneficium rogo, 'by a right of my own, I ask of you this kindness,' i.e. 'I ask you with reference to this kindness.'
Fortuna belli artem victos quoque docet, 'fortune teaches the vanquished also (with reference to) the art of war.'
Te atque alios partum ut celaret suum, 'in order that she might escape the notice of you and others with reference to her labour.'

Obs. 1 Another way of explaining this construction is by regarding both accusatives as denoting the object of the verb, one denoting the person, as the nearer object, the other indicating the thing, as the

272   SYNTAX OF THE ACCUSATIVE.

more remote object; thus, *Posce Deos veniam,* 'ask: *whom?* the gods: for *what?* pardon.' *Dedocebo te istos mores,* 'I will unteach: *whom?* you: *what?* those customs of yours.' *Iter quod habebant, omnes celat,* 'he conceals: *what?* the journey which he was undertaking: from *whom?* from all men.' But that the accusative of the thing is an accusative of reference is shown by the consideration already mentioned (144), that it remains in the accusative when the verb becomes passive, whereas the accusative of the object becomes the subject of the passive verb; thus we may say, *Scito, me non esse rogatum sententiam,* 'know that I was not asked (with reference to) my opinion.' *Omnes belli artes edoctus,* 'thoroughly taught (with reference to) all the arts of war.' It is to be observed, however, that in some phrases there seems to be an option as to which of the accusatives is to be regarded as the case of reference; the accusative denoting the thing must be retained when it is a pronoun or adjective with a general signification, as *multa, plura, &c.*; as *multa ostentis, multa extis admonemur.* But *we say pecunia a me exigitur* rather than *exigor pecuniam.*

Obs. 2 A prepositional phrase is very often substituted for the accusative of reference with the verbs now under consideration; thus we may have *celare, consulere, dicere, interrogare, monere aliquem de aliqua re; contendere, exigere, flagitare, petere, postulare, precari aliquid ab aliquo; percontari, quaerere, scitari, sciscitari aliquid ex aliquo.* With *celo* we may have a dative of the person both when it is used in the active, as *Ut tegat hoc coletque viris* (Ovid, *Fast.* IV. 149, where some read *viros*), and also with the passive, as *Id Alcibiadi celari non potuit* (Corn. Nep. *Alcib.* 5).

(b) An accusative of reference is used with all kinds of verbs, and with certain participles and adjectives, to denote the part of the subject or object to which the predication has immediate relation; as

Omnia Mercurio similis, vocemque coloremque, 'like Mercury in all respects, both in voice and complexion.'

So also we have *fractus membra,* 'broken down in reference to his limbs,' *odoratus capillos,* 'perfumed as to his hair,' *aeger pedes,* 'infirm in his feet,' &c.

Obs. This construction, which is sometimes called the *accusativus Graecus* because it is a common Greek idiom, is chiefly confined to the poets; for the prose writers more usually employ the ablative, as *aeger pedibus, &c.*; and even Virgil has in the same line *micat auribus et tremit artus,* 'he quivers in *his* ears and trembles as to *his* limbs.' But the best prose writers use the accusative in certain phrases; as *magnam* or *maximam partem,* 'in regard to a great or the greatest part;' *cetera, reliqua,* 'for the rest;' *id temporis, id aetatis, id genus, &c.*

(c) In the poets the passive of verbs, signifying to put on or take off something from the person, such as *induor, exuor, cingor, accingor, discingor, amicior, inducor*, take an accusative of reference to denote the thing put on or off; as

Protinus induitur faciem vultumque Dianae, 'she immediately clothes herself with the face and looks of Diana.'

Obs. 1. We have a similar idiom in such phrases as *moveri Cyclopa*, 'to represent a Cyclops in dancing,' i.e. 'to move oneself with reference to a Cyclops.' See § 143, *obs.* 2.

Obs. 2. The passive participle is often used with the accusative; as *Dido Sidoniam chlamydem circumdata*, 'Dido clothed in a Sidonian cloak;' *pueri laevo suspensi loculos tabulamque lacerto*, 'boys having their bags and tablet hanging from their left arm.'

(d) The accusative of reference may assume an interjectional form, whether an interjection is used or not; as

Proh deum fidem! 'O for (having regard to) the plighted faith of the Gods!'

O fallacem hominum spem fragilemque fortunam! 'O for the deceitful hopes, and precarious fortune of men!'

Testes egregios! 'O for such noble witnesses!'

Obs. The accusative of time, space, measurement, &c. will be discussed separately.

§ 3. *The Genitive.*

147 A study of the Greek language enables us to see that each of the cases had originally a simple meaning; thus, the accusative signified the end of motion or action; the genitive or ablative, which were identical, denoted the origin of motion; and the dative implied rest or presence. Consequently, the accusative would be expressed in English by the preposition 'to' or 'unto' in the sense of 'towards,' or by the mere oblique case; the genitive or ablative, which are really the same case, by the prepositions 'of' or 'from;' and the dative by 'at,' or by 'to,' in its limiting sense of 'for.' In the Latin language, idiomatic usage has introduced considerable confusion in the genitive, ablative, and dative; for while the genitive and ablative have been divided into two distinct cases, with significations more or less inconsistent, the dative has been separated from all connexion with prepositions signifying locality or rest, and those have been transferred to the ablative, which ought to convey a strong expression of separation and movement. The only words which preserve the original use of the cases are the proper names of places and the words which have been mentioned above (128, VII. (b)), to which may be added the adjectives in compounds like *meridie, postridie,* for *medii die, posteri die.* And even here an alteration in the forms has led to a want of discrimination, and we find practical rules which assign differences of construction to differences of declension. Under these circumstances we cannot treat the Latin genitive, dative, and ablative with reference throughout to their primitive and proper meaning, but must be content to enumerate the idiomatic usages to which they are applicable.

The genitive in Latin, for which the most general rule is that it may be used when 'of' is employed in English to signify partition, possession, quantity, or relation, and when 'at' or 'for' means price or value stated indefinitely, may be considered in the following arrangement of idiomatic constructions.

(A) *Genitive of Possession.*

148 (a) A genitive of possession stands after another noun, and denotes to whom or what the object belongs, or from whom it proceeds; as

Honor est virtutis praemium, 'honour is the reward of virtue.'

Assidua eminentia fortunae comes est invidia, 'envy is the constant companion of eminent fortune.'

Obs. 1 A genitive of possession is used after the quasi-prepositions *instar, causa, gratia, ergo,* which must be regarded as substantives; as *Plato est mihi instar omnium,* 'Plato is in my judgment as good as all the rest taken together.' *Sophistae appellabantur, qui ostentationis aut quaestus causa philosophabantur,* 'those were called Sophists who philosophized for the sake of ostentation or gain.'

Obs. 2 The possessive pronouns *meus, tuus, suus,* are generally used instead of the genitive of possession of the corresponding personal pronouns; thus we say *liber meus,* 'the book belonging to me;' *comitia tua,* 'the election which concerns you;' and these pronouns are used instead of the genitive with *causa* in the case just mentioned; as *tua causa hoc facio,* 'I do this for your sake,' i.e. 'for the sake of you.' In the same way we say *Ciceronis opera factum est,* 'it was done by the exertions of Cicero;' or *mea opera factum est,* 'it was done by my exertions;' or with a genitive agreeing with the presumed genitive of the pronoun, *mea unius opera factum est,* 'it was done by the exertions of me alone.'

Obs. 3 The possessive genitive may stand without its governing noun if this precedes in a corresponding member of the sentence, especially if it is combined with another genitive, as *flebat pater de filii*

mortis, de patris filius, 'the father wept for his son's death, the son for his father's.' And here also the possessive pronoun is considered as equivalent to the genitive; thus, *meo judicio stare malo, quam omnium reliquorum,* 'I would rather stand by my own judgment, than by that of all other men.'

Obs. 4 The possessive genitive is expressed alone, when the governing noun may be taken for granted; thus the word *aedes,* 'a temple,' is presumed in the genitive denoting a divinity, as *ventum erat ad Vestae,* 'they came to Vesta's,' scil. temple. So in some parts of England we say, 'are you coming to mine?' i.e. 'to my house.' Occasionally we have the same omission of the governing noun when it denotes a wife, son, daughter, or dependant; as *Pisonis Verania,* 'Piso's Verania,' i.e. his wife; *Hasdrubal Gisgonis,* 'Gisgo's Hasdrubal,' i.e. his son; *Flaccus Claudii,* 'Claudius' Flaccus,' i.e. his slave or freedman.

Obs. 5 The possessive genitive may bear different meanings, to be determined by the context, thus *Ciceronis libri,* 'the books of Cicero,' may mean either what he possessed in his library, or what he published as an author; *injurias praetoris,* 'the wrong doings of the praetor,' i.e. what he did; *injuriae civium,* 'the wrongs of the citizens,' i.e. what they suffered.

(b) A genitive of possession may stand after *sum, facio,* or *fio,* to denote the being, making, or becoming the property of something else; as

Pecus est Meliboei, 'the flock belongs to Meliboeus.'

Omnia, quae mulieris sunt, viri fiunt dotis nomine, 'all things, which *are the property* of a woman, *become the property* of her husband, under the name of dowry.'

Tyrus urbs mare vicinum suae ditionis fecit, 'the city Tyre made the neighbouring sea belong to its dominion.'

(D) *Genitive of Quality.*

149 (a) The genitive of possession is often used specially to denote what is suitable or proper, i.e. belonging in a moral sense, and is then called 'the genitive of quality;' as

Est boni judicis ex parvis rebus conjecturam facere, 'it belongs to a good judge (it is his property or characteristic) to form a conjecture from trivial circumstances.'

Negavit moris esse Graecorum, ut in convivio virorum mulieres accumberent, 'he said it was inconsistent with, did not belong to, the custom of the Greeks, that women should take their places in a party of men.'

Nihil est tam angusti animi tamque parvi, quam amare divitias, 'nothing belongs so much to a narrow and trivial mind as the love of riches.'

Obs. 1 We may sometimes make this genitive dependent immediately on such words as *munus, officium, proprium,* as *sapientis est proprium, nihil quod paenitere possit facere,* 'it is the characteristic of a wise man to do nothing that he can regret.' And we never say, *mei est,* 'it is proper to me,' &c., but *meum est, tuum est,* &c.

Obs. 2 In the case of adjectives of the third declension the genitive of quality is used after the substantive verb, instead of the nominative neuter; thus we say, *stultum est hoc facere,* 'it is foolish (or the part of a fool) to do this;' but we say, *insipientis est, impudentis est,* not *insipiens est, impudens est.*

(b) The quality of a particular person or thing is described by a genitive either immediately following the main noun, or predicated through the copulative verb; but this genitive must always be accompanied by an epithet; thus,

Claudius erat somni brevissimi, 'Claudius was a man of very little sleep,' i. e. a man who slept very little.

Plurimarum palmarum vetus gladiator, 'an old gladiator, a man of very many victories,' i. e. who had obtained very many prizes.

Non multi cibi accipies hospitem, sed multi joci, 'you will receive as your guest a man not of large appetite, but of many jokes.'

And this genitive may be placed on a parallel footing with a primary predicate; as

Natura humana imbecilla atque aevi brevis est, 'human nature is feeble, and of a short existence.'

Obs. 1 For this use of the genitive of quality, it is not uncommon to substitute the ablative, especially when we can express it by 'he had, he possessed,' a certain quality; thus, *Cato singulari fuit prudentia et industria,* 'Cato was a man of (he possessed) extraordinary prudence and industry.' In some phrases we must use the ablative, because the genitive would refer us to the other signification of this construction; thus we must say, *esse bono animo, esse genere atque animo regio,* 'to have a good courage,' 'to possess the rank and feelings of a prince;' because *est boni animi* means 'it belongs to, is the characteristic of a good courage,' &c.; i. e. the former indicates the existing state, and the latter the whole character.

Obs. 2 This genitive or ablative of quality is generally subjoined to an appellative noun, as *vir magni ingenii,* 'a man of great ability,' and this is our English idiom; but the general noun is occasionally omitted, and we have such phrases as *T. Manlius, priscae ac nimis durae severitatis, ita locutus fertur,* 'Titus Manlius, (a man) of old-fashioned and excessively harsh severity, is said to have spoken thus.'

Obs. 3 In speaking of qualities of the soul we may substitute *est in aliquo* for the genitive or ablative of quality, as *est in te summa sapientia,* for *summa es sapientia.*

(C) *Genitive of the Object* (1) *with Substantives.*

150 By a further application of the genitive of possession, it denotes the object affected, rather than the thing as belonging to the subject and proceeding from it; and this use of the genitive, which is very extensive, is found both with substantives or adjectives and with verbs.

The nouns which are followed by the genitive of the object are mostly those which denote an activity, especially an activity of the mind; thus we have

Insitus est nobis amor patriae, 'there is implanted in us a love of our country,' i.e. of which our country is the object.

Jucunda est memoria praeteritorum malorum, 'the memory of past misfortunes (i.e. of which they are the object) is pleasant.'

Iphicrates ipso adspectu cuivis injiciebat admirationem sui, 'Iphicrates, by his mere appearance, inspired every one with an admiration of himself (i.e. of which he was the object).'

Obs. 1 In translating this genitive into English we are often obliged to use some other preposition than 'of;' thus *aditus laudis* is 'the approach *to* honour;' *consolatio rerum adversarum* is 'consolation *in* misfortune;' *desiderium urbis,* 'a longing *for* the city;' *maeror funeris,* 'sorrow *on account* of death;' *remedium irae,* 'a remedy *against* anger.'

Obs. 2 In some cases the same expression may signify either the possession or the object; thus *metus hostium,* 'the fear of the enemy,' may signify either 'the fear which the enemies *feel,*' which is the subjective or possessive genitive; or, 'the fear which the enemies *cause,*' which is the objective genitive; and the context alone can determine which is intended.

Obs. 3 The genitives *mei, tui, sui, nostri, vestri* after a substantive do not admit of this ambiguity, but must denote either the genitive of the object or the genitive of partition; thus *amor meus* is 'my love,' 'that which I feel;' but *amor mei* is 'the love of me,' i.e. 'of which I am the object;' *pars mea* is 'my part,' 'that which belongs to me,' but *pars mei* is 'a part of me,' i.e. 'taken from me.' There are, however, few instances in which the possessives are used instead of the objective genitive of the personal pronoun, as *neque negligentia tua neque id odio fecit tuo*, 'he did it neither from neglect nor from hatred of you.'

Obs. 4. The possessive and objective genitive may occur together with the same noun, as *Crassi defensio Vatinii*, 'Cramus' defence of Vatinius,' i. e. 'the defence proceeding from Crassus, and of which Vatinius was the object.' And here the distinction between the personal pronoun and the possessive is immediately applicable; as *grata mihi vehementer memoria nostri tua*, 'your memory of us is extremely agreeable. In some cases a genitive may depend on another genitive, as *causa intermissionis litterarum*, 'the cause of the interruption of the correspondence;' but in these cases we must guard against any ambiguity.

(D) *Genitive of the Object (2) with Adjectives.*

151. All relative adjectives, i. e. those which require a substantive to define their meaning, are followed by a genitive of the object. These are

(a) Adjectives denoting desire or fear, ignorance or knowledge, remembrance or forgetfulness; thus,

Est natura hominum novitatis avida, 'the nature of man is eagerly desirous of novelty.'
Memor esto brevis aevi, 'be mindful of a short life.'
Ignarus rerum omnium, 'ignorant of all things.'

(b) Verbal adjectives in *-ax* and participles; but this construction is more common in poetry than in prose; thus we have

Tenax propositi vir, 'a man firm in his purpose.'
Amans reipublicae civis, 'a citizen attached to the commonwealth.'
Patiens laboris atque frigoris, 'capable of enduring labour and cold.'

(c) Adjectives which denote power over a thing, and participation in it, or the reverse; thus,

Compos mentis, 'having the full control of his mind.'
Expers rationis, 'devoid of reason.'
Impotens irae, 'unable to keep down his anger.'
Particeps consiliorum, 'a sharer in his counsels.'

(d) Adjectives denoting plenty or deficiency in anything; especially *plenus, inops, pauper, egenus, indigus, sterilis*; as

Italia plena est Graecarum artium, 'Italy is full of Greek arts.'

(c) Adjectives denoting profusion or the contrary; as
Prodigus aeris, 'lavish of money.'
Parcissimus somni, 'most sparing of sleep.'

Obs. 1 Some adjectives are so regularly used with the genitive of the object, so as to form a sort of compound; thus we have *juris* (also *jure*) *consultus,* for 'a man learned in the law;' so also *juris prudens,* &c. The poets with reference to this have such phrases as *insanientis sapientiae consultus, rerum prudens,* &c.

Obs. 2 Instead of the genitive we may have a prepositional phrase, as *prudens in jure civili, rudis ad pedestre certamen.*

Obs. 3 Adjectives of class (d), except those especially mentioned, take the ablative as well as the genitive.

(E) *Genitive of the Object* (3) *with Verbs.*

152 (a) The genitive of the object is used generally with verbs of remembering, reminding, and forgetting, as *memini, admoneo, reminiscor, recordor,* and *obliviscor*; but they sometimes take an accusative, especially when they denote to have a thing in the memory, to have knowledge of a thing, or the reverse, rather than to call it to mind or think of it; thus we find

Stultum est eorum meminisse, propter quae tui obliviscéris, 'it is foolish to remember those things, on account of which you are forgetful of yourself.'

But, *Antipatrum tu probe meministi,* 'you retain Antipater in your recollection, you still remember him.'

Homines non modo res praeclarissimas obliviscuntur, sed etiam nefarias suspicantur, 'men not only forget (are continually forgetful of) the most illustrious actions, but they even suspect wickednesses.'

Catilina admonebat alium egestatis, alium cupiditatis suae, 'Catiline reminded one of his wants, another of his passions.'

Obs. 1 *Recordor,* 'I think of,' almost always governs the accusative; and we have also the ablative with *de*; as *de illis lacrimis recordor, quas pro me saepe et multum profudistis,* 'I think of those tears, which you have often and abundantly shed for me.' Similarly we have *de illo ne meminisse quidem volo,* 'I do not even wish to have a recollection concerning him.' The poets use *obliviscor* with an accusative of the person; as *quisquis es, amissos hinc jam obliviscere Graios*, 'whoever you are, from this time forth forget the Greeks whom you have lost.'

Obs. 2 Besides *moneo, admoneo, commonefio*, the impersonal phrase *venit mihi in mentem* takes a genitive of the object; as *non minus saepe Quintio venit in mentem potestatis, quam aequitatis tuae*, 'Quintius thinks as often of your justice, as of your power.' But the ablative with *de* is often used after *moneo, rogo, hortor*, &c.; and we may also have the accusative of an adjective or pronoun, as *illud te moneo*, 'I warn you in reference to that' (see above, 146, (b)).

(b) The genitive of the object to denote the *thing*, as well as an accusative to denote the *person*, is used with the impersonal verbs *pudet, piget, taedet, paenitet, miseret*; denoting shame, weariness, pity, and sorrow; thus,

Pudet me hujus facti, 'it shames me (I am ashamed) of this action,' i.e. 'a shame of this action causes me shame.'

Me non solum piget stultitiae meae, sed etiam pudet, 'I am not only weary of my folly, but even ashamed of it.'

Dum me civitatis morum piget taedetque, 'while I am vexed and wearied with the principles of the commonwealth.'

Nostri nosmet paenitet, 'we are not satisfied with ourselves.'

Miseret me tui, 'I feel pity for you.'

Obs. 1 The personal verbs *misereor* and *misereo* also take a genitive of the object; but *miseror* and *commiseror* are construed with the accusative. Thus, *Qui misereri mei debent, non desinunt inviders*, 'those who ought to pity me, do not cease from envying me.' *Agesilaus tantum abfuit ab insolentia gloriae, ut commiseratus sit fortunam Graeciae*, 'Agesilaus was so far removed from the arrogance of fame, that he pitied the fortune of Greece.'

Obs. 2 The verbs *angor, excrucior, pendeo* take the genitive *animi* more frequently than the ablative *animo*; e.g. *video te animi angi*, 'I see that you are vexed in your mind.' We have also the singular expression *rerum suarum satagere*, 'to have enough of one's own affairs.'

(c) To this class belong the impersonal phrases *rē-fert = rei fert*, 'it contributes to the interest,' and *interest*, 'it is concerned about the business,' where *rei* is understood in the sense, in which the Latin verb is used as a substantive in English. With these phrases we have either a G. of the person or persons interested, or the possessive pronouns *meī, tuī, suī, nostrī, vestrī*, agreeing with the dative *rei*, expressed in *re-fert* and understood in *interest*, and therefore put for *meae, tuae, suae, nostrae, vestrae*, just as *posthāc* is written for *posthaec*. Thus we have, in the same sentence,

Caesar dicere solebat non tam suâ quam rei-publicae interesse, ut salvus esset, 'Cæsar used to say that it was not so much for his interest as for that of the state, that he should be safe.'

Quid tua id refert? 'what concern is that of yours?' i.e. 'what does it make for your business or interest?'

The *degree* of the interest implied in these phrases is sometimes expressed by the adverbs *magnopere, magis, maxime, minime,* sometimes by the accusatives *nihil, multum, plus, tantum,* sometimes by the genitives *parvi, magni, tanti, quanti* (below, 156); as

Plurimum refert compositionis quae quibus anteponas, 'it is of very great importance for the right arrangement of words, which you put first and which second.'

Illud mea magni interest, te ut videam, 'it is of vast importance to me that I should see you.'

The *thing* wherein the interest consists, is expressed by the accusative with the infinitive, by the subjunctive with *ut* (as in the last example) or *ne*, by an indirect question, or by the mere infinitive; as

Vestra interest, commilitones, ne imperatorem pessimi faciant, 'it is for your interest, fellow-soldiers, that the worst of men should not appoint the emperor.'

Theodori nihil interest, humine an sublime putrescat, 'it is of no consequence to Theodorus, whether he moulders away on the ground, or on high.'

Interest omnium recte fucere, 'it is the interest of all to act rightly.'

The thing which constitutes the interest, may also be expressed generally by a neuter pronoun, even the relative; as

Tua quod nihil refert, percontari desinas, 'desist from inquiring about that which does not concern you.'

The *relation* in which a thing is of importance is expressed by the accusative with *ad;* as

Magni ad honorem nostrum refert, me quam primum ad urbem venire, 'it is of great importance in reference to my honour that I should come to the city as soon as possible.'

(d) Verbs of accusing, condemning, and acquitting take a genitive of the object, as well as an accusative of the person; as

282   SYNTAX OF THE GENITIVE.

Qui alterum incusat probri se ipsum intueatur oportet, 'he who accuses another of wickedness ought to look at himself.'
Themistocles absens proditionis damnatus est, 'Themistocles was condemned of treason in his absence.'
Miltiades, capitis absolutus, pecunia multatus est, 'Miltiades, having been acquitted of the capital charge, was fined in a sum of money.'

Obs. 1 This genitive is sometimes explained by a reference to the ablative *crimine*, which may also be expressed; as *damnatus est crimine repetundarum, ceteris criminibus absolutus*, 'he was condemned on the charge of extortion (lit. of money to be refunded), but acquitted on the other counts in the indictment.' The ablative with *de* may stand instead of the genitive of the specific charge, as *accusabat amicum de ambitu*, 'he accused his friend of bribery;' and we may say indifferently *damnatus repetundarum* or *de repetundis.*

Obs. 2 The punishment is also expressed in the ablative or genitive, as *damnari decem millibus aeris, damnari octupli, damnare aliquem capitis* or *capite.*

Obs. 3 Verbs implying rather than expressing accusation, &c. are construed sometimes with the genitive of the object, as *interrogare aliquem ambitus; judicatus pecuniae; nullius probri compertus; tenetur furti.*

Obs. 4 The genitive of the object is sometimes used by the poets instead of the ablative of separation after verbs of abstaining, as *desine mollium querelarum*, 'desist from tender complaints;' *abstineto irarum*, 'abstain from outbreaks of passion;' *tempus desistere pugnae*, 'it is time to desist from the fight.' This is simply a Graecism.

(F) Genitive of Partition.

153 When a certain part of a given whole is to be taken, the whole is expressed in the genitive. Accordingly, the genitive of partition stands,

(1) after numerals, and especially ordinals;

(2) after substantives, adjectives, and pronouns which denote the part of a whole, as *nemo, multi, pauci, quotusquisque, uter, uterque, alteruter, alius, ullus, nullus, solus, quisquam*;

(3) after superlatives, and generally after all nouns which represent the part of a divided whole.

Thus we have

Tarquinius Superbus septimus atque ultimus regum Romanorum fuit, 'Tarquin the tyrannical was the seventh and last of the Roman kings.'

Elephanto nulla belluarum prudentior est, 'no one of beasts is more sagacious than the elephant.'

Animalium alia rationis expertia sunt, alia ratione utentia, 'of animals some are devoid of reason, others enjoy reason.'

Graecorum oratorum praestantissimi sunt ii qui Athenis vixerunt, 'of Greek orators the most excellent are those who lived at Athens.'

Obs. 1 Instead of the genitive of partition we may have the ablative with *de, ex*, or the accusative with *inter*, when a particular object is to be selected from a number; as *Themistocles de servis suis quem habuit fidelissimum ad Regem misit; acerrimus ex omnibus nostris sensibus est sensus videndi; inter maxima vitia, nullum est frequentius quam ingrati animi*.

Obs. 2 The Latin idiom sometimes requires a genitive of partition, when the English idiom does not admit it; as *nihil mali*, where we say 'nothing wrong.' On the contrary, we use a genitive of partition where the Latin idiom requires an apposition of the same case, as in the phrases *quot estis*, 'how many *of you* are there?' *trecenti conjuravimus*, 'three hundred *of us* have conspired;' *perpauci supersumus*, 'very few *of us* survive;' *quum tam pauci sitis*, 'since there are so few *of you*.' This is especially the case in such phrases as *qui multi, qui pauci, qui nulli*; e.g. *amici tui, quos multos habes*, 'your friends, *of whom* you have many;' similarly with demonstratives, as *Caninius quaerit, num ferias quaedam piscatorum essent, quod eos nullos videret*, 'Caninius asked, whether the fishermen were keeping a kind of holiday, that he saw none *of them*.'

Obs. 3 A neuter adjective may be used in the genitive of partition after *aliquid, nihil*, &c. if the adjective is of the second declension; but if it is of the third declension, where the neuter is not distinctly expressed in the genitive, it is made to agree with the partitive word; thus we have both *aliquid bonum* and *aliquid boni*, 'something good,' both *nihil novum* and *nihil novi*, 'nothing new;' but only *aliquid triste, nihil gratius*, and the like. If, however, adjectives of both forms concur, they may both stand in the genitive of partition; as *si quidquam in vobis, non dico civilis, sed humani esset*, 'if there were in you anything at all not only of the citizen, but of the man.'

(G) *Genitive of Quantity.*

154. (a) The genitive of quantity may be regarded as an application of the genitive of partition; and it stands after words

denoting a mass or a part, such as *acervus, copia, grex, multitudo, pars, pondus, vis;* thus we have

Acervus tritici, 'a heap of corn.'
Amphora vini, 'a jar of wine.'
Cohors militum mercenariorum, 'a battalion of mercenary soldiers.'
Copia omnium rerum, 'an abundance of all things.'
Magnum pondus argenti, 'a great weight of silver.'
Magna pars hominum, 'a great part of men.'

(b) The genitive of quantity stands after neuter adjectives and pronouns used substantively to denote a certain number; as

Tantum cibi et potionis, 'so much of meat and drink.'
Plus aerumnae quam delectationis, 'more of trouble than amusement.'
Quod operae curaeque in litteris ponis, 'the amount of labour and care which you bestow upon literature.'

Obs. The genitive of partition in *aliquid boni, nihil novi,* &c. is scarcely distinguishable from these genitives of quantity.

(c) The genitive of quantity is used after the adverbs *sat, satis, abunde, parum, partim, affatim;* as

Satis eloquentiae, sapientiae parum, 'enough of eloquence, but too little wisdom.'
Abunde potentiae gloriaeque, 'an ample amount of power and glory.'

Obs. To this idiom belong the phrases *quoad ejus fieri potest,* 'to such an amount of it as is possible;' *eo audaciae progressus est,* 'he advanced to such a pitch of boldness;' *eo miseriarum ventum est,* 'we came to such a pitch of distress.' So also the genitive after adverbs of place and time; as *ubi terrarum?* 'where in the earth?' *nusquam gentium,* 'nowhere in the world;' *minime gentium,* 'in nowise;' *interea loci* or *locorum,* 'meanwhile,' &c.

(H) *Genitive of Number.*

155 Another application of the genitive of partition is used with numbers to express size, duration, or age, and this is called the genitive of number from the numerals in which it is specially ex-

pressed; it is either dependent directly on the main noun, or connected with it through *esse;* thus,

Caesar contra hostem pedum quindecim fossam fieri jubet, 'Caesar orders a ditch of fifteen foot (wide) to be made opposite to the enemy.'

Dies tempus est viginti quattuor horarum, 'a day is a period of twenty-four hours.'

Xerxis classis fuit mille et ducentarum navium longarum, 'the fleet of Xerxes consisted of 1200 ships of war.'

Hamilcar in Hispaniam secum ducit filium Hannibalem annorum novem, 'Hamilcar takes with him to Spain his son Hannibal (a boy) of nine years.'

(I) *Genitive of Price or Value.*

156 With verbs of estimating, buying and selling, such as *aestimo, duco, facio, sto, consto, emo, vendo, veneo,* we have a genitive of price, to denote indefinite estimation, expressed by the general words *magni, pluris, plurimi, parvi, minoris, minimi, tanti, tantidem, quanti, quantivis, quanticunque,* with or without *pretii;* as

Magni ejus opera aestimata est in proelio, 'his services in the battle were rated at a high value.'

Ille finis amicitiae est deterrimus, ut quanti quisque se ipse faciat, tanti fiat ab amicis, 'that end of friendship is worst, that every man should be estimated by his friends at the value which he sets upon himself.'

Vendo meum frumentum non pluris quam ceteri; fortasse etiam minoris, quum major est copia, 'I sell my corn for no higher price than the rest of the farmers, perhaps at even less, when there is greater abundance.'

Obs. 1 The genitives *multi* and *majoris* are not used in this idiom, but *magni* and *pluris.* In the colloquial style, the genitive of price appears also in the words *flocci,* 'at a lock of wool;' *nauci,* 'at a nutshell;' *pili,* 'at a hair;' *teruncii,* 'at three ounces;' *assis,* 'at an as.'

Obs. 2 The genitive of price is also found in the phrases *aequi bonique facere, boni consulere aliquid,* 'to put up with something;' *pensi aliquid habere,* 'to take thought about something.'

Obs. 3 The phrase *tanti est* does not merely mean 'it is worth so much, it is of such importance,' but also 'it is worth the trouble,' or 'the evil must be borne;' as *est mihi tanti hujus invidiae tempestatem subire, dummodo a vobis belli periculum depellatur*, 'I am ready to bear the whole weight of this unpopularity, provided the danger of war may be averted from you.'

Obs. 4 The ablatives *magno, plurimo, parvo, minimo, nihilo* are used instead of the genitive of price; as *quanti oryza empta est ? parvo*, 'for, or at, how much was the rice bought? for a small sum.' We also say *rem pro nihilo habere, ducere, putare*.

(K.) *Genitive of Relation.*

157 The genitive of relation, which is so common in Greek, is used in Latin chiefly by the poets, and the later prose writers, like Tacitus, who aimed at poetical diction; thus we have

Vetus militiae, scientiae caerimoniarumque, regnandi, laborum, 'experienced in warfare, in religious knowledge and ceremonies, in reigning, in labours.'

Modicus voluptatis, 'moderate in regard to his pleasure.'
Integer vitae, 'upright in regard to his life.'
Maturus aevi, 'of ripe age in regard to his life.'
Ambiguus futuri, 'doubtful with regard to the future.'
Lassus maris atque viae, 'weary with regard to voyages and journeys.'

Obs. The ablative with *de* or *in* may be substituted for this genitive.

§ 4. *The Dative.*

158 The dative in Latin may generally be used when we prefix 'to' or 'for' to a noun to imply limitation or destination. There are two principal applications of this case; it is either (A) the dative of the person or thing interested or concerned, that is, of the object to or for which the action takes place, and to which its effect is limited; or it is (B) the dative of the thing, which is the destination or purpose of the action. These two may be called the proper uses of the dative, and may occur in the same sentence; but the dative is also used (C) improperly, or in a sense inconsistent with its general application, to supply the place of some phrase with a preposition.

(A) *Dative of Limitation.*

159. (a) The dative of limitation is used with adjectives which denote that which is advantageous or disadvantageous, agreeable or disagreeable, suitable or unsuitable, known or unknown, friendly or unfriendly, near or distant, with a necessary reference to something else; thus,

Virtus fructuosa est aliis, ipsi laboriosa, 'virtue is profitable to others, laborious to itself.'

Siculi Verri inimici infestique sunt, 'the Sicilians are ill-disposed to Verres, and in open opposition to him.'

Dis carus ipsis, 'dear to the gods themselves.'

Nihil est naturae hominis accommodatius beneficentia et liberalitate, 'nothing is better suited to the nature of man than beneficence and liberality.'

Mors est terribilis iis quorum cum vita omnia extinguuntur, 'death is terrible to those, with whose life all things are extinguished.'

Obs. 1 With some of these adjectives a phrase with a preposition is substituted for the dative to express a definite object; thus *aptus, habilis, idoneus, paratus, commodus, promptus ad aliquam rem,* is the proper phrase to express an aptitude for a certain employment; and to express 'towards a person' we say *crudelis, durus, injuriosus, iniquus in aliquem,* or *gratus, ingratus, pius, impius erga aliquem.*

Obs. 2 With *aequalis, affinis, communis, par, dispar, similis, dissimilis, superstes* we may use the genitive as well as the dative; with *similis* (*consimilis, adsimilis*) and *dissimilis* we have more frequently the genitive of the names of gods and men, as *similis patris,* though we may have *Deo similis;* we have always the genitive in such phrases as *similis mei, tui, &c.;* and *verisimile* is more common than *vero simile; communis* may take a genitive with another genitive of the object and a prepositional phrase; as *hoc commune est potentiae cupidorum cum otiosis,* 'this is common to those desirous of power with the indolent.'

Obs. 3 *Proprius* has much more frequently a genitive than a dative, which is never found with it in Cicero; its opposite *alienus* has not only the genitive and dative, but also the ablative with or without *ab;* thus we may say *alienum huic causae, alienum dignitatis, alienum amicitia nostra, alienum ab hoc instituto.*

Obs. 4 Some of the adjectives, referred to in the rule, are used as substantives, e.g. we have *amicus,* 'a friend;' *aemulus,* 'a rival;' *aequalis,* 'a contemporary;' *necessarius, propinquus,* 'a relative;' *supplex,* 'a suppliant;' *vicinus,* 'a neighbour;'. and these have of course a genitive of the object (above, 151). Accordingly, while we say *amicus veritatis*, 'a friend of the truth,' we say *amicus alicui*, 'friendly to some one;' and while we say *Curius, qui Ciceronis amicus est*, 'Curius, who is Cicero's friend,' we say *Curius, qui Ciceroni amicissimus est*, 'Curius, who is most friendly to Cicero.'

Obs. 5 Adverbs of this class, as *convenienter, congruenter, constanter, obsequenter*, are construed with the dative; as *naturae convenienter vivere*, 'to live in a manner suited to nature.'

Obs. The poets use the dative instead of *atque* in expressions of identity; as *invitum qui servat idem facit occidenti*, 'he who saves another against his will, does the same as the person who kills him.' This seems to be a Greek idiom.

(b) A dative of limitation is used with predicative substantives to denote to whom or what the predicate specially refers; as

Ego huic causae patronus exstiti, 'I came forward as the patron for this cause (i.e. on behalf of it, for its especial advantage).'

Avaritia multis causa maximorum malorum fuit, 'avarice has been to many the cause of the greatest evils (has caused them in the case of many persons).'

(c) A dative of limitation may be used with any verbs which admit or imply the question, 'to or for what is the thing done?' (This is called the *dativus commodi* or *incommodi*); as

Venus nupsit Vulcano, 'Venus put on the veil (i.e. became a bride, was married) for Vulcan.'

Non scholae discimus sed vitae, 'we do not learn for the school, but for life.'

Liber is existimandus est, qui nulli turpitudini servit, 'he is to be considered free, who is the slave of no baseness.'

Imperat aut servit collecta pecunia cuique, 'a store of money is to every one a master or a slave.'

Non solum nobis divites esse volumus, sed liberis, propinquis, amicis, maximeque reipublicae, 'we wish to be rich not for (the advantage of) ourselves alone, but for our children, our relatives, our friends, and, most of all, for the state.'

Obs. The datives *mihi, nobis, tibi, vobis*, are used with a sense of special limitation to a particular person, to express the aspect under which the act presents itself to his mind; as *quid mihi Celsus agit ? haec vobis illorum per biduum militia fuit*, 'this you see was their military service for two days.' Such a dative is called *Dativus Ethicus*.

(d) A dative of limitation is regularly and properly used after verbs of giving or assigning (*do, dedo, dico, addico, tribuo, commodo,* &c.) to denote the recipient. The name of the case (*dativus*) is derived from this usage, which however is only one form of the dative of limitation; thus,

Quid vis tibi dari in manum? 'what do you wish to be given to you into your hand?'

Ubi te socordiae atque ignaviae dedideris, nequidquam deos implores, 'when you have given up yourself to indolence and sloth, you would in vain call upon the gods.'

(e) A dative of limitation is regularly used with the verb *sum* to denote the recipient as possessor, so that *est mihi* is quite equivalent to *habeo*; thus,

Dives est, cui tanta possessio est, ut nihil optet amplius, 'he is rich to whom there is (who has) so large a possession, that he desires nothing farther.'

Est mihi namque domi pater, est injusta noverca, 'I have in fact a father at home, I have a severe step-mother.'

Obs. 1 In speaking of the properties of the soul, we do not say *est mihi*, 'I have,' but *est in me,* e.g. *erat in Bruto summa eloquentia*, not *erat Bruto*.

Obs. 2 In the expressions *est mihi nomen, nomen mihi datur, inditur, imponitur*, the name is generally expressed in the dative, more rarely in the genitive; e.g. *Scipio, cui Africano nomen ex virtute fuit. Leges quibus duodecim tabulis nomen est. In campis, quibus nomen Raudius erat, decertavere.* But, *Q. Metello Macedonici nomen inditum est.* In foreign names, when it is of importance to give the right form, the nominative is used.

Obs. 3 The phrase *aliquid mihi volenti est,* 'something is to me wishing it,' 'I like something' (Sall. *Jug.* 84; Liv. xxi. 50; Tacit. *Ann.* i. 59; *Hist.* iii. 43), is merely a Graecism (*Greek Grammar,* p. 495 (gg)).

(f) A dative of limitation is used after a number of verbs compounded with prepositions (*ad-, ante-, con-, in-, inter-, ob-, post-, prae-, re-, sub-, super-*), if the verb has a secondary meaning in which the primary force of the preposition is lost, so that 'to' or 'for' can be introduced into the English translation; as,

Iniquissimam pacem justissimo bello antefero, 'I prefer the most unjust peace to the most righteous war.'

Vix resisto dolori, 'I can scarcely offer resistance to my sorrow.'

Omnibus negotiis non interfuit solum, sed etiam praefuit, 'he was not only present at all the business, but was even its principal manager' (cf. *est mihi = habeo*).
Subjiciunt se homines imperio alterius et potestati de causis pluribus, 'men submit themselves to the commands and control of another from various causes.'
Exercitum exercitibus, duces ducibus comparare, 'to compare armies to armies, generals to generals.'

Obs. 1 Compounds of *sum*, as *adesse*, 'to stand by, assist,' *deesse*, 'to be wanting,' *prodesse*, 'to be profitable,' *obesse*, 'to be hurtful,' &c., are among the regular applications of this rule.

Obs. 2 If the force of the preposition is clearly felt, it is subjoined with its case to the compound verb instead of the dative, as in *adhaeret navis ad scopulum; inhaeret sententia in animo; sceritas inest in vultu; concurrere, congredi cum hoste;* or a different preposition is introduced, as in *obversari ante oculos, obrepere in mentem.*

Obs. 3 In some cases it is optional whether we use the dative or the prepositional phrase; as in *abdicare aliquid alicui* or *ab aliquo;* in others the prepositional construction is much the more common; thus we say more frequently, *adhibere diligentiam ad aliquam rem,* than *alicui rei; conjungere se cum aliquo,* than *alicui; conferre* and *comparare aliquem cum aliquo,* rather than *alicui.* And we say, *communicare aliquid cum aliquo,* not *alicui; in oratore inest omnis sententia* not *oratori; vide quid intersit inter hominem et belluam,* not *homini et belluas.* Similarly we say *eripere alicui aliquid,* 'to take away something from somebody,' but *eripere aliquem ex miseriis,* 'to snatch a person from wretchedness;' *detrahere alicui pallium,* 'to take away a man's cloak,' but *detrahere de laudibus alicujus, de senatu, de teste,* 'to detract from a man's praises, from the senate, from a witness,' because in the latter instances the force of the preposition is distinctly felt.

(g) A dative of limitation is used after many verbs, which denote an action or affection of the mind limited to a particular person or thing, though, in many cases, the corresponding English verbs imply an accusative of the immediate object. Thus we have the dative with verbs of speaking well or ill (*benedico, maledico, convitior, blandior*), of threatening (*minor, minitor*), forgiving (*ignosco*), being enraged (*irascor, succenseo*), envying (*invideo*), healing (*medeor*), sparing (*parco*), hurting (*noceo*), patronizing (*patrocinor*), persuading (*persuadeo*), eagerly pursuing (*studeo, vaco*), trusting and distrusting (*fido, confido, credo, diffido*), indulging (*indulgeo*), obeying (*obsequor, obtempero, obedio, pareo*), &c.; thus we have:

Cui benedixit unquam bono! 'what good man did he ever speak well of?'

Utrique mortem est minitatus, 'he threatened death to both.'

Inscitiae meae et stultitiae ignoscas, 'may you pardon my ignorance and folly.'

Irasci amicis non temere soleo, 'I am not wont to be angry with my friends inconsiderately.'

Invident homines maxime paribus aut inferioribus, 'men envy most frequently their equals or inferiors.'

Afflictae et perditae reipublicae medeor, 'I apply remedies to the dejected and ruined state.'

Parcere subjectis et debellare superbos, 'to spare those who yield, and to fight it out with the proud.'

Non licet sui commodi causa nocere alteri, 'it is not allowed to do harm to another for the sake of one's own advantage.'

Videor prudentiae tuae diffidere, 'I seem to distrust your prudence.'

Obsequor voluntati tuae, 'I comply with your wishes.'

Sero sentiunt frustra se aut pecuniae studuisse aut imperiis aut gloriae, 'they perceive too late that they have vainly devoted themselves to money, or power, or glory.'

Obs. 1 Although we may say *invidere bonis, invidere laudibus,* it is also good Latin to say *invidere alicui aliquid* or *aliqua re. Persuadeo,* 'I induce,' takes the dative of the person, and expresses the advice which is successfully recommended by *ut* or *ne* with the subjunctive, or by the accusative of an adjective or pronoun, or by the accusative with the infinitive; as *Themistocles persuasit populo ut classis centum navium aedificaretur. Hoc quum mihi non solum confirmasset sed etiam persuasisset. Sic te tibi persuadere velim, mihi neminem esse cariorem te.* For 'I am persuaded,' we must not say *persuadeor* or *persuasus sum,* but *hoc mihi persuadetur,* or *persuasum mihi est,* or *persuasissimum mihi est,* or *mihi persuasum habeo* (which occurs, however, only in Caes. B. G. III. 2) case *aliquid, de aliqua re. Suadeo,* which signifies 'to advise,' as distinguished from *persuadeo,* which means 'to advise successfully' (cf. Cic. *Phil.* II. 11: *An C. Trebonio persuasi? cui ne suadere quidem ausus essem*), is usually construed with a dative of the person, and an accusative of the thing.

Obs. 2 We must carefully distinguish between *vaco aliqua re,* 'I am without, am devoid of something,' and *vaco alicui rei,* 'I have leisure to engage in something, I spend my time about it, I am earnestly occupied with it,' as in *itinere huic uni vacabat,* 'on the journey he paid exclusive attention to this.'

(B) *Dative of Destination.*

160 A dative of the destination, object, or purpose, is used with the verbs *sum* and *fio* signifying 'to prove,' 'tend,' or 'turn out;' with *do, duco, tribuo, verto,* signifying 'to esteem, or attribute;' with *habeo,* signifying 'to treat;' and with those which denote giving, taking, coming or sending. And these verbs have frequently a dative of limitation also; thus,

Exitio est avidis mare nautis, 'the sea is *for* a destruction *to* greedy sailors,' (i. e. is destined to destroy them, their destruction is its destination).

Ampla domus saepe fit domino dedecori, 'a large house often proves a disgrace to its owner, (is destined to disgrace him).'

Ne sibi vitio verterent quod abesset a patria, 'not to impute it to him as (for) a fault that he was absent from his country.'

Quando tu me bene merentem tibi habes despicatui, 'since you treat me, who have been so kind to you, with contempt.'

Virtus sola nec dono datur neque accipitur, 'virtue alone is neither given nor received as (for) a present.'

Pausanias venit Atticis auxilio, 'Pausanias came to the Athenians as (for) an aid,' i. e. 'with the view of aiding them.'

Obs. 1 The dative of destination is generally expressed by certain words which are specially used in this way; thus we say *have res tibi erit* (*fiet*) *decori, dedecori, detrimento, impedimento, laudi, lucro, odio, oneri, pignori, praesidio, probro, quaestui, usui,* and the like. Other phrases to be noticed are such as *est mihi cordi,* 'I am anxious about it;' *erit mihi curas,* 'I will take care of it;' *cui bono fuerit,* 'whose interest it would serve' (to whom it would be for good); *dono dari, muneri mittere, pignori relinquere, dare crimini* or *vitio, ducere laudi, tribuere ignaviae, vertere crimini* or *vitio ; habere aliquem derisui, despicatui ; habere aliquid relligioni ; habere aliquid quaestui.* Some of these are found in the examples given above.

Obs. 2 The dative of destination is used regularly with the name of certain functionaries to indicate the purpose of their office or employment, as *decemviri legibus scribendis ; triumvir aere* (*aeri*) *flando, feriundo ; triumvir reipublicae constituendae.*

(C) *Dative instead of a prepositional phrase.*

161 The Latin dative is sometimes used improperly, that is, in a sense inconsistent with its primary meaning and general usage, and when we should expect *a* (*ab*) or *cum* with the ablative, or *ad* or *in* with the accusative. These exceptional usages, which are found generally in the poets, must have sprung from an absolute or adverbial use of the case, like some similar application of the Greek dative (*Greek Grammar*, pp. 488, 492).

(a) The dative is used after passive verbs to denote the agent, instead of the ablative with *a* (*ab*); as

Carmina quae scribuntur aquae potoribus, 'poems which are written by the drinkers of water.'

Barbarus hic ego sum, quia non intelligor ulli, 'I am a barbarian here, for I am not understood by any one.'

When this idiom occurs in prose we can generally see traces of the original force of the dative; thus we must not explain *haec res mihi probatur* by *haec res a me probatur*, because we can say in the active *probare alicui rem*, 'to recommend or make good a thing to somebody;' so, *dissimillimis bestiis communiter cibus quaeritur* presumes not so much the agency as the interest of the agent; and *res mihi tota provisa est* means that the business is regarded as completed to or for the agent. The dative of the agent with gerunds and gerundives is simply a dative of limitation depending on the substantive verb, and whether we say *scribendum est mihi* or *mihi Chremes exorandus est*, we must render it by, 'it-is-for-me to write' (i.e. writing is for me), and 'it-is-for-me to entreat Chremes' (i.e. the entreating of Chremes is for me). (See below, 185.)

(b) The poets sometimes use the dative instead of the ablative of separation; as

Eripe te morae, 'tear yourself from delay,' i.e. when there are inducements to tarry, as at Tusculum, lay them aside, tear yourself from them.'

Similarly we may say *distare, dissentire alicui*, 'to be distant or dissent from somebody,' for *ab aliquo*.

(c) The dative is used instead of the ablative with *cum* in some few cases and by the poets; for instance we have *pugnare alicui* for *pugnare cum aliquo;* as

Placitone etiam pugnabis amori? 'will you even struggle with the love of which you now approve?'

Similarly *misceo* takes a dative instead of the ablative with *cum;* as

Vulnera supplevit lacrimis, fletumque cruori miscuit, 'she filled up the wounds with tears and mixed weeping with the gore.'

The use of *confero, contendo, comparo* with the dative, though explicable from the preposition in composition (above 159, (f)), approximates to this poetical idiom.

(d) The dative is used by the poets instead of the accusative with *ad* or *in* to denote the direction of motion; as

It clamor caelo, 'the shouting rises to the sky,' i.e. *ad caelum; spolia conjiciunt igni,* 'they throw the spoils on the fire,' i.e. *in ignem.*

So also when *in* with the accusative denotes the end; as

Bello animos accendit agrestes, 'she inflamed to war the rustic minds,' i.e. *in bellum,* as another poet says, *in proelia mentes accendit.*

§ 5. *The Ablative.*

162 If we except the use of the ablative in predications of space or time (below, 168), and its idiomatic use with certain prepositions (below, 169), we may divide the applications of this case, as it appears in Latin (B), into three main subdivisions; it is

(A) The ablative of immediate determination, or the case which determines the instrument, the cause, the manner, or condition of an action;

(B) The ablative of circumstance, or the case which defines the contemporary or antecedent circumstances of an action;

(C) The ablative of the object, or the case which expresses that which the action requires for its completion. The Latin ablative may therefore be rendered by the English prepositions 'by,' 'with,' 'in,' 'from,' 'at,' in different applications, regulated by the verb on which it depends.

(A) *Ablative of Immediate Determination.*

163 (a) The ablative determines the *instrument* or means with or by which an act is effected; as

Hi jaculis, illi certant defendere saxis, 'these endeavour to defend themselves *with* darts, the others *with* stones.'

Medici graviores morbos asperis remediis curant, 'physicians cure more urgent diseases *with (by means of)* severe remedies.'

SYNTAX OF THE ABLATIVE. 295

Obs. 1 If a man is represented as the instrument we cannot use the ablative, but must employ the accusative with *per;* so *bellum per legatos gessit,* 'he carried on the war by means of his lieutenants,' not *legatis.*

Obs. 2 If an accompaniment rather than an instrument is implied we must use *cum* with the ablative, as *Cimonem semper pedisequi cum numis secuti sunt,* 'servants *with* money (i.e. carrying it) always followed Cimon;' *magna cum cura atque diligentia scripsit,* 'he wrote *with* (i. e. calling in and employing) great care and diligence;' for the instruments and means were his pen and paper.

(b) The ablative determines the *cause* by or through which an act is done; as

Metu supplicii aut mortis multi vim tormentorum pertulerunt, 'many have endured the force of tortures through fear of punishment or death.'

Servius Tullius regnare coepit non jussu, sed voluntate atque concessu civium, 'Servius Tullius began to reign, not by (in consequence of) the orders, but by the will and permission of the citizens.'

Obs. 1 To this use belong the ablatives *causa, gratia, ergo, quo consilio, qua mente,* &c. A participle is often used with the ablative *amore, caritate, ira, libidine, odio, spe, studio,* &c., denoting affections of the mind, when the mere ablative is not sufficiently definite; as *ductus amore, incensus ira, inflammatus odio, impulsus spe et cupiditate, coactus metu, captus misericordia.*

Obs. 2 We must here repeat the general rule that *a* (*ab*) must be used with the ablative when we express not the cause but the agent (128, VI. (d)); as *Pompeius a Caesare victus est,* 'Pompey was conquered by Caesar.'

Obs. 3 The ablative of the *cause* appears as an ablative of *origin* after the participles *cretus, creatus, editus, genitus, natus, ortus, satus, prodilus;* as *P. Africanus fidem fecit non sanguine humano sed stirpe divina satum se esse.* But the prepositions *a* (*ab*) and *de* may stand with these participles; as *satos Curetas ab imbri,* or *Ilia cum Lauso de Numitore sati.* To this class belong the expressions *natus loco nobili, ignobili, humili, obscuro,* unless they represent the locative use of the ablative.

(c) The ablative determines the *manner* in which an act is done, and this is the regular construction of the substantives, which in themselves denote the way or manner (as *modo, more, ritu, ratione, consuetudine*); the accompanying circumstance is stated in the genitive of possession, or by means of an adjective; as

Miltiades summa aequitate rem Chersonesi constituit, 'Miltiades settled the affairs of the Chersonesus with the greatest equity' (i.e. that was the way or manner of his administration).

Apis more modoque carmina fingo, 'I mould my poems after the manner and practice of a bee.'

More Carneadeo disputare, 'to dispute in the manner of Carneades.'

Fieri nullo modo (pacto) potest, 'it cannot be done in any way.'

(d) The ablative determines the *reference* or relation under which an action is considered; as

Atticus usum pecuniae non magnitudine, sed ratione metiri solitus est, 'Atticus was accustomed to estimate the use of money not in reference to its amount, but in reference to its application.'

Natura tu illi pater es, consiliis ego, 'you are his father by (in regard to) nature, I with reference to my counsels.'

Contremisco tota mente et omnibus artubus, 'I tremble in (as to) my whole mind and all my limbs.'

Obs. 1 It will be observed that this usage corresponds exactly to one form of the accusative of reference (above, 146 (b), *Obs.*), which is used by the poet; and it has been mentioned that Virgil has both cases in one line: *micat auribus et tremit artus.*

Obs. 2 The ablative of *reference* is found in the limiting phrases, *ea lege, ea conditione, tua pace dixerim, bona tua venia, meo jure, optimo jure, mea quidem sententia, more majorum, omnium judicio;* also in expressions like *cognomine Barcas, natione Syrus, natu major, natu minimus,* &c.

(e) The ablative determines the *comparison*, in regard to which a certain degree of a quality is predicated; in other words, it is used after adjectives in the comparative degree instead of the subject connected with the comparative by the particle *quam.* This usage is in fact only a special application of the ablative of *reference,* which has just been mentioned; for *amoris simulatio est pejor odio* means, 'the pretence of love is worse in reference or relative to hatred.' Thus we have

Nihil est otiosa senectute jucundius, 'nothing is more pleasant than tranquil old age.'

Tullus Hostilius fuit Romulo ferocior, 'Tullus Hostilius was more savage than Romulus.'

SYNTAX OF THE ABLATIVE.

Nullum officium referenda gratia magis est necessarium, 'no duty is more necessary than that of returning a favour.'

Obs. 1 The explanation of the ablative of comparison as an ablative of reference is best shown by its use in relative propositions; e. g. *Hortensius quo nemo fuit doctior,* 'Hortensius, in relation to (in comparison with) whom no one was more learned.' *Attalus quo graviorem inimicum non habui,* 'Attalus, in relation to whom I never had a bitterer enemy.' *Avaritia qua nulla major pestis humano generi inferri potuit,* 'avarice, as compared with which no greater pest could have been inflicted on the human race.'

Obs. 2 As the word, which stands in the ablative of comparison, must be the subject, as distinguished from the predicate of a proposition, this construction is admissible only in the following cases:

(α) The object compared may be in the nom., voc., or accus. with the infinitive, as *O matre pulcra filia pulcrior,* or *nemo dubitabit solem esse majorem luna,* where we might have *majorem quam lunam.*

(β) The object compared may be an accusative with an adjective in the comparative degree; as *nunquam ego vidi hominem Phormione callidiorem,* because we could resolve this into *qui fuerit callidior quam Phormio.* But when a gen. or dat. is used with such an adjective, the construction with *quam* is more common; as *haec sunt verba Varronis, quam fuit Claudius doctioris,* rather than *Varronis doctioris Claudio.* Horace, however, writes: *Panis egeo, jam mellitis potiore placentis,* 'I need bread, now more desirable than honied cakes.'

(γ) The ablative of comparison stands regularly after comparative adverbs; as *opinione celerius, dicto citius, justo longius, plus aequo, solito tardius;* also in such phrases as *nemo te melius intelligit.*

(δ) The ablative of comparison may follow *plus, minus, amplius,* but generally the numerical expression is appended without *quam;* thus we have *Amplius sunt sex menses,* 'they are more than six months.' *Quid si tandem amplius biennium est?* 'what if it is more than two years?' *Plus quingentos colaphos infregit misero mihi,* 'he inflicted more than 500 buffets on poor me!' *Quis dubitat, exarsisses Romanos quum plus ducentorum annorum morem solveremus?* 'who doubts that the Romans were exasperated when we broke up a custom of more than 200 years?'

Obs. 3 The ablative of comparison cannot be used when two predicates are compared; thus we must say *pestis fuit minacior quam periculosior,* not *minacior periculosiore;* nor can it be used in a comparison of two subjects in the genitive or dative; thus we may say *Miltiades amicior fuit civium libertati quam suae dominationi,* not *sua dominatione.*

(ε) The ablative determines the *quantity* by which one thing exceeds another; as

Turres denis pedibus, quam muri, altiores sunt, 'the towers are higher by ten feet each than the wall.'

Pompeius biennio quam Cicero major fuit, 'Pompey was older than Cicero by two years.'

Obs. This ablative of quantity is found regularly in the adverbial expressions, *quo,* 'the more,' *eo,* 'by that,' *quanto,* 'by how much,' *tanto,* 'by so much,' *multo,* 'by much,' *aliquanto,* 'by something considerable,' *paullo,* 'by a little,' *nihilo,* 'by nothing.' The last will only express the ablative of quantity; if we wish to express the cause we must use the phrase *nulla alia re* or *in nulla alia re.*

(g) The ablative determines the *price,* when it is expressed by a substantive, and in connexion either with verbs of buying, selling, &c., or with adjectives like *carus, vilis, venalis;* as

Viginti talentis unam orationem Isocrates vendidit, 'Isocrates sold one speech for 20 talents.'

Multorum sanguine et vulneribus ea Poenis victoria stetit, 'that victory cost the Carthaginians the blood and wounds of many men.'

Quod non opus est asse carum est, 'that which you do not require is dear at a penny.'

Obs. 1. It is to be observed that this rule applies to the *price* as distinguished from the *value,* which is expressed in the genitive; as *emere denario quod mille denarium est,* 'to buy for a denarius that which is worth 1000 denarii.'

Obs. 2. The general expression of the price is given in the adverbs *care, carius, carissime, vilissime,* or by the ablatives *magno, permagno, plurimo, parvo, vili, nimio, minimo, dimidio;* but in some cases we have the genitive, as in *quanti, tanti, pluris, minoris, tantidem* (see above, 150).

(h) The ablative, accompanied by an adjective, determines the *quality* of a thing; and is either connected immediately with the subject which it describes, or predicated through the copulative verb; thus we have

Caesar traditur fuisse excelsa statura, colore candido, nigris oculis, valetudine prospera, 'Caesar is said to have been of lofty stature, fair complexion, black eyes, and sound constitution.'

Obs. On the genitive of quality see above (149). The ablative is more common, because the genitive is sometimes ambiguous. In adjectives of the third declension the ablative is, on this account, so much more common than the genitive, that it even follows a genitive of quality in the same sentence, when there is a change of declension; thus we have *Thyus, homo maximi corporis terribilique facie.*

(B) *Ablative of Circumstance.*

164 The ablative of circumstance, or ablative absolute, as it is commonly called, is a construction in which both subject and predicate stand in the ablative case without any conjunction or copula, and which defines a concomitant or antecedent circumstance of time, cause, condition or assumption. In order to use this ablative of circumstance the following rules must be observed:

(a) The predicate of the ablative sentence must be a substantive, an adjective, or a participle; in other words, if the subordinate sentence represented includes the primary predicate in a verb, it must be changed into the corresponding participle; thus,

for *quum puer essem*, 'when I was a boy,' we may write *me puero*, 'I being a boy.'

for *quum caelum serenum est*, 'when the sky is clear,' we may write *caelo sereno*, 'the sky being clear.'

for *quum natura reluctatur*, 'when nature resists,' we may write *natura reluctante*, 'nature resisting.'

for *postquam Augustus mortuus est*, 'after Augustus was dead,' we may write *Augusto mortuo*, 'Augustus being dead.'

for *quum Caesar profecturus esset*, 'when Caesar was about to start,' we may write *Caesare profecturo*, 'Caesar being about to start.'

(b) The subject of the ablative sentence must not appear in the main sentence, either as subject, or in an oblique case. Thus we may say,

Augustus natus est Cicerone et Antonio consulibus; iisdem consulibus Catilinae conjuratio erupit, 'Augustus was born, Cicero and Antonius being consuls (in their consulship); the same men being consuls (in the same consulship) the conspiracy of Catiline broke out,'

because *Augustus*, the subject of the first sentence, and *conjuratio*, the subject of the second, are different respectively from *Cicero* and *Antonius*, who are the subjects of the first absolute sentence, and from *iidem*, which is the subject of the second absolute sentence.

On the other hand we could not render the sentence, 'as Dionysius feared the razor of his barber, he burnt off the hair with red-hot coals,' by *Dionysio cultros tonsorios metuente, candenti carbone sibi adurebat capillum*, because *Dionysius* is the subject of *adurebat* no less than of *metuo*, implied in *metuente*. We must therefore express the circumstance either by *Dionysius, quod cultros tonsorios metuebat*, or *Dionysius, cultros metuens tonsorios, candenti carbone sibi adurebat capillum*.

Similarly, if the subject of the dependent sentence appears before in an oblique case, we cannot use the ablative of circumstance; thus, if we had to express in Latin, 'after Cæsar was dead the greatest honours were paid to him,' we could not render this by, *Caesare mortuo, summi ei honores habiti sunt*, but must write, *Caesari mortuo summi honores habiti sunt.*

If, however, the subordinate sentence, though it has the same subject as the main verb, can be expressed passively, so that its object becomes its subject, the subject will of course be different, and the ablative of circumstance may be employed; thus the sentence, 'Xerxes having carried on the war in Greece unprosperously, began to be an object of contempt even to his own subjects,' may be rendered either by *Xerxes, quum bellum in Graecia infeliciter gessisset*, or, *bello in Graecia infeliciter gesto, etiam suis contemptui esse coepit.*

Obs. 1 The predicate of the ablative absolute is most frequently expressed by a participle; but as the Latin language has no present participle of the substantive verb, a noun representing the primary predicate is often appended without any copula, as in *Cicerone et Antonio consulibus, te auctore, duce Cicerone, caelo sereno, aestu magno, summa hominum frequentia*, &c.

Obs. 2. A negative may be attached to the predicate; as *me non invito*, 'when I was not unwilling.'

Obs. 3 The participles of impersonal verbs may be used in the ablative of circumstance without any subject; thus from *auditum est, cognitum est*, we may have *audito*, 'it having been heard,' *cognito*, 'it having been known' (see below, 182, (e), *Obs.* 1).

(C) *Ablative of the Object.*

165 (a) An ablative of the object is used with the adjectives, *dignus*, 'worthy,' *indignus*, 'unworthy,' *contentus*, 'contented,' *fretus*, 'relying,' *praeditus*, 'endued;' as

Dignus es odio, 'you are worthy of hatred.'

Sorte tua contentus abi, 'depart contented with your lot.'

Haec scripsi ad te liberius, fretus conscientia officii mei, 'I have written these things to you the more freely, relying on the consciousness of my friendship.'

Homo parvis opibus et facultatibus praeditus, 'a man endued with small means and resources.'

Obs. In the poets *dignus* and *indignus* are sometimes construed with the genitive, as *Descendam magnorum haud unquam indignus avorum,* 'I shall come down never unworthy of great ancestors.' We may also have an infinitive after *dignus,* as *Lyricorum Horatius fere solus dignus legi,* 'Horace almost the only one of the lyric poets who is worth reading;' but this is rare.

(b) An ablative of the object is used after adjectives denoting plenty or want, burdening and disburdening, exemption, liberation, aversion, separation, and the like; such as *abundans, differtus, refertus, distentus, plenus, dives, locuples, fertilis, gravis, onustus, inanis, nudus, orbus, vacuus, liber, immunis, purus, alienus, extorris;* thus we have

Graeci homines non solum ingenio et doctrina sed etiam otio studioque abundantes, 'the Greeks, men abounding not only in genius and learning, but also in leisure and devotion to this pursuit.'

Neque hoc di alienum ducunt majestate sua, 'nor do the gods consider this at variance with their majesty.'

Extorrem patria et domo effecit ut ubivis tutius quam in meo regno essem, 'he has brought it to pass that being banished from my country and my home, I should be safer any where than in my own kingdom.'

Obs. 1 *Plenus, fertilis* and *dives* are also used with the genitive; this is the common construction of *plenus* in the best writers; and the participles *refertus* and *completus* are used with the genitive when persons are signified.

Obs. 2 *Liber* always has *ab* with the ablative when persons are denoted, as *locus liber ab arbitris;* otherwise generally the ablative only.

Obs. 3 *Alienus* has *ab* with the ablative when it signifies 'averse,' as *alienus a litteris;* also when persons are denoted; but it has the dative in the sense 'inconvenient,' 'unfavourable' (see above, 159, *Obs.* 3).

Obs. 4 *Inanis* and *immunis* have also the genitive. This is rarely the construction of *alienus;* but we have *non alienus joci, alienus paris.*

Obs. 5 The vocative *macte* (i. e. *magis aucte*), plur. *macti*, in the phrase *macte virtute esto* (below, 166, *Obs.* 2), belongs to this rule.

(c) An ablative of the object is used with verbs of the same signification as the adjectives just mentioned, that is, with verbs of abundance and want, of requiring and doing without, of burdening and disburdening, of liberation and separation; such as *abundo, redundo, fluo, affluo, diffluo, careo, egeo, indigeo, vaco, supersedeo, orbo, augeo, compleo, impleo, onero, gravo, afficio, levo, libero, arceo, disto, prohibeo*, &c.; thus we have

Amore abundas, Antipho, 'you are rich in love, Antipho.'

Miser est, qui in vitiosa et flagitiosa vita affluit voluptatibus, 'he is wretched, who in a vicious and criminal life abounds in pleasures.'

Malo virum qui pecunia egeat, quam pecuniam quae viro, 'I would rather have a man who should want money, than money that should lack a man.'

Caesar proelio supersedere statuit, 'Caesar resolved to abstain from, decline, do without a battle.'

Sarmentis et virgultis fossas complent, 'they fill up the trenches with twigs and brushwood.'

Consilio et auctoritate non modo non orbari sed etiam augeri senectus solet, 'old age is accustomed not only not to be deprived of, but even to increase in, wisdom and authority.'

Omnium rerum natura cognita, levamur superstitione, liberamur mortis metu, 'when the nature of the universe has been learned, we are relieved from superstition, and set free from the fear of death.'

Itinere exercitum prohibere conantur, 'they endeavour to hinder the army from marching.'

Obs. 1 With *egeo*, and still more frequently with *indigeo*, we have a genitive instead of the ablative, especially when we imply a requirement rather than a need; as *jam illa non tam artis indigent quam laboris,* 'now these things do not require skill so much as labour.'

Obs. 2 *Impleor* is sometimes used with the genitive; as *implentur veteris Bacchi pinguisque ferinae,* 'they are filled with old wine and fat venison.'

Obs. 3 The verb *afficio aliquem aliqua re* is used in a number of phrases where we employ the phrase 'to confer a benefit,' or 'inflict an injury,' as *afficere aliquem beneficio, gaudio, dolore, praemio, honore, injuria, poenis.*

Obs. 4 With some of these verbs the ablative is as frequently used with, as without, a preposition. With *prohibeo* and *arceo* we have generally the ablative alone, as *prohibere aliquem usu urbis, arcere ali-*

quem tecto; with verbs of liberating, &c. the ablative is more common, except when a person is designated, as *te ab eo vindico ac libero*, 'I rescue and free you from him;' with verbs of difference, alienation, and distance, the preposition is generally used, as *differre ab aliquo, distare ab aliquo, alienare* or *abalienare aliquem ab aliqua re;* with verbs of shrinking or abstaining both constructions are common, as *abhorrere* or *abstinere aliqua re* and *ab aliqua*. The poets sometimes use the dative improperly after verbs of this class, as *paullum sepultae distat inertiae celata virtus,* for *a sepulta inertia; eripe te morae* for *a mora* (see above, 161 (b)).

(d) An ablative of the object is used with the expression *opus est,* 'there is need,' which belongs really to the same class as the verbs which have just been mentioned; but *opus* is sometimes also predicated directly of the thing required; thus we may say

Auctoritate nobis opus est et consilio et gratia, 'we have need (there is need to us) of authority, counsel, and popularity;' and

Dux mihi et auctor opus est, 'a leader and adviser is a necessity to me.'

Obs. 1 As the word *opus* in the second construction is really a primary predicate, we may say *opus mihi est liber* and *libri mihi opus sunt.* The impersonal construction is required in such phrases as *quid opus est armis?* 'what need is there for arms?' *nihil opus est simulatione,* 'there is no need of false pretences.'

Obs. 2 When the object of *opus est* is expressed by a sentence, we may have either the accusative with the infinitive, the subjunctive with *ut*, the supine in *-tu*, or a perfect passive participle; as *Haec fieri et oportet et opus est,* 'it is both proper and necessary that these things should be done.' *Nunc tibi opus est, aegram ut te assimules,* 'now it is necessary that you should pretend to be sick.' *Ita dictu opus est,* 'it is necessary that it should be so spoken.' *Priusquam incipias consulto, et ubi consulueris mature facto opus est,* 'before you begin there is a need for deliberation; and when you have deliberated speedy execution is required.'

(e) An ablative of the object is used idiomatically after the following deponent verbs:

(α) *Potior,* 'I am master of,' 'I possess,' takes the ablative of abundance; as

Egressi optatā potiuntur Troes arenā, 'the Trojans having landed possess the wished-for shore.'

(β) *Fungor, (defungor, perfungor,)* which includes the root of *fug-io*, 'I flee,' as *jungo* involves the root of *jug-um*, signifies 'I make myself quit of, go through, get rid of, discharge, or perform,' and thus governs the ablative of liberation; as

Justitiae fungutur officiis, 'let him discharge [himself from] the duties of justice.'

Hannibal multis variisque perfunctus laboribus anno acquievit septuagesimo, 'Hannibal, having gone through many and various labours, rested in his 70th year.'

(γ) *Utor,* 'I use *(abutor),*' and *fruor,* 'I enjoy,' are correlative terms, (as appears from the compound *usufructus*) and take the ablative of abundance, like *potior;* as

Hannibal, quum victoriâ posset uti, frui maluit, 'Hannibal, though he was in a situation to get profit from his victory, preferred to enjoy it.'

(δ) *Vescor* and *pascor,* 'I take food for myself,' are followed by an abl. of the materials; as

Di nec escis nec potionibus vescuntur, 'the gods do not live on meat or drink.'

Frondibus et victu pascuntur simplicis herbae, 'they feed on boughs and a diet of plain grass.'

(ε) *Dignor,* 'I think worthy,' takes an ablative on the same principle as the adjective *dignus;* as

Haud equidem tali me dignor honore, 'I do not think myself worthy of (do not estimate myself at) such an honour.'

(ζ) *Nitor,* when it signifies 'I am supported by,' takes the abl. of the instrument (163 (a)); as

Nititur hastâ, 'he is supported by a spear.'

(η) *Glorior,* 'I boast of, pride myself in,' takes an ablative of the cause (163 (b)); as

Nominibus veterum gloriantur, 'they boast of the names of the ancients.'

Obs. 1 *Potior* takes the genitive as well as the ablative, as *Romani signorum et armorum potiti sunt,* 'the Romans became masters of the standards and arms.' This is the only construction allowable in the phrase *rerum potiri,* 'to become master of the state.'

Obs. 2 *Fungor, fruor, potior, utor (abutor), vescor,* are sometimes construed with the accusative, but chiefly in older Latin.

Obs. 3 *Nitor* takes the ablative with *in* when it signifies 'I lean or depend on;' as in *vita Pompeii nitebatur salus civitatis,* 'the safety of the state depended on Pompey.'

SYNTAX OF THE VOCATIVE.   305

Obs. 4 *Glorior* often takes the ablative with *de* or *in*; as *Quis de misera vita potest gloriari?* 'who can take pride in a miserable life?' *In virtute recte gloriamur*, 'we rightly take pride in virtue.'

Obs. 5 *Ven-eo* for *venum-eo*, 'I go for sale,' i.e. 'I am sold,' and *vapulo*, 'I howl or cry out (οἰμώζω) for pain,' i.e. 'I am beaten,' are considered as passive verbs, and take the ablative of the agent with *ab* (128, VII. (d)); as *Respondit se malle a cive spoliari quam ab hoste venire*, 'he replied that he would rather be robbed by a fellow-citizen than be sold by an enemy;' *Testis rogatus est, an ab reo fustibus vapulasset*, 'the witness was asked whether he had been beaten with clubs by the defendant.'

§ 6. *The Vocative and its Substitutes.*

166 (1) The vocative is the case of allocution, exhortation, or exclamation. In the poets it is frequently used with the interjection *O*; in prose this interjection is not prefixed in merely addressing a person, but is reserved for exclamations of joy, anger or surprise. In prose the vocative does not stand first in the sentence, except in solemn addresses, and in expressions of strong emotion; thus we have

Recte te, Cyre, beatum ferunt, quoniam virtuti tuae fortuna conjuncta est, 'they rightly call you happy, O Cyrus, because good fortune was combined with your virtue.'

Obs. 1 If an adjective or participle is added to the vocative it is properly in the same case, as

Maecenas, atavis edite regibus.

There are rare instances to the contrary, as

Succinctus patriâ quondam, Crispine, papyro.

Obs. 2 By a very singular usage, the vocative of the adjective is made to agree with the nominative *tu*, as

Stemmate quod Tusco ramum millesime ducis,
Censorem fatuum vel quod trabeate salutas?
(PERS. III. 27, 28).

This is regularly the case in the idiomatic use of *macte* = *magis aucte*; thus we have *macte virtute esto,* 'increase in virtue' (Hor. I. Serm. ii. 31); *macte novâ virtute puer,* 'go on and prosper in your young valour' (Virg. Æn. IX. 641). And even in an oblique sentence, as *juberem [te] macte virtute esse* (Liv. II. 12).

(2) (a) In addresses the most common substitute for the vocative is the nominative; as *audi tu, populus Albanus* (Liv. I. 24). But in exclamations the vocative and accusative are used indifferently after *O, heu,* and *proh*; as

O formose puer, nimium ne crede colori, 'O beautiful boy, trust not too much to your complexion;' but,

O fortunatos nimium agricolas, 'O too fortunate husbandmen.' *Heu pietas, heu prisca fides,* 'Ah! piety, ah! old-fashioned faith;' but, *heu stirpem invisam,* 'ah! hated race.' *Proh Deûm atque hominum fidem,* 'alas for our reliance on gods and men!' but, *proh sancte Jupiter,* 'Oh! hallowed Jupiter!'

(b) *Hei* and *vae* are followed by the dative of limitation; as *hei mihi!* 'ah! woe's me;' *vae misero mihi,* 'alas! for me wretched.'

(c) *En* (*ecce*), which calls attention to an object, takes the nominative as a sort of exclamation, but the accusative as an object to be looked at; thus

Ecce ubi Italiae tellus, 'here is the land of Italy for you.' *En quattuor aras,* 'see these four altars.'

§ 7. *Differences of Case with the same Verb.*

167 Among the difficulties created by the syntax of government in Latin, one of the most frequent arises from the effect produced on the case of the dependent noun by modifications in the meaning or application of the governing verb. This point will therefore require a separate examination.

(a) Verbs compounded with *ad, in, ob* and *sub,* which retain in the composite form a reference to the position or motion indicated by the prefix, are sometimes construed with an accusative or dative, but more frequently there is an additional preposition connected with the dependent noun (see above, 159, (f)). Thus we have both *accedere muris* and *muros,* 'to approach the walls;' both *adjacere mari* and *mare,* 'to lie near the sea;' both *adnare navibus* and *naves,* 'to swim to the ships;' both *illabi animis* and *illabi animos,* 'to glide into, descend upon, inspire the minds of men;' both *incessit me* and *incessit mihi cura,* 'an anxious thought came upon me;' both *timor invadit mihi* and *me,* 'fear attacked me;' *subire muro,* 'to go under the wall,' and *subit mentem,* 'it comes into my mind.' Generally, however, the use of the accusative belongs rather to poetical diction, and the prose-writers repeat the preposition or a similar one before the noun, as *accedere ad urbem* or *in urbem; adstare ad tumulum, invadere in aliquem, in fortunas alicujus.*

(b) Verbs compounded with *ante* and *prae*, especially *antecedo, antesto,* and *praesto,* which signify superiority or pre-eminence, are construed with the accusative as well as with the dative; as

Difficile est, quum praestare ceteris concupieris, servare aequitatem, 'it is difficult, when you have felt a longing to excel all others, to preserve equity.'

Praestate virtute peditem, ut honore atque ordine praestatis, 'excel the foot-soldiers in valour, as you excel them in honour and civic rank.'

Natura hominis pecudibus ceterisque bestiis antecedit, 'the nature of man is superior to cattle and other beasts.'

Populus Romanus cunctas nationes fortitudine antecedit, 'the Roman people is superior to all nations put together in fortitude.'

Obs. To this class we may add several compounds of *cello,* especially *excello,* but the usual construction is *excellere praeter ceteros* or *inter ceteros*.

(c) Several verbs, which denote behaviour towards another person, are construed sometimes with the dative and sometimes with the accusative; such verbs are, *adulor, aemulor, allatro, attendo, ausculto, blandior, despero, illudo, insulto, medicor, obtrecto, praestolor;* as

Mihi ausculta: vide ne tibi desis, 'listen to me: see that you are not wanting to yourself.'

Nisi me auscultas, atque hoc, ut dico, facis, 'unless you mind me, and do this as I tell you.'

Obs. 1 We have sometimes other constructions with these verbs. Thus we may say not only *desperare suis fortunis* or *desperare pacem,* but *desperare de fide alicujus;* and not only *obtrectare laudibus,* or, more rarely, *laudes alicujus,* but *Themistocles et Aristides obtrectarunt inter se*.

Obs. 2 We do not find *audire alicui* in good writers, but *dicto audientem esse alicui* is a good phrase.

(d) Certain verbs which signify giving or imparting are sometimes construed with the dative of the person and the accusative of the thing, sometimes with the accusative of the person and the ablative of the thing; such are *adspergo, circumdo, circumfundo, dono, exuo, impertio, induo, inspergo, intercludo;* thus

Non pauca suis adjutoribus large effuseque donabat, 'he gave liberally and lavishly not a few gifts to those who helped him.'

308   VERBS WITH DIFFERENT CASES.

Tarentini hunc civitate ceterisque praemiis donarunt, 'the Tarentines presented this man with the franchise and the other privileges.'

Similarly we may say, *adspergere labeculam alicui* and *adspergere vitae splendorem maculis; circumdare sibi cancellos,* and *circumdare oppidum vallo et fossa; impertire alicui salutem plurimam,* and *impertire aliquem salute; induere sibi torquem,* and *indutum esse duabus personis; intercludere multitudini fugam* and *intercludere aliquem commeatu.*

Obs. 1   In Cicero we do not find *exuere alicui aliquid,* but *exuere aliquem armis, bonis omnibus, castris; exuere omnem humanitatem, nurres, personam.*

Obs. 2   We find *interdicere alicui aliquid;* and not *alicurus aliqua re,* but *alicui aliqua re.* The phrase *interdicitur mihi aqua et igni* is good, but the student should avoid *interdicor aqua et igni.*

(e) Either the dative or the ablative may be used with the verbs *acquiesco, confido, insisto, insuesco, supersedeo.* Thus we may have *acquiescere rei,* but Cicero has *acquiescere re,* and more frequently *acquiescere in aliqua re;* we may have *confidere virtuti* and *confidere corporis firmitate; insistere via,* and, in Cicero, *insistere vestigiis alicujus* or *in vestigiis; insuescers re* and *rei; occumbere morti* and *morte,* also *mortem; supersedere itineri;* but in Cicero more usually with the ablative; as *supersedere labore,* 'to sit on the other side and away from it, to do without it' (see above, 165, (c)).

(f) The following verbs have a different construction according to their different significations:

Animadvertere aliquid, 'to remark something;' *animadvertere in aliquem,* 'to punish somebody.'

Cavere alicui (sibi), 'to provide for the security of somebody or oneself;' *cavere alicui aliquid,* 'to give security to some one;' *cavere aliquem* and *ab aliquo,* 'to be on one's guard against some one;' *cavere aliqua re* or *de aliqua re,* 'to get security by pledge about something.'

Constare sibi or *secum,* 'to be consistent with oneself;' *constat inter omnes,* 'it is universally admitted;' *constat magno,* 'it costs a good deal.'

Consulere alicui, 'to give advice to some one;' *consulere rei,* 'to provide for something;' *consulere aliquem,* 'to ask the opinion or advice of some one;' *consulere boni,* 'to take in good part;' *consulere graviter in aliquem,* 'to take severe measures against somebody;' *consulere in medium, in commune,* 'to provide for the common good.'

Convenire alicui rei, 'to suit something;' *cum aliqua re,* 'to agree with something;' *convenire aliquem,* 'to have an interview with somebody;' *convenimus* or *convenit mihi tecum,* 'we are agreed;' *convenit inter omnes,* 'all agree.'

Cupere aliquid, 'to desire something;' *cupere alicui* or *cupere causa alicujus,* 'to wish well to somebody.'

Dare alicui litteras, 'to give a letter to somebody;' *dare litteras ad aliquem,* 'to despatch a letter to somebody.'

Facere ad aliquid, 'to contribute to a thing, to avail or profit it;' *facere alicui,* 'to suit or be becoming to something;' *facere magni,* 'to esteem highly;' *facere aliquid aliquo* or *alicui,* 'to do something with a person or thing' (as *quid fecistis scipione,* 'what have you done with the stick?'); *facere cum aliquo* or *ab aliquo,* 'to favour somebody;' *facere contra, adversus aliquem,* 'to be opposed to somebody.'

Feneror or *fenero tibi,* 'I lend money to you;' *feneror a te,* 'I borrow money from you.'

Horrere aliquid, 'to be afraid of something;' *horrere alicui,* 'to be afraid for somebody.'

Imponere alicui aliquid, 'to put something on somebody,' (e. g. *clitellas bori*); *imponere aliquid in cervices alicujus,* 'to lay something on somebody's shoulders;' *imponere alicui,* 'to trick, deceive, impose upon somebody.'

Incumbere rei, 'to lean upon a thing, as a support;' *incumbere in aliquam rem,* 'to apply oneself diligently to some pursuit;' but the dative alone is also used in this sense.

Interesse rei or *in aliqua re,* 'to be present at a certain transaction;' *hoc interest inter hominem et belluam,* 'this is the difference between a man and a beast;' *mea interest, omnium interest,* 'it is for my interest, for the interest of all.'

Manere apud aliquem, 'to remain with some one;' *manet mihi,* 'it remains for me;' *manet me,* 'it awaits me (I may expect its coming).'

Merere aliquid, 'to earn something' (*quid mereas, ut Epicureus esse desinas?* 'what would you take to leave off being an Epicurean philosopher?'); *merere stipendia,* 'to serve as a soldier;' *mereri de aliquo,* 'to deserve well of somebody.'

Metuere aliquem, 'to fear somebody;' *metuere aliquid ab aliquo,* 'to fear something from somebody;' *metuere alicui,* 'to fear for somebody, on somebody's account.'

Moderari alicui rei, 'to bridle something, control it,' e.g. *irae, animo; moderari aliquid,* 'to guide something,' e.g. *rempublicam, navem.*

Petere aliquem lapide, &c. 'to aim at somebody with a stone, &c.;' *petere aliquid ab aliquo,* 'to ask something from somebody.'

Praestare alicui et aliquem, 'to excel somebody;' *praestare rem* (e.g. *culpam, damnum*), 'to make good, be answerable for something;' *praestare aliquem tutum ab aliqua re,* 'to make a person safe from something;' *praestare se virum,* 'to show oneself a man.'

Prospicere aliquid, 'to foresee something;' *prospicere alicui,* 'to provide or take care for somebody.'

Quaerere aliquem or *aliquid,* 'to seek some person or thing,' 'go in search of, look for;' *quaerere ex aliquo,* 'to put a question to some one,' 'to ask,' 'to inquire.'

Recipere aliquem, 'to take back some one;' *recipere se aliquo,* 'to betake oneself somewhither;' *recipere se,* absolutely, 'to recover spirit or courage, to be emboldened;' *recipere alicui,* 'to pledge oneself, to give a solemn promise to some one' (the full phrase being *recipio ad me* or *in me*).

Renuntiare alicui rem, 'to announce a circumstance to some one;' *renuntiare rei,* 'to renounce a thing, to give it up;' *renuntiare aliquem consulem,* 'formally to declare some one consul.'

Respondere alicui, 'to give an answer to some one;' *respondere rei* (e.g. *votis, exspectationi*), 'to answer, or correspond to something;' *respondere alicui* or *ad aliquid* (e.g. *ad crimina, criminibus*), 'to make answer to, refute something;' *respondere de jure,* 'to give a legal opinion.'

Solvere alicui aliquid, 'to pay something to somebody;' *solvere aliquem aliqua re,* 'to set a person free from something;' *solvere aliquid* (*fidem, vota,* &c.), 'to make good or perform something.'

Temperare sibi or *rei alicui,* 'to restrain oneself or something' (e.g. *irae, linguae*); *temperare rempublicam institutis et legibus,* 'to regulate the state by institutions and laws;' *temperare alicui* or *ab aliqua re,* 'to spare, forbear, refrain from something' (e.g. *lacrimis* or *a lacrimis*).

Timere alicui, 'to fear, be anxious for some one;' *timere aliquem* and *ab aliquo*, 'to fear some one;' *timere de aliqua re*, 'to be fearful about something.'

Vacare alicui rei, 'to give up one's time to something;' *vacare aliqua re* or *ab aliqua re*, 'to be free from something,' e. g. *vacare culpa*; *vacat* or *vocat mihi*, 'I have time.'

Valere, 'to be worth,' with the accusative or ablative, as *valere denos sestertios* or *denis sestertiis*; *valere apud aliquem*, 'to have weight or influence with some one;' *valere ab aliqua re*, 'to be strong, on the side of (above 109, (a)) something,' e. g. *ab oculis, a pecunia*.

§ 8. *The Cases in definitions of Space and Time.*

(A) *Definitions of Space.*

168. It has been already mentioned that the original force of the cases, as indicating motion to or from and rest at a place, is preserved only in the proper names of places, and in a limited number of words (128, VII. (b), 147). And even here, as has been mentioned, there is such a confusion in the forms of the cases that a difference of declension and number is supposed to require a different rule of construction, the genitive acting as locative in the singular number of the first and second declensions, and the ablative both as the locative and as the case of removal in the third declension, and in the plural number of all declensions. The etymological or philological fact is simply this: that the locative or case of rest ended in *-i*, and corresponded, more or less exactly, to the dative in all declensions; but the loss of the genitive *-s* in the first declension led to the confusion of the genitive and dative, and therefore *Romae = Romāī* was the only possible form for the case signifying 'at Rome;' the loss of the genitive *-s*, and of the characteristic *-o* in the second declension led to the confusion of the genitive and locative, and *Corinthi = Corintho-is*, 'of Corinth,' became confused with *Corinthi = Corintho-i*, 'at Corinth,' the usual dative *Corintho = Corintho-i* being confused with the ablative *Corintho = Corintho-d*; and in the third declension the dative in *-i*, which is generally distinguished from the ablative in *-ĕ*, was not only confused with it in some regular uses of the dative, as in *triumvir aere flando* for *aeri flando*, *postquam est morte datus* for *morti datus*, *si suffuderit ore ruborem* for *ori*, but also in some uses

of the dative as a locative in common words, as *linguis micat ore trisulcis* (see *Varronianus*, pp. 335, 336). That this was the case in the names of towns also is clear from the fact that we have *Karthagini*, 'at Carthage,' in good MSS. of Livy. In the plural the dative is universally identified with the ablative, and the locative is of course swept away in the confusion. It will be remembered also that the prepositions of rest are always construed with the ablative. The following rules, then, for the syntax of the cases in definitions of place, must be regarded as referring to the usual forms of the Latin language, and not to the original case-endings or their proper signification.

(1) (a) In answer to the question 'where? at what place?' the names of cities stand in the genitive, if the words belong to the first or second declension and are in the singular number, but in the ablative if they belong to the third declension, or are in the plural number; as

Ut Romae consules, sic Carthagine quotannis bini reges creabuntur, 'as at Rome two consuls, so at Carthage two kings were every year created.'

Artemisia Mausoli, Cariae regis, uxor, nobile illud Halicarnassi fecit sepulcrum, 'Artemisia, the wife of Mausolus, king of Caria, made that famous sepulchre at Halicarnassus.'

Cur Delphis oracula jam non eduntur? 'why are oracles no longer delivered at Delphi?'

Obs. If the word *urbs* is placed in apposition with the name of the city thus used in the genitive (locative) the explanatory word will stand in the ablative; as *Antiochiae, celebri quondam urbe et copiosa*, 'at Antioch, formerly a populous and opulent city;' *Corinthi, Achaiae urbe*, 'at Corinth, a city of Achaia.'

(b) In answer to the question 'whither? to what place?' all names of cities stand in the accusative; in answer to the question 'whence? from what place?' all names of cities stand in the ablative; as

Quum Athenas tanquam mercaturam bonarum artium profectus sis, turpe est inanem redire, 'seeing that you have set out for Athens, as it were the mart of all accomplishments, it is disgraceful that you should return empty.'

Timoleon arcessivit colonos Corintho, 'Timoleon sent for husbandmen (colonists) from Corinth.'

(c) While the names of cities are thus used without prepositions, the names of islands may be construed either with prepositions or without, and the preposition generally accompanies the names of countries, mountains, and estates; as

Lacedaemonii Pausaniam cum classe Cyprum atque Hellespontum miserunt, 'the Lacedemonians sent Pausanias with a fleet to Cyprus and the Hellespont.'

Pompeius magnam ex Cycladibus insulis et Corcyra classem coegerat, 'Pompey had collected a great fleet from the Cyclades and Corcyra.'

Pueri in Formiano videntur hiematuri, 'the boys seem likely to pass the winter on my Formian estate.'

Ad Amanum iter feci, 'I marched to mount Amanus.'

Obs. 1 The lesser islands are generally construed without a preposition, and the greater islands, which constituted provinces, as *Sardinia, Sicilia, Britannia,* generally require a preposition in the cases mentioned. The preposition is occasionally omitted with the names *Chersonesus* and *Hellespontus,* often with *Ægyptus,* and sometimes with *Macedonia.*

Obs. 2 The prepositions *ad, ab, ex,* and *in* are sometimes used with the names of cities, but then *ad* signifies 'in the neighbourhood of,' or 'as far as;' *ab* and *ex* mean 'from the distance of,' or serve to define a noun; and *in* generally stands by the names of those towns which are really the names of the inhabitants; thus we have *bellum ad Mutinam gerebatur,* 'the war was going on in the neighbourhood of Mutina;' *Cæsar in Gallias contendit, et ad Genevam pervenit,* 'Cæsar set out for Gaul and got as far as Geneva;' *non tibi a Corintho nec a Tarquiniis bellum moliri necesse est,* 'it is not necessary for you to enter on a war from the distance of Corinth or Tarquinii;' *legati ab Ardea,* 'Ardean ambassadors;' in *Philippis,* 'at Philippi,' i.e. 'among the Philippians.'

(d) The words *domus, rus, bellum, militia, humus* are in certain connexions construed like the names of cities; thus we may say

Domum Pompeii venit, 'he came to the house of Pompey.'

Caesaris virtus domi fuit militiaeque cognita, 'Cæsar's excellence was known both at home and abroad.'

Cibaria domo attulit, 'he brought provisions from home.'

Similarly we say *domi meae, tuae, suae,* 'in my, your, his house;' *domum redire,* 'to return home;' *domo proficisci,* 'to leave home;' *ruri vivere,* 'to live in the country;' *rus proficisci,* 'to go into the country;' *rure redire,* 'to return from the country;' *humi jacere*, 'to lie on the ground;' *humo oculis attollere*, 'to raise one's eyes from the ground.' With regard to *domus*, however, while *domi* means 'at home,' *in domo* means 'in the house,' as *in domo furtum factum est ab eo qui domi fuit*, 'a theft was committed in the house by one who was at home there.' And we have generally *in domo* instead of *domi*, when the word is accompanied by an adjective or the name of the owner, as *in domo regali*, 'in a royal house;' *in domo Caesaris*, 'in the house of Caesar.'

(e) General designations of place are regularly expressed by means of the prepositions *in, ad, ex, per*, and others.

Obs. 1 Some general designations of place, answering to the question 'where?' are expressed in the ablative without a preposition, as *mari, terra, loco;* and this is the regular construction of those which have the adjective *totus* prefixed; thus we have *terra marique*, 'by land and sea;' *hoc loco*, 'in this place;' *eodem loco*, 'in the same place;' *meliore loco*, 'in a better place;' *tota urbe*, 'in the whole city;' *toto orbe terrarum*, 'in the whole world;' *tota Asia*, 'all through Asia;' *tota Sicilia*, 'all over Sicily;' *tota Perside*, 'throughout Persia.'

Obs. 2 The poets sometimes construe the names of countries in the same way as the names of cities; e.g. *Italiam fato profugus Laviniaque venit littora.*

(2) (a) In answer to the question 'how long?' 'how high?' 'how broad?' 'how thick?' the measure is generally given in the accusative; as

Babylon sexaginta millia passuum complexa est, muris ducenos pedes altis, quinquagenos latis, 'Babylon comprised sixty miles, with walls two hundred feet high and fifty feet in breadth.'

Ab hac regula mihi non licet transversum, ut aiunt, digitum discedere, 'from this rule it is not permitted me to diverge a finger-breadth.'

Hercyniae sileae longitudo novem dierum iter expedito patet, 'the length of the Hercynian forest extends to a journey of nine days for a lightly equipped traveller.'

Obs. 1 After a substantive the extent may be described by a genitive of number (above, 155); as *in palatio Neronis columna centum viginti pedum stabat*.

Obs. 2 Although the accusative is much more common with adjectives of extension, we occasionally find a genitive or ablative; as *fossam viginti pedum latam duxit; fossam sex cubitis altam, duodecim latam duxit Antiochus*.

(b) In answer to the question 'how far off?' we have either the accusative of extension (a) or the ablative of quantity (above, 163, (f)); as

Tertio post die Romani amnem transgressi sunt, et duo millia ferme et quingentos passus ab hoste posuerant castra, 'on the third day after the Romans crossed the river, and placed their camp about two miles and five hundred paces from the enemy.'

Caesar ab exploratoribus certior factus est Ariovisti copias a nostris millibus passuum viginti quattuor abesse, 'Cæsar was informed by the scouts that the forces of Ariovistus were distant twenty-four miles from our army.'

Obs. 1 The distance is often expressed by the genitives *bidui, tridui, quatridui,* with which we may understand *itinere,* e.g. *bidui,* sc. *itinere,* 'at the distance of two days' journey.'

Obs. 2 If the distance is given with reference to the mile-stones, it is usual to mention the number with *ad,* e.g. *ad quartum a Cremona lapidem,* 'at the fourth mile-stone from Cremona.'

(B) *Definitions of Time.*

(a) In answer to the question 'when?' 'at what time?' the noun expressing the time is regularly put in the ablative without a preposition; as

Hora sexta Caesar profectus est, 'Cæsar set out at the third hour.'

Qua nocte natus Alexander est, eadem Dianae Ephesiae templum deflagravit, 'the temple of the Ephesian Diana was burnt down on the same night on which Alexander was born.'

Arabes campos et montes hieme et aestate peragrant, 'the Arabs traverse plains and mountains in the winter and summer.'

Obs. 1 In the same way we may say *prima aetate,* 'in my earliest age;' *meo consulatu,* 'in my consulship;' *anno proximo,* 'next year;' *nocte superiore,* 'last night;' *tertia vigilia,* 'in the third watch;' *nostra memoria,* 'in our memory;' *die festo,* 'on a holiday;' *ludis Juventatis,* 'at the games of Juventas;' *solis occasu,* 'at sun-rise;' *bello Punico,* 'in the Carthaginian war;' also *bello,* 'in war-time;' *tumultu,* 'at a time of tumult' (Cic. *Phil.* VIII. 1), though in these instances the preposition *in* is commonly used. On the contrary we always use the prepositions *circa, prope, in, per, de, cum, sub* when the time *when* must be more nearly defined, as *de tertia vigilia,* 'from the third watch going onwards;' *per hoc tempus,* 'through this period;' *sub noctem,* 'just before night;' *prope, circa, lucem,* 'near day-break;' *cum prima luce,* 'at the first dawn;' *in tempore,* 'at the right time;' *in tali tempore,* 'under such circumstances;' *bis in hora,* 'twice in the hour,' for the preposition must be used when the question is 'how often in a given time?'

Obs. 2 That the ablative in these usages, as in the adverbial phrases *mane, noctu, horlie, pridie, postridie, perendie,* &c. is a corrupted form of the locative is clear not only from the case of the adjective involved in *mertilis (medii die), quotidie,* &c., but also from the expressions *die septimi, die noni, die proximi, die crastini,* which actually occur (*Varron.* p. 327).

Obs. 3 In counting the date from the foundation of Rome we either say *anno ab urbe condita,* or *anno post urbem conditam,* or *anno urbis,* or *anno* (e.g. *trecentesimo altero) quam condita Roma erat.*

(b) In answer to the question 'how long?' the noun expressing the time is used in the accusative; thus

Augustus non amplius, quum plurimum, quam septem horas dormiebat, 'Augustus did not sleep more, when he slept most, than for seven hours.'

Pericles quadraginta annos praefuit Athenis, 'Pericles ruled at Athens (through, during) forty years.'

Improborum animi sollicitudinibus noctes atque dies exeduntur, 'the minds of the wicked are eaten up with anxieties by night and day' (i.e. all through the night and day).

Obs. 1 The use of the ablative to express duration of time is rare in the best authors, though it is occasionally found, as *tota aestate Nilus Aegyptum obrutam oppletamque tenet* (Cic. *N. D.* ii. 52); *pugnatum est continenter horis quinque* (Caes. *B. C.* i. 46); *nocte pluit tota, redeunt spectacula mane* (in a line attributed to Virgil). But this is not uncommon in the later writers, as *octoginta annis vixit* (Seneca, *Ep.* 93); *Caligula vixit annis undetriginta, imperavit triennio et decem mensibus, diebusque octo* (Sueton. *Calig.* 59).

Obs. 2 The preposition *per* is often used to express duration of time; *per annos quattuor et viginti primo Punico bello classibus certatum est cum Poenis.*

Obs. 3 In answer to the question 'since when?' we may have either the accusative alone, or the accusative with *intra,* as *Lacedaemonii septingentos jam annos amplius nunquam mutatis moribus vivunt; invicti Germani qui intra annos quattuordecim tectum non subierint.*

Obs. 4 In answer to the question 'within how long a period of future time?' we have either the ablative alone or *intra,* with the accusative; as *Clodius respondit, triduo Milonem, ad summum quadriduo periturum; intra vicesimum diem dictatura se abdicavit.*

Obs. 5 In answer to the question 'how long a time previously?' we have *ante* with the accusative; *abhinc* with the accusative or ablative; or the ablative with *hic* or *ille*; *ante annum et quattuor menses; Demosthenes qui abhinc annos prope trecentos fuit; comitia jam abhinc triginta diebus erant habita; his annis quadringentis Romae rex fuit; ante hos annos quadringentos regnabat; respondit, ut paucis illis diebus argentum misisset Lilybaeum.*

Obs. 6 In answer to the question 'how long?' either before or since, we have the ablative with *ante* or *post* used adverbially; as *paucis ante diebus, multis annis post* or *post annis.*

Obs. 7 In answer to the question 'for how long a time?' we have the accusative with *in*; as *Sardianis Tiberius, quantum aerario aut fisco pendebant, in quinquennium remisit.*

(c) In answer to the question 'how old?' the noun expressing the age is used in the accusative with the participle *natus*, or in the ablative or genitive with the comparatives *major, minor*; as

Decessit Alexander mensem unum, annos tres et triginta natus, 'Alexander died, aged thirty-three years and one month.'

Julius Caesar sanxit, ne quis civis major annis viginti, minorve quadraginta, plus triennio continuo Italia abesset, 'Julius Caesar decreed that no citizen older than twenty or younger than forty years should be absent from Italy more than three years together.'

Cautum est Pompeia lege ne quis capiat magistratum minor triginta annorum, 'it was laid down in the Pompeian law that no one should hold an office who was younger than thirty years.'

Obs. The age of a man may be expressed by the genitive alone, as *Cato primum stipendium meruit annorum decem septemque,* 'Cato served his first campaign when seventeen years old.' We may also use the ordinal in such phrases as *annum aetatis agebat vicesimum,* 'he was in the twentieth year of his age.'

§ 9. *The Cases when construed with Prepositions.*

169 The general meanings and distinctions of the prepositions have been already stated (above 109), and the general rules for the cases which they govern have been given in memorial lines (above 127). It remains, however, that their usage as supplements to the cases should be properly classified and illustrated by examples. It will be observed that, though several of the prepositions denote rest in a place, the dative or locative, as the proper case of rest, is never used with a preposition in classical Latin, but this usage has been usurped by the ablative, which, as we have seen, appears as a corruption of the locative. There are traces in some inscriptions of the use of *cum* with a form *quem* or *quen*, which seems to be a locative analogous to *palam, partim, saltim* and the like (cf. *quon-dam = quo-dam tempore, olim*, &c.), and *coram = co-ore* may be another example of the same usage; but in ordinary Latin the regular prepositions are used only with the accusative, the ablative, or both of these cases; and the few other particles, which seem to serve as prepositions and govern the genitive or ablative, must be regarded as words which have not quite lost their original value as nouns, and which take the genitive of possession (above 148, Obs. 1), or the ablative of reference (162, (d)). These *quasi-prepositions* are the following:

(a) *Palam*, 'openly before, in the presence of,' takes the ablative; as

Centurio rem creditori palam populo solvit, 'the centurion paid the debt to his creditor openly before the people.'

(β) *Clam*, 'without the knowledge of,' generally takes the ablative; as

Clam uxore mea et filia, 'without the knowledge of my wife and daughter.'

In the comedians *clam* takes also the genitive, dative, and accusative, and the accusative is construed with the synonym *clanculum*.

(γ) *Procul*, 'far from,' takes the ablative; as *fusis Tuscis, haud procul Ticino flumine*, 'the Tuscans having been routed not far from the river Ticinus.'

(δ) *Simul*, 'together with,' takes the ablative; as *pontifices et augures septemviris simul et sodalibus Augustalibus*, 'the pontifices and augurs together with the seven commissioners and the board of Augustales.'

(ε) *Coram*, 'in the presence of,' takes the ablative; as *cantabit vacuus coram latrone viator*, 'the traveller, if he has no money in his pocket, will sing in the presence of the robber.'

(ζ) *Tenus*, 'as far as, up or down to,' takes the ablative singular, but the genitive, or more rarely the ablative, plural, and always follows its case; as *capulo tenus*, 'up to the hilt,' *crurum tenus*, 'down to the legs.'

(η) *Instar*, 'after the likeness of,' *ergo*, 'on account of,' *gratia*, 'for the sake of,' are followed by the genitive like the Greek δίκην,

CASES WITH PREPOSITIONS. 319

ἕνεκα, and χάριν, to which they correspond; as *instar montis equus,* 'a horse like a mountain,' (ὄρους δίκην); *donatur virtutis ergo,* 'he is rewarded on account of his virtue,' (ἀρετῆς ἕνεκα); *majorum dolorum effugiendorum gratia,* 'for the sake of avoiding greater evils,' (ἀποφυγῆς χάριν).

The regular prepositions will be most conveniently discussed in alphabetical order, and in three classes according as they are construed (A) with the accusative only; (B) with the ablative only; (C) with the accusative and ablative.

(A) *Prepositions construed with the Accusative only.*

AD signifies (1) 'to' of motion or destination; as *Antonius legiones quattuor ad urbem* (to the city) *adducere cogitabat.* Cic. ad div. XII. 23.

Litteras dare ad aliquem, (to be taken to him; as *Fortasse discedens ad te aliquid dabo.* Cic. Att. X. 8 fin.). *Eamus ad me,* 'let us go to me,' i. e. to my house. Ter. Eun. III. 5. 64.

(2) 'to' or 'towards' of direction; as *Pars Galliae vergit ad Septentriones* (towards the north). Cæsar, B. G. I. 1.

(3) 'towards' of time; as *Quum magnam partem noctis vigilassem, ad lucem* (towards morning) *arcte et graviter dormire coepi.* Cic. ad div. I. 28. *Nos hic te ad mensem Januarium* (towards January, by or about that time) *expectamus.* Cic. Att. L 3.

(4) 'at' or 'near;' as *Fatum fuit exercitum populi Romani ad lacum Trasimenum* (at or near the lake) *interire.* Cic. ad div. II. 8.

(5) 'with' (in the house of), or 'before' (in the presence of), in much the same sense as *apud;* as *Curio fuit ad me* (with me) *sane diu.* Cic. Att. X. 10. *Patrum superbiam ad plebem* (before the people) *criminatus maxime in consulare imperium invehebatur.* Liv. III. 9.

(6) 'at,' in the sense of habitual employment; as *Servos ad remum* (slaves employed at the oar) *cum stipendio nostro dabamus.* Liv. XXXIV. 6.

(7) 'at,' of an occurrence or its announcement; as *Feminam ferunt ad primum conspectum redeuntis filii* (at the first sight of her returning son, i. e. when she saw him) *gaudio nimio exanimatam.* Liv. XXII. 7. *Ad famam obsidionis* (at the news of the

blockade, when it was announced) *delectus haberi coeptus est.* Liv.
IX. 7.

(8) 'to the number or amount of,' in an estimate; as *Manlius
protulit spolia hostium caesorum ad triginta* (to the number of
thirty), *dona imperatorum ad quadraginta* (to the number of forty).
Liv. VI. 20.

(9) 'in strict accordance with,' in giving a standard of measurement; as *Ad perpendiculum* (by the plummet, in strict accordance with the vertical line) *columnas exigere.* Cic. *Verr.* I. 51.
Obsides ad numerum (in strict accordance with the prescribed number) *frumentumque miserunt.* Caes. *B. G.* v. 20. *Britannis utuntur
taleis ferreis ad certum pondus* (in accordance with a certain
weight) *examinatis.* Caes. *B. G.* v. 12. To this use belongs the
phrase *ad fistulam saltare,* 'to dance to (in strict accordance with)
the notes of the flute;' *ad amussim,* 'in strict measurement;' also
ad verbum, 'word for word,'—'word measured against word'—in
accordance with the standard of verbal accuracy; as *Est ad verbum ediscendus* (to be learned word for word) *libellus.* Cic. *Acad.*
IV. 44. *Fabellas Latinas ad verbum* (word for word) *de Graecis
expressas non inviti legunt.* Cic. *Fin.* I. 2.

(10) 'in comparison with;' as *Laelium Decimum cognovimus
virum bonum et non illitteratum, sed nihil ad Persium* (nothing in
comparison with Persius). Cic. *de Orat.* II. 6.

(11) 'with reference to,' 'as to,' 'in point of:' *Faciam id
quod est ad severitutem* (in point of) *lenius, ad communem utilitatem*
(with reference to) *utilius.* Cic. *Cat.* I. 5.

(12) 'in addition to,' 'besides;' *Ad reliquos labores* (in addition to my other labours) *etiam hanc molestiam assumo.* Cic. *Planc.* I.
So also *ad id quod; ad hoc,* &c.

(13) 'for,' 'on account of,' 'with a view to;' as *Argentum dabitur ei ad nuptias* (for, with a view to the marriage). Ter. *Heaut.*
IV. 5, 29. This is particularly common with gerunds and gerundives (below, 186, 190).

(14) 'for the purpose of meeting or averting,' 'against;' as
*Mirari licet, quas sint animadversa à medicis herbarum genera ad
morsus bestiarum* (as a remedy against), *ad oculorum morbos, ad
vulnera.*

ADVERSUS or ADVERSUM signifies (1) 'opposite to,' 'in presence of;' 'facing,' 'face to face;' as *Ara Aio Loquenti adversus eum locum* (opposite to that place) *consecrata est.* Cic. Div. I. 45. *Neque adversus* (in front) *neque ab tergo aut lateribus tutus est.* Sallust. Orat. I. *Sed nunc peropust aut hunc cum ipsa aut de illa me adversum hunc* (face to face with him) *loqui.* Ter. Andr. I. 5, 28.

(2) 'against,' 'contrary to;' as *Hostis legitimus adversus quem* (against whom) *jus feciale est.*

(3) 'towards,' 'in regard to;' as *Pietas est justitia adversum deos* (towards, in regard to the gods).

ANTE signifies 'before,' either in space or time; as *Quod est ante pedes* (before his feet) *nemo spectat.* Cic. Div. II. 13. *Democritus causam explicat cur ante lucem* (before daylight) *galli canant.* Cic. Div. II. 26. If it follows an ablative *ante* is an adverb; as *multis diebus ante,* or *multis ante diebus,* 'many days before.'

APUD signifies (1) 'in the house of;' as *Neoptolemus apud Lycomedem* (in the house of Lycomedes) *erat educatus.* Cic. Lael. 2. Hence, *vix sum apud me* (in my senses). Ter. Andr. V. 4. 34.

(2) 'in the presence of,' e. g. before judges; as *Curio causam contra me apud centumviros* (before the centumviri, not *coram centumviris*) *pro fratribus Cosris dixit.* Cic. de Orat. II. 23.

(3) 'among;' as *Legationis jus apud omnes gentes* (among all nations) *sanctum esse consuevit.* Corn. Nep. 16, 5.

(4) 'in' an author; as *Videtisne ut apud Homerum* (in Homer, i. e. in his poems) *saepissime Nestor de virtutibus suis praedicet.* Cic. Cat. 10.

CIRCA, 'about,' (1) of space; as *Collatiam, et quidquid circa Collatiam* (in the neighbourhood of Collatin) *agri erat, Sabinis ademptum.* Liv. I. 38.

(2) 'of time;' as *Postero die circa eandem horam* (about, nearly at, the same hour) *in eundem locum rex copias admovit.* Liv. XXXI. 9.

CIRCITER, 'about' (1) of space; as *Loca haec circiter* (in the neighbourhood of these places). Plaut. Cistellaria, IV. 2, 7.

(2) 'of time;' as *Nos circiter Kalendas* (about the first of the month) *aut in Formiano erimus aut in Pompeiano.* Cic. Att. II. 4.

(3) 'of numbers;' as *Milites dies circiter quindecim* (in about fifteen days) *iter fecerunt.* Caes. *B. G.* I. 15.

CIRCUM, 'around,' of space only; as *Terra circum arem* (around its axis) *se summa celeritate convertit.* Cic. *Acad.* II. 39. *Exercitus in foro et in omnibus templis quae circum forum* (round the forum) *sunt, collocatus est.* Cic. *Opt. gen. or.* IV. *Naevius pueros circum amicos* (round to the houses of his friends) *misit.* Cic. *Quint.* 0.

CIS, CITRA, 'on this side,' 'short of;' as *Clusini audiebant, saepe a Gallis cis Padum ultraque* (on this, i.e. the southern and the other side of the Po) *legiones Etruscorum fusas.* Liv. V. 35. *Decretum est ut Antonius exercitum citra flumen Rubiconem* (on this side of the Rubicon) *educeret.* Cic. *Phil.* VI. 3. *Natura posuit acutam vocem a postrema syllaba non citra tertiam* (not within three syllables from the end, not nearer to the end than the antepenultima). Cic. *Or.* 18. *Notum est Atticos citra morem* (contrary to the custom) *gentium Graeciae ceterarum dixisse.* Aul. Gell. II. 4. *Capparis in desertis agris citra rustici operam* (without the labour of the agriculturist) *convalescit.* Colum. XI. 3, 35. The last two usages are confined to the later writers.

CONTRA, 'opposite to,' 'against,' (1) in a merely local sense; as *Libo insulam, quae contra Brundusinum portum* (opposite to, over against) *est, occuparit.* Caes. *B. C.* III. 23.

(2) in a moral sense; as *Hoc non pro me sed contra me* (against me, in opposition to me) *est.* Cic. *de Orat.* III. 20. *Contra omnium opinionem* (contrary to the opinion of all). Caes. *B. G.* VI. 30. *Communis utilitatis derelictio contra naturam* (contrary to nature) *est.* Cic. *de Off.* III. 6.

ERGA signifies (1) 'over against' in a merely local sense; as *Tonstricem Suram novisti, nostras quae modo erga aedes habet* (lives over against our house). Plaut. *Truc.* II. 4, 52. This sense is rare.

(2) 'towards,' 'in relation to,' of feelings whether friendly or the reverse; as *Praecipiunt ut eodem modo erga amicum* (towards a friend) *affecti simus, quo erga nosmetipsos.* Cic. *Lael.* 10. *Hamilcaris perpetuum odium erga Romanos* (against the Romans) *maxime concitasse videtur secundum bellum Poenicum.* Corn. Nep. XXII. 4.

EXTRA, 'outside of,' 'beyond,' sometimes 'except,' 'without;' as *Apud Germanos nullum habent infamiam quae extra fines* (beyond the borders) *cujusque civitatis fiunt.* Caes. *B. G.* VI. 23. *Manlius adversus edictum patris extra ordinem* (out of his proper rank) *in hostem pugnavit.* Liv. VII. 7. *Extra ducem* (except the leader) *paucosque praeterea reliqui in ipso bello erant rapaces.* Cic. *ad div.* VII. 3. *Mehercule extra jocum* (without a joke) *homo bellus est.* Cic. *ad div.* VIII. 16.

INFRA signifies 'below,' 'beneath,' (1) in space; as *Infra Saturnum* (below, i. e. nearer to the earth than, the planet Saturn) *Jovis stella fertur.* Cic. *N. D.* II. 20.

(2) 'less than,' of magnitude; as *Uri sunt magnitudine paulo infra elephantos* (below, less than elephants). Caes. *B. G.* VII. 28.

(3) 'within,' 'less than,' of time; as *Ova incubari infra decem dies* (in less than ten days after they are laid) *editu utilissimum.* Plin. *N. H.* X. 54; also 'nearer to our time than;' as *Homerus multis annis fuit ante Romulum, si quidem non ante superiorem Lycurgum* (not nearer to our time than Lycurgus, who came above, i. e. before Romulus) *fuit.* Cic. *Brut.* 10.

(4) of a lower place at table; as *Accubueram hora nona apud Volumnium, et quidem supra me Atticus, infra* (below me, in the next place at table) *Verrius, familiares tui.* Cic. *ad div.* IX. 26.

(5) 'inferior to;' as *Tuce tu, quem ego esse infra infimos omnes puto homines* (below, inferior to, more despicable than all the lowest of men). Ter. *Eun.* III. 2, 26. *Sapientia et animi magnitudinem complectitur, et ut omnia, quae homini accedant, infra se* (below itself in worth) *posita judicet.* Cic. *Fin.* III. 7.

INTER signifies 'between,' 'among,' 'in the midst of,' (1) of space; as *Ager Tarquiniorum, qui inter urbem ac Tiberim fuit* (which lay between the city and the Tiber), *consecratus Marti, Martius deinde campus fuit.* Liv. II. 5.

(2) of time, 'during,' 'at,' 'in the course of;' as *Inter coenam* (at, in the course of supper). Cic. *Phil.* II. 25; *ad Q. Fr.* III. 1, 6. *Inter tot annos* (in the course of so many years). Cic. p. *Quint.* 14.

(3) in the company of many others; as *Furere apud sanos et quasi inter sobrios* (in the midst of sober persons) *bacchari vinolentus videtur.* Cic. *Orat.* 28.

(4) of reciprocity or mutual action; as *Neque solum colent inter se* (one another) *et diligent, sed etiam verebuntur.* Cic. *Lael.*

324   CASES WITH PREPOSITIONS.

22. *Vis ergo inter nos* (between ourselves, one with the other) *quid possit uterque viciasim experiamur ?* Virg. *Ecl.* III. 28.

INTRA, 'within,' (1) of space; as *Antiochum Romani intra montem Taurum* (in the regions bounded by mount Taurus) *regnare jusserunt.* Cic. *Sext.* 27; cf. Aul. Gell. *N. A.* XII. 13.

(2) of time: *Dimidiam partem nationum subegit solus intra viginti dies* (within twenty days, in a less period of time). Plaut. *Curcul.* III. 1. 77.

(3) of mutual action, like *inter*; as *Picae meditantes intra se* (among themselves, with one another). Plin. *N. H.* X. 42.

JUXTA (in old Latin *juxtim*) signifies (1) 'near;' as *Atticus sepultus est juxta viam Appiam* (near the Appian road). Corn. Nep. *Att.* ad fin. *Juxtim Numicium flumen* (near the river Numicius) *obtruncatus.* Sisenna, ap. *Non.* II. 451.

(2) 'next to,' 'next after;' as *Juxta divinas relligiones* (next to the obligations of religion) *fides humana colitur.* Liv. IX. 9.

(3) 'closely following,' 'in accordance with' (*secundum*); as *Iones juxta praeceptum Themistoclis* (in accordance with, conformably to, the injunction of Themistocles) *pugnae se paulatim subtrahere coeperunt.* Justin. II. 12, fin.

(4) 'along with,' 'combined with;' as *Periculosiores sunt inimicitiae juxta libertatem* (alongside of liberty, when combined with liberty, i. e. among free men, in a free state). Tacit. *Germ.* 21.

OB signifies (1) 'to,' 'in the direction of;' as *ob Romam* (towards Rome) *noctu legiones ducere coepit.* Ennius ap. *Fest.* p. 178. *Hicine est ille Telamon...cujus ob os* (to or towards whose face) *Graii ora obvertebant sua.* Ennius ap. Cic. *Tusc.* III. 18. This usage is obsolete.

(2) 'before,' 'in front of,' with a notion of backwards and forwards; only with *oculos*; as *Nunc demum experior prius ob oculos mihi* (before my eyes) *caliginem obstitisse.* Plaut. *Mil.* II. 5. 51.

(3) 'on account of,' 'for the sake of;' as *qui ob aliquod emolumentum suum* (on account of some advantage of their own) *cupidius aliquid dicere videntur, iis credi non convenit.* Cic. *Font.* 8. Hence *ob rem,* 'for the sake of something real,' as opposed to

frustra; thus, *Id frustra an ob rem* (to the purpose) *faciam, in vestra manu situm.* Sall. *Jug.* 31.

PENES signifies 'in the power' or 'possession of;' as *Servi centum dies penes accusatorem* (in the power of, under the control of, the accuser) *fuere.* Cic. *Mil.* 22, fin. *Fides ejus rei penes auctores erit* (shall rest with the writers, i.e. 'I refer you to them for it). Sall. *Jug.* 17; Sen. *Qu. N.* IV. 3; Plin. *N. II.* XVII. 12.

PER signifies (1) 'through' either of space or time; as *Mihi quidem videtur Brutus noster jam vel coronam auream per forum* (through the forum) *ferre posse.* Cic. *Att.* XIV. 10. *Post impetratam studiis meis quietem, quae per viginti annos* (through a period of twenty years) *erudiendis juvenibus impenderam.* Quintil. *I. O. prooem.*

(2) 'through,' 'by means of,' 'with,' of the instrument; as *Plura sunt detrimenta publicis rebus, quam adjumenta per homines eloquentissimos* (by means of the most eloquent men) *importata.* Cic. *de Orat.* I. 9.

(3) 'in the way of,' so that the whole phrase is equivalent to an adverb, or represented by an ablative of the manner; as *Versus saepe in oratione per imprudentiam* (unawares) *dicimus.* Cic. *Orat.* 56. Similarly, we have *per negligentiam, per jocum, per iram, per vim, per contumeliam,* and in the poets even with a neuter adjective, as *per subitum,* 'suddenly,' *per tacitum,* 'silently.' Cf. the Greek phrases διὰ τάχους, 'swiftly,' διὰ τέλους, 'completely,' &c. (*Greek Grammar,* p. 511).

(4) 'on account of,' 'owing to;' *Neque per aetatem* (owing to his age) *etiam potis erat.* Ter. *Eun.* I. 2, 32.

(5) 'as far as depends on,' in permissive phrases; as *Per me* (as far as I am concerned) *vel stertas licet, inquit Carneades.* Cic. *Acad.* IV. 29. *Eum nihil delectabat, quod aut per naturam* (as far as nature was concerned) *fas esset aut per leges* (so far as depended on the laws) *liceret.* Cic. *Mil,* 16.

(6) 'without depending on anything else,' with the pronouns *se, te;* as *Nihil audacter ipsos per se* (of themselves, by themselves alone, without help or assistance) *sine P. Sulla facere potuisse.* Cic. *Sull.* 24. *Satis per te* (of yourself alone) *tibi consulis.* Hor. 1 *Epist.* XVII. 1. That *per se* does not mean 'on its own account' is clear from Cic. *Lael.* 21, where we have both *per se* and *propter se.*

(7) 'by,' 'for the sake of,' 'in the name of,' in adjurations, sometimes with a word interposed between the preposition and its case; as *Per ego te deos* (by the gods, in the name of the gods) *oro.* Ter. *Andr.* v. 1, 15.

PONE, 'behind,' only of space; as *Ti. Sempronius aedes P. Africani pone Veteres* (sc. *tabernas*, behind, at the back of, the old shops) *ad Vortumni signum emit.* Liv. XLIV. 16. *Pone nos recede* (retire behind us). Plaut. *Poen.* IV. 2, 34.

POST signifies (1) 'after,' 'since,' of time; *Sexennio post Veios captos* (six years after the taking of Veii). Cic. *Div.* I. 44. *Maxima post hominum memoriam classis* ('the greatest fleet since the world began, i.e. in the memory of man'). Also as an adverb in such phrases as *multis annis post*, 'many years after,' &c.

(2) 'behind,' of space, which is more rare than the temporal use of the word; as *Vercassivellaunus post montem* (behind the mountain) *se occultavit.* Caes. *B. G.* VII. 83. *Quum ab Ægina Megaram versus navigarem post me* (behind me) *erat Ægina, ante Megara.*

PRAETER signifies (1) 'by the side of;' as *Aretho, navigabilis amnis, praeter ipsa Ambraciae moenia* (close to the walls of Ambracia) *fluebat.* Liv. XXXVIII. 3.

(2) 'besides,' 'except;' as *Britanniam non temere praeter mercatores* (except merchants) *adit quisquam, neque iis ipsis praeter oram maritimam* (except the sea-coast) *notum est.* Caes. *B. G.* IV. 20.

(3) 'beyond,' 'more than;' as *Gustatus dulcitudine praeter ceteros sensus* (beyond the other senses) *movetur.* Cic. *de Orat.* III. 25.

(4) 'contrary to;' as *Lentulus praeter consuetudinem* (contrary to his custom) *proxima nocte vigilarat.* Cic. *Cat.* III. 3.

(5) 'immediately before' with *oculos* and *ora* (like *ob*) or *pedes;* as *Servi praeter oculos Lollii* (before the eyes of Lollius) *haec omnia ferebant.* Cic. *Verr.* III. 25, § 62. *Praeter suorum ora* (before the faces of their own friends). Tac. *Hist.* IV. 30. *Mustela murem mihi abstulit praeter pedes* (before my feet). Plaut. *Stich.* III. 2, 7.

PROPE 'signifies,' (1) 'near' of place; as *Quum plebs prope ripam Anienis* (near the bank of the Anio) *ad tertium milliarium consedisset, M. Valerius dicendo sedavit discordiam.* Cic. *Brut.* 14.

Sometimes with *a* and the ablative; as, *Prope a meis aedibus* (near my house). Cic. *Pis.* 11.

(2) 'about' of time; as *Prope Kalendas Sextiles* (about the first day of August) *puto me Laodiceae futurum.* Cic. *ad div.* III. 5.

(3) 'near' of a circumstance or event; as, *Prope secessionem plebis* (near a secession of the commons, i.e. it nearly happened) *res venit.* Liv. VI. 42.

PROPTER signifies (1) 'near' of place; as *Vir clarissimus, qui propter te* (by your side) *sedet.* Cic. *Pis.* 3. *Vulcanus tenuit insulas propter Siciliam* (close by Sicily). Cic. *Nat. Deor.* III. 22. *Fluvius Eurotas propter Lacedaemonem* (close to Lacedæmon) *fluit.* Cic. *Invent.* II. 31. Cf. *praeter* (1).

(2) 'on account of,' 'by reason of;' as *Verre praetore homines nocentissimi propter pecuniam* (on account of money, i.e. for bribes) *judicio sunt liberati.* Cic. *Verr.* A. 1. 3. *Ex castris in oppidum propter timorem* (for fear, on account of fear) *sese recipiunt.* Cæs. *B. C.* 35. Where it will be remarked that *propter timorem* merely gives the reason why they so acted; but *prae timore* would imply that under the influence of fear they could do nothing else, so that the fear in the one case is represented as a *cause*, in the other as an *obstacle*.

SECUNDUM, properly 'following,' signifies (1) 'immediately after or behind,' 'next to;' as *Proxime et secundum deos* (next to the gods) *homines hominibus maxime utiles esse possunt.* Cic. *de Off.* II. 3. *Marcellus pugione vulnus accepit in capite secundum aurem* (immediately behind the ear). Cic. *ad div.* IV. 12.

(2) 'along, by the side of;' as *Secundum flumen* (along the river) *paucae equitum stationes videbantur.* Cæs. *B. G.* II. 18.

(3) 'during' of time; as *Secundum quietem* (during his sleep) *visus Alexandro dicitur draco is, quem mater Olympias alebat.* Cic. *Div.* II. 60.

(4) 'according to;' as *Finis bonorum est secundum naturam* (according to, in accordance with nature) *vivere.* Cic. *Fin.* V. 9.

(5) 'in favour of;' as *Nec cogat ante horam decimam de absente secundum praesentem* (in favour of the party who was present) *judicare.* Cic. *Verr.* II. 17. Some writers use *secus* with the accusative as the opposite of *secundum;* for instance, we have *Chamaeleuce nascitur secus fluvios* (away from rivers). Plin. *N. H.* XXIV. 15. *Secus*

riam stare (to stand away from the road). Cat. *R. R.* XXI. 2, and the like.

SUPRA signifies (1) 'above' of place or situation; as *Si essent qui sub terra semper habitavissent, neque exissent unquam supra terram* (above the surface of the earth). Cic. *N. D.* II. 37. *Exercitus qui supra Suessulam* (above Suessula) *Nolae praesideret.* Liv. XXIII. 32.

(2) 'farther back,' 'before' of time; as *Paulo supra hanc memoriam* (a little before the present age) *servi et clientes una (cum dominis) cremabantur.* Caes. *B. G.* VI. 19.

(3) 'superior to,' of that which is more ancient or better or more powerful; as *Supra septingentesimum annum* (more than 700 years back). Liv. *Praef. Ratio recta supra hominem* (more than human) *putanda est deoque tribuenda.* Cic. *N. D.* II. 13.

(4) 'more than;' as *Karthaginiensium sociorumque caesa eo die supra millia viginti* (more than 20,000). Liv. XXX. 35.

(5) 'overhanging,' of that which is imminent, threatening, and troublesome, with *caput*; as *Quum hostes supra caput sint* (when the enemy are overhanging our heads, are in a threatening attitude) *discedi ab armis, leges ferri placet.* Liv. III. 17. *Clamor supra caput hostilis* (the threatening clamour of the enemy) *captam urbem ostendit.* Liv. IV. 22. *Dux hostium cum exercitu supra caput est* (is over our heads, i. e. is threatening us). Sall. *Cat.* 56. *Ecce supra caput* (here we have over our heads) *homo levis ac sordidus.* Cic. *ad Quint. Fr.* I. 2.

TRANS signifies 'on the other side of, across,' especially of rivers, seas, and mountains; as *Cogito aliquando trans Tiberim* (on the other side of the Tiber) *hortus aliquos parare.* Cic. *Att.* XII. 10. *Caelum non animum mutant qui trans mare* (across the sea) *currunt.* Hor. 1 *Epist.* XI. 780. *Tusci prius cis Apenninum ad inferum mare, postea trans Apenninum* (beyond the Apennines) *colonias miserunt.* Liv. V. 33.

VERSUS signifies 'towards,' 'in the direction of,' and always follows its case; as *Quum Brundisium versus* (in the direction of Brundisium) *iret ad Caesarem.* Cic. *ad div.* XI. 27. It is often used with other prepositions, as *ad* or *in*; thus *Ad Oceanum versus* (towards the Ocean). Caes. *B. G.* VI. 32. *In Italiam versus* (in the direction of Italy). Cic. *ad div.* IV. 12. See *Adversus.*

ULTRA signifies 'beyond' (1) of place; as *Antiochus prope extra orbem terrae ultra juga Tauri* (beyond the ridges of Taurus) *exactus est.* Liv. XXXVIII. 8.

(2) of time; as *Ultra promissum tempus* (beyond, longer than, the promised time) *abesse queror.* Ovid. *Her.* II. 2.

(3) of degree; as *Julius Caesar laboris ultra fidem* (beyond all belief) *patiens erat.* Sueton. *Caes.* 57.

It is regularly opposed to *citra: Sunt certi denique fines quos ultra citraque* (beyond or short of which) *nequit consistere rectum.* Hor. 1 *Serm.* L 107.

(B) *Prepositions construed with the Ablative only.*

A, AB, ABS are merely different forms of the same preposition, employed according to certain prescriptions, more or less depending on the sound; thus, *a* stands generally before consonants, and *ab* before vowels and *h*; but in keeping their accounts the Romans said, e. g. *ab Longo pecuniam accepi* not *a Longo* (see Velius Longus, p. 2224). In the text of Cicero, *Orat.* 47, we find: *una praepositio est ABS eaque nunc tantum in accepti tabulis manet, et ne iis quidem omnium: in reliquo sermone mutata est,* where we ought to prefer the older reading *ab';* and in Horace, 2 *Serm.* III. 69, we have *scribe decem* A *Nerio,* where we ought perhaps to read AB *Nerio.* So also we have *Conditiones pacis Romae* AB *senatu* et A *populo peti debere.* Caes. *B. C.* III. 10. *Puer* AB *janua prospiciens,* Corn. Nep. XXIII. 12. *Abs* is used before *q* and *t,* as *abs quivis* (Ter. *Adelph.* II. 3, 1), *abs te* (Ter. *Phorm.* IV. 3, 12). This preposition, however written, denotes, as we have seen above (109 (a)), separation or removal from the side or surface of an object; and, according to the following applications, it signifies:

(1) 'from,' of the starting point in space or time; as *Animadversum est longius a vallo* (from the rampart) *esse aciem Pompeii progressam.* Caes. *B. C.* III. 85. *A prima aetate* (from my earliest age) *me et omnis ars et maxime philosophia delectavit.* Cic. *ad div.* IV. 4. So also *a teneris, a puero, a pueris, ab adolescentia, ab ineunte astute. Verti igitur me a Minturnis* (from Minturnae) *Arpinum versus.* Cic. *Att.* XVI. 10. *Nec velim, quasi decurso spatio, ad carceres a calce* (from the winning-post back again to the starting-post) *revocari.* Cic. *Senect.* 23. *Atticus Junium familiam a stirpe*

(from its first beginning) *ad hanc aetatem ordine enumeravit.* Corn. Nep. XXV. 18. *Camillum secundum a Romulo* (after Romulus) *conditorem urbis Romanae ferebant.* Liv. VII. 1. *Charmadas repetebat rhetoras usque a Corace* (as far back as Corax). Cic. *de Orat.* I. 20. *Ab hora tertia bibebatur* (they commenced drinking at the third hour). Cic. *Phil.* II. 41. *Quartus a victoria* (from the time of the victory) *mensis.* Tac. *Hist.* II. 95. *Haec a principio* (from the beginning) *tibi praecipiens.* Cic. *ad Qu. F.* II. 3.

(2) 'from,' of the order or arrangement; as *Dactylus, si est proximus a postremo* (next to the last), *parum volubiliter venit ad postremum.* Cic. *Orat.* 64. *Sacerdos ejus deae majestate imperio et potentia secundus a rege* (second counting from, next to the king) *consensu gentis illius habetur.* Hirtius, *B. A.* 06.

(3) 'from,' of the origin from which any thing proceeds; as *Caesar reperiebat plerosque Belgas esse ortos ab Germanis* (sprung from the Germans). Caes. *B. G.* II. 4. *Levior est plaga ab amico* (when it comes from a friend) *quam a debitore* (when it comes from a debtor). Cic. *ad div.* IX. 16. *Pharos est turris, quae nomen ab insula* (from the island as the origin of the name) *accepit.* Caes. *B. C.* III. 112. *Annulos Graece a digitis* (from, after the finger, by the name δακτύλιος, derived from δάκτυλος) *appellavere.* Plin. *N. H.* XXXIII. 1. But *de* and *ex* are sometimes used in giving the derivatives of a name; see, e.g. Ovid. *Met.* I. 447. Caes. *B. G.* VII. 73. Hence in keeping their accounts the Romans said *scribere ab aliquo, solvere ab aliquo,* to denote the person from whom the money was derived; thus, *Non modo non recusare, sed etiam hoc dicere, se ab me* (with money derived from me, with my money) *quodammodo dare.* Cic. *Att.* V. 21, § 11.

(4) 'by,' of the agent considered as the origin of the action, generally (like the Greek ὑπό, with the genitive) with passive and neuter verbs; as *Eratosthenes a Serapione et ab Hipparcho reprehenditur* (Eratosthenes is censured by Serapion and Hipparchus). Cic. *Att.* II. 6. *Immunitates ab Antonio civitatibus, sacerdotia, regna, venierunt* (immunities, priesthoods, kingdoms were sold to the states by Antony). Cic. *Phil.* XII. 5. See above, 165 (c), Obs. 5.

(5) 'from,' 'of,' 'through,' 'out of,' as the cause of the action; as *Illud certe scio me ab singulari amore ac benevolentia* (from, out of, the most complete affection and kindness) *quaecunque scribo tibi scribere.* Cic. *Att.* IX. 6.

CASES WITH PREPOSITIONS. 331

(6) 'from,' 'against,' 'away from,' 'out of the power of,' with an idea of removal or separation; as *Tu, Juppiter, hunc a tuis aris, a tectis urbis, a moenibus, a vita fortunisque civium arcebis* (thou, O Jupiter, wilt keep off this man from thy altars, from the houses and walls of the city, from the lives and fortunes of the citizens). Cic. *Cat.* I. *ad fin. Tarentini pugnabant ut, recuperata urbe ab Romanis* (out of the power of the Romans), *arcem etiam liberarent.* Liv. XXVI. 39. *Teneras defendo a frigore* (against the cold) *myrtos.* Virgil, *Ecl.* VII. 6.

(7) 'away from,' 'unconnected with,' 'foreign to;' as *Non ab re fuerit* (it would not be foreign to the subject) *subtexere quae evenerint.* Sueton. *August.* 94.

(8) 'from or on the side of,' 'in respect to,' 'in point of;' as *Antonius ab equitatu* (in point of cavalry) *primus esse dicebatur.* Cic. *ad div.* X. 15. *Imparati sumus quum a militibus* (in respect to soldiers) *tum a pecunia* (in point of money). Cic. *Att.* VII. 15. *Est nonnulla in Catone et Lysia similitudo; sed ille Graecus ab omni laude* (in regard to every excellence) *felicior.* Cic. *Brut.* 16. *M. Crassus fuit mediocriter a doctrina* (in point of learning) *instructus, angustius etiam a natura* (in regard to natural abilities). *Ibid.* 66. *Isthmus duo maria ab occasu et ortu solis* (on the side of the west and the east) *finitima faucibus dirimit.* Liv. XLV. 28. *Gallia attingit ab Sequanis et Helvetiis* (from the side of the Sequani and Helvetii) *flumen Rhenum.* Caes. *B. G.* I. 1. *Panaetius requirit Juppiterne cornicem a laeva* (on the left), *cornum a destra* (on the right) *canere jussisset.* Cic. *Div.* I. 7. *Horatius Cocles a tergo* (behind him, in his rear) *pontem interscindi jussit.* Cic. *Leges,* II. 4. *Principes utrinque pugnam ciebant, ab Sabinis* (on the side of the Sabines) *Curtius, ab Romanis* (on the side of the Romans) *Hostilius.* Liv. I. 12. *Perfugae coacti sunt cum eis pugnare, ad quos transierant, ab hisque stare* (to stand on the side of those) *quos reliquerant.* Corn. Nep. XIV. 6. Hence we have the ablative with *ab* in designations of employments, with a suppressed *puer, servus, libertus, minister, procurator,* or the like; as *Sextius Paccius Sex. Pompeii a potione* (sc. *puer,* 'his cup-bearer'); *Eumolpus Caesaris a supellectile* (Caesar's master of the wardrobe); *Antiochus Ti. Claudi Caesaris a bibliotheca* (his librarian).

ABSQUE signifies 'without,' but only in the older writers and in the phrase *absque eo esset,* when we denote the conditional absence of something; as *Absque te esset* (without you, but for you), *hodie nunquam ad solem occasum viverem.* Plaut. *Men.* v. 7. 35. In the only passage quoted as an authority for *absque = sine* (namely, Cic. *Att.* L 19), the common preposition is substituted by Oudendorp (*ad* 1. *de Invent.* 36), Orelli (*ad loc.*), and Hand (*Tursell.* L p. 68).

CUM signifies (1) 'with,' of society or mutual agency; as *Sex menses cum Antiocho philosopho fui* (I spent six months in his company). Cic. *Brut.* 91. *Omnia secum* (along with himself, in his company or train) *armentarius Afer agit.* Virgil, *Georg.* III. 343. *Nihil est turpius quam cum eo* (with him, of mutual agency) *bellum gerere, quicum* (with whom, in whose society) *familiariter vixeris.* Cic. *Lael.* 21. *Mihi nihil erat cum Cornificio* (I had nothing to do with Cornificius, we had no mutual transactions). Cic. *Att.* XII. 17. *Quid mihi cum ista summa sanctimonia!* (what have I to do with that wonderful conscientiousness?). Cic. *Quint.* 17.

(2) 'at,' 'with,' of coincidence in time; as *Pariter cum vita* (at the same time with our life) *sensus amittitur.* Cic. *Tusc.* I. 11. *Cum prima luce* (at the first dawn) *Pomponii domum venisse dicitur.* Cic. *de Off.* III. 32.

(3) 'with,' of an accompaniment of any kind; as *In cella concordiae cum gladiis* (armed with swords, with swords by their sides) *homines collocati stant.* Cic. *Phil.* II. 8. *Ut reniret Lampsacum cum magna calamitate et prope pernicie civitatis* (with, i. e. bringing with him, great calamity and almost the ruin of the state). Cic. *Verr.* III. 24. *Fictas fabulas, e quibus utilitas nulla elici potest, cum voluptate* (with pleasure, i. e. not without pleasure, with that concomitant of our reading) *legimus.* Cic. *Fin.* V. 19. *Quum Isocrates videret oratores cum severitate* (with critical severity) *audiri, poetas autem cum voluptate* (with pleasure). Cic. *Orat.* 52. *Semper equidem magno cum metu* (under the influence of great apprehension) *incipio dicere.* Cic. *Cluent.* 18.

Obs. The difference between this usage and the more ablative of immediate determination (above, 163) is easily seen from such a passage as the following: *Si et ferro interfectus ille, et tu inimicus ejus cum gladio cruento comprehensus es* (Cic. *de Orat.* II. 10, § 170). For *ferro* is clearly the ablative of the instrument with which the man was slain ; but *cum gladio* merely indicates the accompaniment, the fact that the man was found *with* a sword, that he had a sword about him. Similarly, in the passages from Cicero quoted above in which we have *cum voluptate, cum metu,* it is clear that the acts described are represented as *accompanied* by the emotions of pleasure or fear, not as caused by them or in any way qualified by them, as if we had *metu examimari, territare, trepidare* or the like. So also when Pliny says of the centurion Vinnius Valens that he was accustomed *vehicula cum culeis onusta donec exinanirentur sustinere* (*N. H.* VII. 20 § 82), he does not mean 'carts loaded with sacks,' but 'loaded carts together with sacks;' intimating an addition to the weight, and not merely that with which the carts were loaded; and when Plautus writes (*Men.* v. 4. 14) *magna cum cura illum curari volo*, he implies not 'I wish him to be cared for with great care,' but 'I wish him to be cared for, and, in addition, I wish great care to be used.'

DE denotes separation or removal from the surface of an object in a downward direction, and it has the following special significations:

(1) 'from,' down from; as *De digito annulum detraho* (I take the ring from—down to the point of and away from—my finger), Ter. *Heaut.* IV. 1, 37. *Praetor de sella* (down from his chair, which was placed on a tribunal) *surrexit atque abiit. Itaque cum de foro* (away from the forum, because we should speak of going up to the market-place) *discessimus.* But immediately before we have *cives Romani a me nusquam discedere* (the citizens nowhere left my side). Cic. *Verr.* IV. 65. *Manum de tabula* (take the hand away from the picture, i.e. down from it, because it is lifted while painting). Cic. *ad div.* VII. 25.

(2) 'from,' 'out of,' especially with reference to taking a part from its whole, or the contents from that which contains; as *Rex Ariobarzanes a me* (from me) *equitatum, cohortesque de meo exercitu* (out of my army) *postulabat.* Cic. *ad div.* XV. 2. *Catilinae ferrum de manibus* (out of his hands) *extorsimus.* Cic. *Cat.* II. 1. Some MSS. have *e manibus*, which would signify the completed result, as *de manibus* denotes the act itself. *Non soleo duo parietes de eadem fidelia* (out of the same paint-pot) *dealbare.* Cic. *ad div.* VII. 29. *Ita est perscriptum senatus-consultum ut a me* (by me as the agent) *de scripto* (from the document,—of the contents) *dicta sententia est.* Cic. *ad div.* X. 13. *Assentior Crasso, ne de C. Laelii aut arte aut gloria detraham* (that I may not take anything from the skill or renown of Laelius). Cic. *de Orat.* I. 9. *Dictator C. Marcius Rutilus primus de plebe* (from the number of the plebeians) *dictus est.* Liv. VII. 17. *Licinius nescio qui de Circo Maximo* (from the Circus Maximus, i.e. from the number of those who lived there). Cic. *Mil.* 24. *Scripseras velle te bene evenire quod de Crasso* (from Crassus, i.e. from out of his possessions) *domum emissem.*

Cic. ad div. v. 6. *Ut decerneret Senatus, ut stipendium miles de publico* (from out of the public treasury) *acciperet, quum ante id tempus de suo* (from, out of his own resources) *quisque functus eo munere esset.* Liv. IV. 59. *Clodius proscripsit se per omnes dies comitiales de caelo servaturum* (that he would take observations from, i.e. of the signs exhibited by, and coming down from the sky). Cic. *Att.* IV. 3. Hence: *De caelo tactus quercus* (oaks touched from the sky, i.e. struck or blasted by lightning descending from the sky). Virg. *Ecl.* I. 17. *P. Messalla consul de Pompeio quaesivit* (inquired of Pompey, got or sought the answer out of him). Cic. *Att.* I. 14.

(3) 'in the midst of,' 'while it is or was still such a period,' in speaking of time; as *Surgunt de nocte latrones* (get up while it is still night). Hor. 1 *Epist.* II. 32. *Coeperunt epulari de die* (they began to banquet in the middle of the day). Liv. XXIII. 8.

(4) 'about,' 'concerning,' of a subject or cause of action which might be selected from many others; as *Regulus nuper librum de vita filii* (about the life of his son) *recitavit. Credas non de puero scriptum sed a puero* (you would believe that the boy was not the subject but the author of it). Plin. *Epist.* IV. 7. *Cum duobus ducibus de imperio* (about, for the empire) *in Italia decertatum, Pyrrho et Hannibale.* Cic. *Lael.* 8. *De benevolentia* (in regard to benevolence), *quam quisque habeat erga nos, illud est in officio, ut ei plurimum tribuamus a quo plurimum diligimur.* Cic. *de Off.* I. 15. *Helvetii omnium rerum inopia adducti, legatos de deditione* (on the subject of, with a view to) *ad eum miserunt.* Caesar, *B. G.* I. 27. There are many idiomatic phrases with this preposition; as *De improviso,* 'of a sudden.' Cic. *Rosc. Am.* 53. *De integro,* 'afresh.' Cic. *Att.* XIII. 51. *De industria,* 'on purpose.' Cic. *de Off.* I. 7. *De meo consilio,* 'by my advice.' Cic. *Att.* 3. *De publico consilio,* 'by the public authority.' Cic. *Inv.* I. 1, 3. *De Jovis sententia,* 'by the counsel of Jupiter.' Cic. *Tusc.* II. 14.

E and EX are different forms of the same preposition, the latter, which is the full form, being used before both vowels, and consonants, and the former being employed before consonants only. The primary meaning of *ex* is separation or motion from the interior of an object. It therefore signifies:

(1) 'Out of,' of place; as *Ex tortuosis locis et inclusis* (from within flexuous and confined places) *referuntur ampliores soni.*

Cic. *N. D.* II. 57. *Ampius conatus est tollere pecunias Epheso ex fano Dianae* (from Ephesus out of the temple of Diana). Cæs. *B. C.* III. 105. *Pulsis e foro bonis omnibus* (all the good having been driven out of the forum). Cic. *Pis.* 13. And so metaphorically; as *Ex vita discedo tanquam ex hospitio, non tanquam ex domo.* Cic. *Sen.* 23.

(2) 'out of,' from among a number; as *Ex Massiliensium classe* (from among the fleet) *quinque naves sunt depressae, ex reliquis* (out of the remainder) *una praemissa Massiliam.* Cæs. *B. C.* II. 7. *M. Calidius non fuit orator unus e multis* (one out of many, an ordinary example of oratory); *potius inter multos prope singularis fuit.* Cic. *Brut.* 79.

(3) 'from or out of,' with reference to the origin, the materials, or the cause; as *Circe erat e Perseide* (from, of her mother). *Oceani filia, nata.* Cic. *N. D.* III. 19. *Ennius in sepulcro Scipionum putatur constitutus e marmore* (of marble, as the material). Cic. *Arch.* 9. *Majores ex minima tenuissimaque republica* (out of— with nothing to start from but—a very small and feeble commonwealth) *maximam et florentissimam nobis reliquerunt.* Cic. *Sext. Rosc.* 18. *Ex ea re* (out of that thing, as the cause), *quid fiat vide.* Ter. *Andr.* II. 3. 11. *Demetrius, vir et ex republica* (by, in consequence of his administration) *Athenis et ex doctrina* (by reason of his learning) *nobilis et clarus, Phalereus vocitatus est.* Cic. *Rabir. Post.* 9. *Dionysius Stoicus, quum ex renibus* (from the kidneys, as the source of the pain, i.e. by reason of that part of his body) *laboraret, clamitabat falsa esse omnia quae antea de dolore ipse sensisset.* Cic. *Tusc.* II. 25.

(4) 'immediately after,' or 'upon,' of time; as *Ex Kalendis Januariis* (ever since the first of January) *ad hanc horam invigilavi reipublicae.* Cic. *Phil.* XIV. 7. *Germani statim e somno* (immediately after sleep, i.e. as soon as they got up) *lavantur.* Tac. *Germ.* 22. *Cotta ex consulatu* (immediately after his consulship) *est profectus in Galliam.* Cic. *Brut.* 92. *Oppidum Remorum ex itinere* (immediately after their march) *Belgae oppugnare coeperunt.* Cæs. *B. G.* II. 6.

(5) 'in accordance with,' from, as from a mould or model; thus: *Facis ex tua dignitate et e republica* (you act in accordance with your dignity and the interests of the state). Cic. *ad Brut.* 2. *Vulgus ex veritate* (in accordance with the truth) *pauca, ex opinione*

(by the standard of common opinion) *multa aestimat.* Cic. *Sext. Rosc.* 10. *Ridicule etiam illud P. Nasica censori Porcio Catoni, quum ille,* '*Ex tui animi sententia tu uxorem habes?*' '*Non hercle,*' *inquit,* '*ex mei animi sententia.*' Cic. *de Orat.* II. 64, § 260. In this last passage the joke consists in the two idiomatic applications of *ex animi sententia,* 'according to the intention of my mind.' The censor asked Nasica: 'tell me on your solemn declaration'—*dic vere et fide*—'whether you are married or not?' (cf. *de Off.* III. 29: *quod ex animi tui sententia juraris*). The answer means: 'My wife is not according to the wish of my heart.' The preposition *ex* is used in a number of adverbial phrases; as *ex adverso,* 'opposite,' *e regione,* 'over against,' *ex animo,* 'sincerely,' *ex improviso,* 'suddenly,' *ex tempore,* 'on the spur of the moment,' *ex usu,* 'profitably,' *e re mea,* 'for my interest,' *ex toto,* 'entirely,' *e vestigio,* 'on the spot,' *e re nata* (also *pro re nata*), 'according to the circumstances,' *ex parte,* 'in part,' *heres ex asse,* 'heir to the whole property,' *ex occulto,* 'secretly,' *ex insidiis,* 'by stratagem,' *ex insperato,* 'unexpectedly,' *ex integro,* 'afresh,' *ex aequo,* 'on an equal footing,' *ex contrario,* 'on the contrary,' *ex equo,* 'on horseback,' &c.

PRÆ signifies (1) 'before' of place or position; as *Villa a tergo potius quam prae se flumen habeat* (let the villa have a river rather behind than in front of it). Columella, I. 5, 4. *Hercules prae se armentum agens* (driving the herd before him) *nando trajecit.* Liv. I. 7. Hence the phrase *prae se ferre* or *gerere,* 'to carry before oneself,' i.e. 'to display, or exhibit;' as *Fiduciam orator prae se ferat* (let the orator display confidence). Quint. *I. O.* V. 13, § 51. *Prae se quandam gerit utilitatem* (displays, has the appearance of, a sort of usefulness). Cic. *Invent.* II. 52.

(2) 'for,' 'on account of,' with reference to some obstacle which stands in the way; as *Solem prae jaculorum multitudine* (owing to the number of missiles) *non videbitis.* Cic. *Tusc.* I. 42. *Sed finis sit; neque enim prae lacrimis* (for tears—owing to my tears) *jam loqui possum.* Cic. *Mil.* 38. Similarly: *Prae moerore.* Cic. *Planc.* 41, 99. *Prae fletu et dolore.* Cic. *Att.* XI. 7. *Prae gaudio.* Ter. *Heaut.* II. 3. 67. *Prae amore.* Ter. *Eun.* I. 2. 18. *Prae tremore.* Plaut. *Rud.* II. 6. 41.

(3) 'in comparison with,' of an object held forth by way of contrast; as *Gallis prae magnitudine corporum suorum* (in compa-

rison with the size of their bodies) *brevitas nostra contemptui est.* Caes. *B. G.* II. 30. *Romam prae sua Capua* (in comparison with their own Capua) *irridebunt atque contemnent.* Cic. *Agrar.* II. 35.

PRO signifies (1) 'before,' of place; as *Pro muro* (before the wall) *dies noctesque agitare.* Sallust, *Jug.* 94. *Caesar legiones pro castris* (before the camp) *constituit.* Caes. *B. G.* VII. 70. *Augustus bifariam laudatus est, pro aede divi Julii* (in front of the temple of the deified Julius) *a Tiberio, et pro veteribus rostris* (in front of the old tribunal) *a Druso, Tiberii filio.* Suet. *Aug.* 100. *Dictator miris pro concione* (before the assembly, i. e. in a public speech) *Manlii Torquati pugnam laudibus tulit.* Liv. VII. 10.

(2) 'for,' 'on behalf of, in favour or defence of;' as *Convenit dimicare pro legibus, pro libertate, pro patria* (to fight for the laws, for liberty, for our country). Cic. *Tusc.* IV. 19.

(3) 'instead of,' as a return or equivalent for; as *Italico bello Sicilia Romanis non pro penaria cella, sed pro aerario fuit* (not in the place of a granary, but a treasury). Cic. *Verr.* II. 2. *Tu ausus es pro nihilo prae tua praeda* (in the light of nothing as compared with your plunder) *tot res sanctissimas ducere?* Cic. *Verr.* II. 16. *Minas pro ambobus* (in exchange for, as the price of both) *viginti dedi.* Ter. *Eun.* I. 2. 85. *Ego te pro istis dictis et factis ulciscar* (I will requite you for those words and deeds). *Ibid.* v. 4. 19.

(4) 'in proportion to,' 'according to;' as *Permissum uti pro tempore atque periculo* (in proportion to the exigency and danger) *exercitum compararent.* Sall. *Cat.* 29. *Haec pro tuo ingenio* (as far as your abilities allow) *considera.* Cic. *ad div.* XVI. 1. Hence *pro re nata* (according to circumstances). Cic. *Att.* VII. 6.

SINE signifies 'without,' as the opposite of *cum*; as *Homo sine re, sine fide, sine spe, sine sede, sine fortunis* (without money, credit, hope, a fixed abode, or property). Cic. *Cael.* 32. *Nulla dies sine linea* ('no day without a stroke of the brush,' a proverb from the industry of Apelles). Plin. *N. H.* XXXV. 10. 84. *Sine periculo* (without incurring a risk). Ter. *Heaut.* II. 3. 73. *Sine fraude* (without hurt or harm). Liv. I. 24. Horat. 2 *Carm.* XIX. 20. *Sine dolo malo* (without any evil design). Liv. XXXVIII. 11.

(C) *Prepositions construed with the Accusative and Ablative.*

IN corresponds in usage to the Greek prepositions εἰς and ἐν. When construed with the accusative it answers to εἰς governing the same case; when construed with the ablative it answers to ἐν governing the dative. It also performs some of the functions of ἀνά, which is identical in origin with the other two.

(a) With the accusative, *in* signifies (1) 'into,' 'unto,' 'up to,' of motion or direction; as *Proba vita via est in caelum et in coetum eorum, qui jam vixerunt* (the road to heaven and to the company of those who have already lived in the same way). Cic. *Somn. Scip.* 3.

(2) 'into the middle of something;' as *Codrus se in medios immisit hostes* (into the midst of the enemy). Cic. *Tusc.* I. 48. *Homo optutum negotium sibi in sinum delatum esse dicebat* (he said it had come into his bosom, under his complete control). Cic. *Verr.* I. 50. Hence of a close fight: *Pugna jam in manus* (to a close grapple), *jam ad gladios venerat.* Liv. II. 46.

(3) 'to,' 'till,' or 'unto,' of time; as *Studebat in coenae tempus* (he studied till supper-time). Plin. *Epist.* III. 5.

(4) 'by,' of distributive time; as *In dies* (by days, i. e. every day). Cic. *Phil.* I. 2. *In horas* (Horat. 2 *Serm.* VII. 10), or *in singulas horas* (every hour). Liv. II. 12.

(5) 'for,' of future time; as *Ad coenam hominem in hortos invitavit in posterum diem* (he invited the man to his country-house to dinner for the following day). Cic. *de Off.* III. 14.

(6) 'to,' of extent or magnitude; as *Lautumiae Syracusanae sunt opus ingens, totum ex saxo in mirandam altitudinem* (to a wonderful depth) *presso.* Cic. *Verr.* V. 27. *In dimidiam partem* (to the extent of one half) *decoquenda.* Colum. XII. 24. *Nec puer Iliaca quisquam de gente Latinos in tantum* (to such an extent) *tollet avos.* Virg. Æn. VI. 875.

(7) 'into,' of division; as *Stoici diviserunt naturam hominis in animum et corpus* (into soul and body). Cic. *Fin.* IV. 7.

(8) 'towards,' of a local aspect; as *In meridiem spectet* (let it look to the south). Cato, *R. R.* I. 1. More commonly *ad meridiem, ad septemtriones.* Cic. *N. D.* II. 19.

(9) 'towards' or 'against,' of feelings, relations, or actions; as *T. Manlius fuit perindulgens in patrem* (towards his father), *idem*

acerbe severus in filium (against his son). Cic. *de Off.* III. 31. *In consules designatos* (against the consuls elect) *legem senatus decrevit.* Cic. *Cluent.* 49. *Majores nostri de servis in dominos* (against their masters) *quaeri noluerunt.* Cic. *Part.* 34.

(10) 'for,' of the object or motive; as *Deletam urbem cernimus eorum quorum in gratiam* (for whose gratification) *Saguntum deleverat Hannibal.* Liv. XXVIII. 39. *Puerum conspexi olera et pisciculos ferre in coenam seni* (for the old man's supper). Ter. *Andr.* II. 2. 31.

(11) 'after,' 'according to;' as *Cur paucis centurionibus in modum servorum* (after the manner of slaves) *obedirent.* Tac. *Ann.* I. 17.

(12) 'over;' as *In filium* (over my son) *quam habebam potestatem, ea usus sum.* Cic. *Invent.* II. 17.

(b) With the ablative, *In* signifies (1) 'in,' 'within;' as *Deus intelligentiam in animo* (in the soul), *animum conclusit in corpore.* Cic. *Univ.* 3.

(2) 'in the midst of,' 'among;' as *In Persis* (among the Persians) *augurantur et divinant Magi.* Cic. *Div.* I. 41. *Dolor in maximis malis ducitur* (is reckoned among the greatest evils). Cic. *Leg.* I. 11.

(3) 'upon;' as *Verres coronam habebat unam in capite* (on his head), *alteram in collo* (on his neck). Cic. *Verr.* V. 11.

(4) 'at,' 'upon,' of a time or occasion; as *Q. Mucii janua in ejus infirmissima valetudine* (at the time of his most infirm health) *maxima quotidie frequentia civium celebratur.* Cic. *de Orat.* I. 45. *Plerumque in summo periculo* (in a case of great danger) *timor misericordiam non recipit.* Caes. *B. G.* VII. 26.

(5) 'in,' 'during,' of time; as *In hoc spatio* (during this time) *et in iis post aedilitatem annis* (in those years after my aedileship) *et praetor primus et incredibili voluntate sum factus.* Cic. *Brut.* 93.

(6) 'in,' 'within,' of a period; as *Credo potis esse te Massici montis uberrimos quattuor fructus ebibere in una hora* (within the space of one hour). Plaut. *Pseud.* V. 2. 10. *Crassum semel ait in vita* (in the course of his life) *risisse Lucilius.* Cic. *Fin.* V. 30.

(7) 'on account of,' as the present cause of something; as *In quo oratore* (on account of what orator) *homines exhorrescunt? quem*

stupefacti dicentem intuentur! in quo exclamant? (who causes them to cry out?) Cic. *de Orat.* III. 14.

We have a number of adverbial phrases with *in* and the ablative; as *in praesentia,* 'at present,' *in tempore,* 'at the right time,' *in loco,* 'in the proper place,' *in confesso est,* 'it is admitted,' *in difficili est,* 'it is difficult,' *in aere alieno est,* 'he is in debt,' *in libris est,* 'he is at his books,' *in culpa est,* 'he is in fault,' *in more est,* 'it is customary,' *in periculo, in ambiguo, in incerto est,* 'it is hazardous, doubtful, uncertain,' and the like.

SUB denotes 'motion under' with the accusative, and 'rest under' with the ablative.

(a) With the accusative *sub* signifies (1) 'motion under,' in space; as *Milites Caesaris sub montem succedunt* (go under the mountain). Caesar, *B. C.* I. 45. So also of objects which fall under the senses; as *Res quaedam ita sunt parvae, ut sub sensum cadere non possint* (that they cannot be brought within the reach of the senses). Cic. *Acad.* I. 8. Similarly of that which is brought under any one's control: *Miltiades insulas quas Cyclades nominantur sub Atheniensium redegit potestatem* (reduced under the power of the Athenians). Corn. Nep. I. 2.

(2) 'about,' of time; as *Pompeius sub noctem* (about nightfall) *naves solvit.* Caes. *B. C.* I. 28.

(3) 'immediately after,' of time; as *Redditae sunt litterae tuae Cornuto, quum is recitasset litteras Lepidi. Sub eas* (immediately after them) *statim recitatae sunt tuae.* Cic. *ad div.* X. 16.

(b) With the ablative *sub* signifies (1) 'under,' of rest under an object in space; as *Caesar hostem sub muro* (under the wall) *sistere cogit.* Caes. *B. C.* I. 45. So of objects which are under the senses; as *Jam lucisrebat omniaque sub oculis* (visible to the eyes) *erant.* Liv. IV. 28. Similarly of that which is under one's control; as *Antigenis sub imperio* (under his command) *erat phalanx Macedonum.* Corn. Nep. XVIII. 7. Compare with these the three passages under (a).

(2) 'at,' of time; as *Sub exitu anni* (at the end of the year) *comitia habita sunt.* Liv. VI. 18.

SUBTER is used only in reference to space, and signifies

(a) With the accusative, 'beneath,' with a sense of motion; as *Cupiditatem subter praecordia locavit* (he placed passionate desire under the diaphragm). Cic. *Tusc.* I. 10.

(b) With the ablative, 'beneath,' with an implication of rest; as *Virtus omnia, quae cadere in hominem possunt, subter se* (beneath itself) *habet.* Cic. *Tusc.* v. 1.

SUPER denotes 'motion above' with the accusative, and 'rest above' with the ablative.

(a) With the accusative *super* signifies (1) 'motion above,' of place; as *Demetrius super terras tumulum* (on the top of the mound of earth) *noluit quid stutui, nisi columellam, tribus cubitis ne altiorem.* Cic. *Leg.* II. 26.

(2) 'over,' in the sense of during; as *Vespasianus super coenam* (over his supper, during that meal) *multa joco transigebat.* Sueton. *Vesp.* 22.

(3) 'beyond,' 'besides,' 'in addition;' as *In Bruttiis Punicum exercitum super morbum* (in addition to the pestilence) *etiam fames adfecit.* Liv. XXVIII. 46.

(b) With the ablative *super* signifies (1) 'rest above,' of place; as *Districtus ensis cui super impia cervice pendet* (hangs above his impious neck). Horace, 3 Carm. I. 17.

(2) 'about,' 'concerning;' as *Hac super re* (about this matter) *scribam ad te Rhegii.* Cic. *Att.* XVI. 6.

CHAPTER III.

TENSES AND MOODS OF VERBS.

§ 1. *Construction of the Tenses in the Finite Moods.*

170 A COMPLETE system of tenses includes three pairs of verb-forms. For a predication of tense must refer either to the time of speaking, which does not need definition, or to some other point of time, which has to be defined. In the former case, the tense is called *definite* or *determinate*; in the latter, *indefinite* or *indeterminate*. Now, besides this, every predication of tense must express either *simultaneity*, i.e. at the same time, or at the present; *posteriority*, i.e. afterwards, or in the future; or *anteriority*, i.e. *before*, or in the past. According to this view of the matter, which is fully established by the Greek language (see *Complete Greek Grammar*, articles 422 and following), the Latin system of tenses is defective. For the perfect has to serve both as the definite tense of anteriority, and as the indefinite tense of posteriority. Thus we have:

Definite Tenses.

Simultaneity: *scribo*, 'I am writing'—*at* the present time.
Posteriority: *scribam*, 'I shall write'—*after* the present time.
Anteriority: *scripsi*, 'I have written'—*before* the present time.

Indefinite Tenses.

Simultaneity: *scribebam*, 'I was writing'—*at* a given time.
Posteriority: *scripsi*, 'I wrote'—*after* a given time.
Anteriority: *scripseram*, 'I had written'—*before* a given time.

Moreover, as we have seen, in all cases where there is no future in *-bo*, the tense used for the expression of definite posteriority is really the present subjunctive, and denotes, as will be shown directly, rather probability than futurity.

TENSES. 343

Obs. Although the reduplicated form corresponds to the true preterite in Greek, which is also involved in the compound preterite with *fui* appended, whereas the perfect in *-vi* answers to the Greek aorist in *-σα*, there is practically no difference in the syntactical usage of these forms, and their absolute identity is farther developed in the sameness of their person-endings, which is probably a subsequent accommodation. Nor is there any difference in use between the two forms of the future.

(A) *Indicative and Imperative.*

171 (*a*) As the imperative differs from the present indicative only in a weakening or extension of the person-endings, we may consider the two moods together as far as their tenses are concerned. The following examples will show the usage of the tenses in the indicative mood.

I. Present: *Deus mundum conservat,* 'God preserves (i.e. is still continuing to preserve) the world.'

Jamdudum ausculto, 'I am all this while continuing to listen,' i.e. I have long been doing so.

Zeno aliter judicat, 'Zeno determines otherwise,' i.e. in an extant record of his sentiments, or in a passage now before us.

II. Imperfect: *Socrates dicebat* (or *dicere solebat*) *omnes in eo quod scirent satis esse eloquentes,* 'Socrates was saying or used to say (at a specified time, namely, while he lived and spoke) that all men were sufficiently eloquent in that wherein they had knowledge.'

Romae quotannis bini consules creabantur, 'every year two consuls at a time used to be created at Rome,' i.e. it was a continued custom.

Proelio se expediebant, 'they were preparing themselves for the battle,' i.e. they began to do so at the specified time.

III. Perfect (*a*) as aorist, or historical perfect: *Vixit inaequalis clarum ut mutaret in horas,* 'he lived so inconsistently (a mere statement of a past occurrence) that he changed the fashion of his robe every hour.'

With an imperfect following: *Quo tempore Philippus Graeciam evertit, etiam tum Athenae gloriâ litterarum et artium florebant,* 'at the time when Philip overthrew Greece (a mere statement of a past occurrence, happening at a specified time, and subsequent to prior events expressed or presumed), even then (at the time) Athens was flourishing in the renown of literature and art.'

344   SYNTAX OF VERBS.

(b) As a true perfect, expressing the continuance of an action up to the present time, and its completion now: *Ille potens sui laetusque degit, cui licet in diem dixisse—Vixi,* 'he lives master of himself and happy, who can say, at the end of every day—I have lived,' i. e. I have completed a period of living; compare this with the first example of the aorist perfect, and with the converse saying of the Emperor Titus: *diem perdidi,* 'I have lost a day.' So also: *fuimus Troes, fuit Ilium et ingens gloria Dardanidum,* 'we have been'—but are no more. Sometimes this usage is fully explained by the context; as *is mos usque ad hoc tempus permansit,* 'that custom has continued up to this day.'

Obs. The present may sometimes be used instead of the imperfect or historical perfect, and even in the same sentence with the other tense; as *Eo postquam Caesar pervenit, obsides, arma, servos qui ad eos perfugissent poposcit: dum ea conquiruntur et conferuntur, noctu intermissa circiter hominum millia IV. ex castris Helvetiorum egressi ad Rhenum finesque Germanorum contenderunt,* where *conquiruntur* and *conferuntur* are used instead of the imperfect by the side of the historical perfect. *Expectabant omnes, quo tandem Verres progressurus esset, quum repente proripi hominem ac deligari jubet,* where *jubet* is used instead of the historical perfect by the side of the imperfect.

IV. Pluperfect: *Quum esset Demosthenes, multi oratores magni et clari fuerunt, et antea fuerant, nec postea defecerunt,* 'they were at the time when Demosthenes flourished, they had been before, and were not wanting afterwards,' (where the expression of anteriority stands between historical statements of fact).

Quum ego illum vidi, jam consilium mutaverat, 'when I saw him he had already changed his mind' (the change was anterior to my seeing him).

Irruerant Danai et tectum omne tenebant, 'the Greeks had rushed in (previously) and were occupying (at the time) all the building.'

Daphnis sub ilice consederat, compulerantque greges Corydon et Thyrsis in unum; huc mihi caper deerraverat; atque ego Daphnin adspicio, 'Daphnis had already taken his seat under the oak; Corydon and Thyrsis had already driven their flocks together; my he-goat had wandered to this spot; and as a consequence of this previous state of things, I see' (i. e. I saw, according to the last observation) 'Daphnis.'

V. Future: *Tu bibes Caecubam uvam*, 'you shall drink the Caecuban wine' (which conveys a permission or a promise).

Quando veritas ullum inveniet parem? 'when will Truth find any one equal to him?' (where the whole of future time is excluded from the range of choice).

Illo tempore Respublica florebit, 'at that time the Commonwealth will flourish' (where a subsequent event is predicted).

Obs. Students will observe that the Latin language can carry the future indicative through all the members of a period, whereas in English the sign of the future is expressed only in the leading sentence. Thus we say: *proferto beati erimus, quum corporibus relictis cupiditatum erimus expertes*, 'truly we shall be happy, when having left our bodies we are, i. e. shall be, free from passionate desire;' *naturam si sequemur ducem, nunquam aberrabimus,* 'if we follow nature as our guide, we shall never go wrong;' *ut voles me esse, ita ero,* 'I will be, as you wish.'

The general meaning of the different moods has been already given (Part I. 70, (b)), and the above instances will sufficiently illustrate the use of the indicative.

(β) The imperative mood of the second person is either a direct command or an intreaty, and in some verbs, which are limited to this mood, it has become a mere interjection (104, h). *Fac* and *cura* are often used periphrastically with *ut*. The third person of the imperative is generally employed in laws, in imitations of the legal style, and in prohibitions with *ne*. The following are examples:

Patres conscripti, subvenite misero mihi, ite obviam injuriae, 'O Senators, patrician and elected, assist unhappy me, go forth to meet wrong-doing.'

Fac venias or *ut venias*, 'make a point of coming.'

Cura ut valeas, 'take care of your health.'

Regio imperio duo sunto, iique consules appellantor, 'let there be two with kingly authority, and let them be called consuls.'

Servus meus Sticho liber esto, 'let my slave Sticho be free' (in a will).

Ter uncti transnanto Tiberim somno quibus est opus alto, 'let those who need sound sleep anoint themselves and swim thrice across the Tiber' (in an imitation of the style of laws and medical prescriptions).

Et ille, 'Audite vero, audite,' inquit, 'and he says, "Hear ye, hear ye"' (in a ludicrous imitation of scholastic pomposity. Cic. de Orat. II. 7, 28).

Nocturna sacrificia ne sunto, 'let there be no sacrifices by night.'

(B) *Subjunctive.*

172 The tenses of the subjunctive are used as follows:

I. The present is a kind of future, for it denotes the *probable* occurrence of something *after* the time of speaking. Hence, while it is so nearly identical with the form which in most verbs is used for the future, the subjunctive has no simple future in the active, and no future at all in the passive voice. The learner must particularly observe that the possibility, expressed by the subjunctive in Latin, is always hypothetical, and that the direct statement of permission or power must always be made by *licet* or *possum* with the infinitive mood (see 177, (c), *Obs.* 2). Thus described the present subjunctive is (a) *optative,* (b) *deliberative,* (c) *hortative,* (d) *potential,* (e) *conditional* or (f) *dependent,* in each case with a presumption of possibility, as the following examples will show.

(a) *Optative;* with or without *utinam,* and in negative wishes with *ne; as salvus sis,* or *utinam salvus sis,* 'may you be well'— which is not only desired but possible; *ne sis patruus mihi,* 'I wish you would not act as an uncle to me'—abstain from the harshness which you may avoid. (Optative without ἄν in Greek.)

(b) *Deliberative; as eloquar an sileam?* 'shall I speak out or hold my tongue?' (Conjunctive in Greek.)

(c) *Hortative; as imitemur majores nostros,* 'let us imitate our ancestors.' (Conjunctive in Greek.)

(d) *Potential;* either in the apodosis or second clause of a conditional sentence (128, XVI. 3); as *ego, si Scipionis desiderio me moveri negem, mentiar,* 'if I deny (i. e. shall deny) that I am affected by a longing for Scipio, I shall speak falsely,' where there is a mere assumption; similarly, *tu si hic sis, aliter sentias,* 'if you were,—which you are not but might be—in my situation, you would think otherwise:' or by itself without an expressed condition; as *dicat aliquis,* 'some one may here say.' Also in interrogatives; as *quis dubitet?* 'who would doubt?' (Greek Optative with ἄν.)

(e) *Conditional;* either in the protasis or first clause of the conditional sentence; as in the examples just given: or followed by a future indicative; as *si quid habeat, dabit* (128, XVI. 2); or by itself, as containing a supposition; thus, *vendat aedes vir bonus propter aliqua vitia*, 'suppose a good man sells a house on account of some fault,' and so on through the passage (Cic. *de Officiis*, III. 13); (Greek optative with εἰ and without ἄν). The conditional may amount to an optative; as *O mihi praeteritos referat si Jupiter annos*, 'O if Jupiter would only give me back the years that are gone!' (Virg. *Æn.* VIII. 560.) (So also in Greek: *Gr. Gr.* Art. 516 *b.*)

(f) *Dependent;* with *ut* or *ne* or some relative word after the present, the true perfect, and future of the main clause; as *scribo, scripsi, scribam, ut discas*, 'I am writing, I have written, I shall write, to the end that you may learn;' *danda opera est, ut ea res ne obsit reipublicae*, 'care must be taken, to the end that the business in question may do no harm to the state.' (Greek conjunctive after ἵνα, ὅπως, ὡς, and sometimes the future indicative with ὅπως.)

II. The imperfect indicates that the probable occurrence is past and must be foregone; it is:

(a) *Optative*, to imply that the wish cannot now be realized; as *utinam salvus esses*, 'I wish you were (what you are not) in good health;' *illud utinam ne vere scriberem*, 'I wish I was not writing that sentiment with truth.' If *non* is used for *ne* it must be closely connected with the predicative word. (Greek indicative with εἰ, εἰ γάρ, εἴθε: *Gr. Gr.* Art. 517.)

(b) *Hortative*, chiefly *in oratione obliqua; as imitarentur majores suos*, 'let them, he said, imitate their ancestors.'

(c) *Potential;* either in the apodosis (128, XVI. 4, (a)); as *si scirem, dicerem*, 'if I knew (which is not the case), I would speak:' or by itself; as *nollem factum*, 'I would not like it done.' (Greek imperfect indicative with ἄν.)

(d) *Conditional*, in the protasis of the last case, and sometimes followed by the imperfect indicative; as *si non alium longe jactaret odorem, laurus erat*, 'if it did not emit a widely different smell, it were a laurel.' (Greek imperfect indicative with εἰ, and without ἄν.) *O si*, with the imperfect subjunctive, might express an impossible wish.

(e) *Dependent*, with *ut* or *ne*, or some relative word, after the imperfect, aorist perfect, and pluperfect of the main clause; as

348   SYNTAX OF VERBS.

scribebam, scripsi, scripseram, ut disceres, 'I was writing, I wrote, I had written to the end that you might learn.' (Greek optative after ἵνα, ὅπως, ὡς.)

III. The perfect subjunctive is sometimes called the *futurum exactum*, and referred to the indicative; but all its functions are as a tense of the subjunctive mood. As the subjunctive itself is a kind of future, it is quite natural that the perfect subjunctive should be a sort of future perfect, and in fact it does correspond, in the protasis, to the Greek aorist conjunctive; as *si quid feceris* = ἐάν τι ποιήσῃς, 'if you shall have done anything.' It is:

(a) *Potential*, either as the apodosis of a simple future, present, or perfect, or perfect subjunctive; or by itself; thus we have in an apodosis, *quum tu haec leges, ego fortasse eum convenero,* 'when you read these words, I shall perhaps have had a meeting with him;' *si pergis, abiero,* 'if you go on, I shall be off at once;' *si plane occidimus, ego omnibus meis exitio fuero,* 'if we have altogether fallen, I shall have been (i. e. I shall prove in the result) a destruction to all my friends;' *qui Antonium oppresserit, is bellum confecerit,* 'he who shall have overthrown Antony, will, by that very act, have put an end to the war.' By itself, *ego de me videro,* 'I shall be found to have looked after myself;' *tu invita mulieres; ego accivero pueros,* 'do you invite the ladies; I will, before that, send for the boys,' i. e. 'I shall have done it, ere you have finished your part of the business;' *hoc sine ulla dubitatione confirmaverim,* 'I shall have said this without the least hesitation,' in reference to a statement which he is actually about to make. Also in interrogations; as *quis tulerit Gracchos de seditione querentes!* 'who will, for a moment, tolerate the Gracchi complaining of sedition?'

(b) *Conditional,* either as the protasis, in the case just mentioned, and with a perfect or simple future in the apodosis, or by itself; thus we have, *si quis bona carmina condiderit, si quis opprobriis dignum latraverit, solventur risu tabulae, tu missus abibis,* 'if any one shall have made good verses, if any one shall have inveighed against a man worthy of reproach, laughter will do away with the severity of the sentence, and you will get off with impunity;' *dixerit Epicurus,* 'suppose Epicurus shall have said.'

(c) *Dependent,* after past and future tenses; as *Hortensius ardebat dicendi cupiditate sic, ut in nullo unquam flagrantius studium viderim*, 'Hortensius was inflamed with a desire for oratorical distinction to such an extent, that I have never seen greater eagerness in any one;' *Epaminondas paupertatem adeo facile perpessus est, ut de republicâ nihil praeter gloriam ceperit*, 'Epaminondas bore poverty so easily, that he took nothing from the state except glory;' *adnitar, ne frustra vos hanc spem de me conceperitis*, 'I will do my best, to the end that you may not have conceived this hope about me in vain.'

(d) *Prohibitive*, when a single act is forbidden, just as the aorist of the conjunctive is used in Greek; *ne dixeris*, 'do not say at all;' *tu ne quaesieris*, 'have done with inquiring[1].'

IV. The pluperfect subjunctive is:

(a) *Optative*, to imply that the wish could not have been realized; as *utinam ne Phormioni id suadere in mentem incidisset*, 'I wish it had never come into Phormio's head (as it did), to recommend that course;' *hoc utinam tibi a principio placuisset*, 'I wish you had liked this from the first.'

(b) *Potential*, in the apodosis to another pluperfect (128, XVI. 4, (b)); as *si voluissem plura, non negasses*, 'if I had wished for more (which I did not), you would not have refused;' but the protasis is sometimes not expressed; as *summôsses omnes*, 'you would have put aside all competitors'—if you had had my assistance.

(c) *Conditional*, in the protasis to the former case, and sometimes with the perfect or pluperfect of the indicative in the apodosis; as *Antoni gladios potuit contemnere, si sic omnia dixisset*, 'he had it in his power to despise (as an historical fact) the swords of Antony, if he had (which he had not) spoken every thing in this strain;' *me truncus illapsus cerebro sustulerat, nisi Faunus ictum dextrâ levâsset*, 'if Faunus had not parried the blow with his right hand, the trunk of a tree, having fallen on my head, had slain me on the spot.' We have even the imperfect indicative in the apodosis to the pluperfect subjunctive, as in Tac. *Ann*. XII. 39: *nec ideo fugam sistebat, ni legiones proelium excepissent*, 'nor did this stop the flight, had not the legions taken up the battle.' In most instances, however, this construction must be regarded as indirect,

---

[1] See *Gr. Gr.* art. 427, (a₁). Bishop Andrewes on Matt. iii. 7, 8: 'the word is not *bring forth at this time, now;* then it should be *vessiste*, in the present; but it is... *venisate*, in the aorist...It signifies rather *have done bringing forth*, than *bring forth presently*.' (Vol. I. p. 430).

and the true apodosis has to be supplied from the terms of the main clause (below, 203, (β)).

(d) *Dependent*, after an historical perfect; as *Sol Phaethonti dixit se facturum esse, quicquid optasset,* 'the Sun said to Phaethon that he would perform whatever wish he had conceived.'

V. The future subjunctive, which occurs only in the active, is found in dependent sentences after the present and perfect indicative or subjunctive, and the imperative; as *quotusquisque tam patiens est, ut velit discere quod in usu non sit habiturus,* 'how few there are so patient as to be willing to learn what they are not likely to want;' *defectiones solis praedictae sunt quae, quantae, quando futurae sint,* 'it has been predicted of what kind, to what extent, and when there will be eclipses of the sun;' *quid sit futurum cras, fuge quaerere,* 'avoid asking what is likely to take place tomorrow.'

§ 2. *Distinctive uses of the Indicative and Subjunctive.*

173 The great difficulty in Latin composition is the correct employment of the indicative and subjunctive moods, especially after relatives and relative particles. The simplest way of dealing with the subject is to consider as separate questions: (I) When *must* we use the indicative? (II) When *must* we use the subjunctive? (III) When *may* we use either mood, and with what difference of signification?

174 I. (a) We *must* use the indicative in all direct statements; as *silvestrem tenui musam meditaris avend,* 'you are practising woodland music on a slender reed.'

(b) We *must* use the indicative in all relative sentences, whenever the antecedent *is* definite, so that the clause describes or serves as an epithet; as *de iis autem, quos ipsi vidimus, neminem fere praetermittimus eorum, quos aliquando dicentes vidimus,* 'of those, however, whom we have seen ourselves, we pass over scarcely any one of them, whom we have at some time or other seen speaking.'

Obs. 1 It is to be observed that the antecedent may be definite, and the relative sentence descriptive, although all the particulars in the description may not be fixed; thus: *quidquid id est, timeo Danaos et dona ferentes,* 'whatever that particular, definite thing—the wooden horse—may be, I fear the Greeks even when they offer us gifts.'

Obs. 2 A definite antecedent is presumed, and therefore the indicative is used, in such idiomatic phrases as *quae tua est virtus*, 'such is your virtue;' *quod scribis*, 'as to what you write.'

(c) We *must* use the indicative after *ut* in all mere comparisons; as *ut orator de iis rebus..., ut heri Crassus dicebat, optime potest dicere*, 'as an orator, as Crassus was saying yesterday, can speak best' (Cic. *de Orat.* II. 9, 37).

175 II. (a) We *must* use the subjunctive in all expressions of supposition or possibility, as opposed to statements of fact; consequently, in all the optative, potential, and prohibitory clauses, which have been given under the separate tenses.

(b) We *must* use the subjunctive after relatives and relative particles, whenever the antecedent is vague or indefinite, so that the clause does not define or describe, but is dependent for its meaning on something in the main sentence. Thus the subjunctive appears:

(1) In all dependent questions after relatives, interrogatives, and the particles enumerated above, where other examples are given (108, (c)); as *quis haec fecit?* 'who did these things?' but, *nescio, quis haec fecerit*, 'I know not who has done these things;' *saepe ne utile quidem est scire quid futurum sit*, 'it is often not even profitable to know what is about to be.'

Obs. Nescio quis is often used either as a parenthesis or as a periphrasis for the nominative, and is therefore followed by the indicative mood; as *nescio quid majus nascitur Iliade*, 'some poem (I know not exactly what) is coming forth, which will surpass the Iliad;' *nescio quis teneros oculus mihi fascinat agnos*, 'some evil eye (I know not whose), is bewitching the lambs to my sorrow' (see 174, Obs. 1). That *nescio quis* was regarded as equivalent even rhythmically to a single word is shown by its position in such lines as

Summa leves hinc *nescio qua* dulcedine laetas.
(Virg. *Georg.* IV. 55)—

for Virgil carefully abstains from making the third foot consist in a single word. In Virgil, *Ecl.* III. 106, some MSS. and editions read:

Dic, quibus in terris inscripti nomina regum
Nascuntur flores.

which, if it stands, must be a direct question; 'tell me—in what lands do such flowers grow?' but the true reading is *nascuntur*, as we have in the preceding line: *dic, quibus in terris pateat;* and the question in each case is indirect.

SYNTAX OF VERBS.

(2) In all sentences connected by *ne* or *ut* with verbs of fearing; as

Metuo ne dum minuere velim laborem, augeam, 'I fear, lest, while I am wishing to lessen my trouble, I shall increase it.'

Adulatores, si quem laudant, vereri se dicunt, ut illius facta verbis consequi possint, 'flatterers, if they praise any one, say they fear that they will not be able to express his actions in their words.'

(3) In all final sentences, i.e. those which express an end, purpose or result, after the conjunctions mentioned above (112, (G)), and the relative pronoun used as a substitute for them; as

Edimus ut vivamus; non vivimus ut edamus, 'we eat to the end that we may live, we do not live in order that we may eat.'

Legem brevem esse oportet, quo facilius ab imperitis teneatur, 'a law ought to be short in order that it may the more easily be remembered by the unlearned.'

Nihil tam difficile est quin quaerendo investigari possit, 'nothing is so difficult, that it cannot be discovered by inquiry.'

Parmenio regem deterrere voluit quominus medicamentum biberet, 'Parmenio wished to deter the king, to the end that he should not drink the medicine.'

Clusini legatos Romam, qui auxilium a senatu peterent, misere, 'the people of Clusium sent ambassadors to Rome, to the end, or with the view, that they should ask assistance from the senate.'

(4) In all illative or intensive sentences, after *ut* or *qui*, whether the antecedent precedes or not, provided only that we can render *qui* by ' such or such a kind that ;' as

Epaminondas fuit disertus (or *tam disertus*), *ut nemo ei par esset*, 'Epaminondas was so eloquent, that no one was a match for him.'

Nunc dicis aliquid quod ad rem pertineat, 'now you are saying something of such a kind that (*tale ut*) it pertains to the subject.'

Obs. To this rule belong all such phrases as *quis sum cujus aures laedi nefas sit ?* = *num talis sum ut, &c.*; *major sum quam cui possit fortuna nocere* = *major quam talis ut mihi, &c.*; *nemo est qui nesciat* = *nemo est talis ut nesciat; non est quod invideas* = *non est tale ut invideas; non quo haberem quod scriberem, sed, &c.* = *non ita ut haberem, &c.*; *inventi sunt multi, qui parati essent* = *tales ut parati essent ; quis est qui non oderit ?* = *talis ut non oderit; o fortunate adolescens, qui inveneris* = *o tali fortuna, ut inveneris;* and after *dignus, indignus, aptus, idoneus, unus, solus*, the relative presumes a construction in which *talis ut* might occur;

INDICATIVE AND SUBJUNCTIVE.

as *indignus eras qui faceres injuriam = non conveniebat dignitati tuae ut faceres, non talis eras ut faceres*. With regard to such phrases as *est qui, sunt qui*, it is to be remarked that if the phrase *est qui* or *sunt qui* is to be taken as one word equivalent to 'some one,' 'some person,' it will be followed by the indicative like *nescio quis* (above, 173, (b), (1), *Obs*.): but if it means 'there is a person or there are persons so constituted or qualified as to do such and such things,' it must be followed by the subjunctive; thus we have *sunt quos curriculo pulverem Olympicum collegisse juvat*, 'some persons delight in the chariot-races at Olympia;' but, *sunt qui censeant una animum et corpus occidere*, 'there are some persons so constituted that (*tales ut*) they think that the soul and body perish together.'

(5) In oblique narration, when the relative sentence contains the words or reasons of others; as

Socrates accusatus est, quod corrumperet juventutem, 'Socrates was accused of corrupting the young men' (i. e. the accuser said so).

Aristides ob eam causam expulsus est patriâ, quod praeter modum justus esset, 'Aristides was expelled from his country simply because, as they said, he was too just.'

And especially in relative sentences dependent on an accusative with an infinitive, although, in the direct sentence, the verbs following the relative would stand in the indicative (128, XI.; below, 205, (5)); compare the direct and oblique expression of the same sentiments in Cicero and Quintilian:

| An earum rerum *est*, quae *sciuntur*; oratoris omnis actio opinionibus non scientiâ *continetur*; nam et apud eos *dicimus* qui *nesciunt*, et ea *dicimus* quae *nescimus* ipsi. (*De Oratore*, II. 7.) | Artem earum rerum *esse quae sciantur*; oratoris omnem actionem opinione non scientiâ *contineri*; quia et apud eos *dicat* qui *nesciant*, et ipse *dicat* aliquando quod *nesciat*. (*Inst. Orat.* II. 17, 37.) |

(6) In narratives, when repeated action is signified by the relative sentence (see *Gr. Gr.* Art. 380); as

Ut quisque maxime laboraret locus, aut ipse occurrebat aut aliquos mittebat (Caes. *B. G.* VII. 17, § 4), 'as each post was most in peril, (so often) he either came up himself, or sent others.'

Quemcunque lictor jussu consulis prehendisset, tribunus mitti jubebat (Liv. III. 11), 'as often as the lictor had seized a man, so often the tribune ordered him to be let go.'

But *quoties* takes the indicative, e.g. Virg. Æn. XII. 483: *quoties oculos conjecit in hostem.*

(7) In comparisons, after *quasi, tanquam, ac si, ceu, velut,* signifying 'just as if,' and *dummodo, dum, modo,* signifying ' provided only,' when possibility, as distinguished from reality, is supposed or assumed; as

Quasi id curem! 'just as if I care for that!'
Tanquam Asia sit clausa, sic nihil perfertur ad nos, 'just as if Asia were closed, no news reaches us.'
Oderint, dum metuant, 'let them hate, provided only they fear.'
Dummodo ne quid imminuat ejus gloriae, quam consecuti sumus, 'provided only that it detracts nothing from that renown, which we have obtained.'

176 III. We *may* use either the indicative or the subjunctive in the following cases, but with the distinctions of meaning which will be indicated.

(1) In conditional sentences, after *si, nisi,* &c., the indicative expresses possibility without any uncertainty, but the subjunctive expresses uncertainty, mere assumption, or impossibility (128, XVI.). In such phrases as *nemo saltat sobrius, nisi forte insanit,* 'no one dances when sober, unless perchance he is deranged,' the possibility is taken for granted. And thus *fortasse,* 'perhaps,' always takes the indicative, but *forsitan* and *forsan,* with the same meaning, though a different application, are always followed by the subjunctive and frequently by the perfect; thus, *ego fortasse vaticinor,* 'perhaps I am prophesying,' where the possibility is assured; but *forsitan quaeratis,* 'you may perhaps ask,' *forsitan aliquis dixerit,* 'some one may perchance have said,' where there is a mere assumption, as in *quaerat, dixerit aliquis* (above, 172, L (d); III. (b)).

(2) In temporal sentences, (a) *quum* or *ubi* or *ut,* 'when,' *postquam,* 'after,' and *simulac,* 'as soon as,' are always followed by the indicative, when a particular or definite time is denoted; as

Qui non propulsat injuriam a suis, quum potest, injuste facit, 'he acts unjustly who does not repel injury from his friends, when (i.e. on those definite occasions when) he has the power.'
Ut sumus in Ponto ter frigore constitit Ister, 'since we have been in Pontus the Danube has stood frozen three times.'
Ubi is finem fecit, 'when he made an end.'

But the imperfect or pluperfect of the subjunctive is always used after *quum* or *ubi*, 'when,' if we wish to indicate not only the time, but a necessarily antecedent circumstance. In this case we may often render the phrase by the English participle; as *quum videret*, 'seeing' or 'upon seeing;' *quum vidisset*, 'having seen' or 'in consequence of his having seen.' Thus,

In Cumano quum essem, venit ad me Hortensius, 'during my stay in his neighbourhood, as a sort of consequence of my being there, Hortensius came to see me.'

Alexander, quum interemisset Clitum, vix manus a se abstinuit, 'Alexander, having killed Clitus, as a result or consequence, was all but laying violent hands on himself.'

Id ubi dixisset, hastam emittebat, 'having first said this' or 'as soon as ever he had said this, he proceeded to throw his spear.'

See below, 200, (γ).

(b) *Antequam* and *priusquam* are used with the indicative when there is merely a mark of tense and no hypothetical connexion, but we have the subjunctive when the preceding event is supposed to be in some sort the cause of the subsequent; thus,

Tempestas minatur antequam surgat, 'a tempest threatens before it rises' (but if there is to be a tempest at all, it must rise).

Medico priusquam conetur aegro adhibere medicinam, natura corporis cognoscenda est, 'the physician must learn the nature of the body before he attempts to give medicine to the sick' (where a condition is involved).

But, *Omnia experiri certum est priusquam pereo*, 'I am resolved to try every thing before I am ruined' (a consummation which I hope to avoid).

Neque prius fugere destiterunt, quam ad Rhenum pervenerunt, 'they did not leave off running away, until they got to the Rhine' (a mere mark of time).

And we may say either *antequam dicam* or *antequam dicere instituo* after a future (cf. Cic. Philipp. L 1, with pro *Murena*, I. 1), because the latter is a periphrasis of the subjunctive present.

See below, 200, (δ).

(c) *Donec, quoad*, 'until,' 'as long as,' and *dum*, 'until,' 'while,' 'as long as,' take the indicative when they merely indicate continuance in time; but if they imply a cause or condition, and so approximate to the other meaning of *dum*, they are followed by the subjunctive; as

350   SYNTAX OF VERBS.

Priami dum regna manebant, 'while, as long as, during the time that, the kingdom of Priam lasted:'

Milo in senatu fuit illo die, quoad senatus dimissus est, 'Milo was in the senate on that day until the senate was adjourned.'

Donec rediit Marcellus, silentium fuit, 'the silence lasted until Marcellus returned.'

But, *Haud desinam donec perfecero,* 'I will not leave off until I shall have accomplished it' (I will do so only on that proviso).

Tertia dum regnantem riderit aetas, 'until the third age shall have seen him reigning.'

Exspectas fortasse dum haec dicat, 'you are waiting perhaps until he says this' (it is the condition or cause of your patience).

(3) In causal sentences, (a) *quum,* 'since,' ' because,' is followed by a subjunctive when the circumstances are intimately connected, so that the sentence may be rendered by our participle (as above, 176, (2)); but it takes the indicative when the cause is introduced as an independent fact; thus,

Quum vita sine amicis insidiarum et metus plena sit, ratio ipsa monet amicitias comparare, 'since life without friends is (or ' life being') full of treachery and fear, reason itself warns us to form friendships.'

But, *Gratulor tibi, quum apud Dolabellam tantum vales,* 'I congratulate you, because (as a fact) you have so much influence with Dolabella.'

(b) *Quod, quia, quoniam, quandoquidem,* which are much more frequently used than *quum* in the case just mentioned, take the indicative except in the case stated above, (175, (b), (3)), when the cause is assigned as the opinion of some other person, so that the sentence is oblique; thus, *Fecisti mihi pergratum quod Serapionis librum mihi misisti,* 'you have obliged me by sending the book of Serapion:' but, *Hic tu me accusas quod me afflictem,* 'here you accuse me because (as you say) I afflict myself.'

(c) *Quippe qui,* and *ut* or *utpote qui* generally take the subjunctive; as *Plato a Dionysio violatus erat, quippe quem venumdari jussisset,* 'Plato had been ill used by Dionysius, for he had ordered him to be sold.'

(4) In concessive sentences we may have either an extreme supposition or the statement of a fact; in the latter case we have

the indicative, in the former the subjunctive is used. *Quamquam*, 'although,' *utut*, 'however much,' are generally and properly followed by the indicative; *etsi*, *etiamsi*, *tametsi*, 'even if,' take the indicative, when the possibility of the extreme supposition is taken for granted; but the subjunctive when the supposition is conceived as impossible; *licet*, 'it is allowable,' *quamvis* or *quantumvis*, 'as much as you please,' and *ut*, 'however much,' properly and regularly take the subjunctive, although the last is used parenthetically with the indicative in some few instances, chiefly in the poets, who also use *quanquam* in the sense of *quamvis* with the subjunctive. Thus we have

Romani, quanquam fessi erant, tamen procedunt, 'the Romans, although they were tired, nevertheless advance.'

Dis quanquam geniti essent, 'although born of the gods.' (Virg. Æn. VI. 394.)

Tametsi viciase debeo, tamen de meo jure decedam, 'although I ought to have gained the day, nevertheless I will relinquish my rights.'

Cur Siculi te defensorem habere nolint, etiamsi taceant, satis dicunt; verum non tacent, 'the Sicilians sufficiently declare, even though they were silent, why they would not like to have you for their advocate; but they are not silent.'

Fremant omnes licet; dicam quod sentio, 'although all exclaim against it (they may all do so, it is allowed), I will nevertheless say what I think.'

Quod turpe est, id, quamvis occultetur, tamen honestum fieri nullo modo potest, 'that which is disgraceful, let it be concealed as much as you please, still can never become honourable.'

Pollio amat nostram (quamvis est rustica) musam, 'Pollio loves our muse,—albeit she is as countrified as you please.'

Ut fueris dignior, non competitor in culpâ est, 'you may have been as much more worthy as you please, still your competitor is not in fault.'

§ 3. *Construction of the Infinitive, Participles and other Verbals.*

(1) *Infinitive.*

177 The infinitive, which expresses the mere action of the verb, may be considered as a noun, undeclined but used either as the subject of a proposition, or as the object of certain verbs; and when the infinitive has a subject of its own, this is put in the accusative, unless it is attracted into the case governed by the finite verb on which it depends.

(a) The infinitive, with all that belongs to it, is sometimes the subject of a copulative verb, the predicate being some noun in the nominative case; as

Diligere parentes prima naturae lex est, 'to love one's parents is the first law of nature.'

Apud Persas summa laus est fortiter pugnare, 'among the Persians to fight bravely is the highest excellence.'

(b) The infinitive sentence is the subject of all verbs of an impersonal nature whether the copula is expressed or included; as

Victorem parcere victis aequum est, 'that a conqueror should spare the vanquished is a right thing.'

Ad salutem civium inventas esse leges constat, 'that laws were invented for the safety of citizens is an established point.'

Obs. If the impersonal verb is followed by a dative and an adjective, the latter may either agree with the dative or be in the accus. after the infin.; thus we may say either *licet illis esse beatis* or *beatos.* When the gen. follows *est,* the accus. is resumed by the adjective; see Cic. *Brut.* 56.

(c) The infinitive is the object of all verbs of seeing, hearing, knowing, thinking, saying, &c.; as

Audio te contumeliose de me dicere, 'I hear that you are speaking of me in an insulting manner.'

Ego tibi hoc confirmo, nihilo te nunc majore in discrimine esse, 'I assure you of this, that you are not now in any greater danger.'

(d) The infinitive appears as the necessary supplement to those verbs which contain no complete predication in themselves, for instance, those which express will, obligation, power, necessity, commencement, custom, or cessation; as

Malo beneficii mei oblivisci, quam periculi vestri meminisse, 'I rather wish to forget my kindness, than remember your danger.'

Quae fortuita sunt, certa esse non possunt, 'those things which are casual, cannot be certain.'

(e) The infinitive with the personal or reflexive pronoun follows a verb of believing, hoping, promising, and in the last two

INFINITIVE, PARTICIPLES, &c. 359

cases we have generally the future active participle without the substantive verb; as

Credo me tibi esse carissimum, 'I believe that I am most dear to you.'

Spero me propediem istuc venturum esse (or without *esse*), 'I hope that I shall soon come to the place where you are.'

Cæsar pollicetur se iis auxilio futurum, 'Cæsar promises that he will assist them.'

Obs. 1 The accusative of personal pronouns may be omitted before the infinitive when the subject is the same, and the poets even imitate the Greek construction and place the predicate after *esse* in the nom.; as *Rettulit Ajax esse Jovis pronepos,* 'Ajax declared that he was the great grandson of Jupiter;' like the Greek ἔφασκεν Διὸς εἶναι, though the more common construction is, *se pronepotem esse.* So also, *Phaselus ille quem videtis, hospites, ait fuisse navium celerrimus,* 'that skiff, which ye see, O strangers, says that it was the swiftest of vessels.' After verbs of *wishing* and *endeavouring,* the pronoun is generally omitted, and the nominative retained when the subject is the same; as *eruditus fieri cupio,* 'I desire to be learned.' After *volo* and *nolo* in particular the past passive participle is used with or without *esse,* to denote the complete accomplishment of the wish; as *Corinthum exstinctam esse volo,* 'I would have Corinth destroyed;' *id factum nollem,* 'I would rather not have that done.'

Obs. 2 In most cases the tense of the infinitive is that of the dependent verb in English; as *arbitror te dixisse,* 'I presume that you said;' *promittebat se venturum,* 'he promised that he would come;' *audio hominem laudatum iri,* 'I hear that the man will be praised.' Sometimes the future is expressed by a periphrasis of *fore* or *futurum esse* for a continuous state, and *futurum fuisse* for a contingent futurity; as *spero fore ut contingat id nobis,* 'I hope it will so happen that this may fall to our lot;' *ignorabat futurum fuisse ut urbs dederetur,* 'he knew not that it would have come to pass that the city would be given up.' But after verbs expressing possibility or obligation, the past tense is expressed by the main verb, and the infinitive is always present; thus we say *licuit mihi ire,* 'it was allowed to me to go' = 'I might have gone;' *facere potui,* 'I had the power to do it' = 'I could have done it;' *oportuit te dicere,* 'it behoved you to speak' = 'you ought to have spoken.' Although *spero* is generally followed by the future, according to the rule (above, (e)), there are some few instances in which it takes the present infinitive; as *Spero nostram amicitiam non egere testibus.* Cic. *ad div.* ll. 2. *Magnitudine poenae reliquos deterrere sperans.* Cæs. *B. C.* lll. 8.

Obs. 3 We have an infinitive of the passive voice after *coeptus sum* and *desitus sum*; as *Desiderari coepta est Epaminondae diligentia,* 'the diligence of Epaminondas began (was begun) to be missed.' *Papirius is, qui primus Papisius vocari est desitus,* 'that Papirius, who was the first who left off (was left off) being called Papisius.' We have also sometimes a passive infinitive after *solitus sum.*

Obs. 4 We occasionally find the present participle instead of the infinitive, after *audire, videre,* and *facere* (in the sense 'to introduce or exhibit in writing'); as *Heraclitum studiose audivi contra Antiochum disserentem,* 'I have heard Heraclitus eagerly reasoning against Antiochus.' *Xenophon facit Socratem disputantem, formam Dei quaeri non oportere,* 'Xenophon introduces Socrates arguing that the form of the Deity ought not to be inquired into.'

Obs. 5 Verbs of seeing, &c. (above, (c)) do not take the infinitive in an indirect interrogation; thus we say *ex his intelligitur, quanta Ciceronis fuerit auctoritas* (above, 128, XII.), not *quantam Ciceronis fuisse auctoritatem.* But it is good Latin to say *Quantam censes Ciceronis fuisse auctoritatem,* because in this case *quantam* is a mere predicate.

Obs. 6 If the dependent infinitive has an accusative of the object as well as an accusative of the subject, and if the context is not sufficient to remove all ambiguity, the active construction is changed into the passive; thus we say *Clitarchus narravit Darium ab Alexandro superatum esse,* not *Darium superasse Alexandrum.* But the context shows that *Amazones* is the subject in *Constat magnam Asiae partem tenuisse Amazones.*

178 Whenever we wish to express the *end* rather than the *object* of an action, that is, whenever the preposition 'to' prefixed to an English infinitive means 'to the end that,' or 'in order to,' we must use *ut* with the subjunctive instead of the infinitive in Latin. Thus, as a general rule, we have *ut* with the subjunctive after verbs of *asking, commanding, advising, intending,* and *effecting;* as

Id agit ut se conservet, 'he does his best to (i.e. to the end that he may) preserve himself.'

Te oro et hortor ut diligens sis, 'I beg and exhort you to (i.e. to the end or intent that you may) be diligent.'

Obs. 1 Some verbs belonging to this class take the infinitive as well as the subjunctive with *ut,* but with a difference of meaning: thus when *moneo* or *admoneo* signifies 'to inform or remind' it takes the infinitive; as *moneo te hoc falsum esse,* 'I apprize you that this is false;' but we have *moneo ut quiescas,* 'I exhort you to be quiet.' *Persuadeo,* 'I convince,' takes the infinitive; as *persuasit mihi hoc verum esse,* 'he convinced me that this was true;' but when it means 'I induce' it is followed by the final sentence with *ut;* as *quis tibi persuasit ut hoc faceres?* 'who so far persuaded you that you did this?' i.e. 'who induced you to do it?' *Jubeo,* 'I order,' takes the infinitive because it expresses the thing commanded rather than the purpose; it may however have the subjunctive with *ut,* when it is used absolutely in the sense 'I give orders,' and this is generally the case with all other verbs of commanding. *Fac,* 'suppose,' and *efficio,* 'I prove,' take the infinitive, but *facio,* 'I effect, accomplish, bring it to pass,' is so regularly used with the final clause that *facio ut* is often a mere periphrasis for a verb of action; as *faciunt inviti ut dent = dant inviti*, 'they give unwillingly;' *libenter ac saepe fecerunt ut laudarent*, 'they often and willingly praised.' The same is the case with many verbs expressing a result, a consequence, a contingency, as *fit ut, fieri potest ut, accidit ut, accedit ut, sequitur ut*, &c.

Obs. 2 Some verbs of willingness or permission, which usually take the infinitive, and some verbs of asking and advising, take the subjunctive without *ut*; this is particularly the case with *fac, velim, nolim, malim, licet, necesse est*, and *oportet; as tu velim animo sapienti sis*, 'I wish you to be wise.'

179 Whenever we wish to express the *object* or *reference* of an emotion with some indication of the *cause*, we use *quod* with the finite verb instead of the infinitive. This is particularly the case with verbs of grief, joy, surprise and admiration, and the sense is sometimes strengthened by a demonstrative antecedent; as

Doleo quod stomacharis, 'I am sorry that (or 'because') you are angry.'

Illud est admiratione dignum, quod captivos retinendos censuit, 'that is particularly worthy of admiration, namely, that he advised the retention of the prisoners.'

But *gaudeo, doleo, miror* may also take the infinitive (e.g. Cic. *Att.* XV. 27; VI. 3; *ad div.* L 7), and there is only a shade of difference between the objective and causal construction.

180 There are three cases in which the infinitive may be used without the support of any finite verb:

(a) In the oblique narration, where it may even appear in relative sentences; as *se quoque, quum transiret mare, non Ciliciam aut Lydiam, quippe tanti belli exiguam hanc esse mercedem, sed Persepolim*, &c., *imperio suo destinasse*, where *scripsit* or *dixit* is to be supplied.

(b) As an equivalent to the present or imperfect indicative, which is probably a result of the oblique narration, the main verb being tacitly supposed; thus, *ingenium ejus haud absurdum; posse versus facere*, &c., 'it is reported that her abilities were the reverse of contemptible; that is, she could make verses, &c.;' *postquam in aedes irruperunt, diversi regem quaerere,* 'after they broke into the palace [we are told], they went in different directions to seek the king.'

Obs. The ellipsis of *coepit, coeperunt,* which is given in most Grammars, is not always applicable, and seems not to be founded in truth.

(c) In exclamations the accusative is used with the infinitive, as a merely objective sentence, just as the accusative alone is used with interjections (168); thus, *adeone hominem esse infelicem quenquam,* 'could any man at all be so unlucky!'

(2) *Participles.*

181 The participle, which must be regarded as a verb used adjectively, retains the verbal meaning of its tenses, so far as they are distinguished in this form, and governs the same case as its verb, except when it has assumed a secondary and attributive meaning; thus,

Dionysius cultros metuens tonsorios candenti carbone sibi adurebat capillum, 'Dionysius fearing the barber's razor used to burn his hair with red hot charcoal.'

Caesar aggressus Pompeianos ex vallo deturbavit, 'Caesar having attacked the Pompeians, drove them from the rampart.'

Quid nimis grave est in homines tanti facinoris convictos? 'what is too severe for men convicted of so great a crime?'

Atticus liberalitate utens nullas inimicitias gessit, 'Atticus, employing liberality, cherished no enmity.'

Obs. 1 When the present participle does not signify an action but a condition it becomes a mere adjective and is followed by a genitive (see above, 151). On the other hand, a verbal noun may take the case of the verb from which it is formed; as *Quid tibi istunc tactio est?* 'what have you to do with touching that man?' *Quid tibi hanc receptio ad te rei meum virum?* 'what right have you to receive my husband into your house?' This usage seems, however, to be confined to interrogations.

Obs. 2 As the passive voice has no present participle, and as only deponent verbs have a past participle with an active signification, it is obvious that the application of the Latin participle to the expression of subordinate ideas must be very limited. And the want of a definite article leaves us no outward means of distinguishing between the participle as an epithet or description, and the same word as a causal, concessive, or hypothetical term. Hence, while on the one hand it is generally more convenient to substitute a complete sentence with some conjunction for the participle, as used in Greek, on the other hand, the Latin participle easily passes into a mere adjective, and, from that, becomes fixed in use as a substantive. Thus the active participles *adolescens, parens,* and *sapiens* are constantly used as substantives; *secundus,* 'following,' is always an adjective, 'second,' i. e. 'following in time or order,' and is generally used in a metaphorical or applied sense, as *secundus ventus,* 'a fair wind,' i.e. 'one which follows the ship,' *secundas res,* 'fair, favouring, prosperous circumstances.' It is used properly in Virgil, *Æn.* 1. 156 : *curru secundo,* 'the chariot which follows them,' i.e. the steeds. The passive participles *acutus, arguus,* &c., are almost always employed as epithets, and the neuters *commentum, consultum, dictum, furtum, placitum, praeceptum, scriptum,* &c., are to all intents and purposes substantives. And some of the participles in -*ns* have their degrees of comparison like the ordinary adjectives.

182 The participle is used in its proper or verbal sense,

(a) As a secondary predicate or apposition to the subject, which may be resolved into a parallel verb with a copulative conjunction; as

Lex est voluntas Dei, imperans honesta, prohibens contraria, 'law is the will of God, and it commands what is virtuous, and prohibits the contrary.'

(b) As a tertiary predicate or apposition to the object, which may also be resolved as in the former case; but here the participle is in the perfect passive, and precedes in the resolved construction; as

Triginta tyranni plurimorum bona publicata inter se diviserunt, 'the thirty tyrants confiscated and divided among themselves the property of very many persons.'

Antiocho bellum a Romanis denuntiatum est, quod ille facile susceptum infeliciter gessit, 'the Romans declared war against Antiochus, which he undertook without hesitation but carried on unfortunately.'

(c) In temporal sentences; as

Domum reversus, litteras inveni tuas, 'when I got home, I found your letter.'

(d) In final sentences; as

Pergit ad Hammonem consulturus oraculum, 'he goes to Jupiter Hammon, for the purpose of consulting the oracle.'

(e) In causal sentences; as

Aer eueffins huc et illuc ventos efficit, 'the air by rushing to and fro (i.e. because it does so) produces winds.'

(f) In concessive sentences, sometimes with *quamvis,* &c. added; as

Caesarem milites, quamvis recusantem, ultro in Africam sunt secuti, 'the soldiers went so far as to accompany Cæsar to Africa, although he refused to have them.'

304   SYNTAX OF VERBS.

(g) In the ablative absolute, as hypothetical, temporal, causal, or concessive; as

Tarquinio regnante, 'when Tarquin was king.'

Antonius, repudiata Octavia, Cleopatram duxit uxorem, 'Antony, having divorced Octavia (i.e. after he had done so), married Cleopatra.'

Comprehendi non poterat, tot Persarum millibus laturis opem regi, 'he could not be taken, because so many thousand Persians were likely to assist their king.'

Proposita sibi morte, 'although death was set before him.'

Obs. 1 In some passive participles the ablative absolute is used impersonally to denote the previous state of things which caused or suggested the main action; as *Alexander, audito Darium appropinquare, &c.,* 'Alexander, it being heard (i.e. intelligence having been brought) that Darius was drawing near, &c.'

The participles generally used in this way are *audito, cognito, comperto, desperato, nunciato, edicto.*

Obs. 2 Some passive participles are used in the neuter accus. after *habeo,* to form a periphrastic perfect, as in many of the modern languages; such are *cognitum, comprehensum, constitutum, deliberatum, exploratum, perspectum, persuasum, &c.*; as *hoc cognitum habeo = hoc cognovi.* All these, except *persuasum,* may agree with the object of the verb; as *Omnes habeo cognitos sensus adolescentis,* 'I have learnt all the feelings of the young man.'

(3) *Gerunds and Gerundives.*

183 The participle in *-ndus* is really only another form of that in *-ns*; it is therefore present in tense and active in signification; as

Volvenda dies, en, attulit ultro, 'time rolling on has brought it to you unexpectedly.' (Virg. Æn. IX. 7.)

Quae ante conditam condendamve urbem traduntur, 'traditions derived from a period when the city was neither built nor building.' (Liv. *Præfat.*)

184 The participle in *-ndus* is generally found as a substitute for some use of the infinitive active (above, 70, (o), *Obs.* 2); and it is called the *gerundium* or *gerund,* when it governs the case of the verb, and the *gerundivum* or *gerundive,* when it agrees with the object; thus in *consilium capiendi urbem* we have a *gerund,* but in *consilium urbis capiendae,* a *gerundive,* and both phrases mean 'the design of taking the city.' This *gerundive* is merely

an attraction; for *dandus* = *dans*, means 'giving;' *ad dandum opes* means 'for giving riches;' and this is attracted into the case of the object in *ad opes dandus*, 'for riches-giving.' with precisely the same signification.

185 This attraction always takes place in the nominative after the impersonal *est*, in the sense of 'it is the duty, part, obligation, or destiny,' so that the verb becomes personal; in such a phrase as *sapientis est seipsum nosse*, 'it is the part of a wise man to know himself,' we should not think of inserting the *gerund* or *gerundive*; and we might say also, *est Romanorum delere Carthaginem*, 'it is the part of the Romans to destroy Carthage;' but if, instead of the genitive with the infinitive, we had the dative of the person, the only allowable construction would be that of the attracted *gerund* or *gerundive: delenda vobis est Carthago*, 'Carthage is for you to destroy,' = 'you ought to destroy it.' This would commonly be rendered 'Carthage is to be destroyed,' and, from our idiom, it has been supposed that the participle in *-ndus* is future and passive. But it is often a matter of indifference in English, whether we use the active or passive infinitive; thus, 'he is a man to love,' = 'he is a man to be loved;' 'I give you this to eat,' = 'I give you this to be eaten,' &c.; and this is the reason why a similar interchange has been erroneously presumed in Latin. No one can doubt that the *gerund* is active; but if *vivendum est* = *vivere est* = *oportet vivere*, there can be no reason why the *gerundive* should not be active also; for they are used sometimes in the very same sentence; as *nunc est bibendum, nunc pede libero pulsanda tellus*, 'now we must drink, now we must beat the ground with free foot;' and the *gerundive* and active infinitive are used indifferently, though the former is preferred, after verbs which express that a thing is given out, commissioned, or undertaken to be done; such as *do, trado, permitto, accipio*; thus we may have *Antigonus Eumenem mortuum propinquis sepeliendum tradidit*, 'Antigonus gave up the dead body of Eumenes to his friends for burial' (i.e. 'to bury'). (Corn. Nep. *Eumen*. 13); or, *tristitium et metus tradam protervis in mare Creticum portare ventis*, 'I will give up sorrow and fear to the wanton winds for transportation (i.e. 'to carry') to the Cretan sea.' (Hor. 1 *Carm*. xxvi. 1.)

186 The gerund in *-dum*, as it is called, is always dependent on prepositions, and mostly on *ad* or *inter*; as

Locus ad agendum amplissimus, 'a place most honourable to plead in.'

If the verb of the gerund requires an accusative, the gerundive is commonly preferred; as *ad tolerandos labores,* 'for enduring labours,' because *tolero* is transitive.

187 The gerund in *-di* is always used as a genitive after substantives implying *desire, design, hope, power, cause,* &c.; and after relative adjectives which require a genitive to complete their meaning; as

Innatus amor habendi, 'a natural desire of possessing stores.'
Studiosus erat audiendi, 'he was very fond of hearing.'

If the verb of the gerund requires an accusative, the gerundive is preferred; as *consuetudo hominum immolandorum,* 'the custom of sacrificing human beings,' because *immolo* is transitive. The gerundive *repetundus* is used only in the gen. and abl. pl. to agree with *pecuniarum* and *pecuniis,* expressed or understood (generally the former in Cicero), and in the sense of 'extortion, illegal exaction;' as *legem de pecuniis repetundis tulit,* 'he brought in a law about extortion,' i.e. 'concerning money to be redemanded and refunded' (see Tacit. *Ann.* XIII. 33, and cf. *Varron.* p. 430).

188 The gerund in *-do* is either dative or ablative. (a) When dative, it usually follows adjectives and verbs, to signify limitation or design; the adjectives most generally used with the dative of the gerund are *accommodatus, aptus, ineptus, bonus, habilis, idoneus, par, utilis,* and *inutilis;* after which, however, the gerund in *-dum* with *ad* may be substituted for the dative; thus we have both *utilis bibendo* and *utilis ad bibendum,* 'useful for drinking;' the verbs used with this gerund are generally *sum* and its compounds; as *non solvendo est,* 'he is insolvent;' *scribendo adfuerunt,* 'they were present at the drawing up of the decree.'

(b) When ablative, the gerund in *-do* either denotes the instrument, in which case, of course, no preposition is necessary; as

Alitur vitium viritque tegendo, 'the disease is nourished and lives by concealment;'

or it is an ablative depending on *ab, de, ex,* or *in;* as

Aristotelem non deterruit a scribendo amplitudo Platonis, 'the grandeur of Plato did not deter Aristotle from writing.'

Summa voluptas ex discendo capitur, 'the greatest pleasure is derived from learning.'

If the verb of the gerund requires an accusative case, the *gerundive* is preferred to the gerund in *-do*, whether it be dative or ablative; as

Tresviri reipublicae constituendae, 'a board of three commissioners for settling the constitution.'

Consul placandis dis dat operam, 'the consul pays attention to the appeasing of the gods.'

Fortitudo in laboribus periculisque subeundis cernitur, 'courage is manifested in undergoing toils and dangers.'

(4) Supines.

169 The supine in *-tum* is generally used after verbs of motion. It may be changed, without any difference of meaning, into the final subjunctive with *ut*; thus,

Spectatum veniunt, veniunt spectentur ut ipsae, 'they come to see (we might say also *ut spectent*); they come that they may be seen themselves.'

Obs. 1 The synonymous substitutions for the supine in *-tum* will appear from the equivalence of the following usages:

1. Venerunt legati *petitum pacem*.
2. .... *petituri pacem*.
3. .... *ad petendum pacem* (this is rare).
4. .... *ad pacem petendam*.
5. .... *pacem petendi causa*.
6. .... *pacis petendae causa*.
7. .... *ut pacem peterent*.
8. .... *qui pacem peterent*.

Obs. 2 The various expressions after which the supine in *-tum* is regularly used may be seen in the following examples:

Coriolanus in Volscos *exulatum abiit*. Liv. II. 35. Galli gallinacei cum sole *eunt cubitum*. Plin. x. 21. Themistocles Argos *habitatum concessit*. Corn. Nep. II. 8. Eumenes Antigonum in Mediam *hiematum coëgit redire*; ipse in finitima regione Persidis *hiematum* copias divisit. Corn. Nep. xviii. 8. Totius fere Galliæ legati ad Cæsarem *gratulatum convenerunt*. Cæs. *B. G.* I. 10. Lacedæmonii Agesilaum *bellatum miserunt* in Asiam. Corn. Nep. ix. 2. Athenienses *miserunt* Delphos *consultum*, quidnam facerent de rebus suis. Corn. Nep. IL 2. Fabius Pictor Delphos ad oraculum *missus est sciscitatum*, quibus precibus suppliciisque deos possent placare. Liv. xxII. 57. Porsena *praedatum milites* trans Tiberim aliis atque aliis locis *trajecit*. Liv. II. 11. Stultitia est, *venatum ducere invitas canes.* Plaut. *Stich.* 1. 2. 82. *Nulli negare soleo, si quis eorum me rocat. Ib.* 1. 3. 28. *Dumnorix propinquas suas nuptum in alias civitates collocavit.* Cæs. *B. G.* 1. 18. *Augustus filiam Juliam primum Marcello, deinde Marco Agrippæ nuptum dedit.* Suet. *Aug.* 63. *Spectatum admissi risum teneatis amici.* Hor. *Ars Poet.* 5.

Obs. 3 We have seen (70, 83) that the supine in *-tum* is regularly used with the passive *iri* to form the future passive of verbs, and that some compounds, as *venumdo*, also contain it; there are other paraphrases, such as *perditum eo, ultum eo,* which add little to the meaning of the verbs *perdo, ulciscor.*

Obs. 4 The poets sometimes use the common infinitive instead of the supine in *-tum;* as *pecus egit visere montes.* (Hor. 1 *Carm.* II. 7.)

190 The supine in *-tu* is used after *fas, nefas, opus,* and certain adjectives denoting quality, as *facilis, difficilis, dignus, indignus, jucundus, injucundus, acerbus, honestus, mirabilis, turpis, utilis;* but only a certain number of supines are used in this way, such as the following: *auditu, cognitu, dictu, exitu, factu, intellectu, gustatu, inceptu, inventu, memoratu, scitu, visu;* thus we have

Nefas est dictu, miseram fuisse Fabii Maximi senectutem, 'it is wrong to say that the old age of Fabius Maximus was miserable.'

Quid est tam jucundum cognitu et auditu, quam sapientibus sententiis gravibusque verbis ornata oratio? 'What is so pleasant to apprehend and hear as a speech embellished with wise sentiments and weighty words?'

Non longius quam quod scitu opus est in narrando procedetur, 'the narrative will not be carried on farther than is necessary for information.'

Pleraque dictu quam re sunt faciliora, 'most things are easier in the saying than in the doing '(i. e. more easily said than done).'

Quod factu foedum est, idem est et dictu turpe, 'that which it is abominable to do, it is also disgraceful to speak.'

Obs. 1 This supine, like that in *-tum,* may be changed into the gerund in *-dum* with *ad*; compare *quid est tam jucundum auditu* (Cic. *de Orat.* 1. 8) with *verba ad audiendum jucunda* (Id. *Ibid.* 1. 49). A dative in *-tui* is occasionally found with much the same meaning (above, 53, (a)).

Obs. 2 The poets use the infinitive instead of the supine in *-tu;* thus we have *cereus in vitium flecti; mortem spernere nobilis; opprobria fingere sævus; facilis legi, &c.*

CHAPTER IV.

SYNTAX OF SENTENCES.

§ 1. *Definitions.*

191 In speaking hitherto of the details of Latin Syntax, we have addressed ourselves to the task of determining the functions of nouns and verbs according as their different inflexions contribute to the machinery of the simple sentence. It is true that any discussion of the moods and tenses of the verb must lead to some mention of the different kinds of sentences which they assist in forming; and in a less detailed exposition of Latin Syntax, it might be sufficient to enumerate the different classes of these accessory propositions, with references to the rules in which mention has been made of their essential elements. The student, however, who wishes to take a comprehensive view of Latin construction, and to use it as an exercise of his logical faculties, must make a fresh start from a knowledge of the facts which have been presented to him in the preceding chapters; and instead of contenting himself with rules for the use of separate words, he must learn to classify and analyse the different kinds of sentences, to recognize them when he finds them in the pages of the best authors, and to construct them himself, when he attempts to express his meaning in the Latin language.

192 Connected sentences are either *co-ordinate*, or one of them is *subordinate* to the other. This distinction will be best illustrated by the two different kinds of *Hypothetical Propositions*. For in logic all propositions are regarded according to their *substance* as either *Categorical* or *Hypothetical*. Categorical propositions contain a direct assertion or predication, either *unqualified*, as *Deus est bonus*, 'God is good;' or *qualified*, as *homo prudentissimus fallī*

potest, 'the wisest man may be deceived.' *Hypothetical* propositions consist of two sentences, and they are either *conditional* or *disjunctive.* If the hypothetical proposition is *conditional,* it consists of a categorical proposition and an adverbial sentence dependent on it; as *si quid habet, dat,* 'if he has any thing, he gives it.' If the hypothetical proposition is *disjunctive,* both its members are categorical, but they are rendered hypothetical by the conjunction which connects them, as *vel habet vel non habet,* 'he either has or has not;' and if the conditional particle is then applied, the inference may also be disjunctive, as *aut dat aut non dat,* 'he either gives or does not give.' Now the adverbial sentence in the conditional hypothetical is dependent on the main or categorical sentence; its construction is regulated by the construction of the main sentence; it is therefore called subordinate; and the discussion of conditional propositions belongs to the doctrine of subordinate sentences. On the other hand, the two constituent sentences in the disjunctive hypothetical stand on an equal footing; the construction of the one does not depend on the construction of the other; they are therefore called co-ordinates, and their discussion belongs to the doctrine of co-ordinate sentences.

193 This distinction will give us the following classification.

(A) Co-ordinate sentences are

(a) *Copulative,* in which two or more sentences stand on the same footing, and the one is regarded as merely added or appended to the other.

(b) *Disjunctive,* in which there are two or more distinct alternatives, without any clause to indicate the consequence.

(c) *Adversative,* in which the predication of the subsequent clause is opposed to that of the first, but not dependent on it in construction.

(d) *Distributive,* which are generally in some sense adversative also, and in which a main sentence is divided or repeated in two or more co-ordinate and distributed parts.

(e) *Distinctive,* in which different subjects or objects are indicated by a parallel use of nouns or pronouns.

(f) *Comparative,* in which the subject or predicate of one sentence is compared with the subject or predicate of another.

CO-ORDINATE SENTENCES.

(B) Subordinate sentences are

(a) *Conditional*, which consist of a sentence containing 'if,' 'provided that, &c.,' and called a *protasis;* and a sentence giving the result of the condition, and called an *apodosis*.

(b) *Definitive*, in which a relative sentence defines or describes some antecedent in the main sentence, and thus performs the part of an epithet.

(c) *Subjunctive*, in which a relative sentence conveys a secondary predication with regard to something already predicated in the main sentence, and thus performs the part of an adverb.

(d) *Temporal*, which are supplementary to the tenses of the verb.

(e) *Objective*, which are supplementary to the cases of the noun.

(f) *Illative* or *consecutive*, when they follow a former predication as a consequence.

(g) *Final*, when they declare the end of what is predicated.

(h) *Causal*, when they declare the cause of what is asserted.

(i) *Concessive*, when they strengthen or limit by an admission.

(A) *Co-ordinate Sentences.*

§ 2. (a) *Copulative Sentences.*

194 The usage of the conjunctions, by means of which copulative sentences are constructed, has been fully discussed above (pp. 191 sqq.). Here we have to examine and analyse the logical structure of the sentences themselves; and with this view the following circumstances must be considered.

(a) Copulative sentences are expressed in three ways: (1) by a mere juxtaposition of words or sentences, as *veni, vidi, vici,* 'I came (and) I saw, (and) I conquered;' and *quae res sensibus percipiuntur, eas cernimus, audimus, gustamus, olfacimus, tangimus,* 'we see, (and) hear, (and) taste, (and) smell, (and) touch the objects of the senses:' (2) by inserting a copulative conjunction before the appended words and sentences, or the last of them; as *quamvis reus sum et panem candidum edo,* 'I am as guilty as you please, and still I eat white bread;' and *auctoritate tua nobis opus est, et*

372   SYNTAX OF SENTENCES.

consilio et etiam gratia, 'we need your authority, and your advice, and, in addition, your popularity;' (3) by inverting some word or words in the first clause, which presume and require correlative expressions in the following copulative sentence or sentences; such are *et—et, -que—-que, tum—tum, quum—quum, tum—quum, tamquam, non solum—sed etiam, partim—partim, primum—deinde—tum—postremo,* &c.; thus: *tu multis de causis vellem me convenire potuisses; primum, ut te viderem; deinde, ut tibi possem praesens gratulari; tum, ut quibus de rebus vellemus, te tuis ego meis, inter nos communicaremus; postremo, ut amicitia nostra confirmaretur vehementius,* 'for many reasons I wish you could have had an interview with me, *first,* to have the pleasure of seeing you; *then,* that I might personally express my congratulations; *again,* that we might confer together on such of our mutual affairs as we wished; *lastly,* that our friendship might be the more strongly confirmed.'

Obs. 1 The most common cases of the omission of the copulative particle, or *asyndeton,* as it is called, are those in which we wish to give animation and energy to our words, as in the celebrated announcement of Cæsar's victory quoted above; the enumeration of colleagues in office, as *Cn. Pompeio, M. Crasso, consulibus;* in examples, as *inferis iuxta fortitudinem sæpe dicimus, ut in equis, in leonibus,* Cic. *de Off.* I. 16; in enumerations of classes of persons and things opposed to one another, as *Democritus albis et alia discernere non poterat, at vero bona, mala; æqua, iniqua; honesta, turpia; utilia, inutilia; magna, parva poterat,* Cic. *Tusc.* V. 39; similarly we have side by side *primus, postremus; fanda, nefanda; publica, privata; ultro, citro;* such phrases as *Patres, Conscripti* (above, p. 192); and formal statements, such as *quidquid dare, facere oportet; æquum, bonum; sarta, tecta,* &c.

Obs. 2 Instead of omitting the copulative particle, we may produce a similar effect of emphasis and animation, by repeating some word common to all the copulative sentences; this is called *anaphora,* and is found in words of various kinds; as adverbs: *si recte Cato judicavit, non recte frumentarius ille, non recte ædium pestilentium venditor tacuit* (Cic. *de Off.* III. 16); personal pronouns: *nos deorum immortalium templa, nos muros,* &c., *nos leges,* &c., *defendimus* (Cic. *Phil.* VIII. 3); conditional particles: *si loca, si fana, si campum, si canes, si equos consuetudine adamare solemus, quantum id in hominum consuetudine facilius fieri potest?* (Cic. *Fin.* I. 20); adversative particles: *promisit, sed difficulter, sed subductis superciliis, sed malignis verbis* (Sen. *Benef.* I. 1).

Obs. 3 When the copulative sentence assumes the correlative form, *non modo (solum)—sed,* and the second member includes a negative, the negative is presumed but not expressed in the first clause; thus: *Philosophi quidam sublata assensione omnem et motum animorum et actionem rerum sustulerunt, quod non modo* (not only *not*) *recte fieri, sed omnino fieri non potest.* Cic. *Acad.* IV. 19. *Dolere non modo summum* (not only not the chief evil), *sed ne malum quidem case maximae auctoritate philosophi affirmant.* Cic. *de Off.* III. 19. *Epicurus cupiditates quasdam, quod essent plane inanes, neque necessitatem modo* (and not only did not belong to necessity), *sed ne naturam quidem attingerent, funditus ejiciendas putavit.* Cic. *Tusc.* v. 33. *Praedonum a Chalcide naves non modo Sunium superare* (not only did not dare to double Cape Sunium), *sed ne extra fretum Euripi committere aperto mari se audebant.* Liv. XXXI. 22. *Camillorum, &c., virtutes non solum in moribus nostris* (are not only not found in our habits of life), *sed vix jam in libris reperiuntur.* Cic. *Cael.* 17.

(β) In whatever way copulative sentences are expressed, their original basis is the same as that of the relative construed with its antecedent. For it is an established fact in philology that the relative was primarily a demonstrative pronoun denoting relative proximity, and there are languages which express the strongest form of the relative sentence either by the correlative of two pronouns expressing nearness, or by placing one of these in the relative clause (*New Cratylus*, § 148). While therefore the omission of the copulative conjunction stands on precisely the same footing as all other cases of *asyndeton*, we have the oldest form of the relative sentence, when the enumeration is expressed by a repetition of the same demonstrative or relative pronoun; as in *et homines et viri*, or *hominesque virique;* and we have the ordinary form of the relative sentence, when a relative is opposed to a demonstrative particle; as *hominesque et equi*, which means '*where* (there are) men, *there* (opposite to them, for *et* = ἄντα, ἀντί, *New Cratylus*, § 194) horses.'

Obs. This analysis of the copulative sentence has its special value in Latin, for it is well known that the relative is often really equivalent to the copulative conjunction with a demonstrative pronoun; thus in *Infima conditio est servorum, quibus non male praecipiunt, qui ita jubent uti ut mercenariis* (Cic. *de Off.* I. 13), the relative sentence is equivalent to *Et non male praecipiunt, qui jubent iis uti, ut mercenariis.* Similarly in *Grave ipsius conscientiae pondus est, qua sublata jacent omnia* (Cic. *Nat. Deor.* II. 33), the relative sentence is equivalent to *Et hac sublata, jacent omnia.* And so in a number of examples.

§ 3. (b) *Disjunctive Sentences.*

195 Although copulative and disjunctive sentences seem to be constructed in a perfectly similar manner, there is an essential difference in their logical value. For while, as we have seen, the copulative sentence may be reduced ultimately to that form of the

relative sentence which constitutes the conditional proposition, with both the assumption and consequence stated, the disjunctive sentences oppose two assumptions as alternatives, without stating the consequence of either (above, 192). Accordingly, while *homines-que et equi* means, 'where there are men, there are also horses,' the disjunctive sentence *vel homines, vel equi* implies, 'you may choose horses, you may choose men,' and the disjunctive sentence, *aut homines aut equi* presumes, 'where there are men, there are not horses,' for, as we have seen, *aut* and *haud* are the same word.

Obs. The examples given above (p. 194) of the disjunctive conjunctions *vel, aut,* and *ve* render it unnecessary to illustrate their use here. It must be remarked, however, that the concessive force of *vel,* which is seen in the disjunctive sentence, is really preserved by this particle, when it is said to mean 'even' or when it introduces an example. In both cases it may be rendered by 'take, if you please.' In the former usage, it is especially combined with superlatives, as *vel optime, fructus vel optimus,* which may be rendered 'if you like, in the best manner,' 'produce, if you please, of the best kind.' That it is not properly rendered 'even' is shown by its occasional combination in this use with *etiam;* as *De rebus nostris antis, vel etiam nimium multis,* 'enough, if you please, even too much of our affairs.' Cic. *ad Div.* IV. 14. That it has a concessive value is clear from such passages as *Per me vel stertas licet,* 'as far as depends on me, you may snore, if you please.' Cic. *Acad.* II. 19. *Quam sis morosus vel ex hoc intelligi potest, quod, &c.,* 'how morose you are, may, if you please, be understood from this, because, &c.' Precisely the same is its real force when it means 'for example,' for there it denotes, 'take this instance, if you like it;' thus, *Amant te omnes mulieres—vel illae quae here pallio me reprehenderunt,* 'take for instance those who pulled me by my cloak yesterday.' Plaut. *Mil. Gl.* I. 1. 59.

§ 4. (c) *Adversative Sentences.*

196 Adversative sentences are constructed by means of the adversative conjunctions (*sed, autem, verum,* &c., which have been discussed above (p. 196)). The logical value of these co-ordinate propositions is to a certain extent dependent on the particle which is used. Generally, however, the second clause is supposed to contain some predication essentially different from that which is conveyed by the former sentence. The difference may amount to a statement of something inconsistent with what has gone before, or it may be merely that distinction which is marked in the introduction of the second proposition of a syllogism. Thus, if we describe any one as *ingeniosus homo, sed (ut, verum) in omni vita inconstans,* we concede his ability, while we oppose to it the very

CO-ORDINATE SENTENCES. 375

different and inconsistent fact that he was fickle in all his actions. Here the particle used (generally *sed*, another form of *si*, and *sine*) means 'but' in the sense of our adversative conjunction (originally *be-outan*, 'without'). But if we say *nunc quod agitur agamus ; agitur autem liberine vivamus an mortem obeamus*, we mean, 'let us attend to the business before us; but the business before us is whether we are to live in freedom or to die.' Here the particle used (generally *autem*) means 'but,' in the sense of our 'now' or 'however,' and we naturally expect a third clause beginning with 'therefore.' In the former use of the adversative sentence, its construction is sometimes copulative in Latin ; or we have *-que, et*, or *ac*, where we use 'but' in English. This occurs when the former sentence is negative, and the adversative sentence affirmative. Thus we have, *nostrorum militum impetum hostes ferre non potuerunt ac terga verterunt* (Caes. *B. G.* IV. 33), 'the enemy could not withstand the attack of our men, but turned their backs.' Here the Greek would use the strongest adversative particle ἀλλά. The relative pronoun which, as we have seen, takes the place of the copulative conjunction, is also used in Latin as a substitute for the adversative particle, and even in those cases where the first clause is affirmative ; thus in *Romani nutu vocibusque hostes, si introire vellent, vocare coeperunt, quorum progredi ausus est nemo* (Caes. *B. G.* V. 43), *quorum* is used for *sed eorum*, 'but no one of them dared to do so.' Similarly in *nulla res vehementius rempublicam continet, quam fides, quae nulla esse potest, nisi erit necessaria solutio rerum creditorum* (Cic. *de Off.* II. 24), *quae* is used for *sed ea* or *ea autem*, 'this, however, cannot exist, unless the payment of what is trusted shall be necessary.'

§ 5. (d) *Distributive Sentences.*

197 Distributive sentences are constructed (*a*) by the opposition of the concessive *quidem* to the adversative *sed*; or (*β*) by means of the indicative pronouns *hic* and *ille* (62) ; or (γ) by a repetition of distributive words, as *pars, alius*, &c.

(*a*) When we have the opposition of *quidem* to *sed*, corresponding to the Greek μέν—δέ, it is the usual practice of the best writers to insert a pronoun immediately before *quidem* in order to emphasize the word of which the predicate is conceded; thus,

Oratorius exercitationes non tu quidem reliquisti, sed certe philosophiam illis anteposuisti (Cic. *de Fato*, 2), 'you, it must be admitted, have not abandoned the practice of oratory, but you have certainly preferred philosophy to those exercises.' *Domitius nulla ille quidem arte, sed Latine tamen et multa cum libertate dicebat* (Cic. *Brut.* 77), 'Domitius, it must be owned, did not speak with much art, but still he spoke good Latin, and with much freedom.' *Tuus dolor humanus is quidem, sed magnopere moderandus* (Cic. *Att.* XII. 10), 'your grief, it must be confessed, is prompted by the feelings of humanity, but it is by all means to be moderated.' *Libri scripti inconsiderate ab optimis quidem viris, sed non satis eruditis* (Cic. *Tusc. Disp.* I. 3), 'books written inconsiderately by men who were no doubt excellent in their moral character, but who were not sufficiently learned.' *Ludo et joco uti illo quidem licet, sed tum quum gravibus seriisque rebus satisfecerimus* (Cic. *de Off.* I. 29), 'one may indeed indulge in sport and joke, but only when we have adequately dealt with affairs of weight and seriousness.' *Cyri vitam et disciplinam legunt, praeclaram illam quidem, sed non tam aptam rebus nostris* (Cic. *Brut.* 29), 'they read the Cyropaedia, an admirable work it must be allowed, but not so well suited to our business.' The omission of the pronoun before *quidem* is of rare occurrence, but we have such constructions as *Proposuit quidem legem, sed minutissimis litteris et angusto loco* (Sueton. *Cal.* 41). And the merely adversative sentence without *quidem* has sometimes a distributive sense; as *Ennius esse deos censet, sed eos non curare opinatur, quid agat humanum genus* (Cic. *de Div.* I. 58), where we might insert *ille quidem* without altering the signification.

(*β*) When the distribution has reference to persons or things, already mentioned separately, the pronoun *hic*, 'this here,' is generally used to indicate the last-mentioned; *ille*, 'that other,' to indicate that which was named first; as *Caesar beneficiis atque munificentia magnus habebatur, integritate vitae Cato; ille* (the former—Caesar) *mansuetudine et misericordia clarus factus, huic* (to the latter —Cato) *severitas dignitatem addiderat* (Sall. *Cat.* 54). But *hic* and *ille* may mean, conversely, the *first* and the *second* terms in the enumeration, because in the idea, though not in the retrospective order, the first is nearer than the second; as *Melior tutiorque est certa pax, quam sperata victoria; haec* (the first-mentioned, peace) in *tua*, *illa* (the second, victory) in *deorum potestate est* (Liv. xxx. 30).

(γ) When the distribution has reference to things already mentioned in the aggregate, the enumeration of the particulars is expressed by a repetition of distributive words; thus we have *pars —pars*; as *Ceteri deserti ab ducibus pars* (in part, some of them) *transitione, pars* (others of them) *fuga dissipati sunt* (Liv. XXVIII. 10). *Multitudo pars* (some of the multitude) *procurrit in vias, pars* (others) *in vestibulis stat, pars* (others) *ex tectis fenestrisque prospectant, et quid rei sit rogitant* (Liv. XXIV. 21), where it will be observed that it is optional whether we use the singular or the plural verb with *pars* in a distributive sentence. Similarly we have *pars —quidam*; as *Cherusci instant cedentibus collectosque in orbem pars* (some of them) *congressi, quidam* (certain of the number) *eminus proturbant* (Tac. Ann. 1L. 11). Also *alii—alii* or *alter—alter*; as *Illi ad deprecandum periculum proferebant, alii* (some of them) *purpuram Tyriam, tus alii* (others), *gemmas alii* (others), *vina nonnulli* (some few) *Graeca* (Cic. Verr. VII. 56). *Duas filias harum altera* (one of the two) *occisa, altera* (the other) *capta est* (Cæsar, B. G. I. 53). Sometimes the distribution is expressed in a single sentence, as when we have *Discedebant alius in aliam partem (alius alio)*, 'they separated one to one side, one to the other.' So also *Aliter cum aliis loqueris*, 'you speak differently to different people.' *Haec aliter ab aliis definiuntur*, 'these things are defined by different persons in different manners.' Sometimes the distribution is expressed without an enumeration of parts by the mere pronoun *quisque*; as *Neque mirum, ubi vos separatim sibi quisque* (each of you for himself) *consilium capitis* (Sall. Cat. 52). *Infensus miles memoria laborum se quisque* (each of the soldiers), *ultione et sanguine explebant* (Tac. Ann. IV. 25). *Quisque suos patimur Manes* (Virg. Æn. VL. 743). So also we have *hic et hic, hic et ille, ille et ille*, 'this and that,' 'one or two.'

§ 6. (e) *Distinctive Sentences.*

198 As the distributive sentence is often in a certain sense adversative, so the distinctive sentence may approximate in logical value to the distributive. But the distributive is of wider application than the adversative, and the distinctive than the distributive. The main instrument in the construction of a distinctive sentence

378   SYNTAX OF SENTENCES.

in Latin is the pronoun, and a discussion of this form of the co-ordinate sentence resolves itself into an examination of the syntax of the different demonstrative and indefinite pronouns; but although the Latin language is much more precise in this respect than the English, it sometimes omits the pronoun where we should insert it; it dispenses with the verb when distinctive nouns are used; and it often repeats the same word where we should use some distinctive expression. It will be convenient, before we investigate the syntax of the different pronouns, which are used as substitutes for nouns in distinctive sentences, to consider those cases in which the pronoun or verb is omitted, and in which the same word, whether noun or pronoun, is repeated to mark a distinctive relation.

(a) *Omission of the Pronoun or Verb.*

199 (aa) The pronoun is not inserted, as in English, when there are distinctive genitives in reference to the same noun; as *Perspicuum est benevolentiae vim esse magnam, metus* (that of fear, i.e. *vim metus*) *imbecillam.* Cic. *de Off.* II. 8.

(bb) The same verb is not repeated in distinctive sentences, even though a different person or number would be required; thus we have *Abi rus ergo hinc: ibi ego te* (i.e. *feram*, 'I will put up with you'), *tu me feres.* Ter. *Heaut.* IV. 2. 4. *In Hyrcania plebs publicos alit canes, optimates domesticos* (i.e. *canes alunt,* 'rear dogs in their houses'). Cic. *Tusc. Disp.* I. 45.

(β) *Repetition of Distinctive Words.*

200 (aa) The same noun is repeated, when mutuality or correspondence is signified; as *Placet Stoicis homines hominum causa esse generatos* (Cic. *de Off.* III. 17), 'it is the opinion of the Stoics that men have been created for the sake of one another.' *Ad Vadimonis lacum Etrusci, lege sacrata coacto exercitu, quum vir virum legisset* (each man having chosen his mate), *dimicarunt.* Liv. IX. 39.

(bb) More frequently the same pronominal word is repeated in this sense; as *Sergius Virginiusque noxii ambo alter in alterum causam conferunt* (lay the blame upon one another, i.e. the one upon the other). Liv. v. 11. *Nihil aliud in judicium venit, nisi uter utri insidias fecerit* (which of the two plotted against the other). Cic. *Mil.* 12. *Magni est judicis statuere quid quemque cuique praestare oportet* (what every man ought to do for his neighbour, i. e. every man for every man). Cic. *de Off.* III. 17. *Alius alio gravius atque ornatius de mea salute dixit* (every successive speaker outstript the previous speaker in the dignity and eloquence with which he enlarged on my safety). Cic. *Sext.* 34. *Equites sine duce relicti alii alia* (one in one way, another in another) *in civitates suas dilapsi sunt.* Liv. XLIV. 43.

(γ) *Use of the Distinctive Pronouns.*

201 The signification of the pronouns has been already given (above, Part I. Chap. III.); but it belongs to the syntax of co-ordinate sentences to illustrate by examples the construction of the demonstrative and indefinite pronouns, which are used as the vehicles of distinctive reference.

(aa) *Is.*

The pronouns, which are most especially distinctive, are *is* and its two derivatives *idem* and *ipse*, corresponding, as we have seen (above, 63), to the three usages of the Greek αὐτός. In its most ordinary use, *is* is either the correlative of *qui* in a definite sentence, as *A me ii contenderunt, qui apud me et amicitia et dignitate plurimum possunt* (Cic. *Rosc. Am.* 1), 'I was applied to by the particular persons, who have the greatest influence with me on grounds of friendship or worthiness;' or it is a mere pronoun of reference; as *Omitto Isocratem discipulosque ejus, Ephorum et Naucratem* (Cic. *Or.* 51), 'I omit Isocrates and his scholars (the scholars of the person in particular just mentioned) Ephorus and Naucrates.' In regard to the former usage, the *is* sometimes introduces not *qui*, but *quicunque* or *siquis*; as *Eam fortunam quaecunque erit tua* (Cic. *Mil.* 36). *Ex ea facilitate, si quam habet* (Cic. *Div. in Caecil.* 13). As a pronoun of reference *is* becomes emphatically distinctive, when it is used by itself with a copulative or disjunctive conjunction, so that *et is, et is quidem, atque is,* or *isque*, means 'and that too,' and *nec is* means 'and that not;' as in the following examples: *Exempla quaeruntur et ea* (and those) *non antiqua* (Cic. *Verr.* III. 90). *Epicurus una in domo et ea quidem* (and that too) *angusta quam magnos quantaque amoris conspiratione consentientes tenuit amicorum greges!* (Cic. *Fin.* I. 20). *Uno atque eo facili* (and that an easy one) *proelio caesi ad Antium hostes* (Liv. IV. 57). *Unam rem explicabo eamque maximam* (Cic. *Fin.* I. 8), 'I will explain one circumstance, and that a point of the greatest importance.' *Galli legionem nec eam plenissimam* (and that not a very complete one) *propter paucitatem despiciebant* (Caes. B. G. III. 2). If the distinction added belongs to the general predication, we have *et id* or *idque;* as *Crassum cognovi studiis optimis deditum idque a puero* (Cic. *ad div.* XIII. 10), 'I have known Crassus to be devoted to the best pursuits, and that too (i.e. the circumstance that he was so devoted) from his boyhood.' We have also *sed is* in a similar sense; as *Severitatem in senectute probo, sed eam modicam* (Cic. *Sen.* 18). The distinctive sentence with *is* sometimes stands by itself and independently of the context. In this case it begins the sentence; as *P. Annius Asellus mortuus est C. Sacerdote praetore. Is quum haberet unicam filiam, eam bonis suis heredem instituit* (Cic. *Verr.* I. 41). In this case the proper name of the person referred to is sometimes repeated in the distinctive sentence, and we write, for instance, *is Piso* (Sall. *Cat.* 19), much in the same way as we should write in Greek ὁ Πίσων. We have also *is est* and *id est* in the sense 'I mean to speak of.'

(bb) *Idem.*

Besides its common use in expressions of identity, where we say 'the same,' *idem* is employed distinctively when we introduce some adverbial phrase denoting correspondence ('also,' 'likewise,' 'at the same time,' 'in the same manner') or contrast ('still,' 'on the other hand,' 'notwithstanding'); as *Nihil utile, quod non idem honestum* (Cic. *de Off.* III. 7), 'nothing is useful, which is not also (at the same time) virtuous.' *Etiam patriae hoc munus debere videtis, ut ea, quae salva per te est, per te eundem sit ornata* (Cic. *Leg.* I. 2), 'you seem to owe this good service to your country, that being saved by you, it should be adorned by you also.' *Inventi multi sunt, qui vitam profundere pro patria parati essent, iidem* (still, notwithstanding, on the other hand) *gloriae jacturam ne minimam quidem facere vellent* (Id. *ibid.* I. 24). *Epicurus, quum optimam et praestantissimam naturam dei dicat esse, negat idem esse in deo gratiam* (Cic. *N. D.* I. 43), 'Epicurus, although he says that the nature of God is the best and most excellent, denies all the while that there is any feeling of favour in the Deity.'

(cc) *Ipse.*

We may use *ipse* either alone or with an immediate reference to the personal or reflexive pronouns. In the former case, it denotes

(1) the most emphatic or exclusive distinction, as when the Pythagoreans said of their master: *Ipse dixit* (αὐτὸς ἔφα) (Cic. *N. D.* I. 5, § 10), 'he said it himself,' 'you have his own authority for it;' or (2) spontaneity; as *Ipsae lacte domum referent distenta capellae ubera* (Virg. *Ecl.* IV. 21), which Horace (*Epod.* XVI. 49) expresses thus: *Injussae veniunt ad mulctra capellae;* or (3) exact measurement, especially of time; as *Triginta dies erant ipsi, quum has dabam litteras, per quos nullas a vobis acceperam* (Cic. *Att.* III. 21), 'exactly thirty days had elapsed;' *nunc ipsum ea lego, ea scribo, ut ii qui mecum sunt difficilius otium ferant, quam ego laborem* (Cic. *Att.* XII. 40), 'at this particular time I read and write such things that those who are with me find it more difficult to endure their leisure than I do to bear my toil.' When *ipse* is used with immediate reference to the personal or reflexive pronouns, it admits of two constructions; it is used in the nominative with a personal or reflexive pronoun in an oblique case, if we wish to intimate that the agency is confined to the subject of the sentence; thus we say, *Non egeo medicina, me ipse consolor* (Cic. *Lael.* 3), 'I need no medicine;' 'I console myself,' i.e. 'I need no external or foreign consolation;' 'I alone minister consolation to myself.' *Valvae clausae repagulis subito se ipsae aperuerunt* (Cic. *N. D.* II. 3), 'the doors, though shut and bolted, suddenly opened themselves by their own agency.' *Non potest exercitum is imperator continere, qui se ipse non continet* (Cic. *pro leg. Manil.* 13), 'the general, who does not by his own efforts keep himself under control, cannot control his army.' But if we wish to intimate that the results of the action are confined to the subject, we put *ipse* in the same oblique case with the reflexive pronoun; thus we say, *Sensim tardeve potius nosmet ipsos cognoscimus* (Cic. *Fin.* V. 15), 'we get to know our very selves gradually, or rather slowly,' i.e. 'it is only with reference to ourselves that this knowledge is so difficult.' We find, however, that *ipse* is used in the nominative in a sort of redundant manner, where we should expect it to be in the same case with the reflexive pronoun; but here the distinctive value of the pronoun is very apparent; thus we say *Ipse sibi inimicus est* (Cic. *Fin.* V. 10), 'he is his own enemy,' i.e. 'he has no other enemy.' *Secum ipsi loquuntur* (Cic. *R. P.* I. 17), 'they soliloquize,' i.e. 'there are no other speakers.' *Crassus et Antonius ex scriptis cognosci ipsi suis non potuerunt* (Cic. *de Orat.* II. 2), 'Crassus and Antonius could not be learnt from their own writing in their distinctive characteristics.'

382   SYNTAX OF SENTENCES.

(dd) *Se, suus.*

The reflexive pronoun, which is thus used with *ipse*, is the regular vehicle of a distinctive reference to the main subject of a sentence.

(1) Properly the reflexive is the pronoun of distinctive reference to the nominative of the main sentence; thus, *Id ea de causa Caesar fecit, ne se* (i.e. Caesar himself) *occupatum opprimerent. Exposuit, cur ea res parum sibi* (i.e. to Caesar) *placeret. Accusat amicos, quod se* (himself, i.e. Caesar) *non adjuverint. Ariovistus respondet, si quid Caesar se* (him, the speaker, Ariovistus) *velit, illum* (Caesar) *ad se* (Ariovistus) *venire oportere.* Caesar, *B. G.* I. 34. *Tum si dormienti ulem ille visus est rogare, ut quoniam sibi* (the murdered man, whose ghost asked the question) *vivo non subvenisset, mortem suam* (his, the ghostly speaker's death) *ne inultam esse pateretur.* Cic. *de Div.* I. 27.

(2) *Se, suus* are also used, whenever there is an expression of reciprocal or mutual action; in the former case it is often combined with *ipse*, as we have seen above; thus we have *Ipse se quisque diligit* (Cic. *Am.* 21), 'every man loves himself.' *Bestiis homines uti possunt ad suam utilitatem* (Cic. *Fin.* III. 20), 'men may make use of the lower animals for their own requirements' (i.e. of the men who use them). *Etiam feras inter se partus et educatio conciliat* (Cic. *Rosc. Am.* 22), 'birth and education bind even wild beasts to one another.' *Veri amici non solum colent inter se et diligent, sed etiam verebuntur* (Cic. *Am.* 22), 'true friends will not only serve and love one another, but will also feel mutual respect.'

(3) We may use *se, suus,* even without any distinctive reflexion to the subject, if there is an emphatic reference to any person or thing in the sentence, where we introduce the phrase ' his, her, its own,' in English; thus, *Hannibalem sui cives e civitate ejecerunt* (Cic. *pro Sext.* 68), 'his own citizens banished Hannibal.' *Si ceteris recte facta sua prosunt, mihi mea ne quando obsint providete* (Cic. *Cat.* III. 12), ' if their own good deeds are advantageous to others, take care that mine be not at any time injurious to me.' *Cui proposita est conservatio sui, necesse est huic quoque partes sui caras esse* (Cic. *Fin.* V. 13), 'it is necessary that the parts of himself should be dear to the man, who has proposed to himself his own

preservation.' Sometimes it may appear doubtful whether we ought to use *suus* or *ejus*. Thus, while we have *Dicaearchum cum Aristarcho, aequali et condiscipulo suo, omittamus* (Cic. *Tusc.* I. 18), we have in a sentence apparently very similar, *Omitto Isocratem discipulosque ejus Ephorum et Naucratem* (Cic. *Or.* 51). But in the former the use of the preposition *cum* conveys an idea of accompaniment which makes the reference emphatic; 'let us pass over Dicaearchus, and with him his own scholar Aristarchus;' but in the second case, we merely say, 'I pass over Isocrates and his scholars (the scholars of that particular rhetorician) Ephorus and Naucrates.' Similarly we have *Fabius a me diligitur propter summam suam humanitatem et observantiam* (Cic. *ad Div.* XV. 14), where the writer intimates that the politeness and attention of Fabius were peculiarly his own; but in a precisely similar sentence we find, *Pisonem nostrum merito ejus amo plurimum* (Cic. *ad Div.* XIV. 2), because there is no emphasis in the attribution of merit to Piso.

Obs. 1 *Se, suus* may be used in a reflexive sense, though they do not refer to the nominative of the main sentence, but to the word which constitutes the real rather than the grammatical subject of the general proposition; thus, *Jam inde ab initio Faustulo spes fuerat, regiam stirpem apud se educari* (Liv. I. 5), because *Faustulo spes fuerat* is quite equivalent to *Faustulus speraverat*. *A Caesare valde liberaliter invitor sibi ut sim legatus* (Cic. *Att.* 18), because *a Caesare invitor* is quite equivalent to *Caesar me invitat*.

Obs. 2 In a dependent sentence, the reflexive pronoun may refer to either of two nouns in the main sentence, or there may be two reflexive pronouns referring respectively to the two nouns previously introduced; thus we may say, *Hortensius ex Verre quaesivit, cur suos* (i. e. *Hortensii*) *familiarissimos rejici passus esset* (Cic. *Verr.* I. 7), because the direct interrogative would have been *Cur meos familiarissimos rejici passus es?* Again we may say, *Livius Salinator Q. Fabium Maximum rogavit, ut meminisset opera sua* (i. e. *Lirii*) *se* (i. e. *Fabium*) *Tarentum recepisse* (Cic. *de Or.* II. 67), because the direct sentence would have been *Memento opera mea te Tarentum recepisse*.

Obs. 3 Sometimes the necessity for a distinctive reference obliges the writer to use *is* with reference to the nominative of the main sentence, and *se, suus* with reference to the subordinate word; thus we find such sentences as the following: *Helvetii persuadent Rauracis et Tulingis, uti, eodem usi consilio, oppidis suis vicisque* (i. e. *Rauracorum et Tulingorum*) *exustis, una cum iis* (i. e. *Helvetiis*) *proficiscantur* (Caes. *B. G.* I. 5), because there would be a confusion if the reflexive were used after the appropriation of *suis* in the absolute sentence.

Obs. 4 Even in a purely dependent sentence and *in oratione obliqua* we may have *is* for *se* when a new subject is interposed; as *Audistis nuper dicere legatos Tyndaritanos, Mercurium, qui meris anniversariis apud eos* (i. e. *Tyndaritanos*) *coleretur, Verris imperio esse sublatum* (Cic. *Verr.* IV. 39), because the new subject of the infinitive, *Mercurium*, intervenes between the main subject and the pronoun of distinctive reference. On the other hand, we have the reflexive instead of *is*, even when there is no dependent sentence, if the pronoun of reference immediately follows the main subject, though it may be grammatically dependent on a verb containing another subject; as *Chrysogonus hunc sibi* (i. e. *Chrysogono*) *ex animo scrupulum, qui se* (i. e. *Chrysogonum*) *noctes diesque stimulat ac pungit, ut evellatis postulat* (Cic. *Rosc. Am.* 2). Hence we have such phrases as *quantum in se est;* and hence too *se* is used with reference to an indefinite subject; as *Negligere, quod de se quisque sentiat, non solum arrogantis, est sed etiam omnino dissoluti* (Cic. *de Off.* L 28), 'to neglect (i. e. that any one should neglect) what everybody thinks about oneself (i. e. about himself, with reference to the indefinite person, who is supposed to be negligent), is not only the part of an arrogant, but of an absolutely dissolute person.'

(cc) *Hic.*

Besides their use in distributive sentences (above, 197, (*β*)), *hic* and *ille* are employed, with *iste*, in an indicative sense, which contributes to the formation of distinctive sentences. *Hic*, in particular, is used (*a*) to denote that which is present in space or time; as *Opus vel in hac magnificentia urbis conspiciendum* (Liv. VI. 4), 'a work worthy of notice even in the present magnificence of the city' — 'the splendour which it has reached in our time.' *Qui vituperare haec volunt, Chrysogonum tantum posse queruntur* (Cic. pro *Rosc. Am.* 48), 'those who desire to find fault with the existing state of things, complain that Chrysogonus has so much power.' *Hic* is also used (*β*) to denote that which follows in the sentence; as *Libertas pauperis haec est* (Juven. III. 299), 'the liberty of a poor man is as follows,' and then we have an account of his miserable condition. *Hic* is also used (*γ*) as the definite antecedent to a relative, instead of *is*, either to denote relative proximity, as *Haec quae a nobis hoc quadriduo disputata sunt* (Cic. *Tusc.* IV. 38), 'these things which have been discussed by us in the last four days;' or to give a marked emphasis, as *Quos ego campos antea nitidissimos viridissimosque vidissem, hos vastatos nunc atque desertos videbam* (Cic. *Verr.* III. 18), 'the very plains, which I had previously seen in the highest cultivation and fertility, these I now saw laid waste and desolate.'

(ff) *Iste.*

Iste is the indicative pronoun of the second person, and is properly used with reference to the person addressed.

(α) It is often directly referred to *tu* and *tuus*; as *De istis rebus exspecto tuas litteras* (Cic. *Att.* II. 5), 'I expect a letter from you respecting what is going on where you are.' *Quaevis mallem causa fuisset, quam ista quam dicis* (Cic. *de Orat.* II. 4), 'I would rather it were any cause than that which you mention.' And in this way it is directly opposed to *hic*; as *Iisdem hic sapiens, de quo loquor, oculis, quibus iste vester terram, mare, intuebitur* (Cic. *Acad.* IV. 33), 'this philosopher, of whom *I* am speaking, will gaze on the earth and sea, with the same eyes as that man, whom *you* mention.' Hence, in a law-court, *hic* is the client of the speaker, *iste*, 'the person before you (the judges)' is the other party.

(β) *Iste* may be used to distinguish the words of the speaker, when, having been uttered, they are, as it were, transferred to the hearer, and left to his consideration; as *Utinam tibi istam mentem dii immortales duint* (Cic. *Cat.* I. 9), 'I wish the gods would give you such a mind as that which I have mentioned.' *Fructum istum laudis in alia tempora reservemus* (Cic. *Verr.* I. 11). That it differs from *hic* in this idiomatic usage merely by implying a transference for the moment of that which really belongs to the speaker, may be seen from such passages as the following, in which the two pronouns are used together: *Si quid noristi rectius istis, candidus imperti; si non, his utere mecum* (Hor. 1 *Epist.* VI. 67), 'if you know anything more correct than what I have mentioned—what is now before you—candidly impart it; if not, join me in acting on these principles of mine.'

(gg) *Ille.*

(α) As opposed to *hic*, denoting that which is before our eyes, *ille* indicates that which is absent or unseen; thus, *Si illos, quos jam videre non possumus, negligis, ne his quidem, quos vides, consuli putas oportere* (Cic. *pro Rab.* 11), 'if you neglect *those*, whom we can no longer see, you do not think that regard ought to be paid even to *these* whom you see.'

(β) As opposed to *iste*, which is frequently used in expressing contempt, *ille* often denotes distinction or eminence; as *Alexander ille magnus*, 'that well-known Alexander the Great;' *Medea illa*, 'the notorious Medea.'

(γ) As referring to that which follows in the sentence, *ille* is used much in the same way as *hic*, with this exception, that *hic* denotes that which is immediately introduced, but *ille*, that which is either new, or remarkable, or well-known; thus, *Nonne, quum multa alia mirabilia, tum illud imprimis?* (Cic. *de Div.* I. 10), 'while many other things are wonderful, is not that particular circumstance especially so?' Hence we find *hoc Thrasybuli*, 'the following remark of Thrasybulus,' *illud Pherecydis*, 'that memorable saying of Pherecydes.'

(δ) *Ille* is often repeated when an emphatic distinction is intended, as in the following passage (Cic. *de Orat.* I. 41): *nisi ille prius, qui illa tenet, habeat illam scientiam.*

(hh) *Alter, alius.*

Alius, which is merely another form of *ille* = *ollus* (62, Obs. 4), is used to denote an indefinite number of persons or things different from the object or objects mentioned; but *alter* is confined to those cases in which only one other person or thing is mentioned. Thus while we say *alii plures* (Hor. 1 *Serm.* VI. 110), 'several other persons,' we say *unus atque item alter* (Ter. *Andr.* I. 1), 'one, and then one other;' *solus aut cum altero* (Cic. *Att.* XI. 15), 'alone or with one other person;' *ne te sit ditior alter* (Hor. 1 *Serm.* I. 40), 'that no single person besides should be richer.' So while we have *Fonteius Antoni, non ut magis alter, amicus* (Hor. 1 *Serm.* V. 32), where only two are compared, we have *Ut non magis quisquam alius* (Hor. 2 *Serm.* VIII. 40), where we exclude all other persons from the comparison. Hence we have such phrases as *alter Nero*, 'a second Nero,' &c., where we mean a second person of the same kind. But *alius* alone is used when we imply a difference or diversity.

(ii) *Uterque, ambo, quisque.*

Uterque and *ambo* refer to both of two persons or things, and *quisque* includes every one of a given number. But although *uterque* and *ambo* imply both of two, *uterque* means, 'both the one and the other,' and intimates a distinction of act or condition at the particular time, whereas *ambo* means 'both together;' as the following example will sufficiently show (Ter. *Adelph.* I. 2. 50):

> Curemus æquam *uterque* partem; tu *alterum*,
> Ego *alterum*: nam *ambos* curare propemodum
> Reposcere illum est quem dedisti.

'Let *both the one and the other of us* take an equal share in the business; do you look to one of them; let me look to the other; for to concern yourself with *both together* is almost to demand back again the boy whom you gave me.' *Quisque* on the other hand signifies 'each' or 'every one' of a larger number taken separately; as *Quam quisque norit artem in hac se exerceat* (Cic. *Tusc.* I. 18), 'let each one practise the art in which he (as distinguished from other men) excels.' *Ut quisque maxime ad suum commodum refert quaecunque agit, ita minime est vir bonus* (Cic. *Leges,* I. 18), 'in proportion as each man refers all his actions to his own interest, in the same proportion is he deficient in goodness.' *Non quantum quisque prosit, sed quanti quisque sit, ponderandum est* (Cic. *Brut.* 79, § 257), 'we must estimate, not what is the usefulness, but what is the value of each man taken by himself.' From this function of marking the individual and distinguishing him from a considerable number, *quisque* is specially used with superlatives; as *Ex philosophis optimus et gravissimus quisque confitetur multa se ignorare* (Cic. *Tusc.* III. 28), 'of the general mass of philosophers, every one, who is most distinguished by his excellence and power, confesses that he is ignorant of many things.' As the ordinal belongs to the same class as the superlatives we have *quisque* also in this combination, and *primus quisque* means that which on each occasion is first, i.e. in succession; as *Primum quidque consideremus* (Cic. *N.D.* I. 27), 'let us consider each circumstance in its order.' So also *tertius quisque, quartus quisque,* &c. 'every third,' 'every fourth;' but 'every other' is expressed by *alternus,* as *alternis diebus* 'every other day.' In accordance with the same usage we have *quisque* with *quotus;* and *quotus quisque* means ' what number is each of a long series counted by?' as *Quotus quisque philosophorum invenitur, qui sit ita moratus ut ratio postulat?* (Cic. *Tusc.* II. 4), 'what of a given number is each philosopher, who is so constituted in his character as nature requires?'—e.g. is he one in five, one in fifty, or one in five hundred? and this amounts to the exclamatory inference: 'how few philosophers there are who are so qualified.' It has been already mentioned (above 69, *Obs.* 2), that *quisquis* is occasionally used for *quisque,* and that in this case the neuter is written *quicquid* instead of *quidquid.*

(kk) *Quis, quispiam; aliquis, aliquispiam.*

The opposition between 'some' and 'any' is expressed in Latin by prefixing the syllables *ali-* (a relic of the indicative pronoun *ille* or *alius*) to the indefinite *quis* or *quispiam*, *ali-quispiam*, however, being of very rare occurrence. We have *quis* convertible with *quispiam* in such phrases as *dicat quis, dicat quispiam,* 'suppose any one were to say,' by the side of *dicat aliquis,* 'suppose some one were to say;' we have *quis* in preference to *quispiam* after relatives, and in interrogative, conditional, or final sentences; as *Illis promissis standum non est, quae coactus quis metu, quae deceptus dolo promisit* (Cic. *de Off.* I. 10). *Num quis irascitur pueris, quorum aetas nondum novit rerum discrimina?* (Sen. *de Ira*, II. 9.) *Galli legibus sanctum habent, ut si quis quid de republica a finitimis rumore acceperit, uti ad magistratum deferat* (Caes. *B. G.* VI. 20). *Fieri potest, ut recte quis sentiat, et id, quod sentit, polite eloqui non possit* (Cic. *Tusc.* I. 3). *Id ego arbitror apprimis in vita esse utile, ut ne quid nimis* (Ter. *Andr.* I. 1. 34). In all these passages we must translate *quis* by 'any;' but if in similar constructions we wish to express the meaning of '*some*' we must use *aliquis* even after *si* or *ne*, as *Si aliquid de summa gravitate Pompeius, si multum de cupiditate Caesar remisisset, pacem stabilem nobis habere licuisset* (Cic. *Phil.* XIII. 1), 'if Pompey had given up somewhat of his high dignity, if Caesar had given up much of his ambition, we might have had durable peace.' *Timebat Pompeius omnia, ne vos aliquid timeretis* (Cic. *pro Mil.* 24), 'Pompey feared all things, that you might not have some particular object of fear.' The difference between *quispiam* and *aliquis* may be seen by such passages as the following: *Si de rebus rusticis agricola quispiam, aut etiam, id quod multi, medicus de morbis, aut de pingendo pictor aliquis diserte dixerit aut scripserit, non idcirco illius artis putanda sit eloquentia* (Cic. *de Orat.* II. 9, § 38), 'if *any person* versed in agriculture shall have written or spoken with eloquence on rural affairs, or even any physician, as many have done, on diseases, or if *some* painter shall have so discussed painting, eloquence would not therefore be considered as belonging to the particular art which was so illustrated.' The difference between *quispiam* and *quisque* may be seen by comparing the two following passages of Caesar: *Quoties quaeque cohors procurreret, ab ea parte magnus hostium numerus cadebat* (*B. G.* V. 34), 'as often as *each* or *every* cohort rushed forward, a great number of the enemy fell on that side.' *Quum quaepiam cohors ex orbe excesserat, hostes fugiebant* (B. G. 1. 35), 'when any cohort had left the circle, the enemy fled.' *Aliquis* and *quispiam* may occur in the same phrase; as *Forsitan aliquis aliquando ejusmodi quidpiam fecerit* (Cic. *Verr.* II. 32), 'some one may at some time have done any thing of that kind.'

(11) *Quivis, quilibet, quisquam, ullus.*

If we wish to speak of 'any' person or thing with an unrestricted liberty of selection, we must write *quivis* or *quilibet*. If we wish to speak of 'any' person or thing, in an exclusive sense, we must use *quisquam* substantively, and *ullus* as an adjective. The distinction between *quivis* or *quilibet* and *quisquam* or *ullus* is clearly given in such oppositions as the following: *Cuivis potest accidere quod cuiquam potest* (Publ. Syrus, ap. *Sen. de Tranqu.* XI. 8), 'what may happen to any one at all, may happen to any one you please.' The distinction between *quivis* or *quilibet* and *aliquis* appears in such passages as, *Dummodo doleat aliquid doleat quidlibet* (Afranius, ap. *Cic. Tusc. Disp.* IV. 25), 'provided he only suffers *some* pain let him suffer *any thing you please.*' The near approximation in meaning between *quisquam* and *quispiam* appears in such passages as the following: *Nego esse quicquam a testibus dictum, quod aut vestrum cuipiam esset obscurum, aut cujusquam oratoris eloquentiam quaereret* (Cic. *Verr.* I. 10), 'I deny that anything *at all* has been said by the witnesses, such that it should be obscure to *any one* of you, or should require the eloquence of any orator at all.' *Ne suspicari quidem possumus, quenquam horum ab amico quidpiam contendisse, quod contra rempublicam esset* (Cic. *Am.* 11), 'we cannot even suspect that *any one at all* of these has sought *anything* from a friend, of such a nature as to be against the commonwealth.' That *quisquam* and *ullus* are used in the same sense may be seen by comparing *Si quisquam est, ille sapiens fuit* (Cic. *Am.* 2) with *Si tempus est ullum jure hominis necandi, certe illud est non modo justum, verum etiam necessarium* (Cic. *pro Mil.* 4). Although *ullus* is generally used as an adjective, in the place of *quisquam*, which is not completely inflected and has no feminine (above, 68, *Obs.* 1), we sometimes find *ullus* used without a noun; as *Tu me existimas ab ullo malle mea legi probarique, quam a te!* (Cic. *Att.* IV. 5). Conversely we may have *scriptor quis-*

quam, quisquam Gallus, &c.; thus, *Quasi vero quisquam vir excellenti animo optabilius quidquam arbitretur, quam se a suis civibus reipublicae causa diligi* (Cic. *Tusc.* 3).

§ 7. (f) *Comparative Sentences.*

202 Comparative sentences, which express either the identity or the difference in kind and degree of two subjects or predicates, are constructed in the former case by means of the correlation of certain adverbs, and in the latter case by a comparative adjective either followed by *quam* or by the ablative case of the noun indicating the standard of comparison.

(a) When the comparison presumes an identity or dissimilarity in the same degree of comparison it may be expressed by the following uses of relatives, and correlative adverbs.

(aa) We may have *ut, uti,* 'as,' with *itidem, sic, into modo, sic item* or *sic contra,* as in the following examples: *Ut* filium bonum patri esse oportet, *itidem* ego sum patri. Plaut. *Amph.* III. 4. 9. *Ut* vos hic, *itidem* illic apud vos meus servatur filius. Id. *Capt.* II. 2. 11. *Ut* in urbe retinenda tunc, *sic* nunc in Italia non relinquenda testificabar sententiam meam. Cic. *Att.* VIII. 1. Ariovistus respondit: *Ut* sibi concedi non oporteret, si in nostros fines impetum faceret, *sic item* nos esse iniquos, quod in suo jure se interpellaremus. Caes. *B. G.* I. 44. *Ut* hi miseri, *sic contra* illi beati, quos nulli metus terrent. Cic. *Tusc.* V. 6. Non ille *ut* plerique, sed *into modo, ut* tu, distincte, graviter, ornate dicebat. Cic. *N. D.* I. 21. *Ut* optasti, *ita* est. Cic. *Fam.* II. 10. *Uti* initium, *sic* finis est. Sall. *Jug.* II.

(bb) In the expressions *ut fit, ut est, ut opinor, ut dico, ut scriptum est, ut videtur,* &c., we must regard the whole of the correlative sentence as the antecedent of *ut;* thus we have, Qui in sua re fuisset egentissimus erat, *ut fit,* insolens in aliena. Cic. *Sex. Rosc.* 8. Si vero improbus fuerit, *ut est,* duces cum captivum in triumpho. Cic. *Fam.* V. 11. Triginta dies tibi ad decedendum lego, *ut opinor,* Cornelia constituti sunt. *Ib.* III. 6. Antonius illa dicendi mysteria enunciet. *Ut videtur,* inquit Sulpicius. Cic. *Or.* I. 47. His consulibus, *ut* in veteribus commentariis *scriptum est,* Naevius est mortuus. Cic. *Brut.* 15. Erat hoc, *ut dico,* factitatum semper. Cic. *Verr.* VII. 24.

(cc) An identity of relation between two predicates may be

CO-ORDINATE SENTENCES. 391

definitely expressed by *quemadmodum* or *quomodo*, either alone or with *ita* or *sic* as the antecedent; thus we have, Si *quemadmodum* soles de ceteris rebus, quum ex te quaeruntur, *sic* de amicitia disputaris. Cic. *Am.* 4. Necesse est, *quo* tu me *modo* esse voles, *ita* esse, mater. Plaut. *Cist.* I. 1. 48. Ut *quemadmodum* gubernatores optimi vim tempestatis, *sic* illi fortunae impetum superare non possent. Cic. *Q. Fr.* I. 1. Nos in Senatu, *quemadmodum* spero, dignitatem nostram, ut potest in tanta hominum perfidia, retinebimus. Cic. *Fam.* I. 2. *Quomodo* hominum inter homines juris esse vincula putant Stoici, *sic* homini nihil juris esse cum bestiis. Cic. *Fin.* III. 20. Postulatio brevis, et, *quomodo* mihi persuadeo, aliquanto aequior. Cic. *Sex. Rosc.* II.

(dd) Similarity or dissimilarity, when the predication is in the positive degree, may be expressed by *atque*, *ac*, after the adjectives, and adverbs mentioned above (p. 173). This idiom has been already explained, but for the sake of method some additional examples are here subjoined: Hostes inter se jactabant, *similem* Romae pavorem fore, *ac* bello Gallico fuerit. Liv. VI. 28. Hannibal Minucium Rufum, magistrum equitum, *pari ac* dictatorem imperio, dolo productum in praelium fugavit. Corn. Nep. XXIII. 5. Agrippa Menenius erat vir omni vita *pariter* Patribus *ac* plebi carus. Liv. II. 33. Civibus victis ut parceretur, *aeque ac* pro mea salute laboravi. Cic. *Fam.* XL 28. Ostendant milites, se *juxta* hieme *atque* aestate bella gerere posse. Liv. V. 6. Virtus *eadem* in homine ac deo est. Cic. *Leg.* I. 8. Equi non *item* sunt spectandi, *atque* habendi. Varr. II. 7, 15. Miltiades cum *totidem* navibus, *atque* erat profectus, Athenas rediit. Corn. Nep. I. 17. Desiderium absentium nihil *perinde ac* vicinitas acuit. Plin. *Ep.* VI. 1. Honos *talis* paucis est delatus, *ac* mihi. Cic. *Vatin.* 4. Posteaquam mihi renuntiatum est de obitu Tulliae, filiae tuae, sane quam pro eo, ac debui, graviter molesteque tuli. *Sulpicius* in Cic. *Fam.* IV. 5. Dissimulatio est, quum *alia* dicuntur, *ac* sentias. Cic. *Or.* II. 67. Stoici multa falsa esse dicunt, longeque *aliter* se habere, *ac* sensibus videantur. Cic. *Acad.* II. 31. Tecum agam, Servi, non *secus*, *ac* si meus esses frater. Cic. *Mur.* 4. Vides, omnia fere *contra*, *ac* dicta sint, evenisse. Cic. *Div.* II. 24. Verres inter alios *contrarium* decernebat, *ac* proximis paullo ante decreverat. Cic. *Verr.* I. 46. *Simul atque* natum animal est, gaudet voluptate, et eam appetit, ut bonum. Cic. *Fin.* II. 10.

(ee) A negation of dissimilarity is expressed by *nihil aliud, non aliud, quid aliud*, &c., followed by *quam*, if *nihil aliud* means 'nothing different in kind;' by *atque, ac*, if *nihil aliud* is equivalent to *idem*; and by *nisi*, or *praeter*, if *nihil aliud nisi* means *non unum* or *tantum*; in the last case *aliud* may be omitted. The following examples will illustrate these distinctions: Virtus est *nihil aliud, quam* in se perfecta et ad summum perducta natura. Cic. *Leg.* I. 8. Lysander *nihil aliud* molitus est, *quam* ut omnes civitates in sua teneret potestate. Corn. Nep. VI. 1. Militiae causam *nullam aliam* invenietis, *quam* ne quid agi de commodis vestris posset. Liv. v. 2. *Non aliud* malorum levamentum esse dicebant, *quam* si linquerent castra infausta. Tac. I. 30. Difficile est in Asia, Cilicia, Syria, regnisque interiorum nationum ita versari vestrum imperatorem, ut *nihil aliud*, *quam* de hoste ac de laude cogitet. Cic. *Manil.* 22. Si essent omnia mihi solutissima, tamen in republica *non alius* essem, *atque* nunc sum. Cic. *ad div.* I. 9. 61. Bellum ita suscipiatur, ut *nihil aliud*, *nisi* pax quaesita esse videntur. Cic. *Off.* I. 23. Erat historia *nihil aliud*, *nisi* annalium confectio. Cic. *Or.* II. 12. Philosophia, omnium mater artium, *quid est aliud*, *nisi*, ut Plato ait, donum, ut ego, inventum deorum? Cic. *Tusc.* I. 26. *Non alia* fuit *ulla* causa intermissionis litterarum, *nisi* quod, ubi esses, plane nesciebam. Cic. *ad div.* VII. 12. Rogavit, num *quid aliud* ferret, *praeter* arcam. Cic. *Or.* II. 69.

(ff) Adverbs of comparison are changed into correlative pronouns, if quality, magnitude, and number, are distinctly compared; in other words, we do not say *tam bonus* or *malus*, *tam magnus*, *tam multi*, but *talis, tantus, tot*, with their correlatives; thus, *Quales* sumus, *tales* esse videamur. Cic. *Off.* II. 13. At si quis est *talis*, *quales* esse omnes oportebat, qui me vehementer accuset, quod tam capitalem hostem non comprehenderim potius, quam emiserim: non est ista mea culpa, sed temporum. Cic. *Cat.* II. 2. *Tanta* contentione decertavi, *quanta* nunquam antea ulla in causa. Cic. *ad div.* V. 8. Amicitia *tantas* opportunitates habet, *quantas* non queo dicere. Cic. *Lael.* 6. In sua quisque navi dicit se *tantum* habuisse nauturum, *quantum* oportuerit. Cic. *Verr.* V. 39. *Quot* homines, *tot* causae. Cic. *Or.* II. 31. Quid miserius, quam eum, qui *tot* annos, *quot* habet, designatus consul fuerit, fieri consulem non posse? Cic. *Att.* IV. 8.

(gg) The highest degree of a quality, magnitude, or number, is expressed by *quam* or *quantus* with the superlative and the verb *possum*, which, however, may be omitted even with a superlative adverb. Thus we have, Jugurtha *quam maximas* potest copias armat. Sall. *Jug.* 13. Gallinæ avesque reliquæ cubilia sibi nidosque construunt, eosque *quam possunt mollissime* substernunt, ut quam facillime ova serventur. Cic. *N. D.* II. 52. Hannibal medio Etruriæ agro prædatum profectus, *quantam maximam* vastitatem *potest* cædibus incendiisque consuli procul ostendit. Liv. XXII. 3. Mihi nihil fuit optatius, quam ut *quam gratissimus* erga te esse cognoscerer. Cic. *ad div.* I. 5. Definitio est oratio, quæ, quid sit id, de quo agitur, ostendit *quam brevissime.* Cic. *Or.* 33. Tam sum amicus reipublicæ, *quam qui maxime.* Cic. *ad div.* IV. 2. Gratissimum mihi feceris, si huic commendationi meæ tantum tribueris, *quantum* cui *tribuisti plurimum.* Ibid. XIII. 22. Grata ea res, ut *quae maxime* senatui unquam, fuit. Liv. V. 25. Cæsar sit pro prætore eo jure, *quo qui optimo.* Cic. *Phil.* V. 16.

(β) When a difference of degree is implied in the comparison, we have the three following forms of the comparative sentence.

(aa) A comparative or superlative adjective is introduced in both clauses, which are placed on an equal footing by the opposition of *quo—eo, quanto—tanto* with the comparatives, and of *ut quisque —ita* with the superlatives, as in the following examples: *Quo major* est in animis præstantia et *divinior, eo majore* indigent diligentia. Cic. *Tusc.* IV. 27. Duæ ad Luceriam ferebant viæ, altera aperta, sed *quanto tutior, tanto* fere *longior,* altera per furculas Caudinas brevior. Liv. IX. 2. *Quo quisque* est *sollertior* et *ingeniosior, hoc* docet *iracundius* et *laboriosius.* Cic. *Q. Rosc.* 11. *Quanto perditior* quisque est, *tanto acrius* urget. Hor. *Serm.* I. 2. 15. In morbis corporis *ut quisque* est *difficillimus, ita* medicus *nobilissimus* atque *optimus* quæritur. Cic. *Cluent.* 21. *Ut quisque* est vir *optimus, ita difficillime* esse alios improbos suspicatur. Cic. *Q. Fr.* I. 1. 4. *Ut quisque optime* dicit, *ita maxime* dicendi facultatem, variosque eventus orationis timet. Cic. *Or.* I. 26.

(bb) A comparative is introduced into the first clause only, and the object compared is introduced by *quam;* thus, *Minus* dixi, *quam* volui de te. Plaut. *Capt.* II. 3. 70. *Segnius* homines bona, *quam* mala sentiunt. Liv. XXX. 21. *Meliora* sunt ea, quæ natura,

quam illa, quæ arte perfecta sunt. Cic. *N. D.* II. 34. Nihil præstabilius viro, *quam* periculis patriam liberare. Cic. *Mil.* 35.

(cc) This *quam* is omitted after the neuters *plus, amplius,
minus, longius,* when the standard of comparison is a definite number or magnitude (163, (e), δ); thus we have, Nec enim *plus
decem millia* hominum erant. Liv. XLII. 8. Cominius cum equi-
tibus venerat, qui numero non *amplius* erant *quingenti.* Cæs. *B. G.*
VIII. 10. Constabat, non *minus ducentos* Carthaginiensium equites fuisse. Rex, qua sex mensibus iter fecerat, eadem *minus
diebus triginta* in Asiam reversus est. Corn. Nep. II. 5. Spatium, quod non est *amplius pedum, DC.* Cæs. *B. G.* I. 38. Cæsar
certior est factus, magnas Gallorum copias non *longius millia passuum* octo ab hibernis suis afuisse. *Ib.* V. 53.

(dd) We have an ablative with *pro,* when the standard of
comparison is an expectation rather than the object itself, as in the
following examples: Prœlium atrocius, *quam pro numero* pugnau-
tium, editur. Liv. XXI. 29. In quiete utrique consuli dicitur visa
species viri *majoris, quam pro humano habitu,* augustiorisque. Liv.
VIII. 6. Minor *caedes, quam pro tanta victoria,* fuit. Liv. x. 14.
Suevi frumenta ceterosque fructus *patientius, quam pro solita Germanorum inertia,* laborant. Tac. *Ger.* XLV.

(ee) The object compared is expressed by the ablative alone
(above, 163, (e)), if it is implied that the quality is possessed by that
object, though not in the same degree; thus, *Elephanto* beluarum
nulla *prudentior* est. Cic. *N. D.* I. 35. Tunica *proprior pallio*
est. Plaut. *Trin.* v. 2. 30. *Vilius* argentum est *auro, virtutibus*
aurum. Hor. *Ep.* I. 1. 52. Sapientia humana omnia *inferiora virtute* ducit. Cic. *Tusc.* IV. 20. Quid est in homine *ratione divinius?*
Cic. *Leg.* I. 7. Non ego hac nocte *longiorem* vidi. Plaut. *Amph.* I.
1. 123. O matre pulcra filia *pulcrior.* Hor. 1 *Carm.* I. 16.

Obs. This construction is particularly common with the ablatives
solito, justo, aequo, dicto, spe, exspectatione, opinione, when we wish
to express that the degree is higher than what is customary, right,
proper, or than our words, thoughts, hopes, expectations, or opinions
(163, (e) γ); thus we say, Seditionem *solito magis* metuendam Manlius
faciebat. Liv. VI. 14. Non verendum est, ne *plus aequo* quid in amicitiam congeratur. Cic. *Lael.* 16. Cæsar *opinione celerius* venturus
esse dicitur. Cic. *ad div.* XIV. 23. Lævinus consul *serius spe* omnium Romam venit. Liv. XXVI. 26. Servilius consul *minus opinione*
sua efficiebat. Cæs. *B. C.* III. 21.

B. *Subordinate Sentences.*

§ 8. (a) *Conditional Sentences.*

203 It has been mentioned above (192) that the conditional sentence is that form of the hypothetical, in which a categorical proposition has an adverbial sentence dependent on it. This adverbial sentence is really of the nature of a relative clause, to which the categorical sentence furnishes the antecedent. Though it is most usually expressed by means of the particle *si*, the inflected relative may be used in the same sense; for *qui haec fecerit, bonus erit* is quite equivalent to *si quis haec fecerit, bonus erit*. But the proper meaning of *si* itself is 'in whatever case;' and its correlative or antecedent may be occasionally expressed by *ita* or *sic*, as Hoc ipsum *ita* justum est, quod recte fit, *si* est voluntarium (Cic. *de Off.* I. 9), 'this very thing is just on the condition that it is rightly done in those cases in which it is voluntary.' Patres decreverunt, ut quum populus regem jussisset, id *sic* ratum esset, *si* Patres auctores fierent (Liv. I. 17), 'that should be determined on the condition that (in those cases in which) the Senate recommended it.'

Obs. That the conditional clause is really relative is shown also by the structure of the optative sentence, which is expressed not only by *si* and *ni* or *utinam* (above, 172, (1), (e) 128, XIV. *Obs.*), but also by *qui*, as in the phrase: *qui illum Dii omnes perduint* (Ter. *Phorm.* I. 2. 73. Plaut. *Men.* III. 1, 6. cf. Cic. *Att.* IV. 7).

The four different kinds of conditional propositions are given and explained in 128. XVI; and the usage of the different moods and tenses is discussed in the preceding chapter. It only remains to show the various forms in which the Latin idiom exhibits the connexion between the *protasis* or conditional clause and the main clause or *apodosis*.

(α) Regularly and properly the *apodosis* appears as the direct antecedent or correlative of the conditional clause, as in the following examples: *Si fato omnia fiunt,* nihil nos admonere potest, ut cautiores simus. Cic. *Div.* II. 8. Dies affert, vel hora potius, *nisi provisum est,* magnas saepe clades. Cic. *Phil.* III. 1. Ante misissem ad te literas, *si genus scribendi invenirem.* Cic. *ad div.* VI. 10 med. Non possem vivere, *nisi in literis viverem.* Cic. *ibid.* IX. 26.

(β) Sometimes, however, the *apodosis* must be supplied from the terms of the main sentence, which, as it is expressed, stands in an indirect relation to the conditional clause. This is really the case when an indicative takes the place of the subjunctive in the apodosis to a past tense of that mood (above, Ch. III. 172; IV. (c)). The following examples will explain this indirect construction: *Occasio egregie rei gerendae fuit, si* (Furius) *protinus de via ad contra oppugnanda duxisset.* Liv. XXXI. 21. *Admonebat me res, ut hoc quoque loco intermissionem eloquentiae deplorarem: ni vererer, ne de me ipso aliquid viderer queri.* Cic. *Off.* II. 19. *Praeclare viceramus, nisi spoliatum, inermem, fugientem Lepidus recepisset Antonium.* Cic. *ad div.* XII. 10. *Pons sublicius iter paene hostibus dedit, ni unus vir fuisset,* Horatius Cocles. Liv. II. 10. *Ipsos inter se legiones octava et quintadecuma ferrum parabant; ni miles nonanus preces et adversum aspernantis minas interjecisset.* Tac. I. 23. *Trudebantur in paludem, ni Caesar productas legiones instruxisset.* Ib. 63. *Cucina circumveniebatur, ni prima legio sese opposuisset.* Ib. 65. *Stesichorus si tenuisset modum,* videtur aemulari proximus Homerum potuisse. Quint. X. 1. 62. Here the true apodosis in the first example would be, *res egregie gesta esset;* in the second, *et deplorassem;* in the fourth, *paene dedit* implies *et dedisset;* in the fifth, the *ferrum parabant* leads us to the apodosis, *et decertassent;* in the sixth, the consequence is not the imperfect *trudebantur,* 'they were in the act of being thrust,' but *et trusi essent,* which must be supplied; the same remark applies to the seventh example, where we must add, *et circumventus esset,* and the full form of the last example would be, *Stesichorus videtur aemulari proximus Homerum potuisse, et proximus aemulatus esset, si tenuisset modum.* In the third example, as in those given above (172. IV. (c)), it is possible to understand the pluperfect indicative as the real apodosis to *recepisset,* but the implied meaning is expressed most clearly, if we add to *viceramus* the phrase, *et victoria frueremur.*

(γ) The apodosis is omitted altogether, if the conditional clause amounts to the expression of a wish (above, 172. I. (c)), in which case the result is that which we would do, if the wish were realized. And this omission also takes place when the apodosis would be expressed by the same verb as that of the conditional clause, in a sentence dependent on some expression of attempting, expecting, wondering, or the like. The following examples illustrate the latter usage: *Circumfunduntur ex reliquis hostes partibus, si quem aditum reperire possent.* Caes. *B. G.* VI. 37. *Palus erat non magna inter nostrum atque hostium exercitum. Hanc si nostri transirent,* hostes exspectabant. *Ib.* II. 9. Helvetii, *si perrumpere possent,* conati, operis munitione et militum concursu et telis repulsi, hoc conatu destiterunt. *Ib.* I. 8. Tentata res est, *si primo impetu capi Ardea posset.* Liv. I. 57. Te adeunt fere omnes, *si quid velis.* Cic. *ad div.* III. 9. Mirabar, *si tu mihi quicquam adferres novi.* Ter. *Phorm.* III. 2. 5. If we examine these passages, we shall see that in the first we must supply *ut reperirent aliquem aditum;* in the second, the enemies' expectation would be clearly expressed if we added *quid facturi essent nostri;* in the third and fourth the full phrases would be *conati perrumpere si possent;* and *capere Ardeam, si capi posset;* in the fifth we must insert *ut discant;* and in the last the meaning is *mirabar, quid novi adferres, si quid adferres.*

(δ) The conditional particle may be occasionally omitted, if the construction is otherwise complete and obvious, as in the following examples: *Unum cognoris,* omnes noris. Ter. *Phorm.* II. 1. 35. cf. I. 4. 9. *Decies centena dedisses huic parco, paucis contento;* quinque diebus nihil erat in loculis. Hor. *Serm.* I. 3. 15. *Dedisses huic animo* (Corellii Rufi) *par corpus;* fecisset, quod optabat. Plin. *Ep.* I. 12.

(ε) The conditional particle may be added to the comparative particles, *ut, velut, ac, quam,* and it forms one word with *quam* in *quasi,* but it is generally omitted after *tanquam.* Thus we have, Milites, quis impugnandus agger, *ut si* murum succederent, gravibus superne ictibus conflictabantur. Tac. *Ann.* II. 20. Sequani absentis Ariovisti crudelitatem, *velut si* coram adesset, horrebant. Caes. *B. G.* I. 32. Egnatii absentis rem ut tuears, atque a te peto, *ac si* mea negotia essent. Cic. *Fam.* XIII. 43. Deleta est Ausonum gens perinde *ac si* internecivo bello certasset. Liv. IX. 25. Quidam idcirco deum esse non putant, quia non apparet, nec cernitur: proinde, *quasi* nostram ipsam mentem videre possimus. Cic. *Mil.* 31. Stultissimum est, in luctu capillum sibi evellere, *quasi* calvitio maeror levetur. Cic. *Tusc.* III. 26. Parvi primo ortu sic jacent, *tamquam* omnino sine animo sint. Cic. *Fin.* V. 15. Antonium Plancum sic contemnit, *tamquam si* illi aqua et igni interdictum sit. Cic. *Phil.* VI. 4.

Obs. On the distinction between *nisi* and *si non,* see p. 201.

§ 9 (b). *Definitive Sentences.*

204 The rules for the construction of the relative pronoun have been fully given (above, 141); and it has been shown

SYNTAX OF SENTENCES.

(above, 194, (β), Obs. 196) that the relative may be used for the demonstrative combined with a copulative or adversative particle. In this place, however, it is necessary to direct the student's attention to those cases in which the relative with the indicative mood represents the functions of the defining adjective (above, 123, 8, (b); 128, x., (a)), and especially to those forms of the defining sentence in which the relative seems to be in itself conditional or indefinite.

The distinction between the definitive and the subjunctive sentence should be obvious to every one who can recognize the difference between an epithet and a predicate (above, 124). It is clear that this distinction does not consist in the meaning of the epithet or predicate used, but in the construction of the word which for the time being serves to define or predicate. As is well known, the most indefinite of all the pronouns may be used as the subject of a sentence, and we have seen that these pronouns, no less than the demonstratives, contribute to the machinery of the distinctive sentence. Although therefore the relative word may be vague or indefinite in itself, or may have the conditional particle prefixed, it will still form a definitive sentence, if it serves as the attribute or qualification of some single term and is used with the indicative mood. If we say 'a possible contingency,' 'an uncertain amount,' 'however large a sum,' &c., it is manifest that these vague attributes are, in point of syntax, as completely epithets, qualifications, or defining expressions as the most precise and distinct adjectives would have been, and, conversely, that a different construction would convert the most definite expressions into predicates or even adverbs. The student then will see that we have definitive sentences in all the following uses of the relative or relative particles with the indicative mood.

(a) The relative or relative particle with *si* may introduce a definitive sentence; thus, Errant, *si qui* in bello omnes secundos rerum proventus exspectant. Cæs. *B. G.* VII. 29. Tu melius existimare videris de ea, *si quam* nunc habemus, facultate. Cic. *Brut.* 87. Nuda fero Alpium cacumina sunt, et *si quid* est pabuli, obruunt nives. Liv. XXI. 37. Summum bonum est, vivere seligentem, quæ secundum naturam sunt, et *si quae* contra naturam sunt, rejicientem. Cic. *Fin.* III. 9. Jam non tam mihi videntur injuriam facere, *si qui* hæc disputant, quam *si cujus* aures ad hanc disputationem patent. Cic. *ad div.* III. 6.—Studiose equidem utor poëtis nostris, sed *sicubi* illi defecerunt, verti multa de Græcis, ne quo ornamento careret Latina oratio. Cic. *Tusc.* II. 11.

Obs. If the verb is subjunctive the nature of the sentence is of course changed; thus in the following passages the sentences dependent on *sicunde* and *si quando* are conditional and not definitive: Tentabantur urbes, *sicunde* spem aliquam ne ostendisset. Livy, XXVI. 38. Utinam, inquit Pontius Samnis, tum essem natus, *si quando* Romani dona accipere cœpissent! Cic. *de Off.* II. 21.

(β) The vague relatives and relative particles *quicunque*, 'whoever,' *ubicunque*, 'wherever,' *undecunque*, 'whencesoever,' *quocunque*, 'whithersoever,' *quandocunque*, 'whensoever,' *utcunque*, 'howsoever,' *quantuscunque*, 'how great soever,' *quotcunque*, 'how many soever,' are used with the indicative in adjectival sentences; thus, *Quoscunque de te queri audivi, quacunque ratione potui, placavi.* Cic. *Quint. Fr.* I. 2. *Quemcunque hæc pars perditorum lætatum morte Cæsaris putabit, hunc in hostium numero habebit.* Cic. *Att.* XIV. 13. Hoc mementote, *quoscunque* locos attingam, unde ridicula ducantur, ex iisdem locis fere etiam graves sententias posse duci. Cic. *Or.* II. 61. Quod *quibuscunque* verbis dixeris, facetum tamen est, re continetur; quod mutatis verbis, salem amittit, in verbis habet leporem omnem. Cic. *Or.* II. 62. Nihil est virtute amabilius, quam qui adeptus erit, *ubicunque* erit gentium, a nobis diligetur. Cic. *Nat. Deor.* I. 44. *Ubicunque* Patricius habitat, ibi carcer privatus est. Liv. VI. 36. Non *undecunque* causa fluxit, ibi culpa est. Quint. VII. 3. 33. Hæc novi judicii forma terret oculos, qui, *quocunque* inciderunt, veterem consuetudinem fori, et pristinum morem judiciorum requirunt. Cic. *Mil.* 1. Verres *quacunque* iter fecit, ejusmodi fuit, ut non legatus populi Romani, sed ut quædam calamitas pervadere videretur. Cic. *Verr.* I. 16. *Quandocunque* ista gens (Græcorum) suas literas dabit, omnia corrumpet. Plin. *N. H.* XXVIII. 1 med. Orator *utcunque* se adfectum videri et animum audientium moveri volet, ita certum vocis admovebit sonum. Cic. *Or.* XVII. Hoc, *quantumcunque* est, quod certe maximum est, totum est tuum. Cic. *Marcell.* 2. Homines benevolos, *qualescunque* sunt, grave est insequi contumelia. Cic. *Att.* XIV. 14. But the following sentences are conditional: Debeo, *quantumcunque* possim, in eo elaborare, ut &c. Cic. *Fin.* I. 4. *Quotcunque* Senatus creverit, populusve jusserit, tot sunto. Cic. *Leg.* III. 3.

(γ) The same sense of vagueness may be conveyed in a definitive clause by the reduplicated pronouns and particles, *quisquis*, *ubiubi, undeunde, quoquo, utut, quantus quantus, quotquot;* thus, *Quisquis* homo huc profecto venerit, pugnos *edet.* Plaut. *Amph.* I. 1. 152. Omnia mala ingerebat (Hecuba), *quemquem* adspexerat. *Id. Men.* v. 1. 17. *Quisquis* honos tumuli, *quidquid* solamen humandi est, Largior. Virg. *Æn.* x. 193. Plus certe attulit huic populo dignitatis, *quisquis* ille est, si modo est aliquis, qui non illustravit modo, sed etiam genuit in hac urbe dicendi copiam, quam illi, qui Ligurum castella expugnaverunt. Cic. *Brut.* 73. *Quidquid* erit, tibi erit. Cic. *ad div.* II. 10. In amicitia *quidquid* est, id verum et voluntarium est. Cic. *Lael.* VIII. Nunc *ubiubi* sit animus, certe quidem in te est. Cic. *Tusc.* I. 29. *Quoquo* hic spectabit, eo tu spectato simul. Plaut. *Pseud.* III. 2. 69. Id, *utut* est, etsi dedecorum est, patiar. Plaut. *Bacch.* v. 2. 73. *Quantiquanti,* bene emitur, quod necesse est. Cic. *Att.* XII. 24. Tu, *quantus quantus,* nil nisi sapientia es. Ter. *Ad.* III. 3. 40. Si leges duae, aut si plures, aut *quotquot* erunt, conservari non possunt, quia discrepant inter se, ea maxime conservanda putatur, quæ ad maximas res pertinere videtur. Cic. *Inv.* II. 49.

Obs. The particles *quamris* and *quantumvis,* though apparently synonymous with *quantusquantus,* are used with the subjunctive mood, and constitute a concessive sentence, thus, Ista, *quantumris* exigua sint, in majus excedunt. Sen. *Ep.* 85. Illa mali generis vincla quæ, *quamvis* robusta sint, propter sterilitatem fructu carant, emendantur insitione facta. *Colum.* IV. 22.

§ 10. (c) *Subjunctive Sentences.*

205 The subjunctive sentence, properly so called, is a special characteristic of Latin syntax, at least so far as concerns the uniform employment of the subjunctive mood. Its general effect is to express by means of the relative clause a number of adverbial or predicative phrases. The predicative or adverbial nature of the subjunctive sentence is most plainly seen in the use of the subjunctive after *sunt qui, inveniuntur qui, reperiuntur qui,* &c.; for here *qui = talis ut* (175), (4), *Obs.*), and this meaning may be conveyed by the predicative adjective (140), (b)). Even relative clauses which would otherwise be definitive, become subject to the operation of this rule when they are found included in an oblique or predicative sentence. Thus in the example given above (p. 242), *Socrates dicebat omnes in eo, quod scirent, satis esse eloquentes,* it is clear that we should have written *omnes in eo, quod sciunt, satis sunt eloquentes,* if we had been expressing the thought as our own, for

SUBORDINATE SENTENCES. 401

quod sciunt is strictly a definitive clause; but the objective sentence formed by the accusative with the infinitive is itself predicative, because the accusative constitutes a secondary predicate (above, 125). By a kind of attraction therefore the included relative clause assumes the dependent or subjunctive form.

Subjunctive sentences may be divided into the following classes:

(a) The indirect interrogative.

Whenever a direct question is made dependent on another sentence—in other words, when it becomes indirect or oblique—the verb is necessarily in the subjunctive mood (above, 126, xII.).

(aa) The indirect interrogative is dependent on a main sentence expressive of seeing, hearing, feeling, supposing, thinking, knowing, learning, saying, certainty, uncertainty, likelihood, wonder, &c. Thus: *Videamus* primum, *deorumne* providentia mundus *regatur*; deinde *consulantne* rebus humanis. Cic. *Nat. Deor.* III. 25. *Sentiet, qui* vir *siem.* Ter. *Eun.* I. 1. 21. *Qua sint* illæ sorores dignitate, potes ex his pueris *suspicari.* Cic. *Inv.* II. 1. Ad ferendum dolorem placide et sedate plurimum proficit, toto pectore, ut dicitur, *cogitare, quam* id honestum *sit.* Cic. *Tusc.* II. 24. *Disce, quid sit* vivere. Ter. *Heaut.* v. 2. 18. *Qualis sit* animus, ipse animus *nescit.* Cic. *Tusc.* I. 22. Credo te *audisse, ut* me *circumstiterint* judices. Cic. *Att.* I. 6. Cæsar *docebat, ut* omni tempore totius Galliæ principatum Ædui *tenuissent.* Cæs. *B. G.* I. 43. *Videmus, ut* luna accessu et recessu suo solis lumen *accipiat.* Cic. *Or.* III. 45. *Quid* quæque nox, aut dies *ferat, incertum est.* Liv. III. 27. *Mirum est, ut* animus agitatione, motuque corporis *excitetur.* Plin. *Ep.* I. 6. *Verisimile non est, ut* Heius religioni suæ monumentisque majorum pecuniam *anteponeret.* Cic. *Verr.* IV. 6. Postrema syllaba brevis, an longa *sit,* ne in versu quidem *refert.* Cic. *Or.* 64, § 217. *Quaeritur, cur* doctissimi homines de maximis rebus *dissentiant.* Cic. *Or.* III. 29. Iphicrates quum *interrogaretur, utrum* pluris patrem, matremne *faceret;* matrem, inquit. Corn. Nep. xi. 3.

(bb) The indirect interrogative is dependent on a verb expressive of fear, anxiety, or doubt; and in this usage *vereor, timeo, metuo ut* mean 'I fear that it will not be so;' but *vereor, timeo, metuo ne* mean 'I fear that it will be so.' That this construction is that of the indirect interrogative with verbs of seeing, considering, &c. is clear from the fact that these verbs, when they express not only uncertainty but anxiety, may be followed by *ne;* thus: Vide, *ne* superbi *sit,* aspernari Cæsaris liberalitatem. Cic. *ad div.* IV. 9. Si vita in exsilio tibi commodior esse videatur, cogitandum tamen est, *ne* tutior non *sit. Ib.* Accordingly we might, if it were necessary, add to the verb of fearing some participle, as *cogitans, cogitantes,* to express the uncertainty on which the apprehension rested. The following are examples of the usage: Omnes labores te excipere video. *Timeo, ut sustineas. Ib.* XIV. 2. De amicitia tua etsi non dubitabam, tamen, *ut* incorrupta *maneret*, *laborabam. Ib.* XI. 28. *Timebam, ne evenirent* ea, quæ acciderunt. *Ib.* VI. 21. Non vereor, *ne* mea vita modestia parum *valitura sit* contra falsos rumores. *Ib.* XI. 28. *Verebamini, ne* non id *facerem*, quod recepissem semel. Ter. *Phorm.* v. 7. 8. *Dubito, an* idem nunc tibi, quod tunc mihi, *suadeam.* Plin. *Ep.* VI. 27. De Baiis nonnulli *dubitant, an* Cæsar per Sardiniam *veniat.* Illud enim adhuc prædium suum non inspexit. Cic. *ad div.* IX. 7. *Vereor, quid sit.* Cic. *Att.* VII. 7. Recessum tuum *quomodo acciperent* homines, *quam* probabilis necessitas *futura esset, vereor* etiam nunc. Cic. *ad div.* VIII. 10.

(cc) The indirect interrogative is dependent on a noun expressing an apprehension, a reason, or a thought. Thus: *Pavor ceperat milites, ne* mortiferum *esset* vulnus Scipionis. Liv. XXIV. 42. *Cura incesserat* patres, *ne* plebs tribunos militum ex plebe *crearet. Ib.* IV. 50. Difficile dictu est, quænam *causa sit, cur* (ea?) quæ maxime sensus nostros impellunt voluptate, et specie prima acerrime commoveant, ab iis celerrime fastidio quodam et satietate *abalienemur.* Cic. *Or.* III. 25. Me quidem Athenæ non tam operibus magnificis delectant, quam *recordatione* summorum virorum, *ubi* quisque habitare, *ubi* sedere, *ubi* disputare *sit solitus.* Cic. *Leg.* II. 2.

(β) The relative predication.

The manner in which the subjunctive sentence with the relative serves as a secondary predication, may be seen by an examination of the following examples:

(aa) The relative sentence may be a secondary predication of the *end.* Clusini legatos Romam, *qui* auxilium ab senatu *peterent,* misere. Liv. v. 35. In Germania quum bellum civitas aut illatum defendit, aut infert, magistratus, *qui* et bello *praesint*, ut vitæ necisque habeant potestatem, deliguntur. Cæs. *B. G.* vi. 23.

(bb) The relative sentence may be a secondary predication of the *cause*: O magna vis veritatis, *quae* contra hominum ingenia facile se ipsa *defendat!* Cic. *Cael.* 26. Nunquam laudari satis digne possit philosophia, *cui qui pareat*, omne tempus ætatis sine molestia *possit* degere. Cic. *Sen.* 1. Magna est Pelopis culpa, *qui* non *erudierit* filium, nec *docuerit*, quatenus esset quidque curandum. Cic. *Tusc.* I. 44. Actio maluimus iter facere pedibus, *qui* incommode *navigassemus*. Cic. *Att.* v. 9. Tarquinio quid impudentius, *qui* bellum *gereret* cum iis, qui ejus non tulerunt superbiam! Cic. *Tusc.* III. 12.

(cc) The relative sentence may be a secondary predication of the *consequence*, or the relative may be rendered by *talis ut*, 'such that' (above, 175, (b), 3): *Qui post factam injuriam se expurget*, parum mihi prosit. Ter. *Hec.* v. 1. 16. Vendat ædes vir bonus propter aliqua vitia, *quae* ipse *norit*, ceteri *ignorent.* Cic. *Off.* III. 13. Excellentibus ingeniis citius defuerit ars, *qua* civem *regant*, quam qua hostes *superent.* Liv. II. 43. Incidunt sæpe multæ causæ, *quæ conturbent* animos utilitatis specie. Cic. *Off.* III. 10. Sæpe vidimus fractos pudore, *qui* ratione nulla *vincerentur.* Cic. *Tusc.* II. 21. Natura est, *quae contineat* mundum omnem, eumque *tueatur.* Cic. *Nat. Deor.* II. 11. Nunc id dicam, *quod* tacitus tu mihi *assentiare.* Cic. *Caecil.* 7. Duo tum excellebant oratores, *qui* me imitandi cupiditate *excitarent*, Cotta et Hortensius. Cic. *Brut.* 92.

Obs. There are two special illustrations of the use of *qui* with the subjunctive to introduce a predication of the consequence; the first is when *is sum qui*, 'I am such a person as,' is used as an abbreviated form of the illative or consecutive sentence; thus, Ego *is sum, qui* Cæsari concedi *putem* utilius esse, quod postulat, quam signa conferri. Cic. *Att.* vii. 8. Num tu *is es, qui* in disputando non tuum judicium *sequare*, sed auctoritate aliorum *pareas?* Cic. *Leg.* I. 13. Non *is sum, qui*, quidquid videtur, tale *dicam* esse, quale videatur. Cic. *Acad.* II. 7. In corpore si quid *ejusmodi est, quod* reliquo corpori *noceat*, uri secarique patimur. Cic. *Phil.* viii. 5.

The other case is when *est qui*, *invenitur qui* and the like are similarly used to introduce a special qualification (above, 205); thus, *Sunt, qui* (= tales ut) duos tantum in Sacro monte creatos tribunos esse *dicant.* Liv. II. 33. *Fuit, qui* (= talis ut) *suaderet*, adpellationem mensis Augusti in Septembrem transferendam. Suet. *Aug.* 100. *Inventus est, qui*

(= talis ut) flammis *imponeret manus*. Sen. *Ep.* 76. *Qui* (= tales ut) se ultro morti *offerant*, facilius *reperiuntur*, quam *qui* dolorem patienter *ferant*. Caes. *B. G.* VII. 72. Est aliquis, *qui* (= talis ut) se inspici, aestimari *fastidiat*. Liv. VI. 41. But if *sunt qui*, &c., merely contains the definite statement, 'there are certain persons who,' the sentence is definitive, and the indicative must be used, as we have explained above (173, (b), (4), *Obs.*), and as the following examples will show: Insularum (Rheni) pars magna a feris barbariaque nationibus incolitur, ex quibus *sunt*, *qui* piscibus atque ovis avium vivere *aestimantur*. Caes. *B. G.* IV. 10. Sunt, *qui* officia lucis noctisque *perverunt*, nec ante *diducunt* oculos, quam apperture nox coepit. Sen. *Ep.* 122. Tum primum *reperta sunt*, quae per tot annos rempublicam *exederant*. Tac. II. 27. Sunt principes consilii publici; *sunt* (alii), qui eorum sectam *sequuntur*. Cic. *Sext.* 45. *Sunt*, quibus e ramo frondea *facta* cara *est*. Ovid, *Fast.* III. 527. *Est deus occultos qui vetat esse dulces*. Tibull. I. 9, 24. *Eum to esse finge*, *qui sum ego*. Cic. *Fam.* III. 12. *Multa sunt quae dici possunt*. Cic. *Cluent*. 60. *Sunt permulti viri, qui valetudinis causa in his locis conveniunt*. Cic. *ad div.* IX. 14.

(dd) The relative sentence may be a secondary predication of the *concession*, or the relative may be rendered by 'although' with the demonstrative pronoun: Mihi permirum videtur, quemquam exstare, qui etiam nunc credat Chaldaeis, *quorum* praedicta quotidie *videat* re et eventis refelli. Cic. *Div.* II. 47. Neque est boni, neque liberalis parentis, *quem procrearit* et *eduxerit*, eum non et vestire et ornare. Cic. *Or.* II. 28. Quis est, qui C. Fabricii, Manii Curii non cum caritate aliqua et benevolentia memoriam usurpet, *quos* nunquam *viderit?* Cic. *Lael.* 8. Sapiens posteritatem ipsam, *cujus sensum habiturus* non *sit*, ad se putat pertinere. Cic. *Tusc.* I. 38.

(ee) The relative sentence may be a secondary predication of the condition, or *qui* may be rendered by 'if any one' (above, 203); thus, Errat longe, mea quidem sententia, *qui* imperium *credat* gravius esse aut stabilius, vi quod fit, quam illud, quod amicitia adjungitur. Ter. *Ad.* I. 1. 40.

(γ) The reference to a conception or supposition.

The relative is followed by the subjunctive, when it does not merely define a fact but refers to some conception, so that *qui* may be rendered, 'who, as it is, or was understood;' as in the following examples: Recte Socrates exsecrari cum solebat, *qui* primus utilitatem a natura *sejunxisset*. Cic. *Leg.* I. 12. In Hispania prorogatum veteribus praetoribus est imperium cum exercitibus, *quos haberent*. Liv. XL. 18. Mos est Athenis, laudari in concione eos, *qui sint* in præliis interfecti. Cic. *Or.* 44. Hannibal tabernas argentarias, *quae* circa forum Romanum tunc *essent*, jussit venire. Liv. XXVI. 11. Themistocli fuit optabilius oblivisci posse potius, *quod* mominisse *nollet*, quam *quod* semel *audisset, vidissetve*, meminisse. Cic. *Or.* II. 74. Erat Hortensio memoria tanta, ut, *quae* secum *commentatus esset*, ea sine scripto verbis eisdem redderet, *quibus cogitavisset*. Cic. *Brut.* 88. Quid me reducem esse voluistis? An, ut inspectante me expellerentur ii, *per quos essem restitutus*? Cic. *Mil.* 37. Multa in silva Hercynia genera ferarum nasci constat, *quae* reliquis in locis *visa* non *sint*. Cæs. *B. G.* VI. 25. Ego me minus diu senem esse mallem, quam, esse senem ante, quam *essem*. Cic. *Sen.* 19.

(δ) The oblique narration.

The relative is followed by the subjunctive even in a definitive sentence, if this is included in an objective sentence dependent on a verb of speaking or thinking, so that there is, as in the case just considered, a reference, however tacit, to the words or thoughts of another. (Above, 126, XL.)

In the oblique narrative (*obliqua oratio*), the dependent infinitive expresses the main verb of the direct narrative (*oratio directa*), but the relative sentences and those parts of the main sentence which denote a wish or a command, a condition or a cause, exhibit the verbs in the subjunctive mood; as in the following examples: Legatos ad Cæsarem mittunt (milites): *sese paratos esse* portas aperire, *quae*que *imperaverit* facere et L. Domitium in ejus potestatem *tradere*. Cæs. *B. C.* I. 20. Legationi Ariovistus respondit: *Si* quid *ipsi* a Cæsare opus *esset, sese* ad *eum venturum fuisse; si* quid *ille a se velit, illum ad se* venire *oportere*. Ib. *B. G.* I. 34. Theopompus et Timæus de Alcibiade prædicarunt, quum Athenis, splendidissima civitate, natus *esset*, omnes splendore ac dignitate *superasse;* postquam inde expulsus Thebas *venerit*, adeo studiis eorum *inservisse*, ut nemo eum labore corporisque viribus *posset* æquiparare. Corn. Nep. VII. 11. Hirri necessarii fidem imploraruut Pompeii: *Praestaret, quod* proficiscenti *recepisset*. Cæs. *B. C.* III. 22. Pyrrho adelto a Tarentinis in Italiam a Dodonæo Jove data dictio erat: *caveat* Acherusiam aquam Pandosiamque urbem: ibi fatis ejus *terminum duri*. Liv. VIII. 24. Athenis lege sanctum est: ne quis sepulcrum *faceret* operosius, quam quod decem homines *effecerint* triduo. Cic. *Leg.* II. 26. Addit hæc (Milo): Fortes et sapientes viros non tam præmia sequi solere recte factorum, quam ipsa recte facta; se nihil in vita, nisi præclarum fecisse, siquidem nihil *sit* præstabilius viro, quam periculis patriam liberare; beatos esse, quibus ea res honori *fuerit* a suis civibus; nec tamen eos miseros, qui beneficio cives suos *vicerint:* sed tamen ex omnibus præmiis virtutis, *si esset* habenda ratio præmiorum, amplissimum esse præmium gloriam; esse hanc unam, quæ brevitatem vitæ posteritatis memoria *consolaretur;* quæ *efficeret,* ut absentes *adessemus,* mortui *viveremus:* hanc denique esse, cujus gradibus etiam homines in cœlum *viderentur* adscendere. Cic. *Mil.* 35. Cæsar scribit Labieno, *si* reipublicæ commodo facere *posset,* cum legione ad fines Nerviorum *veniat.* Cæs. *B. G.* v. 46. Cæsar orat et postulat: Rempublicam *suscipiant* atque una secum *administrent: sin* timore *defugiant,* illis so oneri non futurum et per se rempublicam administraturum. Id. *B. C.* I. 32. Eleus Hippias quum Olympiam venisset, gloriatus est, nihil esse ulla in arte rerum omnium, quod ipse *nesciret;* nec solum has artes, quibus liberales doctrinæ atque ingenuæ *continerentur,* sed annulum, quem *haberet,* pallium, quo *amictus,* soccos, quibus *indutus esset,* se sua manu confecisse. Cic. *Or.* III. 32. Socratem solitum aiunt dicere, perfectum sibi opus esse, *si* quis satis *esset* concitatus cohortatione sua ad studium cognoscendæ percipiendæque virtutis: quibus enim id persuasum *esset,* ut nihil *mallent* se esse, quam bonos viros, iis reliquam facilem esse doctrinam. Id. *ibid.* L 47. Legationi Ariovistus respondit: So neque sine exercitu ea cas partes Galliæ venire audere, quas Cæsar *possideret,* neque exercitum sine magno sumptu atque emolimento in unum locum contrahere posse; sibi autem mirum videri, quid in sua Gallia, quam bello *vicisset,* aut Cæsari, aut omnino populo Romano negotii *esset.* Cæs. *B. G.* I. 34. Cato mirari se aiebat, quod non *rideret* haruspex, haruspicem quum *vidisset.* Cic. *Div.* II. 24.

Obs. 1 Interrogations, and those relative sentences which are copulative rather than definitive, have their verbs in the infinitive in the oblique narration; but if the verbs would have been subjunctive in the *oratio recta,* this mood *is* retained. The following examples will illustrate this rule: Haud mirum esse Superbo inditum Romæ cognomen. *An quisquam superbius esse,* quam ludificari sic omne nomen Latinum? *Cui non adparere,* adfectare eum imperium in Latinos? Liv. I. 50. Plebs fremit: *Quid se vivere, quid* in parte civium *censeri,* si quod duorum hominum virtute partum sit, id obtinere universi non possint? Liv. VII. 18. Tribuni militum nihil temere agendum existimabant:

SUBORDINATE SENTENCES. 407

Quid esse levius aut turpius, quam, auctore hoste, de summis rebus capere consilium? Cæs. *B.G.* v. 28. Tum jussa Messalinæ prætendi, et labare defensio. Cur enim *neminem alium delectum,* qui sævienti, impudicæ vocem præberet? Puniendos rerum atrocium ministros, ubi pretia scelerum adepti, scelera ipsa aliis delegunt. Tac. *Ann.* xiii. 43. Cur enim *differri nuptias suas? formam* scilicet *displicere, et triumphales avos? an fecunditatem* et verum animum *timeri,* ne uxor saltim injurias Patrum, iram populi adversus superbiam avaritiamque matris aperiat? Tac. *Ann.* xiv. 1. *Quantum interesse* inter moderationem antiquorum et novam superbiam crudelitatemque. Liv. viii. 33. Unumquemque nostrum censent philosophi mundi esse partem; *ex quo illud* natura *consequi,* ut communem utilitatem nostrae anteponamus. Cic. *Fin.* iii. 19. Fama est, aram esse in vestibulo templi Laciniæ Junonis, *cujus cinerem* nullo unquam moveri vento. Liv. xxiv. 3. Themistocles apud Lacedæmonios liberrime professus est, Athenienses suo consilio deos patrios maris sepsisse. Nam illorum urbem ut propugnaculum oppositam esse barbaris, *apud quam* jam bis *classes regias fecisse* naufragium. Corn. Nep. ii. 7. Quod vero ad amicitiam populi Romani attulissent, id iis eripi, quis pati possent? Cæs. *B.G.* i. 43. Sextius Liciniusque primores Patrum interrogando fatigabant: *Auderentne* postulare, ut quum bina jugera agri plebi dividerentur, ipsis plus quingenta jugera habere liceret? Liv. vi. 36. Si bonum virum ducerent, *quid ita* pro malo ac noxio *damnassent?* si noxium comperissent, *quid ita,* male credito priore consulatu, alterum *crederent?* Liv. xxvii. 34. Singulos sibi olim Reges fuisse, nunc binos imponi; e *quibus* Legatos in sanguinem, Procurator in bona *sæviret.* Tac. *Agr.* 15.

Obs. 2. The indicative is retained after relatives in the *oratio obliqua,* when the relative clause introduces a statement or explanation from the narrator rather than the supposed speaker, and when it is intimated that the statement so introduced is an absolute fact, not merely an opinion or assertion of the person whose words are quoted. Thus we have, Cæsari nuntiatur, Sulmonenses, quod oppidum a Corfinio septem millium intervallo *abest,* cupere ea facere, quæ vellet, sed a Q. Lucretio, Senatore, et Attio Peligno prohiberi, qui id oppidum septem cohortium præsidio *tenebant.* Cæs. *B.C.* i. 18. Juris interpretes contendunt, tribunos vetere jurejurando plebis, quum primum eam potestatem *creavit, sacrosanctos esse.* Liv. iii. 55. Atticum ipsum vere gloriantem audivi, se nunquam cum sorore fuisse in simultate, *quam* prope æqualem *habebat.* Corn. Nep. xxv. 17. Cogitavit (Gaius) etiam de Homeri carminibus abolendis. Cur enim sibi non licere, dicens, quod Platoni *licuit,* qui eum e civitate, quam *constituebat,* ejecerit? Suet. *Calig.* 34. Cæsar per exploratores certior factus est, ex ea parte vici, quam Gallis *concesserat,* omnes noctu discessisse, montesque, qui impenderent, a maxima multitudine teneri. Cæs. *B.C.* iii. 2. Perseus cohortatus est milites ad bellum. Omnia, quæ regia cura præparanda *fuerant,* plena cumulataque habere Macedonas. Liv. xlii. 52.

Obs. 3. The following may be taken as an example of the manner in which the *oratio obliqua* may be reduced or restored to the *oratio recta.*

SYNTAX OF SENTENCES.

Liv. III. 17. *Oratio recta.*
Quid hoc rei est, inquit, tribuni? Ap. Herdonii ductu et auspicio rempublicam everruri estis? Tam felix vobis corrumpendis fuit qui servitia vestra non commovit auctor? Quum hostes supra caput sint, discedi ab armis, legesque ferri placuit?

Oratio obliqua.
clamans: Quid hoc rei esset? Ap. Herdonii ductu et auspicio rempublicam everruros esse? Tam felicem eis corrumpendis fuisse, qui servitia eorum non commovisset auctor? Quum hostes supra caput essent, discedi ab armis, legesque ferri placere?

Inde ad multitudinem oratione versa:

Si vos urbis, Quirites, si vestri nulla cura tangit, at vos vereamini Deos Patrios ab hostibus captos. Jupiter Optimus Maximus, Juno regina, et Minerva, alii Dii Deaeque obsidentur: castra servorum publicos vestros penates tenent. Haec vobis forma sanae civitatis videtur? Tantum hostium non solum intra muros est, sed in arce, supra forum, curiamque. Comitia interim in foro sunt; senatus in curia est; velut quum otium superat, senator sententiam dicit; alii Quirites suffragium ineunt. Non, quidquid Patrum plebisque est, consules, tribunos, Deos hominesque omnes armatos opem ferre, in Capitolium currere, liberare ac pacare augustissimam illam domum Jovis Optimi maximi decuit? Romule pater, tu mentem tuam, qua quondam arcem ab his iisdem Sabinis auro captam recepisti, da stirpi tuae; jube hanc ingredi viam, quam tu dux, quam tuus ingressus exercitus est. Primus, en, ego consul, quantum mortalis Deum possum, te ac tua vestigia sequar.

Si vos urbis, si ipsorum nulla cura tangat; at verentur Deos patrios ab hostibus captos. Jovem Optimum Maximum, Junonem reginam, et Minervam, alios Deos Deasque obsideri: castra servorum publicos populi Romani penates tenere. Hanc eis formam sanae civitatis videri? Tantum hostium non solum intra muros esse, sed in arce, supra forum, curiamque: comitia interim in foro (esse); senatum in curia esse: velut quum otium superet, senatorem sententiam dicere: alios Quirites suffragium inire. Non, quidquid Patrum plebisque esset, consules, tribunos, Deos hominesque omnes armatos opem ferre, in Capitolium currere, liberare ac pacare augustissimam illam domum Jovis Optimi Maximi decuisse? Tum precibus ad Romulum patrem versus oravit: Mentem suam, qua quondam arcem ab iisdem Sabinis auro captam recepisset, daret stirpi suae: juberet eam ingredi viam, quam ipse dux, quam ipsius ingressus exercitus esset. Primum se consulem, quantum mortalis Deum posset, eum atque ejus vestigia secuturum.

Ultimum orationis fuit:

Ego arma capio, voco omnes Quirites ad arma. Si quis impediet, jam ego consularis imperii, jam tribuniciae potestatis, sacratarumque legum oblitus, quisquis ille erit,

Se arma capere, vocare omnes Quirites ad arma; si quis impediat, jam se consularis imperii, jam tribuniciae potestatis, sacratarumque legum oblitum, quisquis ille sit, ubi-

ubicunque *erit*, in Capitolio, in foro pro hoste habebo. *Jubeta*, tribuni, quoniam in Ap. Herdonium *retalis*, in P. Valerium consulem sumi arma. *Audebo ego* in tribunis, quod princeps familiae *meae* ausus in regibus *est*.

cunque *sit*, in Capitolio, in foro, pro hoste *habiturum*. *Juberent* tribuni quoniam in Ap. Herdonium *retarent*, in P. Valerium consulem sumi arma: *ausurum se* in tribunis, quod princeps familiae *suae* ausus in regibus *esset*.

§ 11. (d) *Temporal Sentences.*

206 Temporal sentences are differently expressed according to the differences of the time denoted.

(a) *Contemporary acts* are denoted by *quum, quando, ut, ubi, simulac, dum* with the indicative (176, 2, (a)); by the participle in agreement with the subject (182, (c)); or in the ablative absolute (182, (g)). Thus: *Tum, quum* in Asia res magnas permulti amiserant, scimus, Romae, solutione impedita, fidem concidisse. Cic. *Manil.* 7. Quid ogeris, *tunc* apparebit, *quum* animam *ages*. Sen. *Ep.* 26. *Ubi* satur sum, nulla crepitant intestina: *quando* esurio, tum crepant. Plaut. *Men.* v. 5. 57. Haec *dum* Romae geruntur, Quintius interea de saltu agroque communi a servis communibus vi detruditur. Cic. *Quint.* 6. *Dum* hominum genus erit, qui accuset eos, non deerit: *dum* civitas erit, judicia fient. Cic. *S. Rosc.* 32. *Simul ac primum* Verri occasio visa est, consulem deseruit. Cic. *Verr.* I. 13. Fuit quoddam tempus, *quum* in agris homines passim bestiarum more vagabantur. Cic. *Inv.* I. 2. Nunquam obliviscar *noctis illius, quum* tibi vigilanti pollicebar, &c. Hence also, Fuit, *quum* hoc dici poterat: Patricius enim eras et a liberatoribus patriae ortus. Liv. VII. 32. Ille *ubi* videt, me tam facile victum quaerere, *ibi* homo coepit me obsecrare, ut sibi liceret discere id de me. Ter. *Eun.* II. 2. 29. Hae *ubi* filio nuntiata sunt, statim exanimatus ad aedes contendit. Cic. *Verr.* I. 26. *Ubi primum* illuxit, abire sine certamine cupiunt. Liv. x. 35. Varro *ut* advenit, extemplo Hostilius legionem unam signa in urbem ferre jussit. Liv. XXVII. 24. *Ut* ab urbe discessi, nullum adhuc intermisi diem, quin aliquid ad te literarum darem. Cic. *Att.* VIII. 15. Pompeius *ut* me *primum* decedens ex Syria vidit, complexus et gratulans meo beneficio patriam se visurum esse dixit. Cic. *Phil.* II. 5. *Dum* ea Romae geruntur, jam Sutrium ab Etruscis *obsidebatur*. Liv. IX. 33. Haec *dum* nostri *colligunt*, rex ipse e manibus *effugit*. Cic. *Manil.* 9. *Dum* elephanti *trajiciuntur*, interim Hannibal Numidas equites quingentos ad castra Romana *miserat* speculatum. Liv. XXI. 29. *Dum*

Sulla in aliis rebus *erat occupatus, erant* interea, qui suis vulneribus
mederentur. Cic. *S. Rosc.* 32. In has clades incidimus, *dum* metui,
quam cari esse et diligi, malumus. Cic. *Off.* II. 8. (See Heindorf.
ad *Hor. Serm.* p. 127.) *Hipparchus,* Pisistrati filius, in Marathonia
pugna cecidit, arma contra patriam *ferens.* Cic. *Att.* IX. 10. Ne
mente quidem recte uti possumus, multo cibo et potione *impleti.* Cic.
Tusc. V. 35. Socratis morti illacrimare soleo, Platonem *legens.* Cic.
N. D. III. 33. Pleraeque scribuntur orationes, *habitae* jam, non ut
habeantur. Cic. *Brut.* 24. Alit lectio ingenium, et studio *fatigatum*
reficit. Sen. *Ep.* 84. *Arunti Quintio Cincinnato* nuntiatum est, cum
dictatorem esse factum. Cic. *Sen.* 16. Tiberius, *trajecturus* Rhenum,
commeatum omnem non ante transmisit, quam explorasset vehicu-
lorum onera. Suet. *Tib.* 18. Nihil affirmo, *dubitans* plerumque et
mihi ipso *diffidens.* Cic. *Div.* II. 3. Æduorum milites legatis
Cæsaris renuntiant, se Biturigum perfidiam *veritos* revertisse. Cæs.
B. G. VII. 5. Hostes, hanc *adepti* victoriam, in perpetuum se fore
victores confidebant. *Ibid.* V. 39. *Mendaci homini* no verum quidem *dicenti* credere solemus. Cic. *Div.* II. 70. Ut oculus, sic animus, se non *videns,* alia cernit. Cic. *Tusc.* I. 27. Scripta tua, Varro,
jam diu *exspectans,* non audeo tamen flagitare. Cic. *Acad.* I. 1.
Crastino die *oriente sole* redite in pugnam. Liv. III. 2. Dionysius prior decessit *florente regno.* Corn. Nep. XXI. 2. Artes innu-
merabiles repertæ sunt, *docente natura.* Cic. *Leg.* L. 8. Maximas
virtutes jacere omnes necesse est, *voluptate dominante.* Cic. *Fin.* II.
35. Nihil præcepta atque artes valent, *nisi adjuvante natura.*
Quint. *Proœm.* 26. Solon et Pisistratus *Servio Tullio regnante*
viguerunt. Cic. *Brut.* 10. *Sole orto* Volsci firmiore se munimento
ab Romanis circumvallatos, quam a se urbem viderunt. Liv. IV. 9.
Tarquinius Turnum *oblato falso crimine* oppressit. Liv. I. 51.
Dione Syracusis *interfecto* Dionysius rursus Syracusarum potitus
est. Corn. Nep. XX. 2. *Regibus exactis* consules creati sunt. Liv. IV.
4. Quænam sollicitudo vexaret impios, *sublato* suppliciorum *metu?*
Cic. *Leg.* I. 14. Deserere Rheni ripam, *irrupturis* tam *infestis
nationibus,* non conducit. Tac. *Hist.* II. 32. Res, *quum* hæc *scribebam,* erat in extremum adducta discrimen. Cic. *ad div.* XII. 6.
Credo *tum, quum* Sicilia *florebat* opibus et copiis, magna artificia
fuisse in ea insula. Cic. *Verr.* IV. 21. *Quum redeo,* Hortensius
venerat et ad Terentiam salutatum deverterat. Cic. *Att.* X. 16.
Fabius prætor *quum primum* Crotæ litus *adtigit,* nuntios circa civitates misit, ut armis absisterent. Liv. XXXVII. 60. Dionysius

tyrannus ea ipsa, quæ concupierat, ne tum quidem, *quum* omnia so
posse *censebat*, consequebatur. Cic. *Tusc.* II. 20.

But we have *quum* with the imperfect subjunctive, if a necessary
connexion is presumed between the contemporaneous events. Thus,
Quum Lacedæmonii *quererentur*, opus nihilo minus fieri: interim
reliqui legati sunt consecuti. Corn. Nep. II. 7. Plura *quum* scribere *vellem*, nuntiatum est mihi, vim parari. Sall. *Cat.* 35. *Quum*
per colloquia principum succedens muris parum *proficeret:* postremo
ingressus urbem precibus evicit, ut permitterent se Romanis. Liv.
XXXVIII. 9. Epistolam *quum* a te avide *exspectarem* ad vesperum,
ut soleo: ecce tibi nuntius, pueros venisse Roma. Cic. *Att.* II. 9.
Hæc *quum moliretur* Alcibiades, eodem tempore Critias cœterique
tyranni Atheniensium certos homines ad Lysandrum in Asiam miserunt. Corn. Nep. VII. 10. We have the subjunctive with *quum*
in the oblique narration; thus, Herculem Prodicium dicunt, *quum
primum* pubesceret, exisse in solitudinem. Cic. *Off.* I. 32. Also
when the time is dependent on the expression of a wish. Thus,
Utinam *diem* illum videam, *quum* tibi gratias agam. Cic. *Att.* III.
1. Utinam tunc essem natus, *quando* Romani dona accipere cœpissent! Cic. *Off.* II. 21.

(β) *Repeated acts* are denoted by *quoties, quum, uti si*, or some
other particle with the present, perfect, or future tense; and the
pluperfect indicative is often used with relatives or relative particles when the main verb implies repetition and is used in the
imperfect (175, 5). The best writers, as Cicero, Cæsar, and Sallust,
generally prefer the indicative mood, or treat the subordinate sentence as definitive. Thus we have: Consul non unius anni, sed
quoties bonus atque fidus judex honestum *præstulit* utili. Hor. 4
Carm. IX. 40. *Quoties* te Roma tuo *reddet* Aquino, me quoque
convelle a Cumis. Juv. III. 318. *Quamcunque in partem* equites
impetum *fecerant*, hostes loco cedere *cogebantur*. Cæs. *B. C.* II. 41.
Quum quæpiam cohors ex orbe *excesserat*, hostes fugiebant. Cæs.
B. G. V. 34. Numidæ *si* a persequendo hostes deterrere *nequive-
rant*, disjectos a tergo et lateribus *circumveniebant; sin* opportunior
fugæ collis quam campi *fuerant*, Numidarum equi facile *evadebant*.
Sall. *Jug.* 50. But these authors sometimes regard the circumstances as necessarily connected, and therefore use the subjunctive
in this construction. The following are examples of this use of
the subjunctive: *Quoties* quæque cohors *procurreret*, ab ea parte

magnus hostium numerus cadebat. Caes. *B. G.* v. 34. Id fecialis *ubi dixisset*, hastam in fines eorum mittebat. Liv. l. 32. See also above, 175, (6).

(γ) *Subsequent acts* are denoted by *quum, simul*, or *postquam* with the indicative unless it is intended to imply that there is a necessary connexion—as of cause and effect—with the preceding circumstance; and then we have the subjunctive in the dependent clause (above, 176, 2, (a)). Thus we have the indicative in such passages as the following: *Quum* diutius in negotio cumque *fueram*, ad Capuam revertebar. Cic. *Verr.* v. 61. *Quum* Pompeius in Hispania bellum acerrimum et maximum *gesserat*, quo jure Gaditana civitas esset nesciebat? Cic. *Balb.* 6. *Quum* ver esse *coeperat*, ejus initium Verres non a Favonio notabat, sed *quum* rosam *riderat*, tunc incipere ver arbitrabatur. Cic. *Verr.* v. 10. *Poenus posteaquam* obstinatos *vidit*, obsidere inde atque oppugnare parat. Liv. xxiii. 17. But we have the subjunctive in the following cases: Epaminondas *quum vicisset* Lacedaemonios apud Mantineam atque ipse gravi vulnere exanimari se *videret*, quaesivit salvusne esset clipeus. Cic. *Fin.* ii. 30. *Simul* ego tribunus vocare tribus in suffragium *coepero*, tu statim consul sacramento juniores adiges, et in castra educes. Liv. iv. 5. *Posteaquam* mihi nihil de adventu tuo *scriberetur*, verebar, ne id ita caderet, ne *ante, quam* tu in provinciam *venisses*, ego de provincia decederem. Cic. *ad div.* ii. 19. His de rebus multa disputata sunt quondam in Hortensii villa, quum eo Catulus et Lucullus nosque ipsi *postridie* venissemus, *quam* apud Catulum *fuissemus*. Cic. *Acad.* ii. 3. *Postquam* Juba ante portas diu multumque primo minis pro imperio *egisset* cum Zamensibus... ubi eos in sententia perstare animadvertit, tertio polit ab eis, ut sibi conjuges liberosque redderent. Hirt. *B. Afr.* 91.

(δ) *Continued acts* are denoted by *donec, quoad, dum*, with the indicative, if the time only is signified, but with the subjunctive, if a condition or necessary connexion is implied. Thus:

(aa) Ægroto *dum* anima *est*, spes esse dicitur. Cic. *Att.* ix. 10. Catilina erat unus timendus tam diu, *dum* mœnibus urbis *continebatur*. Cic. *Cat.* iii. 7. Hoc feci. *dum licuit*. Cic. *Phil.* iii. 13. Tiberius Gracchus tam diu laudabitur, *dum* memoria rerum Romanarum *manebit*. Cic. *Off.* ii. 12. *Donec eris* felix, multos numerabis amicos: tempora si fuerint nubila, solus eris. Ovid, *Trist.* i. 8. 5. Cato *quoad vixit*, virtutum laude crevit. Corn. Nep.

SUBORDINATE SENTENCES. 413

XXIV. 2. Redemptio mansit usque ad eum finem, *dum* indices *rejecti sunt.* Cic. *Verr.* A. 1. 6. Delibera hoc, *dum redeo.* Ter. *Ad.* II. 1. 42. Saltim, *dum,* quid de Hispaniis agamus, *scitur,* exspecta. Cic. *Att.* X. 9. Julius Caesar exanimis aliquamdiu jacuit, *donec* lecticae impositum tres servuli domum *rettulerunt.* Suet. *Caes.* 82. Epaminondas ferrum usque eo retinuit, *quoad renuntiatum est,* vicisse Boeotios. Corn. Nep. XV. 9.

(bb) Elephanti in trajiciendo nihil trepidabant, *donec* continenti velut ponte *agerentur.* Liv. XXI. 28. Quantus amor bestiarum est in educandis custodiendisque iis, quas procrearunt, usque ad eum finem, *dum possint* se ipsae defendere! Cic. *Nat. Deor.* II. 51. Exspectate, *dum* consul aut dictator *fiat* Kaeso, quem privatum viribus et audacia regnantem videtis. Liv. III. 11. Rhenus servat nomen et violentiam cursus, qua Germaniam praevehitur, donec Oceano *misceatur.* Tac. *Ann.* II. 6. Multis Patrum orantibus, ponerent odia in perniciem itura, mansere infensi ac minitantes (consules), *donec* magistratu *abirent. Ibid.* v. 11, cf. II. 34. Domi certum est obsidere, *donec* redierit. Ter. *Ad.* IV. 6. Perseus in castris Romanis progredi prae turba occurrentium ad spectaculum non poterat, *donec* consul lictores *misisset,* qui submovendo iter ad praetorium facerent. Liv. XLV. 7, cf. Tac. *Hist.* I. 35, III. 10. *Quoad percentum sit eo,* quo sumpta navis est, non domini est navis, sed navigantium. Cic. *Off.* III. 23.

(cc) Latrones, *dum sit,* quod rapiant, quod auferant, nihil sibi defuturum arbitrantur. Cic. *Phil.* IV. 4. Caesar ex eo tempore, *dum* ad flumen Varum *veniatur,* se frumentum militibus daturum pollicetur. Caes. *B. C.* I. 87. Me amicissime admones, ut me integrum, *quoad possim,* servem. Cic. *Att.* VII. 26. Nihil puto tibi esse utilius, quam ibidem opperiri, *quoad* scire *possis,* quid tibi agendum sit. Cic. *ad div.* VI. 20.

(e) *Previous acts* are denoted by *antequam* or *priusquam*, with the indicative, if time only is indicated; but with the subjunctive if a conditional turn is given to the sentence (above, 176, 2, (b)). Thus: Non prius sum conatus misericordiam aliis commovere, *quam* misericordia *sum ipse captus.* Cic. *Or.* II. 47. Membris utimur *prius, quam didicimus,* cujus ea utilitatis causa habeamus. Cic. *Fin.* III. 20. *Ante, quam opprimit* lux, majoraque hostium agmina *obsepiunt* iter, erumpamus. Liv. XXII. 50. Memmius

414   SYNTAX OF SENTENCES.

pridie, quam ego Athenas *veni*, Mitylenas profectus erat. Cic. *Att.* v. 11. Tragœdi quotidie, *antequam pronuntient*, vocem sensim excitant. Cic. *Or.* I. 59. In omnibus negotiis *prius, quam aggrediare*, adhibenda est præparatio diligens. Cic. *Off.* I. 21. *Ante* videmus fulgurationem, *quam* sonum *audiamus.* Sen. *Nat. Quaes.* II. 12. Si quis de cœlo servavit, non habitis comitiis, sed *prius, quam habeantur*, debet nuntiare. Cic. *Phil.* II. 32. Ægyptii quamvis carnificinam *prius* subierint, *quam* ibim, aut aspidem, aut felem, aut canem, aut crocodilum *violent.* Cic. *Tusc.* V. 27. Hannibal omnia et in prœlio apud Zamam, et ante aciem, *priusquam excederet* pugna, erat expertus. Liv. XXX. 35. Aristides interfuit pugnæ navali apud Salamina, quæ facta est *prius, quam pœna* (exsilii) *liberaretur.* Corn. Nep. III. 2. Cæsar ad Pompeii castra pervenit *prius, quam* Pompeius sentire *posset.* Cæs. *B. C.* III. 67. Providentia est, per quam animus futurum aliquid videt, antequam *factum sit.* Cic. *Inv.* II. 54. Sæpe magna indoles virtutis, *priusquam* reipublicæ prodesse *potuisset*, exstincta fuit. Cic. *Ph.* V. 18. Scis, me quodam tempore Metapontum venisse, neque ad hospitem *ante* divertisse, *quam* Pythagoræ ipsum illum locum, ubi vitam ediderat, sedemque *viderim.* Cic. *Fin.* v. 2.

§ 12.   (c) *Objective Sentences.*

207 Objective sentences are expressed either by the oblique case of the object followed by the infinitive mood (128, VIII.), or by the conjunction *quod* with a finite verb. The construction of the accusative with the infinitive has been sufficiently illustrated above (177). The other form of the objective sentence, which approaches very nearly to the force of the causal sentence, admits of the following distinctions: (a) If the statement introduced by *quod*, i. e. 'that' or 'because,' is regarded as a fact or as stated only by the subject of the main sentence, the verb is in the indicative mood; (b) but if the statement is supposed to rest on the opinion or assertion of some other person, the verb is subjunctive, as in the *oratio obliqua.* Thus we have,

(a) Gratulor tibi, *quod* ex provincia salvum te ad nos *recepisti*. Cic. *ad div.* XIII. 73.

(b) Sæpenumero admirari soleo, M. Cato, *quod* nunquam senectutem tibi gravem esse *senserim.* Cic. *Sen.* 2.   Quum contemplor animo, reperio quatuor causas, cur senectus misera videatur: unam *quod avocet* a rebus gerendis; alteram, *quod corpus faciat* infirmius; tertiam, *quod privet* omnibus fere voluptatibus; quartam, *quod* haud procul *absit* a morte. Cic. *Sen.* 5. Video mihi gratum fecisse Siculis, *quod* corum injurias meo labore, miseriis, periculo *sim persecutus.* Cic. *Verr.* II. 6. Laudat Africanum Panætius, *quod fuerit* abstinens. Cic. *Off.* II. 22. Phalereus Demetrius Periclem vituperat, *quod* tantam pecuniam in præclara illa propylæa *conjecerit. Ibid.* II. 17.

The cases in which *quod* with a finite verb is preferred to an infinitive with the accusative are as follows:

(aa) When we use 'that' of a fact, but not of one perceived or directly asserted. Thus, Mitto, *quod* invidiam, *quod* omnes mens tempestates *subieris.* Cic. *ad div.* xv. 4, 27. Habet hoc optimum in se generosus animus, *quod concitatur* ad honesta. Sen. *Ep.* 39. Addo, *quod* ingenuas didicisse fideliter artes, *emollit* mores, nec *sinit* esse feros. Ov. *Pont.* II. 9. Num reprehendis, *quod* libertus patronum *juvabat* cum, qui tum in miseriis erat? Cic. *Verr.* L. 47.

(bb) When we have an impersonal verb in the main sentence, or when the nominative case is a neuter pronoun, or some general expression, as *ea res.* Thus, *Relinquitur* illud, *quod* vociferari non *destitit,* non debuisse, quum prætor esset, suum negotium agere. Cic. *Flac.* 34. Hoc *cecidit* mihi peropportune, *quod* transactis jam meis partibus, ad Antonium audiendum *venistis.* Cic. *Or.* II. 4. Eumeni multum *detraxit* inter Macedones viventi, *quod alienæ erat* civitatis. Corn. Nep. XVIII. 1. Non ea res me *deterruit,* quominus literas ad te mitterem, *quod* tu nullas ad me *miseras,* sed *quia* nihil, quod scriberem, in tantis malis reperiebam. Cic. *ad div.* VI. 22. *Accedit, quod* patrem plus etiam, quam non modo tu, sed quam ipse scit, *amo.* Cic. *Att.* XIII. 21. *Accedit, quod* tibi certamen *est* tecum. Plin. *Ep.* VIII. 24. Huc *accedit, quod* paullo tamen occultior ac tectior vestra ista cupiditas *esset* (= esse debebat). Cic. *Sext. Rosc.* 36. *Vitium est, quod* quidam nimis magnum studium multamque operam in res obscuras atque difficiles *conferunt,* easdomque non necessarias. Cic. *Off.* I. 6. Multa sunt admirabilia, sed nihil magis, quam *quod* ita stabilis *est* mundus, atque ita *cohaeret* ad permanendum, ut nihil ne excogitari quidem possit aptius. Cic. *Nat. Deor.* II. 45.

(cc) When 'that' expresses the cause of grief, joy, wonder, congratulation, complaint, or the like. Thus, *Dolet* mihi, *quod stomacharis.* Cic. *Brut.* 17. *Gaudeo, quod* to *interpellari.* Cic. *Leg.* III. 1. Tibi *gratulor quod* te summa laus *prosecuta est.* Cic. *ad div.* XV. 14. Hannibal unus Antiocho, Magis *mirari* se, aiebat, *quod* non jam in Asia *essent* Romani, quam venturos dubitare. Liv. XXXVI. 41. Falso *queritur* de natura sua genus humanum, *quod*, imbecilla atque ævi brevis, forte potius quam virtute *regatur.* Sall. *Jug.* 1.

Obs. 1 *Quum* is sometimes used for *quod*, especially in the last case (above, 170, 3, (a)). Thus we have Tibi gratias ago, *quum* tantum litteræ meæ potuerunt. Cic. *ad div.* XIII. 24. Gratulor tibi, *quum* tantum vales apud Dolabellam. *Ib.* IX. 14. Gratissimum fecisti, *quum* eum indignum eā fortunā amicum nobis quam servum esse maluisti. *Ib.* XVI. 16. Nemini, *quum* mihi deripere videlare, quod cum istis potius viverem, quam nobiscum. *Ib.* VII. 28. Jovi Diisque ago gratias merito magnas, *quoni* te reducem tuo patri reddiderunt, *quomque* ex miseriis plurimis me exemerunt. Plaut. *Capt.* V. 1. 1.

Obs. 2 In the sense 'so far as,' *quod* is the objective apposition to the whole sentence, and in this usage is followed by the subjunctive. Suæ cuique utilitati, *quod* sine alterius injuria fiat, serviendum est. Cic. *ad div.* V. 2. Epicurus se unus, *quod* sciam, sapientem profiteri est ausus. Cic. *Fin.* II. 3. Aristides unus post hominum memoriam, *quod* quidem nos audierimus, cognomine Justus appellatus est. Corn. Nep. III. 1.

§ 13. (Γ) *Illative Sentences.*

208 Illative, intensive, or consecutive sentences are expressed by *ut* with the subjunctive in an affirmative sense, or by *ut non, ut nihil*, negatively, after intensive words, as *tantus, talis, tot, adeo, ita, sic, usque eo*, or with some such word implied in the former sentence (175, (b), 3). Thus, Siciliam Verres per triennium *ita* vexavit ac perdidit, *ut* ea restitui in antiquum statum nullo modo *possit.* Cic. *Verr.* A. I. 4. Hortensius ardebat dicendi cupiditate *sic ut* in nullo unquam flagrantius studium *viderim.* Cic. *Brut.* 88. Epaminondas paupertatem *adeo* facile perpessus est, *ut* de republica nihil, præter gloriam, *ceperit.* Corn. Nep. XV. 3. Piso *eo usque* corruptionis profectus est, *ut* sermone vulgi parens legionum *haberetur.* Tac. *Ann.* II. 55. *Eo* rem jam adducam, *ut* nihil divinatione opus *sit.* Cic. *Sext. Rosc.* 34. *Talis* est ordo actionum adhibendus *ut* in vita omnia *sint* apta inter se et convenientia. Cic. *Off.* I. 14. Atticus quum *tanta* prosperitate usus esset valetudinis, *ut* annos

triginta medicina non *indiguisset*, nactus est morbum. Corn. Nep.
xxv. 21. Hæc quum viderem *tot* vestigiis impressa, *ut* in his
errari non *posset*, non adscripsi, quod tua non referret. Cic.
Fam. v. 20. Arboribus consita Italia est, *ut* tota pomarium *videatur.* Varr. *R. R.* i. 2. Romani ex loco superiore strage ac ruina
fudere Gallos, *ut* nunquam postea nec pars nec universi *tentaverint* tale pugnæ genus. Liv. v. 49.

Obs. 1 After a comparative we may have *quam ut* in an illative
sense; thus, Isocrates *majore* mihi Ingenio videtur *esse*, *quam ut* cum
orationibus Lysiæ *comparetur.* Cic. *Or.* 13. Chabrias vivebat laute et
indulgebat sibi *liberalius, quam ut* invidiam vulgi *posset* effugere. Corn.
Nep. xii. 13.

Obs. 2 After *tantum abest* we may have two sentences with *ut*, of
which the first represents the subject of *abest*, and the second is the consequence of *tantum*. Thus, *Tantum abest, ut* nostra *miremur, ut usque
eo difficiles* et morosi *simus, ut* nobis non *satisfaciat* ipse Demoetheues.
Cic. *Or.* 30. *Tantum abest, ut enervetur* oratio compositione verborum,
ut aliter in ea vis esse non *possit. Ibid.* 68. *Tantum abfuit, ut* civilis
certaminis terror externus *cohiberet, ut contra* eo violentior potestas tribunicia *esset*. Liv. vi. 31.

Obs. 3 *Ut* with the subjunctive seems to represent the subject of such
impersonal verbs as *fit, accidit, evenit, non venit, est* ('it takes place'),
abest ('it is far from happening'), *contingit, relinquitur, restat, sequitur,
reliquum est, extremum est, accedit, mos est, consuetudo est, convenit, fas
est, jus est:* and as in this case the negative is *non*, never *ne*, we must
refer these verbs to the class of illative rather than of final sentences.
The following are examples: *Fieri* non potest, *ut* quis Romæ *sit*, quum
est Athenis. Quint. v. 9, 5. Plerisque *accidit, ut* præsidio litterarum
diligentiam in perdiscendo ac memoriam *remittant. Cæs. B.G.* vi. 14. Forte
evenit, ut in Privernati *essemus.* Cic. *Or.* ii. 55. Volo hoc oratori *contingat, ut,* quum auditurum sit, eum cræ dicturum, locus in subselliis *occupetur, complentur* tribunal. Cic. *Brut.* 84. Apud Romanos nunquam
fere *usu venit, ut* in magno discrimine non et proximi ventem *mutarent.*
Liv. vi. 20. *Est, ut* plerique philosophi nulla *tradant* præcepta dicendi,
et *habeant* paratum tamen, quid de quaque re dicant. Cic. *Or.* ii. 36.
Esto, ut hi *sint* optimates, quiqui integri sunt et bene de rebus domesticis constituti. Cic. *Sext.* 45. Ne ille longe *aberit, ut* argumentis
credat philosophorum. Cic. *Acad.* ii. 36. *Abest, ut* Milonem *deseram.*
Apul. *Met.* ii. 3. *Restat, ut* his *respondeam*, qui sermonibus ejusmodi
nolint personas tam graves illigari. Cic. *Acad.* ii. 2. *Relinquitur, ut*, si
vincimur in Hispania, *quiescamus.* Cic. *Att.* x. 8. *Reliquum est, ut*
nihil a te *petam*, nisi, ut ad eam voluntatem, quam tua sponte erga Cæcinam habiturus *esses*, tantus cumulus accedat commendatione mea, quanti
me a te fieri intelligo. Cic. *ad div.* vi. 9. *Sequitur, ut doceam,* omnia
subjecta esse naturæ eaque ab ea pulcherrime geri. Cic. *N. D.* ii. 32.
Si hæc enuntiatio non vera est, *sequitur, ut* falsa *sit*. Cic. *Fat.* 12.
Accedit, ut eo facilius animus *evadat* ex hoc aëre, quod nihil est animo

velocius. Cic. *Tusc.* I. 19. *Eo accedebat, ut* in caritate civium nihil spei reponenti metu regnum *tutandum esset*. Liv. I. 49. *Mos est* hominum, *ut nolint*, eundem pluribus rebus excellere. Cic. *Brut.* 21. Qui *convenit, ut* tibi Aricina natus ignobilis *rideatur*, quam tu eodem materno genere soleas gloriari? Cic. *Phil.* III. 6. *Expedit* omnibus, *ut* singulae civitates sua jura et suas leges *habeant.* Just. xxxiv. 1. Caesari Ariovistus respondit: *jus esse* belli, *ut*, qui vicissent, iis, quos vicissent, quemadmodum vellent, *imperarent.* Caes. *B. G.* I. 36.

§ 14. (g) *Final Sentences.*

209 Final sentences, which declare the end of what is predicated, are expressed by *ut* or *quo* affirmatively, and by *ne, ut ne, quominus,* and *quin* negatively, followed in every case by the subjunctive (128. xiii.; 175, (b), (2)). Sometimes this sentence is contained in a future participle (182, (b)), or conveyed by the gerund with *ad* (186), or the supine in *-tum* (189), or introduced by a relative (205, (β), (aa)). These latter usages have been sufficiently discussed. It is only necessary in this place to classify the final sentences which are expressed by means of the final conjunctions (above, p. 202).

(a) *Ut* and *ne.*

(aa) *Ut* is used to denote the end, when a purpose or object is distinctly expressed, and it is sometimes introduced by *idcirco;* thus, Legum *idcirco* omnes servi sumus, *ut* liberi esse possimus. Cic. *Cluent.* 53. Romani ab aratro abduxerunt Cincinnatum, *ut* dictator *esset.* Cic. *Fin.* II. 4. *Ne* nimium multi poenam capitis *subirent, idcirco* illa sortitio comparata est. Cic. *Cluent.* 46. Illos *idcirco* non commemoro, *ne* de miseriis meorum necessariorum conquerens, homines, quos nolo, *videar* offendere. Cic. *ad div.* xiii. 8.

(bb) *Ut* denotes the end after verbs of wishing, willing, commanding, endeavouring, and the like; thus, Phaëton *ut* curru patris *tolleretur optavit.* Cic. *Off.* III. 25. Equidem *vellem, ut* aliquando *redires.* Cic. *Fam.* vii. 31. Caesar Dolabellae *dixit, ut* ad me *scriberet, ut* in Italiam quam primum *venirem.* Cic. *Att.* II. 7. Deliberantibus Atheniensibus Pythia *respondit, ut* moenibus ligneis se *munirent.* Corn. Nep. II. 2. Caesar per litteras Trebonio *mandarerat, ne* per vim Massiliam expugnari *pateretur.* Caes. *B. C.* II. 13. Sol *efficit, ut* omnia *floreant.* Cic. *Nat. Deor.* II. 15. *Habet hoc* virtus, *ut* viros fortes species ejus et pulchritudo etiam in hoste posita *delectet.* Cic. *Pis.* 32. Tribuni plebis *postulant, ut* sacrosancti *habeantur.* Liv. III. 19.

(cc) *Ut* is similarly used to denote the end or object after verbs of expecting, persuading, constraining, and the like; thus, *Magno opere te hortor, mi Cicero, ut non solum orationes meas, sed hos etiam de philosophia libros studiose legas.* Cic. *Off.* I. 1. *Te illud admoneo, ut quotidie mediteris, resistendum esse iracundiæ.* Cic. *Quint. Fr.* I. 1, 13. *Huic persuadet, uti ad hostes transeat.* Cæs. *B. G.* III. 18. *Impellimur natura, ut prodesse velimus quam plurimis, imprimis docendo.* Cic. *Fin.* XIII. 20. *Senatus P. Lentulum, ut se abdicaret prætura, coëgit.* Cic. *Cat.* IV. 8. *Opera danda est, ut verbis utamur quam usitatissimis et quam maxime aptis, id est, rem declarantibus.* Cic. *Fin.* V. 20. *Ante senectutem curavi, ut bene viverem; in senectute, ut bene moriar.* Sen. *Ep.* 61. *Consulere vivi ac prospicere debemus, ut liberorum nostrorum solitudo et pueritia quam firmissimo præsidio munita sit.* Cic. *Verr.* I. 58.

(β) *Quo* and *quominus.*

Quo = *ut eo* is used to denote the end when there is an implication of the means, by which it may be effected; and in this form of the final sentence we have often an adjective or adverb in the comparative degree (see, e. g. Ter. *Phorm.* 1. 2. 54). This is always the case in the negative form, and *quo minus* = *ut eo minus* expresses the negative end or purpose after verbs signifying to hinder or refuse (above, p. 203). Thus we have In *funeribus Atheniensium sublata erat celebritas virorum ac mulierum, quo lamentatio minueretur.* Cic. *Leg.* II. 26. *Ager non semel aratur, sed novatur et iteratur, quo meliores fœtus possit et grandiores edere.* Cic. *Or.* II. 30. *Medico puto aliquid dandum esse, quo sit studiosior.* Cic. *ad div.* XVI. 4. *Rebus terrenis multa externa, quo minus perficiantur, possunt obsistere.* Cic. *Nat. Deor.* II. 13. *Nihil impedit, quo minus id, quod maxime placeat, facere possimus.* Cic. *Fin.* I. 10. *Mors non deterret sapientem, quominus in omne tempus reipublicæ suisque consulat.* Cic. *Tusc.* I. 38. *Præter quercum Dodoneam nihil desideramus, quominus Epirum ipsam possidere videamur.* Cic. *Att.* II. 4. *Nihil de me tulistis, quo minus in civium essem numero.* Cic. *Dom.* 31. *Nemini civi ulla, quo minus adesset, satis justa excusatio est visa.* Cic. *Pis.* 15. *Quæ relligio C. Mario fuerat, quo minus C. Glauciam prætorem occideret, ea nos relligione in privato Lentulo liberamur.* Cic. *Cat.* III. 16.

(7) *Quin.*

As we have seen above (p. 203), *quin* denotes the negation of a consequence after a sentence which is in itself negative. Its usages may be divided into two classes—the negation of a doubt, and the absolute negation.

(aa) *Quin* ('but that') is used after *non dubito, non dubium est, quis dubitat? = nemo dubitat.* Thus, *Non dubitari debet, quin fuerint ante Homerum poëtæ.* Cic. *Brut.* 18. *Non debes dubitare, quin, aut aliqua republica, sis futurus,* qui esse debes; aut perdita, non afflictiore conditione, quam ceteri. Cic. *Fam.* VI. 1. Jus jurandum, patri datum, ita conservavi, ut *nemini dubium esse deboat, quin* reliquo tempore eadem mente *sim futurus.* Corn. Nep. XXIII. 2. *Quis dubitet, quin* in virtute divitiæ positae sint? Cic. *Par.* VI. 2.

(bb) *Quin* ('so, such that—not') is used generally after an absolute negation in the main sentence, or when it contains a question equivalent to an absolute negation. Thus, Cleanthes *negat ullum esse* cibum *tam* gravem, *quin* is die et nocte *concoquatur.* Cic. *Nat. Deor.* II. 9. Ego *nihil prætermisi,* quantum facere potui, *quin* Pompeium a Cæsaris conjunctione *avocarem.* Cic. *Phil.* II. 10. *Nemo* Lilybæi fuit, *quin viderit; nemo* in Sicilia, *quin audierit.* Cic. *Verr.* V. 54. *Nego* ullam gemmam aut margaritam fuisse, *quin quaesierit, inspexerit, abstulerit. Ib.* IV. 1. Dies vero *nullus* est, *quin* hic Satrius domum meam *ventitet.* Cic. *Att.* I. 1. Literas ad te *nunquam* habui, cui darem, *quin dederim.* Cic. *Fam.* XII. 19. *Quis est, quin cernat,* quanta vis sit in sensibus? Cic. *Acad.* II. 7. *Nihil est, quin* male narrando *possit* depravari. Ter. *Phorm.* IV. 4. 17. *Non possum* facere, *quin* quotidie ad te *mittam* literas. Cic. *Att.* XII. 27. *Non possum quin exclamem.* Plaut. *Trin.* III. 2. 79. Non potest, *quin obsit.* Plaut. *Mil.* III. 1. 7. Prorsus *nihil* abest, *quin* ego *sim* miserrimus. Cic. *Att.* XI. 13. Haud multum abfuit, *quin* interficeretur. Liv. XLII. 44. Aberit *non* longe, *quin* hoc a me decerni *velit.* Cic. *Att.* IX. 9. Causæ *nihil* erat, *quin* secus *judicaret* ipse de re Quintius. Cic. *Quint.* 9. *Quid est* causæ, *quin* decemviri coloniam in Janiculum *possint* deducere? Cic. *Agr.* II. 27. *Non* est in nostra potestate, *quin* illa *eveniant,* quorum causæ fuerint. Cic. *Fat.* 19.

Obs. 1 If the negation in the final clause is emphatic we must have *ut non* instead of *quin.* Thus, Neque ullo modo facere possum, *ut non* sim popularis. Cic. *Agr.* IX. 9. Fieri non potest, *ut* eum tu in provincia *non* cognoris. Cic. *Verr.* II. 77.

Obs. 2 If the main sentence and the final clause have the same subject, we may translate the latter by the participle with the preposition 'without.' Thus, Timoleontem mator post fratris necem *nunquam* adspexit, *quin* eum fratricidam implumque *compellaret*. Corn. Nep. xx. 1 ('without calling him a fratricide and unnatural monster'). *Nulli* ex itinere excedere licebat, *quin* ab equitatu Cæsaris *exciperentur*. Cæs. *B. C.* 1. 79 ('no one could fall out on the march, without being cut off by Cæsar's cavalry').

§ 15. (h) *Causal Sentences.*

210 Causal sentences explain the cause of what is asserted, and are expressed by the relative (above, 205 (β), (bb)), by the participle (182, (c)), by *quia, quod, quoniam, quando, quandoquidem, siquidem,* followed by the indicative (176, (3), (b)), by *quum,* generally followed by the subjunctive (176, (3), (a)), and by *qui, ut qui, quippe qui* most frequently with the subjunctive (170, (3), (c)). The conjunctions *nam* and *enim* form distinct and independent clauses, which are not even co-ordinate sentences, unless these particles are connected with adversative or copulative conjunctions. These usages in their general application have been sufficiently illustrated above (pp. 199, 200). It will be observed that, when relative particles are used, the causal sentence is a modification either of the temporal sentence, in its application to contemporary acts (200, (a)), or of the objective sentence, when the antecedent is expressed or distinctly implied. But in the causal application of the temporal sentence we have the indicative only when the contemporary occurrence is regarded as in itself the explanation of the fact, and here we generally have *quoniam* (= *quum jam*), *quando* or *quandoquidem*, rather than *quum.* Thus, *Quoniam* tu ita vis, nimium me gratum esse concedam. Cic. *Planc.* 33. *Quando* artibus, inquit, honestis, nullus in urbe locus [est], res hodie minor est here quam fuit, atque eadem cras deteret exiguis aliquid, proponimus illuc ire. Juv. III. 21. Deos quæso, ut sit superstes, *quandoquidem* ipse est ingenio bono. Ter. *Andr.* III. 2. 7. On the other hand, we have the subjunctive, and generally with *quum* when the idea of time is subordinated to that of dependence on the circumstance mentioned in the main clause, as the following examples will show: *Quum* solitudo et vita sine amicis insidiarum et metus plena *sit*, ratio ipsa monet amicitias comparare. Cic. *Fin.* I. 20. Dionysius *quum* in communibus suggestis consistere non *auderet*, concionari ex turri alta solebat. Cic. *Tusc.* v. 20. Socratis ingenium variosque

422   SYNTAX OF SENTENCES.

sermones immortalitati scriptis suis Plato tradidit, *quum* ipse litteram Socrates nullam *reliquisset.* Cic. *Or.* III. 16. De pietate Attici quid plura commemorem, *quum* hoc ipsum vere gloriantem *audierim* in funere matris suæ, se nunquam cum ea in gratiam rediisse. Corn. Nep. XXV. 17. Aliæ in historia leges observandæ, aliæ in poëmate, *quippe quum* in illa ad veritatem *referantur,* in hoc ad delectationem pleraque. Cic. *Leg.* I. 1. Percrebuerat ea tempestate pravissimus mos, *quum* plerique orbi fictis adoptionibus *adasciscerent* filios. Tac. *Ann.* XV. 19. Munatius Plancus, tribunus plebis, quotidie meam potentiam criminabatur, *quum diceret,* senatum, non quod sontiret, sed quod ego vellem, decernere. Cic. *Mil.* 5. Contendi cum P. Clodio, *quum* ego publicam causam, ille suam *defenderet.* C. Anton. in Cic. *Att.* XIV. 13. The immediate reference of *quod* or *quia* to an antecedent expressed or implied in the main sentence is shown by such passages as the following: *Hoc uno præstamus vel maxime feris, quod colloquimur* inter nos, et *quod* exprimere dicendo sensa *possumus.* Cic. *Or.* I. 8. Dupliciter delectatus sum tuis literis, et *quod* ipse risi, et *quod* te *intelleri* jam posse ridere. Cic. ad *div.* IX. 20. Aristides nonne *ob eam causam* expulsus est patria, *quod* præter modum justus *esset?* Cic. *Tusc.* v. 36. Alcibiades ostendit, Lacedæmonios *eo* nolle confligere classe, *quod* pedestribus copiis plus, quam navibus *valerent.* Corn. Nep. VII. 8. Eram otiosus in Tusculano *propterea, quod* discipulos obviam *miseram.* Cic. *ad div.* IX. 18. Recordatione nostræ amicitiæ *sic* fruor, ut beate vixisse videar, *quia* cum Scipione *vixerim.* Cic. *Lael.* 4. *Quia* scripseras te proficisci cogitare, *eo* te hærere censebam. Cic. *Att.* X. 15.

§ 16. (i) *Concessive Sentences.*

211 Concessive sentences, which strengthen or limit by an admission, are expressed by the participle with or without *quamvis* or *quamquam* (182, (d)), by *qui* with the subjunctive (205, (β), (dd)), by *quanquam* and *utut* generally with the indicative (176, (4)), by *etsi, tametsi, etiamsi,* with either the indicative or subjunctive, according to the rule for the use of *si* in conditional propositions (128, XVI, 176, (4)), and by *quamvis, quantumvis, licet, ut, quum,* with the subjunctive only (176, (4)). The use of the concessive conjunctions has been sufficiently illustrated above (pp. 202, 357). When *quum* is used as a concessive particle, it is followed by the indicative, if the temporal meaning prevails; as Has tabulas Marcellus, *quum* omnia profana fecit ('at the time when he profaned everything, although he was at that time profaning everything'), non attigit. Cic. *Verr.* IV. 55. But more frequently the subjunctive is used to indicate the dependence of the secondary predication. Thus we have, Drucatia, Alpinus amnis, *quum aquae vim vehat ingentem, non tamen navium patiens est.* Liv. XXI. 31. Marcelli, Scipionis, Mummii domus *quum* honore et virtute *florerent,* signis et tabulis pictis emnt vacuae. Cic. *Verr.* I. 24. Phocion fuit perpetuo pauper, *quum divitissimus esse posset.* Corn. Nep. XIX. 1. Toto praelio, *quum* ab hora septima ad vesperam *pugnatum sit,* aversum hostem videre nemo potuit. Caes. *B. G.* I. 26.

§ 17. *Figures of Speech.*

212 In order to complete the subject of Syntax, it will be convenient here to enumerate the different figures of speech which have been defined and exemplified by rhetoricians. The writers on oratory treat of *figurae sententiarum* as well as *figurae dictionis.* The grammarian is concerned only with the latter, which may be divided into the following classes: (A) Figures of Syntax; (B) Figures of Style.

(A) *Figures of Syntax.*

The figures of syntax are the following:

(a) Figures of excess:

(aa) *Pleonasm,* or accumulation of words either in a single phrase, as *audivi auribus, vidi oculis;* or in co-ordinate sentences, as *gaudeo vehementerque laetor, oro te atque obsecro, &c.*

(bb) *Polysyndeton,* or superabundance of conjunctions, as *Fatique, fortunasque virum, moresque manusque.*

Obs. 1 This figure is regularly adopted in some cases. For instance, two or more epithets in agreement with the same substantive require the intervention of a copulative conjunction, unless one of them is so closely connected with the substantive as to form only one idea with it. Thus we must not say *multae graves causae, multa magna incommoda,* though we omit the conjunction in English, but we must say *multae et graves causae, multa et magna incommoda.* On the other hand we may say *navis oneraria maxima, agrestis duplex amiculum,* because *navis oneraria* is a particular kind of ship, and *duplex amiculum* a particular kind of garment. We may also say *multi fortissimi atque optimi viri* (Cic. *ad div.* V. 17), because the included epithets indicate a special and distinguished class of men. We find occasionally such phrases as *externos multos claros viros* (Cic. *ad div.* VI. 24); *militare honestum funus* (Corn. Nep. XVIII. 13); but these are exceptional usages, and should not be imitated.

Obs. 2 In the case of three or more nouns, the best writers either omit the conjunction or insert it between each. For instance, they would either write *amicitiam summa fide, constantia, justitia servavit;* or, *summa fide et constantia et justitia.* And similarly with verbs.

(cc) *Parenthesis,* when a new sentence is inserted, as *Credo equidem (nec vana fides) genus esse deorum.*

(b) Figures of defect:

(aa) *Ellipsis,* when some word, easily supplied, is omitted, as *Scite enim Chrysippus* (scil. *dicit*); *Non est solvendo* (scil. *aptus*).

(bb) *Zeugma,* when the same word is made to do double duty, or to represent some other word of similar meaning in a corresponding sentence; as *Si legatus imperii terminos, obsequium erga imperatorem exiit,* where with *terminos* we must supply *accessit,* the corresponding word to *exiit.*

(cc) *Asyndeton,* or deficiency of conjunctions; as *Rex, miles, plebs, negat illud. Quid dicam de utilitate litterarum! Erudiunt, ornant, oblectant, consolantur.*

(c) Figures of the context:

(aa) *Hyperbaton,* when a word is out of its place in the sentence; as *Vina bonis quas deinde cadis onerarat Acestes, littore Trinacrio, dederatque abeuntibus, heros dividit.*

(bb) *Hypallage,* when the cases are changed; as *Necdum illis labra admovi,* for *necdum illa labris admovi.*

(cc) *Enallage,* when there is a change of number, person, or tense; as *Ni faciat* for *Ni faceret.*

(dd) *Anastrophe,* when the order of successive words is changed; as *Italiam contra* for *contra Italiam.*

(B) *Figures of Style.*

The figures of style are (1) *Tropes,* which consist in single words; (2) *Figures,* in the limited sense of that term, which consist in propositions:

(1) Tropes are as follows:

(a) *Metaphora* or *Translatio,* a contracted simile; as *Segetes sitiunt.*

(b) *Metonymia*, when a thing is expressed by means of some circumstances connected with it; as *Vulcanus* for *ignis*; *Mars* for *bellum*; *Lego Horatium* for *opera Horatii*.

(c) *Synecdoche*, when a part is put for the whole; as *Decem aestates vixi sub hoc tecto*, where *aestates* is put for *annos* and *tecto* for *domo*.

(d) *Antonomasia*, when a descriptive word or phrase is substituted for a proper name; as *Poenus tulit victoriam* for *Hannibal*; *Romanae eloquentiae princeps* for *Cicero*.

(e) *Catachresis*, when for want of a specific term we use some word in an improper sense; as *aedificare naves* for *construere*; *vir gregis* for *dux gregis*, &c.

(f) *Hyperbole*, when there is an exaggeration; as *Currit ocior euro*.

(g) *Litotes*, when we mean more than we say; as *Non equidem laudo sed neque sperno tua munera* for *vitupero quidem ea sed accipio*.

(h) *Metalepsis* combines several tropes in one; as *Hinc movet Euphrates, illinc Germania bellum* for *Mesopotamiae et Germaniae incolae bellum capessunt*.

(i) *Allegoria*, when there is a continuation of tropes; as *Sine Cerere et Baccho friget Venus* for *amor alget sine pane et vino*.

(k) *Ironia* says one thing and means another; as *Egregiam laudem* when we mean *culpam*; *bone custos* when we mean *perfide pastor*, &c.

(l) *Sarcasmus*, when there is a bitter and sneering jest; as *Satia te sanguine, Cyre!* addressed to the head of Cyrus by Tomyris.

(m) *Onomatopoeia*, when we coin words to imitate a particular sound; as *Torva Mimalloneis implebant cornua bombis*.

(n) *Antiphrasis*, when we signify something by its contrary; as *Auri sacra fames* when *sacra* means 'accursed;' *Euxinus*, 'the hospitable,' applied to a sea where strangers were murdered; &c.

(2) Figures, specially so called, are as follows:

(a) Figures of words of the same sound.

(aa) *Epizeuxis* is a repetition of the same word; as *Litterae, litterae, inquam, solae me delectant.*

(bb) *Epanaphora*, where several members of the proposition begin with the same word; as *Litterae me puerum aluerunt, litterae me juvenem ab infamia libidinum servarunt, litterae virum in rep. administranda adjuverunt, litterae senectutis imbecillitatem consolabuntur.*

(cc) *Antistrophe*, where several members end with the same word; as *Nascimur dolore, degimus vitam dolore, finimus dolore.*

(dd) *Symploce* combines the last two figures; as *Quam bene, Caune, tuo poteram nurus esse parenti: quam bene, Caune, meo poteras gener esse parenti.*

(ee) *Anadiplosis* begins a clause with the last word of the preceding; as *Pierides, vos haec facietis maxima, Gallo, Gallo, cujus amor tantum mihi crescit in horas.*

(ff) *Epanalepsis* begins and ends with the same word; as *Pauper amet caute, timeat maledicere pauper.*

(gg) *Epanodos* changes the place of the same word in successive clauses; as *Crudelis tu quoque mater: crudelis mater magis, an puer improbus ille: improbus ille puer, crudelis tu quoque mater.*

(hh) *Antanaclasis* varies the sense of a repeated word; as *Hic* (i. e. Orestes) *sustulit* (i. e. interfecit) *matrem; ille* (i. e. Æneas) *sustulit* (i. e. portavit humeris) *patrem.*

(ii) *Ploce* repeats a proper name in a general or attributive sense; as *Ex illo Corydon Corydon est tempore nobis*, 'Corydon is truly what his character would lead me to expect;' *In hac victoria Caesar erat Caesar*, i.e. 'a most clement conqueror.'

(kk) *Climax* is continual gradation with a repetition of the preceding word; as *Studia mihi litterarum doctrinam, doctrina gloriam, gloria invidiam et obtrectationem comparavit.*

(b) Figures of words of a similar sound.

(aa) *Paregmenon* consists in the introduction of words derived from the preceding; as *Servitium lepidum! tecum servio servus!*

(bb) *Paronomasia* consists in a slight change of the preceding word; as *Inceptio est amentium haud amantium.*

(cc) *Homoeoteleuton*, when the clauses end similarly; as *Num putas fieri posse, ut, qui litterarum studiis teneatur, libidinum vinculis obstringatur.*

(dd) *Parechesis* is a play on repeated syllables; as *O fortunatam natam me consule Romam.*

(c) Figures of words for explanation.

(aa) *Hypotyposis* draws a vivid picture; as *Videbar videre alios intrantes, alios exeuntes, &c.*

(bb) *Paradiastole* explains by adding an opposition; as *Fortuna obumbrat virtutem, tamen non obruit eam.*

(cc) *Antimetabole* or *Metathesis* opposes by repeating the same words in a contrary order; as *Poema est pictura loquens, pictura est mutum poema.*

(dd) *Enantiosis* or *Antithesis* places opposites in a sort of symmetry or equilibrium; as *Alba ligustra cadunt, vaccinia nigra leguntur.*

(ee) *Synoeceiosis* combines two contraries with the same subject; as *Tam quod adest desit, quam quod non adsit avaro.*

(ff) *Oxymoron* contrasts a noun with its epithet; as *Ars iners; concordia discors;* &c.

PART III.

PROSODY, OR QUANTITY AND METRE.

CHAPTER I.

QUANTITY.

§ 1. *General rules of Quantity.*

213 PROSODY, which, in its original meaning as a Greek word (προσῳδία), denotes accentuation, is used in Latin Grammar to signify that part of the subject which teaches the quantity of syllables and the laws of metre.

214 By 'quantity' we understand the condition of a syllable in regard to the time occupied by its pronunciation. We say that it is a short syllable (*syllaba brevis, syllaba correpta*) if it occupies only one *mora* or time, and a long syllable (*syllaba longa, syllaba producta*) if it occupies two such *moras* or times (below, 232). When a syllable is sometimes long and sometimes short it is called common or doubtful (*syllaba anceps*). A short syllable is marked with a semicircle open above, as in *brĕvĭbŭs*; a long syllable is marked by a horizontal line, as in *cēlārūnt*; and both marks are placed over a common or doubtful syllable, as in *tĕnēbrāē*.

215 The quantity of a syllable is supposed to reside in its vowel, which may be either long or short by *nature;* and in the latter case it may be lengthened by *position*.

216 A syllable is long by nature, when it is represented by a diphthong or two vowels pronounced as one, when its original form was a diphthong, and when it involves the absorption of one or more syllables or of a consonant. Thus the penultima or last syllable but one is long in *Caesar, coena, aurum*; similarly we have *ĭl-līdo* from *laedo, pūnio* from *poena, explōdo* from *plaudo, obēdio* from *audio, Samarīa* from Σαμαρεία, *Ilithȳia* from Εἰλείθυια, *musēum* from μουσεῖον, *cōgo* from *co-igo* (*ago*), *ōtium* from *opitium, mālvolo* and *mālo* for *măgis vŏlo, jūnior* for *jŭvĕnior, sūmo* for *su-imo* (*emo*), *tibīcen* for *tibii-cen, bōbus* for *bŏvĭbus, suspītio* for *suspĭcĭtio, sētius* for *sĕcĭtius, novĭtius* for *novī-ĭtius, pōno* for *po-sino*, and the like.

Exceptions:

(1) The diphthong *ae* is sometimes shortened before a vowel, especially in the preposition *prae* and in Greek words; as *Ver praĕit aestatem. Longior antiquis visa Maĕōtis hiemps. Insulaĕ Ionio in magno.* But this quantity of *ae* is not always observed even in the same word, and we have *Regna Thoas habuĭt Maēōtĭdĕ clarus in ora.*

(2) The Greek diphthong *ει* is generally represented by *ī* or *ē* (above, 3, (3), *Obs.* 5); but we have sometimes *ĕ* for this diphthong, as in *platĕa, chorĕa* by the side of *platēa, chorēa.*

217 A syllable is short by nature when it consists in a single vowel, which does not represent any absorption either of a consonant or of another vowel. And this may generally be inferred when the following syllable begins with a vowel or *h*, as in *mĕ-us, pī-us, delicĭ-ae, tŭ-us, cor-rŭĕt, rebŏat, trăho, vĕho, prŏhibeo.* The fact that a vowel is short by nature before a single consonant may be learned from experience guided by etymology.

The exceptions to the general rule that a vowel before another vowel or *h* is short, are as follows:

(1) The former vowel is long in the old genitives of the first declension, as *aulāī, pictāī.* Also in the genitives and datives in *ēi* from nouns in *es*, as *dīēi, speciēī*; but if a consonant precedes the *e* this vowel may be short, as in *fidĕī, rĕī, spĕī*, the two former of which, however, sometimes follow the general rule for the lengthening of the penultima.

(2) The *i* is long in *fīo* for *fuio*, unless *-er-* follows; thus we have *fīem, fīet, fīunt*, but *fĭerem, fĭeri*, as in the line *Omnia nunc fĭunt, fĭĕri quae posse negabam.*

(3) Genitives in *-ius* have the *i* long, but this is often shortened by the poets, who write e.g. both *illīus* and *illĭus*; except in *alīus,*

which being contracted from *ali-ius* is always long. In *alterīus* the penultima is generally short, though it is occasionally lengthened by the poets. In *ējus, hūjus*, the *i* is hardened into *j*, and the previous syllable lengthened accordingly.

(4) We have *a* long before the termination *-ius* in *Gāīŭs*; as *Pervigil in pluma Gāīŭs, ecce, jacet.* Also in the vocative *Gāī*; as *Quod debes, Gāī, redde, inquit Phoebus.* Similarly we have *Pompēī* from *Pompēius*; but the poets also write *Pompēī* as a dissyllable; thus, *Pompēī meorum prime sodalium.*

(5) The interjection *O!* is common before a vowel; and the penultima of *ŏhe* may be either long or short. But *e* in *ĕheu* is always long.

(6) In Greek words the *e* or *i* of the penultima generally represents the diphthong *ει*, and is therefore long; as in *panacēa, elegīa, Ænēas, Alexandrīa,* and *āēr, ēōs, hērōus, Menelāus, Brisēis,* retain their Greek quantity. But in some Greek words the *e* or *i* or *y* is common; thus we have both *Academīa* and *Academĭa,* both *Dīana* and *Dĭana,* both *Gerȳon* and *Gerўon,* both *Orīon* and in later poets *Orĭon.*

Obs. Some considerations, which belong rather to comparative philology than to Latin Grammar, may assist the student in determining whether a vowel is in its nature short or long. He will recognize an originally single or unaffected vowel of articulation, in the change from *a* to *i* and *e*, as in *ŏd-no, ce-ci-ni, con-cent-us, făcio, con-fī-cio, con-fec-tus* (*Varron.* p. 309), also in the change from *a* or *e* or *i* to *o*, as *pars, portio; fero, fors; mens, memĭni, mŏneo; disco* (= *dic-sco*), *dĭ-dĭci, dŏcro; terra, extorris* &c. (Ibid. p. 311). And with regard to *o* in particular he will notice that when this letter is secondary or derivative, it is generally short, even though the primitive form may give a long 1 or *ū*; thus we have *hŏdie* for *hĭdie* (cf. *prĭdie, postrĭdie*) *hŏmo* by the side of *hūmanus* (where the comparison of other languages shows that *ū* is the original letter), and probably *mŏdo* for *mī dato,* 'give' or 'grant me.' Some such consideration as this justifies the later poets (e.g. Prudentius, *Apotheos.* 194; *Cathem.* L 33) in making the first syllable of *sŏcors* and *sŏcordia* short, although the original form of the prefix was *sē*; and we accept this quantity without any direct authority from poets of the classical age.

218. A vowel which is short by nature becomes long by position, when it stands before two or more consonants or before the double letters $j = di$, $x = cs$ or gs, and $z = ds$; as in *mēns, exēmplum, vēlt, mājor, lēx, gāza.*

QUANTITY. 431

The following special cases require to be noticed:

(1) When a word ends with a short vowel, and the next word begins with two consonants, this is not generally regarded as a position affecting the quantity of the final vowel; but the final vowel very rarely remains short before *sc, sp, sq, st, x, z*, at the beginning of the word following; thus we have *Ferte citi ferrum, date tela, scandite muros. Occultā spoliā, et plures de pace triumphos.* But on the other hand we have *Ponitĕ spem. Praemiā scribae. Nemorosā Zacynthus.*

(2) The letter *h* is not counted as a consonant, and therefore makes no position; thus we have *Serpĭt humi tutus.*

(3) The combination *qu* is regarded as a single letter, which does not affect the quantity of the preceding short vowel; thus we have *Gratius ex ipso fonte bibuntur āquae.*

(4) Compounds with *jugum*, e.g. *bijugus, quadrijugus*, leave a short vowel before *j*; as *Quadrījugum currum.* Hence we have the contraction *bīgae, quadrīgae.*

Obs. The comic poets neglect the rule of position.

219 When a short vowel stands before a mute and liquid, this combination of consonants does not necessarily constitute a position, and the vowel may remain short. In Latin, however, this exception to the rule of position is practically confined to those cases in which the consonant is followed by *r*, and to some few instances where it is followed by *l*; as *pătris, tenĕbrae, mediŏcris, vĕpres, volŭcris, pŏples, assĕcla.* That the vowel in these cases may be either long or short appears from lines in which both quantities are exhibited by the same word; as *Nātum ante ora pātris, pătrem qui obtruncat ad aras. Et primo similis volūcri, mox vera volŭcris.* In Greek words the Greek quantity is observed, and we may have a short vowel in *Ătlas, Prŏcne, Cŷgnus, Tĕcmessa*, &c.

The following remarks must be noticed:

(1) The weak position created by the mute followed by a liquid does not affect the quantity of a vowel naturally long; thus we have only *mātris* from *māter, arātrum* from *arāre*, and *salūbris* from *salūs.*

(2) The position is not weak, when there are two liquids, as in *ōmnes*; or a *liquid* before a mute, as in *părtem*; or when the mute and liquid belong to different syllables, as in *ōb-luo.*

220 Derived words retain the quantity of their primitives; thus we have *ămīcus, ămīcitia, inīmīcitias,* by the side of *āmo* and *āmor;* we have *scrība, conscrībere* from *scrībo; valētudo* from *valēre; profīciscor* from *făcio; insīdeo* from *vĭdeo,* &c.

Obs. Some words, which seem to deviate from this rule, are either falsely derived from the assumed primitive, as *mălentus,* which does not come from *mŏles* but from *mălus,* and *cōma,* which has nothing to do with *cōmo = co-imo (emo);* or there has been strengthening of the root in one of the forms, which has lengthened the syllable naturally short; this must be the explanation of *lex, lĕgis, rex, rēgis* by the side of *lĕgo, rĕgo; păx, păcis* by the side of *păco; dux, dŭcis* by the side of *dūco; vōco* from *vox, vōcis; dīco (-are)* and *dīcax* by the side of *dīco; lūcerna* by the side of *lūceo; lăbor (-oris)* and *lābo (-are)* by the side of *lābor (-i); nătus* by the side of *nāta; sŏpor* by the side of *sōpio; stătio, stăbilis* by the side of *stāre* and *stăturus,* &c. Thus too *fīdo, fīdus, infīdus, fīducia* have a long I; but the I is short in *fĭdes, fĭdelis, perfĭdus, perfĭdia.*

221 Compounds retain the quantity of the simple words which they involve; as *caedo, oc-cīdo; cădo, occĭdo* (above, 216). But there are some few exceptions, as *juro, pejĕro; nŏtum, agnĭtum, cognĭtum; nūbo, pronūbus; sōpitus, semisōpitus, sī, quandō, sīquidem, quandŏquidem.*

§ 2. *Quantity of the Middle Syllables.*

(α) *Middle Syllables of Nouns and Pronouns.*

222 (aa) A vowel is always long before the termination -*rum* of the gen. pl.; thus we have *musārum, diērum, dominōrum, illārum, istōrum.*

(bb) If the vowel before -*bus* or -*bis* in the dat. abl. is *a, e,* or *o,* it is always long; thus we have *duābus, deābus, diēbus, duōbus, nōbis, vōbis;* if the vowel is *i* or *u* it is short; thus we have *artĭbus, artŭbus, partĭbus, partŭbus;* except in the case of *būbus, būbus* for *bovĭbus.*

(β) *Middle Syllables of Verbs.*

223 (aa) Dissyllabic perfects and supines have the penultima long, except when one vowel stands before another; thus we have *vīdi, ēgi, ēmi; vīsum, actum, emptum,* from *vĭdeo, ăgo, ĕmo;* but *rŭi, rŭitum* from *ruo,* are exceptions.

(1) Seven dissyllabic perfects and eight dissyllabic supines have the penultima short; these are remembered by the following rhymes:

Short are: *bĭbi, dĕdi, fĭdi,*
Tŭli, stĕti, stĭti, scĭdi;
Dătum, ĭtum, lĭtum, quĭtum,
Rŭtum, rŭtum, sătum, sĭtum.

(2) The supine *stĭtum* from *sto* has the penultima long, and *stĭtum* from *sisto* has the penultima short. We have both *citum* and *cĭtum* from *cio* and *cieo* (above, pp. 103, 130).

(bb) Reduplicated perfects have the penultima short, as in *cecĭni, cecĭdi, tetĭgi, didĭci.*

Exceptions:

We have *cecĭdi* from *caedo*, and in some cases, as in *cucurri, fefelli, pependi, spopondi,* the penultima is long by position.

(cc) Polysyllabic perfects in -ri or -si, and polysyllabic supines in -tum or -sum, have the penultima long; as in *amāvi, divīsi, solūtum, divīsum.*

(dd) Perfects in -ui of the first, second, and fourth conjugations, and the corresponding supines in -itum, have both the penultima and the antepenultima short; as *dŏmo, dŏmŭi, dŏmĭtum; mŏneo, mŏnŭi, mŏnĭtum; sŏno, sŏnŭi, sŏnĭtum; gigno* (for *gigeno*), *gĕnŭi, gĕnĭtum; pōno* (for *po-sĭno), pŏsŭi, pŏsĭtum.*

Obs. *Praebeo, praebui, praebitum* is not an exception to this rule, for the full form is *praehibeo*, which is merely a compound of *habeo.* The same may be said of *debeo, debui, debitum*, which in one sense at least is a contraction of *dehibeo.*

(ee) Supines in -ĭtum which are not formed from perfects in -ŭi, have the penultima short, as *fugĭtum, cognĭtum.*

Obs. The later poets make an exception to this in *recensitus*, which has its penultima long in Claudian, *Eutrop.* II. 60: *Prisca recensitis evolvite saecula fastis;* and Prudentius has *recensītus, Apoth.* 1069: *stirps recensīta numerandus sanguinis haeres.* But it is clear that *censitor* is only another form of *censor*, and as we have *censtor, censtom,* and *ancensto* in Oscan, for *censor, censum,* and *non censitus* (*Varron,* pp. 149, 150), we may conclude that this participle originally and properly followed the rule, and that the lengthening of the *i* is a misconception on the part of those later writers. Accordingly the other quantity is given above, 103, 130.

224 The quantity of the penultima is fixed in many of the inflexions of the verb. Thus the student has seen that a vowel is always long before the endings -*bam,* -*bas,* -*bat,* &c., -*bo,* -*bis,*

-bit, &c., and before *-runt* or *-re* in the perfect; that the penultima is always long in *-amus*, *-atis*, *-emus*, *-etis;* and in the infinitives of the first three conjugations. The following cases must be noticed:

(1) The *a* is short in all inflexions of *do* except *das* and *da;* thus we have *circumdămus*, *circumdăbam*, *circumdăbo*, and it is even represented by a short *u* in the occasional forms *duim* (*creduim, perduim*).

(2) The penultima of the third person plural of the perfect indicative is occasionally shortened by the poets; as *Longa decem menses tulĕrunt fastidia matres. Di tibi divitias dedĕrunt artemque fruendi. Obstupui, stetĕruntque comae, et vox faucibus haesit.*

(3) The terminations *-imus, -itis*, have the penultima short in the first, second, and fourth conjugations; but the *i* is long in the present tense of the third conjugation, and in all present subjunctives; thus we have *audīmus, audītis, sīmus, sītis, velīmus, velītis*.

(4) Although we have always *erĭmus, erĭtis* in the future indicative, we have no authority for a short penultima in *fuerimus, fueritis*, or in the first and second persons plural of the perfect subjunctive of ordinary verbs; on the contrary we have several instances of the *i* being long; as *fecerīmus* (Catull. v. 10), *transierītis* (Ovid, *Epist. Pont.* IV. 5, 6), *contigerītis* (Id. *ibid.* IV. 5, 16), &c.

§ 3. *Quantity of the final Syllable.*

225 (*a*) *Monosyllabic Words.*

(aa) Monosyllabic words, which end in a vowel or *h* are long; as *ā, dē, mē, sē, ei, ōh, prō* and *prōh*.

Except the enclitics; as *-cĕ, -nĕ, -quĕ, -tĕ, -vĕ, -ptĕ, -psĕ*.

(bb) Monosyllabic words, which end in a single consonant and are not nouns, are short; as *ăd, sĕd, ŭt, vĭl, ăb, ŏb*.

Except *cūr, quīn, sīn, ēn, nōn, crās*, and the adverbs in *c*, as *hīc, hūc, sīc*.

(cc) Monosyllabic nouns are long; as *sōl, vēr, mōs, ūs, fūr, jūs, rōs, plūs, pār, vās, lār, pēs, būs, ōs* (*ōris*).

But *mĕl, fĕl, vĭr, cŏr, lăc, ŏs* (*ossis*) are short.

(dd) *Hic* in the nom. is either long or short; *hōc*, whether nominative or ablative, is long.

QUANTITY.   435

(ee) The imperatives dīc from dīco, dūc from dūco, fāc from fācio, fĕr from fĕro, which are the usual forms¹, retain the quantity of their verbs; ĕs from sum is short; ēs for ĕdĭs from edo, is long. Fīs, vīs, and sīs are long.

(β) *Polysyllabic Words ending in a Vowel.*

226 (aa) The final a is regularly short; as in musă, regnă, lampadă. The following are the only exceptions:

(1) In the ablative sing. of the first declension; as musā.

(2) In the voc. of nouns in -as; as in Ænĕā, Pallā, from Æneas, -eae, Pallas, -antis.

(3) In the imperative of the first conjugation; as in amā.

(4) In undeclinable words; as in contrā, extrā, intrā, frustrā, ergā, anteā, posteā, intereā, quadragintā. But of these ită, quiă, ejă, and pută, ‘for example,’ have short ă.

(bb) The final e is short; as in patrĕ, currĕ, nempĕ, propĕ, facilĕ, legerĕ, amaverĕ. The following are the only exceptions:

(1) The ablatives of the e declension; as diē (hodiē, pridiē, postridiē, &c.), rē (quārē, quādērē), fidē, speciē. Together with famē from fames.

(2) The imperatives of the second conjugation; as monē. But of these some dissyllables are made short by the poets, as cavĕ, habĕ, valĕ, vidĕ, tacĕ.

(3) The adverbs in ē from adjectives of the second declension, as doctē, miserē, altē, together with ferē, fermē, and the interjection ohē. But benĕ, malĕ, infernĕ and supernĕ are short.

(4) The Greek words, in which e represents η, either in the nom. singular feminine, in the voc. masc., or in the nom. plur. neut.; as crambē, Atridē, Tempē.

(cc) The final i is long; as in pueri, patri, fructui, misi, legi, rideri. The following are the only exceptions:

(1) Greek datives and vocatives; as Paridi, Alexi, and ōli when it is used as a dissyllable.

¹ In ordinary Latin the apocope of the final e in these imperatives is invariable in the simple forms, and in those compounds, as edūc, effēr, calefac, which do not change the root-vowel; but we have confĭce, perfĭce, &c., where there is the usual change from a to i, and face, dice, dice are found in the poets. From scio we have only the fuller form scito and generally scitote.

28—2

(2) The particles *nĭsĭ* and *quăsĭ*.

(3) The following, in which the final *i* is common; *mihī̆, tibī̆, sibī̆, ibī̆, ŭbī̆*, and the compounds of *uti*, which generally follow the exigencies of the verse; thus we have *utŭtī*, but *sĭcŭtī*. In *utĭnam* and *utĭque, necubī̆, sicubī̆, ubīvis, ubīnam*, the *i* is always short; it is long in *ibĭdem, ubĭque, utrobĭque*; and common in *ubĭcunque*.

(dd) The final *o* is invariably long in the dat. abl. of the second declension, as *domĭnō, regnō, bonō*; and in Greek nouns in *o* (ω), as *Iō, Echō*; it is generally long in adverbs and other particles in *o*, as *adeō, ergō, porrō, quandō, idcircō, omnīnō*. It is common in the nom. of the third declension and in the first person of verbs; as *virgō, canō*. The following special cases deserve notice.

(1) The adverbs *cĭtŏ, modŏ* (with its compounds *tantummŏdo, dummŏdo*), *quomŏdŏ* (when written as one word), *immŏ, illicŏ;* the pronoun *egŏ;* the numerals *duŏ, octŏ;* the imperative *cedŏ;* and the obsolete preposition *endŏ* for *in*, have a short *o*.

(2) The poets of the silver age shorten the *o* in the adverbs *ergo, quando, porro, postremo, sero*, and the ablative of the gerund, as *vigilando*. But adverbs which can be referred to an inflected form are always long; as *quo, eo, paullo, multo, tanto, quanto, falso, merito, subito, profecto*, &c.

(ee) The final *u* is always long, as in *cornū, diū;* and *y*, which occurs in a very few Greek words, is always short, as in *molў*.

(γ) *Polysyllabic Words ending in a Consonant.*

227 (aa) The endings *d, t, l, n, r* are short, as *apŭd, capŭt, semĕl, carmĕn, amŏr*. This rule holds without exception in Latin words; the only deviations are the following Greek nouns:

(1) Masculine and feminine nouns in *n;* as *Tītān, Salamīn, Actaeōn.*

(2) Nouns in *-er* increasing in the genitive; as *aethēr, charactēr.*

(3) Accusatives in *-an* or *-en* for *-αν, -ην;* as *Aenean, crambēn.*

Obs. Greek nouns in *-or* are short, as *Hectŏr, Nestŏr, rhetŏr*, though the original forms have *-ωρ*.

QUANTITY. 437

(bb) The ending -as is long, as in mensis, aetās, amās; except in andis, gen. anātis; in the Greek nouns in -as, gen. -ădis, as Ilias, and the Greek accusatives, as lampadăs, heroăs.

(cc) The ending -es is long, as in nubēs, dūces, dūcēs, amēs, quotiēs.

The following are the exceptions to the general rule:

(1) The compounds of es from sum, as adĕs, abĕs, potĕs.
(2) The preposition penĕs.
(3) Nominatives in -ĕs which have a gen. in -ĕtis, -ĭtis, -ĭdis, as segĕs, milĕs, obsĕs; but of these Cerēs, ariēs, abiēs, pariēs, have the termination long; as also the compounds of pes, as bipĕs, tripĕs, quadrupĕs.
(4) Greek nominatives plural, as cratērĕs, Arcadĕs.
(5) Greek neuters in -es, as Cynosargĕs, hippomanĕs.

(dd) The ending -is is short, as in ignis, dŭcis, dŭcis, tristis, sanguis. The following are the exceptions:

(1) Datives and ablatives plural in -is, as musis, pueris, nobis, vobis.
(2) Accusatives plural of the third declension (above, 29), as omnis, civis.
(3) The adverbs gratis, foris.
(4) The second person singular of the present indicative of -i verbs, as audīs, venīs; of the forms adsīs, possīs, &c. mavīs, malīs, &c.; and often in the second person singular of the perfect subjunctive, as amaverīs.
(5) The nominatives Quirīs, Samnis, Salamīs, Eleusīs, Simoīs.

(ee) The ending -os is long, as in honōs, multōs, illōs. The exceptions are only ŏs, gen. ossis, exŏs, compŏs, impŏs, and Greek words in -os, as Delŏs nom., Erinnyŏs gen.

(ff) The ending -us is short, as in dominŭs, senatŭs, tempŭs, vetŭs, fontibŭs, scribimŭs, tenŭs, funditŭs.

The following are exceptions:

(1) The nom. sing. in -ūs, when the genitive has a long ū in the penultima, as virtūs, virtūtis; palūs, palūdis; tellūs, tellūris.
(2) The gen. sing. and nom. acc. voc. pl. of the -u nouns; as gen. sing. fructūs for fructuis; nom. acc. voc. pl. fructūs for fructues.

(3) Greek nom. in *-us* for *-ous*, as *Panthūs, Melampūs* (but we have *Œdĭpūs, (Ædĭpi*), and genitives of nouns in *-o* for *-ōs*, as *Sapphūs*.

(gg) The ending *-ys* occurs only in Greek words, and is short, as in *Cotўs*.

§ 4. *Quantity of the connecting Vowel in Compounds.*

228 The following are the rules for the quantity of the connecting vowel, i. e. of the termination of the preceding word, in compounds.

(a) If the first part of the compound is a complete word, its final syllable retains its proper quantity, thus we have *rēpublĭcā, jurējurando, usūcapio, quantīvis*, &c. The exceptional cases of *nĭsĭ, sīquidem, quandoquĭdem*, and other particles, have been already mentioned.

(β) If the first part of the compound is abbreviated by the omission of a syllable, the vowel of connexion retains the quantity of the original word; thus from *venēnum facio* we have *venēficus*.

Obs. In compounds of *facio* with verbs, the connecting *e* is generally short, but it is long in *arēfacio, patēfacio*.

(γ) If the first part of the compound drops its final consonant, the preceding vowel is short, unless the final consonant is *i*, and then the vowel is long; thus we have *quāsi* for *quam-si*, *āperio* for *ad-perio, ōperio* for *ob-perio, ā-moenus* for *ad-moenus, ōmitto* for *ob-mitto*, &c.; but *dĭ-ripio* for *dis-rapio, trā-do* for *trans-do*. In accordance with this the masculine *īdem* has the *i* long because it stands for *is-dem;* but *ĭ-dem* has the *i* short, because it represents *id-dem*, as the following line shows:

Per quod quis peccat, per *ĭdem* punitur et *īdem*.

(δ) If the first part of the compound is an uninflected form, the vowel of connexion is a short *i, o*, or *u*, as in *causīdĭcus, viŏlentus, Trojĭgena*. The quantity of the *o* in *sacrosanctus* is doubtful.

Obs. In Greek nouns we have *ŏ* or *ō* according as the original letter was o or ω; thus we have *Minŏtaurus*, but *Argŏnauta*.

(ε) Prepositional prefixes ending in a consonant are short before a vowel; as in *ădigo, ăbigo, sŭbigo, praetĕreo;* but monosyllables ending in a vowel, and dissyllables in *a* and *o*, are long before a consonant; as in ăvoco, dētraho, ējungo, vēcors, vēsanus, contrādico, contrōversus, intrōduco, retrōcedo.

Obs. We must except so- in sŏcors, sŏcordia, for the reasons given above (217, (5), *Obs.*). And long vowels are shortened before other vowels, as in deŭrum, soŭreum, prŏavus, retrŏngo, or sometimes they coalesce and form one syllable with a following e or i, as deĕram for dēĕram, dĕinde for dĕinde, prŏinde for prŏinde, dēmo for dēimo, cŏgo for cŏago, &c. We must also except dīrimo and dĭsertus from the above rule.

(ζ) The following cases of prefixes require special notice.

(1) *Pro* is short in Greek words, but generally long in Latin; thus we have prŏdi, prŏgenies, prōlabor by the side of Prŏmetheus, &c. But the Greek words prologus and propola have the first syllable long, and pro is short in the Latin words prŏcella, prŏfanus, prŏfecto, prŏfestus, prŏficiscor, prŏfiteor, prŏfugus, prŏfundus, prŏhibeo, prŏnepos; and common in prŏcumbo, prŏcuro, prŏfugio, prŏfundo, prŏpago, prŏpello, prŏpino.

(2) *Re-* before a single consonant or a mute and liquid and red- before a vowel are short, as in rĕfero, rĕdimo, rĕtineo, rĕcludo; and re- is long before sc, sp, st, as in rēscribo, rēspicio, rēstinguo, &c. But red- is retained before l, to which it is assimilated, in rellĭgĭo, rellĭquiae; and we have either an assimilated d or the first letter of a reduplicated perfect in reccĭdi, repperi, rettuli.

Obs. The first syllable of the impersonal rēfert is the dative rei (above, 152, (c)).

(3) If the first word is a numeral it is generally shortened, as in duŏdecim, dŭcenti, quadrĭpes, bĭpes, trĭceps, trĭvium; but we have sēdecim, bīduum, trīduum.

§ 5. *Quantity of Syllables as affected by Metre.*

229 The measurement or quantity of vowels is affected also by the following rules applicable to contiguous or final syllables in a metrical line. The first five of these rules are known by the names of certain figures.

I. *Synaloepha*, or the elision of a final vowel or diphthong before a vowel or h at the beginning of the following word; as

Sērd nīmīs vīt' ēst crāstīnă, vīv' hŏdīe,

for vītă, vīvĕ.

This rule does not apply to the interjections *heu* and *o*, and is sometimes neglected by the poets; as

Ter sunt cōnātī impōnĕrĕ Peliō Ossam.

From this line we see that the hiatus shortens the final long vowel of *Peliō*, because it stands in the *thesis* of the metre (231), but the final long vowel of *conati* retains its quantity because it stands in the *ictus* or *arsis* of the foot.

II. *Ecthlipsis*, or the elision of a final *m* with its vowel before a vowel or *h*; as

mōnstr' hŏrrēnd' infōrm' ingēns, cūi lūmĕn ădēmptūm,

for *monstrum horrendum, informe.*

The oldest poets used sometimes to omit a final *s* before a consonant, so that -*us* became *ŭ'*; as *volitō vivŭ' pĕr ōrā virŭm* for *vivus:* see the examples in 245.

III. *Synaeresis*, or the contraction of two syllables into one; as

Seu lentō fuĕrint alveāriī rimīnă texta,

as if it were written *alvyaria*,

Seclāqu' intĕxūnt ăbiĕte costas,

as if it were written *abyete.*

Obs. Less usual examples of *synizesis* are the following: *connūbia = connubja* (Lucret. III. 741), *connūbiu = connubjo* (Virg. Æn. I. 73); *ebulliat = ebulljat* (Pers. II. 10); *principium = principjum* (Hor. 3 Carm. VI. 5); *tenuis = tenvis* (Lucret. I. 875); *duarum = dvarum* (Ter. Heaut. II. 3. 85); *duellica = dvellica* (Lucret. II. 661); *tuas = tvas* (Ter. Andr. I. 5. 61).

IV. *Dialysis*, or the resolution of one syllable into two; as

Dēbuĕrānt fūsōs ēvŏlŭissĕ sŭōs,

for *evolvisse.*

V. *Caesura* (237), when, in consequence of the last syllable belonging to a fresh foot or metre of which it receives the *ictus* (231), a single consonant is allowed to make it long by position;

Pectŏrĭbŭs inhīans spirantiă consulit extā.

VI. The last syllable of every verse is common.

CHAPTER II.

METRE.

§ 1. *Metrical Feet.*

230 RHYTHM (*numerus*) is the harmonious proportion, which results from the methodical arrangement of words according to their long and short syllables; and from a recurrence of an emphasis or stress at intervals. If the rhythm is not regulated by fixed laws it is called prosaic (*solutae orationis numerus*). If the emphasis recurs according to a definite measure, the *rhythm* becomes *metre* (*metrum*). Every recurrence of the emphasis is termed a *metre*, and those collections of metres, which recur as distinct wholes, are called verses or lines (*versus*).

231 The emphasis, on which the metre depends, is called the *ictus*, because the time was marked by a stamp of the foot; hence the old Latin metre, or Saturnian verse, was termed *tripudiatio—triplex pedis pulsatio;* and Horace says (3 *Carm.* XVIII. 15), *gaudet invisam pepulisse fossor ter pede terram,* 'the labourer delights to have beaten the hated earth with the three blows of his foot,' i. e. to dance in the old fashion. When the emphatic and unemphatic parts of the metre are contradistinguished, they are called the *arsis* (ἄρσις) and *thesis* (θέσις) respectively, i.e. the raising and sinking of the voice.

232 Every short syllable, which is the unit of metre or measurement, is considered as one *mora* or 'time;' and every long syllable consists of two such *morae*. According to this principle, long syllables are resolved, short syllables combined, and rhythms calculated.

233 When a rhythm is considered as the element of the verse, it is called a 'foot' (*pes*), and the division of verses into feet is called scanning or scansion (*scansio*, i. e. ascending or climbing up by steps, whence a *scale* in music, from *scāla*, 'a ladder').

The following are all the combinations of long and short syllables, which are called feet, and which have distinctive names:

Of two Syllables:

Pyrrhichius	⏑⏑	two *morae*.
Iambus	⏑−	three ——
Trochaeus or *Choreus*	} −⏑	do.
Spondaeus	−−	four *morae*.

Of three Syllables:

Tribrachys	⏑⏑⏑	three *morae*.
Dactylus	−⏑⏑	four ——
Anapaestus	⏑⏑−	do.
Amphibrachys	⏑−⏑	do.
Creticus or *Amphimacer*	} −⏑−	five *morae*.
Bacchius	⏑−−	do.
Antibacchius	−−⏑	do.
Molossus	−−−	six *morae*.

Of four Syllables:

Proceleusmaticus	⏑⏑⏑⏑	four *morae*.
Paeon primus	−⏑⏑⏑	five ——
—— *secundus*	⏑−⏑⏑	do.
—— *tertius*	⏑⏑−⏑	do.
—— *quartus*	⏑⏑⏑−	do.
Ionicus a minore	⏑⏑−−	six *morae*.
—— *a majore*	−−⏑⏑	do.
Diiambus	⏑−⏑−	do.
Ditrochaeus	−⏑−⏑	do.
Chorianibus (i. e. *Choreus* or *Trochaeus + iambus*)	} −⏑⏑−	do.
Antispastus	⏑−−⏑	do.
Epitritus primus	⏑−−−	seven *morae*.

Epitritus secundus	$-\cup--$	seven *morae*.
—— *tertius*	$--\cup-$	do.
—— *quartus*	$---\cup$	do.
Dispondaeus	$----$	eight *morae*.

Although it is necessary that the student should know this nomenclature, he must be assured from the first that it points to an erroneous classification, and that it will not help him to understand the first principles of Greek or Latin metre.

234. There are only two kinds of proper feet or distinct and primitive rhythms.

(a) The equal rhythms, consisting of four *morae*, in which one long syllable is opposed to two short, so that the ratio is $\frac{2}{2}$; these are

Dactylus, 'the dactyl,' $-\cup\cup$; as *mūnĕrā*;
Anapaestus, 'the anapaest,' $\cup\cup-$; as *lăpĭdēs*.

(b) The double rhythms, consisting of three *morae*, in which a long and a short syllable are opposed, so that the ratio is $\frac{2}{1}$; these are

Trochaeus, 'the trochee,' $-\cup$; as *mūsă;*
Iambus, 'the iambus,' $\cup-$; as *ămās*.

To these may be added the representative feet; i. e. the *spondaeus* or 'spondee,' which represents (232) the equal rhythm by two long syllables, as *dīcūnt*, and the *tribrachys* or 'tribrach,' which represents the double rhythm by three short syllables, as *brĕvĭbŭs*.

235. If in any verse the regular course of the rhythm is preceded by an unemphatic syllable, whether long or short, this is called an *anacrusis*, or 'back stroke,' and if the *anacrusis* extends to three or four *morae*, it is called a *basis* or 'pedestal.' It is customary to mark the onward course of the ictus by the acute accent, the *anacrusis* by the grave, and the *basis* by the two accents crossing one another. The divisions of the feet are marked by vertical lines, and the change of rhythm in the middle of the verse by two vertical lines.

236. All verses, except the dactylic and the old Saturnian trochaics, reckon the metre by a double foot or *dipodia*, as it is called, and have only one ictus to the pair of feet.

237 It is essential to the harmony of a line that some one or more of its feet should be divided between two different words. This division is called *caesura* or 'cutting.' There are two kinds of *caesura*—the *masculine, strong,* or *monosyllabic caesura,* when only the first syllable of the foot is in the preceding word; and the *feminine, weak,* or *trochaic caesura,* where the first two syllables of a dactyl are in the preceding word, and the remaining short syllable in the word which follows. Thus in the following line we have *strong caesuras* in the third and fourth feet, and *weak caesuras* in the first and second places:

Arma vir-|umque | ca|no Tro-|jae qui | primus ab oris.

If a word is so placed in a verse as to coincide with a metrical foot, we have a *diaeresis,* which is the opposite of the *caesura;* thus there is a *diaeresis* in the first and fifth feet of the following line of Virgil:

Lumina | labentem caelo quae | ducitis | annum.

238 Half a foot is technically called a *hemimer* (ἡμιμερές), and *caesuras,* which take place in the middle of the second, third, fourth and fifth feet respectively, are called *trihemimeral, penthemimeral, hephthemimeral* and *ennehemimeral caesuras.*

239 If a metre terminates in a *hemimer,* it is called *catalectic* or 'interrupted;' if it is completed, it is called *acatalectic* or 'uninterrupted.'

If the supposed or prescribed metre is redundant by a *hemimer,* the term *hypercatalectic* is applied. Two catalectic forms are so common that they are often called feet; these are the *choriambus* or dactylic trihemimer; as *extāte|rūs*||, which may be termed the dactylic dimeter catalectic; and the *creticus* or trochaic trihemimer; as *īffē|rūnt*||, which may be termed the trochaic monometer catalectic.

§ 2. *Equal Rhythms.*

A. *Dactylic Verse.*

240 (a) *Hexameter* or *Heroic Verse.* The only dactylic rhythm, which appears in long systems of single lines, is called the Hexameter, because it contains six metres or repetitions of the ictus. The first four metres may be either dactyls or spondees, but the fifth must generally be a dactyl, and the sixth must always be a spondee, or, according to 229, vi., a trochee. The following are examples:

Pāstō| rēs ŏvĭ|ūm tĕnĕ|rōs dē|pĕllĭt⁀ĕ| fŏetūs‖.
Tū nĭhĭl | ĭnvī|tā̆ dī|cēs făcĭ|ās⁀ĕ Mĭ|nērvā‖.

Obs. 1 In these verses there is generally, as in the examples, a penthemimeral caesura, and often a hephthemimeral caesura also. In fact, the former must occur, unless there is a caesura in the fourth foot. And even then the absence of the penthemimeral caesura is comparatively rare, e.g. in such lines as the following verse of Catullus:

Eumenides quibus | anguino|o redimita capillo.

Obs. 2 If there is a strong hephthemimeral but a weak penthemimeral caesura, there is generally also a strong trihemimeral caesura; as

Non un|quam gravis | aere do|mum mihi dextra redibat.
Funer|a super exuvi|as ename|nque relictum.

and we have rarely a weak penthemimeral without a strong trihemimeral caesura, or vice versa; as

Degene|rem⁀que Ne|optole|mum nar|rare memento
Armen,tarius | Afer algū tec|tumque lare⁀mque.

Weak caesuras very seldom follow in succession; but we have occasionally such lines as

Daphnin ad | astra fe|remus a|mavit nos quoque Daphnin.
Una Eu|rusque No|tusque ru|ens cre|berque pro|cellis.
Antiqu|a e ce|dro Ita|lusque po|terque Sa|binus
Satur|nusque se|nex Ja|nique bi|frontis i|mago.

Obs. 3 The third foot rarely makes a *diaeresis*; as

Montibus audiri fragor | et resonantia longe;

for this divides the hexameter into two trimeters: and it must not consist of a single word; for the exception in the line of Virgil,

Summa leves hinc | nescio | qua dulcedine laetas,

is only apparent, since *nescio qua* is regarded as constituting one word equivalent to an indefinite pronoun (above, 175, (b)).

Obs. 4 The second foot is very rarely comprised in a single word, as in the line of Virgil,

Scilicet | omnibus | est labor impendendus et omnes;

except when *inter* or *intra* is followed by a monosyllabic pronoun; as

Talibus | inter | se dictis ad tecta subibant,

for then the connexion of the words produces a *quasi-caesura*.

Obs. 5 The fourth foot is not comprised in a single word, unless it is preceded by a word of two short syllables, as in the line

Exisum Euboicae latus | ingens | rupis in antrum,

or by a monosyllable connected in syntax or sense with the words which follow; as in the lines

Et sine lite loquax cum | Palladis | alita cornix
Et graviter frendens sic | satis | ora resolvit.

Obs. 6 The word preceding the dactyl of the fifth foot must not be a *trochius*, as it is called, that is, a trisyllable consisting of one short and two long syllables, such as *dēdĕrănt*, unless a monosyllable precedes; as in the line

Pallentes hederas et āmāntēs | littora myrtos.

Obs. 7 If the fifth foot is a spondee, which is rarely the case, the fourth must be a dactyl; as

Cōnstĭtĭt | ātque ŏcŭlīs Phrȳgĭ|a āgmĭnă | cīrcŭm|spēxĭt||.
Clārā dĕ|ăm sŏbŏ|lēs māg|năm Jŏvĭs | īncrĕ|mēntŭm||.

Obs. 8 Words of more than three syllables and monosyllables are rarely found at the end of hexameter lines; and the strong ennehemimeral cæsura is not often found in the last dactyl, unless the concluding word is a quadrisyllable, when it is of course inevitable; thus we rarely find such lines as

Per connubia nostra per incep|tos hyme|naeos.
Sternitur exanimisque tremens pro|cumbit bu|mi bos.
Nec saturare fimo pingui pude'at sola | nova.

But the older writers, as Ennius, very often have lines resembling the cadence of the first two; there are at least twenty-six lines in Lucretius which end in a monosyllable; in Horace's Satires there are fifty-five lines with monosyllabic endings, and at least nine with a strong ennehemimeral cæsura; but these poets are not to be imitated in all respects by the modern writer of hexameters. Words of five and six syllables at the end of the line are also very rare; as in Virgil's

Quarum quae forma pulcherrima | Deio|peia,

and Horace's

Quisquis luxuria tristive su|perstiti|ona|.

With regard to the final monosyllable, it is not so objectionable, if another monosyllable precedes; as in Horace's line

Principibus placuisse viris non ultima | laus est|.

Obs. 9 It is desirable to avoid hexameters, which rhyme at the middle and end. These verses are called *Leonine*, from Leonius a monk of Paris, who first regularly introduced them. But solitary instances have been noticed in the best classical poets; thus we have in Virgil:

Limus ut hic du|rescit | et haec ut cera li|quescit|.

in Ovid:

Si Trojae | fatis | aliquid restare pu|tatis|.

Obs. 10 In consecutive lines, the sense must be carried on from one verse to another, and the pauses and cæsuras must be varied. If the pause falls after the first word in a line, the word thus separated is generally a dactyl, a trochee or a choriambus. A spondaic word is rarely found by itself, but this may be allowed, if there is a special emphasis, as in the lines of Virgil:

Extinctum Nymphae crudeli funere Daphnin
Flebant: | vos coryli testes et flumina Nymphis.

The following description of the horse from the third *Georgic* will exemplify the manner in which Virgil varies the caesuras and pauses in his hexameters:

Sin ad bella ma|gis studi|um tur|masque fe|roces,
Aut Al|phea ro|tis prae|labi flumina Pisae,
Et Jovis in luco cur|rus agi|tare volantis;
Primus e|qui labor | est ani|mos atque arma videre
Bellan|tum, litu|osque pa|ti, trac|tuque gementem
Ferre ro|tam, et stabu|lo fre|nos au|dire sonantis;
Tum magis atque mu|gis blan|dis gau|dere magistri
Laudibus, || et plau|sae soni|tum cer|vicis amare.
Atque haec jam pri|mo de|pulsus ab ubere matris
Audeat, || inque vi|cem det | mollibus ora capistris
Invalidus, || etiamque tre|mens, eti|am inscius aevi.
At, tribus exac|tis, ubi | quarta accesserit aestas,
Carpere mox gy|rum incipi|at, gradi|busque sonare
Compositis; || sinu|atque al|terna volumina crurum;
Sitque laboranti similis; || tum cursibus auras,
Tum vocet, || ac, per aperta vo|lans, ceu liber habenis,
Æquora, || vix sum|ma ves|tigia ponat arena.

241 (b) *Elegiac Verse.* Not only does custom require that the dactyl should be represented by a spondee at the end of an hexameter verse, but the ictus alone may suffice for the close of a set of dactyls.

This is regularly the case with the dactylic trimeter catalectic or *penthemimer;* and a class of poems, called *Elegiac*, is written in complete hexameter lines followed alternately by pairs of these interrupted trimeters, which are erroneously called *Pentameters.* Example:

Grātŭlŏr | Ēchălī|ăm tĭtă̄|lĭs ăc|cēdĕrē | vēstrĭs||
Vīctō|rēm vīc|tae || succŭbū|īssĕ quĕ|rōr||.

Obs. 1 The penthemimers of the elegiac must be kept distinct, and we must not imitate Catullus, who frequently has an elision at the end of the first penthemimer.

Obs. 2 The last word of the line should be an iambus, and either a verb, a substantive, or pronoun; it should not be preceded by an elision; and the word preceding it should not be a monosyllable. There are exceptions to these rules, but they are not to be imitated. For example, a word of four or five syllables is more frequently found at the end than a trisyllable, and a very emphatic adjective may terminate the pentameter.

Obs. 3 The first penthemimer seldom ends with an iambic word, but when this is the case the first foot is generally a spondee, as in the line

Pascebatque suas || *ipse senator oves.*

But there are not unfrequent exceptions to this; thus we have in the same narrative (Ovid, *Fasti*, II. 98—108) the following instances in close succession:

At tibi | *nave tua* || *tutius aequor erat.*
Reddidit | *icta suos* || *pollice chorda sonos.*

Obs. 4 The first penthemimer more frequently begins with a dactyl than a spondee, and a spondaic word at the beginning of the line is to be avoided.

The two spondees in the example above are not to be imitated; they are required in the special case by the antithesis.

Obs. 5 The first penthemimer should not end in a monosyllable, unless it is proceded by a word of one long or two short syllables; as in the lines

A pecoris lux est || *ista notata metu.*
Saepe tibi pater est || *saepe legendus avus.*

Obs. 6 The first penthemimer should not begin with a spondee which has a real pause after it; but this objection does not apply to the case when the first word, though followed by a vocative or other parenthetical member, belongs in sense to the end of the line; as

Vellem, Maeonide, || *pectus inesse tuum.*

Obs. 7 The final syllables of the penthemimers may rhyme; as

Comas virgine|as || *hasta recurva co|mas|.*

But Leonine Verses are to be avoided, and perhaps the difference of quantity prevented the perception of a true rhyme in Ovid's line

Quaerebant | *flavos* | *per nemus omne* | *favos|.*

242 (c) *Glyconic Verse.* The dactyl and spondee, which terminate the hexameter verse, appear as a separate dipodia, which is called the *Adonius,* and always, as we shall see, terminates the Sapphic stanza; as

Tĕrrălt | ărbĕm||.

If the second dactyl is retained, and a basis prefixed, the line is called a *Glyconeus;* as

Sīc tē || *dīvă pŏ|tēns Cўprī||.*

If the *Adonius* has a basis prefixed it is called a *Pherecrateus*; as

$$Cr\bar{a}t\bar{o} \parallel P\bar{y}rrh\check{a} \; s\check{u}b \mid \bar{a}ntr\bar{o} \parallel.$$

The Glyconic verse is used by Catullus with a Pherecrateus after every third (34 [32]) or fifth line (61 [59]).

243 (d) *Choriambic Verse.* The dactyl and long syllable, which form the end of the pentameter, appear as a catalectic dipodia by the side of complete pairs of feet. Thus, in the lesser *Asclepiadean* verse, we have two dipodiæ with the basis prefixed, the former dipodia appearing as a trihemimer or *choriambus;* and in the great Asclepiadean verse the complete dipodia is preceded by two *choriambi*, or catalectic dimeters. Examples:

$$M\stackrel{a}{a}sc\bar{e}\mid n\bar{a}s \; \bar{a}t\bar{a}\mid v\bar{\imath}s \parallel \bar{e}l\bar{\imath}t\bar{\imath}\mid r\bar{e}g\bar{\imath}b\bar{u}s \parallel.$$

$$T\stackrel{u}{u} \; n\bar{e} \mid qu\bar{a}es\bar{\imath}\bar{e}\mid r\bar{\imath}s \parallel sc\bar{\imath}r\bar{e} \; n\bar{e}\mid f\bar{a}s \parallel qu\bar{e}m \; m\bar{\imath}h\bar{\imath}\mid qu\bar{e}m \; t\bar{\imath}b\bar{\imath}\parallel.$$

The shorter *Asclepiadean* is used by itself, or alternately with *Glyconei* (Hor. 1 *Carm.* III.), or with a *Glyconeus* after every third line (Hor. 4 *Carm.* XII.), or in couplets followed by a *Pherecrateus* (243, *Obs.*) and *Glyconeus* (Hor. 1 *Carm.* V.), between which *hiatus* is not allowable.

244 There are other kinds of dactylic verse, which are less common; thus, we have the *Tetrameter;* as

$$A\bar{u}t \; \bar{E}ph\bar{e}\mid s\bar{o}n \; b\bar{\imath}m\bar{a}\mid r\bar{\imath}s\bar{e} \; C\bar{o}\mid r\bar{\imath}nth\bar{\imath}\parallel.$$
$$M\bar{\imath}ns\bar{o}\mid r\bar{\imath}m \; c\bar{o}h\bar{\imath}\mid b\bar{e}nt \; \bar{A}r\mid ch\bar{y}t\bar{a}\parallel.$$

And the penthemimer occurs as a separate verse;

$$P\bar{u}lv\bar{\imath}s \; \bar{e}t \mid \bar{u}mbr\bar{a} \; s\bar{u}\mid m\bar{u}s\parallel.$$

B. *Anapæstic Verse.*

245 (a) *Anapæstic Dimeter.* The commonest anapæstic system is the dimeter, which consists of successive pairs of feet, the whole system being counted as one line until it is broken by a basis, or by a catalectic dimeter, which is termed a *paroemiac*. The dactyl and spondee may take the place of the anapæst, except in the last foot of the dimeter, where the dactyl is not used by Seneca. Example:

450   METRE.

Ŭndă ĭg|nī' clā́rĭ || mīrtū|tĭbŭ' clām||
Dīcī|tŭs: Fūm̄ || dĭctă' Prō|mĕ̄theŭs||
Clēpsī|sĕt dŏlō||, poēnās|quē Jŏvī||
Fūto ĕx|pĕndī||sĕt sŭprē|mō||.

Obs. The *Pherecrateus* was formed by omitting two *morae* at the beginning of the paroemiac (see *Theatre of the Greeks*, Ed. vii. 170).

246 (b) *Ionic a minore.* If the thesis in the anapaestic dipodia is represented by a single long syllable, it is usual to term this metre *Ionicus a minore*, in contradistinction to a certain form of the choriambic rhythm *cum anacrusi*, which was called the *Ionicus a majore.* Four of these imperfect anapaestic dipodia form a verse in Horace; thus,

Mīsĕ̄rā|rŭm ĕst || nĕc āmō|rī || dărĕ̄ lū̄|dŭm || nĕquĕ̄ dū̄|lcī||.

§ 3. Double Rhythms.

A. Trochaic Verse.

247 (a) *Ithyphallic Metre.* The trochee is a dactyl with the last *mora* omitted. The simplest and oldest form of the trochaic metre is the *ithyphallicus*, or *tripudiatio*, generally called the *Saturnian verse*, in which the ictus occurred thrice. This metre always appears in two sets of three feet with an anacrusis. It was very rude, and the substitutions for the trochee were extremely arbitrary, as the following examples will show :

Dăbū̄nt mă|lŭ̄m Mĕ|tēllī || Nǣviī|ō pō|ētae||.
Fūn|dĭt fūlgāt prō|stē̆rnīt || māxĭ̄|mā̆s lĕgĭ|ōnē̆s||.
Nŏ|vĕm Jŏ|vĭs cōn|cŏrdĭ̄s || fīlĭ|ae sŏ|rōrē̆s||.

248 (b) *Hipponactean Verse.* The trochaic metre is generally counted by pairs of feet, each having but one ictus, i.e. on the first syllable. If a long syllable is added to a trochee, the *trihemimer* which results is called *dimeter catalectic*, and is also designated as a *creticus*; as crē̆dĭ|dī|'. When the last syllable is resolved, it is termed *paeon primus*, as dīvĭtĭbŭ̄s; if the first syllable is resolved, it is called *paeon quartus*, as mărĭtī|mŏs||. The

METRE.   451

paeon secundus, as *ămăbĭmŭs*, and the *paeon tertius*, as *stĭmŭlătŭs*, correspond in the number of *morae*, but not in rhythm, to the true cretic measure. The Greeks considered the *Cretic* and *Paeonic* metres as constituting a special class of rhythms, which they designated as *hemiolian*, i. e. 'one and half,' because the ratio of the arsis to the thesis was 3/2: and the *Cretic*, and, by implication, the *trochaic dipodia*, were reckoned as equivalent rhythmically to the dactyl, because, at the end of a line, $\perp \cup - = \perp \cup \cup$. The *trochaic dipodia*, which plays an important part in metrical systems, is generally regarded as = *trochee + spondee* by the Augustan poets. If the *ithyphallic* is increased by a long syllable, the verse is called *dimeter catalectic*; as

$$Trādĭ|tūr \; dĭ|ēs \; dĭ|ē\|.$$

And if an *ithyphallic*, added to a *trochaic dipodia cum anacrusi*, follows this dimeter, the metre is termed *Hipponactean*; as

$$Nōn \; ĕbŭr \; n\breve{e}|que \; a\bar{u}r\bar{e}|\bar{u}m\|$$
$$M\bar{e}|\bar{a} \; r\breve{e}|n\bar{\imath}d\bar{e}t \; \| \; \bar{\imath}n \; d\breve{u}|m\bar{o} \; l\bar{a}|c\bar{u}n\bar{a}r\|.$$

249 (c) *Tetrameter Catalectic.* If the dimeter catalectic is added to a complete dimeter, the verse becomes *tetrameter catalectic*, —a form which was much used by the dramatists. A tribrach may stand everywhere for the trochee, and in the even places a spondee; the older poets, who follow the colloquial pronunciation, put a spondee, a dactyl, or an anapaest in any place; as

$$\bar{E}m\bar{o}|r\bar{\imath} \; n\bar{o}\|l\bar{o} \; s\bar{e}d \; | \; \bar{\imath}ss\breve{e} \; \|\| \; m\bar{o}rt\bar{u}|\bar{a}m \; n\bar{\imath}l \; \| \; \bar{u}es\bar{\imath}t|m\bar{u}|\bar{\imath}|.$$
$$\bar{E}g\bar{o} \; quŭm \; | \; g\bar{e}n\bar{u}\bar{\imath} \; \| \; t\bar{u}m \; m\bar{o}r\bar{\imath}|t\bar{u}r\bar{a}m \; \||\| \; sc\bar{\imath}v\bar{\imath} \; et \; | \; e\bar{\imath} \; re\bar{\imath} \; \| \; s\bar{u}s\bar{t}\bar{u}|l\bar{\imath}\|\|.$$
$$N\bar{a}m \; s\bar{\imath}p\bar{\imath}|\bar{e}ns \; v\bar{\imath}r\|t\bar{u}t\breve{e} \; h\breve{o}|n\bar{o}r\bar{e}m \; \||\| \; pr\breve{a}em\bar{\imath}|um \; ha\bar{u}d \; pr\bar{a}\bar{e}\|t\bar{a}m \; p\breve{e}t\bar{\imath}t\|.$$
$$\bar{E}cqu\bar{\imath}d \; | \; v\bar{\imath}d\bar{e}\bar{o}? \; \| \; f\bar{e}rr\breve{o} \; | \; s\bar{e}pt\breve{u}s \; \||\| \; p\bar{a}x\bar{\imath}|d\bar{e}t \; s\bar{\imath}|d\bar{e}s \; s\breve{a}cr\bar{\imath}s\|\|.$$

B. *Iambic Verse.*

250 The iambus always appears in *dipodiae*, the second member of which received the ictus. A tribrach may be substituted

29—2

for the iambus in any place of the longer verses, or a spondee in the odd places.

251 (a) *Dimeter Acatalectic.* This verse consists of four feet; the first and third may be spondees; the first a dactyl, and the second a tribrach; as in the following examples:

Ĭnār|sĭt āes|tŭō|stŭs||.

Vĕl hār|dŭs ē||rēptūs | lŭpō||.

Ĭmbrĕs | nĭvēs||quĕ cŭm|pătrūĭt||.

Fōrtĭ | sĕquā||mŭr pĕc|tōrĕ||.

Vĭdē|rĕ prŏpĕ|rāntĕs | dŏmŭm||.

Āst ĕgŏ | vĭcĭs||sĭm rĭ|sĕrō||.

252 (b) *Trimeter Acatalectic.* This verse, which is also called the *Senarius*, may consist of six iambi, which is the case in Horace's xvith *Epode*, and admits tribrachs any where but in the last foot, spondees in the odd places, dactyls in the first and third, and an anapæst in the first foot; as

Sŭĭs | ĕt ĭp|sa Rō|ma vī|rĭbus rŭĭt||.

Ālĭtĭ|bŭs āt||quĕ cănĭ|bŭs hŏmĭ||cĭdam Hĕc|tŏrĕm||.

Cānĭdĭ|ă brĕvĭ|bŭs im|plĭcā||tă vĭ pĕrŭs||.

Pŏsĭtŭs|quĕ vēr||nās dĭ|tĭs ēx||āmēn dŏmŭs||.

Ŏptāt | quĭē||tēm Pĕlŏ|pĭs ĭn||fĭdĭ pătĕr||.

If the last word in the line is a trisyllable, the fifth foot ought to be an iambus or a tribrachys. The second of the above examples is one of some twenty exceptions to the rule. There ought to be a penthemimeral or hephthemimeral cæsura; if possible, the former, as in the above examples.

Obs. If trimeters follow a dactylic hexameter, or dimeters follow trimeters, the poem is called an *Epodos.* Horace has a book of such poems.

253 (c) *The Scazon.* If the last foot of the senarius is a spondee, the line is called a *scazon,* or "halting line.' The second, fourth, and fifth feet must then be iambi; as

Nĕc fōn|tĕ lă||brā prō|lŭī || căbăl|līnō||.

254. (d) *Tetrameter Catalectic.* If we add a catalectic metre to the senarius, we have a tetrameter catalectic; as

Sĕd ĭn | dĭēm ĭs‖tŭc Pār|mĭ⁴no ĕst ‖ fŏrtās|ĭs quŏd ‖ mĭnărĭĕ‖.
Ĕt ĭn|sŏlĕn‖tĭr āes|tŭăs ‖ vĕlŭt | mĭnŭ‖tă mūg|nŏ‖.

§ 4. *Asynartete Rhythms.*

255. If rhythms of different kinds are put together, the verse is called *asynartete* (ἀσυνάρτητος), or 'unconnected.' The most common of these combinations are dactyls mixed with trochaic dipodiæ; and if the trochees follow the dactyls, the verse is termed *logaoedic*.

256. (a) *Sapphic Verse.* The ordinary Sapphic stanza consists of three asynartete lines followed by an *Adonius* (242). The first three lines are made up of a dactyl flanked by two trochaic dipodiæ, in each of which the second foot is a spondee; the metre therefore stands thus:

$$\_ \cup | \_ \_ \| \_ \cup \cup \| \_ \cup | \_ \_ \|\| \text{ (ter)}$$
$$\_ \cup \cup | \_ \_ \|\|$$

Jām sǎt' tĕs tĕr‖rĭs nĭvĭs ‖ ātquĕ | dīrāe‖‖
Grāndĭ|nĭs mī‖sĭt pătĕr ‖ ĕt rŭ|bēntĕ‖‖
Dēxt⁴|rā ǎl|crās jăcŭ‖lātŭs | ārcĕs|¹|
Tērrŭĭt | ūrbĕm‖‖.

Obs. 1. We must always have either a strong cæsura after the fifth syllable, as in the specimen just given, or at least a weak cæsura after the sixth syllable, as in the line

Quem virum aut he|rōa ly|ra vel acri.

The former is much the more usual.

Obs. 2. The last word of the third line sometimes makes a false cæsura with the *Adonius*, as in the following examples from Horace:

Labitur ripa Jove non probante u-
xorius amnis.
Thracio bacchante magis sub inter-
lunia vento.
Grosphe nec gemmis neque purpura ve-
nale nec auro.

Obs. 3. There may be an hypermeter at the end of a Sapphic line; as

Dissidens plebi numero beator-um
Eximit virtus.

Obs. 4 The later poets, such as Seneca and Boethius, introduce the *Adonius* after any number of Sapphic lines, or omit it altogether. For example, in Seneca's *Medea*, 652—669, there are 17 Sapphic lines followed by an *Adonius*; and in the *Hippolytus*, 274—329, fifty-one Sapphic verses are followed at once by a system of Anapæstic dimeters.

257 There is a longer form of the Sapphic line, in which the first trochaic dipodia is followed by a choriambus, or incomplete dactylic dimeter, which precedes the usual dactyl; and there is also a shorter form in which the first trochaic dipodia is omitted. The two appear together in an ode of Horace; thus,

$$L\bar{y}d\bar{\imath}\bar{a} \parallel d\bar{\imath}c\ p\check{e}r \mid \bar{o}mn\bar{e}s \parallel.$$

$$T\bar{e} \ d\bar{e}\mid\bar{o}s \ \bar{e}\mid r\bar{o} \ S\bar{y}b\bar{a}\mid r\bar{\imath}n \parallel c\bar{u}r \ pr\check{o}p\check{e}r\mid\bar{e}s \ \bar{o}\mid m\bar{a}nd\bar{o}\parallel\mid.$$

258 If the dactyl in the former of these lines is preceded by a basis and followed by an ithyphallicus instead of a dipodia, the verse is called the *Phalaecian hendecasyllable*; as

$$P\bar{a}ss\bar{e}r \parallel d\bar{\imath}l\bar{\imath}ct\parallel \bar{a}e \ m\check{e}\mid \bar{a}e \ p\bar{u}\mid \check{e}ll\bar{a}\check{e}\parallel\mid.$$

259 (b) *Alcaic Verse.* If we call the trochaic dipodia A, the dactylic B, and the anacrusis x, the Alcaic stanza of four lines will consist of two lines containing x + A + B, followed by x + 2A and B + A; thus,

  x   A.   B.
$$V\bar{\imath}\mid d\bar{e}s \ \bar{u}t \mid \bar{a}lt\bar{a} \parallel st\bar{e}t \ n\bar{\imath}v\check{e} \mid c\bar{a}nd\bar{\imath}d\bar{u}m\parallel.$$

  x   A.   B.
$$S\bar{o}\mid r\bar{a}ct\check{e} \mid n\bar{e}c \ j\bar{a}m \parallel s\bar{u}st\bar{\imath}n\check{e}\mid \bar{\imath}nt \ \bar{o}n\bar{u}s\parallel.$$

  x   2 A.
$$S\bar{\imath}\mid l\check{v}\bar{a}e \ l\bar{a}\mid b\bar{o}r\bar{a}n\mid t\bar{e}s \ g\check{e}\mid l\bar{u}qu\check{e}\parallel.$$

     B.   A.
$$Fl\bar{u}m\bar{\imath}n\bar{a} \mid c\bar{o}nstit\check{e}\parallel r\bar{\imath}nt \ \bar{a}\mid c\bar{u}t\bar{o}.$$

Obs. 1 There can be no cæsura between A and B in the first two lines, unless there is an elision; as

$$Qu\bar{\imath}s \mid d\bar{e}v\mid \bar{u}m \ sc\bar{o}r\parallel tum \ \bar{e}l\bar{\imath}c\mid \bar{e}t \ d\bar{o}m\bar{o}\parallel.$$

There are very few examples of such lines as

Hostile aratrum exercitus insolens.
Mentemque lymphatam Mareoticu.

METRE.   455

Obs. 2 The anacrusis is rarely a short syllable, but this occurs sometimes, as in the first line above; and there are only fifteen instances in Horace in which a monosyllable terminates the trochaic dipodia; and then the anacrusis is also a monosyllabic word; as in the line

Nīl | Claudī|aē nōn || pēr̄f ī́cī|ent mānūs|.

Still more rare is a monosyllable at the end of the dactylic dipodia; as

Nē | fōrtē | crēdās || īntēr|tūra quaē|.

But *et* with an elision preceding is not uncommon; as

Fortuna saevo laeta negotio et.

Obs. 3 The anacrusis of the third line is most frequently a long syllable; but Horace has ten instances to the contrary.

Obs. 4 The third line does not begin with a word of four syllables unless an elision follows; as

Funalia et vectes et arcus.

Two disyllables at the beginning of the third line must be avoided altogether. And Horace has only the following instance of a monosyllable followed by a cretic:

Hunc Lebio snerare plectro.

Obs. 5 The third line must not end with a monosyllable, except it be *et* or *in* with an elision; nor with two disyllables, or a word of four syllables, though Horace has three instances of a quadrisyllable and eight of two disyllables in the first and second books of his Odes, which are not so exact as the third and fourth books.

Obs. 6 As a general rule the trochaic dimeter contained in the third line ought to have a penthemimeral caesura. Hence the best rhythm is three words of three syllables each, or equivalent substitutions; as

Dḗ sccndē | Cōreī|nō jū|bēntē |.
Nār|rātūr | ēt prīs|cī Ca|tōnīs|.
Dē|mīssā |tēmpēs|tūs ab | Eūrō|.
Ō | māgnī | Carthā|gō prō|brōsīs|.

The following may also be imitated:

Dū|mētā | nātālēmque | sīlvām|.
Sīl|vaē lā|bōrān|tēs gē|luque|.
Pōr|tūs Alēxān|drēā | sūpplēx|.
Nōn ērū|bēscēn|dīs ad|hīrīt|.
Dē|lēnīt | ūsūs | nēc Falērnā|.

Obs. 7 A short syllable at the end of the first three lines, with a vowel at the beginning of the following line, must be avoided, and there are two instances in Horace of an hypermeter and ecthlipsis at the end of the third line:

Sors | exi|tūra et | nōs in dētērn'·um
Exsĭlĭum—
Cūm | pāre | dēlā|běntĭs Ētrūsc'·um
In mare.

Obs. 8 The fourth line should not have a diæresis after both the dactyls, and we should generally avoid a weak cæsura in the second dactyl, though we have such lines as the following in Horace:

O Thali|arche, me|rum diota.
Jupiter | ipse ru|ens tumultu.
Stesichor|ique gra|ves camoenæ.
Quas caret | ora cru|ore nostro.

Occasional examples are found in which the last line is made up of only two words; as

Divitias operosiores.
Progeniem vitiosiorem.

But these will naturally be of rare occurrence. The best rhythms for the last line consist of three words or their natural substitutes; as in the following:

D-decorum pretiosus emptor.
Missilibus melior sagittis.
Hesperiæ mala luctuosæ.
Gaudia luminibus remotis.
Pocula prætereuntis lympha.
Tempus Amazonia securi.

Or the resolved lines corresponding to these in rhythmical cadence; as

De tenero meditatur ungui.
Ille dies Latio tenebris.
Dura fugæ mala dura belli.
Pertulit Ausoniæ ad urbes.
Ducit opes animumque ferro.
Prælia conjugibus loquenda.

260 (c) *Archilochian Verse.* This is a dactylic tetrameter followed by an *ithyphallicus*; as

Sōlvĭtūr | ācrĭs hĭ|ēmps grā|tā vĭcē || vēr|ĭs | ĕt Fā|vōnī|||.

261 (d) *Elegiambus.* This is composed of a dactylic penthemimer and iambic dimeter; as

Dēsĭnǎt | ĭmpărī|bǎs ‖ cĕrtā|rĕ sŭb|mŏtǐs | pŭdŏr.

262 (e) *Iambelegus.* This is the reverse of the preceding, and consists of an iambic dimeter followed by a dactylic penthemimer; as

Tū vī'nā Tōr|quātō | mōre |'! cōnsŭlĕ | prĭssā mē'ō||.

263 (f) *Galliambicus.* Catullus in his *Attis* introduces a measure, which is called *Galliambic* from its use by the Galli, or priests of Cybele, and from the practice of scanning it as an iambic rhythm. It is really a sort of spurious trochaic metre, made up of a trochaic dipodia preceded and followed by a *paeon tertius*, and finished off by a cretic, or *paeon quartus*. As the second and fourth elements are equivalent to the first and third only in the assumed relation of the four *paeons* (248), the verse is really asynartete. It is scanned according to the following scheme:

```
        1.              2.              3.              4.
   Paeon tertius.  Trochaic dipodia.  Paeon tertius.  Paeon quartus.
   ∪ ∪ ⏌ ∪    |    ⏌ ∪ – –    |    ∪ ∪ ⏌ ∪    |    ⏌ ∪ ∪ –
       –      |       ∪ ∪     |       ∪ ∪     |       ⏌ ∪ –
```

Super alta | vectus Attis | celeri ra|te maria
Dea magna | dea Cybelle | dea domina|Dindymi
Itaque ut do|mnum Cybelles | tetigere |lassulae
Laevumque | pecoris hostem | stimulans i|ta loquitur.

264 The Greeks, from whom the Romans derived most of their metres, made great use also of the *Antispastic rhythm*, ∪–|–∪ (Gr. Gr. art. 672 sqq.), which is not used by the Latin poets. They also counted by rhythms in the ratio $\frac{4}{3}$, which they called *epitrites* (ἐπίτριτοι). These were the reverse of the *paeon*, and contained three long syllables and one short; according to the place of the short syllable, the epitrite was called first, second, third or fourth. The fourth epitrite, – – – ∪, which was also termed the *antispast of seven times* (ἀντισπαστικὴ ἑπτάσημος), or *monogenes* (μονογενής), is alluded to by Cic. (de Orat. I. 59. 251, according to the excellent emendation of the Baron von Bunau), as a rhetorical rhythm.

§ 5. *Comic Metres.*

265 The subject of the Latin Comic Metres cannot be discussed without inquiries into the colloquial pronunciation of the language, which are beyond the scope of a practical work like the present.

Besides this, it has not yet been determined by the eminent scholars, who have paid special attention to the subject, how far the accent of the spoken language was allowed to influence the structure of dramatic verse. And it is certain that eventually Latin verses were constructed with a substitution of accent for quantity. In a practical grammar, therefore, it will be sufficient to give a few specimens of the manner in which the Latin Comedians constructed the lines of most frequent occurrence in their dialogues.

The most common metres in the Latin Comedies are the (a) *Iambic Trimeter Acatalectic* or *Senarius;* (b) the *Iambic Tetrameter Catalectic,* called also the *Septenarius* or *Comicus quadratus;* (c) the *Iambic Tetrameter Acatalectic,* called also *Octonarius* or *Boiscius* from its inventor *Boiscus;* (d) the *Trochaic Tetrameter Catalectic,* called, like the corresponding iambic verse, *Septenarius* and *quadratus;* (e) the *Trochaic Tetrameter Acatalectic* or *Octonarius;* and (f) the *Bacchiac* verso.

(a) *Iambic Trimeter Acatalectic.*

266 The following is an average specimen of the *Iambic Senarius,* as employed by the Comedians (Ter. *Andr.* IV. 1, 31):

PA. *Iúmo etiam, quó | tu minus scis aérumnas meás, |*
Haec nuptiaé | non adparé|bantur mihí; |
Nec postulá|bat nunc quisquam úx|orem duré. |
CH. *Scio: tu code|tus tua volún|tate es.* PA. *mané. |*
Nondum etiam scis. | CH. *Scio equidem dúc|turunu esse té. |*
PA. *Cur me enicás! | hoc audi. Núm|quam destitit |*
Insture, ut dí|cerem me dúc|turum patrí; |
Suadere, ord|re, usque adeo dó|nec perpulit. |
CH. *Quis homo istuc!* PA. *Dá|vos.* CH. *Davos! quémob|rem ?*
PA. *Nescio: |*
Nisi [ni] mihi [mi] deos [dyos] fuise|e iratos, qui uús|cultuverím. |

METRE. 459

(b) *Iambic Tetrameter Catalectic.*

267 The following is a specimen of the *Iambic Septenarius* (Ter. *Hecyr.* v. 2. 2 b):

L. *At haec amí|cae erunt, ubi quí|mob|rem advenerís | resciscent.*
PH. *At eásdem amí|cas fore tibí | promitto, rem úbi | cognorint: Num illas errô|re et te simúl | suspitiô|ne exsolves.*
B. *Perii, pudét | Philumenaé: | tus sequimini in|tro húc ambae.*
L. *Quid'st mihi quod mú,lim quam quod hinc | intelligo êlcenire? Ut gratiam íne|am sine meó | dispendio ét | mihi prosim. Nam si'st ut haéc | nunc Pamphílúm | vere ab sè segr|egarit, Scit se nobili|tatem ex eá | re nactum et glór|iam esse: Refert gratiam el i unayue nós | sibi opera ami|cós jungit.*

(c) *Iambic Tetrameter Acatalectic.*

268 The following is a specimen of the *Iambic Octonarius* (Ter. *Andr.* I. 3. 1):

Enimvero, Dá|ve, nil locús | segnitiae néque | socordidé, | Quantum intellé|i modo sens | sententiám | de nuptils: | Quae si nón dá|tu providén|tur, me aut erúm | pessum dabúnt: | Nec quid agám cér|tumst: Pamphilúm|ne adjutem, an aús|cultem sent. | Si illum relín|quo, ejus vitae time|o; sin opitu lor, húju& minds; Cui verba dáre | difficilest: prí|mum jam de amó|re hoc comperít; | Me infensus sér|eat, ne quam fáciam | in nuptils | fallaciám, | Si senserit, | perii, aut quam libi|tum fuerit cau|eam ceperít, | Qua jure quá | me injurid | praecipitem in pis|trinum dubit. |

(d) *Trochaic Tetrameter Catalectic.*

269 The following is a specimen of the *Trochaic Septenarius* (Plautus, *Captivi*, v. 3. 1):

PH. *Hégio, assum | sí quid me vis | impera.* HE. *Hic gna|túm meum Tuó patri ait se | véndidisse | sèx minis in | 'Alide. |*
PH. *Qáum diu id fac|túm'st? ST. Hic annus | incipit vi|céni- mus.*
PH. *Fálso memorat. | ST. Aút ego, aut tu. | Ném tibi quad|- rimulum | Tlus pater pe|cúliarem | párvolum pue|ró dedit. |*
PH. *Quid erat ei no|mén? Si vera | dícis, memora | dúm mihi.*

460   METRE.

St. *Paégnium vocì|tátu'st; post vos | índidistis | Týndaro.*
Ph. *Cúr ego te non | nóvi!* St. *Quia mos | ést oblivis|ci hóminibus.*
Néque novisse | cújus nihíli | sit faciunda | grátia.

(e) *Trochaic Tetrameter Acatalectic.*

270 The following is a specimen of the *Trochaic Octonarius* (Plautus, *Bacchides*, IV. 3. 1):

*Pétulans, protervo|o, íracundo | ánimo, indómito, in|cógitato
Sine modo et mo|déstia sum, | sine bono ju|re átque honore,
'Incredíbilis | ímposque animi, | ínamabilis, in|lépidus vivo,
Málevolente in|génio natus. | póstremo id mist | quód volo aliis.*

(f) *Bacchiac Verse.*

271 The following is a specimen of the *Bacchiac Verse*, mixed as it often is with *Cretics* (Plautus, *Menaechmi*, IV. 2. 1):

Ut hóc ultimúr mox|umé mo|rs | móro | molésto|que múl|tum: (Bacchiac):
'Atque utí | quíque sunt | óptumi, | máxumi: | mórem habent | húncce | (Cretic)
Cliéntis | sibi ómnes | volúnt es'se múltos; | (Bacch. with Iambus);
Bonine an | malí sint, | id hauíd quae|rítúnt: Bacch. with Iamlms):
Rés magis | quaéritur, | quám cliem'tám fides | quójusmodi | clúeat. | (Cretic).
Sí quis est | paúper at'|que haúd malus, | néquam habetur; |
Sis malus | díves est. | ís cliens | frúgi habetur. |
(Cretics with Trochaic dipodia).

§ 6. *Accentual and rhyming Verses.*

272 (a) The substitution of accent for quantity, which took place in the middle of the third century, will be sufficiently exemplified by the following verses on the martyrdom of Marcellinus and Petrus in the reign of Diocletian (Fleetwood, *Syll. Inscr. Monum. Christ.* p. 449):

*Dúas quaedam réferuntur Rómae natae féminae;
'Una dicta ést Lucílla, Fírmininaque áltera;
Véram puris rétinentes Chrísti fidem córdibus.
Quaé propinqui tér beati Mártyris Tibúrtii,
'Ad illius desidentes sácrosanctum túmulum,
Déi gratas vigilando dúcebant excúbias.*

Quíbus ipse cúm beatís sémet comitántibus,
Márcellíno átque Pétro mániféste rétulit
Pér sopórem, úbi sacra jácuissent córpora
'Eorúndem flectorum, átque simul ádmonet,
'Ut euntes ábsque mora íllis statim adferant,
'Et in crypta súum prope cárent corpus pónere.

In these imitations of the *trochaic Septenarius* it will be observed that the ictus always corresponds to the accent (above, 3, (6)), except in the word *ducebant*. An approximation to this kind of versification is cited as early as the time of Julius Cæsar, whose soldiers, according to Suetonius (*Jul. Caesar*, 51), sang thus at his triumph over the Gauls:

'Urbani servâte uxores moéchum calvum addúcimus.
Aúrum in Gallia effútuisti: at hic sumpsisti mútuum.

Here also the accent corresponds to the ictus except in the first word.

273 (b) The tendency to *homoeoteleuton* or rhyme, which was common enough in the oldest Latin verse (see Ennius, *apud Cic. Tusc.* I. 35, 44; *de Offic.* I. 12; Anonym. *ap. Cic. Tusc.* I. 28; *Orat.* III. 38; Plaut. *Capt.* I. 1. 17; *Cas.* II. 7. 1; *Cistell.* II. 1. 48; *Mil. Glor.* II. 1. 1), and which the classical poets generally, but not always, avoided, was allowed to prevail, when accent had superseded quantity, and Christian poets in the middle ages used this substitute for the resources of the old metrical system with no inconsiderable success. The following stanzas from the celebrated hymn *de Novissimo judicio*, by Thomas of Celano, a Minorite of the 13th century, furnish one of the most pleasing specimens:

Júdex ergo quúm sedebit
Quidquid latet, apparebit
Nil inultum rémanebit.
Quid sum miser túnc dicturus?
Quém patronum rógaturus?
Quúm vix justus sit securus?

Occasional practice in writing these rhyming trochaics will contribute to extend the student's command over the Latin language, if he is careful to observe the classical usages of quantity and metre, which are signally neglected in most of these sacred Latin poems.

§ 7. *Poetic Style as connected with Metre.*

274 Elaborate treatises have been written on the style, diction, and idiom of Latin poetry. The most important of these works is Juni's (*Artis Poeticæ Latinæ Libri* IV. Hake, 1774), which has also appeared in an English adaptation (*Art of Latin Poetry.* Cambridge, 1828). And the student, who wishes to pursue the subject, may have recourse to one of these books. Most of the grammatical forms peculiar to poetry, have been noticed in their proper places. Here it will be sufficient to adduce a few particulars respecting those forms and constructions, which are adopted to obviate some difficulty of metre.

(a) Obsolete forms are sometimes used to help the scansion; thus we have genitives in *āī* for *æ;* imperf. in *-ibam* for *-iebam,* and even in *-ibo* for *-iam,* and infinitives in *-ier* for *-i; olli* for *illi;* and *indu-* for *in-* in compounds, as *induperator* for *imperator.* These and other archaisms are generally confined to epic verse.

(b) Syllables are contracted when the metre requires it; thus we have always **ī** for *ii* in *dī* for *dii,* and in the gen. sing. of substantives in Virgil and Horace; and *ûm* is written for either *-orum* or for *-ium* in the gen. plur.; *u* is written for *ui* and *e* for *ei,* as in *cunctantis juvenem fide; parce metu;* we have *-asse, -assem, -esse, -essem* for *-aviæe, -aviæem, -evisem;* also *-aro, -oro* for *-avero, -overo;* and in particular words we have contractions of contiguous short syllables, as *rēice* for *rēiice, compostus* for *compositus, puertia* for *pueritia,* and even when the second syllable is long, as *asperis* for *asperis* (Virg. *Æn.* II. 379). On the contrary, we have resolutions, as *navita* for *nauta, silua* for *silva, alituum* for *alitum.*

(c) Prepositions are separated from their cases; as *argutos inter strepere ansor olores* (Virg. *Ed.* IX. 36); and prepositions and other separable words are divided by what is called *tmesis* from the rest of the compound, as *inque salutatum linquo* (Virg. *Æn.* IX. 288); *argento post omnis ponas* (Hor. l Serm. i. 86); *septem subjecta trioni* (Virg. *Georg.* III. 381); *quae me cunque vocant terræ* (Virg. *Æn.* L 614).

(d) Græcisms are occasionally introduced; thus the gen. is used as an ablative (above, 153, *Obs.* 4), and the participle is used as an infin. in an objective sentence, e. g. *sensit medios delapsus in hostes,* Virg. *Æn.* II. 377 (cf. above, 177, *Obs.* 1).

(e) The order of the words, in Latin as in other poetry, is often affected by the exigencies of the metre, but a study of the best authors will correct the natural tendency to take undue liberties in this respect.

APPENDIX I.

CLASSIC AUTHORS.

The best writers of Latin are called *auctores classici*, i.e. 'authors of the first class,' a phrase derived from the *comitia centuriata*, which divided the Roman people into classes according to their wealth (Aul. Gel. xix. 8). They are also subdivided, according to the old mythological arrangement, into authors of the golden and silver age respectively. The period during which the Latin language flourished in full perfection was little more than three hundred years, that is, from about 200 B.C. to about 100 A.D. The Christian æra indicates the line of demarcation between the golden and silver ages of Latinity.

A. *Golden Age.*

T. Maccius Plautus (254-184 B.C.); b. at Sarsina in Umbria: 20 Comedies.

P. Terentius Afer (195-159 B.C.); b. at Carthage: 6 Comedies.

M. Terentius Varro (116-28 B.C.); b. at Rome: 3 books on Agriculture; 6 books on the Latin Language.

M. Tullius Cicero (106-43 B.C.); b. at Arpinum, in the Volscian territory: Rhetorical and Philosophical Works; Orations; Epistles.

C. Julius Cæsar (100-44 B.C.); b. at Rome: History.

T. Lucretius Carus (95-52 B.C.); b. at Rome: Philosophical Poetry.

C. Valerius Catullus (87-47 B.C.); b. at Verona: Lyric and Elegiac Poetry.

Cornelius Nepos (1-30 B.C.); b. at Verona: Lives of Cato and Atticus. The other biographies ascribed to him were written by Æmilius Probus in the reign of Theodosius.

C. Sallustius Crispus (86-34 B.C.); b. at Amiternum, in the Sabine territory: histories of the rebellion of Catiline and the war with Jugurtha.

P. Virgilius (or rather *Vergilius*) Maro (70-19 B.C.); b. at Andes near Mantua, in Cisalpine Gaul: 10 books of *Bucolics*, 4 of *Georgics*, and 12 of the *Æneid.*

Q. Horatius Flaccus (65-8 B.C.); b. at Venusia in Apulia: 4 books of *Odes*, 1 book of *Epodes*, 2 of *Satires*, and 2 of *Epistles* in verse.

Albius Tibullus (54?-18 B.C.); b. at Pedum near Tibur in Latium: Elegiac Poetry.
Sex. Aurelius Propertius (51?-19 B.C.); b. in Umbria: Elegiac Poetry.
Titus Livius (59-19 B.C.); b. at Padua in Cisalpine Gaul: History.
P. Ovidius Naso (43 B.C.-18 A.D.); b. at Sulmo, in the territory of the Peligni: Elegiac Poetry, and Mythology in verse.
M. Vitruvius Pollio (?); Architecture.
M. Manilius (also *Manilius* or *Mallius*) (?): Astronomy in verse.

B. Silver Age.

T. Phaedrus (?): Fables.
M. Annaeus Seneca, father of L. Seneca, and grandfather of Lucan (60 B.C.-30 A.D.): Rhetoric.
Velleius Paterculus (killed A.D. 31): History.
L. Julius Moderatus Columella (?): Agriculture.
A. Persius Flaccus (A.D. 38-65): 6 Satires.
C. Silius Italicus (A.D. 25-100): Epic Poetry.
L. Annaeus Seneca (killed A.D. 65): Philosophy.
M. Annaeus Lucanus (A.D. 38-65): Epic Poetry.
C. Plinius Secundus (A.D. 23-79): Natural History.
Valerius Maximus (?): Anecdotes.
C. Valerius Flaccus (ob. A.D. 88): Epic Poetry.
Q. Curtius Rufus (?): Life of Alexander the Great.
M. Fabius Quintilianus (ob. A.D. 88): Rhetoric.
P. Papinius Statius (ob. A.D. 95): Poetry of various kinds.
M. Valerius Martialis (?): Epigrams.
D. Junius Juvenalis (about A.D. 95): 16 Satires.
L. Annaeus Florus (do.): History.
C. Cornelius Tacitus (cos. A.D. 97): History, Biography, and Rhetoric.
C. Plinius Caecilius Secundus, nephew of the older Pliny (about A.D. 95): Epistles and Oratory.
C. Suetonius Tranquillus (do.): Biographies.
Pomponius Mela (?): Geography.

The nature of the ancient Roman language, before the classical age, may be seen from the subjoined short specimens of old Latinity.

(a) *Royal Laws.*

Romulus; about 750 B.C.

Sei parentem puer verbasit, ast ole plorasit, puer diveis parentom sacer estud.

(Si parentem puer verberarit, ast ille ploraverit, puer Divis parentum sacer esto.)

APPENDIX I.   465

Numa; about 700 B.C.

Sei qui hemonem loebesum dolo sciens mortei duit, paricidas estod.
(Si quis hominem liberum dolo sciens morti det, parricida esto.)

(b) *Tribunitian Law;* 493 B.C.

Sei qui aliuta faxit, ipsos Jovei sacer estod; et sei qui im, quei eo plebei scito sacer siet, ocisit, paricidas ne estod.
(Si quis aliter fecerit, ipse Jovi sacer esto; et si quis eum, qui eo plebis scito sacer sit, occiderit, parricida ne sit.)

(c) *XII. Tables;* 450 B.C.

Sei qui in jous vocatus nec it, antestamino; igitur im capito; si calvitur pedemve struit, manum endo jacito.
(Si quis in jus vocatus non it, antestare; inde eum capito; si moritur fugitve, manum injicito.)

(d) *Tiburtine Inscription;* about 320 B.C.

Nos animum nostrum non indoucebamus ita facta esse, propter ea quod scibamus ea vos merito nostro facere non potuisse: neque vos dignos esse quoi ea faceretis, neque id vobeis neque rei poplicae vestrae oitile esse facere.

(Nos animum nostrum non inducebamus ita facta esse, propterea quod sciebamus ea vos merito nostro facere non potuisse: neque vos dignos esse qui ea faceretis, neque id vobis neque reipublicae vestrae utile esse facere.)

(e) *Epitaph on L. Cornelius Scipio;* about 260 B.C.

L. Cornelio' L. F. Scipio. Aidiles. Cosol. Cesor.
Hone oino' ploirumé con|séntiánt Románi
Duonóro' óptimó' | fúíse víro'
Lúciom Scipiónem. | Fílios Barbáti
Cósol Cénsor Aidíles | hic fúet apúd vos.
Hec cépit Córsica' A|lóriá'que úrbe'.
Dédet témpestátebus | aidé' meréto.

(L. Cornelius L. F. Scipio Ædilis, Consul, Censor.

Hunc unum plurimi consentiunt Romani
Bonorum optimum fuisse virum
L. Scipionem. Filius Barbati
Consul, Censor, Ædilis hic fuit apud vos.
Hic cepit Corsicam, Aleriamque urbem.
Dedit tempestatibus aedem merito.)

(f) *The Columna Rostrata;* about 260 B.C.

En eodem magistratud bene rem navebos marid consol primos ceset, socios clasesque navales primos ornavet paravetque, cumque eis navebos clasels Poenicas omneis et maxsumas copias Cartaciniensis, præsented sumod dictatored olorom, in altod marid pucnad vicet.

(In eodem magistratu bene rem navibus mari consul primus gessit, socios classesque navales primus ornavit paravitque, cumque iis navibus classes Punicas omnes et maximas copias Carthaginiensem, præsente summo Dictatore illorum, in alto mari pugnâ vicit.)

(g) *Silian Law;* 244 B.C.

Si quis magistratus adversus hæc d. m. pondera modiosque vasaque publica modica, majora minorave faxit jusseritve fieri, dolumve adduit quo ea fiant, eum quis volet magistratus multare, dum minore parti familias taxat, liceto.

(Si quis magistratus adversus hæc, dolo malo, pondera modiosque vasaque publica modica, majora minorave fecerit jusseritve fieri, dolumve addat, quo ea fiant, eum quicunque volet magistratus multare, dum minore parte familiæ æstimet, liceto.)

(h) *Livius Andronicus;* about 240 B.C.

Tum autem lascívom Nerei simum pecús
Ludens ad cántum classim lústrat navium.

(i) *Cn. Naevius;* about 230 B.C.

Mortáles immortáles—flére si forét fas
Flerént divæ Caménæ—Navium poétam.
Itaque póstquam ést Orcíno—tráditús thesaúro
Oblíti súnt Románi—loquiér Latína língua.

(k) *Q. Ennius;* about 200 B.C.

Pellitur e medio sapientia, vei geritur res,
Spernitur orator bonus, horridu' miles amatur;
Haut docteis dicteis certanteis, sed malo dicteis,
Miscent inter sese inimicitias agitanteis
Non ex joure manu' consertum, sed magi' ferro
Rem repetunt, regnumque petunt, vadunt solidâ vei.

(Tollitur e medio sapientia, vi geritur · res,
Spernitur orator bonus, horridus miles amatur;
Haud doctis dictis certantes, sed maledictis,
Miscent inter sese inimicitias agitanteis
Non ex jure manum consertum, sed magis ferro
Rem repetunt, regnumque petunt, vadunt solidâ vi.)

APPENDIX I.

(l) *M. Pacuvius;* about 190 B.C.

Jám profectióne læti píscium lasciviam
'Intuentur, néc tuendi cápere satietás potest.
Interea prope jam óccidento sóle inhorrescit mare,
Ténebræ conduplicántur, noctisque ét nimbum occrecét nigror,
Flámma inter nubés coruscat, cælum tonitru cóntrémit,
Grándo mixta imbri largifico súbita præcipitáns cadit,
Undique omnes vénti erumpunt, sævi existunt túrbines.

(m) *Senatus Consultum de Bacchanalibus;* 186 B.C.

Haice utei in coventionid exdeicatis ne minus trinum noundinum,
Senatuosque sententiam utei scienteis esetis, eorum sententia ita fuit.
Sei ques esent, quei arvorsum ead fecisent, quam suprad scriptum est,
eeis rem capitalem faciendam censuere, atque utei hoce in tabolam
ahenam incideretis.

(Hæc uti in contione edicatis, intra trinundinum, Senatus sententiam
uti scientes esetis, eorum sententia ita fuit. Si qui esent, qui adversus ea fecissent, quam supra scriptum est, iis rem capitalem faciendam
consuerunt, atque uti hoc in tabulam æneam incideretis.)

(n) *L. Attius;* about 140 B.C.

Adde huc quod mihi portento cælestum patér
Prodigium misit, regni stábilimen meí,
Agnum inter pécudes auroá clarum comá
Quondam Thyéstes clepere esso aúsum e rogiá,
Qua in re adjutricem conjugém cepit sibí.

(o) *C. Lucilius;* about 120 B.C.

(1) Virtus, Albine, est pretium persolvere verum,
Queis in versamur, queis vivimu' rebu', potesse:
Virtus est homini, scire id, quod quæque habeat res;
Virtus scire homini rectum, utile, quid sit honestum;
Virtus, quærendæ rei finem scire modumque.

(2) O lapatho, ut jactare nocesest, cognitu' cui sis!
In quo Lælio' clamores σοφός ille solebat
Edere, compellans gumias ex ordine nostros!
O Publi! O gurges Galloni! es homo miser, inquit:
Cœnasti in vitá nunquam bene, quum omnia in istá
Consumis squillá atque acipensere cum decumano.
Lælio' præclare, et recte σοφός, illaque vero.

APPENDIX II.

ABBREVIATIONS.

(a) *Praenomina.*

A.	Aulus.	P.	Publius.
C. or G.	Caius or Gaius.	Q.	Quintus.
CN.	Cneius or Gnæus.	SER.	Servius.
D.	Decimus.	SEX.	Sextus.
K.	Kæso.	SP.	Spurius.
L.	Lucius.	T.	Titus.
M.	Marcus.	TI.	Tiberius.
M'.	Manius.		

Woman's names are expressed by inverted characters; as ↃGaia.

(b) *Titles.*

ÆD. CUR. Ædilis Curulis.
COS. Consul.—COSS. Consules v. Consulibus.
COS. DES. Consul designatus.
D. Divus.
III VIRI A. A. A. F. F. Tresviri auro, argento, ære, flando, feriundo.
III VIR R. C. Triumvir reipublicæ constituendæ.
IMP. Imperator.
P. C. Patres, Conscripti.
P. M. Pontifex Maximus.
PRO. Proconsul.
S. P. Q. R. Senatus Populusque Romanus.
TR. PL. Tribunus Plebis.
X. V. Decemvir.
XV. V. S. F. Quindecimviri sacris faciundis.

(c) *Sepulcral.*

F. C. Faciundum curavit.
H. C. E. Hic conditus est.

H. S. E.   Hic situs est.
Ob.   Obiit.
P. C.   Ponendum curavit.
V.   Vixit.

(d) *Miscellaneous.*

A.   Absolvo.—C. Condemno.
N. L.   Non liquet.
A. P.   Antiquam legem probo.
V. R.   Uti rogas.
(These are the forms of voting on trials, laws and elections.)
A. U. C.   Anno Urbis Conditæ.
D. D.   Dono dedit.
DD.   Dederunt.
D. D. D.   Dat, dicat, dedicat.
D. M.   Dis manibus.
D. O. M.   Deo Optimo Maximo.
F.   Filius.
F. F. F.   Felix, faustum, fortunatum.
L.   Libertas.
M. P.   Mille Passuum.
N.   Nepos.
S. C.   Senatus Consultum.
S. P. D.   Salutem plurimam dicit.
S. T. E. Q. V. R. E. E. Q. V.   Si tu exercituusque valetis, bene est, ego quoque valeo.
Tr. pot.   Tribunicia Potestate.

(e) *Modern Latin.*

A. C. or A. D.   Anno Christi or Anno Domini.
a. C. n. p. C. n.   ante⎱ Christum natum.
             post⎰
C. P. P. C.   Collatis pecuniis ponendum curaverunt.
Cet.   Cetera.
Cf.   Confer or Conferatur.
Coll.   Collato or Collatis.
Cod. Codd.   Codex, Codices.
Del.   Dele or Deleatur.
Ed. Edd.   Editio, Editiones.
e. g.   exempli gratiâ.
etc. or &c.   Et cetera.
h. e.   hoc est.
J. C.   Jesus Christus.

Ictus.   Juris consultus.
ibid.   ibidem.—id. idem.
i.e.   id est.—i.q.   idem quod.
L. or Lib.   Liber.
L. B.   Lectori benevolo.
l.c.   loco citato.—l.l.   loco laudato.
leg.   lege.
L. S.   locus sigilli.
MSS.   Manuscripti.
N.B.   nota bene.
N.T.   Novum Testamentum.
Obs.   Observa.
P. S.   Postscriptum.
sc.   scilicet.
sq. and sqq.   sequenti and sequentibus.
vid.   vide.
viz.   videlicet.
V. col.   Vir celeberrimus.
V. cl.   Vir clarissimus.
V.D.M.   Verbi divini Minister.
V.T.   Vetus Testamentum.

(f) *Academical or Scholastic.*

A. B. or AA. B.   Artium Baccalaureus.
A. M. or AA. M.   Artium Magister.
D.   Doctor.
J. U. D.   Juris utriusque Doctor.
LL. B.   Legum Baccalaureus.
LL. D.   Legum Doctor.
M. B.   Medicinæ Baccalaureus.
M. D.   Medicinæ Doctor.
Mus. D.   Musicæ Doctor.
S. T. B.   Sanctæ Theologiæ Baccalaureus.
S. T. P.   Sanctæ Theologiæ Professor; which is the same as
S. T. D.   Sanctæ Theologiæ Doctor.

Max. ma. mi. min. are affixed to the names of boys in Classical Schools to denote *maximus natu, major natu*, &c.

The University titles require a few words of explanation. It was always supposed that the University gave two kinds of *Degrees* or certificates of proficiency—in *Arts* and in the *Faculties*. The inferior or preparatory degree in each department was that of *Bachelor, baccalaureus*, a barbarous title derived from the French *bas Chevalier*, which primarily denoted a Knight Bachelor, one who sat at the same table with the Bannerets, but, being of inferior rank, was *mis arrière et plus bas assis;* hence, it came to denote the unfinished apprentice, the unmarried man, and the demi-graduate. The complete degree in *Arts* was that of *Magister* or 'Master;' in the *Faculties*, that of *Doctor* or 'Teacher;' two titles equivalent to one another, and to the common designation of *Professor* or claimant of complete knowledge. The *Arts*, which were supposed to require seven years' study, and which were seven in number, are enumerated in the following lines:

Gram. [grammatica] loquitur; *Dia.* [dialectica] vera docet; *Rhet.* [rhetorica] verba colorat;
Mus. [musica] canit; *Ar.* [arithmetica] numerat; *G.* [geometria] ponderat; *As.* [astronomia] colit astra.

The arts, enumerated in the first line, were called the *Trivium;* those in the second the *Quadrivium;* it is remarkable, however, that the first of the latter four, *Music*, is a kind of faculty, which has Bachelors and Doctors of its own. The regular faculties are three: *Divinity, Law,* and *Medicine,* the first and highest of which is supposed to include all the arts.

APPENDIX III.
GENERAL INFORMATION.

(*a*) *Names of Persons.*

THE Roman names of men were generally three, (1) the *Praenomen* or designation of the individual, which was one of those mentioned above, Appendix II. (a); (2) the *Nomen* or name of the *gens* or clan, which properly was an adjective in *-ius*, as *Cornelius, Tullius*; (3) the *Cognomen* or name of the *familia* or branch of the clan, to which the individual belonged, as *Scipio, Cicero*, and this was generally the characteristic designation of the person, quality, or pursuits of some ancestor, so that it corresponded to our surname. In common intercourse, the *nomen* or gentile name was taken for granted, and *C. Caesar* would be a sufficient designation of *Gāius Jūlius Caesar*. The *Praenomen* alone was used in familiar addresses. And women were known by a feminine form of the gentile name; thus *Cornelia* the mother of the *Gracchi*, was called by the gentile name of her father *P. Scipio*. Besides the three regular names, two others are occasionally found,—the *Agnomen* or surname of distinction, and the adoptive *Agnomen*, which referred to the family left by the party adopted; thus *P. Cornelius Scipio* was called *Africanus*, from his conquest of Carthage, and the Emperor Augustus, who was originally *C. Octavius*, when adopted by *C. Julius Caesar*, was called *C. Julius Caesar Octavianus*, to which the *Agnomen* of *Augustus* was subsequently added.

(b) *Epistolary Forms.*

A Latin epistle always begins with the address and greeting, and, if it has a date, this is appended, together with any supplementary expressions of friendship, at the end of the letter. Thus, Cic. *ad div.* IV. 12, begins, Ser. *Sulpicius M. Ciceroni S. D.*, and ends, *Vale. D. pr. Kal. Jun. Athenis*, i. e. *datum pridie Kalendas Junias:* and sometimes the year is added, as (*ad Attic.* I. 18): *Vale. XI. Kal. Febr. Q. Metello, L. Afranio coss.* Common endings are, *cura ut valeas;* and, *me velim, ut facis, diligas;* and the like.

Obs. In epistolary style the imperfect and pluperfect are used for the present and perfect, because a reference is presumed to the time when the letter would be received. Thus, *Nihil habebam quod scriberem. Neque enim novi quidquam audieram et ad tuas omnes rescripseram pridie* (Cic. *ad Att.* IX. 10, init.).

APPENDIX III.   473

(c) *The Seven Hills of Rome, the Tribes, and the Kings.*

(1) The three hills nearest to the river, and the four more inland, will be remembered by the following lines, which enumerate the two sets of hills by their directions up the river:

Collis *Aventini*, dein celsa *Palatia* fulgent,
Transque Forum surgit *Capitoli* immobile saxum;
Caelius, Esquiliae, dictusque a *Vimine* collis,
Ultimaque ad Campum tendunt juga longa *Quirini*.

(2) The three original tribes, the *Tities* or *Sabines*, who occupied the *Quirinalis* and *Capitolium*, the *Ramnes* or *Romans*, who were settled on the *Palatinus*, and the *Luceres* or *Latins*, who held the *Caelius*, may be remembered by a line of Propertius:

Hinc *Tities*, Ramnesque viri, *Luceres*que coloni.

(3) The seven kings of Rome were
Romulus ante omnes: post hunc *Numa, Tullus* et *Ancus;*
Tarquinius Priscus, dein *Servius* atque *Superbus*.

(d) *Mythology.*

(1) The twelve principal gods were, according to Ennius,
Vesta, Minerva, Ceres, Juno, Diana, Venus, Mars,
Mercurius, Jovi', Neptunus, Vulcanus, Apollo.

(2) The nine *Pierides* or Muses were
Calliope, Urania, Euterpe, Polyhymnia, Clio,
Terpsichore, atque Erato, cum Melpomeneque Thalia.

(3) *Thalia* was also counted one of the Graces; the other two being *Aglaia* and *Euphrosyne*.

(4) The three *Parcae* or Fates were *Clōthō*, 'who spins the thread of life,' *Lăchĕsis*, 'who rules our lot,' and *Atrŏpos*, 'the unchanging destiny.' The Etruscans substituted *Nursia = ne-vertia*, 'the unturning,' for the last of the three, and considered her as the goddess of Fortune.

Net *Clotho, Lachesis* sortitur, et *Atropos* occat.

(5) The six rivers of Tartarus were
Styx, Acheron, Lethe, Phlegethon, Cocytus, Avernus.

(e) *The Roman Winds.*

North, *Aquilo* or *Boreas;* North-East, *Caecias;* East, *Eurus* or *Subsolanus;* South-East, *Vulturnus;* South, *Auster* or *Notus;* South-West, *Africus* or *Libs* (*Libis*); West, *Favōnius* or *Zephȳrus;* North-West, *Cōrus* (or *Caurus*), *Argestes*, and, in Gallia Narbonensis, *Circius*.

The general directions of the winds are given in the following memorial lines:

Asper ab axe ruit *Boreas*, furit *Eurus* ab ortu.
Auster amat medium solem, *Zephyrusque* cadentem.
Flant *Subsolanus*, *Vulturnus*, et *Eurus* ab ortu.
Circius occasum *Zephyrusque Favonius* adflant.
E solis medio surgunt *Notus*, *Africus*, *Auster;*
Conveniunt *Aquilo*, *Boreas* et *Caurus* ab ursa.

(f) *Days of the Week.*

The seven days of the week were called from the planet which ruled the first hour of each; the Latin names are preserved in French:

1. Sunday,   *Dies Solis*, also *Dies Dominicus*, or the 'Lord's day' (*Dimanche*).
2. Monday,   *Dies Lunae* (*Lundi*).
3. Tuesday,   *Dies Martis* (*Mardi*).
4. Wednesday, *Dies Mercurii* (*Mercredi*).
5. Thursday,   *Dies Jovis* (*Jeudi*).
6. Friday,   *Dies Veneris* (*Vendredi*).
7. Saturday,   *Dies Saturni* or *Dies Sabbati* (*Samedi*).

(g) *The twelve Signs of the Zodiac.*

Sunt Aries, Taurus, Gemini, Cancer, Leo, Virgo,
Libraque, Scorpius, Arcitenens, Caper, Amphora, Pisces.

(h) *The four Seasons of the Year.*

Ver, Æstas, Auctumnus, Hiemps dominantur in anno.
Æstas a Geminis, Auctumnus Virgine surgit;
Bruma Sagittifero, Ver Piscibus incipit esse.

(i) *Names of Relationship and Affinity.*

Agnati patris, cognati matris habentur.
Dic *patruos* patris fratres, *amitasque* sorores;
Frater *avunculus* est, soror est *matertera* matris.
Quos generant fratres natos, dices *patrueles;*
Sed *consobrinos* dic, quos peperere sorores.
Quos soror et frater gignunt, dices *amitinos.*
Vir natae *gener* est, *nurus* est pro conjuge nati.
Uxoris genitor *socer* est, socrusque genitrix.
Vitricus haud verus pater est, materque *noverca.*
Ipse viri frater *levir*, sed *fratria* fratris
Uxor; *glos* uxor fratris, soror atque mariti.

APPENDIX IV.

DISTINCTIONS OF WORDS IN MEMORIAL VERSES.

(a) *Differences of Quantity.*

1. *Sternitur arbor ăcer, fueris si viribus ācer.*
'The *maple* tree is cut down, if you shall have been *vigorous* in strength.'

2. *Ānus pars hominis, sed femina fit ănus annis.*
'The *ănus* is a part of a man, but a woman becomes *ānus*, "old," by years.'

3. *Mel vaga condit ăpis; deus est Ægyptius Āpis.*
'The roving *bee* stores honey; *Apis* is an Egyptian god.'

4. *Est hăra porcorum brevis, at non āra deorum.*
'The *hăra* or *sty* of pigs has short *a*; not so the *āra* or *altar* of gods.'

5. *Dum sinet hora cănes; effeto corpore cānes;*
   Grandaevique cănis candescunt tempora cānis.
'While time permits, you will *sing*; your body being exhausted you are *grey*; and the skin of the aged *dog* is white with *grey* hairs.'

6. *Silva vetus cecĭdit, ferro quam nemo cecīdit.*
'An old wood *fell*, which no one *felled* with an axe.'

7. *Fert ancilla cŏlum, penetrat res humida cōlum.*
'A maid-servant carries a *distaff*, liquid matter penetrates a *strainer*.'

8. *Cōmas virgineas, hasta recurva, cŏmas.*
'Mayest thou, O bent spear, part (i. e. put in order) the virgin's *hair*' (referring to the *hasta caelibaris*. Ovid, *Fasti*, II. 560). *Cŏmo* is contracted from *co-ĕmo* (90, (1), p. 117).

APPENDIX IV.

9. *Si vis cŏmes mihi, mores indue cŏmes.*
'If you would be a companion to me, put on affable manners.'

10. *Lucrandī cupīdo damno est sua saepe cupīdo.*
'His own desire is often detrimental to one desirous of gain.'

11. *Oblītus decŏris violat praecepta decŏris.*
'He who is forgetful of honour violates the laws of beauty.'

12. *Dĕdĕre cor divis par est qui tanta dĕdēre.*
'It is right to give up our heart to the gods who have given us so much.'

13. *Carmina dīcantur, Domino dum templa dīcantur.*
'Let poems be recited, while temples are dedicated to the Lord.'

14. *Solvere diffīdit, nodum qui diffīdit ense.*
'He has no confidence in untying the knot, who has cut it with his sword.'

15. *Sanus ĕdit carnem; carmen doctissimus ĕdit.*
'A healthy man eats meat; a most learned man gives out, i.e. publishes, a poem.'

16. *Edūcat hic catulos, ut eos edŭcat in apros.*
'This man trains whelps, that he may lead them out against wild boars.'

17. *Si tibi non est aes, ĕs inops, et pinguia non ĕs.*
'If you have not money, you are poor, and do not eat dainties.'

18. *Nos precor excūsā, male sit si excŭsā moneta.*
'Prithee excuse us, if the money is badly coined.'

19. *Fābŭla sermonis, fābŭla est faba parvula dicta.*
'A fable belongs to language, but a little bean is called fābula.'

20. *Fīdĕ sed ante vīdē; qui fīdit, nec bene vīdit,*
Fallitur. Ergo vīdē, ne cupias fīde.
'Trust, but look first; he who trusts and has not well considered, is deceived. Therefore consider, lest you be inveigled by confidence.'

21. *Fallit saepe frĕtum placido nimis aequore frētum.*
'The sea often deceives one who relies too much on its smooth surface.'

22. *Fūgĕre hi; fūgēre est melius, ne fuste fūgēre.*
'These have run away; it is better to run away, lest you be driven away with a stick.'

23. *Per quod quis peccat, per idem max plectitur idem.*
'By what a man sins, by the same thing the same man is soon punished' (above, p. 438).

24. *Difficilis labor est, cujus sub pondere labor.*
'It is a difficult *labour*, under the weight of which *I am sinking*.'

25. *Laevus erit, cui dextra manus non praebeat usum; Levis adhuc puer est; levis autem lingua puellae.*
'A man is *left-handed*, if his right hand is unserviceable; the boy is still *smooth;* but the tongue of the girl is *light*.'

26. *Ut lepōres canibus, sunt omnia capta lepōre.*
'As *hares* are caught by dogs, so all things are captivated by *beauty*.' (See Lucret. 1. 14, v. 1258.)

27. *Tange lyram digitis, dum liram vomere duco.*
'Touch the *lyre* with your fingers, while I draw a *furrow* with the plough.'

28. *Cernis triste mālum, fractum jam turbine mălum? Māla măli mălo meruit măla maxima mundo. Mălo ego māla mea bona quam māla frangere mălā.*
'Do you see this sad *disaster*,—the mast (*mălus*) already broken by the whirlwind?'
'The *jaw-bone* of a *bad man* with an *apple* (*mălum*) earned the greatest *evils* for the world.'
'I would rather break with my *jaw good apples* than *bad*.'

29. *Mānĕ domi, mi Fusce, mănĕ, visure sodales.*
'*Remain* at home in the *morning*, my dear Fuscus, being about to see friends.'

30. *Matrōna augusta est mulier, sed Matrōna flumen.*
'A *Matron* is a dignified lady, but the *Marne* is a river.'

31. *Es praeclarus homo, miseris si miseris aurum.*
'You are a noble man, if you *shall have sent* gold to the *poor*.'

32. *Nitĕre, parve puer, cupiunque nitĕre.*
'*Strive*, little boy, whoever you are that desire to *shine*.'

33. *Sit nōta nōta: nōtus ventus, sed nōtus amicus.*
'Let the *mark* be *known*; the *south* is a wind, but a friend is *known*.'

34. *Oblīta quae fuco rubet, est oblīta decoris.*
'She who is red from being *daubed* with paint is *forgetful* of beauty.'

APPENDIX IV.

35. *Occĭdit latro, verum sol occĭdit almus.*
'The robber murders, but the balmy sun sets.'

36. *Oppĕrior Fabium, qui longo opĕritur amĭctu.*
'I am waiting for Fabius, who is clad in a long robe.'

37. *Os (ōris) mandat, sed os (ossis) mandĭtur ōre.*
'The mouth commands, but a bone is eaten with the mouth.'

38. *Quaeque pălus stagnat; fixus stat pālus acutus.*
'Every marsh is stagnant; the sharp stake stands firm.'

39. *Uxōris pārĕre si pārĕre, pārăre marīti est.*
'It is the part of the wife to bear children and obey; of the husband to provide.'

40. *Gaudet uterque pārens, si filius est bonus pārens.*
'Both parents rejoice, if the boy is properly obedient.'

41. *Pendĕre vult justus, sed non pendĕre malignus.*
'The honest man wishes to pay, but the scoundrel wishes not to be hanged.'

42. *Perfĭdus absque fĭde est; contra est perfĭdus amīcus.*
'The perfidious is without faith; on the contrary the friend is thoroughly trusty.'

43. *Ludo pĭlā: pīlum torquetur: pīla columna est.*
'Play at ball: the javelin is hurled: the pillar is a column.'

44. *Pro reti et regione plăga est, pro verbere plāga.*
'Plăga means a net or a region: plāga is a blow.'

45. *Sunt cives urbis pōpulus, est pōpulus arbor.*
'The inhabitants of a city are a people: the poplar is a tree.'

46. *Si vitare pōtes, ne plurima pocula pōtes.*
'If you can avoid it, drink not very many cups.'

47. *Haud mihi prŏfecta est bene res ex urbe prŏfecto.*
'The business did not turn out well for me having departed from the city.'

48. *Quae probus ille rĕfert, nostrā cognoscere rĕfert.*
'It is for our interest to know what that good man is telling us.'

49. *Decrĕtum relĕgat, qui sontem ex urbe relēgat.*
'Let him, who is banishing the guilty from the city, read again his decree.'

APPENDIX IV. 479

50. *Si qua sĭdĕ sĕdĕs, atque est tibi commoda sĕdes,
Illa sĕdĕ sĕdĕ, nec sĭdĕ ubi sĭdere non est.*

'If you are *sitting* on any *seat*, and your *seat* is convenient, remain *sitting* on that *seat*, and do not *settle*, where it is not possible to *settle*.'

51. *Est in veste sĭnus, sĭnus vas lactis habetur.*

'The bosom-*folds* are in the dress; the *sinus* is a bowl of milk.'

52. *Tam cito suffōcat laqueus, quam suffōcat ignis.*

'The halter *strangles* as quick as the fire *suffocates*.'

53. *Trĭbula grana terunt; trĭbuli nascuntur in agris.*

'*Threshing machines* bruise grain; *caltrops* grow in the fields.'

54. *Ne sit ŭti censes; opus est melioribus ŭti.*

'Let it not be as you determine; it is necessary to *use* better plans.'

55. *Si transire vĕlis maris undas, utere vēlis.*

'If you *wish* to cross the waves of the sea, make use of *sails*.'

56. *Merx nummis vēnit; vĕnit huc aliunde profectus.*

'Merchandise *is sold* for money; he *comes* hither, having started from some other place.'

57. *Vēnĭmus hesternā, ast hodiernā luce vĕnĭmus.*

'We *came* yesterday, but we *are coming* to-day.'

58. *Nil prosunt vires, ni probitate vires.*

'*Strength* is of no avail, unless you *are strong* in honesty.'

(b) *Differences of Form, Construction, or Gender.*

59. *Cantat acanthis avis, sed floret acanthus in agris.*

'The *goldfinch* is a bird which sings; but the *acanthus* blooms in the fields.'

60. *Qui fert arma humeris, armo dux fertur equino.*

'The general, who carries *arms* on his shoulders, is carried on the horse's *back*.'

61. *Vexat asilus equos; miseros excipit asylum.*

'The *gad-fly* torments horses; the *sanctuary* is wont to receive the wretched.'

62. *Qui sculpit caelat; qui servat condita celat.*

'He who engraves, *carves*; he who keeps secrets, *conceals*.'

63. *Haec cassis galea est; hi casses retia signant.*
'This *cassis* (*f.*) is a *helmet*; these *casses* (*m.*) mean *nets*.'

64. *Cēdo facit cessi; cecīdi, cādo; caedo, cecīdi.*
'*Cēdo*, I yield, makes *cessi*; *cădo*, I fall, *cecĭdi*; *caedo*, I cut, *cecīdi*.'

65. *Clava ferit, clavus firmat, clavisque recludit.*
'The *club* strikes, the *nail* fastens, and the *key* opens.'

66. *Consule doctores, si tu tibi consulis ipsi.*
'*Consult* your teachers, if you *provide for* your *interests*.' This is only a difference of construction (above, p. 308).

67. *Fuste dŏlat furem, dŏluit qui dōlia perdens.*
'He *beats* the thief with a stick, who *grieved* at losing his *wine-jars*.'

68. *Haec ficus (ficūs vel fici) est fructus et arbor;
Hic ficus (fici) malus est in corpore morbus.*
'This *fig* (*f.*) is a fruit and a tree; this *ficus* (*m.*) or tumour is a bad disease in the body.'

69. *Frontem dic capitis, frondem dic arboris esse.*
'Say that *frons, frontis*, "a brow," belongs to the head; but *frons, frondis*, "a bough," to a tree.'

70. *Non licet asse mihi, qui me non asse licetur.*
'He is not *valued* by me at a penny, who does not *value* me at a penny.'

71. *Merx venit; mercesque vēnit, quaesita labore.*
'*Merchandise* is *sold*; and *wages* come being gained by labour.'

72. *Prunus habet prunum, prunam ignis, et arva pruīnam.*
'The *plum-tree* has the *plum*, the fire a *hot-coal*, and the fields the *hoar-frost*.'

73. *Spondet vas (vădis), at vas (vāsis) continet escam.*
'The *surety* (*m.*) promises, but the *vessel* (*n.*) contains food.'

(c) *Synonyms, or different Words with similar Meanings.*

74. *Est cutis in carne, est detracta e corpore pellis.*
'*Cutis* is the skin attached to the flesh, *pellis* is the *hide* stript off the body.'

APPENDIX IV.   481

75.   *Sanguis inest venis, cruor est e corpore fusus.*

'Blood is in the veins; gore is shed from the body.' This distinction is clearly seen in the following passage of Tacitus, Ann. xii. 47 : *mox ubi sanguis in artus extremos suffuderit, levi ictu cruorem eliciunt atque invicem lambunt.*

76.   *Armus brutorum est, humerus rationis fruentium; Tergum est animorum; belua tergus habet.*

'The *armus* is the shoulder of brutes, the *humerus*, that of rational beings: the *tergum* is the hinder part of anything; a beast has *tergus* (*tergoris*), a hide.' The first statement is proved by Ovid, Metam. x. 699, where it is said of Hippomenes turned into a lion, *ex humeris armi fiunt.* But the distinction is not always observed. In the case of a horse, the *armi* were not only the *withers*, but the *flanks* (Virg. Æn. vi. 882. Hor. 1 Sat. vi. 106). *Tergum* is only the hinder part, or the part turned away; whence such phrases as *terga vertere, dare,* 'to turn one's back to the enemy, to run away;' and *a tergo, post tergum,* 'behind.' The back, considered as part of the body, is *dorsum*.

77.   *Ungula conculcat; lacerat, tenet, arripit unguis.*

'The *hoof* tramples; the *nail, claw,* or *talon* tears, holds, seizes.'

78.   *Pistor habet furnum, fornace hypocausta calescunt.*

'The baker has an oven, the stove-rooms of baths are warmed by furnaces.'

79.   *Fructus arboribus, fruges nascuntur in agris.*

'Fruits grow on trees, corn in the fields.' This is only true of *fructus* as opposed to *fruges*, for both of them may be used as general designations of produce—*id quo fruimur*.

80.   *Ales hirundo canit; nat hirudo; vernat arundo.*

'The *swallow* is a bird which twitters; the *leech* swims; the *reed* grows green.'

81.   *Alga venit pelago, sed nascitur ulva palude.*

'The *sea-weed* comes from the sea, but the *sedge* grows in the marsh.'

82.   *Prōra prior, puppis pars ultima, at ima carina.*

'The *prow* is the front part of a ship, the *stern* the hind part, and the *keel* the lowest part.'

83.   *Cōminus ense feris, jacit eadis ēminus hasta.*

'You strike *close at hand* (cum manu) with a sword; you fall by a spear thrown from a distance (e manu).'

D. L. G.   31

84. *Forfice sartores; tonsores forpice gaudent;*
   At faber ignitum forcipe prenulis opus.

'Tailors delight in scissors, barbers in curling-irons; but the smith takes the ignited iron with a *pair of tongs*.'

85. *Vallamus propris castrum, sepimus ovile.*

'We properly *intrench* a camp, but *hedge-in* a sheep-fold.'

86. *Consortes fortuna eadem; socios labor idem;*
   Sed caros faciunt schola, ludus, mensa sodales.

'The same fortune makes *partners*; the same toil, *comrades*; but the school, the game, the table, make dear *associates*.'

87. *Vir comis multos comites sibi jungit eundo;*
   Unum collegas efficit officium.

'A courteous man joins to himself many *companions* (*comes* from *cum eo*) in his journey; a common occupation makes *colleagues*.'

88. *Dele quod scriptum est, sed flammam extingue lucernas.*

'*Blot out* what is written, but *quench* the flame of the lamp.'

89. *Quod non est simulo, dissimuloque quod est.*

'I *feign* what is not, and *conceal falsely* what is.'

90. *Vas caput, at nummos tantum praes praestat amici.*

'A *bail* kindly makes good the person, but a *surety* money only.' The word *vas* is included in *praes*, as is proved by the old form *praevides* for *praedes* (*Varron.* p. 146). The distinction between these words may also be recollected by the lines of Ausonius (*Idyll.* XII. 100):

   Quis subit in pœnam capitali judicio? Vas,
   Quod si lis fuerit nummaria, quis dabitur? Praes.

If we do not speak of 'a surety in a strictly legal sense, we use the general term *sponsor*, e.g. Cic. *ad div.* VI. 18.

91. *Hasta teres dici, sphaera rotunda potest.*

'A spear may be called *rounded*, but a sphere *round*.' The proper meaning of *rotundus* is 'circular,' like a wheel (*rota*), and thus it is opposed to *quadratus*, in Hor. 1 *Epist.* I. 100: *mutat quadrata rotundis*. But it is constantly used to denote that which is globular or spherical, as in Cic. *Somn. Scip.* 3: *stellas globosas et rotundas*. The proper meaning of *teres* is 'cylindrical,' i.e. prolonged rotundity (*ter-it*, 'going rounded'). Hence it is properly applied to the trunk of a tree (Virg. *Æn.* VI. 207; *Ecl.* VIII. 16), or to a rounded stick, such as a spear-shaft (Liv. XXI. 8. Virg. *Æn.* VII. 65), a wand (Ovid, *Met.* II. 735), or a spindle (Ovid, *Met.* VI. 22).

APPENDIX IV. 493

It is also applied in its proper sense to cords, which are approximate cylinders (*teres strophium*, Catull. LXIII. 65; *teres zona*, Ovid, *Fast.* II. 320; *teres habenu fundas* Virg. *Æn.* XI. 579; *teretes laquei*, Sen. *Hippol.* 45; *teretes plagae*, Hor. 1 *Carm.* L. 28). With less precision *teres* is applied to the long tapering neck (Virg. *Æn.* VIII. 633), or the slender well-turned leg (Hor. 2 *Carm.* IV. 6n.). From the idea of elongation implied in the word *teres* is used to denote a smaller as opposed to a larger circle or opening. Hence as the phrase *os rotundum* (Hor. *Ars poet.* 323) is applied to the large round opening in the Greek tragic mask, which is also called *hiatus* (Juv. III. 175, cf. Pers. v. 3: *fabula seu maesto ponatur hianda tragoedo*), Persius calls the man who cultivated a refined and unpretending style, *ore teres modico* (v. 15). We have the same reference to the smaller opening in Cicero's phrase: *Atticorum aures teretes*, 'the delicately susceptible ears of the Athenians' (*Orat.* 9), and in his opposition of *teres* to *plenus* in speaking of style (*de Orat.* III. 52, § 199). When *teres* is applied to a sphere, along with *rotundus* (Hor. 2 *Serm.* VII. 86: *in se ipso totus, teres atque rotundus, externi ne quid valeat per leve morari.* Cf. Auson. *Idyll.* XVI. 4), it seems to imply smoothness as an attribute of complete and polished roundness.

92.   *Lingua cibum gustat, qui bene cunque sapit.*

'The tongue *tastes* any food, which *has* a good *savour*.'

93.   *Sunt aetate senes, veteres vixere priores.*

'Men are *old* in age; the *ancients* lived before us.' *Senex* properly denotes a man of advanced longevity, who, however, is still living; and *vetus* refers to the length of time during which a person or thing has lasted. There is nothing therefore to hinder the application of *vetus* to *senex*, and we find such passages as Tibull. I. 8. 50:

In veteres esto dura puella senes.

Ter. *Eun.* IV. 4. 21: *Hic est vetus, vietus, veternosus senex.* But although *vetus* may be applied to *senex*, it is only in later writers that we have *senex* in that sense of *vetus*, in which it denotes a lapse of time not limited to the life of a single man, and the student must remark as special exceptions the passage in Persius in which Aristophanes is designated as *praegrandis senex* (1. 124), because he was the most illustrious representative of the old Comedy (*comoedia prisca*, Hor. 1 *Serm.* IV. 2; *comoedia vetus*, Id. *Ars poet.* 281), and the use of *senium* by Statius (*Silv.* I. 3. 38, *venerabile locorum senium*) to denote antiquity in general. With a

31—2

484   APPENDIX IV.

genitive *retus* may signify 'experienced' (*gnarus*), as in *filius*, IV.
33: *gnarus belli veteresque laborum* (cf. Tac. *Ann.* VL 44); and
though *antiquus* is a stronger word in reference to time which has
long ago passed away (e. g. Cic. *Phil.* v. 47), we very often find
retus and *antiquus* side by side in writers of the silver age as
nearly synonymous words (see Juv. VI. 21; XV. 33. Tac. *Dial.* 15.
Plin. *Ep.* III. 6; *Paneg.* XL 4).

94.   *Ne sit securus, qui non est tutus ab hoste.*
'Let him not be secure (i. e. free from care; *se-curus = sine curâ*), who
is not *safe* from the enemy.'

95.   *Tarquinius Patribus Conscriptos addere jussit.*
'Tarquin directed the addition of *Conscripti* or Plebeian knights to the
Patres or Patricians,' i. e. the heads of the original burgesses of
Rome. Accordingly the address *Patres, Conscripti*, must be ren-
dered *not*, 'Conscript Fathers,' but, 'Fathers and Conscripts,' or
'Patricians and elected Senators:' the *et* being omitted as in
Populus Romanus, Quirites, 'Burgesses of Ramnian and Sabine
origin;' and such phrases as *sarta, tecta*, 'sound in wall and roof,'
&c. (above, 112, *Obs.* 1).

96.   *Poplicolam populus non plebs agrestis amabat.*
'Poplicola was a favourite with the *populus* or old burgesses of Rome,
and not with the *plebs* or citizens of inferior franchise, who were
imported from the country' (Niebuhr, L p. 530, n. 1172).

97.   *Deliciae procêrum, procêro corpore, Kaeso*
        Militiae atque domi clarus et amplus erat.
'Kæso, the delight of the *nobles*, a man of *tall* stature, was *illustrious*
and *distinguished* both in foreign service and at home.' The oldest
names of the patricians or *patres* seem to have been *celêres* or
'horsemen' (ἱππόβοται), and *procêres* or 'wooers.' The latter word,
formed, like *celêres*, from the original designation *proci patricii*,
'patrician suitors' (Fest. p. 249, ed. Müller), denotes that they had
the right of intermarriage (*jus connubii*), which was denied to all
but *prers* of the original burgesses. *Procêrus* comes from *procello*,
as *obs-citrus* from *os-cello*, and denotes remarkable growth. *Clarus*
and *amplus* are the most usual terms for personal distinction in
the old Roman state: the former, which is connected with the same
root as κλέος, κλύω, *in-clǐtus, glôria* (compare such phrases as
clare dixit, 'he spoke loud,' Hor. 1 *Epist.* XVI. 59), signifies 'much
spoken about;' and *vir clarissimus* amounts to our phrase 'most
illustrious;' *amplus* from *amb*- (above, 111), as *circulus* from *circum*,

APPENDIX IV. 485

denotes size or circumference—that which fills the eyes—but is used as all but a synonym for *clarus*; thus we have such phrases as *maximâ cum gratiâ et gloriâ ad summam amplitudinem pervenit* (Cic. Brut. 81, 281); *is mihi videtur amplissimus, qui suâ virtute in altiorem locum pervenit* (Cic. Rosc. Am. 30); *majestas est amplitudo ac dignitas civitatis* (Cic. de Orat, II. 39, 164); *auctoritas et amplitudo hominum* (Cic. Rosc. Am. 1); *domus clari hominis* is described as *ampla domus* (Cic. de Offic. 1. 39, 139); and *amplus* and *gloriosus* are used as parallel predicates (Liv. xxviii. 42). On the use of *amplus* as a synonym of *magnus*, see below, 111.

98. *Actirè perdo, passivè amittere possum.*

Although both *perdo* and *amitto* signify 'I lose,' the former may also mean 'I destroy.' According to the etymology, *a-mitto* is 'I send away,' 'I part with;' but *per-do* is 'I cause to go through and out of,' in which sense it is the active of *per-eo*, 'I go through and out of,' just as *inter-ficio* and *inter-imo*, 'I make or take from the midst of,' are opposed to *inter-eo*, 'I go from between or away.'

99. *Ultro polliceor, promitto saepe rogatus.*

Polliceor is 'I make a free offer,' generally of good things; *promitto*, 'I promise what may be asked or expected from me,' whether good or evil.

100. *Quid, nisi mens infensa, infestam torqueat hastam?*

'What except an *angry* mind could hurl the *hostile* spear?' These words are constantly confused by modern Latinists. If we compare *in-fensus* with *of-fensus*, from *ob-fendo*, we shall see that the former is connected with *in-fendo*, and implies an unfriendly or angry disposition of the mind; so that it corresponds to *inimicus, iratus*. If, on the other hand, we compare *in-festus* with *mani-festus* and *fest-ino*, we shall see that it comes from *in-fero*, and implies some outward opposition and attack; so that it is a synonym of *adversus, hostilis*. This will be seen in a passage of Livy, where the two words occur together (II. 6): *concitat calcaribus equum atque in ipsum* INFESTUS *consulem dirigit...Adeoque* INFENSIS *animis concurrerunt, ut...duabus haerentes hastis moribundi ex equis lapsi sint*, 'he spurs his horse and urges him *straight against* (*full tilt against*) the consul himself; and they met with such *angry* minds that they fell dying from their horses, sticking to the two spears fixed in them.'

101. *Collige mater-iam; patr-iam tu, dilige, civis.*

'*Collect materials*; do you, O citizen, *love* your *native land*.' Although *mater-ia* (of which *materia-is* = *materies* is an extension; above, 28, *Obs.*) is derived from *mater*, 'a mother,' just in the same way as *patr-ia* comes from *pater*, the above line shows that their meaning is absolutely different; for while *materia* denotes the 'mother-stuff' or 'materials' of which any thing is composed, so that the work seems to proceed or be born from it, *patr-ia* is the country to which we belong by inheritance, and which is our common parent. The same example shows the difference of two compounds of *lego*, 'I call, pick up or gather.' *Col-ligo* expresses the result of gathering, namely, *collection; di-ligo* selection in gathering, choice, preference, love. Similarly, *emo*, 'I take for myself,' 'I buy,' becomes in a secondary form *amo*, 'I love.' The compound *intel-ligo*, 'I discriminate,' i.e. 'I understand,' is very different from *inter-imo*, 'I take from the midst,' i.e. 'I destroy.' The next example gives another use of *lego*. The student will also notice the widely different significations of the similarly formed words *patri-monium*, 'patrimony,' 'inheritance,' and *matri-monium*, 'matrimony,' 'marriage.'

102.   *Sit pietas coluisse Deum, coluisse parentes;*
       Relligio populum obstringit formidine caeli.

'Let *piety* or *duty* be defined as an affectionate reverence for God and our parents; religious scruples bind the popular mind with a fear of heaven.' The ancients placed our *duty* to God and to our parents on the same or a similar footing (see Pindar, *Pyth.* VI. 19, and the note); and *piare* is to perform any act of duty or worship; hence the epithet *pius* is constantly applied to Æneas, because he carried his father out of danger on his shoulders (*senior parens pia sarcina nati*, Ovid, *Heroid.* VII. 107). But *relligio* involves a much more complicated notion. It is not derived from *re-ligare*, 'to bind back,' according to the usual notion, but from *reli-gere*, 'to make careful gathering,' so that *re-ligens* might be a synonym of *di-ligens*, and an opposite of *neg-ligens*. Similarly, *op-tio* comes, not from *op-tare*, but from *op-tum*, as *lec-tio* from *lec-tum;* and *rebellio* comes, not from *rebell-are*, but from *rebellia*. Thus *relligio*, according to its primary meaning, is 'perpetually thoughtful care; dwelling upon a subject, and continually recurring to it;' and in its application it is: (1) 'religious worship;' (2) 'religious scruple,' especially in the plural; (3) by substituting the cause for the effect, it is 'guilt causing religious scruple or fear,' or 'the divine curse and consequent remorse or oppression of the conscience caused by a sense of violated religious scruples:' in the second and third sense

APPENDIX IV.   487

it is used in a curious connexion with the words *violare* and *expiare* in three passages of Cicero which have never been compared by any lexicographer or commentator. Cic. *Philipp.* l. 6. 13 : 'an me censetis, P. C., docreturum fuisse, ut parentalia cum supplicationibus miscerentur, ut *inexpiabiles relligiones* (curses) in rempublicam inducerentur ?;' *Tuscul. Disput.* l. 12. 27: 'cærimoniis sepulcrorum, quas neo tantâ curâ coluissent, nec *violatas tam inexpiabili relligione* (curse) *sanxissent ;' ad Atticum,* l. 17. 16 : 'quare et illa, quæ violata, expiabuntur; et hæc nostra, quæ sunt sanctissime conservata, suam *relligionem* (scrupulous observance) obtinebunt.'

103.   *Nôsse potes populum, sed scis quid agatur in urbe;*
       Sontibus ignoscis; notos agnoscis amicos;
       Et cognoscis eum, qui non tibi cognitus erat.

Novi means, 'I know,' or 'am acquainted with' a person or thing: but *scio* means, 'I know' or 'have knowledge of' a reality or fact; thus we have in the same passage of Livy, l. 54: quod utriusque populi vires *nôsset, sciretque* invisam profecto superbiam regiam civibus esse, 'because *he was acquainted* with the strength of both the Romans and the Gabinians, and *knew* for a fact that the royal tyranny was hateful to the citizens.' *Ignosco* is, 'I take no knowledge, overlook, pardon ;' *agnosco* is, 'I recognise or acknowledge' what I knew before; and *cognosco,* 'I learn, or become acquainted with the unknown.'

104.   *Credulus expectans: filos præstolor amicos.*

'You, being credulous, are *expecting,* or *looking out, in hope and desire;* I am *waiting for* friends on whom I can rely.' *Expecto* merely denotes definite or indefinite hope or expectation; as in the *rusticus expectat* of Horace ; but *præstolor* presumes an appointment.

105.   *Dulcia delectant gustantem; suavia odore;*
       Jucunda exhilarant animum; sed grata probantur
       A gratis; quae visa placent loca, amoena vocamus.

Although both *dulcis* and *suavis* are used generally to signify 'sweet,' the former more properly denotes that which is agreeable to the palate (γλυκύς); the latter that which is pleasant to the smell (ἡδύς); thus we have *suavis dulcior* *sed, μέλιτος γλυκίων; but *suave olens, ἡδύοσμος.* In general, *dulcis* denotes a more lasting, and *suavis* a more transient gratification ; and while *suavis* means that which is agreeable at a particular time, *dulcis* is used to express whatever is permanently dear and charming in love and friendship. *Jucundus* is properly a participle for *juviscundus,* and is applied to that, *quod juvat et cordi est*, that which causes mental pleasure and satisfaction. *Gratus* is that which is welcome or acceptable, although it may not be productive of any pleasure at the moment; as Forcellini says: *grata, sunt quae habere nos praestat, licet jucunda non sint*; e. g. in Cic. *Att.* III. 24: *haec scriptae etsi* JUCUNDA *non est, mihi tamen* GRATA *est. Ad Div.* v. 15: *amor tuus* GRATUS *et optatus; dicerem* JUCUNDUM *nisi hoc verbum in tempus perdidissem*. Hence *gratus* is used as a synonym for *acceptus*. Cic. *Tusc.* v. 15: *id* GRATUM ACCEPTUMque *habendum*. *Amoenus* is that which charms the sight with a sense of cheerfulness and beauty. That it is properly applied to denote the beauties of nature may be inferred from its use in this sense by Ennius (Vahlen, p. 10):

> *Nam me visus homo pulcher per amoena salicta*
> *Et ripas raptare locosque novos.*

Similarly, Cic. *Leg.* II. 3: *hac insula nihil est amoenius*. That in this sense it denotes a really inherent natural beauty, as distinguished from the pleasure which the landscape is calculated to afford to an individual, is clear from its opposition to *dulcis* in the passage of Horace (1 *Epist.* XVI. 5):

> *Hae latebrae dulces, etiam, si credis, amoenae,*

'these retreats pleasant to me, still more, if you believe me, charming in themselves.' At the same time *amoenus* signifies that which is ornamental rather than useful; Livy says (XXII. 15): *consita omnia magis amoenis quam necessariis fructibus;* and Tacitus opposes *amoenitas* to *usus*; *Ann.* XIV. 31: *dum amoenitati prius quam usui consulitur*.

106.   *Dividimus muros et moenia pandimus urbis.*

'We make a breach in the walls, and disclose the *collective buildings* of the city' (see Niebuhr, *H. R.* II. note 80).

107.   *Omnibus in rebus remur ratione sagaci;*
        Rem petit unusquisque; reos respublica punit;
        Irrita ne facias, rationem ponere par est.

'In *all things* we *think* by means of *sagacious reason*. Every one seeks for *wealth;* the re-public or common-*wealth* punishes the *culprits*. That you may not make things of *no avail*, it is proper to send in an *account*.' There are no words in the Latin tongue which are so much or so vaguely used as *res* and *ratio*, which are connected by the verb *re-or*, ('I think,' i. e. propose a *res* to my mind), derived from *res*, and furnishing a derivation for *ratio* from its participle *rá-tus*.

APPENDIX IV.

The memorial lines give some of the principal distinctions of meaning: but the following definition extends to every use of the two words: *res* = *ri-is* is probably for *kra-is*, from *kir* the old Latin for 'a hand' (Varro, *L. L.* IV. 26); and is therefore equivalent to the Greek χρέος, χρεία, χρῆμα, from χείρ; compare *laena* with χλαῖνα, *luridus* with χλωρός, &c. Consequently *res* is that which is handled, and means whatever is or may be an object of thought or action. But *ratio* is a derivative in *-tio* from the verb *reor*, and therefore, like other derivatives of the same kind, implies the action of the verb, and may be defined as the *mode* or *act of thinking*. Thus, whereas *res* or *res familiaris* is 'property,' *ratio* is the account kept; whereas *res* or *respublica* is the state objectively, *ratio* is the mode of governing; and in general if *res* is the outer world (as in *natura rerum*, &c.), *ratio* is the inner reason which deals with its theory. The participle *ratus* means 'determined;' whence *irritus* means 'made of no effect.' And *reus* means a person accused or impeached, because *res*, in a legal sense, means the object of controversy, the *thing* or *matter* under dispute. In Cicero (*de Orat.* II. 15), *rerum ratio* or 'history,' as the arrangement of facts (§ 63), is opposed to *verborum ratio* or 'style,' as the arrangement of words (§ 64).

108. *Planitiem dicas regionis et aequora campi;*
Æquora pontus habet; ponto licet esse profundo;
Et mare proruptum pelago premit area somni.

'You may speak of the *level surface* of a region and of the *wide expanse* of a field; the *main sea* has an *expanse*; it may also be deep; and the *flood* rushing forth covers the lands with a roaring *sheet of water.*' *Planities* means the absence of hills, and therefore is applicable only to the land; *aequor* implies horizontal expansion, and is therefore applicable either to land or sea; *pontus* properly refers to the depth of the sea; *mare* to the mass of water, as opposed to dry land; and *pelagus* to the extended sheet of water as opposed to the surface of the land.

109. *Praesentes timeo casus, metuoque futuros.*
Formidare licet fures, regesque severi.
Attonitus trepido, tremulos pavor occupat artus.

Metus means a cautious fear of future and even distant objects; *timor* means a vehement fear of near or approaching dangers, which takes away or at least perturbs the senses. Thus, while *metus*, which is opposed to *spes*, looks forward to dangers while still absent and perhaps only possible, *timor*, which is opposed to *fiducia* and *animus*, regards a peril as imminent or present. *Metus* therefore is a fearful expectation, as a sort of intellectual prescience of coming evil; but *timor* is cowardly display or fear in its most urgent form. These fundamental distinctions are given by Cicero, who says (*Tusc. Disp.* IV. 37, § 80): 'si *spes* est exspectatio boni, mali exspectationem esse necesse est metum.' And (*l. l.* IV. 8, § 19): '*timor* est metus mali appropinquantis.' And the opposition of the two words is sufficiently illustrated by the following passages; Virg. *Æn.* VIII. 556: 'vota *metu* duplicant matres, propiusque periclo it *timor*, et major Martis jam apparet imago.' Liv. XLV. 26, § 7: 'quom major a Romanis *metus timorem* a principibus suis vicissot' (because the Romans were absent). Hence Horace speaks of the *reges timendi*, but the tyrant says of his subjects who regard him with constant and cautious fear to offend: *oderint dum metuant*. In this sense of constant or abiding apprehension *metuo* approaches to *vereor* as *timeo* does to *formido*. But *vereor* comes a step nearer to *timeo*, as the following passage will show (Liv. XXXIX. 37): '*veremur* quidem vos, Romani, et, si ita vultis, etiam *timemus*; sed plus etiam *veremur* et *timemus* Deos immortales.' That the object of *vereor*, though absent and even distant, is regarded as constantly present to the mind, is clear from the words attributed to Cato (Cic. *Sen.* VI. 18): 'de Karthagine *vereri* non ante desinam, quam illam excisam esse cognovero.' For this reason *vereor* is used to denote the abiding sense of respect, honour, and dutiful submission; and the relationship and opposition of *vereor* and *metuo* is well shown by such a passage as the following; Cic. *Sen.* XI. 37: 'Appius tenebat non modo auctoritatem sed etiam imperium in suos; *metuebant* servi, *verebantur* liberi.' What *vereor* is to *metuo*, *formido* is to *timeo*, i. e. it expresses a permanence of the feeling. Being derived from *forma* it plainly expresses the sense of being haunted by a present picture of the dreaded object; and Shakspeare gives us the force of the term when he says (*Midsummer Night's Dream*, v. 1):

> In the night *imagining some fear*,
> How easy is a bush supposed a bear.

When Cicero tells us (*Tusc.* IV. 8 fin.) 'Stoici definiunt *formidinem* metum permanentem,' he states the truth, but his definition would have been more exact if he had substituted *timor* for *metus*. That *formidare* implies being haunted by some perpetual *timor* is well shown by the passage of Horace (*Serm.* 1. 77), to which tacit reference is made in the above lines; namely:

An vigilare metu exanimem, nocturnaque diesque
Formidare malos fures, incendia.

And that *formido*, like all play of the imagination, may arise from imperfect knowledge, is distinctly alleged by Cicero, *Fin.* I. 19: 'ex ignorantia rerum ipsa horribiles existunt saepe *formidines.*' Any of the forms of apprehension expressed by *metuo, timeo, terror* and *formido* may produce an effect on the nervous system; if this merely quickens the pulse or produces paleness and an expression of anxiety in the face, the word *paveo* denotes the result; if it goes farther and makes the teeth chatter and the limbs tremble, *trepido* is the statement of the effect. The latter speaks for itself. That *paveo* expresses rather the effect of fear than fear itself, is shown strikingly by the following passages; Ovid, *Metam.* IX. 111, 112:

> Pallentemque metu, fluviumque ipsumque timentem,
> Tradidit Aonidae paridam Calydonia Nessa.

Id. *Fast.* III. 362:

> Sollicitae mentes speque metuque pavent.

And that *pavor* may arise from astonishment as well as from fear is shown by Liv. VII. 34, § 8: 'admiratione *paventibus* cunctis.'

110. *Dat male sales dicax; ludit bona dicta facetus.*

This line expresses in its strongest form the distinction between *dicax* and *facetus.* Cicero says (*Orator*, 26, § 87) that there are two kinds of *sales*—*unum facetiarum, alterum dicacitatis.* The former comprises all kinds of harmless and good-humoured wit and raillery; the latter, which is sometimes termed *sales* in the narrower sense of that word, includes the different varieties of the severe and biting jest. Thus *facetus* implies that the witty man does not indulge in coarseness, scurrility, caricature or personality; he does not lay himself out to obtain the character of a joker of jokes; and introduces his pleasantries only on suitable occasions. On the other hand, *dicax* necessarily implies that wit, which is exercised at the expense of another, and is used as a ready means of turning an opponent into ridicule. Cicero, who says that Demosthenes was rather *facetus* than *dicax*, remarks at the same time that, while it requires more art to be *facetus*, the *dicax* exhibits a more excitable and passionate temperament (*Orator*, 26, § 90: 'Demosthenes non tam *dicax* fuit quam *facetus.* Est autem illud acrioris ingenii, hoc majoris artis'). The various forms of elegant and inoffensive pleasantry which are included under the more general term *facetiae*, are *lepos*, 'light and gentle humour;' *festivitas*, 'innocent merriment;' and *urbanitas*, 'subdued and polished irony.' Sharp, satirical, and ill-humoured wit, which is known generally as *dicacitas* and *sales*, may sometimes degenerate into *cavillatio*, or jeering mockery; but while in *sales* we consider only the piquancy of the saying, and while *dicacitas*, in disregarding the feelings of another, does this really for the sake of the joke, *cavillatio* makes the attack on another the main object, and cares nothing for the goodness or badness of the witticism, which is made the pretence of the personality; so that *cavillatio* may exist without any real *dicacitas*, as Cicero says of Piso (*Att.* 1. 13), that he was '*cavillator* genere illo moroso, quod etiam sine *dicacitate* ridetur, *facie magis quam facetiis* ridiculus.' The sayings of the *facetus* may be termed *dicta* or *bon mots*; the sarcasms of the *dicax* may be termed *dicteria*.

III. *Multa donuit numerum, sed copia larga redundat;*
Bellua deformis caeta est, immania, et ingens;
Grandia ne tenues; ne parci magna sequantur.

In these lines the Latin words denoting magnitude are placed together so as to show the different shades of meaning with which they are used. *Multus*, which, in the plural implies number rather than magnitude, properly and in the singular denotes a superiority or excess in relative size or quantity. The distinction is clearly given in the advice to students: *ne multa, sed multum*, i. e. 'do not read many books, but read a great deal—do not hastily peruse a number of authors, but bestow much time upon your studies.' The root of the word is contained in the comparative *mel-ior*, for which the older Romans said *mel-ius*, i.e. *mul-tus* (Fest. p. 122); and there can be no doubt that we have the simplest form of the word in *mal-us*, which in common Latin has passed from its original signification of excess in quantity to that of difficulty and badness, just as we have in Greek the co-ordinate adverbs μάλα and μόλις. The primary meaning is retained in the adverb *male*, which is often used as a synonym for *valde* or *nimis* in the best authors (*Varronianus*, p. 393). As *multus* and *multi* denote relative excess or superiority in quantity or number, so *largus* denotes abundance or redundance of a particular thing in regard to that which might circumscribe or contain it. For *multus* is 'much,' as placed by the side of something of the same kind; but *largus* is 'plentiful' or 'copious,' with regard to the limits which might be imposed upon the increase of the object. Hence we have such phrases as *largi copia lactis* (Virg. *Georg.* III. 308); *quum sol terras larga luce compleverit* (Cic. *N. D.* II. 19) in the same sense as *largus liquidi fons luminis*,

aetherius sol (Lucret. v. 281); *largus imber* (Virg. Georg. L 23);
largne opes (Ovid, A. A. III. 408); and the like. Hence *largus*, as a
moral epithet, implies a man who is munificent in his gifts; and
Cicero says (*de Off.* II. 16, § 53), *duo sunt genera largorum, alteri
prodigi, alteri liberales.* The same sense is borne by the derived
verb *largior*, which means to 'give in abundance, to bestow largely;
lavishly and liberally.' The epithets *vastus, immanis*, and *ingens*
are used to denote an excess in size which destroys our perceptions
of beauty and proportion. The primary meaning of *vastus* is 'wide-
spread, empty, void.' It is a synonym of *vacuus*, and probably contains the same root. Thus Livy says in one passage (XXIII. 30),
urbs vastа a defensoribus; and in another (XLII. 63), *moenia vacua
defensoribus;* and Tacitus says of Vitellius (III. 84), *in palatium
regreditur vastum desertumque* (cf. Liv. XXVIII. 11. Cic. *Rull.* II. 26,
Curtius, IX. 40), and immediately afterwards, *terret solitudo et
tacentes loci; tentat clausa; inhorrescit vacuis. Im-manis* and
in-gens are negative expressions denoting, the former that the
excessive magnitude is beyond what is good, and the latter that it
is contrary to nature. In their usual applications, *vastus, immanis*
and *ingens* are used indifferently to denote that which is 'huge,'
'big,' 'overgrown,' 'unshapely,' and 'enormous.' Thus Cicero says
(*N. D.* L 35), 'Elephanto nulla belluarum prudentior; at figura
quæ *vastior?*' Similarly (*de Div.* L 34): 'bellua vasta et *immanis;*'
and (*Verr.* V. 40) '*ingens immanis*que præda.' The general word
to signify that a thing is great in itself, without any implication of
excess or enormity, is *magnus*, which in its positive degree may be
used to denote the attribute of greatness or distinction acquired by
an individual, as *Cn. Pompeius Magnus*, and which in its comparative and superlative *major* and *maximus*, with *natu* expressed or
understood, denotes the permanent relation of the elder and eldest
of the name to their younger namesakes. That *magnus* is distinguished from *ingens* and *immanis* is shown by the following examples,
from which it may be seen that *magnus* does not, like these ex-
aggerative words, convey any idea of excessive magnitude. Ter.
Eun. III. 1. 1: *Magnus* vero agere gratias Thais mihi. *Ingentes.*
Sen. *Ir.* L 16: Non enim *magnitudo* est sed *immanitas.* The adjective *amplus*, which has been already noticed in another reference
(above, 97), is often used in connexion with *magnus*, to which it
bears much the same relation as our 'big' does to our 'great;' thus
we have, Cic. *ad Qu. Fr.* L 1: theatrum *magnitudine amplissimum.*
Cic. *Inv.* L 5, § 6: civilis rationis *magna* et *ampla* pars et arti-
ficiosa eloquentia. The regular opposite of *magnus* is *parvus*, as

intimated in the above memorial lines. Thus Virgil says (*Ecl.* I. 24): *sic parvis componere magna solebam.* Sall. *Jug.* 10: *concordia res parvae crescunt, discordia maximae dilabuntur.* Similarly we have a regular opposition between *grandis* (from the root *gra-*, 'grow,' found in *gra-men*, &c.), which denotes an increased size with reference to the former condition of the object or to other things of the same kind, and *tenuis* (of the same origin as our word 'thin'), which implies a diminution of the original bulk, or a meagreness when compared with other objects of the same class. Thus we find in Horace, 1 *Carm.* vi. 9, *conamur tenues grandia;* and Cicero in distinguishing the three kinds of orators puts in the first class the *grandiloqui*, or 'lofty speakers;' in the second the *tenues*, or 'plain and unadorned speakers;' and between them the *medii*, or 'orators of the mixed style' (*Orat.* 6). The adjective *minutus* seems also to bear the same relation to *parvus* that *grandis* does to *magnus.* At least Cicero says (*de Orat.* III. 45, § 169): *abutimur saepe etiam verbo non tam eleganter quam in transferendo; sed, etiamsi licentius tamen interdum non impudenter: ut quum grandem orationem pro magna, minutum animum pro parvo dicimus.* Other synonyms of *tenuis* are *exiguus, exilis,* and *pusillus.* Like *magnus, grandis* is used to signify advanced age, but with reference rather to the same person than to others of the same name. Thus we have Cic. *Senect.* 4: *bella gerebat ut adolescens quum plane grandis erat.* Ovid, *Met.* vi. 321: *grandior aevo genitor.* Whence the compound *grandaevus.* And while *natu major* means older than some other person, *natu grandior* (Cic. *Inv.* I. 24) means advanced in age as compared with one's former self. It is curious that while our 'great' corresponds to *magnus,* and our 'grand' to *grandis,* we combine the two in the word 'great grandfather.'

112. *Vir bonus est frugi; Nequam malus. Usque reclamat*
    Noxa reo culpae, quem fraus et noxia produnt.
    Nil sibi vir justus, nisi verum orabit et aequum;
    Sed vitium vetitumque nefas in crimina ducunt.
    Peccatum opprobrio est: facinus memorabile patrat
    Qui scelere obstrictus fas juraque proterit. At qui
    Flagitium peperit turpatur nomine pravo.

These lines contain the principal Latin words denoting moral rectitude and its contraries, which require to be distinguished by the student. The commonest expression for 'good' and 'bad' are *bonus* and *malus.* The former (anciently written *duonus*) signified primarily 'manly vigour' (cf. δύναμαι and the Celtic *duine* 'a man;' *Neo-*

Crat. § 202); the latter, as we have seen, contains a root denoting excess in magnitude, and its comparative *melior* has actually been attached to *bonus*, to which in its secondary sense *malus* is directly opposed, as the derivative *malignus* is to *benignus*. To express that a man was 'good for something,' 'good for nothing,' the Romans used the terms *frugi* and *nequam*. The former, however, was understood to imply not usefulness only, but a considerable amount of positive excellence (Cic. *Tusc.* III. 8), and *Frugi* was the cognomen of a branch of the Calpurnian family. When the word is used in a special sense it denotes moderation and sobriety. Thus it is coupled with *modestus* (Brutus *ad Cic.* VI.), with *temperans* (Terent. *Heaut.* III. 3. 19), and *pudicus* (Hor. 2 *Serm.* v. 77). *Nequam*, for which *nihili* is sometimes used (Plaut. *Asin.* v. 2. 9), denotes not only negative worthlessness, but positive vice, especially with reference to prodigality and intemperance, and in this special sense the substantive *nequitia* is also used (Cic. *Cluent.* 51). *Culpa*, which seems to be connected with *calvor* 'to frustrate,' and perhaps with the Greek κλέπ-τω 'to deceive,' when used to denote the fault itself approaches in meaning to *delictum*, with this difference, that *culpa* denotes 'blameable negligence' and *delictum* 'wrongful omission.' But *culpa* also denotes the blame imputed in consequence of a certain act, and we have such phrases as *culpa delicti* (Cic. *Rabir.* 1, 2), *extra culpam causamque ponere* (Cic. *Univ.* 13 init.). The jurists distinguish *culpa* from *dolus*, which means 'deliberate wrong-doing.' The primary meaning of the latter word is 'painstaking' (cf. *dolor*, τολ-μάω, &c.), and to give the word a bad sense it was originally the practice to add the epithet *malus* (see Fest. p. 69. Cæsar, *B. C.* II. 14). To be *sine culpa*, 'without negligence,' is *diligentiam praestare* in a sale; to be *sine dolo*, 'without intentional fraud,' is *bonam fidem praestare* (Proc. *Dig.* XVIII. 1. 68). The primary meaning of *dolus* is involved in *sedulitas*, 'an absence of the sense of toil,' as in Ovid, *Fast.* IV. 4. 34: *et non sentitur sedulitate labor*. And we have the secondary meaning of *dolus*, or that of *dolus malus*, when *sedulo* signifies 'truly,' as in Plaut. *Capt.* IV. 2. 106, *quippe quando nil mihi credis quod ego dico sedulo*. In old legal Latin *sine dolo*, or *se dolo*, 'without intentional wrong,' and *sine fraude* or *se fraude*, 'without actual loss or detriment,' are used as parallel expressions. And in this old sense *sine fraude* is found in the best writers (e. g. Hor. 2 *Carm.* XIX. 20). But *fraus* with or without *mala* is most frequently used to denote the guilty cause of loss or harm, and it is often found as an exact synonym of *dolus* in the sense of 'deceit.' In Hor. 1 *Carm.* III. 28, *ignem fraude mala gentibus intulit*, the word is used to signify the κακὴ τέχνη or guilty wiles of Prometheus. Latin scholars have always found a great difficulty in distinguishing between *noxa* and *noxia*. Gesner, in his *Thesaurus*, and Drakenborch, *ad Liv.* II. 54. 10, maintain the identity of the two words. The memorial line gives Fronto's distinction: '*noxa poena est, noxia culpa.*' And the obvious relationship of the two words, as substantive and adjective, shows that this distinction is correct, namely, that *noxia*, like *ob-noxius*, *in-noxius*, is an adjective or secondary word derived from *noxa*. While therefore *noxa* is the thing that hurts or harms, *noxia* is the condition under which a person is *ob-noxius*. Hence while we have both *noxae tibi erit*, 'it will bring punishment upon you,' and *noxiae tibi erit*, 'you will incur blame,' we have always *in noxia esse* or *teneri*, not *in noxa*, 'to be accounted guilty' (e. g. Ter. *Phorm.* II. 1. 36), and *noxae dare* or *dedere*, ' to consign to punishment,' not *noxiae* (e. g. Ovid, *Fast.* I. 359). That Cicero regarded *noxia* as the guilt distinguished from the punishment is clear from his phrase, *noxiae poena par esto* (*Leges*, III. 4 fin.), explained by *in suo vitio quisque plectatur* (ibid. III. 20, § 46). The adjective *obnoxius* is used by good writers to signify 'detected or conscious of a crime;' thus Sallust, *Jug.* 31 : *obnoxiis inimicis*, ' when your enemies' guilt is detected;' *Cat.* 48: *Crasso ex negotiis privatis obnoxii*, ' under obligation to Crassus, at his mercy;' Liv. XXIII. 12: *si reticeam aut superbus aut obnoxius videar*, 'conscious of guilt.' *Innoxius* is predicated of habitual conduct, *innocens* of single acts (Serv. *ad Æn.* X. 301: *innocens re, innoxius animo dicitur*). Hence the former is the stronger word, and we have a climax in Plaut. *Capt.* III. 5. 7 : *decet innocentem servum atque innoxium confidentem esse*. The word *justus* implies a continual observance of the laws of men (*jura*), distinguished from the divine law (*fas*). Although *aequus*, 'brought to a level,' and *justus*, 'strictly in accordance with law,' are often used as synonyms, *aequitas* is occasionally employed, like our ' equity,' to denote that fair and liberal construction of the strict law, which stands between *jus summum* and *indulgentia*, and we have even the phrase *pro aequitate contra jus dicere* (Cic. *de Orat.* i. 56). *Verus*, which is most commonly found in the sense ' true' of statements or professions, is used by the best writers as a synonym for *aequus*, as in the passage imitated above, i. e. Hor. l. *Epist.* XII. 23: *nil Graephus praeter verum orabit et aequum*. So also Hor. 1 *Epist.* l. 11 : *quod verum atque decens curo et rogo et omnis in hoc sum*. Virgil, *Æn.* XII. 693: *me verius unum pro vobis foedus luere et decernere ferro*, 'it is more equitable that I should expiate the treaty in your stead, and decide the strife with my sword.' Cæsar, *B. G.* IV. 8 : *neque verum esse, qui suos fines tueri non potuerint, alienos occupare,* 'nor was it right that those, who could not protect their own territory, should occupy that of others.' Cic. *Tusc.* III. 299, § 93 : *rectum et verum est ut amemus,* 'it is right and proper that we should love.' Liv. XXXII. 33 : *sociorum audiri postulata verum esse,* 'it was right that the demands of the allies should be heard.' Cf. Liv. II. 48; III. 40; XL. 16; Hor. 2 *Serm.* III. 312; 1 *Epist.* VII. 98. It seems that *verus* and *severus* ultimately agree with *jus* in origin as well as signification. *Vitium*, which is connected with *veto* and *vito*, as *prætium* in interpretor, primarily denotes that which is to be shunned and avoided. It involves the *vetitum* in human, and the *nefas* in divine laws, and Horace combines *vetitum nefas* in one expression (1 *Carm.* III. 26). Practically *vitium* is used much in the same way as *culpa; vitupero* is nearly synonymous with *culpo;* and we find *vitio et culpæ dare* in the same passage (Cic. *S. Rosc.* 16 fin.). *Crimen* (from *cerno*) means a distinct and definite accusation, a thing determined by law as wrong, an act charged as wrongful. Thus we have in Ovid, *Trist.* II. 306 :

> Quæcumque irrumpit quo non sinit ire sacerdos,
> Protenus hæc retiâi criminis acta rea est.

Peccatum, from *pecco* = *pecuo*, 'to act like a brute,' conveys the idea of a stupid fault or blunder (cf. Cic. *Paradox.* III. 2. Plaut. *Bacch.* III. 29). Practically it is used as nearly synonymous with *culpa* and *delictum;* thus Plaut. *Epid.* v. 2. 64 : 'mihi ignoscas si quid imprudens culpa peccavi mea.' Cic. *Mur.* 30 : 'fatetur aliquis se peccasse et ejus *delicti* veniam petit.' *Facinus* (for the form cf. *itiner, jecinur*) is a great or bold deed, perpetrated in defiance of the laws. Thus Ter. *Heaut.* II. 2. 73 : 'non fit sine periculo *facinus* magnum et commemorabile.' *Scelus*, literally, 'a thing driven out and excommunicated,' means 'a horrible and atrocious act, such as cannot be tolerated within the limits of a respectable community.' Hence we have such phrases as *scelere contaminare nomen populi Romani; scelere se devincire, obstringere, alligare; sceleribus nefariis coopertus; scelus infestum et immune; scelus detestabile; scelere violare deos immortales,* &c. It is a stronger word even than *facinus;* for Cicero says (*Verr.* VII. 66): '*facinus* est vinciri civem Romanum; *scelus* verberari; prope *parricidium* necari.' A sort of *relligio* or curse (above 102) was attached to the *scelestus* and *sceleratus;* hence both words are used to signify 'unlucky,' the latter especially in funeral inscriptions; as 'parentes sceleratissimi posuerant Mammio suo;' the former in the comic poets, as Plaut. *Cas.* III. 5. 34: '*scelestissimum me esse video.*' *Sceleratus* is also an epithet of places blasted with ill fame in consequence of some horrible, nefarious, or unlucky act; thus we have *sceleratus vicus, campus, scelerata porta*, and the like. In *flagitium*, literally 'cause of outcry, shameful proceeding,' the leading idea is that of the disgrace occasioned by the act; thus we have (Cic. *Att.* XVI. 7): 'factum *flagitii* plenum *et dedecoris.*' The word is very often combined with *facinus*, as the open audacity of a disgraceful act increases the infamy which ensues; thus we have Sall. *Cat.* 14: 'omnium *flagitiorum* atque *facinorum.*' 23: '*flagitiis* atque *facinoribus* coopertus.' Cic. *Cat.* I. 6: 'quod *facinus* a manibus unquam tuis, quod *flagitium* a toto corpus abfuit?' I. 7: 'nullum aliquot jam annis *facinus* exstitit, nisi pro te; nullum *flagitium* sine te.'

APPENDIX V.

ANTIBARBARUS.

THE Latin scholar should not only be able to distinguish those Latin expressions, which, though equally correct, slightly differ in meaning. He should also discriminate between the correct and idiomatic words and phrases, and those which are unusual or inadmissible. Most of the classical and correct idioms of the Latin language have been noticed in the course of the *Grammar*, and attention has been directed to many faulty and objectional phrases or constructions. As, however, this work is especially intended for the use of those who wish to write Latin, it will be desirable to append a list of the solœcisms into which English students are most likely to fall. More than one elaborate treatise, bearing the title of *Antibarbarus*, has been written on this subject. It is to be doubted whether the perusal of one of these works would be likely to remedy the defects which it exemplifies. And it is much better that the young Latinist should be cautioned only against the most usual and probable barbarisms. It is to be observed that the cautions given below with regard to a selection of phrases do not apply to those who use the Latin language as a medium of literary communication. For these persons modern Latin is not a dead language, but admits of new developments within certain limits like any other form of human speech; and to confine the mature scholar to a Ciceronian style is an exploded pedantry. But those, who are still acquiring the habit of writing Latin, cannot be too particular or exact, for it is only from those who have passed the necessary apprenticeship in an imitation of the best models, that we can expect a good and pleasing form of modern Latinity.

A.

Abbreviare, 'to abbreviate,' is not classical; use *per notas scribere* for short-hand writing, *verborum compendia facere* for abbreviations of single words (as *Ictus* for *juris consultus*), and *contrahere*, *in breve cogere*, *in angustum deducere* or *breviare* (Quintil.) for the abridgment of a discourse.

APPENDIX V.

Abdicare magistratum is unclassical; we should say *abdicare se magistratu*. The metaphorical *abdicare se humanitate*, though used by Ruhnken (*Opusc.* I. p. 86), has no classical authority; it should be *humanitatem (omnem) exuere.* Cic. *Att.* XIII. 2; *Ligar.* v. § 14.

Abhinc, which properly refers to past time only (from this time, counting backwards), is sometimes wrongly used with reference to future time or distance in space; in its proper use we must not add *ante;* thus *ante decem annos abhinc* is unclassical.

Abscondere se is not classical; write *abdere se, occultare se.*

Absque, though commonly used for *sine* by modern Latinists in such phrases as *absque vitiis, absque omni dubitatione*, is barbarous, except in the phrase *absque eo esset* (above, p. 331).

Accuratus is an unclassical substitute for *diligens* in the sense of our 'accurate' or 'exact.' So also the adverb *accurate.*

Acquisitio is very late Latin for *comparatio, adeptio.*

Actirus does not occur as a substitute for *gnavus, industrius, strenuus, promptus.*

Ad diem is false Latin for *ante diem.* So also *ad summum*, 'in the highest degree,' for *summum, ad minimum* for *minimum, ad instar* for *instar*, &c.

Adaptare for *accommodare* has no authority.

Adducere scriptorem, 'to quote an author,' is unclassical; of persons we say *producere, citare, laudare, proferre;* of things, *afferre.*

Adhibere vocabulum, 'to use a word,' is not good Latin for *uti.*

Adhuc is frequently confused with *etiam tunc*, and *hactenus* (above, p. 168). Its use with comparatives, as *adhuc fortior*, 'still stronger,' for *etiam fortior*, is not Ciceronian.

Adoptare, e. g. *lectionem*, for *recipere*, is not supported by any good authority.

Advocatus in classical Latin is not the *patronus* or *patronus causae*, i. e. 'the advocate' in our sense, but a friend and abettor.

Aedes in the plur. does not signify 'a temple' without the addition of *deorum, sacrae*, or *divinae.*

Aegritudo means 'trouble of mind,' *aegrotatio*, or *morbus*, 'bodily ailment.'

Aequator is bad Latin for *circulus aequinoctialis*, or *meridianus.*

Aera, 'a period of time,' is very low Latin for *temporum, annorum computatio.*

Aestimabilis is new Latin for *dignus qui magni aestimetur; aestimare* must not be used in the sense of our 'to esteem' without *magni*, nor must we substitute *aestimatio* for *existimatio* or *observantia.*

APPENDIX V. 501

Afferre scriptorem, 'to quote an author,' is not good, but we may say, *afferre locum scriptoris* (above s. *Adducere*).

Agere de aliqua re cannot be said of a book, as *hic liber agit de aliqua re*, but we must say *hic liber est de aliqua re, in hoc libro tractatur aliqua res, disseritur, disputatur de aliqua re*. It is also barbarous to say *agere* for *habere orationem*.

Aggressio is late Latin for *impetus, petitio, incursio, incursus, oppugnatio*, &c.

Aio with *non* is barbarous for *nego*.

Alienatio mentis for *dementia, amentia, furor, stupor*, belongs to the later Latinity.

Alioqui is un-Latin in the sense *alio loco, aliis locis*.

Aliquantus must not be used to signify 'a little,' for it means 'a considerable amount,' and we must not say *aliquanto major*, but *paulo major* for 'greater by a little.'

Alius a is not Latin, although used by Ernesti (*Opusc. Phil.* p. 23); we must write *diversus a*, or repeat the *alius*.

Alloqui aliquem, 'to address a person,' is bad Latin for *adire aliquem, petere ab aliquo*.

Alludere, 'to allude' (in words), is late Latin for *significare, designare, respicere* with or without *tecte*.

Ambire magistratum is not good Latin for *petere mag.* We may say, however, *ambire plebem, cives, patres, amicos*, in the sense 'to canvass.'

Amittere proelium, 'to lose a battle,' is a barbarous substitute for *vinci proelio, inferiorem discedere proelio*.

Animalculum is bad Latin for *bestiola*.

Anne for *annon* or *necne* is barbarous.

Annuus in the sense 'returning yearly' is bad Latin for *anniversarius*, though Wyttenbach (*Opusc.* I. p. 43) uses it so. In means 'continuing through the year,' as *magistratus annui*.

Ante judicem (judicium) vocare aliquem is bad Latin for *in judicium, in jus vocare*.

Antecedens (with *liber, epistola, verbum*) is bad Latin for *superior;* so also *anterior* must not be used for *prior*.

Appendere, 'to hang up,' is bad Latin for *suspendere*, though used by Heyne (*ad Virg. Ecl.* III. 12).

Applausus is a modern substitute for *plausus*.

Apprehendere, 'of mental apprehension,' is late Latin for *percipere, mente comprehendere, intelligere*.

Assecla, assectator, are not classical substitutes for *discipulus, alumnus, qui ab aliquo est, alicujus sententiam sequitur*.

Asserere aliquid is late Latin for *affirmare, dicere, censere;* and so is *assertio* for *sententia, dictum, effatum*.

Assistere alicui, in the sense of our 'assist' is late Latin for *adesse, non deesse alicui*, &c.

Attendere ad aliquem, aliquid is incorrect; we should say *attendere aliquid*, or *animum attendere ad aliquid*. The same remark applies to *attentio* for *attentus animus*.

Attinet me, 'it concerns me,' is bad Latin for *attinet ad me;* and we must not say *quod ad id attinet quod* for *quod* alone. But *quod ad librum attinet* (Cic. *ad div.* VI. 7 *fin.*) is right. It is also wrong to say: 'hac de re multi scripserunt, et, *quod ad Ciceronem attinet*, is quinque libros scripsit' for *et Cicero quidem quinque*, &c.

Attrahere, 'to draw to oneself,' e.g. *nervum, habenas*, is bad Latin for *adducere*.

Auctor is not classical for *scriptor* in the sense of our 'author.'

Audire bene, male is bad Latin for *auditu valere, acri esse auditu; auditu non valere, surdastrum esse*.

Auditus, 'hearing,' is seldom used for *sensus audiendi, aurium*.

Auxiliatrix is late Latin for *adjutrix*.

B.

Bellicosus must be used with *animus, gens*, &c., but *bellicus* with *virtus, laus, gloria;* and *ars militaris* is more common than *ars bellica*.

Bellum cum aliquo, is bad Latin unless there is a verb; 'the war with the Persians,' for instance, is not *bellum cum Persis*, but *bellum Persarum* or *Persicum*.

Bene dicere, 'to bless or praise,' with the accusative, is only found in later Latin.

Bene vivere, 'to live well,' i.e. luxuriously, is unclassical; we must write *laute, molliter, jucunde, liberaliter, magnifice vivere*.

Biblia Sacra is bad Latin for *divinae (sanctae) litterae, libri divini, scriptura sancta, sacri Judaeorum Christianorumque libri*.

Bonum mihi videtur facere aliquid is bad Latin for *mihi videtur, placet, libet*, &c.

Borealis is late Latin for *septentrionalis, ad septentriones vergens, spectans*, &c.

Brachia in the phrase *in brachiis alicujus mori*, 'to die in a person's arms,' is not used for *in alicujus complexu* or *manibus*.

Breve ante tempus, brevi ante tempore are not Latin for *brevi ante* or *nuper*.

Breviter or *brevi* is not Latin for *quid multa? quid plura? ne multa, quid quaeris*, &c.

C.

Cæcutire, 'to be blind,' is later Latin for *cæcum esse, oculis captum esse*.

Calumniosus, calumniose are not the classical expressions; we should write *criminosus, malignus; criminose, per calumniam*.

Calx must not be used to signify 'the end,' unless there is some reference, direct or metaphorical, to the race-course. *In calce, ad calcem libri*, though common in modern Latin, are unsupported by any good authority.

Capacitas ingenii, capax ingenium are bad Latin for *ingenii magnitudo, vis percipiendi, indoles praeclara, ingenium magnum, acre, praestans, &c.*

Capessere opportunam occasionem or *opportunitatem occasionis* is not found in the sense of *occasionem opportunam arripere, capere, non praetermittere*.

Capitalis in the sense of 'distinguished, eminent,' though used by Ruhnken (*Opusc.* I. p. 91), occurs only once in Cicero and Ovid.

Carere, 'to do without,' 'not to require,' is bad Latin for *non opus esse*.

Castigare must be confined to words, and must not be used of personal chastisements; the zeugma in Cic. Tusc. III. 27 does not justify the modern usage.

Catalogus is not good Latin for *index, enumeratio*.

Causa, with the genitive, refers to the future, and we must use *ob* and *propter* with the accusative of the past, and *per* or *prae* of present reasons or obstacles; thus we must not say *tempestatis causa ad te venire non potui*, but *per tempestatem or prae tempestate*; and while we may say *injurias inferendas causa*, we must not write *injurias illatas causa*, but *propter injuriam illatam*.

Celeber, celeberrimus are confined in the best authors to much-frequented places, well-known days, names, or things; accordingly we should not write *vir celeber, celeberrimus*, for *vir clarus, illustris, clarissimus*.

Chorus should not be used for *canticum* to signify the song or poem.

Circumscriptio is bad Latin for *circumlocutio*.

Clima, 'the climate,' is a later expression for *caelum, natura* or *temperatio caeli*.

Coaequalis, coaetaneus, coaevus for 'contemporary' are new Latin terms for *aequalis, ejusdem aetatis, ejusdem temporis*.

Coepi with an infinitive pass. (except *fieri*) must be avoided; we should say *coeptus est laudari, &c.*

Cognitio and *cognitiones* never signify acquired knowledge, which must be expressed by *disciplina, doctrina, eruditio, &c.* The proper

Latin for 'he has not much learning' is *non sunt in eo plurimae litterae, litterarum admodum nihil scit, non valet plurimum a doctrina.*

Coincidere is new Latin for *concurrere.*

Commendatorius must not be written for *commendaticius.*

Commissio, 'a commission,' is bad Latin for *mandatum, negotium.*

Commodare alicui pecuniam is not an allowable phrase for 'to lend money;' we must say, *dare alicui pecuniam mutuam.*

Communicare alicui is late Latin for *communicare cum aliquo.*

Communiter is bad Latin for *vulgo, plerumque,* &c.

Comparative, 'in comparison with,' is without authority for *comparate, ex comparato.*

Compati and *compassio*, as also *condolere* and *condolentia*, in our sense, are very modern words.

Compensatio meritorum is bad Latin for *remuneratio, aequatio, pensatio.*

Compilare librum, of one's own book, is not Latin; for the classical writers add in the accusative that from which the book is derived, and always presume a dishonest or forbidden use of it (see Cic. *Mur.* II.; Hor. I *Serm.* I. fin.).

Concivis, concredere are modern Latin for *civis, credere.*

Condemnare mortis, morti, ad mortem are objectionable phrases. We should write *capitis* or *capite.*

Condemnatio is late Latin for *damnatio.*

Confidens, confidentia, confoederatus are not classical for *fidens, fiducia, foederatus.*

Connatus is late Latin for *ingenitus, ingeneratus, innatus.*

Conscientia bona, 'with a good conscience,' is not a correct phrase for *salvo officio.*

Contentum esse with an infin. following is not classical; we must write *satis habere. Male contentus*, 'ill-satisfied,' is bad Latin for *indignabundus.*

Contradicere alicui, 'to contradict a person,' is not so good Latin as *contra aliquem dicere, alicui obloqui, adversari.* But without the dative *contradicere* is a good classical word (Cic. *Att.* I. 17, § 21. *Verr.* III. 7, § 18. *Rosc. Am.* XXXIII. § 93).

Convenire, 'to agree,' in such phrases as *nos de hac re convenimus*, is bad Latin for *inter nos haec res convenit;* and *convenire cum aliquo* is bad Latin for *convenire aliquem.*

Corporeus, in Cicero, means that which has a body; it is therefore wrong to say *voluptates corporeas* for *vol. corporis; necessitates corporeas* for *usus vitae necessarii, res ad vivendum necessarias.*

Crassus in a metaphorical sense is not good Latin, e. g. *crassum vitium* for *magnum, insigne.*

Creare mundum, creatio mundi, of God, are not Ciceronian; we may write *procreare* and *procreator,* and still better *aedificare, aedificator; efficere, effector; fabricari, fabricator.*

Credere in aliquid, e. g. *in unum Deum,* is modern Latin for *credere aliquid esse,* e. g. *unum esse deum,* or *deum putare.*

Criticus, 'critical,' 'dangerous,' is not Latin; hence we do not say *res criticae, tempora critica,* but *discrimen rerum, tempora periculosa.*

Crucifigere is late Latin for *cruci affigere, suffigere, in crucem tollere, cruce afficere.*

Curare with the acc. and infin. is bad Latin for the construction with *ut* and the subj., or the gerundive; we must write, therefore, not *curo epistolam describi,* but *ut epistola describatur* or *epistolam describendam.*

Curiosus means 'careful,' not 'curious.'

D.

Dare is used barbarously in the following phrases: *dare potestatem alicui,* 'to give a person permission,' for *facere alicui potestatem; dare sententiam,* 'to give one's opinion,' for *ferre sententiam, ferre* or *inire suffragium; dare filiam virum,* 'to give one's daughter a husband,' for *collocare viro filiam, collocare filiam in matrimonio; dare alicui aliquid mutuo* or *feneratio,* 'to lend money,' for *mutuum* or *feneratum.*

Dator, 'a giver,' is poetical for *auctor.*

De is wrongly used in the following phrases: *de die in diem* for *in dies; de hora in horam* for *in horas; de verbo ad verbum* for *totidem verbis, ad verbum, verbis iisdem; de novo* for *de integro.*

Debitum, 'a debt,' is only used with *solvere;* the proper phrase is *aes alienum, pecunia debita.* 'To demand a debt,' is *admonere debitorem, aliquem de pecunia debita appellare.*

Decimus tertius, &c. are not so good as *tertius decimus,* &c.

Declarare bellum is bad Latin for *indicere bellum.*

Deflectere e via, 'to turn out of the way,' is wrong; it should be *de via.*

Delectabilis is an unclassical substitute for *dulcis, suavis, jucundus,* and the like.

Delineatio is late Latin for *adumbratio, brevis descriptio, forma,* &c.

Dependere ab aliquo, 'to depend upon a person' (figuratively), is never used for *pendere ex aliquo.*

Derivare verba is not good Latin for *enodare verba, originem verborum ex aliqua re ducere, repetere, quaerere.*

Descriptio does not mean 'description' in our sense, but 'order,' arrangement;' and *descriptio civitatis* in Cicero (*pro Sext.* 65) is the form or constitution of a government.

Desertum is late Latin for *solitudo, locus desertus, regio deserta.*

Desiderare in the sense 'to wish,' 'to require,' is late Latin for *postulare;* so *desiderium* when used for *postulatum* or *cupiditas.*

Despectui esse is not classical for *despicatui, contemptui esse.*

Dexteritas, applied to the mind, is not supported by authority.

Dicere is not used for *inquam, inquit,* in giving the words of a dialogue.

Dictio in good Latin is rather the act of speaking than a single word, which should be expressed by *verbum, vox, vocabulum.*

Dies is wrongly used in the following phrases: *ante diem* for *ante lucem; diebus nostris* for *nostra memoria; die secundo* (e.g.) *Saturnaliorum,* for *secundis Saturnalibus.*

Diffamare aliquem should not be used in prose for *infamare aliquem, alicui infamiam inferre.*

Dignus with the infin. (e. g. *laudari*) is poetic and unclassical.

Dilabi, 'to slip away,' of time, is not Latin.

Dilectus, 'beloved,' is poetic or belonging to the later prose for *carus, suavis.*

Diligentia means 'care and exactness,' not 'diligence,' or 'industry,' which must be rendered by *industria* when painstaking is implied, by *assiduitas* when perseverance is denoted, by *studium* when zeal and active interest are combined with the effect; and by *opera* when bodily exertion is signified. Similarly, we must not substitute *diligens* for *industrius, assiduus, gnavus, studiosus, laboriosus.*

Diluvies, diluvio, 'a deluge,' is a poetical and later expression for *eluvio, diluvium, inundatio, alluvies.* We may also say *diffundi aquas.*

Dimittere, 'to dismiss,' i. e. from an employment, is unclassical, for *mittere, missum facere:* so also *dimissio* for *missio.*

Dimittere aliquid ex animo, 'to dismiss a thing from one's mind,' is a mere Anglicism.

Disceptare cum aliquo is bad Latin for *certare, contendere cum aliquo.*

Discurrere, 'to discourse,' is late Latin for *disserere, disceptare.* The same verbs are also wrongly represented by *discutere,* in the sense 'to discuss,' and its derivative, *discussio.*

Disertis verbis, 'with clear, expressive words,' is an unauthorized modernism for *ipsis verbis, diserte* (Liv. XXI. 19), *disertissime, aperte* (Cic. *Att.* I. 14), *plane, liquido, omnino* (Cic. *Tusc.* V. 9, § 24), *distincte, dilucide,* and, in the case of persons, *nominatim* (Cic. *Att.* IV. 1, § 9).

Dissitus, though used by the best modern Latinists in the sense of *diver-*

APPENDIX V.

nus, remotus, longinquus, disjunctus (e. g. Muretus, *Op.* II. p. 888: *regiones dissitas*, Hemsterh. *Orat.* p. 4: *quam longe dissitos ac sejunctos fines*) belongs only to the later Latinity.

Ditio, which does not occur in the nom. (above, p. 59. Serv. *ad Virg. Æn.* I. 740) is wrongly used by good modern Latinists (e. g. Muret. I. 14) for *terra, regio*, for it means 'dominion.' It is also wrongly used in its proper sense, but in the plur., by Hemsterh. *Orat.* p. 7.

Diu before *ante* and *post* is barbarous Latin for *multo*.

Diutius est quam octo dies is false Latin for *amplius sunt octo dies* (above, p. 297 (δ)).

Documentum, 'a document,' is modern Latin for *tabula publica, diploma, monumentum*.

Dominium is unclassical for *imperium, dominatus, dominatio*, and barbarous for *terra, ager, &c.*

Donare alicui fidem is bad Latin for *habere alicui fidem* (Cic. *Att.* VIII. 3, § 3).

Drama, dramaticus are late Latin for *fabula, sceniens*.

Dubitare is often used in a barbarous construction. The positive phrases *dubitare, dubium est* must not be followed by *quin*, but by the accus. or infin., or by an indirect interrogative; the negative and interrogative phrases *non dubitare, non dubium est; cave dubites; cur, quid est quod dubites?* must be followed by *quin;* and when in the former case a double interrogative follows, the first interrogative particle may be omitted, as in *dubito mihi faveat an adversetur.*

Dumtaxat with a verb, and *non dumtaxat* for *non solum* are barbarous.

Duratio is modern Latin for *diuturnitas, longinquitas*.

Duumviri, though often used by modern Latinists, is ungrammatical and barbarous (above, p. 62).

E.

E contra, 'on the contrary,' is late Latin for *contra, e (ex) contrario; contra ea*.

Ecquando? 'when?' and *ecquis?* 'who?' are barbarous for *quando?* and *quis?*

Efficacia is late Latin for *efficacitas, efficientia, industria, agendi alacritas, &c.*

Elabi, 'of time,' e. g. *annus elapsus*, is barbarous; we should say *annus praeteritus, peractus, superior, qui effluxit*.

Elementarius must not be used of things, but is applicable to persons (e. g. *puer, tener*) who are still occupied with the mere elements of learning.

Elogium, which properly denotes only an inscription on a monument, is French-Latin (*Éloge*) for *laudatio*.

Emigratio is not classical Latin for *migratio*, and *emigrare* without *ex* and an ablative should not be used for *migrare*, *domicilium mutare*. In Cicero *migrare* with an accus. means 'to transgress,' 'go beyond the bounds of something,' e.g. *migrare jura*, 'to break the laws' (*de Div.* I. 5).

Encomium for *laudatio* is unsupported by authority.

Encyclopaedia is not directly employed by any Latin writer (Quintil. I. 10). We should say *orbis disciplinarum; omnium artium ac disciplinarum doctrina; brevis quaedam omnium artium ac disciplinarum descriptio, quae vulgo encyclopaedia vocatur*.

Enixe, 'earnestly,' is not found for *etiam atque etiam* with *rogare*, *petere*, &c.

Ensis, 'sword,' is only poetical for *gladius*.

Epitaphium is not an authorized substitute for *elogium* or *carmen in sepulcro incisum*.

Est with the infin. act., e.g. *est videre*, 'one may see,' is not classical, and must be avoided.

Evidenter is barbarous for *plane*, *aperte*, *penitus*, *perspicue*.

Exacte is late Latin for *accurate*, *diligenter*.

Exceptio must not be used in the phrase, 'all without exception,' which is *ad unum omnes*.

Excerpere librum is bad Latin for *aliquid e libro excerpere*, and 'extracts' are better called *electa* than *excerpta*.

Excudere without *typis* is bad Latin for *typis imprimere* or *exprimere*.

Exempli causa should be used only with verbs; as *exempli causa paucos nominavi*; if a mere example is cited, we should say *ut* or *velut*.

Experientia, 'experience,' is late Latin for *res*, *rerum usus*, *experta virtus*, *tempus*, &c.; and we must not use *experiri* for 'to learn,' which is *accipere*, *audire*, *cognoscere*.

Exponere, 'to explain,' must not be used for *explanare*, *explicare*, *enarrare*, *interpretari*, nor *expositio* and *expositor* for *enarratio*, and *interpres*. *Exponere se periculo*, 'to expose oneself to danger,' is late Latin for *committere*, *offerre*, *objicere se periculo*, *adire*, *obire*, *subire periculum*.

Exsistere, merely 'to be' is barbarous; for it denotes 'exhibiting oneself in a public and active manner.'

Extrahere librum for *excerpere e libro* is barbarous; so also *extractus* and *extractum* for *epitome*, *summarium*.

Extraordinarius is bad Latin for *singularis*, *insignis*, *eximius*.

F.

Facere is wrongly used in the following phrases: *facere damnum, detrimentum* for *inferre* or *afferre; facere conditiones* for *ferre; facere aes alienum* for *contrahere, suscipere.*

Factum should be written with *bene* not *bonum* in such phrases as *bene factum quod,* 'it is well that,' &c.

Falsitas is late Latin for *mendacium, vanitas, fulmen, falsa.*

Fama must not be used for *rumor* or *fabulae antiquae.*

Familia must not be used for one's wife and children, which should be expressed by *conjux et liberi, mei, tui, sui.*

Festivus, which properly signifies 'merry,' should not be used for *festus, solemnis,* in the sense 'festal,' and *festivitas* is not 'festivity,' but jocose merriment in words.

Fictio and *figmentum* are late Latin for *commentum, fabula, res ficta,* or *opinio ementita,* and *ficticius* is barbarous for *commenticius* or *fictus.*

Finire in Cicero is rather 'to define a limit' than 'to end,' which he expresses by *finem alicujus rei facere* or *afferre, aliquid conficere, terminare* (ad div. III. 13, § 4). *Finire vitam* is not used of natural death.

Finis denotes 'the end,' but e.g. *in fine epistolae* is not so good as *in extrema epistola.*

Firmus is barbarous in *terra firma,* which should be *terra continens.*

Fratricidium is late Latin for *parricidium fraternum, fratris caedes, nex.*

Fugitivi oculi is not supported by authority. Horace says *veloci oculo percurrere.*

Fulcrum should not be used for *firmamentum* (Cic. Att. L. 18, § 6) or *firmum subsidium* (Cic. Sext. 8. § 20).

Funditus is barbarously used for *penitus* with verbs like *cognoscere, perspicere,* &c.

Fungi vita, 'to die,' is a juristic expression, and should be avoided in common prose. *Fungi,* 'to die,' without *vita, fungi dapibus,* 'to feast,' *fungi lacrimis,* 'to weep,' &c. are poetical.

G.

Gaudere aliqua re, in the sense of merely having it, without any sense of pleasure or enjoyment, is not Latin.

Genius in the English sense is barbarous; we must write *ingenium* when mental endowments are intended; 'the genius of the language' is *proprietas, natura sermonis;* 'the genius of the age' is *temporum ratio, hi mores, natura saeculi.*

Genuinus in the English sense belongs to the later Latin; we should write *germanus, probus, verus;* and for *genuinitas* we should say *veritas, auctoritas, fides.*

Gerere se with an adjective (e. g. *modestum, submissum*) is not allowable; we must use the adverb (*modeste, submisse*).

Gesta (plur.) is rarely used for *res gestae.*

Grandiloquentia is modern Latin for *magniloquentia, granditas verborum,* though *grandiloquus* is Ciceronian.

Gratiam agere is not so good as *gratias agere,* 'to return thanks;' on the other hand, *gratiam habere,* 'to feel grateful,' *gratiam referre,* 'to return a favour,' *gratiam deferre,* 'to owe thanks,' are the only allowable expressions.

Gratitudo is a later word for *gratus animus.*

Gustus, 'the taste' (as one of the senses), is unclassical for *gustatus,* and *gustus bonus,* 'a good taste,' for *sensus pulcritudinis,* is altogether barbarous. 'A man of taste' is *homo politus;* 'of the greatest taste,' *vir in omni judicio elegantissimus.*

H.

Habere is often used without a proper regard to the Latin idiom.

Haec habui dicere, 'this is what I had to say,' is a Græcism for *haec habui quae dicerem; nihil habeo tecum facere,* 'I have nothing to do with you,' is an Anglicism for *nihil mihi tecum est;* and so are *habere aliquid in magna copia,* 'to have something in great abundance,' for *habere alicujus rei magnam copiam; habere patientiam cum aliquo,* 'to have patience with some one,' for *patienter aliquem ferre, habere exoptatissimum comitem in aliquo,* 'to have a most welcome companion in some one,' for *habere eum exopt. comitem,* and the like.

Habitare aliquem locum is merely poetical for *habitare in aliquo loco.*

Hactenus for *adhuc,* time, is unclassical.

Haesitanter is new Latin for *cunctanter, haesitans, haesitabundus.*

Heroicus is not used in the modern sense for *fortis.*

Hodiernus, in the sense of 'still living,' is not good Latin for *hic qui nunc est, noster, nunc vivens.*

Hospes and *hospitium* must not be used for *caupo* and *caupona* with reference to places of entertainment where money is demanded and paid.

Hostis is a public, and *inimicus* a private enemy; thus Catiline was *hostis patriae, inimicus Ciceronis.*

Hucusque is unclassical and of rare occurrence for *usque ad hunc locum, usque eo, usque ad id.*

Humaniores litterae is bad Latin, especially on account of the comparative, which is inadmissible; we must write *studia humanitatis et litterarum, litterae antiquae, studia antiquitatis*.

I, J.

Jacere aliquem lapidibus, 'to pelt a person with stones,' is bad Latin for *appetere aliquem lapidibus, jacere lapides in aliquem*.

Idem est cum illo is not a good phrase for *idem est qui ille, atque ille, hic et ille iidem sunt*.

Idiotismus, 'an idiom,' is bad Latin for *proprietas sermonis*.

Illicitus is unclassical for *non, minime licitus, inconcessus, non concessus, nefas*.

Imaginari is a later word for *animo fingere, imaginem cogitatione fingere*, or *depingere, sibi persuadere, conjicere, somniare*, and the like.

Imbibere opinionem, 'to imbibe an opinion,' is bad Latin, but *imbibere*, absolutely, 'to resolve or determine,' is Ciceronian (see e.g. pro Quint. 6 sub fin.).

Immortalis as a title of praise is not applied to persons, but to things, as *gloria, memoria*, &c.

Implorare aliquem aliquid is inadmissible; but we may have *implorare aliquid ab aliquo*, or *aliquid alicujus*, e.g. *patris auxilium*.

Impossibilis, is late Latin for *qui, quae, quod fieri non potest*.

Impostor, imposturа, are later words for *fraudator, fraus*.

Imputare, 'to attribute,' is bad Latin for *tribuere, attribuere, assignare, adscribere;* the proper meaning of *imputare* is 'to charge a person with something,' to consider him your debtor for it, as Tacitus says of the Germans, *nec data imputant nec acceptis obligantur* (*German.* 21).

In Cicerone, &c. is bad Latin for *apud Ciceronem*, &c. In a citation of words and expressions, but it is right when we are speaking of a particular book, as *in Gorgia Platonis*, or when we are speaking of an author's style, of his credibility, or his other peculiarities, as Cic. *Orat.* 71: *in Thucydide orbem modo orationis desidero*. Quintil. IX. 4, § 18: *in Herodoto omnia leniter fluunt*.

Inaestimabilis in the sense 'inestimable,' i.e. of very great value, though used by Liv. xxix. 22, should be avoided as an ambiguous term; for in Cicero (*Fin.* III. 6) it means 'of no esteem or value.'

Inaudita re, 'without a hearing of the cause,' is new Latin for *indicta causa, re inorata* (Cic. *Rosc. Am.* IX. § 26), *causa incognita* (Cic. *Verr.* I. 9). In Cic. *Balb.* 18, *re inaudita* means, 'after the matter had been heard.'

Inauguralis, e.g. *oratio* in our sense is new Latin for *aditialis*.

Includere, 'to include,' e.g. in a packet, is new Latin for *addere, adjungere, conjicere, epistolam in fasciculum.*

Incontentus is barbarous for *non contentus.*

Inde a principio without *jam* prefixed is false Latin: it is also an error, though common in the writings of good modern Latinists, to say *ab eo inde tempore* for *jam inde ab eo tempore.*

Indigestio, in the English sense, is late Latin for *eruditas.*

Indiscretus, 'indiscreet,' is late Latin for *ineptus, imprudens,* &c.

Inelegantia, 'want of taste,' is late Latin for *insulsitas, judicium comptum nulla elegantia.*

Infallibilis is barbarous for *qui falli, errare non potest.*

Informare, 'to inform or instruct,' requires some addition, as *ad humanitatem;* otherwise we must use *erudire, instituere.*

Ingratitudo is late Latin for *ingratus animus.*

Inhabitare is a rare and late word for *habitare.*

Innovatio is late Latin for *instauratio, renovatio.*

Inquisitio in aliquem, as a legal term, is unclassical: we should write *quaestio in aliquem, de aliquo.*

Inserere verba is a later expression for *interponere, includere, intexere, admiscere.*

Inspiratio is late Latin for *afflatus, instinctus divinus.*

Institutio in the sense of 'an institution' (e.g. *institutiones majorum*) is bad Latin for *institutum.*

Instructio, on the other hand, meaning 'instruction,' is bad Latin for *institutio* in its proper sense of *disciplina, doctrina.*

Intellectus, 'understanding, intellect,' is late but not altogether bad Latin for *intelligentia, ratio, cognitio;* it must not, however, be used to denote the signification or sense of a passage.

Intentio, 'the intention,' is late Latin for *consilium, propositum, voluntas.*

Intercedere pro aliquo, 'to intercede for a person,' is bad Latin for *supplicare, deprecari, patere pro aliquo,* but right in the sense of giving security in money matters.

Interlocutor is new Latin for *is qui interloquitur, qui cum altero colloquitur.*

Interludium is a late word for *embolium* or *ludus interpositus, interjectus.*

Internus is unclassical for *interior, intestinus, domesticus,* or, in relation to the mind, with the gen. *animi,* e.g. we should write *dolor intestinus, bellum domesticum, animi tranquillitas.*

Introducere, e.g. *consuetudinem, novi aliquid,* is a rare and unclassical expression for *inducere.*

Introductio, 'the introduction to a book,' is bad Latin for *prooemium, principium.*

Invasio, 'an invasion,' is late Latin for *irruptio, incursio, incursus.*

Invehere in aliquem, 'to inveigh against a person,' is bad Latin for *invehi in aliquem.*

Invincibilis is late Latin for *invictus* or *is qui vinci non potest.*

Invisibilis is unclassical for *occultus, qui cerni non potest.*

Ironice is a later expression for *per ironiam, per irrisionem,* or the like.

Iterare, iterum aliquid facere does not mean 'to repeat continually,' but 'to do a thing twice, for a second time;' continued repetition must be expressed by *repetere, rursus facere.*

J.

Jubere must not be used with a neg. and the accus. c. infin. for *vetare.*

Judicare with the accus. in the judicial sense is barbarous; we must not therefore say *Deus quondam bonosque malosque judicabit,* but *de bonis malisque;* it is, however, correct to say *judicare aliquem (aliquid) ex* or *de* or simply *aliqua re,* 'to judge a person or thing in accordance with something.'

Juramentum, 'an oath,' is late Latin for *jusjurandum.*

Jurisprudentia is late Latin for *juris (civilis) scientia.*

Jusjurandum is not the oath of allegiance (*sacramentum*), but the civil oath in judicial and other matters.

L.

Labor for a work of the intellect is late Latin for *opus.*

Latere aliquem or *alicui,* 'to escape a person's notice,' is unsupported by classical authority and should be avoided, though commonly used by good modern Latinists; the right word is *fugere, fallere, praeterire.*

Latinum as a neuter substantive is barbarous, though we may say *Latinum aliquid vertere (convertere),* or *e Latino in Graecum.*

Latium is never used for *Latini, imperium Romanum.*

Lavacrum is late Latin for the plur. *balneae* or *balnea.*

Lectio, 'a lecture,' is unauthorized Latin for *schola.* Although there is no authority for *lectio* in the sense of 'a various reading,' this expression has become technical among scholars, and cannot now be replaced by *scriptio* or *scriptura.*

Liber must not be used to signify freedom from taxes, military service, &c., which must be expressed by *immunis.*

Liberi does not mean 'young children,' which is expressed by *pueri,* but a second generation of whatever age in contrast to the parents;

accordingly *librorum educatio* would not be good Latin for *disciplina puerilis*.

Librarius, which properly means 'a copyist,' is not good Latin for *bibliopola, librorum redemptor*, or *venditor*.

Linea, 'the line of a book,' is not usual for *versus*.

Litigatio is late Latin for *lis, jurgium, contentio*.

Litteratura is bad Latin for *litterae*, e. g. *Latinae (Romanae, Graecae)*.

Locutio, 'a word,' is late Latin for *vocabulum, verbum, vox*.

Longe is rarely used of time for *diu*, and we rarely find *longe ante, longe post* for *multo*.

Loqui is often used barbarously. *Loqui linguam Latinam* is barbarous for *loqui lingua Latina* or *Latine; ut cum Cicerone loquar* is an unauthorized phrase for *ut Ciceronis verbis utar; loqui bene, bonum, male, malum de aliquo* is unusual for *de aliquo benevole dicere, sermones bonos habere, aliquem laudare, &c.*; and similarly with *mala*.

Ludere, 'to play on a musical instrument,' is barbarous for *canere, cantare*, and so *is ludere personam*, 'to play a part,' for *partes agere (primas, secundas, &c.)*.

Luce meridiana clarius is a modernism for *luce clarius, sole ipso clarius*.

M.

Magnus homo of bodily stature is not usual for *magni corporis homo*.

Majoris aestimare is not classical for *pluris aestimare*.

Manere impunitum, incognitum, &c., 'to remain unpunished, unknown,' &c., is barbarous for *impune, incognitum esse, &c.*

Manuscriptum is new Latin for *liber*, or *codex scriptus, manu scriptus*, or *codex* alone.

Marginalis is a modernism for *in margine adscriptus, in vacua charta additus*.

Materia (-es) ought not to be used for the subject matter, which is *res, argumentum, quaestio*.

Matris frater, soror is contrary to usage for *avunculus, matertera*, and *avunculus* must not be used for 'uncle' by the father's side.

Mediator is late Latin for *conciliator, deprecator, internuntius, sequester, interpres, pacificator*.

Medius should not be used with the genitive following, but in agreement with the noun; thus, *in mediis aedibus*, 'in the middle of the house,' is better than *in medio aedium*, though *medio aedium* occurs in Liv. v. 41.

Memorabilia with a genitive is not Latin for *res memoratu dignae*. For *memorabilia Socratis* we should write *commentarii dictorum factorumque Socratis*.

Mereor laudari is unclassical for *mereor ut lauder*.

Miliare, 'a mile-stone,' is an unsupported form for *milliarium*.

Millio is new Latin for *decies centena millia*, or *decies* alone.

Modernus is not classical for *novus, recens, hodie usitatus, qui nunc est*.

Modus vitae is unclassical for *vivendi ratio, vita, consuetudo, genus vitae*.

Momentum is late Latin for *punctum temporis*.

Monarchia is a later substitute for *civitas quae unius dominatu tenetur; imperium singulare, regium imperium, regnum, tyrannis, unius dominatio*.

Multa pecunia, 'much money,' is bad Latin for *magna pecunia*.

Multoties is later Latin for *saepe, crebro*.

N.

Natio, which denotes the subdivision of a *gens*, must not be used for *populus* to denote a particular nation; we must say *gens Graecorum, natio Atticorum, populus Atheniensium*.

Necnon must not be used for *et* in joining single words.

Negotiator, 'a merchant,' is late Latin for *mercator*.

Neutralis, 'neutral,' is bad Latin for *neutrius partis, medius*.

Nonnihil, 'somewhat,' must not be used for *paulo* with the comparative.

Nota, 'an explanatory note,' is not a good substitute for *annotatio, explicatio, explanatio, scholium* (see Facciolati, *Epist. Phil.* VII. p. 427).

Notitia is bad Latin for 'a notice,' e. g. *historica*, which must be rendered by *res historiae* (e. g.) *veteris;* and for 'acquaintanceship,' 'friendship,' which must be rendered by *amicitia*.

Nullibi is doubtful for *nusquam, nullo loco*.

O.

Obiter is not classical in the sense of *strictim, quasi praeteriens, in transitu, cursim*, although it is constantly so used by modern Latinists.

Obstaculum, obstantia are not to be used for *impedimentum, id quod obstat, impedimento est*.

Obtinere is not 'to obtain,' i. e. get possession of, but 'to retain, keep up, persevere in,' as when Cicero says (*de Orat.* I. 41), *obtinendis atque augendis potentias suae causa*, 'for the sake of maintaining and increasing the power they already possessed.' Similarly, Ter. *Hec.* v.

33—2

4. 20: *at tu morem antiquum atque ingenium obtines*, 'but you stick to the old practice and principles.'

Occupatio is not 'a pursuit,' which must be expressed by *studium*.

Occurrere must not be used of books for *legi*, *inveniri*, *esse*; e.g. *hic locus occurrit in Cicerone* is bad Latin.

Odor and *olfactus*, 'the smell,' as a sense, are the one barbarous and the other unclassical for *odoratus*, *sensus narium*.

Opus habere is unclassical and of rare occurrence for *opus esse*.

Ore tenus is new Latin for *verbis*, *voce*, *orum*.

Oscitantia is new Latin for *oscitatio*, *socordia*, *ignavia*, *negligentia*.

P.

Paenitendus, 'worthy of blame,' is an adjective, and must not be used as a gerundive.

Pagus means 'a district,' and must not be used for *vicus*, 'a village.'

Palatium, 'a palace,' is not used for *domus ampla*, *domus regia*, *aedes regiae*, *domicilium regis*.

Pars virilis in the phrase *pro parte virili* does not mean 'to the best of one's abilities,' in a modest expression, but 'as far as a man can,' 'so far as is allowed to a strong man;' and the expressions *pro virili* and *pro mea virili parte* are not Latin.

Parum must not be used in the sense 'a little;' it always means 'too little.'

Parvus homo is not usual in speaking of stature; we must say *homo humilis* or *brevis staturae*.

Pati damnum, *detrimentum* is not good Latin for *facere*, *contrahere damnum*, *capere detrimentum*, *affici incommodo*, &c. The proper meaning of *pati* is 'to endure,' and it is synonymous with *tolerare* and *ferre*.

Patris frater, *soror* is contrary to usage for *patruus*, *amita*.

Pauper must not be used for *miser* to signify 'poor,' in a compassionate sense.

Peculiaris, which refers only to private or separate property, e.g. that of a child or a slave, is often used erroneously as a synonym for *singularis*, *separatus*, *proprius*, *praecipuus*, or the adverbs *singillatim*, *separatim*.

Pensio, 'a pension,' is new Latin for *stipendium*, *salarium annuum*.

Perfunctorie is late Latin for *leviter*, *celeriter*.

Perpendicularis is a modernism for *rectus*, *directus ad perpendiculum*, or *ad perpendiculum* alone.

Persecutor and *persecutio* are not good words for *vexator*, *vexatio*.

APPENDIX V.   517

Persuasum sibi habere occurs in Cæsar, *B. G.* III. 2 fin., and is a favourite phrase with modern Latinists; but the phrase is so rare that the young student should abstain from imitating it, and should write, instead of this, *mihi persuadeo, mihi persuasi, mihi persuasum est;* at any rate he should avoid altogether *persuasus, -a, -um,* and its superlative *persuasissimus. Me persuaderi patior*, which occurs in Muretus, *Op.* L. 662, is doubly false Latin.

Petitio, 'a petition,' is late Latin for *rogatio, preces, venia*.

Phoenicia is an erroneous form for *Phoenice*.

Placitum is unclassical and of rare occurrence for *sententia, decretum, dogma, praeceptum, quod placet.*

Plenipotentiarius legatus is barbarous for *legatus cum (publica) auctoritate.*

Plures, 'several,' is not classical for *complures*.

Poetaster is new Latin for *malus poeta, poeta nescio quis.*

Pollinctura is bad Latin for *unctio et curatio cadaveris.*

Polus, 'the pole,' is only poetical for *axis* or *vertex caeli.*

Pone, ponamus hoc ita esse, posito ita, are bad phrases for *fac, finge, fingamus ita esse, statue,* and the like.

Populatio, 'population,' and *populosus*, 'populous,' are late Latin for *populi frequentia* and *frequens, celeber.*

Positio verborum, 'position of words,' is bad Latin for *collocatio, ordo verborum*; and *positura* or *positus* is unclassical for *positio, collocatio, situs.*

Possibilis is scarcely allowable for *qui fieri potest* or *qui potest.*

Postscribere is very rarely used for *subscribere, adscribere.*

Potestas (verborum) is late Latin for *vis, significatio.*

Prae gaudio, metu, &c. must be used only in speaking of joy or fear as a *hindrance*, and cannot be used when we speak of them as a *cause* of what happens.

Praecisus signifies 'brief,' 'in few words,' and must not be used to express our 'precise,' i.e. 'exact.'

Praeconcepta opinio is bad Latin for *opinio praejudicata, opinionis commentum,* &c.

Praedictus must not be used for *antea, supra dictus.*

Praeire alicui exemplo (suo), 'to set a person an example,' is bad Latin for *alicui exemplo esse quod sequatur.*

Praejudicium is 'an opinion previously formed about a person or thing' (Cic. *Mur.* XXVIII. § 60), not a prejudice or erroneous idea.

Praeparare, praeparatus are rarely found for *parare, paratus.*

Praesagium, 'a presage,' is rare for *praesagitio, praedictio, praesensio, divinatio.*

APPENDIX V.

Praesens, 'this,' 'the present,' is bad Latin; e.g. we must not write *praesenti hieme* for 'in the present (i. e. this, *hac*) winter.'
Praeternaturalis is new Latin for *portentosus, legibus naturae repugnans.*
Praetextus (-um) is unclassical for *species, simulatio, titulus, causa, &c.*
Pretium, 'a reward,' is unusual for *praemium, insigne.*
Principium, 'a rule or principle,' is bad Latin for *ratio, praeceptum, sententia.*
Pro et contra, 'for and against,' is not Latin.
Prodigalitas, prodigalis are scarcely allowable for *luxuries, prodigus.*
Producere is unclassical for *gignere, efferre, procreare.*
Proficere alicui, 'to profit a person,' is almost barbarous for *alicui prodesse, utile esse, conducere.*
Prolixus, 'long,' 'tedious,' is late Latin for *copiosus, longus, verbosus.*
Promovere studio is modern Latin for *adjuvare, juvare studia, litteras.*
Propria manu is barbarous for *mea, tua, sua manu.*
Protectio and *protector* are late Latin for *patrocinium, tutela, defensio, praesidium; patronus, defensor, tutor.*
Protestari, 'to protest against something,' is barbarous for *contra dicere, adversari, intercedere.*
Publicare, 'to make known,' is unclassical, and *publicatio* is never used for *promulgatio.*
Publice is barbarous for *palam, in publico, sub divo, &c.*
Pusillanimus belongs to late Latin, but we may say *animi pusilli, parvi, &c.*

Q.

Quin after *dubito* is unclassical; see above, under *dubitare.*
Quomodo stas, it? are barbarisms for *quid agis?* Similarly, *quomodo vocaris* for *qui vocaris? quo nomine es? quid tibi nomen est?*
Quoque is often placed wrongly before the word to which it belongs, as *erravit quoque Muretus.*

R.

Ratione temporis, 'in respect of the time,' *ratione habita Platonis*, 'regard being had to Plato,' and such phrases, are barbarous.
Recensere, 'to judge,' 'to review,' and *recensio*, 'a judgment,' 'a review,' are common new Latin substitutes for *judicium facere* or *recognoscere*, and *judicium* or *recognitio.*
Recommendare, recompensare are French-Latin for *commendare, remunerare.*
Reconciliare secum is barbarous for *reconciliare sibi aliquem, redire cum aliquo in gratiam.*

Rectus locus, rectum tempus are barbarous for *opportunus locus, -um tempus*, and *mihi rectum videtur*, 'it seems right to me,' is a mere Anglicism for *mihi videtur*, or the like.

Referre or *rejicere culpam in aliquem* is barbarous for *conferre culpam*.

Regula, 'a rule' (in Grammar), is common, but really inadmissible, for *praeceptum*. There is no plur. *regulae*.

Remittere peccata, 'to forgive sins,' is poetical, and late Latin for *veniam dare, ignoscere peccatis*. In classical Latin we have *remittere poenam*. The same objection applies to *remissio peccatorum*.

Reprobare is late Latin for *improbare*.

Reputatio, 'honour,' 'reputation,' is French-Latin for *existimatio, dignitas*.

Respectu habito with the genitive is barbarous.

Respondere is never used in a dialogue for *inquam*.

Resurgere in the Christian sense is late Latin for *in vitam redire*.

Retego signifies 'to cover carefully' in writers of the silver age (see Casaubon and Ernesti on Sueton. *Octav.* 78); but in the best authors it means 'to uncover:' see *Varronianus*, p. 390.

Revelare, 'to reveal,' is a rare word for *patefacere, aperire, in lucem proferre*.

Revolutio is late Latin for *conversio*.

Rogatio, 'a question,' is barbarous for *interrogatio*.

Romanenses libri, 'Romances,' is new Latin for *Milesiae fabulae*.

Rotundum numerum ponere, 'to put it down in round numbers,' is late Latin for *numerum summatim comprehendere*.

Rudera, ruinae do not mean 'standing,' but 'prostrate ruins;' a ruin partly standing is *parietinae* (Cic. *Tusc.* III. 32), *vestigia diruti muri:* see Duker on Livy, XXVI. 11.

S.

Salvator, salvificator, and the like, are late substitutes for *servator*. For our Saviour we should say *sospitator* (Arnobius, *adv. gent.* I. 42), or *nostrae salutis auctor*, Manutius, *Ep.* II. 1. *Salutaris* is also a suitable word (see Cic. *Fin.* III. 20, § 66, *Juppiter salutaris*).

Sapere aliquid, 'to savour of something,' figuratively, is not sanctioned by usage.

Scholaris is barbarous for *discipulus*.

Scientia is not 'science' (i. e. knowledge reduced to principles) without the addition of some gen. as *medicinae, juris civilis, rei militaris, &c.*; accordingly, we ought not to write *artes et scientiae*, 'arts and sciences,' *academia scientiarum, studiosus scientiarum, &c.*, but *artes et disciplinae, academia optimarum artium, studiosus doctrinae et litterarum, &c.*

Sciolus, 'half-learned,' is late Latin for *semidoctus, leviter eruditus,* or, in jest, *erudiluius.*

Sculptorius is new Latin for *statuarius,* and we should not write *ars sculptoria,* but *ars fingendi, signa fabricandi, statuaria.*

Sectio, 'a small division of a book,' though very common in modern writing, is bad Latin for *pars.*

Secundus, 'second,' is barbarous for *alter* in such phrases as *Cicero erat secundus Demosthenes;* but we might say *secundus a Demosthene.*

Secus must not be used to signify 'wrongly' without *bene* or *recte* preceding; thus we cannot say *haec verba secus vertisti* for *male;* but we may say *nam recte an secus verteris nescio.*

Seducere, 'to lead astray,' is late Latin for *corrumpere, decipere, depravare;* so also *seductio* for *corruptela,* and *seductor* for *corruptor.*

Sensus, 'the meaning of a word or passage,' is unclassical for *notio, sententia* or *intellectus* (Quintil. I. 7).

Sentire dolorem, &c. is unusual for *capere dolorem &c. ex aliqua re.*

Septimana, 'a week,' is very late Latin for *septem dierum spatium, septem dies,* or *hebdomas.*

Serior is not used by the classical writers as a comparative, and only the adverb *serius* is followed by *quam,* as in Cic. *ad div.* xv. 1: *serius quam decuit.* Cæsar (*B. C.* III. 75) has *serissime,* and it occurs also in Pliny; but *admodum sero* is more usual.

Serius of persons in our sense is antiquated for *severus, austerus, gravis.* But *serio,* 'in earnest,' is good Latin.

Sermo, for a public discourse, is rare for *oratio, concio.* It is not idiomatic to say, in giving the meaning of an author, *hic est sermo de*—, but *hic agitur de*—, *hic loquitur* (e.g. Cicero) *de*—.

Sessio, 'a session,' e.g. *senatus,* is barbarous for *consessus, concilium.*

Sine omni spe is bad Latin for *sine ulla spe.*

Singulus hardly ever occurs except in the plural; if we wish e.g. to express 'no single seat,' we must say *nulla una disciplina* (Cic. *Tusc.* IV. 4, § 7); 'this single book' is *hic singularis liber,* 'this single legion' is *haec singularis legio;* on the other hand, *singularis* does not occur for *singuli* in the plural, and to express e.g. 'separate, single words,' we must say *singula verba,* not *singularia;* 'each separate legion' is *singulae legiones,* not *singula quaeque legio;* but 'every fifth year' is not *singulis quinque annis,* but *quinto quoque anno;* and Ruhnken was wrong (*Opusc.* I. 83), when he wrote *e centenis vix singuli* for *vix centesimus quisque,* and in the following passage from the preface to an edition of plays published in single volumes we must substitute the plural throughout: *sin-*

gulae fabulae singulum (singula) *complebunt volumen* (volumina), *ita quidem ut singulo* (singulis) *qui egeant singulum* (singula) *emere possint.*

Societas, 'a society of men,' is barbarous for *sodalitas, coetus, conventus, circulus, congressio.*

Solemnis, 'usual,' is almost barbarous for *usitatus*, and *solemnitas*, 'a solemnity,' is late Latin for *solemnia.*

Solidus in such phrases as *solida doctrina*, or *eruditio*, is not a proper substitute for *accurata, reconlita, subtilis.*

Solummodo is late Latin for *tantummodo, tantum, solum, modo, dumtaxat, &c.*

Somnolentus is late Latin for *somniculosus, somno deditus.*

Specialis, specialiter, in specie are modern Latin for *singularis, praecipuus, proprius; singillatim, separatim, proprie, nominatim.*

Speculatio is late Latin for *investigatio, contemplatio.*

Spicilegium, if used at all, must not be combined with *notarum, annotationum, observationum*, and we must write *in aliquo Scriptore* not *in aliquem Scriptorem.*

Sponte must be accompanied by *mea, tua, sua*, and must not be used alone, as is the practice with the best modern Latinists.

Spurius, 'illegitimate,' is late Latin for *adulterinus, subdititius, subditus, supposititius, non verus, non germanus*, and the like.

Statim atque (ac) is barbarous for *statim ut* (Cic. *ad div.* III. 9, § 10).

Statua means the statue of man, never that of a god, which is *signum, simulacrum.*

Stilus does not denote the language in general, which is *oratio*, or the particular style of an orator or writer, which is *dicendi* or *scribendi genus (ars)*; it refers only to the pen and to the art of writing. Consequently Scheller made a mistake in the very title-page of the book by which he promised to teach the art of writing good Latin, when he called it *Praecepta stili bene Latini*, instead of *Praecepta artis Latine scribendi.*

Strictura, 'a stricture,' or 'severe criticism' (Heyne, *Praef. Virg.* Tom. I. p. vii.) is a barbarous substitute for *judicium, censura, reprehensio.*

Studere, 'to study,' must be followed by *litteris, &c.*; *studium* must not be used in the singular for 'study;' and *studio* must not be substituted for *consulto, dedita* or *data opera, de industria.*

Subactum ingenium must not be used except with a distinct reference to the metaphor involved, as in Cic. *de Orat.* II. 30. As a general epithet *exercitatus* or *cultus* is better.

Subaudire, subintelligere, 'to supply a missing word in the thought,' is quite an unauthorized modernism. The simple *intelligere* is sufficient.

Subjugare is late Latin for *subigere*.

Submittere se legibus is barbarous for *legibus obtemperare*, and *submittere se alicui* is inadmissible for *subjicere se*.

Subordinare is new Latin for *supponere, subjicere*.

Succincte, succinctim is late Latin for *breviter, strictim*.

Sufficienter, 'sufficiently,' is late Latin for *satis, abunde;* likewise *sufficiens* for *quod satis est.*

Summa, 'a sum of money,' is unclassical for *pecunia*.

Superfluus is unclassical and doubtful for *supervacaneus, supervacuus.*

Superscriptio is a barbarism for *titulus, inscriptio*.

Supplicatio is new Latin for *supplex libellus*.

Suspicere aliquem is not an authorized substitute for *suspectum habere*.

Syllabus is a late word for *index.*

T.

Tellus, 'the earth,' as an element, is barbarous for *terra*.

Tempus habere, nullum tempus habere, are barbarous for *otium, vacuum tempus alicui esse; otii, vacui temporis nihil habere, otio carere.*

Tenor, 'the general purport,' is late Latin for *argumentum*.

Terminus, 'a term,' i.e. 'a word,' is barbarous for *vocabulum, verbum, vox*, and 'a technical term' is not *terminus technicus*, but *artis vocabulum*. Nor can *terminus* be used to signify a prescribed period or time, which is *dies data, praefinita, constituta*.

Textus, 'the text of an author,' is not an authorized expression for *verba, oratio, locus*, but it may be used as a technical term with *qui dicitur*.

Theoria is modern Latin for *ratio, ars, disciplina, doctrina*.

Tortura, 'torture,' is late Latin for *tormenta*.

Tractare de aliqua re for *aliquam rem* is barbarous; and there is no authority for the use of *tractatus, tractatio*, in the sense of 'a treatise on some subject.'

Traductio, 'a translation,' is an unauthorized word for *interpretatio*. The same may be said of *versio;* and also of *translatio*, which in classical Latin means 'a metaphor.' The best word for 'to translate' is *reddere, vertere, convertere, exhibere.*

Tumultuosus of men is barbarous for *turbulentus, seditiosus.*

U.

Ubertim is unclassical for *abunde, copiose, &c.* But *uberius* and *uberrime* are good words.

APPENDIX V. 523

Ullibi is new Latin for *usquam, uspiam;* see *Nullibi.*

Ultimus must not be used to signify 'the last,' i. e. immediately preceding; thus we must say, e. g. *anni decem proximi* or *superiores,* not *ultimi.*

Uncinus, 'a hook,' is later Latin for *uncus.*

Undiquaque is barbarous for *undique.*

Unguiculus, in the proverbial phrase *a teneris unguiculis,* should not be used without *ut Graeci dicunt* (Cic. ad div. I. 6), *ut aiunt, ut dicitur.*

Unice must not be used for *unus, solus,* in the sense 'alone.'

Usque huc is barbarous for *usque ad huc.*

Utique, 'by all means,' must not stand by itself in answer to a question; it always requires a verb. This particle is constantly misapplied by modern Latinists.

V.

Vanitas, 'vanity,' 'pride,' is barbarous for *ambitio, jactantia, arrogantia, insolentia,* &c.

Venia sit dicto occurs in Pliny, but the better phrase is *bona venia* or *pace tua dixerim.*

Veracitas is new Latin for *veritas, veri studium.*

Verbo tenus and *de verbo ad verbum* are barbarisms for *verbum e (de) verbo, ad verbum, totidem verbis, eisdem verbis.*

Verisimiliter is late Latin for *probabiliter.*

Vernacula lingua, vernaculus sermo is a modern application of a classical term. Varro, *L. L.* IV. 12, opposes *vernacula vocabula* to *peregrina.*

Vertere, 'to translate,' is a good word, but not with such adverbs as *Latine, Graece, Anglice* for *in Latinam,* &c.

Vice prima, altera, tertia, &c., 'the first, second, third time, &c.' is modern Latin, and so is the common *vice versa* for *vicissim,* and *vice iterata* for *iterum.* Some modern Latinists think they are introducing an elegance when they write *plus vice simplici* for 'more than once :' which is *plus quam semel, semel atque iterum.* In the passage of Horace from which they derive this barbarism (4 *Carm.* XIV. 13) *plus vice simplici* means 'with more than a simple requital or retribution,' as the old scholiast Porphyrius explains it: 'Volt intelligi in vastandis his non tantam solum illis cladem intulisse, quantam ipsi dederant, sed *duplum,* hoc est, eam non simplici vice reddentem.'

Vir must not be used with *juvenis, senex,* like our 'young man,' 'old man.'

Visibilis is late Latin for *adspectabilis, qui sub oculos, adspectum, cadit.*

Visitare, 'to visit,' is not used for *convenire, visere, interviserre*.

Visus, 'the sight,' is rare by itself for *sensus videndi, acies, visus oculorum*.

Vivus, in the phrase *ad vivum aliquid* or *aliquem exprimere*, is without authority for *alicujus vivam imaginem exprimere*.

Vix adhuc is barbarous for *vix dum, vix jam;* so also *vix aliquis* for *vix quisquam*.

Voluptuosus, 'voluptuous,' is unclassical for *voluptarius, voluptatibus affluens*.

Votum, 'the vote or opinion,' is barbarous for *sententia*.

Vox, 'a voice,' is not used for *sententia, suffragium*. Although *vox* in the singular may denote a single word and *voces* several connected words, the singular alone is used to denote 'a sentence,' 'a saying,' as in Cic. *Tusc.* I. 46, § 11 : *Laconis illa vox*.

Vulgaris is not applied to persons in the sense of our 'vulgar,' and *vulgares homines*, though used by Muretus (*ad Cic. Cat.* II. 13) for *vulgus*, is quite inadmissible.

Z.

Zelotypia, though used by Cicero, *Tusc.* IV. 8, § 18, is a Greek word, which may be replaced by the Latin *obtrectatio, aemulatio*.

Zodiacus may be expressed in Latin by *signifer orbis* (Cic. *de Div.* II. 42, § 89; *N. D.* II. 20, § 53) or *duodecim signorum orbis* (Cic. *N. D.* II. 20, § 52).

L. INDEX OF LATIN WORDS AND PHRASES.

A.

a, ab, abs, 160, 319
abiiko, 300
abhinc, 118, 316, 500
absolvo c. gen. 283
aleque, 311
abstineo c. gen. 282
abundans, abundo c. abl. 301, 302
abunde, 172, c. gen. 284
abutor c. abl. 304
ac, atque, 191, with similis, æque, idem,
   talis, pro eo, &c. 301
accedit quod, 415
accedo ad vel in, 306
accerso, arcesso, 134, 136
acessiu, 83
accingor c. acc. 273
accuso, 331, c. gen. 281
acervus, &c. c. gen. 284
Achilles, 19
acquiesco, 308
acutatus, 158, 168, 318
ad, 181, 319; written ar, 186
adeps 185
adhibeo, 300, 309
adhuc, 159, 168, 400
adjaceo, 306
adjuro = adjuvero, 97
aditus laudis, 277
admodum, 171
admoneo c. gen. 279
adno c. dat. et accus. 306
aspergo, 307
adsto, 306
adsum, desum, &c. c. dat. 300
adulor, 307
adversus, 181, 311
advocatus, 300
æmulor, 307
æmulus c. gen. 287

æqualis c. gen. 287
æque ac, 173
æqui boni que facere, &c. 284
æquus and verus, 194
æquus, iniquus, æstimo, existimo, &c.
   8, 223
æra, dat. for æri, 202, 311
æs grave, 64
æstate tota, 316
æstimo, &c., magni, parvi, &c. 284, 301
ætate, 315
affatim, 172, c. gen. 284
affectuum verba, 361
afficio, 302
affinis, 287
affluo, 302
age, 205
aggredior, 270
agnosco, cognosco, ignosco, 287
agricola as neuter adjective, 45
alo, 152
alias, 174
alienus c. abl. et gen. 301
aliquando, 167
aliquanto, 168, 500
alioqui, 174
aliquis, 78, 388
aliquispiam, 78, 389
aliquid boni, aliquid triste, 285
aliter, 174
alius, 45, 74, 377, 386
alius—alium, 337, 378
allatro, 307
almus, 209
alter, 45, 377, 386
alter—alterum, 337, 378
alterutter c. gen. 282
alumnus, 209
amans c. gen. 278
amb-, 187

ambo, uterque, 79, 186
antiquus c. gen. 186
ambio, 301
amicior c. acc. 178
amicus, amo, 186
amorem, 184, 428, 487
amor, 207, 220
amplius, plus without quam, 197
amplus, 282, 193
an, 163
animadverto aliquid, in aliquem, 309
animi pendeo, aeger, excrucior, 280
anno proximo, 315
annon, 164
annuus, 301
ante, 181, 321
antecedo, antesto, praesto, 307
antefero c. dat. 280
antequam, 335
antiquus, 184
aperio, 182, 418
apinae, 53
appellandi verba, 267
appositio, 138
apprime, imprimis, 172
aptus ad aliquid, 287
apud, 181, 321
arbiter, 186
arceo, 302
arefacio, 438
arguo, 186
armenium, 209
armus, humerus, and tergum, 481
artifex, two meanings, 45
as, or libra, its subdivisions, 64
asscia, 301
at, 197
Atropos, 473
atrox, 185
attendo, 302
attinet, 302
audiens dicto, 307
audio, video, facio c. particip. 362
audite, 368
augeo c. abl. 302
ausculto c. dat. et acc. 307
ausim, 89, 153
aut, vel, -ve, 194
autem, 197
ave, 143
avidus c. gen. 278

D.

balneum, 52
belli, 313
bellicosus, bellicus, 502
bello, 315
benedico, 290
bidens, its two meanings, 224
biduum, triduum, &c. 62
bimus, 62
bimestris, 66
blandior, 290
bovem, 494

C.

caerulis, 503
canis, 74
cantillo, 222
capitalis, 503
carus, 503
carmen, 13
castigo, 503
castrum, 53, 211
catervatim, 153
causa, 182, 303
caveo with diff. cases, 308
cavillor, 272, 492
cedo, cette, 143
celeber, 303
celo with dat. and acc. 272
centesimus usura, 65
certo, certe, 154
certiorem aliquem facere, 271
cervix, 53
ceteroqui, 174
cimeterium, 8
cinctutus, 218
cio, cieo, citum, civum, 103
circa, circum, circiter, 182, 321
circumdo c. dat. et acc. 308
circumvenio, 270
cis, citra, 183, 322
clam, 318
clarus, 484
codicillus, 53
coepi, 153
coeptus sum, 339, 503
cognitu, 368
cognitum habeo, 364

INDEX OF LATIN WORDS AND PHRASES.   527

columna, 209
cum, 482
cotemineror c. acc. 280
commodo c. dat. 289
commodus ad aliquid, 287
commoneo, 280
communico aliquid c. aliquo, 290
communis c. gen. vel dat. 287
communis alicujus cum aliquo, 287
comparo c. dat. 291
compleo, 302
complures, 13
compon c. gen. 278
con-, 186
conceditur, 268
condemno, damno, &c. 281
condus, 271
confero, 290, 294
confestim, 158, 168
confido, 308
conjungo me c. aliquo 290
conscribillo, 112
consideratus, 152
consto, with diff. constructions, 308
consulo, with diff. constructions, 308
consultus c. gen. 279
contendo c. dat. 294
contentus, 309
contingit c. dat. 268
continuo, 148, 168
contra, 181, 272
convenienter, &c. c. dat. 288
convenio, with diff. constructions, 309, 304
convivior, 100
convivium, 6
copia, 284
coram, 181, 318
cordi est, 292
corporeus, 124
cervices, cervix, 293
credo c. infin. 329
credulus, 414
crucs, 267
crimen, 100, 197
crimino, 281
crudelis erga aliquem, 287
cruor and sanguis, 481
cui bono fuerit, 192
cujusmodi, 79
cum, 132; cum quam or quum, 317

cunctl, 79
cunque, 77
cupio, with diff. cases, 309
curiosus, 305
cutis and pellis, 180

D.

damnum, 200
de, 180, 181, 333
debeo, 413
decies sestertium, &c. 62
decumanus, 67
defungor, 303
delicium, 51
denarius, 64
denuo, de integro, 170
descriptio, 303
desino, desisto, c. gen. 282
desitum est, 250
despero, with diff. cases, 307
detraho, 292
dextans = decuns, 64
dextrocherium, 218
Diana, quantity, 110
dic, 135
dicax, dicterium, 491
dicor, 267
dicto, 268
dies, 30
diespiter, 30
differtus, 201
dignor, 304
dignus, 300
dignus qui, 352
diligentia, 506
diligo, 286
dimidio, 298
dimidium, dimidia pars, 63
dis-, dir-, 187
direxti, 89
dirimo, disertus, 4
dissingor, 273
dism, 184
dispar c. gen. 287
dissimilis c. gen. 287
distentus, 201
disto c. dat. 293
ditio, 50, 207
do, dedo, &c. c. dat. 181, 191

528   INDEX OF LATIN WORDS AND PHRASES.

do pecuniam meinam, 171; do literas, with diff. constructions, 309; do, wrongly used, 305
doceo, 174
doleo quod, or with the infin. 361
domi, domum, domo, 313
domus, 32
donec, 204, 355
dono, 307
dubito, dubium non est, 307
dubito an, 307
duc, 135
duco, 197
dum, 433
dulcis, 187
dum, 204, 354
dummodo, 354
dumtaxat, 177
duo, 61
durus erga aliquem, 287
duumvir, 61

E.

e, ex, 180, 334
ecce, 306
eccum, eccillum, ellum, 73
edepol, epol, 206
editus a. abl. 295
ego, 301
egredi e castris, modum, 270
ehea, quantity, 430
ejus and suus, 383
en, 306
enim, 109
eo, 109
eo audaciæ ventum est, 284
epiredium, 118
epulum, 52
erepsemus, 89
ergo, 331
ergo, 197, 318
eripio a. dat. 293
est mihi = habeo, 289
et, 191, 373; either omitted between three nouns or verbs, or inserted between all, 473
et non = neque, 193
etiam and quoque, 193
etiamtum, 169, 409
etsi, etiamsi, 201

evado with double nom. 166
e vestigio, 158, 168
excedo, 82
excello præter, 307
excerpta, 104
exigu, 272
existimo, 8
exitu, 368
exuvia, 152
expedit a. dat. 168
expers c. gen. 178
expugnassere, 89
extemplo, 148, 168
exstinxem, 89
exteri, 81
extorris, 300
extra, 183, 332
ennor c. acc. 273

F.

fac, 435
facetus, 191
facinus, 404
facio, officio ut, 362
facio, with diff. cases, 309; wrongly used, 309
facta, 368
facundus, 215
familias, genitive, 16
farl, 153
favonius, favor, 207, 120
faxo, faxim, 89, 153
fecundus, 215
femoror, with diff. cases, 309
fer, 435
fere, ferme, 174
ferunt, 367
festivus, 191, 509
fido, diffido, a. dat. 290
filiacis, 118
fio, 142
fio, with double nom. 166; quantity of, 429
flagitium, 178
flocci, 185
Floralia, 79
fluo, 307
fore ut, 359
forem, 153
formido, 489
fors, fortasse, forsitan, 175

INDEX OF LATIN WORDS AND PHRASES.   529

fraus, 494
fretus, 301
frugi, 494
fruor, 303
frustra, nequidquam, incassum, 175
fungor, 303

G.

Gaius, 8, 18, 130
gaudeo, or laetor, construction of, 361;
  wrongly used, 309
genitus c. abl. 295
gentium, 184
Geryon, quantity, 430
glorior c. abl. 304; de vel in, 305
grandis, 492
gratia, 318
gratulor quod, quum, 415
gratus, 487
gravis c. abl. 301
grex c. gen. 284
gustatu, 368

H.

habeo, wrongly used, 310
habeo c. part. perf. 364
habeor, 267
habilis ad aliquid, 287
haud, 161
haud scio an, 161, 174
hei, 295
hic, haec, hoc, 71, 384
hic et hic, 377
hic and ille, 376
hiemps, 22
hodie, horno, quantity, 430
honestus, 113
horreo, 68
horreo, with diff. cases, 309
hortor ut, 369
humanus, 116
humerus, armus, &c. 481
humi, humo, 181

I, J.

jam, nunc, 165
id temporis, id aetatis, id genus, 273
idem, eadem, idem, 74, 380
idoneus, 287
idus, 63

D. L. G.

igitur, 197
ignarus, 278
illabor, 306
ille, illa, illud, 71, 384; hic and ille, 376
ille et ille, 377
illico, 148, 168
illudo, 307
immanis, 492
immo, 162
immunis c. gen. et abl. 301
impatiens and patiens c. gen. 178
imperitus and peritus c. gen. 278
impertio, 308
impius erga aliquem, 287
impleo c. abl. et gen. 302
impono with diff. constructions, 309
impotens c. gen. 178
improvisus as secondary predicate, 259
imputo, 411
in- negative prefix, 224
in, 181, 138
in, intra, 183
inanis c. gen. et abl. 301
inceptu, 318
incessit me, mihi, 306
incumbo, with diff. cases, 309
indigeo, 301
indignus, 300
indueo, 308
induor c. accus. 273
infensus and infestus, 485
inferi, 51
infitias, 6
infra, 183, 323
ingens, 492
ingratus erga aliquem, 287
iniquus, 8; erg. al. 282
injuriosus erg. al. 287
inops, 178
inquam, inquit, 141, 243, 306
in quinquennium, 317
incipientis est, non incipiens est, 271
irascor with diff. cases, 308
instar, 318
insueco re, rei, 308
insulto, 307
integer c. gen. 285
intellecta, 368
inter, 184, 323
intercludo, interdico, construction of, 308
interea loci, 284

34

intereo, interimo, interficio, 486
interest, 289
interrogo aliquem de aliqua re, 272
interum c. dat. 190; with diff. constructions, 309
intra, 124
invado c. dat. et acc. 306
invenfustar qui, 400, 404
inventa, 368
invideo, 291
Invitus as second predicate, 239
ipse, ipsa, ipsum, 72, 389
iracundus, 215
irascor c. dat. 290
iri, 109, 147
is, ea, id, 74, 379
et is, isque, 379
iste, ista, istud, 73, 184
itaque, 198
item, itidem, identidem, 193
iterum, rursus, 169
jubeo, 360
jucundus, 487
jugera, compounds of, their quantity, 431
junior, 40, 410
juris peritus, prudens, consultus, 240, 279
jussum, 89
juvenis, 94
juvo, 91
juxta, 181, 394
juxta atque, 391

K.

Kalendæ, 65
Karthagini, 'at Carthage,' 312

L.

labor, 207
lætor, or gaudeo, 361
laryus, 493
lætet, 148, 513
lenibat, 107
lepos, 491
levo, 191
liber ab, 301
libero, 303
licet c. dat. 168, 158
lis, 27
locuples c. abl. 301

locus, 114
loco (primo), 315

M.

macte, 301, 304
mæror funeris, 277
magno, parvo, &c. esse, 286
magnopere, 171
magnus, 494
major, maximus natu, 40
maledico, 290
malluvium, 224
malus, 494
maneo with double nom. 266; with diff. cases, 309
mare, pelagus, pontus, 489
materies, 19, 486
matrimonium, 71l, 486
maturus c. gen. 286
meus, tuus, &c. 280
medeor, medicor, 291, 307
mehercule, aurelius fidius, 226
mei, tui, sui, 277
memini, 153, 279
memor, 278
memoratu, 368
mereo, mereor, with diff. cases, 309
meridie, 39, 271
-met, 71
metuo, with diff. cases, 110; with ne, ut, 242, 353, 401
metuo distinguished from timeo, &c. 489
meum est, not mei est, 276
meus, tuus, suus, 277
migro, 408
mihi, dat. eth. 288
militiæ, 313
minime gentium, 184
minor, minitor c. dat. 290
minoris, 298
miror, mirum est, construction, 361
misceo c. dat. 294
misereor, miseror, miseret, 289
moderor with diff. cases, 110
mollem c. gen. 286
modo, 166, 410
mœnia and muri, 488
molestus, 412
moneo, 280, 410
monoculus, 228
morte, dat. for morti, 101

INDEX OF LATIN WORDS AND PHRASES. 531

moveri Cyclope, 973
multi, paucí c. gen. 283
multitudo with plur. verb, 237
multo, 198
multum, 493
mari and montis, 488

N.

nam, 198
nascor, 150
naturalis historia, 249
naics, 295
navel, 283
ne, 161
ne-quidem, 162
necessarius c. gen. 287
necesse est c. dat. 268
nec = ne-quidem, 162
(nec) neque, 190
nemo, 164
nevnon, 193
nefrumlinea, 31
negligo, 161, 227, 486
negotium, 161
nemo c. gen. 283
nequam, 494
nequeo, nequeor, 109
nescio quis, 351
ni, nisi, and si non, 201
nihil c. gen. 283
nihil, (non) aliud quam, atque, &c. 302
nihil gravius, &c. 283
nihilo, 298
nitor, 394
nubo c. dat. 290
noxte superiore, 315
nolo c. part. perf. pass. 359
nomen mihi est, 289
non, 161
non solum, non modo, 177, 372
nonne, 64
nonne, 163
nostri, nostrum, 71
novi and scio, 487
novilius, 6, 117, 190
noxa and noxia, 494
nubo, 283
nullus, 45, 78
num, 163
nunc, 164
nuntius, 117

Nursia, 173
unquam gentium, 284

O.

oh, 314
obedio, 293
obliviscor, 135, 279
obscurus, 484
obsequor, obtempero, pareo c. dat. 290
obsolesco, 188
obtineo, 515
obtrecto c. dat. et accus. 307
occumbo with diff. cases, 308
oli, 163
Œdipus, 438
O, ohe, quantity of, 430
olim, 71, 166
omitto, 186, 438
omnino, 171
omnis, 79
onero, 301
onustus, 301
aperio, 186, 438
oportet, 361
oportuit te dicere, 340
opulentus, &c. 217
opus est, 303
orbus, orbo c. abl. 301, 302
ore, dat. for ori. 311
Orion, quantity of, 430
oro ut, 360
ortus, 295
O si, optat. 347
ovis, exarus, parcus, 152

P.

panis, 175
pænitet c. gen. 280
palam, 318
par c. gen. et dat. 287
paratus ad aliquid, 287
parco c. dat. 290
parcus c. gen. 279
pars, 177
particeps c. gen. 178
partim, 155
parum c. gen. 284
parvo, 308
parvus, 492

532 INDEX OF LATIN WORDS AND PHRASES.

passor c. abl. 304
patefacio, 438
paterfamilias, &c. 16
patiens c. gen. 278
patres conscripti, 484
patrimonium, 211
patronus c. dat. 288
pauci c. gen. 282
paveo, pavor, 489
paullo, 298
peccatum, 494
pejero, 438
pellis and cutis, 480
pensa, 181, 334
penitus, 170
per, 185, 393
percontor aliquid ex aliquo, 272
perdo, 484
pervadio, 316
perfruor, perfungor, 303
perinde ac, 173
perinde quam, 174
peritus, 310
perosus, 142
perpetuo, 167
perquam, 174
persuadeo, 369; persuasum habeo, 364
pertaesus, 142
peto with diff. cases, 310
pietas and religio, 486
piget c. gen. 280
pili, 285
pius erga aliquem, 287
plane, 171
plenus, 279
plult, used personally, 141
plurimus, 298
pluris, 298
polliceor, 107
polliceor c. infin. 350
pomeridianus, 187
pomoerium, 187
Pompei, 430
pondo, 57
pondus, 184
pone, 182, 326
pono = positus, 134, 187, 429
populus and plebs, 484
posco with double accus. 272
possum, 137; potui fuisse, 349
post, 182, 326

postea, postkac, 73, 116
posteri, 81
postliminium, 187
postquam, 354
postridie, 87, 171, 116
postulo, 222; aliquid ab aliquo, 272
postumus, 31
potentes, 213
potior, 303
potissimum, 172
potus, 142
prae, 182, 326
prae, praeter, 184
praebeo, 433
praebao = prohibeo, 187, 433
praeditus, 301
praes and vas, 482
praesertim, 172
praesto, diff. constructions of, 310
praestolor, 307
praesum c. dat. 300
praeter, 326
precor, posco, rogo, &c. 271
primo and primum, 69
primus, as secondary predicate, 259
priusquam, 355
pro, 117; after quam, 394
proinco = prohibeo, 187
proceres, 484
proceres, 484
procul, 318
prodigus c. gen. 279
proh deum fidem, 396
prohibeo, 302, 419
prohibessis, 89
prologus, propolo, 439
prome, 117
prosubus, 437
prope, 326
prope, propemodum, 175
prope, propter, 184
proprius c. gen. 287
propter, 182, 184, 317
prorsus, 171
protinus, 159, 168
prospicio with diff. cases, 310
pie, 71
prudens c. gen. 210, 259; as secondary predicate, 259
pudet c. gen. 280
pugnare pugnam, 170

INDEX OF LATIN WORDS AND PHRASES.   533

pudor, 149
puta, 118

Q.

qu., 2, 431
quadrigati nummi, 64
quaero, 134
quaeso, 183
qualiscunque, 79
quam pro, 394
quam ut, 417
quam omitted after plus, amplius, &c. 297, 394
quamdiu, 304
quamquam, quamvis, quantumvis, 303, 316, 399
quandoquidem, 192, 336, 412
quanti, quanto, 198
quantulus, 80
quantumvis, 316
quasi, 173, 359
quatriduī (biduī, triduī), 218
quem or quos with cum, 317
quemadmodum, quomodo, 391
queo, 109
querimonia, 214
qui, quae, quod, 75
qui = et is, sed is, 373, 376; = si quis, 196, 103; = talis ut, 112, 103; = quamquam is, 103; ut is, 409
qui tuus est erga me amor, &c. 261
qui, 76; for utinam, 198
quia, 200, 336, 414
quicumque, 79; with the Indic. 199
quidem, 376
quilibet, 78
quin, 203, 420
quintana (via), 67
quippe, 163
quippe qui, 326
quis, quae, quid, 76
quis, quispiam, 77, 388
quisquam, 78, 389
quisque, 79, 337, 377, 386
quisque, position of, 251
quisquis, quicunque, quidquid, &c.
quisquis, &c. with the Indic. 400
quitum est, 89
quivis, 78
quivis, quilibet, 78, 389
quo, 202, 418

quoad, 304, 355
quoad ejus fieri potest, 184
quod, 'as far as,' 416
quod, quia, 199, 336, 414
quominus, 203, 419
quondam, 318
quoniam, 76, 200, 336
quoties, 354
quotquot, 400
quotusquisque, &c. 387
quoqueque, 304
quum, 354, 336; 'because,' 336, 416

R.

ratio, 488
re-, 187
reccidī, 439
recensitus, recensetus, quantity of, 433
receptio followed by an accus. 361
recipio, different constructions of, 310
recorder, 370
redundo, 309
refert, 280
refertus, 301
religio, pietas, 486
remedium irae, 277
reminiscor, 370
reses, 31
remuntio, diff. construction of, 310
rear, 148, 188
repeats, 159, 168
reperiantur qui, 400, 404
repetundarum, repetundis, 366
repperi, 439
rerum potiri, 394
res, reus, &c. 488
resisto c. dat. 289
respondeo, diff. construction of, 310
retuli, 439
ergo, 279
rotundus and teres, 482
rudis aī, 179
rudo and rudo, 115
rus, rure, ruri, 318

S.

salio, sapio c. accus. 370
salve, 143

534   INDEX OF LATIN WORDS AND PHRASES.

sanguis and cruor, 481
satis, affatim, abunde, 173
sat, satis c. gen. 284
satius fuit c. dat. 268
satus c. abl. 295
scelus, scelerator, scelestus, 497
sciens, as secondary predicate, 339
scilicet, 161
scio and novi, 487
scisciter, 272
scito, imper. 435
scitu, 368
se-, 288
se, suus, 70, 383
se and sua, 382
se pude, iterum, 63
secundum, 183, 327
secundus, 314, 362
securus, 188, 484
sed, 196, 375
semper, 167
semisopitus, 432
senex and vetus, 483
senior, 50
sequester, 218
servussem, 89
servio c. dat. 288
sestertius, 64
setius, 6, 48, 429
seu (sive), 195
si, optative, 347; conditional, 945; after
    ita or sic, 393; after ut, velut, ac,
    quam, 397
sicanquam, 168
similis c. gen. et dat. 287
similis atque, 391
simul, 318
sine, 337
sino, 134
si non, 201
siquidem, 201, 432
sive, 195
sis = si vis, 205
socors, socordia, 188, 430
sodes = si audes, 205
solitus sum c. infin. pass. 340
solus, 183; c. gen. 282
solvo with diff. cas. 272
spero, 359
sponsor, 482
sponte, 57, 164

statim, 159, 168
statutum, 318
studeo, c. dat. 290
studium, 331
suasi tu, c. dat. 291
suavis, 487
sub, 340
subeo c. dat. et accus. 306
subito, 159, 168
subter, 184, 340
succenseo and suscenseo, 187; c. dat.
    290
sui, sibi, &c. 70, 382
sultis = si vultis, 205
sum, 89
sumentum, 194
sumo, 117, 420
sunt qui, 353, 400
suovetaurilia, 228
super, 345
superi, 51
superadoo, constr. 303, 308
supplex c. gen. 287
supra, 183, 328
surrexe, 83
suscipio, succipio, 187
suscipio, 371
suspicio, 6, 429
suus, 70, 382

T.

tactio, followed by an accus. 362
taedet, 280
talis, &c. 79
tamen, 197
tametsi, tamenetsi, 202, 227
tamquam, 173, 354
tanti, tantidem aestimo, &c. 281
tantum c. gen. 284
tantum abest ut—ut, 417
tempero with diff. cas. 319
tenuis, 493
tenus, 184, 318
teres and rotundus, 482
tergum, tergus, 485
terrarum with ubi, 284
timeo, diff. construction of, 311
timeo ne, ut, 343, 353, 401
timeo, distinguished from metuo, 4 No

INDEX OF LATIN WORDS AND PHRASES. 535

tonitru, 59
trado, 271
trans, 183, 328
trans, 83
trepido, 189
tribuo, 192
trico, 53
tridui, 318
tripudiatio, 441, 450
triumvir not triumviri, 62
triumvir, tres viri reipublicae constituendae, &c. 192, 311, 367
turba c. verb. plur. 247

U.

ubi, 'when,' 409
abl c. gen. 284
aDua, 78, 189
ultra, 184, 329
ultra, 164
ultro tributam, 165
Ulyxes, 19
unciarium fenus, 65
universus, 79
unus, 46
urinor, 148
usque, 167
usque ad, 184
ut, 'that,' 242, 416, 418; 'as,' 351, 390;
  'although,' 357; omitted after certain
  verbs, 361
ut non for quin, 420
uter, 77
uterque, ambo, 79
utilis, &c. c. dat. 287
utinam, 346
utique, 171
utor c. abl. 304
utpote qui, 356
utrum—an, 163

V.

vaco c. dat. et abl. 291, 311
vacuus, 301
vahe, 171
vale, 153
valeo, diff. constructions of, 311
vapulo, 142, 308
vas and prass, 482
vastus, 492
-ve, 104
ve-, vebe-, 188
vecors, vehemens, 188
vectigal, ultrotributam, 165
vel, 194
vel, 'for example,' 374
veneo, 142, 305
veneficus, 438
venit mihi in mentem c. gen. 280
verecundus, 215
vereor ne, ut, 241, 352, 401
vereor, 189
versus, 328
versatus, 218
verum, vero, verumenimvero, 197
verus, 494
vescor c. abl. 304
vestibulum, 188
vestiri, vestrum, 71
veto, 494
vetus c. gen. 286
vetus and senex, 483
vicinus, 287
videor, 367
vigilare noctem, 271
vigilia, abl. 315
vili, 298
vir, 17
vir, virum, 257
vis with plur. verb, 257
visu, 368
vitium, 494
vivere vitam, 270
volo c. part. perf. pass. 339

II. INDEX OF SUBJECTS.

A.

Abbreviations, 468
Ablative, meaning of the term, 11
  plur. in -abus, 16
  in -ubus, 32
  sing. in -i or -e,
  of the agent with a, ab, 238, 295
  of the instrument, 294
  of the cause, 295
  of the manner, 295
  of reference, 296
  of comparison, 296
  of the measure of quantity, 297
  of price, 298
  of quality, 298
  absolute, 299, 410
  of the object, 300
  with prepositions, 339, 318
  with potior, fungor, &c. 303
  of the gerund, 366
Acatalectic, 444
Accents, 9
Accentual verse, 460
Accusative, meaning of the term, 11
  in -am or -im, 27
  of the immediate object, 239, 269
  before the infinitive, 240
  in the figura etymologica, 270
  double, 270
  of reference, 271
  Greek, 272
  with verbs of putting on or off, 272
  interjectional, 273

  with prepositions, 319, 318
  of space or time, 311
Active verbs used as deponents, 141
Additions to the present tense of verbs, 134
Adjectives in -is and -us, 45
  comparison of, 46
  derived, 214
  agreement with substantive, 218
  as secondary or tertiary predicates, 219, 289
  as epithets of the same noun must be joined by a conjunction, 493
Adonius, 448
Adverbs of negation, &c. 116, 161
  of place, 157, 164
  of time, 158, 163
  of manner or degree, 169, 170
Adversative conjunctions, 190, 197
  sentences, 374
Alcaic verse, 454
Alphabet, Latin, 2
Anacrusis, 443
Anapaestic verse, 449
Anomalous nouns, 51
Antibarbarus, 499
Antispastic rhythm, 457
Apposition, 232, 237, 249, 264
Archilochian verse, 456
Arrangement of words in a sentence, 247
Arsis and thesis, 441
Arts and Faculties, 470
Asclepiadean verse, 449
Asynartete rhythm, 453
Attraction of the relative, 263

INDEX OF SUBJECTS.   537

B.

Bacchiac verse, 460
Bachelor, baccalaureus, 471
Basis, 443

C.

Cæsura, 410, 444
Calendar, Roman, 66
Cases, their general distinctions, 11
Catalectic, 444
Causal sentences, 421
Choriambic verse, 449
Classic authors, L 463
Collective nouns, their construction, 157
Comic metres, 431, 457
Comparative sentences, 390
Comparison, degrees of, 46
Compound words, 212
    verbs with a transitive signification, 82
Concessive sentences, 421
Conditional sentences, 145, 395
Conjugations, 85
Conjunctions, copulative, 189, 191
    adversative, 195, 196
    inferential, 190, 197
    causal, 190, 199
    conditional, 190, 201
    concessive, 191, 202
    final, 191, 202
    temporal, 191, 204
Consonantal nouns, 21
    verbs, 109
Co-ordinate sentences, 371
Copulative sentences, 371
Correlative pronouns, 77, 79
Countries, names of, treated as names of towns, 313
Cretic, 451

D.

Dative in -e for -i, 311
    of limitation with adjectives, 287
    of limitation with predicative substantives, 288
    of limitation with verbs (dativus commodi vel incommodi), 288
    with verbs of giving, &c. 289
    with sum for habeo, 289

    with compound verbs, 289
    with verbs denoting an affection of the mind, 290
    of destination, 291
    instead of a prepositional phrase, 292
    of the agent with gerunds and gerundives, 293
    of the gerund, 366
Declensions, 12
Defective verbs (especially), 159
Definitive sentences, 397
Deponent verbs, 142
    used in a passive sense, 141
Derivation of verb-forms, 88
Derivation and composition, 207
Diæresis, 444
Dialysis, 440
Diminutives, their formation, 218
Dipodia, 443
Diphthongs, 7; their quantity, 429
Disjunctive conjunctions, 194, 196
    sentences, 373
Dissyllabic perfects, their quantity, 432
Distinctive pronouns, 74
    sentences, 377
Distributive numerals, 67
    sentences, 375
Double negatives, 162, 193
Doubling, verbs of, 103, 420

E.

Ecthlipsis, 440
Elegiac verse, rules of, 447
Ellipsis, 414
Enclitics, 253
Epistolary addresses, 472
Epistles, imperfect and pluperfect used in, 472
Epithets, two or more, connected by copulative conjunctions, 423
Epode, 452

F.

Fates, 471
Fearing, verbs of, with ut and ne, 343, 352
Feet, metrical, 443
Final sentences, 418

Fractions, how expressed in Latin, 63
Frequentative verbs, formed from nouns, 220
Future, 345

G.

Galliambic verse, 456
Gender of nouns, 12, 16
Genitive in -as of the first declension, 16
    in -i from Greek nouns in -es, 19, 23
    in -i for -ii of the second declension, 18
    in -os for -ei of the third declension, 20
    in -um for -orum of the second declension, 18
    in -um or -ium, 28
    of possession, 274
    of quality, 275
    of the object, 277
    (1) with substantives, 277
    (2) with adjectives, 278
    (3) with verbs, 279
    of partition, 282
    of quantity, 283
    of number, 284
    of price or value, 285
    of relation, 286
    position of the, 340
    of the gerund, 366
Gerund and gerundive, 82, 363
Glyconic verse, 448
Gods, the, 12, 173
Ornate, 173
Greek nouns, 18, 21

H.

Hemimer, 444
Hemiolian rhythms, 481
Hindering or refusing, verbs of, 103, 219
Hexameter, rules of, 444
Hipponactean verse, 450
Hypercatalectic, 444
Hypothetical propositions, 369

I.

Iambic verse, 441, 458
Ictus, 441

Illative sentences, 416
Imperative, 345
    of dico, duco, facio, fero, and scio, 435
Imperfect, 343
Impersonal verbs, 140, 143
Inchoative verbs, 139
Indefinite pronouns, 72, 188
Indicative pronouns, 72, 384
    mood, 343
    and subjunctive, 341, 350
Indirect or oblique interrogation, 343, 401
Infinitive mood, 357
    as neuter substantive, 13
    as subject of the sentence, 358
    with accusative, 210, 268
    after verbs of commanding, &c. 360
Interest of money, 65
Interjections, 205
Interrogative pronouns, 76
    particles, 163
Interrogatives (oblique), 247
Intransitive verbs with the accusative, 270
Ionic a minore (a majore), 450
Islands, construed like the names of towns, 113
Ithyphallic verse, 450

L.

Latinity, modern,
    old, specimens of, 464
Latin language, 1
Letters, classification of, 2
    their subdivisions, 7
Long syllables, 428

M.

Metre, 441
Millions, how expressed in Latin, 61
Money (Roman), 64
Months, names of, as adjectives, 43
    their divisions, 65
Mora, in metre, 441

INDEX OF SUBJECTS. 539

Multiplication expressed by distributives and numeral adverbs, 61
Muses, 473

N.

Names of persons, 468, 473
   of relationship and affinity, 474
Negative particles, 161
Neuter deponents or passives, 135, 139, 152
Nominative, 236
   for the vocative, 305
Numerals, 59
Numeral adverbs, 69

O.

Objective sentences, 414
Oblique narration, 342, 353, 405
Octonarius, 448, 459
Ordinal numbers, 62
Orthography, oldest specimens of, 3

P.

Parm primus, &c. 450, 456
Participles, 362, 410
Patronymics, 213
Perfect, formation of, 133
   indicative, 343
   subjunctive, 348
Pherecrateus, 450
Place, case of, 311
Pleonasm, 423
Pluperfect indicative, 344
   subjunctive, 349
Plural nouns with no singular, 53
Poetic style, 461
Potential tenses, of, 346 sqq.
Predicates, 230
Prepositions, 178, 236, 317
   words used as, 318
Present indicative, 343
   subjunctive, 346
Pronouns, 70
Propositions, their parts, 229
Prosody, 428

Q.

Quantity, 428
   of middle syllable, 432
   of the final syllable, 434
   of syllables as affected by metre, 439
   differences of, in memorial lines, 475
Questions double, what particles employed in, 163

R.

Reflexive pronouns, their use, 70, 383
Relative and interrogative pronouns, 75
   pronoun with indicative mood, 241, 397
   with subjunctive, 241, 400
   agreement with its antecedent, 262
Rhyming verses, 346, 461
Rhythm, 441
Rome, seven hills, tribes, and kings, 473

S.

Sapphic verse, 453
Saturnian verse, 441, 450
Scanning or scansion, 443
Season, 452
Seasons, 474
Semi-consonantal nouns, 27
Senarius, 452, 458
Sentences, different kinds of, 370
Septenarius, 458, 459
Short syllables, 430
Subject of the sentence, 236
Subjunctive and indicative, 241, 350
Subjunctive sentences, 400
Subjunctive with ut the subject of impersonal verbs, 417
Subordinate sentences, 395
Substantive verb, 89
Substantives, derived, 206
Superlative, 46
   with quam, quantus, quisque, 393
Supines, 367

www.ingramcontent.com/pod-product-compliance
Lightning Source LLC
Chambersburg PA
CBHW031940290426
44108CB00011B/629